BEFORE THE FALL

BEFORE THE FALL

AN INSIDE VIEW
OF THE PRE-WATERGATE WHITE HOUSE

WILLIAM SAFIRE

WITH A 2005 PREFACE BY THE AUTHOR

TRANSACTION PUBLISHERS
NEW BRUNSWICK (U.S.A.) AND LONDON (U.K.)

This book is printed on acid-free paper that meets the American National Standard for Permanence of Paper for Printed Library Materials.

Library of Congress Catalog Number: 2005041717
ISBN: 1-4128-0466-3
Printed in the United States of America

Library of Congress Cataloging-in-Publication Data

Safire, William, 1929-
Before the fall : an inside view of the pre-Watergate White House / William Safire.
    p. cm.
Originally published: Garden City, N.Y. : Doubleday, 1975.
Includes index.
ISBN 1-4128-0466-3 (pbk. : acid-free paper)
    1. United States—Politics and government—1969-1974. 2. Nixon, Richard M. (Richard Milhous), 1913-   I. Title.
E855.S23   2005
973.924'092—dc22   2005041717

For Annabel

CONTENTS

VIII: THE NEW MAJORITY

IX: THE PRIVATE MAN

X: MAN IN THE ARENA

LIST OF PLATES

Following page 632

"There has been something crude and heartless and unfeeling in our haste to succeed and be great. Our thought has been 'Let every man look out for himself, let every generation look out for itself,' while we reared giant machinery which made it impossible that any but those who stood at the levers of control should have a chance to look out for themselves. We had not forgotten our morals. We remembered well enough that we had set up a policy which was meant to serve the humblest as well as the most powerful, with an eye single to the standards of justice and fair play, and remembered it with pride. But we were very heedless and in a hurry to be great.

"We have come now to the sober second thought. The scales of heedlessness have fallen from our eyes. We have made up our minds to square every process of our national life again with the standards we so proudly set up at the beginning and have always carried at our hearts . . ."

Woodrow Wilson
Inaugural Address
March 4, 1913

My life was changed in a moment of lucky hesitation.

It was the first day of spring in 1973. Despite what seemed to me to be some minor media flap during the campaign about a bizarre incident at the Watergate building, and despite the intense anti-Vietnam War passions swirling through the country, Richard Nixon had won reelection with a stunning 61 percent of the vote.

Nixon had refused to debate George McGovern, but Bob Haldeman, the White House chief of staff, had told me late in the campaign I could do a written "debate" in the *Washington Post* with McGovern's campaign manager, Frank Mankiewicz. After Nixon's landslide, conservative writers were suddenly in demand; because I had just demonstrated an aptitude for partisan columnizing, both the *New York Times* and *Washington Post* approached me with offers of a job as columnist—the most coveted assignment in journalism. I consulted Stewart Alsop, who was then writing the best column in the business for *Newsweek*. "The Graham family is wonderful to work for," Stew said, "and the *Post* is on the rise, but face it—there is only one *New York Times*."

After choosing the *Times*, I informed Haldeman, whose instant reaction was that it would be a good idea to have a friendly voice on that influential op-editorial page. He directed my fellow speechwriter, Pat Buchanan, to draft a nice note from the president to Arthur O. "Punch" Sulzberger, congratulating him on his acquisition of a contrary view for that liberal page; such a gesture would show that Nixon bore no grudge for his ill treatment by the *Times* editorialists. The chief of staff later told me that Pat drafted the letter but Nixon refused to sign it, preferring to bear his grudge.

I did want to get a traditional farewell note to grace my wall, so I wrote a letter from Nixon to me praising my selfless, dedicated service over the years. A pal of mine in his outer office signed it with the presidential autopen and got the official White House framer to frame it. With that somewhat phony souvenir in hand, I packed up a few belongings and trudged out of my office in room 123 of the Old Executive Office building and crossed the street to the West Wing to say goodbye to a few of the old Nixon hands with whom I had worked since the early '60s.

A Secret Service agent I knew was outside the door to the Oval Office. He shook my hand in farewell and said, "You want to say goodbye to the Old Man? He's inside there with his lawyer."

That's when I hesitated. If I asked to shake hands goodbye, a secretary would have knocked and poked her head in, and Nixon—who knew I intended to write a book about my dozen years through ups and downs with him—would surely wave me in and wish me well, even to work at what he liked to call "that rag." But he wasn't much at small talk, and had made clear he wasn't all that happy at my choice of future newspaper employment. So I shook my head, no, I didn't want to bother him, and kept on going to my car, turning in my parking pass at the gate.

At about that moment of that March morning, I later learned, Nixon was meeting with his counsel, John Dean, later accused of being an architect of the cover-up, who was telling him about the break-in and obstruction of justice that had become, in Dean's phrase, a "cancer on the presidency." Had I gone in, Nixon would probably have told me to listen to the lawyer's worrisome story. He might well have asked me, a former PR man, to make some suggestions about how to handle it, and perhaps to draft a statement in his style, which was my specialty. That fateful Nixon-Dean meeting, of course, was secretly taped, and whatever I would have said would have ultimately made me a grand jury witness, possibly a target of hot-eyed prosecution, and certainly a great embarrassment to the *Times*.

But I walked on past that dark confabulation and out into the sunshine of a spring day. That was some break for me, three decades ago.

In the year afterward, as the Nixon presidency was crumbling, I was getting the hang of column writing by day while writing *Before the Fall* at white heat at night. The title (conceived after the book was finished, which was soon after the Nixon presidency was also finished) was a play on the title of Arthur Miller's *After the Fall*, a play centered on Marilyn Monroe, the phrase in turn evocative of John Milton's *Paradise Lost* dealing with the fall of the angels. I liked the satanic metaphor, though Nixon's post-Watergate political demise, though accurately described by his successor as "our long national nightmare," was not quite on the scale of the banishment of Lucifer from Heaven after rebelling against God's establishment.

The book publisher, who signed up for a look inside an administration that had a full term to run, got cold feet and rejected my manuscript about the president and his men who had been run out of town. That craven bunch tried to wriggle out of the contract by calling it a mishmash, unacceptable because the volume you now hold was "no book at all." I asked my lawyer and lifelong friend, Morton Janklow, to contest the unilateral abrogation of a contract. He arranged for a prestigious and gutsier publisher, Doubleday, to bring out the book exactly as submitted, thereby demonstrating its acceptability. In mediation he won a point about the publisher-friendly "acceptability clause" that he later enshrined in future contracts to protect authors. After that experience, the brilliant and gutsy Janklow founded a literary agency that now represents many of the world's best-selling authors.

Looking back, I'm really glad I wrote *Before the Fall* while all the events were fresh in my mind and at a time when the U.S. political world was in turmoil. It has the little anecdotes, the sidelights and offbeat observations—even scrawled notes and revealing doodles snatched up after meetings—that I would surely have forgotten had this been a memoir written in much-later retrospect with all the false perspective of received wisdom. For that reason, for decades after, I have been urging White House aides, especially speechwriters, to keep little crumpled-up diary notes in the lower right hand drawer of their desks. These moments of drama, poignancy, or humor are the "footnotes to history," in Robert Louis Stevenson's phrase, that cannot be reconstructed from newspaper files or official records, and that become catnip to serious historians. That is why this book became a primary source not just to biographers and historians but to a columnist like me, triggering recollections of moments that would otherwise have receded into the mists. Those nuggets, happy or painful, can help make a point about what is happening in the latest administration.

But loyal aides ask me: What about subpoenas? Won't such scraps of paper supposedly squirreled away be ferreted out and used by investigators to get the boss in trouble? You have to use your head, I tell them; the requirement of history need not include revelations that begin "here's how we obstructed justice." Rather, "here's the way we all reacted the day all the work seemed worthwhile, or on the day the roof fell in." And as most people do not expect, presidents expect their aides to spill the beans, at least most of them. At the first meeting of Nixon's comeback crew in 1965, as recounted herein, Nixon introduced me with, "This is Safire, absolutely trustworthy, worked with us in '60. But watch what you say, he's a writer." After a couple of minutes, none of them watched what they said; later, the only complaints I heard from insiders came from those left out of moments of high drama or intriguing connivance.

I persuaded Nixon and Haldeman to let me make notes at meetings of the Cabinet, State dinners, and similar events (to which I would not be invited otherwise) without suspecting that an ever-whirring taping system was in place recording the events that this book covers. When the tapes that ensnarled Nixon were revealed at the Watergate inquiry, I decided to let what I had noted down stand; so far, no glaring discrepancies between what I scribbled in my bastard shorthand and what appeared in tape transcripts have surfaced; what you read herein was pretty much what was actually said. And because my work was outside the cover-up orbit, much of the reporting has not been covered in published transcripts, even after three decades.

How does Richard Nixon look in retrospect to historians? In general, academics—mostly liberal—consider him the most disapproved-of and most fascinating of twentieth-century presidents. With the passage of time and its inexorable lure of revisionism; with the unprecedented wealth of material that the damnable taping system offered; and especially with the recent, comparable depth of rightist antipathy to the impeached Clinton and the leftist reviling of the wartime, younger Bush—the visceral Nixon-hatred is on the wane. He is no longer the sole target of president bashing.

That's partly because Nixon's foreign policy acumen—demonstrated in détente with the Soviet Union, in the startling China opening, in the use of both of those moves to try to complete an orderly and honorable Vietnam disengagement—is seen to be buttressed by reconsideration of his progressive domestic approach. Working with governmental talents like George Shultz, Pat Moynihan, and Arthur Burns, Nixon's "bright side" presaged much of today's welfare reform, health initiatives, and environmental protection. (Even the partisan passion generated early in his career by Nixon's relentless pursuit of Alger Hiss dissipated to some extent with the conclusive revelations in KGB files of Hiss's spying.) The newest "new Nixon" is also a result of this comeback politician's second comeback; after his precipitous fall, the only U.S. president forced to resign his office refused to crawl into a hole. On the contrary, Nixon wrote his way out of disgrace: a series of serious books, mostly scrawled in longhand on his signature yellow pads, offered purposeful and understandable advice to policymakers. Not surprisingly, they reached a large general audience as well: Nixon books—pro, con, and by—have an audience. (So do plays and movies about him, but those are mostly caricatures.)

His literary output included a memoir far more interesting and profound than that of the dreary product of Johnson, Ford, Carter, the elder Bush, or Clinton. (Reagan, it turns out, could and did write well, but was no memoirist.) Were all these accounts of White House years self-serving? Of course. Still, Nixon's self-defense through policy guidance was at least meaty, equally as revealing of character and rich in detail as Truman's surprisingly solid work (the best presidential autobiography since U.S. Grant, a man of action who once observed, "I am a verb").

During that second comeback, and until his death in 1994, I covered Nixon as an occasional columnist-interviewer, unabashedly asserting my previous connection. Though some old adversaries resisted admitting him to elder-statesmanhood, most Americans accepted him as what he liked to call an "homme serieux"—a politician with no future, therefore safe to listen to for his hard-earned political sagacity. This included a yearly tour d'horizon, ranging from his long-headed views on China policy (he excused much despotism in hope of capitalism's ultimate softening), the Middle East ("we disagree about that, I know, Bill") to gun control ("Guns are an abomination—I can say that, now that I'm not running for anything"). His Super Bowl prognostications were remarkably astute because professional football, like politics, combines strategy, power, and will.

After his death, I continued these "interviews," purporting to converse with him in purgatory, where I placed him to be purged of the sin of imposing wage and price controls. Let me say this about that: I have the Nixon vocabulary and cadence down fairly well, and can guess at what he might think of current events and today's opinionmongers. That's what speechwriters are trained to do. A liberal columnist friend wrote me after one of those imaginary interviews to say he could hear Nixon's voice so well it made his flesh creep, which I took as a compliment as well as a nice play on the Committee to Re-elect the President (which Senator Bob Dole dubbed CREEP).

The alert reader will soon note that the tone of this introduction to the 2005 reissue is gentler and less angrily defensive than the introduction to the 1977 edition, which I now append. At this stage, I'm disinclined to counterattack Nixon's revilers with my hearty railings about their hypocrisy. Why? Not just because the old furies have diminished with the passage of time and the pooling of passions about past presidents; more because of the willingness of a new generation of scholars to make judgments based on an assessment of a political personage's entire life and work, including character, grit, deviousness, foresight, example, and impact.

William Safire

PREFACE TO THE 1977 EDITION

"Two wrongs make two wrongs."

So said former President Richard Nixon to interviewer David Frost in the spring of 1977, on the subject of the double standard that had been applied to his Administration compared with those of his predecessors. But, as he often used to do, Nixon was "acting against the words," in playwright Arthur Miller's phrase, trying to get across a complex message in his mind that must have gone something like this:

I know that two wrongs don't make a right. I know I can't be excused on the grounds that "everybody did it," or at least I shouldn't overtly try to be. But shouldn't you apply the same distrust to my accusers as you apply to me? Shouldn't you try to understand that the continuance of an abuse of power is nowhere nearly as venal as the first, precedent-setting abuse of power? Shouldn't you feel guilty about your passion to punish me when you display such an unwillingness to condemn Roosevelt and Kennedy and Johnson for crimes that were even worse?

Before the Fall was written in 1973 and 1974, after I had left the Nixon White House to take the post of a Washington columnist for the New York *Times*. Looking back now, we can see a time of mass hysteria, of a blood-in-the-eye, let's-get-the-bastards suspension of judgment and perspective that had not erupted since the McCarthy period. Throughout its writing, I kept trying to lean against the winds of Nixon-hatred, to suggest that there might be some extenuation in the truth about the past practices of others, some perspective in the way politics was played before everyone suddenly became aggressively Simon-pure, some balance of judgment available to those willing to apply moral fervor in a moral— that is, single-standard-bearing—way.

Not even this book's original prospective publishers were having any of that. As the national fever rose in 1973, the commercial-editorial faces at William Morrow & Co. fell—they wanted no part of a book that did not join in the general revulsion, and turned down the manuscript of *Before the Fall* on the grounds that it was "not a book." Arbitrators let me keep some part of my author's due, perhaps because the nation's largest publisher—Doubleday—accepted the same manuscript for publication. The political courage of Doubleday editor-in-chief Stuart Richardson was a rarity in those days; the book he brought out—reprinted without a word changed here—was not censored in any way.

We now have the advantage of three years' retrospect. If we knew then what we know now, would the result have been the same?

In examining that question, a battered partisan seeking to be an understanding historian has to work his way through three reactions: anger at personal hypocrisy; fury at having been manipulated by a charge of manipulation; and a long, slow burn at the steady—and after a while, deadening—accumulation of evidence to make the case that the roots of Watergate are to be found in previous administrations. Let's take those reactions in turn.

The hypocrisy rankles. Two little-known vignettes come to mind:

—House impeachment counsel John Doar, certified media hero, wrote the condemnation of Nixon as an abuser of power, citing the "Huston plan" to repress dissidents. Did he know that someday we would find out that in September 1967, then-Assistant Attorney General John Doar wrote the infamous "Doar Plan" to infiltrate dissident groups with community service workers, which was approved unhesitatingly by civil-liberties poseur Ramsey Clark?

—The Senate Watergate Committee, its members household words all, grilled Gulf Oil lobbyist Claude Wild about illegal contributions to the Nixon campaign. As the Senators sat there carefully limiting their question areas, did they know that we would someday hear in an account quoting witness Wild that "every member of the Committee except Erwin" (who was unopposed in his state, and needed no campaign funds) was on the take secretly?

These were minor irritations, caused by—but limited to—the hypocrisy of individuals. After all, it can be argued, evil is no less evil if exposed by men who are less than pure.

The second reaction—fury at having been manipulated, especially with the irony of the charge of manipulation—goes to a more substantive matter. Nixon was driven from office on, essentially, the charge of "cover-up"—the attempt to suppress or doctor information. Lying to the American people.

Yet those in charge of the investigation, and those in the press responsible for digging out the whole truth, came up with what we now know was the partial truth about the abuse of power by the Federal government. Half the truth, in itself, would not be venal but for the fact that the investigators had the information about "the big picture"—and concealed it deliberately.

One example: William Sullivan, an embittered former high official of the FBI, provided the Senate Watergate Committee with a list of "black bag jobs" and other illegal FBI activities that took place in the sixties. The Sullivan memo included the revelation that President Johnson had used the FBI for spying on his political enemies at the 1964 Democratic Convention, and on Republican staffers in the 1968 campaign.

If released in 1973, that memo would have given pause to all those who were acting as if Richard Nixon and his men had invented political sin. But it was not released. It was placed in the committee safe, never published even in the final report—and did not see the light of day until after Nixon's resignation. (The Watergate minority counsel kept it for publication in his own book years later.)

This was, by any definition, a "cover-up"—perhaps not with the sinister ring of "obstruction of justice," but certainly a successful effort to obstruct truth. It is one example of selective release of the facts by partisans or favor curriers who gloried in accusing the Nixon Administration of "manipulation" or "orchestration."

Where was the investigative press in all this? Caught between sources who had an object in mind—getting even with the hated Nixon—and a market of readers with one interest in mind—more fuel to feed the firestorm of protest against a White House cabal.

The deliberate cover-up of the precedents for Watergate did not come about as a result of any liberal establishment conspiracy. To most, it seemed like the right thing to do at the time: any examination of previous power abuses was seen as an attempt to exonerate the Nixon abuses, to play into the hands of the cynical "everybody did it" crowd. The good end (of punishing wrongdoing Nixonites) justified the investigators' means (of denying to the public the information it would ordinarily have the right to know). This might have come with better grace had investigative zealots not been castigating their targets as those who put the ends of national security ahead of the means of protecting constitutional liberties.

It should be noted at this point (or at this time, but never at this point in time) that a handful of genuine civil libertarians did resist the hysteria. Men long scorned by the Nixonites—Nat Hentoff, Murray Kempton, Milton Viorst, Nicholas Von Hoffman—whose own longstanding anti-Nixon credentials were in good order, expressed concern about the anti-libertarian way the self-described civil libertarians were going after the power abusers.

Not by orchestration, then, but in cacophonic concert, public opinion was channeled toward the goal of bringing down the President. Most reporters did not dig for precedents, because editors felt readers were not interested; the sources who did know the whole truth chose to conceal what they knew either for partisan reasons or because they did not want to appear on the side of the "black hats." Ye shall know the half-truth, the sources seemed to say, and the half-truth shall make you free.

The third reaction came more than a year after Nixon's fall, as a mountain of evidence accumulated about the Watergate precedents in earlier administrations. The effect was numbing; most people had had enough of revelations of chicanery at the highest level, and did not want to hear more. Especially since it put to the fire the clay feet of old idols.

The post-Watergate revelations that did so much to explain Watergate were begun by reporter Seymour Hersh, of the New York *Times*, who first wrote of the massive intrusion on the lives of American citizens by the Central Intelligence Agency. This triggered an investigation by a Presidential commission, which shied away from the dirtiest of dirty tricks (assassination attempts on foreign leaders) and in turn led to a Senatorial investigation.

But when Democrats investigate Democrats, the results are not as dramatic—or presented in as horrified a fashion—as when Democrats investigate Republicans. Friends of the late John Kennedy came across evidence of a tie between the late President and the moll of a Mafia chieftain (who happened to be the same hoodlum assigned by the CIA to murder Fidel Castro); this startling White House-Mafia link was discreetly buried in a footnote of a report, almost escaping notice.

But the momentum of the investigation, and the laudable perseverance of portions of the press, pushed the reluctant probers into disgorging episodes in the past that far exceeded—in scope as well as venality—any that so recently shocked the nation.

The most vivid example of Watergate roots was the 1962-65 wiretapping, blackmail, and harassment of the Reverend Martin Luther King, Jr. The original tap was authorized in writing by Attorney General Robert Kennedy; it was carried on into the Johnson Administration with the tacit approval of Attorney General Nicholas Katzenbach; it resulted in thousands of telephone interceptions, the invasion of privacy of hundreds of unsuspecting and unsuspected Americans—all having nothing to do with national security. In the additional surveillance this tapping spawned, Dr. King and his wife were harassed and threatened, and blackmailing eavesdroppers tried to break up their marriage.

All this and more was done by the "good guys," many of whom came before committees (but not on television, as the Nixon men were forced to) to blandly explain how they could not remember those events of the distant past. Mrs. King never sued.

Of course, some of the Congressional "good guys," who preened before the cameras during the Second McCarthy Era of 1973-74, turned out to be the targets of an investigation in 1977. The Koreagate scandal, if properly and vigorously pursued, might discover scores of veteran congressmen on the take—illegally, in direct defiance of Article II of the Constitution—and we shall see where that leads. Even if the self-searching ardor diminishes, we know that some of the legislators loudest in their excoriation of executive venality were pocketing envelopes or being entertained in the grand Agnew tradition.

Which brings us back to the first reaction again, with some of the heat taken out of one's sense of indignation. Perhaps, as Jimmy Carter and other leaders before him have suggested, we would be better off to condemn the sin and not the sinner. In that more charitable mood, and with justice something to be done with sadness rather than lip-smacking vengeance, we can address the question: If we knew then what we know now, would the result have been the same? Knowing that Nixon and his men lied no more than his predecessors; knowing he invaded privacy and abused the intelligence power less than the masters of the Kennedy and Johnson years; and knowing that many of his accusers were draping themselves in a phony cloak of public morality—with that amelioration, with that perspective, would Nixon have been driven out of office?

Of course he would. Not only that, it was right—both morally and practically—for him to have been forced to resign. If the tapes had been running in the

White House of Franklin Roosevelt—and some episode had made them available for inspection—he, too, would have been on the brink of impeachment.

The reason is that hard evidence of lawbreaking by men in power cannot be blinked away when it is forced into public view. When Francis Bacon, Lord Chancellor of England in 1620, was charged with taking money from parties in suits before him, he could not defend himself on the ground that such pocket-lining had been customary for judges of the realm for centuries. It was wrong; he knew it; its previous tolerance offered no protection. Bacon was jailed for four days and then pardoned.

In the same way, the multi-Administration wiretapping, the tradition of "bag jobs" done by the FBI and later assigned to a White House group, the transgressions on individual rights that gathered force over four decades—all these, when exposed by the flipping-over of the fiat rock called Watergate, required expiation. The ones who were caught had to pay, and there were both graveyards and a statute of limitations protecting those who did not get caught in the past.

Richard Nixon will be remembered, as Lord Bacon is, for having been the man in charge when the rules were rightly applied. Nixon's hand-fashioned noose, correctly labeled herein "the goddam tapes," made it possible to change the corrupt toleration of the breaking of those rules; ironically, it was the blundering way Nixon handled the cover-up that will be seen as his great, if unwitting, contribution to the cause of civil liberty.

Nixon's fall was the stuff of history, and will be the subject of historical analysis, revisionism, and re-revisionism for as long as the republic survives. The attacks on him were surely unfair, but the result was surely not unjust. The question is not "Is the President above the law?" (as Lincoln showed, in some situations, he definitely is, and put there by the law) but "Is this President, in this circumstance, justified in stretching the law this far—and has he given us proof of what he did?"

Richard Nixon erred, no more than several predecessors, but then compounded his error again and again, each misstep on inexorably grinding wheels of tape, and so he must bear his disgrace. After the fall, he went to work on his oral and written history, and—one hopes—will justify some of his ways to his countrymen.

But what of the time before the fall? The villains now ten feet tall were then only normal-size staffers who thought they were on their way to a place in history rather than a place in jail. The best metaphor in this book likens the pre-Watergate years to an old movie in which all the bit players later became stars.

Seems like ancient history now, but a look at the dreams and the practices of Richard Nixon and his men as they were riding high—and doing much good, too hurriedly forgotten—can be instructive to the students of power of today and the brokers of power of tomorrow. In the years that now separate us from the first Nixon term, some of us have felt the frustration and outrage described in this introduction, but must grimly agree with the man who once led this nation: two wrongs—or two thousand wrongs done under two previous Presidents—do not make a wrong right.

BEFORE THE FALL

An Inside View of the Pre-Watergate White House

PROLOGUE

PROLOGUE

I first met Richard Nixon in a kitchen in Moscow.

It was "my" kitchen; that is, I was the press agent representing the homebuilder who put up the "typical American house"—then $11,000, plus cost of land—at the American Exhibition in Moscow in 1959. Nikita Khrushchev was being shown around the exhibition by his host, the American Vice President, who was nervously trying to be genial, and the tour was happily disorganized: the two men were wandering around like a couple of politicians at a county fair, stumbled after by the world press corps.

At the RCA color television exhibit, Khrushchev took the opportunity to launch a debate, taunting the Vice President about American consumer gimmickry and aggressive foreign policy. Nixon, the host, was taken aback: he continued to be Mr. Nice Guy as the color tape rolled for rebroadcast back in the United States. Khrushchev clobbered him; Nixon kept trying to placate his guest, but the Russian leader had the upper hand all the way. Because the Vice President was not being the gutfighter people expected him to be, but was being his naturally diplomatic, courteous self on a trip abroad, Nixon's reputation for being a tough bargainer who could "stand up to the Russians" was in danger of being forever dissipated in those twenty minutes of TV debate. Nixon came out of the TV studio sweating profusely, knowing he had "lost," and anxious to find a way to make a comeback.

I slipped out of the control room, went over to my exhibit—which *Pravda* had labeled the "Taj Mahal," because the Soviets could not admit a U.S. tract house was affordable by the average American worker—looped a chain around the fence and the rear bumper of a jeep, and pulled down the fence. There was now no control at all to whatever tour had been planned; to Major Don Hughes, Nixon's military aide, I yelled, "This way to the typical American house!" In a fluid crowd situation like that, any authoritative voice is followed, and Hughes led Nixon, who in turn led Khrushchev, Mikoyan, and Voroshilov over the pulled-down fence into the "typical American house." They all shook hands with my thunderstruck client, Mr. Herbert Sadkin of All-State Properties, Inc., in the walkway carved through the middle of the house, which had been dubbed the "splitnik" because it had been split apart to let crowds walk through. At my signal, a Russian-speaking American guide permitted a crowd of Soviet fairgoers to pour in from the opposite direction: with the crowd of reporters pushing behind the politicians, Nixon and Khrushchev were effectively trapped in the house.

Comprehension of the situation, and the opportunity it offered for a comeback in debate, dawned on the face of the Vice President. He took Khrushchev by the arm and steered him to the railing of the walkway where they could lean into the kitchen. The reporters formed a semicircle behind them, and the "kitchen conference" began between a couple of evenly matched contenders.

Nixon was superb. I was in the kitchen with the woman demonstrator of the equipment, and had the perfect view; listening to the firm, intelligent, nonbelligerent way the American Vice President was handling the blustering Soviet General Secretary made me proud to be on the right side. The problem was this: hardly anybody else could see or hear.

Harrison Salisbury of the New York *Times,* who spoke Russian and could take the pool notes for the press corps, was climbing through the walkway rail into the kitchen; as a Russian guard started to move to stop him, I explained he was the refrigerator demonstrator and the guard hesitated long enough for Salisbury to squeeze in. When I tried the same thing for the AP photographer, holding him out to be the demonstrator for the automatic garbage disposal unit, the guard said, "Which unit is that?" and I was stuck—it was a cheap house, there was no such unit— and the photographer, in desperation, lobbed his Speed Graphic over the heads of Nixon and Khrushchev into the kitchen. I caught it, pushed a button, and lobbed it back; it promptly came back to me, reset, with the screamed imprecation "You had your hand over the aperture, you idiot!" When I tried to compose my picture again, getting in Nixon, Khrushchev, and the washing machine (I was, after all, publicizing the house and its equipment) some bulky Russian bureaucrat that nobody ever heard of had pushed his way through to the front, messing up the three-element composition—there was no way to get the washing machine in without including the damn bureaucrat. I shot the picture again anyway, as Nixon was making a stern gesture tapping the edge of one hand into the other hand's palm, catching Khrushchev looking nonplussed (and the damn bureaucrat with his eyes closed, served him right). I lobbed the AP camera back, narrowly missing the Soviet leader, who was trying to dominate Nixon but kept getting distracted with cameras whizzing past his head, and the AP wirephoto made just about every front page in the world. It is included in this book as Plate 1 following page 56.

Better still, a real photographer, Elliot Erwitt of Magnum Photos, made it into the kitchen later, taking a shot of Nixon jabbing a finger in Khrushchev's chest. The Russians had embargoed photos for a time after that

AP photo was sent showing their man getting the worse of the debate, so I smuggled the negative out of Moscow in my socks the next day; in repayment, Erwitt took a picture of the press agent at work in the kitchen.

With all this going on, I could only listen to snatches of the debate. From the room next to the kitchen, my homebuilder client stage-whispered, "What's he saying?" I listened for a minute to the translation of Khrushchev's riposte, stage-whispering back, "He says, 'You may be my guest, but truth is my mother'—it's an old Russian proverb." "That's no old proverb, he just made it up!" "Look, I only handle your publicity, not his."

Salisbury's notes, which he read to his confrères after the leaders moved on, showed Nixon to have handled the debate with dignity as well as tough-mindedness. When Khrushchev fulminated about American citizens having "the right to buy this house, or to sleep on the pavement at night —and you say we are slaves of Communism!" Nixon came back with a defense of the variety offered by the free enterprise system: "To us, diversity, the right to choose, the fact that we have a thousand different builders, that's the spice of life. We don't want to have a decision made at the top by one government official saying that we will have one type of house. That's the difference . . ." Khrushchev, who was using his temper skillfully, saw that Nixon could out-pious him in the don't-threaten-us department, and backed off; he was impressed with Nixon, and later told Mike Wallace of CBS that he had done all he could to help bring about Nixon's political defeat in 1960.

After the reporters and the crowd had left the house, I went back to the now-historic kitchen, opened the refrigerator, took out a beer and sat down on the range to think things over. I decided to go to work for Nixon, if I could; he didn't get upset when he was caught off guard, he knew how to seize an opportunity, he obviously had respect for—and knew how to play to—the press, he had a sure grasp of issues, and, cornball though it sounds, he made me feel proud of my country. He'd be a good President. I toasted his future and mine with warm beer; I had forgotten to hook up the refrigerator.

That night, at the American Embassy reception, Nixon had a few shots of vodka and loosened up, which I thought showed him to be not as stiff and plastic as reputed; when I introduced myself, he came right to my point with "We really put your kitchen on the map, didn't we?" The man understood self-interest. The episode that day was instructive about public-opinion formation, too. When the story of the kitchen conference was reported in the States, accompanied by the still pictures showing Nixon dominant, the impression was created that Nixon "won." Later, when the television tape of the color-studio debate was played—the first debate, which Nixon really "lost"—the impression did not change. People viewed the TV debate with the mental set that the American Vice President "stood up to the Russians" and the sight of him kowtowing did not cause them to waver. That meant that the writing press would remain important in the coming Age of Television, influencing viewers' opinions of what they saw. Something to remember. Something that Nixon never agreed with, either. "What's on the tube is what counts," he would say. "I've never been able to get anybody in my press operation who understood the power of television."

Six years later, as a private citizen who had been beaten to a political pulp in two elections, Nixon returned to Moscow as lawyer for John Shaheen's oil companies. A Canadian newsman slipped him the fallen Khrushchev's home address; Nixon rose from the dinner table where two Soviet Intourist guides had been assigned to stay with him, asked directions to the men's room, left the restaurant and took a cab to Khrushchev's apartment house, where he was met by two stone-faced, burly women who insisted Khrushchev was not there. Nixon pressed and got nowhere. Frustrated, he left a handwritten letter expressing the hope they could meet and talk again. The note was probably never delivered. If not destroyed, it may be the most interesting document in the Kremlin's file on Richard Nixon.

Seven years after that nonmeeting between nonpersons, Nixon returned to Moscow; this time I came along as Special Assistant to the President of the United States, the ringing title given to senior speechwriters. Times had changed. Nixon was the American President, a recent visitor to Peking where he had skillfully exploited the differences in the Communist world, the man who had reacted to the North Vietnamese last-ditch attempt at victory by mining Haiphong harbor, and in so doing had shown the Soviets that he knew they needed the summit more than he did.

When the Russian leader Nixon was dealing with first walked into the room, I recognized him. Leonid I. Brezhnev was the "damn bureaucrat" whose name nobody knew in 1959, who had elbowed his way into the picture and later pushed his way to the top of the Kremlin hierarchy.

Moscow is used in this prologue as a prism through which we can look at several Nixons: loser, loner, winner, leader, a fighter like Henry Armstrong or Tony Zale, always boring in, always coming back, always seeming as out of date as a metaphor about two long-forgotten middleweights. The fact is, Nixon has been on the national scene longer than any American politician in our history. Franklin D. Roosevelt ran on a major-party national ticket five times (including a Vice Presidential try in 1920); Nixon was the only other American who has matched that, and, like FDR, he won four out of five. He came back again and again. He almost survived.

If you are in your mid-forties, you have been for or against Richard Nixon in national elections, with only one exception, ever since you have been able to vote. He is part of you: a backboard, a mirror, a stimulant, a palliative, an object of your hate or adoration, your grudging respect or mild distaste, but like it or not he is a presence, the presence of the adult postwar generation.

This book is mainly about the active Presidency of Richard Nixon, before the fall; at times it will seem like watching an old movie in which many of the bit players later became stars. By coincidence, the day I left my office in the Executive Office Building happened to be March 21, 1973, the day that John Dean was making his revelations to the President; I recall passing the President's office, wondering if I should stop in to say goodbye, and thinking to hell with it, he was busy and did not care all that much about the departure of one speechwriter.

On political issues and philosophy, we see eye to eye about a great many things, giving much of what I recount here a pro-Nixon "tilt." He is a man worthy of respect, what he likes to call an *homme sérieux*, and yet he is a man deserving of anger, too, for betraying some of the best qualities in himself, a leader magnificent in defeat and vindictive in victory.

In this memoir, which is neither a biography of him nor an autobiography of me nor a narrative history of our times, there is an attempt to figure out what was good and bad about him, what he was trying to do and how well he succeeded, how he used and affected some of the people around him, and an effort not to lose sight of all that went right in examining what went wrong.

Here is the plan of the book. ("Game plan," a phrase that sportscaster Frank Gifford recalls was coined by Coach Vince Lombardi in the Fifties, was frequently used by President Nixon at meetings of the Cabinet Committee on Economic Policy—"Cabcomecopol," to the cognoscenti—and was picked up by economist Paul McCracken to describe the Administration's economic strategy. Bob Haldeman insisted on "game plans" from Jeb Magruder on everything from publicizing a speech to putting together a clipping book, until the President struck it out of a speech draft, with the admonition to me: "Don't use clichés.")

Through each of the ten sections run three strains: the President, the Partisan, the Person, ways of coming at part of the history of our own times through some facets of the man at the center.

As President, Nixon ended the war in Vietnam the way he always intended to—with "honor," that word that sent chalk-squeaking shivers up so many spines—and daringly and realistically reshaped American foreign policy. When history's jury comes in, he may well be best remembered for laying the foundation for what Nehru called "a generation of peace." In economics, the best advice he could muster could not solve the problem of getting inflation and unemployment down at the same time. In race relations, he at first tried to do the right thing but wound up doing the popular thing, which was not always the wrong thing. In returning "power to the people" he did more than he was credited with in decentralizing administrative control, though most of the power he sent out of Washington was snatched from the Congress, and not from the still-growing Executive Branch.

As a partisan, he had a heart too soon made cold, a head too soon made hot. But he was not, as he was widely thought to be, a party partisan; he sought a new alignment across party lines to shape a new majority, succeeded dramatically, and in the success tolerated the hatred and excess that corrupted his re-election and canceled his mandate, causing the Nixon Landslide to land on top of Nixon.

As a person, Richard Nixon is an amalgam of Woodrow Wilson, Niccolò Machiavelli, Teddy Roosevelt, and Shakespeare's Cassius, an idealistic conniver evoking the strenuous life while he thinks too much. Everybody who writes a book centering on Nixon turns amateur psychoanalyst, as I do infrequently, but at least I have been there with pencil in hand a few times when he was rambling along on the couch. The contribution this book seeks to make to the understanding of this man, who understands himself to be somebody else in public than in private, is in the true reports of revealing conversations. Does he enjoy campaigning? "It's something to get through." What motivates most people? "People react to fear, not love—they don't teach that in Sunday School, but it's true." What is it he likes about the business he is in? "Politics is poetry, not prose." An unexpected man. A presence.

About credibility. Whether the reader believes what the book says or not is less important than whether it will help him work out the truth, or as much of an understanding of the situation to be adjudged the whole truth. The us-against-them theme, a conscious effort to explain the reason for some of the excesses, appears in this work unconsciously as well: "critics" and "detractors" are quoted and "supporters" and "defenders" combat them. The controversy that Nixon sought (labeled "polarization" by those who sneered at Lyndon Johnson's stultifying attempts at "consensus") permeates an attempt to understand what was going on—to the extent that even this sentence contains a gratuitous shot at "those who."

The cheap ticket to credibility is phony balance: the generous concession, the open admission of error on minor points, lending credence to a defense of the important matters. Balance is not the author's aim, nor is credibility, nor is persuasion: in the year and a half since leaving the White House, just before the storm broke, I have been trying to figure this thing out for myself, and the only way to do that is to explain the way it was in context, neither in defense nor denunciation. If it helps the reader as well as the writer get a handle on the whys of Watergate it will be useful. Perhaps judgments of Nixon should not be "balanced." Should a baseball slugger who is thrown out at home be denied credit for hitting a triple? Will a "distant replay" show him to have been safe at home after all? The great danger in judging Nixon is to say "on the whole . . ." because he is neither pretty good nor pretty bad, his record not near-failure nor near-great. Nixon is both great and mean, bold and vacillating, with large blind spots in a remarkable farsightedness, and balanced judgments must give way to split decisions. He may be the only genuinely tragic hero in our history, his ruination caused by the flaws in his own character.

Such are the general guidelines of this book. (Working on an economic speech: "Mr. President, FDR once used the word 'yardsticks' in this regard." "Well, float out 'yardsticks,' Bill—and if it doesn't go, the hell with it, use 'guidelines.'") I hope to hang loose, not get overly mechanistic about the sequence of some events, and let the coverage of some themes move back and forth through time.

It is hard for me to realize this, but I have come to the point in life—and to the job in journalism—where, for the first time, I do not have anything to sell. So I Am a Camera, I am telling it like it was, or as nineteenth-century historian Leopold von Ranke put it, "wie es eigentlich gewesen war," how it actually happened. From time to time phrases like that will stud this book to lend sophistication and cachet and to reinforce Henry Kissinger's mistaken notion that I can read German.

Nothing could be more misleading, however, than to rely on the ultimate revelation of all the facts in deciding "how it actually happened," for the men on the scene at the time did not have all the facts, and an important part of what happened occurred because of what *seemed* to be happening. A man who lies, thinking it is the truth, is an honest man, and a man who tells the truth, believing it to be a lie, is a liar. (And even a profundity can be shallow.)

There is a serious purpose in any man's attempt to think through what he has been through, and to report what may be of service to the reader looking for clues toward an understanding of the past five years, but I do not intend to get solemn about it. Haldeman told me in 1968: "You'll be good for us, we're too stiff. I can't remember a joke. I try; I used to be a salesman, I needed jokes, but they would fly right out of my head. A lot of fascinating stuff goes on around here, funny stuff too, and it's lost forever—I only wish I could figure out a way to get it all down." (Oh, did he find a way.) A man wrote Leonard Garment a letter in early 1972 suggesting we give the lie to the rumors being spread by Nixon-haters in 1970 that the Nixon people were planning some kind of Nazi-style putsch, and of course those rumors evaporated as election time approached; Len forwarded it to me with a puckish "Sounds like a good idea to nail this lie—or were we really planning a putsch?" The President to Steve Bull, who had an unwanted politician waiting on the telephone: "Tell him—tell him you can't find me." Julie Eisenhower: "He does not get angry, or blow up, or anything like you read about him. Of course, there was the time when Mother dropped the bowling ball on his toe . . ." And Haldeman of martinet repute recommending a diet of tomato juice with a raw egg in it, with Pat Moynihan adding, "And it makes you act like a sonofabitch for eight hours."

Which brings me to the people around Nixon.

The company a President keeps reveals a good deal about himself, his political techniques, and his Presidency. The men around Nixon at the start were chosen by him to communicate with the powers who could have vetoed his nomination: the center of the Republican Party, wondering if that old slogan that killed Henry Clay, "Clay Can't Win," could be affixed to Richard Nixon. To overcome that fear, Nixon had to warm up to—or at least not offend—many of the people who mistrusted him most in the past. Liberal Kansas Congressman Bob Ellsworth and New York *Herald Tribune* editorial writer Ray Price and liberal Democrat law partner Len Garment made the scene; then, when hard delegate-hunting became the primary need, John Mitchell and Richard Kleindienst surfaced.

Mitchell was reflective of the good and bad in Nixon, and the rise and fall of that oddly romantic, loyal, and benumbed man is chronicled here; as in every case, the sketch is less of the aide than of the aide's effect on, or use by, Richard Nixon. Henry Kissinger is shown here to be an extension of Nixon's mind, and a fierce reinforcer of Nixon's penchant for secrecy, since the "bold stroke" and the leapfrog technique were the essence of the Nixon way of working. "Henry plays a hard game," Nixon once said, with admiration in his voice, because that is the kind of game Nixon liked to play himself, most often through others.

John Connally whistles through here like a Richard Cory, the "top Democrat" Nixon always wanted and could not get (Senator Henry Jackson was offered the Defense post and Hubert Humphrey the UN), exemplar of the man Nixon sometimes wishes he could be. "Every Cabinet should have a future President in it," Nixon told Ehrlichman—as he plucked Connally out of the Texas air, and later chose Elliot Richardson.

Daniel Patrick Moynihan was described by economic adviser Herbert Stein as the "Herbert Hoover of the Harding Cabinet," in the sense that he offered freshness and vitality to a seemingly gray group of men (as Hoover did, in the early Twenties, going on to a change of reputation to dourness later). Nobody, not even cagey, courtly Bryce Harlow, had the self-knowledge Moynihan had: "My half-life will last only until Ehrlichman discovers the Bureau of the Budget and Haldeman produces a telephone directory." Moynihan was an oddity, a concession Nixon made to his own facet of anti-establishment imagination, a flatterer nearly as skillful as Kissinger, a sad wit, an affirmative human being, a ray of hope who knew when to turn himself off and on.

Though Nixon admired and respected Arthur Burns, who was probably his most significant appointment in the long run, he was often annoyed and impatient with the Vermonter's slow, didactic style; with George Shultz, Nixon showed he could adapt to a strong and independent mind who could adapt to Nixon's style. Shultz was the Cabinet member Nixon knew least at the start, but he trusted Arthur Burns's judgment about Shultz, and ol' George lasted the longest of the originals. Shultz was and is a good man, of profound intellect and character, the best of all the Nixon men, a credit to the President who brought him forward and proof that a system does not corrupt an incorruptible man.

Ehrlichman came in as an arrogant man who had the appearance of a good man, and left as a better man with the appearance of an arrogant man. More than any of the men in close, he was a product of Nixon's, and worth observing in studying Nixon's creations. His doodles kept his interest from flagging in many a dull meeting, and a couple of them help enliven this book (as do the powerful abstractions of Elliot Richardson that tell you much about that frequently appointed gentleman, too. "Think of the pressure," Richardson's daughter once said, "only three years to go, and eight more Cabinet posts to fill.").

Doodles remind me of Haldeman. There is the man whose relationship with his President was similar in a way to that of Cathy and Heathcliff in *Wuthering Heights*—Cathy insisted she was not so much in love with Heathcliff, as she *was* Heathcliff—so too did Haldeman see his identity merged with Nixon's. But Haldeman would show what Nixon could conceal. Haldeman could be cruel in person as Nixon could be cruel in the abstract; Haldeman was the one who humiliated Ron Ziegler at meetings with his peers (not until 1973 did Nixon blow up at Ziegler with a shove in public, but that was at a time of great stress). Haldeman was known for his caution—when I asked what the President was currently reading, he would answer with another question, what books did I recommend the President read?—but Bob could also be sensitive and self-mocking, as was Nixon, which brings up the doodles.

"I'm writing this book, sympathetic but not sycophantic," I told him in early 1973. I wanted examples of personal notes the President had written in his own hand, and the permission to use them. But I have to tell you there will be whole chunks of this book the President is not going to like one bit."

"No sweat," Haldeman said. "Adds credibility. The Boss says to cooperate, and he doesn't expect a puff piece, you've disagreed with a lot of stuff along the way. That's what he says now," Haldeman smiled, "but wait'll he reads it—he'll go through the roof."

"Ehrlichman and Richardson gave me their doodles," I began, "which is a kind of interesting way to break things up."

"I know what you're getting at," Haldeman said. "The President does not doodle." My crest fell, and Haldeman nibbled his pencil for a moment. Then he looked at me with a humorously evil expression that spoke volumes about his understanding of image merchants in the throes of manipulation: "*Should* the President doodle?"

The information that I was authoring came as no surprise because when you've written one book, everybody you deal with in politics knows you're going to write another. This has an effect on how closely you are drawn into an inner circle, but Nixon was curiously trusting about what he said with a man in the corner writing it all down, and later I discovered that after 1970 a more trustworthy recorder than me was quietly spinning in the Signal Corps facility in the basement of the Executive Office Building. (Every Christmas, corpsmen in those corridors would build a cardboard-and-cotton Santa Claus, hang it on the door, fix it to an electric eye and boom out a recording of "Merry Christmas! Ho-ho-ho!" to terrified passersby.) I worked with a pencil and a shorthand of my own, never surreptitiously—if Richard Nixon did not want me there to write it all down, he didn't invite me in.

So there are great gaps. I would like to have been able to write firsthand about the handling of the Jordanian crisis, when Syrian tanks rolled across the border to support the Palestinian Arabs in the overthrow of King Hussein, evoking a classic in American diplomatic response—flexing muscles, using Israel, blocking the Soviets, stopping a small war without getting into a big one, but not letting our ally lose—that was Nixon at his best, and I missed it all. The Arab-Israeli war of 1973 took place after I left the White House and I will not pretend to be an insider on that.

Nixon at his worst could have been observed aboard the yacht *Sequoia*, at the time of G. Harrold Carswell's rejection by the Senate, where three men sat around "rubbing each other's sores," in Nixon's too-vivid figure of speech, and working up a rage that the President permitted to explode the next day. But the author wasn't there either.

And I write about China with all the perspective and insight that comes from a member of the staff who was left behind. I really cannot complain about that: Nixon fairly rotated his three senior writers on major trips, and I went on more than my share. Pat Buchanan drew the Peking assignment, since it was felt that a right-winger might best be along to dampen down the conservative reaction. That did not work with columnist William Buckley, who denounced the dealings with the Red Chinese throughout: that sparkling writer did not appreciate it when Bob Haldeman ran into him at a souvenir store in Peking and sweetly inquired, "Doing a little trading with the enemy, Bill?" But I could not ignore the historic China initiative, and so pass along the President's report to the Cabinet afterward verbatim—along with a provocative thought or two about how the Chinese dealings in 1971 affected the Nixon-Kissinger lust for, and sometimes necessary insistence on, secrecy.

Moynihan wrote a book about welfare reform, and John Newhouse a book about the SALT negotiations, absolving me of the need to go into those subjects in detail, and if I can find somebody on whom to unburden reams of dull notes on economic policy, there will be a book on that someday. Not by me.

After the flood of Watergate books, there should be plenty of "inside" books about the Nixon years, and many will be able to be more accurate and detailed than the literature of previous Administrations, for several reasons: the assignment of aides to write "memos for the President's file" on nearly every meeting—though Bill Rogers once cautioned, "The one who writes the notes makes his Boss look like a genius and the other guy look like a plunk"—and, of course, the goddam tapes.

Of course, no book has ever been produced on any Presidency as revealing and as damaging as the Nixon transcripts covering the period in the spring of 1973 when he was scurrying around to find his way out of the Watergate maze. That was Nixon at his weakest, showing his dependency on Haldeman and Ehrlichman, his disloyalty to Colson, his personal squeamishness in not facing up to John Mitchell himself, his moral blind-spot on the subject of eavesdropping. In trying to prove himself innocent of knowledge of the break-in and cover-up of Watergate, Nixon ultimately proved his own willingness to put image ahead of reality, his personal interest ahead of the national interest.

Those transcripts show Nixon's dark side. That side of Nixon was not a surprise to his long-time associates, as much of the material in this book about his feelings about the press indicates, but other facets reassured his friends that the whole man was nobly motivated by what he thought was best for his country. The Nixon of the transcripts was no more the "real" Nixon than the Nixon of the campaign documentary.

This book does not draw on the tapes, because those transcriptions are widely available, and there will be plenty of opportunity to hash them over in other histories. Nobody who worked with Nixon can read most of those tape transcripts without a sinking, disgusted feeling: sometimes they show Nixon to be, in his own words, a "dumb turkey"; at other times a vacillating, abandoned man, and then mean-spirited and vengeful. They show Nixon at his worst (except for that strain of loyalty and compassion that should not always be taken as venal), and the quotes that were immortalized at the conspiracy trial of his aides after his resignation and pardon—showing an arsenal of "smoking guns" which would surely have impeached, indicted and convicted him—are the worst of the worst. To Nixon-haters, Nixon at his worst is ambrosia; to anybody who wants to understand the man and his times, Nixon's dark side is by no means his only side.

What a good idea the goddam tapes must have seemed to be; in Nixon's old age, he could relive every glorious moment, write history as nobody could before—how Churchill would have envied him. And what a terrible idea it was—betraying the confidences of his associates, prolonging Watergate, thrusting the nation into Constitutional conflict—and for what? He was not too lazy to dictate a diary, as the chapter herein about a visit to the Lincoln Memorial shows, yet he wanted to hypnotize historians with the great events he was shaping in a way in which they could not refuse to believe.

The President's decision to tape-record meetings secretly—part of his casual attitude about eavesdropping generally—affects this book in this way: I am under pressure to report with terminological exactitude, uncomfortable or awkward as that may be at times. I often would have liked, as a good ghost is trained to do, to have been able to clean up and straighten out some of the language.

I was formerly an advocate; the pejorative term is "apologist." I do not apologize for having been an apologist. My job and my calling, as I saw it, was first to help refine a point of view, to fit into a framework, making allowances for political compromise; then to clothe that point of view in the most dramatic and persuasive words that came to mind; and then to help promote, project, and advance the man and the Administration that I was a proud part of.

To "know your place" is a good idea in politics. That is not to say "stay in your place" or "hang on to your place," because ambition or boredom may dictate upward or downward mobility, but a sense of place—a feel for one's own position in the control room—is useful in gauging what you should try to do and in setting criteria for a sense of personal satisfaction.

What was I to Richard Nixon, and what did I want to be? Aides can have a variety of ambitions: friend, gadfly, counselor, hatchetman, conscience, philosopher, footstool, amanuensis, spokesman, shoofly, interpreter—these and other roles are available to one who joins a great enterprise at or near the beginning. Available to choose from, not to try to blanket, for the nearer the proximity to the goal, the narrower the need for any individual and the smaller his slice of The Man.

I chose the oxymoronic role of sloganeering philosopher, or creative interpreter; I would like to have been what the Presidentologists call an "intimate adviser," but Haldeman explained once that Nixon considered me too "brittle"—that was the President's word for someone who would not hang tough over the long haul—and too much a loner. No complaints; I am better off in print than in court or in jail.

As Polly Adler would hasten to say, a place is not a niche: it can be a position to operate from, to observe from, and, when the time is ripe, to move from.

I was never a Nixon "intimate" the way Haldeman or Ehrlichman, or even Buchanan or Chapin or Ziegler, was. I was a proven loyalist, however, like Bob Finch and Herb Klein and Peter Flanigan, an Old Nixon Hand who could expect certain privileges of access and could exercise the right to be forthright, and after a time was expected to present an iconoclastic position. Until I discovered in 1973 that I had been wiretapped in 1969, I was sure that my proven loyalty gave me the widest latitude in associating with reporters and political adversaries who were known to Nixon as "them."

Because I believe no serious man can afford to be solemn, and because I enjoy the company of people who treat life more as a joy than a chore, I was generally seen to be "different": as I soft-sold some point of view about Nixon policies, religiously holding to an irreverent tone, I would be asked, "What is a nice Jewish boy like you doing in the Nixon White House?" And when I left to go to work as a columnist for the New York Times, Harrison Salisbury—another man I met in the Moscow kitchen—greeted me with a funny turnaround: "What's a nice Nixon man like you doing at the New York Times?"

He had a point. As a former New Yorker comfortable with the campaigns of Nelson Rockefeller and Jacob Javits, and as a new Washingtonian who enjoyed the company of the "Georgetown set," I could hardly be counted as an example of the Nixon mainstream. And back in New York, as a long-time Nixon loyalist, certified member of the Long March Back, with intense feelings about intellectual snobbery, a receptivity to a new kind of Federalism—and a genuine liking for both Nixon and Agnew—I hardly fit the mold of most people's stereotype of a liberal *Times*man.

In both cases this might have resulted in the status of house pariah, but in fact it has not: the trick in living against the grain of your closest associates is in hanging on grimly but good-humoredly to your own identity. I enjoy the swim upstream: you cover much less distance than a fish swimming with the current, but that fish hardly can tell he's moving and you feel as if you're going very fast.

Since I do not regret "selling" in the past, the reader may wonder if I am still selling, or condoning or justifying, or getting even, in this book. That's for the reader to decide; the intent here is to write about what I have learned and seen others learn about people and processes more than programs and policies; about men who had strength of character and defects in character who acted at times wisely or heroically, at times stupidly or villainously. It is not the whole story, not even all of the story one aide could observe, but it is a start on a side that has not been told. Nor will I burden this book with too many memoranda that made me look omniscient: I keep thinking of my 1971 memo to Haldeman, copy to John Dean, that began: "Why don't we make more of the fact that ours is a scandal-free Administration?"

Because I did not know anything that was going on in regard to bugging and burglary and ultimately Watergate and its concealment, a fairminded person might wonder whether I knew what was going on at all. Such a legitimate wonderment presupposes, however, that Watergate and its roots were "all"—and, hard though it may be to grasp in the midst of its aftermath, dirty tricks and security excesses did not occupy any of the time of most of the men in the White House. Of the men who were involved, during the first term it was considered one seedy but necessary activity in the defense of the nation, while so much else was going on. Nearly every action, in this small section of some men's activities, had a precedent—from the secret recordings in FDR's day to a tax break given Eisenhower on his book to the surveillance of Martin Luther King by the Kennedys—but the "everybody did it" defense, while providing some perspective, pales alongside the fact that nobody else did it so systematically or widely.

The Nixon Administration will never escape Watergate, but nobody who wants to understand what happened in Nixon's Presidency will succeed by becoming transfixed by its subsequent impeachment drama. A great deal more was going on at the time; Nixon and his men were trying to shape great events, not to seize dictatorial power. Perhaps historians will revise the angriest judgments of the mid-Seventies; perhaps the observations of a speechwriter who was sometimes an insider will help round out those judgments.

When Judge Samuel Rosenman, FDR's speechwriter, came down to Washington in 1969, I took him back to one of his old haunts, the Cabinet Room; he remarked at the change of portraits—the ones in his time had been replaced often, and the three men chosen by the current President to inspire his chief associates were Woodrow Wilson, Theodore Roosevelt, and Dwight Eisenhower—but then, misty-eyed, he pointed down to the end of the long table and said, "That's where Bobby Sherwood, Harry Hopkins, and I used to work on speeches. The walkway along the side there was built so the President could wheel himself in and out." He asked if we worked that way, in committee, and I said no—Nixon preferred to work with one writer on a single speech, and rarely in the White House, usually in his personal office across the street in the Old Executive Office Building. He gave a final look around the room and said, "It always seems so much smaller when you come back, from the way you remembered it." It always does.

Since this book is by a speechwriter, there is this danger: episodism. Writers in the Nixon years were not at the center of policymaking or decision (Clark Clifford would arch an eyebrow and Sam Rosenman would have waggled a jowl at this derogation of their powerful function) and would spend most of their time orbiting, holding their patterns, men in waiting, until the moment came. Then, suddenly, they were drawn closer to the center than anyone else, and for three days or a week could get a close-up view of history before being spun out once again to the periphery. That is why a non-intimate can write a fairly intimate memoir.

In the first few months of the Nixon Administration, when some old buildings were being demolished near the White House, there was a "rat scare"—field rats who lived in the foundations of the buildings being torn down were scurrying downtown, frightening people. The Department of Interior put down some poison in key places and soon the problem was solved.

A new problem arose: an animal lover wrote irate letters to just about everybody charging that the rat poison used was killing squirrels, and that the squirrel population of Washington was being decimated by the indiscriminate use of rat poison.

Mindful of the furor that animal lovers raised when President Johnson picked up a beagle by its ears, I checked and received fervent assurances that the rat poison spread was practically mother's milk to squirrels. Double-checking—never trust the bureaucracy—I talked to the White House gardener, a man with no partisan axe to grind, who told me that the only dead squirrel found on the White House grounds lately had been a friendly little fellow that he had known for years and who had died of old age. The gardener was sad about that.

Ron Ziegler, the President's press secretary, was my next stop. In case the question came up in a briefing, I wanted him prepared to refute the charge, and not to treat it as some kind of joke. We went through the documents together and he quickly went to the heart of the matter:

"Got it," Ziegler said briskly. "We're against the rats, we're for the squirrels."

That was Policy. For details, he could send questioners to the proper experts at Agriculture who knew all about poisons. As it happened, Ziegler was never asked the question, but that was no surprise, since we anticipated many questions that reporters never got around to asking.

As the years passed, I thought about the policy on the rats and squirrels: hastily arrived at, simplistic, ignoring all the shades and nuances that should be considered before the "easy answer" was proposed.

After all, both squirrels and rats are rodents. Although some wharf rats are disease carriers and should be exterminated on sight, most field rats live their lives of quiet desperation never interfering with the rat races of men, and indeed playing their necessary ecological role.

Nor is every squirrel a saint. Although their image is that of wisdom and thrift, tucking nuts away for the winter in an animal version of the work ethic, many—especially those in city parks—resort to begging, beginning a cycle of helpless dependency.

As Charles Colson, hatchetman, gutfighter, and one of the men closest to Richard Nixon, said a few months after he left the White House, and a few months before he copped a guilty plea: "I've discovered that all the guys we thought were our friends weren't so good, and all the guys we thought were our enemies aren't so bad."

PART ONE

THE COMEBACK

1. TWENTY BROAD STREET

Drafting a new introduction to the paperback edition of *Six Crises* in early 1968, I suggested some fairly frank language to two-time-loser Dick Nixon about his political depression in 1963, and he made it even franker:

"'No political future' was a fair statement. As a lawyer, I had a good career ahead, but as a political force, as I said at my 'last press conference' in 1962, I was through.

"I wish I could analyze the workings of American democracy and the mystery of public opinion that took a man from 'finished' in 1963 to candidate for the Presidency in 1968. I cannot. Not even a statesman who was also a great historian—Winston Churchill—could adequately explain why, after a decade in political eclipse, he was the one called upon to lead his nation in a time of crisis.

"There is no doubt, however, about what was not the reason for my candidacy today: it was not by dint of my own calculation or efforts. No man, not if he combined the wisdom of Lincoln with the connivance of Machiavelli, could have maneuvered or manipulated his way back into the arena."

Calculation and connivance there was, and a good deal of careful work, but Nixon's fatalism was understandable: after the Goldwater disaster, the rising protest against the Vietnam war, and the vacuum that seemed to exist among potential Republican "new face" candidates there did seem to be a confluence of events and a combination of forces that drew Nixon back from oblivion.

When he came to New York in late 1963, after Warner-Lambert chairman Elmer Bobst arranged for his name to be placed at the head of a prestigious but moribund law firm, Nixon was decidedly "through" as a potential political leader. Bill Rogers recalled those days: "It's hard now to understand how far down he was. He was broke. He had no future in the field he knew best. He was in Rockefeller's state and cut off." Bill and Adele Rogers took Pat and Dick Nixon to dinner at New York's "21" to welcome them; they all got a little high, and the happiest was Pat—glad to be rid of politics, where not even the victories were sweet. Afterward, Rogers did not see too much of his old friend from the Eisenhower days, because he did not want to be drawn into any "Nixon orbit" that might develop: New York was Rockefeller land, and Washington was where Rogers represented the Washington *Post*.

But there always seemed to be "Nixon people" around to help out in areas where the Available Man was called upon for help by local candidates. Charlie McWhorter, his former legislative aide, worked for AT&T in New York and kept in touch; Ned Sullivan, a second cousin of Pat Nixon's, was available for chores; and a variety of lawyers who just seemed to want to keep a loyal hand in kept popping up. I had dropped out of John Lindsay's campaign for Mayor of New York—too many hotshots acting like a palace guard, I thought—and decided to invest some spare time going for the brass ring with Nixon.

The first experience was not good. I rode out to New Jersey with him on October 24, 1965, after he had been asked to speak on behalf of Wayne Dumont, Jr., for Governor. Nixon had been talking to me about winning over the center, reaching out to some intellectuals, but when he got on the stump, out came a flag-waving denunciation of a Rutgers University professor who had said he would welcome a victory of the Viet Cong. To a cheering American Legion audience, Nixon asked: "Does an individual employed by the State have a right to use his position to give aid and comfort to the enemies of the United States in wartime?" and the five hundred Legionnaires and their wives roared back, "No!"

Riding home in a rented limousine—the only fee Nixon charged the men he supported was the travel expense—I asked him why he had dug back to the Fifties that way: Dumont had no chance to win, and an anti-Communist pitch wouldn't even work in California anymore. But he felt good about it: "Oh, I know you and the rest of the intellectuals won't like it—the men back at the firm won't like it either—but somebody had to take 'em on. Imagine a professor teaching that line to kids." I had to admit there was something to be said for a man who said what he thought against all good political calculation, but it turned out that there was an element of political calculation in it, too. The next day, to his "Christmas list" of supporters around the country went a copy of his statement in New Jersey, which was a toned-down version of the stump speech, and this letter:

RICHARD M. NIXON
20 BROAD STREET
NEW YORK, NEW YORK

October 26, 1965

Dear Bill:

On April 23, 1965, Eugene D. Genovese, a professor at Rutgers - a New Jersey state university - speaking at a teach-in on the university campus, stated: "I do not fear or regret the impending Vietcong victory in Vietnam. I welcome it..."

The Republican candidate for Governor, Senator Wayne Dumont, demanded that Professor Genovese be dismissed from his position because of this statement. His Democrat opponent, Governor Hughes, took the opposite position on the ground that Genovese's dismissal would be a violation of his right to free speech.

I thought you might be interested in seeing the statement that I made in support of Senator Dumont's position at Morristown, New Jersey, on Sunday, October 24.

With best wishes,

Sincerely,

Dick

Mr. Bill Safire
375 Park Avenue
New York, New York

I wasn't happy with it; neither was Leonard Garment, Nixon's law partner. Garment was the litigating partner in the firm of Nixon, Mudge, Rose, Guthrie and Alexander—handling cases that went before juries—and had an intuitive grasp of what persuaded people and what turned them away. A liberal, a Democrat, he had been prepared to believe all the stereotypes about Nixon but was surprised by his partner's analytical approach to the nation's problems. Nixon was working on Garment, an atypical Wall Streeter who once played the clarinet in Henry Jerome's band (at a tense moment at the Miami Convention a few years later, I burst into his hotel room to find Garment playing Mozart on his clarinet as a way of clearing his head). Between us, over the months, and with the help of a more conservative young lawyer in the firm, John Sears, we gave some intellectual depth to the position Nixon had taken in his written statement—and, trading, convinced him to adopt a position we believed to be more centrist and sound on a related subject of growing importance, campus dissent.

Nixon would not back away from his position against the specific professor—when it came to matters he identified as support for U.S. troops abroad, he dug in his heels—but at a commencement address at the University of Rochester, he presented it more reasonably: "I believe that any teacher who uses the forum of a university to proclaim that he welcomes victory for the enemy in a shooting war crosses the line between liberty and license. If we are to defend academic freedom from encroachment we must also defend it from its excesses."

After a lot of discussion that seems significant in retrospect, he went on to espouse a position on a subject that was central to his future, the erosion of which ultimately cost him dearly:

> Examine the spectrum of freedom. At one extreme is anarchy—too much freedom, where nobody is really free at all.
>
> At the other end of the spectrum is tyranny—the totalitarian state which stresses order to the exclusion of personal liberty.
>
> In the center is limited freedom, with its very limits posing a kind of defense perimeter against the extremes of anarchy and tyranny.
>
> Here at the points of contact—on the defense perimeter of freedom—is the area of the most difficult choice.
>
> It is easy enough to avoid the choice, to try to escape the tensions along the perimeter by advocating the extreme positions of total control or no control.
>
> The simple answers, the easy solutions, lead to the simple and easy destruction of liberty. The hard choices, the delicate balances along the perimeter of limited freedom, are the ones you will have to face. Not one of us will be right in his choice every time—but we will always be right to face the hard choices as to where to draw the line.
>
> If you agree that a line must be drawn somewhere, as I believe most members of the academic community do, the next question is— where do you draw that line?
>
> I submit that no one person, and no single group has the right or the power to draw that line by itself. Only through the interplay of free discussion can a balance be struck, with each of us willing to speak out on our interpretation of the line that not only limits—but defends —academic freedom.

In the course of working on that speech in his 20 Broad Street office —with its ivory elephants, souvenir gavels, and gifts from potentates met on his Vice Presidential travels—we came across an idea for a contrapuntal line, like one of those that Ted Sorensen did so well for John Kennedy. It didn't quite come off, so I started to move to the next paragraph, but Nixon knew what I was after, and he hung in there—for twenty minutes we worked on a single line. I was surprised; politicians I had known would not do that. Nixon liked a "quotable quote"; he had respect both for language and for President Wilson:

"Woodrow Wilson's distinction between men of thought and men of action can no longer be made. The man of thought who will not act is ineffective; the man of action who will not think is dangerous."

Nixon could not resist sending Garment and myself copies of a conservative criticism he received from former President Dwight David Eisenhower:

DDE

GETTYSBURG
PENNSYLVANIA 17325

June 13, 1966

Dear Dick:

Thank you for your note of the seventh and the text of the talk you made at the University of Rochester. Incidentally, it is one of my favorite institutions; I particularly admire its young president, Wallis.

I agree with almost everything you say—your line of reasoning is sound. Basically you agree that the maximum of human liberty can exist only in an orderly, self-governing society. To determine the correct degree of human liberty on one side and orderliness in our society on the other, has long been a subject of political debate.

For myself I am a bit skeptical about the assertion that teachers and students possess a special freedom in America. Academic freedom is merely one of the freedoms that we enjoy; it is difficult if not impossible to name one that could be completely eliminated without causing the destruction of all. But the specific statement that creates in me a considerable doubt is the one you make near the bottom of page four where you say, ". . . *academic freedom should protect the right of a professor or student to advocate . . . communism. . . .*"

Communism is a very special sort of doctrine in that it openly advocates destruction of the form of government by violence, if necessary, that protects all the freedoms we enjoy. I personally disagree with the Supreme Court decision of some years back that released a lot of Communists convicted under the Smith Act from prison on the theory that it is all right to *advocate* Communism as long as the individual *did not take any overt action to destroy our form of government.* Take for example Tom Paine and George Washington. Obviously Tom Paine had far more to do in bringing about the revolt against Britain than did George Washington, yet under the Supreme Court doctrine of today, Paine would have gone scot-free in the event the revolt failed, while Washington would have been hanged. This is the only statement in your paper with which I disagree.

Possibly, I am just stubborn.

With warm personal regard,

As ever
D.E.

In 1966, Garment's most exciting time with Nixon was spent on the Hill case. The Hill family had sued *Life* magazine for sensationalizing an incident involving their captivity by escaped convicts—an incident made into the play *The Desperate Hours* in 1955. The family had to move away from their neighborhood to escape the publicity; their unwanted notoriety damaged them, and Nixon and Garment fought the case up to the Supreme Court. I was fascinated—the right to privacy had been important to me ever since reading Louis Brandeis' famous article about it—and the fact that Nixon not only chose this case to argue but handled it so well in argument before the Supreme Court was impressive to civil libertarians. Nixon lost the case on a 5–4 decision but won supporters among men close to him who had previously been wary observers. (The Hill family was able to get a substantial out-of-court settlement from *Life.* Nixon wrote a 2,500-word memorandum to Garment after the argument, criticizing his own performance as a lawyer, which—while too complex to go into here— revealed both his introspective bent and grasp of Constitutional issues.)

What fascinated Nixon, however, was not the general right to privacy of the Hill family, but the specific right to privacy *from the press.* The right to privacy from the government (as in wiretaps) did not enter into it, as Sears and I were to discover later.

I was able to sell the North American Newspaper Alliance on syndicating a series of ten articles by Nixon about the issues of the 1966 campaign: Nixon considered this no small breakthrough, for it gave him an outlet in forty important newspapers, especially in the West and South, and provided the income ($10,000) for the salary of Patrick J. Buchanan, the first full-time new Nixon "staffer." Buchanan, then twenty-eight, brought a conservative ideology and a punchy prose style from his job as an editorial writer at the St. Louis *Globe-Democrat,* and also brought a sense of amused wonderment, as if to say, "Do you guys realize what we're doin'?" He called himself "Aide to Richard Nixon" and drafted many of the NANA pieces; a romance between single people bloomed in the law office, which is always a happy sign in a campaign, and five years later Buchanan was to marry Shelly Scarney, a serene and lovely Nixon secretary, with the President in attendance recalling the early days when they had started work together.

At that time, "Campaign '66" was under way, financed and headed by Maurice Stans, formerly Eisenhower's Budget Director (who liked to point out that he was the last man to balance the Federal budget, and would go off every year on a big-game hunting safari); Peter Flanigan, a hard-working investment banker and Old Nixon Hand from the '60 campaign; and law partner Tom Evans, acting as executive officer. We met in the Metropolitan Club off Fifth Avenue, plotting delightedly on green felt tablecloths, with Nixon usually coming in at the end of the meeting to give lift: "You're natural conspirators," he would say with a wink, and in a minor-league way we were.

There are two moments in "Campaign '66" in which I had a part and are worth recording here. One has to do with Nelson Rockefeller, who wanted to run against Lyndon Johnson, and the other has to do with Lyndon Johnson, who wanted to run against Richard Nixon.

2. DEAR NELSON

The relationship between Richard Nixon and Nelson Rockefeller in 1966 was that of a mongoose and a cobra temporarily called upon to work side by side. They had fought before and would fight again, but while Rockefeller was running an uphill race for re-election and Nixon was running around the country supporting Republicans, they agreed to a truce so they could oppose some common enemies.

Nixon had nipped Rockefeller's Presidential bid in the bud in 1959; Rockefeller drove a bargain for his support of the platform at the 1960 Convention with the "Compact of Fifth Avenue" that made Nixon appear to be a suppliant; Rockefeller went through the motions of campaigning for Nixon in 1960, but the Nixon people knew he was dragging a foot; Rockefeller needed Nixon to help stop Goldwater in 1964, which Nixon declined to do; when Nixon came to New York in 1963 to work as a Wall Street lawyer, Rockefeller effectively froze the transplanted Californian out of all state political activity, for fear he would establish a "base." Subtly underscoring these maneuverings of ambitious leaders was the fact that each of them harbored, and in private did not conceal, a hearty personal dislike for the other.

Their strange bedfellowship in 1966 began with a fund-raiser's innocent blunder. Austin Tobin, Jr., a Rockefeller fund-raiser, got the bright idea one summer day to include Richard Nixon's name in a solicitation letter to conservative Republicans. Without checking with anyone else in the Rockefeller entourage, Tobin asked John Shaheen, whom he knew to be a Nixon supporter and law firm client, to see if Nixon would be willing to go on the letterhead.

Nixon told Shaheen that this seemed like a strange way to go about a rapprochement. He remembered an episode when William Miller, Barry Goldwater's running mate in 1964 and a former New York Congressman, came out for Rockefeller for Governor in the early spring of 1966: Jackie Robinson, on the Rockefeller staff, denounced him and demanded that the Governor repudiate his support, which he did, leaving Miller high and dry. Nixon suggested that Shaheen check the matter out with Jack Wells and me. As a known Nixon man on the Rockefeller-for-Governor payroll, I was a likely conduit.

It turned out, as Nixon suspected, that nobody high up knew anything about it. The request for Nixon's support of Rockefeller was discreetly withdrawn. But the idea was intriguing to Wells and William Pfeiffer, a crusty politician managing the Rockefeller campaign. The "Western tier" of New York State was weak, and Syracuse, the state's third largest city, was a hotbed of conservative distaste for the Governor.

As the campaign moved into its last week, the *Daily News's* highly regarded straw poll showed Rockefeller trailing Democrat Frank O'Connor, and the pros knew where much of the weakness lay—among conservative Republicans, especially in and around Onondaga County, the environs of Syracuse.

Until that time, Rockefeller's attitude about Nixon was that he "needed no outside help" and that Nixon, despite his New York residence, was an "outsider." Nixon had respected this and whenever he campaigned in New York for a Congressman and was asked about a Rockefeller endorsement replied, "The Governor has specifically said that he sought no outside help. Of course I will vote as a Republican." This kind of left-handed endorsement made it clear to many Republicans who disliked Rockefeller and liked Nixon that the support for Rockefeller was lukewarm at best.

On Monday, October 31, Jack Wells called me into his corner office at the New York Hilton and laid it on the line:

"Dick Nixon is going to be speaking Wednesday night in Syracuse on behalf of a couple of Congressional candidates. Bill Pfeiffer and I think it would be a good idea for Dick to come out with a strong endorsement of Rockefeller."

"What about the Miller syndrome?"

"We're cured. Think he'll play?"

"For old times' sake?" I asked.

Wells grinned. "See what it would take."

Nixon was speaking in Lodi, New Jersey, that night, and I drove out to hear his speech and to ride back in the car with him. It was Hallowe'en, and the red, white, and blue bunting clashed with the black and orange witches and hobgoblins in the meeting hall, but Dick was in form, with the one-liners working and the crowd enthusiastic.

In the limousine afterward, feet up on the jump seat, he examined the authentic Rockefeller "probe."

"We'd have to watch out for anything like the Miller thing." I assured him that would not be a problem, that I could get a guarantee from Wells that both Rockefeller and Senator Jacob Javits would publicly welcome the endorsement.

The "buttinsky" problem was more difficult. "I've been consistent in campaigning only in those areas that requested me," Nixon said. "Would Nelson be willing to admit that he had changed his mind, and asked me to speak up for him in New York? Won't be easy for him. Let me sleep on it."

Next morning at eight o'clock—this was November 1, one week before Election Day—Nixon called me at home and made these suggestions: If Nixon were to be used for Rockefeller in New York State, he had to be used strongly. A statewide five-minute television appearance would be the answer. In it he would point out that he had campaigned for Congressmen throughout the United States, would press for election of Republican Congressmen in New York State, would stress the necessity of the two-party system and in that context add a strong pitch for Rockefeller and the entire state ticket.

Nixon recognized Rockefeller's difficulty in admitting that he had changed his mind and asked Nixon to campaign for him. With the *Daily News* poll showing Rockefeller trailing O'Connor, this reversal would appear to be a desperation move. Nixon was willing to "voluntarily" come out for Rockefeller provided he was certain that (a) his endorsement would be received with enthusiasm by Rockefeller and Javits, and (b) Rockefeller would help Nixon elect Congressmen in Iowa by helping to finance an Iowa telecast.

That was quite a package—better for Nixon than it was for Rockefeller. Nixon was proposing to come to the rescue in a way that could only be construed as a rescue effort. That would take some pride-swallowing by Rockefeller. Nixon was also proposing to provide a fig leaf by "volunteering" his aid "without being asked," but coupling this with a request for Rockefeller money to help win a few squeaker races for Republicans in Iowa, on the basis that if you wanted help from the party, you should be willing to give help to the party.

I told Nixon I thought Rockefeller would rather spend the rest of his life on a ranch in Venezuela than agree to all of this, but it would be an interesting discussion and was worth a try.

Jack Wells called a meeting in a Hilton room at 10 A.M. Present were Governor Rockefeller, Bill Pfeiffer, William Ronan, with Senator Javits joining us toward the end.

Wells began by carefully protecting my back. "Bill here is an old friend and loyal supporter of Dick Nixon. His firm has been helping us in this campaign. All aboveboard. Yesterday, I asked him to talk to Dick about speaking up for the Governor in Syracuse when he's there tomorrow night. Here's his report."

I pointed out first, and repeated for emphasis, that if Rockefeller wanted to admit publicly that he had asked Nixon to campaign for him in New York State, then Nixon would do whatever Rockefeller requested. If, however, Rockefeller wanted to avoid the appearance of "needing" Nixon, which was understandable, then Nixon would need a graceful way to volunteer his endorsement. In the course of a statewide Congressional telecast, such an endorsement would be natural and could not be interpreted as Nixon "butting in."

Then I laid out the other suggestions. Throughout what I had to say, Bill Ronan—a former professor who served as Rockefeller's right-hand man in government—kept shaking his head. He did not want help from Nixon at all. Pfeiffer, the political pro, registered understanding but no reaction. The Governor sat on the edge of a desk, his legs dangling, looking at the floor glumly. I finished. There was a pause, and Rockefeller said incredulously: "Iowa!"

Wells said that Nixon's Iowa suggestion was for a legitimate party purpose and was quite proper. Pfeiffer was disturbed about the possibility that a focus on Nixon caused by statewide TV would upset a New York *Post* endorsement expected the next day. Ronan kept shaking his head; Rockefeller remained silent.

Senator Javits came in and I went through it again for him. His opinion was expressed crisply, without waiting to hear what others had said: "The Iowa contribution doesn't bother me. But a telecast like that would make Nixon the issue in New York in the closing days, and it would cost more votes than it would gain. What do you say, Nelson?"

"Iowa!" said Rockefeller again, this time in a hoarse whisper. Then he added that he didn't want a controversy about Nixon at the end of the campaign.

Pfeiffer suggested that I ask Nixon simply to speak up for the state ticket in Syracuse "without being asked."

I asked Rockefeller what his reaction would be to that endorsement. Rockefeller sighed and said, "Delighted." Javits said, "I would be willing to go up and down the State of New York saying that Dick Nixon had every right to endorse anybody he pleased, and I was glad that he saw fit to endorse Nelson Rockefeller."

Rockefeller said, "Isn't there anything else we have to worry about?" and I left.

In a subsequent telephone conversation Wells told me that it would be a good idea for Nixon to "be a good soldier" at Syracuse. Although the Iowa request was turned down, he pointed out that Rockefeller had reversed himself on the "outsider" worry and that Nixon would understand why Nelson could not be in the position of asking him for help.

At 6 P.M., November 1, Nixon called me from Minnesota and was briefed on the meeting. He seemed a little testy when told of Javits' sharp reaction but said he could well understand Rockefeller's reluctance to admit any need.

I pointed out that Rockefeller was behind in the polls and recommended that Nixon do what the Rockefeller group had asked, adding that Wells—who supported the original Nixon suggestion at the meeting—in particular wanted Nixon to "be a good soldier."

Nixon said, "Don't say what I am going to do. But you can tell Wells that I will do the right thing." I reported to Wells that Nixon would "do the right thing." Jack seemed relieved.

As Nixon headed toward Syracuse, I ruminated on what I thought was a Rockefeller political mistake. Politics is a business of give and take; in this case, from his side, it was all take and no give. He had good reason not to sponsor Nixon on statewide TV but could have helped those candidates in Iowa. That would have been a compromise showing some understanding of the political life, leaving open the possibility of a warily amicable relationship in the future. But he wanted everything—including protection against having asked for support—and was prepared to give only the assurance of a nonrejection in return.

Nixon took this rebuff in good grace and went on—in New York *Post* reporter Murray Kempton's words—"to sketch his profile in political courage by mentioning Rockefeller's name in Syracuse." It was a full, unstinting endorsement. Nixon had been a good soldier.

Late the next morning, I was at Rockefeller headquarters basking in the glow of party unity when I saw the early edition of the afternoon newspaper, the *World Journal Tribune*—which said that Rockefeller's press spokesman, informed of the Nixon endorsement, reacted coolly. That was not a negotiation rebuff—that was a double-cross.

I ran down the hall, past Wells's and Pfeiffer's offices, and went downstairs to take the subway to 20 Broad Street. There, from Nixon's office, I called Wells.

"Calm down," he growled before I could get started. "I couldn't tell anybody in advance what Nixon would say and how we should react. Now I got to our press people and they're putting out the right story. It'll be on the wires in twenty minutes."

It was. In less than a half hour, Wells called to read me the warm reception that Nixon's Syracuse endorsement of Rockefeller was getting from the Governor, Senator Javits, everybody.

As an afterthought, I mentioned that a little private note from his principal to mine might not go amiss, in the light of the missed signal. The next day, a warm letter arrived expressing the Governor's gratitude.

The idea of a thank-you note turned out to be my biggest contribution to the dealings between the two men. On Tuesday morning, November 8, 1966—which was to be Nixon's first good-news Election Day in exactly ten years—Nixon wrote an intriguing "Dear Nelson" answer to Rockefeller.

He began by replying to the Governor's thank-you note as "thoughtful and gracious but not at all necessary. As we both know from long experience, some of our friends in the press have determined the plots for their political scenarios long in advance. Whenever the dialogue doesn't fit their preconceived notions as to what the participants should be doing and saying at a particular time, they simply change the facts to fit their plots!"

After wishing him well, Nixon put a curious idea forward: "Whatever happens tonight, I recognize that we will probably continue to have different views as to the personalities who should prevail at the Presidential and Vice Presidential level. Completely apart from those differences, I hope that some time during the months ahead we can sit down and have a good talk about foreign policy. I am deeply distressed by the fact that the

Johnson Administration has failed to come up with one single new idea in the field of foreign policy during the three years it has been in office. I also believe that not only in Asia, where we have an immediate problem, but particularly in Europe there are situations which simply cry out for new initiatives.

". . . My suggestion is so way out that nothing may materialize from it, but it would be quite exciting and intriguing if the two of us could sit down, as we did in times gone by, and provide some much needed leadership in the foreign policy area."

Typically, Nixon provided an out for both Rockefeller and himself: "This letter is not being written 'for the record,' but solely in personal terms. If the idea does not appeal to you I, of course, will understand and I am sure we shall both find other areas of interest which will more than take up what time we can devote to such activities."

And, finally, Nixon, who did not jest at scars because he had felt the wounds, closed with this one-pro-to-another paragraph: "When the history of this campaign is written, it will be recorded that win, lose or draw you fought a most gallant battle. It took an incredible amount of courage to look at those unfavorable polls early this year and then to make a horse race out of the contest. There are plenty of people who can put on a good campaign when things are going their way. What separates the men from the boys is that rare ability which you have demonstrated in this contest to fight at your best when the odds were greatest."

To my knowledge, Rockefeller never replied. If he had not rebuffed Nixon's overture, if the two men worked together in the next year on foreign affairs—ah, if only, who's to say what might have happened. But if the Governor had decided to work together with Nixon without absolutely needing to, then he would not be Nelson Rockefeller.

Flashforward to November 1968, aboard *Air Force One* with President-elect Nixon during the interregnum, as he went over Cabinet possibilities. Nelson Rockefeller had been frequently suggested for several posts.

"At Treasury," I said, "what about David Rockefeller—no, you can't have two Rockefellers in the Cabinet."

"Is there a law," Nixon asked without changing expression, "that you have to have one?"

3. TURNING POINT

There is an old pro who scorns the wearing of buttons during campaigns, but who sports this one on Election Night: "Great Job, Kid, Now Get Lost." Dick Nixon's friends wondered whether that would be the attitude of the party toward Nixon after the campaign. Tom Dewey, after 1948, was always warmly welcomed as a Grand Old Supporter, but he knew that if a tinge of suspicion arose that he might become a candidate again, the warmth would surely turn to heat. "We love you, but not for candidate" —would that be the party regulars' attitude toward Nixon?

There was good reason to think so. The Republican National Committee, under Ray Bliss, was being scrupulously correct long before it needed to be: Nixon's campaigning for the Congressional candidates was on his own, with no help offered by the RNC. Bliss, a nonideological technician who replaced Goldwater's Dean Burch after the 1964 debacle, had purchased a half hour of network television on the Sunday before Election Day for a campaign film. Word got out in late October that the film was far too gutty and abrasive, and would likely backfire against Republicans. We tried to get him to assign the time to the one Republican who was campaigning nationally, Richard M. Nixon, who knew how to use a half hour. Bliss would not consider the suggestion; the Romney people, he led us to believe, would never go along with Nixon acting as the party spokesman. (Of course, they were right.)

So Nixon stumped the country, blazing away at Lyndon Johnson on the inflation front ("the high cost of Johnson," "the War on Poverty has become the War on Prosperity") providing a focal point for local races, churning up publicity for Congressional candidates, making friends, giving a national sense of party to a group still wandering in the wilderness after 1964.

But on foreign affairs, Nixon's strongest suit, we were hamstrung: on Vietnam, we didn't have a villain. Nixon could criticize the conduct of the war, but not the war itself; with the nascent peace movement beginning to make noises, any Nixon criticism of the way Johnson was operating in Vietnam could be construed as taking the side of the war critics, which was not where we wanted to be at all. So Nixon remained generally in support, picking up what credit he could for not being partisan beyond the water's edge.

Then LBJ pulled a pre-election rabbit out of his hat: a conference of Asian nations to be held in Manila in mid-October 1966 which he would attend.

A week before he left for Manila, however, Johnson made a tactical political mistake that presaged a much greater error he was to make later in the campaign. He left his "consensus" position to attack the Republican Party as a party of "fear and negativism," which might have gone by as standard political hyperbole, had he not added that Republican gains might cause the nation to "falter and fall back and fail in Vietnam."

As Tom Wicker of the New York *Times* put it, "Richard M. Nixon, the most adept of the Republican issue-makers, lost no time in seizing on Mr. Johnson's invitation to partisan warfare." Nixon did this in the most nonpartisan way—by pointing to the fact that the voices of dissent had been coming from within the Democratic Party, not from the "loyal opposition." But the President's jab opened the way to Nixon's apparently reluctant and unassailable separation from Johnson's position on Vietnam. The difference of the two men's approaches was real—Nixon did not approve of "gradualism"—and now Nixon could permit some of the difference to show without being the one who "undercut" the President on foreign affairs.

But Johnson's plans for a trip to the Manila Conference effectively squelched his Republican opposition. In a September 28 statement, Nixon suggested that Johnson "repudiate" a couple of previously announced positions: that a conference be held in Geneva rather than in Asia for Pacific peace, and that UN Ambassador Arthur Goldberg should stop offering a bombing halt in exchange for a "secret promise" to de-escalate. To my knowledge, no newspaper ran Nixon's statement.

In a Chicago press conference on October 7, Nixon could only damn with faint praise: "The Manila Conference presents President Johnson with his first initiative in the area of foreign policy. That conference must not be made simply the scene of a grandstand play for votes." Nixon did what he could to gently fan the suspicion of political design in the timing of the conference without making any accusations: "The timing was certainly not designed to hurt the Democrats, but who is to say? There might have been other genuine reasons for holding it now." He could not resist an added barb: "This is the first time a President may have figured the best way to help his party is to leave the country."

Proposing that the President come back with a "Pacific Charter" (as a play on FDR's "Atlantic Charter," that set a goal that President Johnson might find hard to achieve), Nixon then tipped off his friends that he would be looking hard and closely at the communiqué which would be issued at the end of the conference: "If [the conference] produces something effective, it will have a massive effect on the election, but I don't believe the electorate will be impressed with any manifesto from Manila which tells us nothing." With that, he declared a moratorium on comment until the President returned to the United States, which would be just before the election. (Nixon enjoyed declaring moratoria; it was one of his favorite locutions, far more impressive than having to say, "I won't have anything to say for a while.")

One October morning, I opened the *Times* in my office in New York's Seagram Building expecting to find a diplomatically ambiguous, carefully drawn document. The news story about the Manila Communiqué was of little interest, so I turned to the official text. I read it, couldn't quite believe it, and read it again.

In essence, Johnson proposed "mutual withdrawal"; now, in retrospect, mutual withdrawal sounds like what we wanted all along. But the U.S. position evolved into mutual withdrawal much later on—only after Vietnamization built up the South's forces. Back in 1966, a mutual withdrawal proposal with no cease-fire guarantee meant that the United States and North Vietnam should get out and let the Viet Cong pulverize the South Vietnamese Government. It meant rejecting the "invasion" concept under which we first became involved, and accepting the "civil war" idea under which we should never have become involved.

Moreover, there was a line in the communiqué that I knew Nixon would spot since "surrendering the initiative" was a frequent criticism he had privately made of Johnson's Vietnam policy: "[allied] military action and support must depend for its size and duration on the intensity and duration of the Communist aggression." That would put us in the position of reacting rather than acting—letting the enemy set the timing for intense action and breathing spells.

I banged out a few pages of a critique and called Pat Buchanan on the road, arranging to meet Nixon in New Jersey. Nixon's criticism would be more newsworthy in the form of a letter to President Johnson, I thought. Buchanan felt that was too gimmicky, and Nixon was not sure, he wanted to look at it first.

In a hotel room in New Jersey, I took my notes along with a series of thoughts from Nixon and a previous statement of Buchanan's and dictated them to Rose Mary Woods in "Letter to the President" form, ending each subject with a complex question. Since few questions were then being asked in the press, I thought the approach might capture attention.

Nixon looked over the draft and shook his head no. The letter format did not appeal to him. And he wanted more time to think about the substance. We agreed to meet back in his law office in New York two days later for a rewrite.

On the morning of November 3, five days before election, Buchanan told reporters there would be an important "Appraisal of Manila" from Nixon that afternoon.

Nixon kept fiddling with it, I kept rewriting passages, and the statement threatened to run longer than the communiqué. There was excitement in the 20 Broad Street office; secretaries Rose Woods, Shelley Scarney, and Anne Volz were typing portions of the manuscript, I was going from one to another with changes, and Buchanan was telling the reporters who came up to the law offices early that we would be ready in plenty of time. I had not seen Nixon under deadline pressure for a long time; I remember thinking then that I wished he would not get so ostentatiously calm, it slowed everything up. But he was determined not to make a foreign-policy mistake.

The analysis was legalistic, properly sober-sided, and ran about 2,500 words, but its essence can be caught in the questions that ran through the text:

1. Does this new Manila proposal for mutual withdrawal by the United States and North Vietnam mean that we are now willing to stand aloof and let the future of the South Vietnamese be determined by the victor of a military contest between the Viet Cong and the Government of South Vietnam?

2. In view of American co-sponsorship of the Manila Communiqué, may we now assume that the United States rejects a return to Geneva as a forum for the peace conference on Asia?

3. Will we, as the communiqué indicates, limit our military response to the fluctuating intensity of Communist aggression? Or shall we move in the other direction as General Eisenhower recommends, and increase the intensity of our military effort to shorten the war and to reduce American and allied casualties?

4. How many more American troops—in addition to this latest 46,000 —do we currently plan to send to fight in Vietnam in 1967? Will the draft quota, which reached a fifteen-year high in October, have to be raised again to meet our troop requirements?

5. Does the Johnson Administration, as is widely predicted, intend to raise taxes after November 8 to pay the rising costs of the war? Or will the President follow the proposed Republican route of cutting nonessential spending to provide the funds for this conflict?

Nixon had one additional question for me: "Do you think this will get any sort of play in the papers?" I said I thought it might if we would only finish it up so that it could make the A.M. deadlines. "Do you suppose," he said, "they would run the text in the New York *Times?*"

That is what I had been thinking about, too. When a story gets front-paged, that's good; but when the New York *Times* runs the full text inside, then the most influential paper is saying, "This is really important; this deserves study; this belongs in the permanent record." Very little of what Nixon had said while Vice President had seen its text run in the *Times*, and nothing since he came to New York in 1963.

I called Harrison Salisbury, the assistant managing editor of the New York *Times*, told him what Nixon was doing, and asked him if the *Times* would consider running the full text. He was polite but pointed out that

this was hardly a document of the nature of the Manila Communiqué itself. I sold as hard as I ever sold anything in my life, appealing to the
Times's sense of political fairness, to their news sense, to their neglect of
Nixon in past weeks, even to our moments together in the Moscow kitchen
(Salisbury took the pool notes there, the reader may recall). He would
not give me any assurances but said he would look it over himself and discuss it with the other editors at the *Times*—if, of course, we put it quickly
into the hands of the *Times* reporter sitting in the outer office at that
moment.

I snatched pages out of the hands of secretaries, stapled them together,
and handed them to Buchanan, who dealt them out to the reporters out
front. It was an eight-point appraisal with—as I look at the mimeographed
handout today—only seven points in it. Either it was numbered wrong or
we left out a crucial paragraph, but there comes a time when you have to
go into production.

The text ran next morning in the New York *Times*. Richard Nixon was
not the only one who recognized the importance thus given his appraisal
of Manila: Lyndon Baines Johnson saw the front page story and went
through the roof of the White House.

Not since Harry Truman lashed out at a music critic had an American
President dumped such abuse on an individual. In a full-fledged news
conference, Johnson zeroed in on Nixon as a "chronic campaigner . . .
never realized what was going on even when he had an official office . . .
in California, you saw what the people did . . . waited in the wings for
Senator Goldwater to stumble . . . an attempt to pick up a precinct or
two or a ward . . ."

It was terrible. But for Nixon, it was wonderful. Ladybird Johnson, who
sat along the wall, kept shaking her head and trying to catch her husband's
eye to stop. Jack Valenti, a top Johnson aide, later told me: "I don't know
what got into him. I never saw him like that in public before. It was so obvious that Nixon had gotten his goat and that he was just playing into
Nixon's hands."

Johnson's press conference remarks that morning in 1966 were widely
interpreted as an outburst of temper, a tirade as unplanned as it was un-
called for. I accepted the conventional wisdom for years but my own
White House service made me wonder—hadn't President Johnson been
briefed on the likely questions that morning? Was he losing his temper
or using it? Didn't he know, as an old pro, that he was only helping
Nixon?

In 1973, I compared notes about the election of 1966 with Bill Moyers,
who was at that time Lyndon Johnson's press secretary, and Joseph Califano, then his chief domestic aide.

Moyers remembers going to Johnson's bedroom that morning to find
the President hopping mad—"not at Nixon," Moyers said, "*but at the
Times for printing the text*. 'Why are they giving all that space to that
chronic campaigner,' the President said, 'don't they know it's all a lot of

politics?' " LBJ felt that the printing of the text was acknowledgment of the seriousness of the analysis—exactly as Nixon had known it. (Odd, how both Johnson and Nixon saw the printing of the text as crucial, and how we advisers—a different generation, perhaps, or too close to the press forest—did not attach that much importance to it.)

Before the press conference, Califano and Moyers went over the likely questions with LBJ, who decided—quite coolly and deliberately by then —that he would attack Nixon as the "chronic campaigner."

If the attack on Nixon at the press conference was not spontaneous but planned—and the testimony of two trusted Johnson men who were there, plus the logic of the situation, attests to that—then the question arises, why?

"Johnson thought that Nixon was the most vulnerable man in American politics—he said so that morning," says Moyers. Califano points out that a Nixon candidacy in 1968 was something that appealed to Johnson, who was already feeling the strain on the Democratic left.

Putting it together in retrospect, my guess is this: Johnson, irritated at the *Times* for treating Nixon so seriously, saw how he could take advantage of the situation politically by making Nixon his opponent. The growing dovecote in the Democratic Party might defect to a Rockefeller or a Romney, or throw away its vote to a splinter party or stay home, but Nixon —characterized as that "chronic campaigner," remembered as a Herblock cartoon—could frighten them back into LBJ's arms. In 1964 LBJ had knifed into traditional Republican strength with horrific visions of a bellicose Goldwater; in 1968 he could hold on to traditional Democratic strength with visions of the Old Nixon. That's why locking horns with Nixon that morning—while scratching an emotional irritation—was a Johnson decision that made political sense.

The irony was that the man LBJ chose as the easiest opponent for himself was the roughest opponent for the man who emerged when Johnson stepped aside in 1968, Hubert Humphrey. In calculating his blast at Nixon, Johnson simply miscalculated a little—the President appeared too tantrum-prone and the challenger too Presidentially calm—and to that extent, LBJ's tactic backfired. But Johnson wanted to run against Nixon in 1968, and this move fit that strategy, an assumption that seems more realistic than jumping to the conclusion that the master manipulator of the U. S. Senate had suddenly and inexplicably lost his political marbles.

As Johnson's heaven-sent tirade was going on, Nixon was being interviewed on film by Mike Wallace of CBS just before leaving in a private plane to New Hampshire. When Nixon got on board, Buchanan had the news of the Presidential press conference. "He *hit* us," said Pat, shaking his head. "Jesus, did he hit us. You'll never believe how he hit us . . ." Buchanan had never before been on the receiving end of a major shot in politics and didn't yet know how to react. Nixon told him to calm down and repeat all he could remember of what the President had said. On the flight up, Nixon sat looking out the window, thinking about how to handle it.

Mike Wallace scrapped the film he had made of Nixon pre-Johnson press conference, and hired a jet to get a fresh interview in New Hampshire. Before that took place, Nixon called me in New York, not to ask advice but to lay out the line: "I'm going to be absolutely cool," he said excitedly. "High road. President is tired, after all, it was a long trip. Not answer in kind. Stick to the issues. No personalities, got that? Bill, it was that text in the *Times* that got to him. But I didn't think he'd go this far. He's wrong, you know—let's make the most of it."

I couldn't figure out if Nixon was being the participant as observer or the observer as participant, but make the most of it is what he did. At the right moment, injured innocence can swing a segment of public opinion, and Richard Nixon had been unfairly attacked with those LBJ thunderbolts from the pinnacle of power. For what? For daring to ask the questions that only a man with a deep understanding of foreign affairs could ask.

Nixon, who had triggered all this with a lengthy printed statement, now swung far away from print to the television medium, where the votes were. He granted every request for television interviews—and this time, when we went back to Ray Bliss and the Republican National Committee about their Sunday half hour, they could not refuse to scrap their questionable film and give the time to the Republican under direct fire from the President.

By making one break by himself—the text of the appraisal in the *Times* —Nixon lucked into the next break and was projected into the limelight of official party spokesman, the number one campaigner, the man who acted like a President when the President did not. Just about every Republican politician around the country who was thinking about 1968 tuned in to that party-purchased half hour. The last they remembered of Nixon was his "last press conference," embittered, less than coherent, a bundle of emotions, in a way like Johnson's most recent press conference. The man they saw now was a happier warrior who knew how to respond to the moment and then—calmly and persuasively—to lay out his arguments in a well-packaged half hour. What other potential candidate could do that?

"This attack isn't going to gag me," Nixon said, in a phrase vaguely reminiscent of the "Checkers" speech fourteen years before, but more low-key, as befits a mature man who cannot be trifled with. "I was never one that could be arm-twisted by anyone and frightened even by the towering temper of Lyndon Johnson." That showed he was a man of courage. "I don't think any American—and I would say no Democrat—has defended our policy in Vietnam more effectively than I have in every capital of the world." Bipartisan patriotism, and in case anybody missed the world-traveler allusion, he went on with: "I defended it in Paris; I have defended it in London; I have defended it in Rome . . ." Republican politicians and delegates-to-be heaved a sigh of relief in the knowledge that, after the unnerving experience with Goldwater's amateurishness, here was Old Pro Nixon who could still touch all the bases.

On election night, Nixon took a suite at the Drake Hotel in New York. Bald John Nidecker handled the invitations—about forty Nixon loyalists showed up. As the returns came in, Nixon walked from room to room with that serious, controlled excitement in him: "It's a sweep, you know— it's a sweep." He went into the bedroom to take a call from Governor Reagan. He came out saying, "He's all right, Ron is—it's a sweep in California too." Forty-four House seats went to the Republicans, more than he had predicted—and more than a few of those seats went Republican because of Nixon's campaigning. The band of loyalists at the Drake didn't feel like such minor-league conspirators anymore. Dick could go all the way.

4. WASHIN' DIRTY DISHES

"Collecting delegates is just like washin' dirty dishes," Peter O'Donnell said, one hand holding an imaginary dishmop, laboriously swabbing an imaginery dish in the other, "you gotta take 'em one by one." All eyes in the room, including Richard Nixon's, watched the Republican state chairman of Texas, who helped capture the 1964 Convention for Goldwater, finish his little pantomime: O'Donnell gently shook the water off the sparkling-clean dish and carefully stacked it on top of the other delegate dishes.

We were in Suite 31-A of the Waldorf Towers, the date January 7, 1967. The spacious rooms were once the home of Herbert Hoover, who had lived there until his death in 1964; Nixon recalled that as a U. S. Senator he came to call on Mr. Hoover here, and had great difficulty getting past the guard. Nixon had specifically asked for this suite over the first weekend of the new year for two days of meetings; he had come to know Mr. Hoover in Boys Club work, admired his stoic way of surviving ignominy and defeat to regain respect in the eyes of most Americans. In a speech after the former President's death, Nixon said Hoover would be remembered "more for what he was than what he did."

I was among the last to arrive. "This is Safire," Nixon said, "absolutely trustworthy, worked with us in '60. But," he added, half in jest, "watch what you say, he's a writer." I took this as an invitation to make notes of the meeting.

Some of the faces were familiar: Peter Flanigan, forty-one, with whom I'd worked in the '60 campaign; Bob Finch, forty-four, newly elected Lieutenant Governor of California (his margin of victory, exceeding Ronald Reagan's, had come as a stunning surprise to Nixon), as close to RN as a son; Tom Evans, thirty-six, from the law firm, who had been the administrative man on the '66 campaign. The faces I did not recognize were Jerry Milbank, forty-six, a fund-raiser for Goldwater with impeccable Wall Street credentials; Fred LaRue, thirty-eight, a soft-spoken Southerner, state chairman of the Mississippi Republicans; and Peter O'Donnell of the dirty dishes simile, forty-two. It was the young group of old pros that Nixon, then fifty-four, wanted; the average age of the seven of us was thirty-nine.

"The purpose of this group," Nixon began, "is to begin planning now to win the nomination. It is important that we keep the existence of this group quiet, not only because of the press, but because we don't want to hurt the feelings of anybody we've left out." This added to a warm organizational feeling; we were the "inner circle" of one of the few men who could actually make it, and Nixon wanted us to know it.

"It is not the purpose of this group to help me on issues," he cautioned, which explained why Len Garment and Bob Ellsworth were not there. "On issues, very briefly, I think we can assume that the Vietnam war will have been ended by the 1968 election. Other issues not so sure of solution, however, include inflation, race, and crime. Johnson's ego, as illustrated by that episode with the portrait, could be an issue too." He moved away from this quickly; he knew what he wanted this group for, and it was not to advise him on matters on which they were inexpert.

"Let's look at the odds as of today.

"Romney is even money to get the nomination. He's got money; he's ahead in the polls, which is important to delegates; but he's never shown an ability to hit big-league pitching.

"Percy and Nixon are two to one. Percy has a good forum in Washington, and he's smart. But he won't have a delegate base, and there's the memory of the '60 platform fight. His problem is that Romney won't roll over and make way when the Eastern Establishment says, 'You're not smart enough for us.' Romney will surprise them—like Warren in '52, he'll hang in there all the way.

"Reagan is four to one. Rocky has no chance at all."

I would have given Rockefeller at least a long-shot chance and stretched the odds a bit on Percy, but Nixon's assessment was fairly close to that of most of the men there. We were more interested in his assessment of his own weakness.

"My biggest problem," Nixon concluded, "is 'Nixon can't win.'" That laid it on the line. Finch added, "If we could convince delegates that Dick could win—then he's in."

We discussed ways to build "winability." I suggested the "inevitability" theme, recalling how other leaders moved inexorably back to power after a period in the wilderness. Nixon pondered that possibility and then warned: "You can't repackage Nixon with PR. Maybe that's okay with a new man, but not with me. I'm a known quantity. That has its benefits— Julie's picture was on all the front pages because it was news.* But it has its drawbacks—the normal image-building won't work with me."

"There's always the dangerous route," said Flanigan, "the primaries."

* Julie Nixon had made her debut in society at the International Debutante Ball on December 30, 1966, escorted by David Eisenhower.

Nixon allowed as how the best way to knock Romney down in the polls was to remove his winner status by beating him in New Hampshire.

But that was a year away, and the nomination could be sewn up before the primaries. "We must stop Romney's bandwagon by showing some delegate strength," said LaRue. "Most delegates think all Nixon has is the South. He doesn't know we can break through in a state like Pennsylvania." The group did not need to be reminded of the "goal line stand" at a recent Governors' Conference when Romney tried to blitz then and there. Nixon men passed among the Governors advising them to stay loose, there was plenty of time to 1968, and we thought in 1967 that the nomination had very nearly been sewn up by Romney in 1966.

Where did that leave us now? "Some say," Nixon started—we all knew that what was coming had to be wrong, because Nixon's "some" and "others" never say anything right—"Some say I should do nothing, because if I try and fail, I could not be kingmaker. I disagree. You cannot be king-maker unless you try to be king—that's what gets you the power to form the deadlock.

"If I were to do nothing, Romney would be nominated. Nobody could stop him in the Midwest. Whoever is running has to start running now, and this group of cynical idealists should be the first to realize it."

That was the word O'Donnell wanted to hear. "We have to have a flag," he said, "run it up, and go into business. Right now, it's somebody against nobody. We've got to start buttonholing delegates. We need a name, a few delegate-getters, an organizer—"

LaRue caught him up short. "Reagan could shoot us down in two minutes." Nixon nodded agreement, observing, "It's the reverse of '64, when the liberals could never get together." Finch said it was our top priority right away to get George Murphy and others to lean on Reagan not to split conservative strength by going for the nomination himself.

"Here's a different game plan," Finch said to Nixon. It was the first time I'd heard that football expression used in politics. "We could lay back and let Reagan be our stalking horse, just the way Rockefeller is using Romney." I saw a big flaw in that: "What if Romney offers Reagan the Vice Presidency—then you have the stalking horses running away with the wagon." "That's a danger," Finch admitted, "but we could offer Reagan the top spot on a silver platter in 1972 if we lost."

Nixon smiled and shook his head. "I'm glad you threw that idea out, and it might even work if Reagan would go for it, but he wouldn't. It's good for us to think the unthinkable, though."

The decision was made to pass the word that Nixon was running. "Don't give out any franchises," was the way he put it, "but get started contacting the power groups in each state."

Peter O'Donnell pressed for Nixon to name a chairman of this group, but I cautioned against it on the basis that it would soon get into print—as soon as there is a boss, there is a story. (Actually, I did not want to see it go to O'Donnell, because of his obvious Goldwater coloration.) Nixon finessed the point by saying "Peter O'Donnell is the nonchairman of a non-existent group." "The Brain Trust?" somebody kidded, and drew a sharp look from RN: "No, no help on the issues. That's something else. Stick to politics."

The specifics began to flow from the "go" signal. Who would be surfaced as the Nixon men? Maury Stans, Fred Seaton, Peter Flanigan, John Davis Lodge, Bob Ellsworth, with Pat Buchanan as press aide. Charley Rhyne to write a letter to "the citizens types." What about polling? We'd need two—one for a prestige name, another for internal use only. Where did we need media contacts? The New York *Times* and *Time* magazine—they were the toughest nuts to crack.

The meeting spilled over to the next day and the campaign seemed to pick up a tempo of its own. Targets were selected. When O'Donnell referred to a Texas politician as "a nut on Communism," Nixon replied evenly: "Go get him—he thinks I'm a nut on Communism." Should we float out a hint that Reagan will be our VP? "Hell, no," answered the most conservative man there, "talk left—Schafer or Percy." Most important: the campaign manager. Who would be out front, full-time, acceptable to the wide party spectrum?

Finch brought up the name of C. Gaylord Parkinson, a California obstetrician and politician who authored the "Eleventh Commandment" in bloody California primary fights: "Thou shalt not speak ill of another Republican." Too quickly, Nixon told Finch to call Herb Klein, his old press secretary who was then editor of the San Diego *Union*, to sound out Parky. (He was soon hired, but the chemistry wasn't right, and along came John Mitchell, whose story is told later.) Before the meeting broke up, just for kicks, Nixon went down the list of states and guessed at his delegate strength in each. There was a moment of tension as I added it up: we had 603 votes on the first ballot. Needed to nominate: 667.*

We had thought we had a fair chance to make it. After going over the state delegations one by one, we realized that Nixon was wrong about one thing—it was no case of even odds for Romney and two to one for us. We were in better shape than anybody—if only we could show Nixon was a winner.

The most important and gutsy decision Nixon then made about his personal plans was to do nothing. To a man, his advisers and staff urged him to capitalize on his 1966 victory by coming out in the open—speeches, appearances, tours, television interviews, the works. He said no: "Let Romney take the point." (In military tactics, the soldier "on the point" of a wedge is the most likely to be shot.) If Nixon had anything, it was a sense of timing, an instinct for the ebb and flow of public boredom in men seeking to pique the public's interest. He had been in the wilderness from 1963 through 1965; he was in the public eye again for a few months in

---

* On the first ballot at the Republican Convention of 1968, Nixon received 690 votes, and the pattern within each state was uncannily the way he had called it eighteen months before. He knew just where his strength was.

1966; now he would recede into the background again for a while, letting them come to him, traveling abroad and stocking up the anecdotes and expertise that would serve him well as primary time neared. Besides, he had a perverse confidence in George Romney: the Michigan Governor, he was sure, could not take the savaging that the press corps reserves for the front runner. Nixon was right on both counts: it is hard, in retrospect, to realize how much nerve it takes to run by not running, and to stick to that strategy for a solid six months as the pressure builds.

Time magazine told us it planned to do a cover story on Nixon in August 1967; the timing was right for us, and the cover might have launched Nixon's next phase into greater public exposure with the kind of boost he needed, but after climbing all over us and the rest of the political landscape, a *Time* editor suddenly pulled the plug—and told us there would be no cover. Nixon was irritated, though he took some pleasure in pointing out to us that he had told us *Time* would never do anything which might be good for Nixon. Then—to his surprise and ours—a stroke of good fortune came our way.

In a political campaign's early stages, it is most useful to know what political leaders are saying privately to reporters—"not for attribution" is the phrase of art. Somebody at Time-Life, who believed that *Time*'s preference for Nelson Rockefeller had prevailed over its editorial judgment, sent Nixon the raw file of correspondents' copy on the Nixon cover. Since it is seven years since then, and time wounds all heels—and because Nixon knew what these politicians were saying then ever since—it might be worth while to look at some of the judgments being expressed by political men who thought they were being anonymous.

Dwight Eisenhower told a "visitor" (Hugh Scott, later the Senate Minority Leader) that Nixon was the best grounded of all the hopefuls in foreign affairs, "but he's certainly being hurt by this 'they say' business." What did Ike mean? "They say he can't win."

A "high-ranking liberal Northeast Republican" (Senator Edward Brooke of Massachusetts) told a reporter "the stigma of being a loser still stays with him." With Nixon as the nominee, "it wouldn't be a contest in '68—it would be a giveaway."

A "conservative Western GOP Senator" (that was Peter Dominick of Colorado, and we needed his support) said, "He's the most qualified man, but can we win with a man who's lost twice?"

A "veteran GOP professional" (Ab Hermann, later Deputy Director of the Republican National Committee) said, not for attribution: "I can't explain it, but I don't like him."

On the other hand, Nixon discovered that some people were saying nice things behind his back: Republican Senator Thruston Morton of Kentucky said: "I think the guy's grown up. He's attained a sense of understanding he didn't have before. To put it bluntly, I like him more than I did in 1960."

Bryce Harlow, former Eisenhower aide, speechwriter and friend to many on Capitol Hill, said, not for attribution: "Nixon is a party loyalist who has stepped up to the tough ones as well as the easy ones." (Soon after, Bryce was brought aboard.)

Besides revealing where some influential Republican figures stood—Everett Dirksen declared Nixon to be "kosher" but Melvin Laird leaked a poll showing Romney would do far better with Democratic voters—the *Time* file contained some helpful stimuli: "Nixon seems devoid of any ideas—and bold new concepts—that could capture the electorate's imagination." Note was made of that, along with this comment from Ronald Reagan's public relations firm: "The one thing that could rejuvenate Nixon would be color TV. In black and white he looks sinister with his black beard."

To have had Nixon, who needed the boost, on *Time*'s cover that fall would have been good, but it was even better to know who our friends were. (Few of us would afterward tell anybody in "group journalism" anything not for attribution that would be embarrassing to have come to the attention of our colleagues.) Certainly the leaking by the *Time* employee was reprehensible—breaking faith with sources and harming the press's ability to carry out its necessary functions—but as the recipient of the leak from the publication put it, "The shoe has been on the other foot often enough." I remember thinking that if I were working for *Time*, I would be furious with the disloyal partisan who gave away corporate secrets to suit that employee's own purposes. Even now, I wonder what I would have done, if I were they, to plug the leak.

Toward the end of 1967, Nixon began talking to people on the telephone without bothering to say hello, and the campaign tempo picked up. Nixon had to lose his loser image in the primaries, so he pretended to enjoy campaigning and plunged into New Hampshire. The phenomenon began that was to continue all that spring of 1968: the pullout of other candidates. George Romney looked at the polls showing him getting less than 10 per cent of the vote against Nixon, and announced he was out of the race. This news was brought to Nixon on the campaign trail by Buchanan, who pulled the candidate into an aircraft's tiny men's room to get away from reporters. Nixon reacted by shaking his head and chiding Buchanan for not checking out the report: "It's not true, you know, Pat. Somebody's kidding." In a sense, he was right—but the man doing the kidding around was Nelson Rockefeller, who was acting as if the starting gate were a revolving door. On March 23, back from campaigning in Wisconsin, Nixon called me to ask why I thought Rockefeller had just pulled out of the race again. Before I could reply, he said, "It was the polls. He has the same figures we have for Oregon's primary. Back in February, they were Nixon thirty-five, Rocky thirty-five, Reagan eight, and just last week they were Nixon forty-seven, Rocky twenty-six, Reagan three. It's all over for him. The only one who can stop us is Reagan." Next day he called again to say, "It would be better for me not to do anything controversial for the time being. I don't want to get into the crossfire between LBJ and

Bobby—let them hit each other, not me. But I don't like this 'secret plan' business."

Earlier that year, he had said, at my urging, that he would "end the war and win the peace in the Pacific." People wanted hope, and there was nothing wrong in promising to do what he intended to do. This was escalated by press reports into a false Nixon quote: "I have a secret plan to end the war." Nixon never said that. To respond to the pressure for a more definite statement on Vietnam, Nixon planned to make a speech on March 31, 1968, on network radio. Between Ray Price, Richard Whalen, and me, and with constant fixes from the candidate, the position was fairly well honed (down to an argument about whether the gains of escalation were outweighed by the "grave risks" or the "heavy costs"). Some early drafts of this speech* carried a suggestion that the United States and South Vietnam adopt a joint command, which I thought was contrary to his Vietnamization emphasis and likely to tie his hands when elected, and he scrapped it. The essence of the Nixon position was to increase the threat of, and the fact of, air and sea pressure, to change "search and destroy" of Viet Cong troops to a more passive approach that I labeled "clear and hold," covering South Vietnamese cities, and to put diplomatic heat on the Soviets and the Chinese to help bring the war to a nonvictorious but honorable conclusion.

The Nixon speech was never given, because President Johnson announced he was going to make a speech that night. He did, and, at the end, dropped his bomb: he was not going to run for re-election.

At the top of the list of "themes that are now out" sent in by Ray Price the morning after was "new leadership"—that, Ray wrote, "becomes a foregone conclusion. Our discussion of new leadership will have to zero in more precisely on the kind of new leadership we will provide," adding about LBJ "we should now be laying whatever groundwork we can for enlisting at least his tacit support in November if the Democratic nominee should turn out to be Kennedy." That is exactly what Nixon was thinking, and would continue to try for until the final weeks of the fall campaign.

Then Robert Kennedy was shot, and two months later Martin Luther King was gunned down, and a kind of shellshock set in around the country. Nixon was told by the Secret Service that he could no longer use the paneled office prepared for him at the "Bible Building," the Park Avenue headquarters formerly the home of the American Bible Society, because he was a setup for a rifle bullet from the building across the street. (Herb Klein took that office, and for the first week felt uncomfortable.)

Nixon gave a good deal of thought to the suggestion that he attend Martin Luther King's funeral. I reminded him of a painful moment in the 1960 campaign, when Jackie Robinson, a supporter of Nixon for President, came to him and pleaded that he at least telephone Dr. King, who

---

* One draft was published in the appendix of *Catch the Falling Flag* by Richard Whalen; there were two more drafts after that one.

had just been jailed. Nixon had said that would be "grandstanding" and declined. Robinson came out of the hotel room, tears in his eyes, shaking his head, ready to blow. I tried to cool him off, but he wanted out, and never again supported Nixon. John Kennedy made the phone call to Dr. King, and since the final election results were so close Nixon's failure to call King became one of the "if-onlies" we entertained ourselves with over the years. Now, in 1968, Nixon said carefully, "Failing to go would present some serious problems." He dialed a call himself and said to the man on the other end, "I'm sitting here with Safire, Garment, and all the libs, talking about the King funeral. What do you think?" The man at the other end, probably John Mitchell, was firmly against Nixon's going. Nixon hung up and said, "There's some feeling that we should not let ourselves become prisoners of the moment. In the long run, politicians who try to capitalize on this could be hurt. There can't be any grandstanding." I said that "grandstanding" was the very word he had used years ago to Jackie Robinson. He repeated, "There will be no grandstanding. I'll go down and pay my respects to Mrs. King quietly." He did, and then went to the funeral, too. But to avoid grandstanding he did not march in the parade.

Nixon liked to walk around a situation, get a lot of differing advice, and do what he liked to call "the right thing, which, you know, is not always the smartest thing politically." Because he measured and calculated beforehand, because he made such an obvious effort not to act impulsively, it was easy for an associate or an observer to assume that to Nixon the "right thing" meant "the smart thing."

On race relations, his instincts were good, neither callous nor patronizing. During the early stages of the campaign, he spoke to Congressman John Anderson of Illinois about an open housing bill, hung up and said delightedly, "We've got a civil rights act. I told a few of the boys it would be a bad thing to make an issue out of this in the campaign." And in a speech about political philosophy, in the part that dealt with the South, he wrote in the words "or the old racist appeals" at the urging of Ray Price:

The new South is no longer prisoner of the past, no longer

or the old racist appeals.

bound by old habits or old grievances∧ The new South is building

a new pride, focusing on the future, pressing forward with

That speech, delivered on May 16, 1968, was called "A New Alignment for American Unity," and deserves a word here because it reflected a Nixon approach to politics and government that was to change after he came into office. In it, he talked about a "new majority" that was already coming into being: "The new majority is not a grouping of power blocs, but an alliance of ideas . . . Many of these men and women belong to the same blocs that formed the old coalitions. But now, thinking independently,

they have all reached a new conclusion about the direction of our nation."
The new direction chosen by these unlikely allies—which included the
traditional Republicans, the Moynihan-Goodwin liberals, the black militants and the progressive South—was away from increased Federal power
and toward more decentralization, more local control, and more personal
freedom. These disparate groups, or blocs, often differed sharply about
the speed of change, but not the direction of change; they often found
each other disagreeable, but did not disagree about the reassertion of
individuality against centralized, bureaucratic authority.

This was hardly sensational new dogma, but it did show some thoughtful commentators that the man likely to be the next President was aware
of some unifying common denominators in a society then appearing to be
coming apart at the seams. He expressed them simply: "People come first,
and government is their servant. The best government is closest to the
people, and most involved with people's lives. Government is formed to
protect the individual's life, property, and rights, and to help the helpless
—not to dominate a person's life or rob him of his self-respect." This was
in the spirit of the times, which was in rebellion against individual powerlessness.

Among the blocs that were making up the new majority, there was one
that Nixon was to become especially identified with, and whose name I
lifted from a speech by former Senator Paul Douglas: "That is the silent
center, the millions of people in the middle of the American political
spectrum who do not demonstrate, who do not picket or protest loudly
. . . a great many 'quiet Americans' have become committed to answers
to social problems that preserve personal freedom . . . As this silent center
has become a part of the new alignment, it has transformed it from a
minority into a majority."

Nixon was talking about what was to be known as the "Silent Majority,"
of course, but his idea was that the majority would not be assembled by
political pandering to bloc votes, the way FDR assembled his coalition of
organized labor, big-city machines, and minorities and the Solid South.
There were national needs—spiritual and philosophic needs—that cut
across the narrow self-interest of each bloc and affected all of them: the
needs of the individuals within each of those old blocs to have a rebirth
of personal freedom and a sense of control of their own destinies. High-
flown? Of course. Ted Sorensen called it a product of a "Nixon mimeograph machine that ran amuck one night," which *Time* magazine reported
with the afterthought that "Nixon, however, has the best-run political
mimeograph that is now in operation." The part about the "new liberals"
thinking along those lines *Time* quickly dismissed: "Moynihan is a big
spender when it comes to Federal funds . . . he is obviously nonaligned
in Nixon's context."

As the strong man in the center of his party, Nixon came to the convention in Miami Beach to take the mantle of leadership. He had it all
wrapped up because he had proven himself to be a party loyalist, was

surely attuned to the issues and equipped for the job of candidate and President, had cast away "loser" forever in the primaries, had trounced an opposition as vacillating as he had been steadfast, and had inspired confidence that he could cool the country down and start taking charge of events. In two and a half years, Richard Nixon had come back to within striking distance of the most powerful office in the world. He took the nomination on the first ballot because he deserved it and could win with it.

5. THE MAN WHO

The campaign for the nomination was over. Nixon left the Republican National Convention to John Mitchell and holed up in Gurney's Inn on Montauk, Long Island, to write his acceptance speech with Ray Price. At the convention in Miami, I was a little glum: not only was I not at Montauk, but not even permitted access to the candidate's inner circle sanctum in Miami—Bob Haldeman, for some reason, had decided I was not "in"—and on top of that, the Governor of Florida, Claude Kirk, whom I was close to, had just bolted from Nixon to Rockefeller and would soon switch again to Reagan. (Alexander Lankler, an ally of Rockefeller's and later Republican state chairman of Maryland, came up to me after the convention and said, "Don't feel so bad—I was supposed to deliver Agnew for Rockefeller.")

A melodramatic, nearly comic secrecy enveloped the first contact of the Nixon political forces with Dr. Henry A. Kissinger. Richard Allen, Nixon's national security adviser, came down to Miami with the Nixon staff to make sure the Republican Convention platform planks on Vietnam and foreign policy generally conformed to Nixon's thinking. Allen arranged to meet with Governor Nelson Rockefeller's security adviser, Henry Kissinger, in the lobby of the Fontainebleau Hotel to exchange plank drafts.

Aware of the hullabaloo around the Rockefeller-Nixon "compact of Fifth Avenue" on the eve of a convention eight years before, the Nixon forces (at conventions, groups always become "forces") were not anxious for the appearance of concessions to Rockefeller. Allen, waiting in the vast Fontainebleau lobby for Kissinger, saw to his horror the narrowed eyes of columnist Robert Novak watching him. Novak knew Allen to be a Nixon adviser, but did not then know Kissinger by sight; when Kissinger came out of the elevator, Allen put on an act of running into an old friend, enthusiastically steering Henry out the front entrance, away from the watching columnist, with Kissinger thinking Allen had gone berserk.

Outside the hotel, the two security advisers started to compare notes but were immediately surprised by Daniel Schorr of CBS, who knew Kissinger but not Allen; the Nixon operative introduced himself as an old student of Kissinger's from Harvard, and the perplexed Kissinger went along with the white lie. When Schorr left, the two advisers made their exchange in a hurry and scurried off in opposite directions; the generalized platform plank did not present a problem, and no reporters had a chance to say the Rockefeller forces extracted concessions from the Nixon men. That convention darting-about was, in a way, symbolic: rule number one had to be "fool the press" for anybody in the national security game.

Mitchell, with Strom Thurmond beside him, turned aside the Reagan challenge—the only one that Nixon had ever been concerned about—and the states sang out their votes to nominate Nixon on the first ballot, reminding me of the Waldorf session eighteen months before, going down the list of states to predict degrees of support. There is no feeling in politics like that of a long-time supporter, standing on the floor of the convention, as I was—or better still, sitting in the room with the Candidate as Pat and Ray were—booting the winner home.

The next night, Frank Shakespeare, a former CBS vice president who ran the television presentation of Nixon and would later head the United States Information Agency, sat in the mobile trailer with Nixon outside Convention Hall as makeup was applied and the final changes were made in the Candidate's speech. Nixon handed his speaking copy to Shakespeare, whose assignment was to place it on the rostrum before the Candidate entered to the expected tumultuous roar. Nixon was conscious of the way to enter a room or hall: "You always have to make an entrance," he once told me, "you have to walk right in and take charge. A lot of politicians never learn that, they mosey in or kind of poke their heads in first—that's all wrong. You have to make sure the door is open, that they're ready for you, and you start striding out a few steps before you get to the doorway—then you sweep in like a leader, and they know you're there." Like Loretta Young did on the opening of her television show, I remember saying, as Nixon shook his head, and gave a look of mock exasperation.

He charged out of the trailer, was surrounded by a phalanx (it is always called a phalanx, after a plan of overlapping shields developed by Philip II of Macedonia) of Secret Service men, and the cocoon was sealed for the safe, swift movement of a celebrity or target through a crowd. If you were inside the cocoon, as Dwight Chapin and other aides were, you were swept along in a fast-moving, thrilling, and unique experience; if you missed the departure of the cocoon, and you had a job to do inside it, or at its destination, then you were in heart-stopping trouble.

That was Shakespeare's situation. As the President left the trailer, Frank double-checked the speech on his lap to see if the pages were in order, then followed along—but to his dismay, in those few seconds, the cocoon had moved out without him. Barriers that had been dropped for a few seconds to let the cocoon in were suddenly again in place, guards with impassive faces were refusing to look at passes, he was outside with the speech in his hand and there was the "Next President of the Yew-Nited States of America" inside the hall, waving his arms, wiggling the "V" sign, and preparing to move forward to the rostrum where he would confidently reach for his speech. Since he would not use a teleprompter, there was no "back-up" to switch to. Nor could he use a copy other than the reading copy without wearing glasses, which he had sworn never to do in public.

Shakespeare, a soft-spoken, mild-mannered man, transformed himself into a raging bully. Finally a Secret Service man recognized him and figured he would do him a favor by letting him in. By that action, Shakespeare made it to the rostrum just in time, and we were not treated to the first acceptance speech in history ad-libbed by a seething candidate.

The 1968 acceptance speech was not as uplifting as the 1960 acceptance, but it was shorter and punchier than the 1972 acceptance. The part I liked best, obviously, was a section I had submitted for another speech months before, and which had gone unused: the "I see" passage, a construction lifted unabashedly from FDR's "I see an America where" speech (which speechwriters Samuel Rosenman and Robert E. Sherwood had borrowed from Robert Ingersoll, who put James Blaine in nomination as the "Plumed Knight").

Nixon had taken the suggested speech construction and changed my draft considerably, so as to conform more closely with his own vision of America's future.

> I see a day when Americans are once again proud of their flag . . . I see a day when the President of the United States is respected and his office is honored because it is worthy of respect and worthy of honor. I see a day when every child in this land, regardless of his background, has a chance for the best education that our wisdom and schools can provide, and an equal chance to go just as high as his talents will take him. I see a day when life in rural America attracts people to the country rather than driving them away. I see a day when we can look back on massive breakthroughs in solving the problems of slums and pollution and traffic . . . I see a day when our senior citizens and millions of others can plan for the future . . . I see a day when we will again have freedom from fear in the world. I see a day when our nation is at peace and the world is at peace and everyone on earth—those who hope, those who aspire, those who crave liberty —will look to America as the shining example of hopes realized and dreams achieved.

Nixon finished the speech with his "train whistle" peroration, taking the audience back to his childhood and reaffirming the American Dream, and when it was over the place dutifully went wild. Afterward, I hit a couple of the parties and left, exhilarated in a depressed kind of way, to go to sleep about midnight.

At one-thirty, Dwight Chapin called: "Did I wake you?" I said no, the phone was ringing, and he said, "Can you come up here? The Boss wants to talk to somebody and nobody's around. Mrs. Nixon is asleep, Rose Woods and Pat Buchanan are both off celebrating, and I'm dying to go out myself. He's too 'up' to sleep—can you sit around with him until he runs out of gas?"

I was dressed and up to the eighteenth-floor penthouse suite of the Hilton Plaza with some alacrity. Chapin nodded me in past the Secret Service men in the hallway and then left, leaving me seated alone opposite a happy, exhausted man. The Candidate—that's how one referred to him at that point—was slumped deep in his easy chair holding a light scotch and water by the top of the glass, waving it gently to tinkle the ice.

"I told Dwight I wanted to talk about the speech, and to get the Old Master up here," Nixon said. I had not yet reached my fortieth birthday, but I lapped up the flattery, and put out of my mind the reason for my presence was that nobody else was around.

"You know, those 'I sees' were yours," he said. He had a habit of reminding his writers that he knew which portions of their draft submissions he used, unlike many public figures who hate to admit, even to themselves, that their speeches did not spring full-blown from their own minds. "I was saving them all these months. Come on now, professionally—what did you think of the speech?"

I said the first half of his acceptance address was a punchy rehash of the stump speech he had been using, but the second half was more interesting. The train whistle was nicely evocative, but his "Let's win it for Ike" line sounded like an old movie with Ronald Reagan and Pat O'Brien about Knute Rockne: "Let's win it for the Gipper."

"Yeah, I know, you intellectuals don't go for that sort of thing. The press won't like it at all, they'll climb the wall. None of them could write a speech like that, one that reaches the folks, and they hate me for it.

"Ike could give a speech like that," he continued, taking slow sips of his scotch, still holding the glass around the rim. "We both started with nothing, and we're both emotional. They call me 'intelligent, cool, with no sincerity'—and then it kills them when I show 'em I know how people feel. I'd like to see Rocky or Romney or Lindsay do a moving thing like that 'impossible dream' part, where I changed my voice." He frowned, thinking about somebody else who could. "Reagan's an actor, but I'd like to see him do that.

"You see, Billyboy"—he never called me that before, or again, but he was feeling congenial and warm all over—"we had an audience of seventy-five million people. They never heard the applause lines before. Now I won't be able to use them on television again, but that was the moment—that was the big chance." I remarked that he really was using one applause line all the time: "The wave of crime must not be the wave of the future." Maybe that was too much—

"Hell with that," he shook his head. "Repeat! Sure we used it before, in the platform statement, too. Billy Graham says, repeat all you like."

I wondered if we could use the Reverend Graham against George Wallace. Nixon shook his head again. "No, that would hurt his ministry. Maybe we could get a thing like 'The Dick Nixon I Know' for a magazine, but nothing political, nothing hard. Reminds me—that magazine Frank Leonard did for us, that was pretty good, hunh? When he uses the acceptance speech in the next edition, tell him to cut it down—just use the last part, not the stump speech . . ."

Nixon was nodding, and his eyes closed for a while, but he still held the dangling glass. I started to leave but he came awake talking, and I went back to my chair.

"You know why we needed Agnew. I gave a lot of thought to Lindsay —surprised?—but what the hell, he'd cut you up. Big gains up North, but Lindsay would lose us Florida, Texas, Kentucky, the Carolinas, Tennessee. Hatfield?—light. Percy?—Boy Scout. Baker?—too new. Agnew's a tough, shrewd Greek. We've got to figure out a way to sell him. He can't give a speech worth a damn, but he's not going to fall apart."

Agnew wears well?

"That's it, he *wears* well. He wears *well*. Get him on press conferences, panel shows, talking about the cities, answering questions, but no set speeches. He's no speechmaker."

He drifted off again for a while; this time I waited, and he opened his eyes to focus on the acceptance speech again. "That last part was poetry," he murmured. "The 'new dawn' phrase was from a Benjamin Franklin quote to George Washington.*

"I wanted to say that a mountaintop is where you can see the dawn first, but it was too long, so I left out the material in between. That's poetry. Let the reader figure out what belongs in between.

"That's what I try to tell Ray. Politics is poetry. Not prose, no matter how good. Mood. Emotion. Oh, you can't do it often, but once in a while, at a historic moment, you need the poetry . . ."

I told him I thought he could really use some shut-eye and he nodded yes, slowly coming to his feet. He walked me to the door of the suite and leaned against the doorjamb, saying to the Secret Service man, "You suppose we could get some ham and cheese sandwiches, and a glass of milk? Been a long day."

Another thought came to his mind about the speech: "I used the thing about the year 2000, and the two hundredth anniversary of the nation, you notice. Like that?" I did. "You think it changes votes?"

I shook my head, and he punched my arm good night. "They won't like the speech, will they, the New York *Times* and those boys," he said, shrugging as if he didn't care. "____ 'em."

---

* The speech's conclusion: "My fellow Americans, the long dark night for America is about to end. The time has come for us to leave the valley of despair and climb the mountain so that we may see the glory of the dawn—a new day for America, and a new dawn for peace and freedom in the world."

PLATE 1. The first and last news photo taken by the author: "The Kitchen Conference." (Wide World Photos)

PLATE 2. "All right, so he isn't a lovable man. Am I a lovable man? Are you a lovable man?" (Drawing by J. Mirachi: © 1972 The New Yorker Magazine, Inc.)

PLATE 3. Author's wife becomes an American citizen. Presiding is Judge John Sirica, a Federal judge, little known at the time.

PLATE 4. Three thorns in the Rose Garden: Ray Price, the author, and
Pat Buchanan.

6. NIXON'S THE ONE

A good campaign hangs loose. A bad campaign never gets together, like Goldwater's in 1964, or never loosens up, like Dewey's in 1948.

Nixon began with an enormous advantage over Hubert Humphrey. First, Nixon was an Out at a time when Ins were unpopular. Next, he had a long lead in the popularity polls, which was helpful in fund-raising. (We had a meeting in the Candidate's hotel room one night; Nixon, in his pajamas, turned to Bob Haldeman and said: "Be sure we outspend them on television, especially in the last three weeks. Remember '60—I never want to be outspent again.") Third, in contrast to Humphrey, he came out of the convention with a united party, hungry to win. Finally, Nixon had an organization tested in the primaries, with most of the personality conflicts long since resolved.

Humphrey had several advantages of his own. He began with much of the traditional Democratic labor support flirting with George Wallace; the unions would soon put a scare into their membership about ol' George, and the momentum of the Democratic campaign was bound to rise. Wallace, who began with 18 per cent in the polls, wound up with half of that in the vote, and most of the switch went to Humphrey, thanks to an all-out drive by organized labor.

Next, allied with the likelihood of a flow away from Wallace, Humphrey had the Democratic habit going for him, which only Eisenhower had been able to overcome in forty years. Also, there was the Presidency on his side, maybe—if Lyndon Johnson wanted to, he could close the gap in a hurry and turn a lopsided campaign into a horse race. For that reason, Humphrey never "declared his independence" of LBJ, as many of his liberal, dovish friends urged him to do—a speech in Salt Lake City was touted as his "break," but his position moved away from Johnson's by a few degrees only, since both candidates saw the election hinging on the same matter.

Nixon, who did nothing in the campaign to raise LBJ's ire on the war, and who kept telling us "say eight years, not five, and attack the Administration, not Johnson," in the end summed up to his writers the strategy of the campaign that was held by the high command in both camps: "If there's war, people will vote for me to end it. If there's peace, they'll vote their pocketbooks—Democratic prosperity."

Naturally, there was suspicion as the campaign drew to a close that Nixon and his supporters tried to block peace efforts; this was not wholly true, though there were enough incriminating leads supplied to the Democrats by the FBI to raise this suspicion, and fresh evidence will be explored in this chapter. Contrariwise, there was suspicion at the Nixon camp that —if provoked—LBJ might give away too much in terms of the U.S. national interest to bring about peace talks, though nobody went quite so far as to think LBJ would sell out our allies in order to gain Humphrey's election. As Nixon told us, "If you give 'em the bombing pause and a coalition government, you give 'em the whole goddam country." LBJ surely did try to make a deal at the end, and he stretched fairly hard—only the decision of President Thieu not to cooperate foiled his effort. But Johnson's motive was only partly partisan politics; there was pride and patriotism in it, too, for a man who wanted the credit for ending the war that had crippled his Presidency.

Humphrey's fourth advantage was a matter of attitude: he was playing to win, and Nixon was playing not to lose. When the two contestants are miles apart (as Goldwater had been in '64 and McGovern was to be in '72), political analysts tend to use football phrases like "catch-up ball" and "punt 'n' pray" to describe desperation tactics. But when the gap is closable, the difference in posture is a significant psychological advantage, and is reflected in press support. (Reporters, being human, like a close race, and tend to root for an underdog on the move.) The Humphrey campaign did not have to try to hang loose; the Nixon campaign, which began that way, had to try hard to end that way.

The account that follows is not intended to be a history of the campaign, which has been done well by in different books by Theodore White and Jules Witcover; it is a campaign collage, a series of impressions of Nixon and his men during the campaign, which may shed some light on how he profited from bitter experience in previous campaigns, and was learning all too well for subsequent campaigns.

Memoirs have a way of getting suffused in the glow of glorification or guilt; this account will be drawn from memoranda and notes set down at the time. There has never been a "diary" of a campaign by the Candidate for President himself, but this technique may bring us fairly close to one. As much as possible, the story will be permitted to tell itself.

Post-Convention: San Diego, California

At Mission Bay, a hotel-recreation complex being developed by friends of Herb Klein in San Diego, the Nixon staff met to change the campaign emphasis. Image-making and delegate-gathering had been the primary efforts of the pre-convention period, but the thrust (we all liked that word) of the campaign now had to center on the issues—financial, "gut,"

and otherwise. As the Candidate put it in a scrawled instruction on one of
Martin Anderson's suggestions for future speeches:

> RN agrees with page 1 completely—This is the point he has been try-
> ing to make—it is time to move away from fighting the old battle of
> image to the new battle of where RN stands—only this way do we
> cut into the Wallace vote.

In such notes, Nixon came to refer to himself in the third person, and
not out of any self-consciousness, or sense of the royal "we." He wrote
often as an observer, watching "RN"—himself—conduct a campaign,
handling himself as a kind of property. The change from "I think" in
memos in 1967 to "RN thinks" in 1968 was disconcerting to recipients at
first, but we soon became accustomed to it, along with the careful avoidance of "RN" as the source of memos. Toward the end of the campaign,
the instructions always came from "DC," which could stand for Dwight
Chapin, his personal aide, or the District of Columbia, our ultimate goal,
but if the memo fell into unfriendly hands, it was less likely to make news
as a "captured document" if it did not have the Candidate's name or
initials on it as author.

At Mission Bay, Nixon's relationship with his senior writers changed
abruptly. No longer were Price, Buchanan, and myself part of the inner-
most inner circle; to organize us, the Candidate brought in James Keogh,
a *Time* editor and the writer of a 1956 biography of Nixon. Keogh was
fifteen years older than any of us, a precise executive with a good grasp of
the care and feeding of "talent." None of the writers liked the idea of having an intermediary between us and the Candidate, but if it had to be,
Keogh was an excellent choice—certainly a better idea than elevating one
of us.

Another writer, Richard Whalen—author of *Founding Father,* the
superb biography of Joseph P. Kennedy, and a writer of many articles for
Fortune magazine—took Keogh's presence as evidence of the isolation of
the Candidate from men of ideas. Both were Time, Inc. veterans and may
have brought a mutual suspicion from their past association, but whatever
the reason, Whalen had the appearance of a man waiting for his fuse to be
lit.

This was promptly accomplished, not by Keogh but by John Mitchell,
who had a few drinks one night and sauntered over to the table where the
writers and Martin Anderson and Richard Allen were seated. Whalen was
fuming, with good reason, because some committee of right-wing defense
experts, ostensibly giving the Candidate advice in an area that Whalen
specialized in, were being brought into the limelight. Mitchell—good-
humoredly, I thought, but Whalen thought insufferably—waved aside his
objections. The idea that John Mitchell, a municipal bond lawyer, should
casually decide on whom the Candidate should listen to on matters of
great import infuriated Whalen, who packed up and left. Anderson tried

to stop him but Keogh did not. (Jim probably figured he would blow up sooner or later, and an early departure was best.) Anderson and I wondered; from Nixon's point of view, there was passion in Whalen, and more experience with the articulation of conservative doctrine than any of us had. Had he stayed, Whalen would have rocked the boat—but what was so bad about that? For his part, Whalen made the choice to leave, rather than to stay, swallow part of his pride, and fight for his ideas on the inside, which I think was a mistake. He missed a lot; later he wrote a book containing many of the memos he wrote to Nixon that he was convinced were never read.

Whalen's departure proved to be a boon for me, however. John Mitchell did not like me, for a reason I did not know until he passed me in the hall one day and muttered, "How are your friends Evans and Novak?" Mitchell was convinced I was the source of leaks to these enterprising columnists, who painted him as the sourpussed *éminence grise* of the rise of Nixon. Whalen, in taking his leave, told Mitchell that he had often talked to Evans and Novak, he was glad he did, and would continue to do so. That got me off the hook. Mitchell apologized and afterward went out of his way to be friendly to me. He saw no objection to my going to the Chicago Democratic Convention as part of the "GOP Listening Post," and I thought it meant he trusted me.

August 28–31, Chicago: Nixonites in Demoland

Nixon thought it would be a good idea to send a small delegation to the Democratic Convention, to take up a public "listening post" in the Conrad Hilton Hotel and put out statements shooting down the more outrageous Democratic claims or allegations. We had a difficult time getting big-name "surrogates," as they later came to be called, to be the spokesmen in the lonely Republican outpost in the midst of the maelstrom of the Democrats' '68 Convention, but finally the Governor of Colorado, John Love—who always seemed to be chairman of some Governors' Conference—agreed to come. He was then teamed up with Don Rumsfeld, a young, dynamic Congressman whose district was in the Chicago suburbs, and given "support" by Buchanan, Bill Timmons (an aide to Congressman Bill Brock who would later be Nixon's assistant for liaison with the Congress), and me.

Pat and I wandered into the Conrad Hilton lobby and were smitten by the smell of the stink bombs (which newspapers referred to as "stench bombs," but a rose by any other name), deposited there by demonstrators who wanted to inflict a degree of discomfort on delegates. I went out to the airport that afternoon to meet our star surrogate and brought him back through a chanting, laughing, snarling mob scene in the lobby; there were signs that said, "Make Love Not War." Governor Love waved gaily at the sign holders and thanked me for being such a good advance man.

After Humphrey was nominated, we of the GOP's Poker Flat put out a statement: "The spectacle of Mayor Daley shouting 'go on home' at Senator Ribicoff is a sure illustration of the fact that a party which cannot unite itself cannot unite the nation." (That wasn't really what Daley had profanely shouted, but it would do.) Pat and I went into Grant Park at twilight and had a good whiff of tear gas, our first such experience, and came coughing back to the suite to find pandemonium—the idea of a band of Nixonites with a good view of the park being at the Democratic headquarters hotel intrigued a lot of reporters. Prizefighter Jose Torres and novelist Norman Mailer were hanging out the window looking at the skull-cracking below. Pat Buchanan looked out as well, saw a police charge and the beatings of young demonstrators, and murmured, "Jesus, we better watch what we say about law and order."

As the horror of that convention was displayed on television, the word came to us from Key Biscayne to sit tight and do nothing—anything we said would detract from the way the Democratic Party was tearing itself apart. We watched Hubert Humphrey make his acceptance speech: "I put it bluntly: rioting, burning, sniping, mugging, traffic in narcotics, and disregard for the law are the advance guard of anarchy—and they must and they will be stopped . . . neither mob violence nor police brutality have any place in America." The Democratic candidate was doing what he had to do—spread-eagling—and it wasn't coming off. He took a light jab at Nixon: "The answer to some who have spoken before does not lie in attacks on our courts, or our laws, or our Attorney General . . ." Then he evoked the memories of FDR, Harry Truman, Adlai Stevenson, and John Kennedy, and courageously—in that crowd—included Lyndon Johnson. He quoted Thomas Wolfe on the promise of America, and Winston Churchill on losing the future by standing in judgment on the past. Humphrey had opened with a good metaphor unconsciously lifted from Nixon's acceptance speech, "a new day," and closed with a realistic line calling on Americans "not to be of one mind, but of one spirit."

At eleven forty-five, Buchanan and I dragged a telephone into the bathroom of Suite 1906 to get away from the noise of the guests trooping through our suite (the local Republicans had provided a pair of long-legged twins as secretary-hostesses who were more of an attraction than Governor Love or Congressman Rumsfeld) to take a call from Nixon.

"Did you write that?" Nixon asked me about Humphrey's speech. I said no, thanks, nothing I ever wrote ran fifty minutes. "He could have gone through that in forty minutes, you know," Nixon said. "He let it drag. Hubert just doesn't know how to talk to that tube."

I allowed as how it was a standard, workmanlike acceptance speech, and I especially liked his "new day." Nixon immediately registered: "You noticed that? He took it from me, from the ending of my speech. No, I'd say it was a below-average acceptance, not as good as the Eisenhower acceptances, for example. Collection of clichés. And all those quotations . . ."

Nixon, speaking from Key Biscayne, cut the generalizing and found a soft spot in the speech: "We're going to crack that Attorney General issue. We got to him. He's taking us on in an area that's bad for him, and that's a mistake. But don't issue any statements. Just let it lie; they're doing plenty to each other."

Buchanan and I went out into the hot Chicago night afterward, mingling with the Grant Park crowd, listening to a speaker yelling into a microphone: "And now I want you to meet a man who called Mayor Daley an asshole long before it was popular!" The green-helmeted troops and the blue-helmeted police were lined up along the street, the tear gas clung to the flower garden, the bayonets and shattered glass gave sharp edges to dulled senses—it was surreal, sickening, frightening.

But all that was nothing to the atrocity that happened later. After refuse had been dumped out of the windows of the hotel, the police came charging up to the floor occupied by the McCarthy "kids." I got off at the wrong floor, found myself among the McCarthy supporters, and saw the devastation and the bloodied heads inflicted by the nightsticks of furious police. I went back to our suite and couldn't get over that. "Imagine invading a political headquarters," I remember saying to Buchanan. "That should be a sanctuary. You can't go into somebody else's headquarters, no matter what."

The rape of the McCarthy suite was covered in the papers, but television was already under criticism for showing too much violence, or even helping to cause it by the stimulating presence of its lights and cameras, and somehow this worst political atrocity of all was not impressed on the national consciousness. Politically, the only thing worse that could happen to the Democratic Party in convention would be for the people on the losing end in Chicago to become the winners four years later in Miami, and the only thing more shocking than to invade a political headquarters in fury would be to invade one in stealth.

September 5, San Francisco: Themes

Since I was developing themes, spending my time on the campaign planes with reporters, and was the only one in the "PR group" who had actually operated a public relations business, Bob Haldeman chose me to be the recipient of a fairly interesting memo that somehow never was passed along to Joe McGinniss for his *The Selling of the President.* Certainly the memo is manipulative, and people who like to profess their shock at attempts to get a political message across will do their thing, but it reveals something of Haldeman's mode of operation, something of what the Candidate wanted to be known, and also a few truths:

September 5, 1968

MEMORANDUM

TO: Bill Safire

FROM: Bob Haldeman

      RN asked that I summarize some of his thoughts regarding the campaign -- and transmit them to you in this form with the request that you make every effort to implement them within your areas of contact or responsibility -- as quickly and as thoroughly as you can.

      As we begin the first week of the campaign, it is essential that we maintain the initiative. This will be primarily the role of the candidate but now is the time for everybody in our organi- zation -- including Surrogates -- other speakers and top staff who talk to press as well as politicos who talk to State and County Chairmen across the country - to have the line and put it out as effectively as possible. Among the points that should be made are the following:

      1. The Come-Back Theme: This has an immense appeal and RN does not believe it has adequately been covered in columns or the press. Find ways to get it out - pointing up the obvious, that RN accomplished this despite the overwhelming opposition of the financial establishment and the press establishment and without huge financial resources, PR gimmicks, etc.

      2. The Calibre of the Nixon Team: This gives us the opportunity to point up the superb RN pre-Convention organization, that it has high intellectual quality, great morale and great loyalty. It will be recalled that one of Johnson's weaknesses is that very few people on his staff are really loyal to him, due to his personal abuse of them. Appparently HHH has real staff problems, too.

      3. The Youth of the RN Organization: Because we have such an outstanding group of young staff members in very key positions - this story should be easily and effectively promoted. Perhaps by emphasizing average age of Nixon staff, or the number of key men under 30, under 40 -- or whatever such statistics might be most telling. Also individual or group features on the young stars of the team, i.e., Buchanan, Price, Anderson, Bell, Gavin, Hart, etc., in R & W; Chapin, Ziegler, Higby, Allan Woods,

etc., in tour operations; the young crew working with Mitchell, Flanigan, et al; and all the young people in the Citizens Operation.

4. The Immense Effect of the RN Acceptance Speech:
It probably had a greater effect in shifting votes than any acceptance speech in the last 25 years. Several have suggested that the story that RN prepared the speech on his own, and did not "try it out" or reveal any of the content to anybody except his secretary, simply hasn't gotten across. This is a very impressive story to the average person who suspects that all politicians are simply parroting the lines their ghosts have written for them. This story should be gotten out broadly. Perhaps one way to bring this off is that when we reprint copies of the Acceptance Speech to distribute to people, a brief paragraph at the outset point out how it was prepared and also the immense effect that it had. Although many will say that we shouldn't build on events of the past, let us not forget that Kennedy made mountains of yardage during the first two years of his Presidency by referring to his Inaugural Address and having the press do likewise. Our people have not yet done an adequate job in this respect as far as this speech is concerned.

5. RN as Party Unifier Even several of the less favorable press men pointed out that the week when we were at Mission Bay plus the swing to the major states was probably one of the major political stories of our time and would have been covered as such had the Czech Revolution not occurred in the same period. This story should be repeated over and over again -- properly embellished -- pointing out that RN fights hard but then is able to unify and bring the best men into the final organization. This will also give a good impression as to how RN will handle the Presidency once the battle is over

6. RN, "the man for the times.": Perhaps most important of all there should be emphasis on RN, "the man for the times." The Churchill analogy is probably appropriate. Churchill was "in the wilderness" as he put it during the '30s but was called back to lead his country in a period of crisis. What we must do is to knock down the idea that , by manipulation and because of political debts that were due RN, he was able to get the nomination. We've got to point out that he won the nomination because of his own strength and not just because of the weakness and confusion of his opponents.

In summary, one weakness of our campaign in the past has been the tendency of our entire staff, and most of our supporters, simply to rely on RN's speeches and activities for our campaign success. We are doing better this time than we have previously, but we can take a leaf out of the Kennedy book and recognize that at least 50% of the credit for his win in 1960 and also for his immensely good press after the 1960 election was due to the fact that his staff and friends were constantly running their own campaigns in his behalf, and not just waiting for him to carry the ball. This must be done at all levels -- on the campaign plane, from the Citizens group in Washington and from the Campaign Headquarters in New York -- as well as by all of our state and local leaders.

- 3 -

Of vital importance is the point that we must play the confident line from now until November, regardless of what developments occur. We are on the offensive and we must stay on the offensive. The Democrats are demoralized, and we must keep them demoralized. We should exude confidence, not cockiness, indicating that we're going to run an all-out campaign and pour it on, but that we do so knowing that we are ahead and that we plan to stay ahead and extend our lead so that we can elect a Republican House and a lot of Republican Senators as well. It is important that all of our major speakers take this line, and particularly important, that those who are on the plane and talking with the press, and the local politicos exude it. It is also important that those who have contact with RN take this line and not come in with long faces any time something goes wrong.

September 5, San Francisco: On the Trail

My first campaign "excerpt" to be prepared for the Republican Presidential Candidate contained a terrible mistake. The secondary boycott of the California grapes, led by Cesar Chavez, was a major issue in that state; Humphrey and the state Democrats were on the grape-pickers' side, Reagan and the California Republicans were in opposition. The instructions, relayed by Finch: I was to prepare a statement condemning the boycott as illegal.

I drafted the statement from some material supplied me by local lawyers, including a line that read, "We have laws on the books to protect workers who wish to organize; we have a National Labor Relations Board to impartially supervise the election . . ." This was wrong. The NLRB Act at that time specifically excluded farm workers. I checked it out with two men on the campaign who should have known it was wrong, but they did not focus on it; as a result, the candidate, depending on his staff, put his foot in his mouth. There was no interest in correcting the mistake; Finch, then Lieutenant Governor of California, suggested a more compassionate and informed statement be issued when we returned to California in two weeks, which I did; but throughout the campaign, whenever a group of angry grape-pickers heckled Nixon at a rally—and they followed us everywhere—I felt a twinge of guilt. And I learned to double-check everything and not to be so trusting of experts.

September 7, Oklahoma City
Signs of Welcome:

Put Nixon
over
The Hump

HHHell NO!

Down the Tube
with
Hube the Cube

Standing at the airport, listening to the Candidate make his stump speech to the crowd outside the hangar, we were dismayed to see a Standard Oil executive jet aircraft taxiing past the speaker's platform, drowning out Nixon's words. The Candidate stopped and glared until the plane went past, then picked up his speech with less enthusiasm. Robert Ellsworth turned to me and said, "There goes the oil depletion allowance."

September 10, Aboard the Aircraft Tricia

The Candidate was unhappy with the way we were handling the economic issue. Maurice Stans had sent him a memo with the best points to make, and Nixon sent this irritated note to Jim Keogh:

> Keogh—
> Get 3 of our writers to
> try a brief excerpt based
> on this—
> Maybe one will be effective.

That same day, two other memos were sent from Nixon to his writers, this time including William Gavin, who specialized in inspirational, uplift stuff, and Richard Moore, an old Nixon friend who provided information about local color. Nixon wrote:

> At an earlier time before the primaries, Safire prepared a memorandum of some of the good Nixon quotes of previous years that he thought might be repeated.

> At this time, I would like the four of you to think back over RN's speeches from the time the primaries began and his stump speech and list those one-liners that ought to be repeated. In this category would be lines like the following: "Rather than more people on welfare rolls, we need more people on payrolls."

> "We must rebuild our cities but we don't need to burn our cities down in order to rebuild them."

> "A party that cannot unite itself cannot unite America."

> You can see what I am driving at. I want real "grabbers." Phrases that people will remember—not cute phrases or gimmicky phrases, but those that will summarize in a sentence a major issue . . .

> A great number of good quotes have been submitted to me in the past couple of weeks. They are useful. However, what all of those who are submitting the quotes overlook is that RN does

not use quotes in his speech as Humphrey did in his acceptance speech. RN likes to use a quote as a parable—as part of a story. The best example is the Sophocles quote and the Guild Hall quote and the one that he used in his acceptance speech with regard to Lincoln leaving Springfield, Illinois.

For example, in presenting a Wilson-Lincoln quote put around it the occasion in which it was made. For example, as Wilson was traveling across the country trying to win support for the League of Nations in a losing cause, he said in a memorable speech, "*quote*". A few hours later he had a stroke which ended his career. The train, with curtains drawn, rode through the night to Washington, D. C., etc., etc.

I do not know, of course, what quote would fit into this kind of anecdote. But the point that I am making is that for speech purposes where RN's style is concerned, I prefer to use parables —not just quotes, because somebody else has said it better than I can say it.

The only man that to date seems to have an understanding of this technique is James Hume. The quotes that he submitted are in that style. What I want is for everybody to think along these lines and to send the quotes into me in a dramatic setting. I am sure Safire would be able to make some suggestions along this line.

If I had about eight or ten of this type that would be enough to last me through the campaign. I have only two or three at this time. This is of high priority and I want anybody who has any gift in this field to get to work on it.

The same applies to humor. Humor is not effective as far as I am concerned unless it is related to an incident—a parable. If any of you took the trouble to listen to Billy Graham's sermon on Sunday you can see the effectiveness of the parable technique. With all of the brilliant people we have working for us I think they should be able to sit down and read some books, speeches, etc., and get me a few more quotes of this type which I can use in an effective way.

For example, I know several quotes from Burke—my recollection is that he might have made one of these statements when he was making a speech to his constituents in a campaign that he lost, at some historic moment in the House of Commons, at Guild Hall, etc., etc. It is this that all of our quote material seems to miss except for the Hume stuff.

Let's get to work on this right away.

One memo from RN to Murray Chotiner, dated September 17, offers a fair, if hard-bitten, approach to political campaigning on the issues, and illustrates the Nixon view of the Humphrey vulnerability:

September 17, 1968

MEMORANDUM

TO: Murray Chotiner

        cc: Bob Haldeman—for whatever distribution he considers appropriate—Agnew, for example—et al

FROM: RN

Among the subjects that might be emphasized by the attack squad are the following:

1. Humphrey would be the most expensive President in U. S. history. During the period he was a Senator he introduced spending bills which did not pass, appropriations for which total at least 100 million dollars and which would have meant that our present budget would be at least 10 billion dollars annually higher than it is. (Agnew and others have done research on this). Be sure we have these figures so that if he tries to deny it we can get specific and not be in hot water.

2. All speakers should ask over and over again for Humphrey to name one issue where he differs from LBJ or the policies of the last four years.

The purpose of this exercise is not to be hard on LBJ but to be hard on Humphrey. Humphrey has said that he offers new leadership—make him indicate those areas where he thinks the old leadership fails. Then follow up by demanding that he indicate where he objected to the policies which he thinks now were mistakes.

3. Humphrey should be nailed on the subjects of steel and textile quotas. These are special issues where I have had to speak out and where Humphrey privately has told the steel and textile operators he is looking at these quotas but publicly has not taken a position. See that some of our friends in the industry nail him down and get him out publicly.

4. Humphrey along the same lines should be nailed on any other subject where his position might prove to be unpopular.

5. Someone should—they can either advocate or defend the provision in the omnibus crime bill which modifies the Supreme Court Decisions—make him either take a position of defense of the Supreme Court and its decisions or one where he criticizes

some of the decisions and advocates legislative action to correct them.

6. Similarly he should be nailed on Administration farm policy. Freeman has been appointed to a major role in his campaign and Humphrey should be put on the record as to whether he approves the Freeman policies and plans to extend them.

It would seem that on all these subjects we should have one or two people among the Humphrey press corps that will ask him the tough questions that press guys never hesitate to ask me.

Some effort should be made to get Humphrey to either endorse or repudiate some of the Southern Senators like Eastland—whose position is basically the same as Thurmond's. Make a list of two or three of them and then have some press guy ask him at a press conference whether he accepts their support and endorses their views.

At a press conference he should be asked whether he endorses the attacks made by O'Brien on RN. We get questions whether I endorse what my campaign people have to say about him and, of course, there should be a single standard.

September 10, Milwaukee, Wisconsin

The Candidate saw a schedule that specified that there would be dancing during dinner. He buzzed for Chapin and announced, "I will not dance. When you're running for sheriff, you dance. Not when you're running for President." Ten minutes later, Chapin's buzzer sounded again, and he scooted up to RN's room. "I'm serious about this dancing thing. I don't dance and I don't wear funny hats. Let's be very clear about that."

September 17, Coming into Salt Lake City

The Mormon Tabernacle in Salt Lake City is the place where politicians love to expound on matters of morality. (Later in the campaign, Hubert Humphrey chose Salt Lake as the site of his Vietnam speech, appearing to declare his independence of Lyndon Johnson, but that was not using the Salt Lake forum in the traditional way.) I drafted an excerpt—that is, a quotable "new" portion of the regular stump speech, to give the traveling press a fresh lead—on one of the articles of faith of the Church of Jesus Christ of Latter-day Saints, "obeying, honoring and sustaining the law."

The draft came back from the Candidate with his scrawl around all the edges. The other writers knew I was reading Nixon's comments because I was turning the page around clockwise. "Add a solid paragraph on role of volunteer groups in reconciliation, respect for law, cities, etc.," he wrote. "If you have nothing better, take the paragraph from RN's acceptance speech." I had drafted a fairly pompous paragraph that troubled the Candidate: "Third, sustaining the law. This goes deepest of all, to the roots of our society." Nixon struck out that line—sounded too much like the "root cause" stuff sociologists used to blame guilt on everybody rather than the guilty. He left in another line: "America has a deep need today to restore a climate of public and private morality that will sustain and uphold our entire system of laws." Alongside this, Nixon wrote a plaintive and characteristic comment:

> P.S.   All this guff is primarily the responsibility of home, church, and voluntary groups—not govt.

September 18, Peoria, Illinois

John Ehrlichman, the tour director, would occasionally say of applause lines that offended the national press traveling with the campaign: "It'll play in Peoria." This was not said in condescension, but in perspective: out there were the folks, the "Nixon people," who appreciated a homespun approach and an appeal to human interest. As a big-city boy myself, I had considered Peoria the equivalent to "Squeedunk," or, as LBJ's Liz Carpenter was fond of citing, "Resume Speed, Texas." This view was changed for me by Senator Everett Dirksen, who said while we were working on a speech together that he had come from Pekin, Illinois, which was kind of a quiet place in his youth—"but for those young rakes that craved excitement, there were, only sixty miles away, the bright lights of Peoria."

RN called Richard Moore and me up to the front of the plane to have a chat about some humor we had suggested for a fund-raising dinner in New York. He was uncertain about a Moore line: "Some people say I never mention my opponent's name. That's not so—I spoke about Larry O'Brien only yesterday." He was feeling the strain, and seemed a little testy, which Dick and I took as an odd compliment, because he rarely let his testiness show to other than intimates. He was down on the press: "You see the way they hate to get up and look at the size of these crowds? Remember —the press is the enemy." I pointed out that the columnists were hitting hard and probably effectively on Agnew—some of his comments were being used to show him as a dangerous buffoon. "You know why they're screaming at Agnew," Nixon replied, "because he's hitting where it hurts." He came around to his need for crowd-stirring lines: "I want more one-liners. 'We want to help our friends who help themselves, and not support those who help our enemies'—that's good. That works. The doormat line was especially good."

On the way out, as we were landing, I asked Nixon if he was enjoying the campaign.

"Never do," he said, looking out at the crowd lined up along the fence, the signs, the mike on the podium, the local politicians waiting to shake hands. "Campaigns are something to get over with."

The Doormat Line

For an excerpt in Indianapolis, where foreign aid was unpopular and patriotism not considered corny, after a denunciation of the way that respect for America had been falling all over the world (a point taken from the 1960 Kennedy campaign) I threw in a "one-liner." The Candidate read the excerpt about how, under new leadership, nobody was going to make a doormat out of the American flag. He read it offhandedly, to be sure the newspapers used it, but he was anxious to get away from the written paragraphs and back to his standard, ad-lib stump speech. To his surprise, there was a roar of approval from the crowd after the doormat line. From then on, for the rest of the campaign, every stump speech had the doormat line; it caused the press to roll up its eyes in derision, but it was a surefire crowd waker-upper. (After the campaign, and after the incident of the shooting down of one of our planes by the North Koreans—which the President wisely ignored—some of my friends sent me a doormat covered by an American flag.)

September 24, New York

RN wrote a memo to the eight men, including myself, responsible for the content of the campaign. It was transcribed dictation which Rose Woods wrote up with no attempt to edit, and it is almost a stream of consciousness.

September 24, 1968

MEMORANDUM

TO: Keogh/Price/Buchanan/Harlow/Gavin/Anderson/Moore

FROM: RN

Here are some general thoughts with regard to excerpts and statements for the next six weeks. I don't think we are yet quite hitting the mark as these comments will indicate.

As a general rule, an excerpt should be no more than 1 to 1-1/2 pages long. It should be meaty and quotable and should be material that I can easily work into a stump speech even if I am speaking outdoors without a podium.

A case in point is the statement for Sioux Falls. Something like this should never be put out as an excerpt for two reasons: (1) It is too long. (2) It is too localized. From now on anything on agriculture should generally just be dropped off as a statement for the local press and let our press give it whatever ride they want. The national press couldn't care less about what we say on Karl Mundt's pet REA project nor on our repeating our agriculture program. In fact, I think the less we speak nationally on agriculture in the next few weeks—the better. Just drop statements off where needed—Harlow knows what we can say—they can just be cleared with Bryce—I won't need to see them.

More often than not a statement dealing with a local subject and zeroing in on a local problem should be dropped off at most stops. This will give enormous local coverage and since it will not require me to include the material in my speech it imposes no burden on me. Just read the advance information sheets and if you see that some place cares about Indians—put out a little statement indicating that we care about Indians, etc. A case in point was the statement Pat Buchanan prepared reacting to the Yippees that broke up the Catholic mass in Milwaukee. As a matter of fact, that statement deserved even a national play. I hope it got out in time to get not only the local press but also to be circulated among our national press.

With regard to our excerpts—they should zero in primarily on the four major themes. If we scatter-gun too much we are not going to have an impact. That is why I repeat we must have at least two excerpts a week which hit some aspect of the law and order theme and one or two a week which hit some aspect of the spending theme and two or three which hit the foreign policy-respect for America theme.

Let me take the spending theme as a case in point. I think a follow up on what we said in Milwaukee would be to find the memorandum that I dictated a couple of weeks ago and if you can't find it—I think you will recall it. In it I said that a survey would show that we could safely make the statement that no member of the Senate had introduced bills calling for more money than Hubert Humphrey. I think we should nail him as the most expensive member of the Senate while he was in the Senate and that he would be the most expensive President in history if he were to be elected. He will have a very difficult time denying this because he would have to say that one of his supporters had introduced more bills—or called for spending more money —than he did.

I think we should start hammering him hard and regularly on the spending theme, particularly in view of the fact that he has introduced so many bills and talks about introducing so many new programs. On this score, it is now time to cost-out Humphrey's programs for spending and then make the charge that already in this campaign—with six weeks left—he has advocated programs which would add _____ millions of dollars annually to the budget. This does not have to be done in too technical a fashion—I don't want a Dun and Bradstreet report on it.

On the law and order theme, I think we should start hammering on the fact that he defends the record of the Administration over the past four years. Demand that he name one instance in which he disagrees with the record of the Administration. Does he disagree with Clark in not using wire tapping—in not going after organized crime—in not enforcing the Narcotics Act. Demand replies. We must keep him on the defensive just as he is trying to put us on the defensive.

Another theme that can be developed is Hubert vs. Hubert. Pick out four or five major issues and use direct quotes where he has contradicted himself. These all don't have to be big issues—of course, Viet Nam offers the most inviting one. Get to work on this one immediately and give me a good excerpt on that one.

Some general guidelines:

Don't be cute or gimmicky—just hit hard with crisp one-liners whenever they are appropriate . . .

Another point that we want to develop is to demand Hubert disassociate himself from any of the Administration's policies with which he disagrees. Ask again and again for him to name in the field of foreign policy, in the field of domestic policy, in the field of law and order where—if at all—he disagrees with the Administration.

I think a good excerpt could be gotten out too on Hubert's not waging a national campaign. Why is he avoiding the South? Challenge him to go South.

Apart from these day to day excerpts, of course, we should drop in regular statements—about two a week from now on—that are meaty, substantive—they will not have any impact on voters but they will impress the press—the piece on the Presidency; merchant marine, etc., are ones in this category.

It seems to me that we should have more of these statements in the bank than currently seems to be the case.

There is no reason why we should not get some rather safe statements on some of these issues, calling in effect for change so that we thereby counter the charge that we are not talking to the issues.

Sometime toward the middle of the week we should all get together and discuss this further but I would like for all of you to have a discussion on this tonight in Seattle and see how we can improve on our program in this respect.

September 25, Seattle, Washington

The next morning, having read that memo, Haldeman, Price, Harlow, Keogh, Buchanan, and I met with Nixon in his room at the Olympic Hotel in Seattle.

A few of the usual, stupid things had been happening that plague every campaign. On the Agnew plane, his "Fat Jap" remark—meant as a friendly salutation to a newsman Agnew knew from Baltimore—was surfaced with political calculation three days after it was made, as the Agnew plane entered Hawaii, with its big Japanese-ancestry population. (Jules Witcover later did a thorough study of that incident, which reflected not a lot of credit on either the press corps or the Vice Presidential candidate.) On a far less important matter, but indicative of a different kind of snafu, was a law-and-order brochure based on a statement about crime in Washington, D.C., that Pat Buchanan had written, and to which I had added some quotable lines. One of the lines was "D.C. should not stand for Disorder and Crime," and that was to be the title of the booklet, nothing inspiring but at least a good headline. However, the man who set the type got it a little bit wrong, and thousands of booklets were printed that read "D.C. Should Not Stand for Crime and Disorder," a ringing non sequitur. We scrapped them. We also scrapped thousands of copies of the new paperback edition of the Earl Mazo-Steve Hess biography of Nixon because Rose Woods and Bob Haldeman felt that the sketch of Nixon on the cover looked too severe.

"We must keep control of the news," RN told us briskly. He had a good night's sleep and was feeling well about the campaign; the meeting was more of a monologue by a man who knew what he wanted and knew how to express it.

RN: "We must keep control of the news and not rely on the other guy falling on his face to make news. I want two or more statements a week dealing with order, two dealing with our credentials in the foreign field—play to our strength—two that have to do with the money side. Very simple: a study of Humphrey reveals that he is the most expensive Senator. If he disagrees he will have to say who has been more expensive.

"Never mention programs specifically. Work up some sharp rhetoric to be included in the basic speech. If you argue specifics, you are against the old ladies and kids. In general, just hit him as a spender.

"A major statement should be made in Florida—St. Petersburg—about Social Security. Not in negative terms, not 'my opponent says'—we should not be reproaching anybody about Social Security. We stand for a program to stop the rise in the cost of living, and we are for an escalator clause tying Social Security to the cost of living.

"On the medical thing: there is a major medical crisis—50,000 doctors and 600,000 medical personnel short. Don't try to match Humphrey. Just make it clear we are for more doctors.

"When Humphrey accuses me of being against Federal aid to education, that's not true. I have been for it for twenty years. Force him to talk about our issues. No peace abroad. No peace at home. Cost of living.

"In order to satisfy the press, we have to be prepared to do a major speech on NATO. It will not go as well as the speech about the Presidency, because you can't talk about Topic A all the time.

"Whenever we get into health, education, welfare—it can't be a question of how much. We will always lose. It is always a question of *how*.

"Let's do a fifteen-minute talk on dissent. Forget ourselves—defend Humphrey. Aim at dissent in colleges, not among Negroes. When dissent becomes destructive, it becomes totalitarianism in reverse. What can a new Administration do? Get across the listening idea. Bring in the expanded democracy speech.

"On Social Security, the people living on pensions are among the forgotten Americans. Keep repeating the basic themes until they run out of your ears.

"Ted Agnew said he only said 'Fat Jap' to a friend of his in the press. I sent him a note: 'Dear Ted: When news is concerned, nobody in the press is a friend—they are all enemies.'

"On Wallace: The way we should take him on is this. He says what he is against. I am saying what I am for. He fears. We hope. He complains about the problems. We have the solutions."

Safire: "Between a spender and a spoiler."

RN: "Maybe. Maybe. I am willing to take the Wallace thing on. But not like a knee-jerk liberal. That will only help him. Never call him a racist, that's a silly damn way to take him on. In the Field poll in California Wallace leveled off at 8 per cent. Don't know why. Maybe less union labor strength.

"Give the press a lot of copy, then they won't have too much to squeal about. As to tone, never name Johnson or Humphrey. Be very careful not to reflect on Johnson. Talk about eight years, not four. Now Johnson is not playing Humphrey's game, so let's not get too biting. Say 'the Administration of which Humphrey was a part.'

"Don't write excerpts in vernacular which I will use. Write hard, crisp copy. Remember: Continue to attack. Don't talk to his terms."

October 4, Atlanta, Georgia

The Regency Hyatt House is a magnificent hotel, built around a central court, with inside balconies leading to glass-enclosed elevators; architecturally, it is a modern adaption of the old part of the Brown Palace Hotel in Denver. Nixon supporter Bo Callaway wanted a letter from RN to the poultry farmers of Georgia. "You might, if you were so inclined," observed gentle Bryce Harlow, "call this a chickenshit assignment."

To get some poultry information, I asked Rose Woods for the Washington number of Bryce's secretary. She wrote it down for me on a slip of paper, adding a touch of thoughtfulness that said something nice about Rose: "Sally Studebaker," the note read, and then the phone number. Underneath, parenthetically, was "Bryce H's secy—re poultry info." Rose explained: "That's in case your wife finds it when she sends your suit to be cleaned."

Humphrey was beginning to move up in our own private polls; organized labor was doing its job of winning back union members to the Democratic fold, and the erosion of the Wallace strength was going Humphrey's way and not ours. The night before, on one of the Q and A television shows, Nixon had taken a jab at the Alabama Governor's best cheer line: "No President of the United States is going to run his car over people. Nobody who talks that way should be President."

I suggested in a long memo to Nixon that we reveal our "secret" strategy —an all-out blazing finish in the last three weeks—and went into detail on how we should do it. Then, when the Humphrey strength began to show in the public polls, we would not appear to be reacting in panic to their momentum.

"This is very perceptive analysis," he wrote on the memo. "Let's go forward with the plan and announcement before the next Gallup poll. Get me if possible dates of next Gallup and Harris. Give me a battle plan on release of R. N. polls (put in here a lot of our sure states, Oregon, etc., where we are winning big.)"

Nixon was worried about the bandwagon effect of polls; a lot of fence-sitting Democrats would go to Humphrey if they felt he really had a chance to win. With a month to go, and with Harlow supplying disturbing intelligence about a bombing halt given him by one of the men meeting with LBJ, Nixon started to worry; his own campaign began to pour it on.

October 11, Dallas, Texas

Nixon's instructions were to draw sharp differences between his position and that of Humphrey's, especially in Texas—to show that there was indeed more than what Wallace was effectively deriding: "not a dime's worth of difference." Wallace had some good slogans. We did not—"Nixon's the One" was innocuous, but not promissory enough—nor did Humphrey have more to offer. The Democrats had started out with "United With Humphrey" but after Chicago that seemed so ludicrous that they dropped it.

In Dallas, Nixon rewrote my excerpt to draw the difference between candidate positions more sharply, and his personal additions are worth scrutiny.

> One candidate advocates concentrating more and more power in the Federal Government; I say it is time for new policies which will move power away from Washington back to the states, local governments and the people.
>
> One candidate defends the present Attorney General and the policies under which we have seen crime go up 9 × as fast as the population. I say, we need a new Attorney General who will launch an all-out battle against organized crime and guarantee the first civil right of every American—the right to be free from domestic violence.

October 12, Key Biscayne, Florida

Alan Greenspan, an economist who with Martin Anderson headed our research department, came out of a meeting on economic policy with an observation that I wrote down: "The carefully thought-through decisions can always be changed; it's the arbitrary decisions that can't be changed."

Nixon, who had told Jim Keogh two weeks before, "Do you really think anybody pays any attention to this intellectual stuff?" now wanted to give a fifteen-minute radio address nearly every night. As Haldeman told us he put it: "Give 'em substance until it runs out of their ears, and then they'll quit their bitching."

At about this point, I noticed how oxymorons have a curious way of popping up in politics. These are phrases in which the adjectives appear to fight the nouns they modify, as in "cruel kindness" or "thunderous silence." We used one in 1966 as the title of the Nixon column: "Loyal Opposition."

I had written a statement denouncing the use of the U.S. mails to purvey salacious, obscene, or pornographic material to children. Not an especially controversial position, in line with Supreme Court decisions, but good to drop off in Salt Lake City. Jim Keogh had okayed the draft statement which—as far as I knew—was in the process of being mimeographed as we flew into Utah. But the system didn't work, and Dwight Chapin came running into our cabin when the plane drew to a stop, blurting without thinking: "I've lost the fuckin' obscenity statement!"

Later in the campaign, after a rousing speech at a rally by a candidate who wanted to fire up the crowd, a local clergyman closed the activities with a prayer. This put a damper on everything; the crowd walked out quietly, causing Nixon to whisper to Haldeman and Chapin: "No more goddam benedictions!"

October 13, Key Biscayne, Florida

The Candidate called the writers and Haldeman into the living room of George Smathers' house, where he was staying.

"In the last three weeks," the Candidate said, "I want to attack them for lying about Social Security payments—that's just a campaign of fear and smear, and we mustn't let them get away with it. It's a lie aimed at the old folks, and what kind of politics is it to scare old people?

"I want to attack their crime statement. That'll make ours look stronger. No more excerpts, only statements that we drop off—intelligence tells us that we can expect hecklers wherever we go, and I don't want to try to read something to an audience that is yelling at us."

Somebody wondered if this speech-a-night routine appeared like we were pressing too hard. "There's a lot of drama to ten speeches in fourteen days," Nixon replied. "Speak up now if you don't like it. What we are fighting, as usual, is the mythology—eighty-five out of the ninety press on the plane is against us.

"Now on dissenters in the colleges. Any violence, I say—cold turkey—expel 'em. We can say an awful lot more about dissent than we do.

"On the volunteer army"—Martin Anderson's pet project—"Bryce, if you're for it, we'll go. Run one on natural resources, too, not so much for the campaign, but for some Senators I'll want to work with later. On the research gap—let's make the U.S. first again. Use that 'first again' line wherever you can. By the way, is there anything left over from our speeches we can give Agnew? Or even something new for him? Try."

He stopped the rapid-fire lecturing and eased up: "Do you suppose anybody listens to radio? Buchanan wrote one of the speeches and never even listened to the darn thing. But it does reach a quarter of a million people. That's a helluva rally. I'm going to use that radio medium afterwards, you'll see. When the President speaks, he'll have an audience."

The radio speeches were a perfect tool: because the speeches were not mere "position papers" but were spoken by the Candidate, they had to be covered in the press. They required little work by the Candidate. He could put on his glasses and in bathrobe and slippers read them into a tape recorder late at night. He knew he was pressing one of his strengths—his resonant, familiar voice—and Haldeman liked to point out that Nixon "won" the Kennedy debates on radio, according to polls—"it was on television RN hadn't done so well."

I told Nixon I was going to suggest he propose a Federal Youth Agency, which was a pretty sound idea and would give us a lead on his youth speech. "Good! Get it out of HEW, that's where they only think about the old folks."

Vietnam came up. "I don't want any advice on that," he told us; he knew his own mind there, repeating, "If you give 'em the bombing pause and a coalition government, you give 'em the whole goddam country."

October 20, New York

Memo from RN, dictated to Rose Woods, typed up rough and sent to Jim Keogh:

"I want to double up next week in terms of a sharp hitting of the major issues . . .

"Cincinnati—strong on law and order. Maybe the idea that law and order is not a code word for racism—but mainly indicating the choice on law and order: a vote for Humphrey is a vote for a policy under which crime will double in the next four years unless we get a change in policy. Sharp. Hard-hitting.

"In the next two weeks we can directly zero in on the difference between HHH and Nixon—cracking hard not only on his record, his defense of [Ramsey] Clark—it might take on his attack of me on the Supreme Court —that I would make appointments that would be conservative and take the court back. Then they can pick up out of the stuff I have used in answering questions on TV, judges who realize it is their responsibility to interpret the laws, not to make the laws. Hitting again that some of the decisions have gone too far in weakening the peace forces as against the criminal forces. Might throw in a word that Potter Stewart has been on the right side of these issues—I agree with him rather than with the Majority (discuss this before using it).

"Columbus, Ohio—Humphrey, the most expensive Senator, will be the most expensive President. Increase in taxes, increase in prices, etc. Or since [Governor James] Rhodes' trademark is jobs, take out the labor speech—15 million new jobs. Maybe Safire could develop this one into 'a vote for Humphrey is a vote to raise your prices and raise your taxes.' Back to the crime excerpt—'A vote for Humphrey is a vote for a policy that has seen crime go up three times as fast as it did under Eisenhower, etc.'

"Toledo—I think this is where HHH made his 'you never had it so good' statement—check that out. If this is so, work up something like this: Who does he tell this to, farmers? What has happened to them? The aged, what has happened to them? Wage earners, less money despite pay increases. Millions who have seen their loved ones killed in Vietnam. Those that have been the victims of crime. Something like that.

"Foreign policy could be hit Tuesday in terms of 'let's look around the world apart from Vietnam.' The danger of war is greater, the prospects for peace lower. We have to have new policies. American respect down, American power down. A vote for HHH is a vote to continue these policies.

"The language style should not be the querulous kind but just hard-hitting and strong. Law and Order. Inflation. Foreign Policy. Peace—Humphrey the uncertain trumpet—he has been on all sides of every issue. That is the greatest risk of war—where a man is on all sides, for that leads to miscalculation."

October 28, Detroit

Humphrey continued to edge up in the polls, and it began to appear that there might be an unprecedented way for him to win. If the states carried by George Wallace denied both major-party candidates the necessary number of votes in the Electoral College, the election would be into the House of Representatives, which would pave the way for a Wallace-Humphrey deal to do in Nixon.

Haldeman, Moore, Finch, Keogh, and I trooped into the Candidate's bedroom at the Sheraton Cadillac Hotel at midnight to talk over the final week. RN was sitting up in bed, wearing bright yellow pajamas, an open bottle of Budweiser beer handy on the nighttable, and his briefcase open with many of its contents spread out on the bed. "That's how Hugh Hefner works," I said and didn't get much of a chuckle. Nixon had turned down a *Playboy* interview.

"I have decided," the Candidate told us, "that the popular vote thing is important." He wanted to be ready for the Humphrey-Wallace Electoral College "deal" contingency by preconditioning public opinion to believe the only fair thing to do would be to elect the candidate who received the highest percentage of the popular vote. "Let's use it in the radio speech about regaining the initiative. Helluva speech," he allowed, then looked at me severely. "You do that speech, Safire? Well, pretty good speech, then." He was feeling pretty good and took another sip of his beer.

"Let's bang away at how Humphrey was afraid to meet the people in the primaries, and now he's afraid to accept the decision of the majority of the people today. There's lots of moxie in the popular vote thing. Don't you agree?" (In 1966 and '67, his most frequent expression at meetings was 'You don't agree, do you?' In '68, it began to change to 'Don't you agree?'; which was unfortunate, since it did not elicit the disagreement he needed.)

"I didn't bring Price and Buchanan in to discuss whether we should hit Wallace on the popular vote, because they cancel each other out on that." (Buchanan did not want to mention Wallace for fear of hurting us with the far-right conservatives; Price long ago had spoken out for an attack on Wallace. In this meeting, Finch and I advised it would be better to hit Wallace as a spoiler than as a racist, and I was assigned to write the popular vote jab into the "regaining the initiative" speech coming up in two days.)

After that was decided, Nixon said, "Let's hit the would-be leaders who stand idly by when draft cards are burned. Kick the weirdos and the beardos on the college campuses—I want to see the violent ones expelled." When I made a face at this, which Nixon did not catch, Haldeman said to me, "If you don't agree, don't just sit there making faces, tell him." So I did—that the harsh anti-demonstrator stuff was a mistake, it made Nixon look mean and helped his opponents sell their caricature of the Old Nixon. The Candidate got the point.

"They tell me to smile more on television," he said, about the criticism he had from campaign headquarters after his appearance on "Face the Nation." "Can you imagine? 'The war in Vietnam is terrible,'" and then he put on a big, fake grin. "I don't know what's the matter with those guys. Bob, are they buying enough TV? We can't let ourselves be out-televised." Haldeman assured him again we were buying all the TV that could be purchased, and that nobody was going to outspend us.

William Casey, Len Hall's law partner in New York and a prodigious writer and publisher of books, had been working with Ray Price on publishing a paperback of all Nixon's recent speeches to be distributed to the press as proof of the campaign's substance. Since I was going to this late meeting (Price was not the type who would insist on presenting it himself just because he had written the lion's share of the speeches in it) I dropped it on the Candidate's bed. He picked up the book—105,000 words—hefted it, and said only "Goddam." He put it aside casually, as if it did not really interest him, but we all knew he was dying to read it in private, so we filed out. "Sock it to 'em!" he said cheerily, a play on his brief "Laugh-In" appearance when he said, "Sock it to *me?*" A moment later, I had to go back in—I had forgotten my notes—and he was avidly reading the book of speeches. I had one more thought to tell him about his speech at Madison Square Garden coming up soon, to be nationally televised: that he should direct himself to the television audience, not the audience in the hall. He shook his head: "You see that rally tonight—the constant heckling? That's why I need cheer lines. Gotta drown 'em out. You can't go into that beautiful, uplifting stuff when they're yelling at you."

October 29, New York City

I wrote a tough blast at Wallace into the radio speech scheduled for tomorrow night, accusing him of "standing in the doorway of the White House to welcome Humphrey," but Keogh and Harlow both felt it should be toned down. The Candidate made his contribution in notes written around the edges of my draft:

> Hubert Humphrey has now adopted a strategy of desperation. He knows he cannot win this election on his own.

> If he becomes President he will owe his election to George Wallace; and the price—

> America will have to pay for this unholy alliance will be four years of hate, division, and despair.

I changed the word "hate" to dissension, less for alliterative purposes than to remove the word from Nixon's discourse entirely. An hour later, I received another note from RN:

> In addition to what I wrote on the bottom—see what the fellows think about whether to add that material along with the following:
> That is why I call upon him to join me in making clear that he will accept the mandate of the American people and will give his support to whichever candidate receives the highest popular vote. Only this way can America be spared the possibility of a Wallace-dictated and Wallace-influenced national Administration.

Again, Harlow and Keogh removed the direct mention of Wallace, but Nixon's message got across: "I say again—the candidate who gets the most votes should be the next President." Humphrey was asked about this and fudged, just as Nixon would have done in his shoes—maybe it scored a point.

On the plane to Albany that day, I talked with RN alone in his cabin, and raised again the need for uplift in his Garden rally speech. "A Garden rally is not an acceptance speech," he replied. "At a convention you can hear a pin drop—but not in a Garden rally. They want to shout. Give me cheer lines."

We talked about the press, and his appearance on "Face the Nation." "I had to crack the *Times* hard on that story they did on Agnew, which was awful. If we lose, Agnew will collect a million bucks—this isn't the Sullivan case where the *Times* only ran an ad, this was an editorial. On 'Face the Nation,' did you see the way [Martin] Agronsky was climbing up the wall? The only way to react when they get together that way is to treat 'em with cold contempt."

He was worried about the polls, showing Humphrey drawing even. "Watch and see—we'll run three ahead of Gallup, five ahead of Harris, if not more. They don't measure the intensity of support." The respected New York *Daily News* poll showed Nixon behind Humphrey by 4 per cent in New York (as it turned out, they were fairly accurate) but the *News* poll had received a black eye two years before in mistakenly predicting Frank O'Connor would defeat Nelson Rockefeller for Governor of New York. "Ask 'Governor' O'Connor about the *News* poll," I said to cheer Nixon up; he bounded out of his chair, went back to the reporters in the rear of the press plane and said, "This is Safire's line, not mine, but ask 'Governor' O'Connor about the *News* poll."

October 31, New York City

A month before, somebody had the great idea of campaigning in the old-fashioned way—from the rear platform of a train, talking to people in small towns in Ohio. It was strictly for television, of course, and it gave a nice change of pace to the writers, who were getting a little jaded by the sameness of the campaign transportation in a jet age. The whole jaunt took just one day, and it was the most bone-rattling, jostling, wearying effort of the entire campaign—how did the old-time politicians do it?

The law and order excerpt came my way—Buchanan was doing something else—so I took the FBI "crime clock" figures and worked them into Nixon's oratory, ticking off the number of robberies and murders, and including the phrase "and one rape every seven minutes." This was rough stuff. When Nixon read it out from the rear end of a train, the traveling press played it as a change in the tenor of the campaign—that he had dropped his dignity and had come out slugging. Goldwater had used something similar in 1964, and McGovern was to use the identical "crime clock" in 1972, but in Nixon's hand it was interpreted as shocking. One of the television commentators, however, kept his perspective: "You really ought to be more careful with those rape figures," he told me privately. "It cuts both ways. For every girl who gets raped, some guy gets laid."

Whistle-stopping was losing its romance for me toward the end of the day, holed up in a tiny compartment banging on a typewriter in my lap, running out to the back of the train to see how the statements were playing at every stop, racing back to board before I was left behind. But then we came to a place called Deshler, Ohio, which made it all worth while.

Dick Moore stood in the twilight in the midst of the crowd observing the signs, as he always did, picking up the local color that the candidate could work into his speech at the next stop. Moore boarded the train with that mystic look a writer gets when he has something delicious to work with, some piece of color that could be more than a gimmick.

In his Madison Square Garden speech on October 31, Nixon went against his own growling about uplift and used it in an ad-lib peroration:

"We need the help of every person in this country." In the 1960 campaign, he never asked for help, and John Kennedy always asked for help from the voters. Nixon learned. "It was brought home to me most by the last whistle-stop tour in the State of Ohio . . . it was late in the day. The ninth appearance. The little town of Deshler. We didn't think there would be much of a crowd and five times as many people as lived in the town were there. There were many signs like those I see here. But one sign held by a teenager said, 'Bring us together again.' My friends, American needs to be brought together . . ."

It didn't get much of a pickup in the papers the next day and Moore was disappointed. I tucked it away—it was one of those things that could come in handy someday.

Nixon's apparent change of heart about "uplift," however—which led him to do the right thing, after making a big point twice of not doing it— taught me something about the man. He would argue against his finer impulses from time to time, using whatever aide was present as a sounding board, and in that convoluted way talk himself around. However, the aide or friend was likely to be convinced that (a) Nixon would never do what he was denouncing and (b) the aide had better not bring that position up again. This was a mistake, but as Nixon moved from a politician with some potential to the Candidate, later to the President, and then to the Most Powerful Leader in the Free World, it became harder for aides to resist the pounding of his prejudices as he got the resentments out of his system, before he took the sensible and usually amelioratory course. (At Tricia's wedding, he even danced for the cameramen, and, as we all know, only candidates for sheriff dance.)

November 1, *Flying Around Texas*

"Drop out a number of statements in Texas," the Candidate instructed us by a note dictated to Rose. "Good rough one on Social Security and Medicare—blasting the fear and smear last minute kind of tactics being used. The cruelest kind of politics—apart from misrepresenting my record, it leads the older people to think that something that could happen will not happen. *That should be dropped every place we go.*

"Three issues of interest to Texas. Oil Depletion. Tidelands Oil. Taft-Hartley. On all of these you have him on one side and Nixon on the other.

"I want Harlow to read the memo on what the Democrats are saying about cutting back the defense economy." This was a reference to our "security gap" speech and its response. Early in the campaign Dick Allen had begun to draft a speech about our defense posture; Ray Price and others who saw an early draft by James Schlesinger (later Secretary of Defense) felt it too hawkish and filled with cold-war rhetoric. Ray gave the Schlesinger draft to a friend at headquarters, who mistakenly sent it to a professor of his at Yale, who happened to be on a Humphrey committee and forwarded it to them. They prepared a response to our charges; then when we finally did come out with our security-gap speech, which was considerably different from the early draft passed to the Democrats, they were ready with a fast, hard comeback. We figured we had been "penetrated," and word was going around that strange clickings were being heard on wires. Some of it was unfounded—the security-gap leak was one—but not all was paranoia.

"Pull out a good lengthy statement on our defense speech," Nixon directed, despite the counterattack that had been effective in the press. "Here is a man that accepts the parity thing—that attacks me because I insist on the U.S. being first. We are going to be first, etc." (In office, Nixon was to accept "parity"—at first, under another word, "sufficiency"—as quickly as John Kennedy had dropped his "missile gap" charge when he became President.) We were worried about being beaten on the defense-security issue in the press, but Nixon was concerned about what he could say on the stump in the two great defense states, Texas and California.

November 3, Los Angeles
Bombing Halt

"As to tone," Nixon had told Harlow and the writing staff earlier, "never name Johnson or Humphrey. Be very careful not to reflect on Johnson. Johnson is not playing Humphrey's game, so let's not get too biting. If you have to, use something like 'the Administration of which our opponent was a part.' I know it's awkward, but I do not want to force Johnson into helping Humphrey."

Again, on October 14, in Key Biscayne, Nixon cautioned the writers to avoid Johnson. I had asked why he wanted comparisons to be made to "the past eight years," which include the popular Kennedy, rather than the Johnson-Humphrey Administration. "Well," he fudged, "that wouldn't be fair to LBJ." I looked at him with an expression of such disbelief that he felt he had to come closer to reality: "Look, I don't want to give LBJ this much"—he held up a finger and marked half of it off with his thumb—"not this much reason to help Humphrey toward the end."

Later, up in my room at the Key Biscayne Hotel, Bryce Harlow—on whose judgment Nixon was relying more heavily as the campaign wound up—explained the relationship between President Johnson and Candidate Nixon: "LBJ hasn't been vindictive in this campaign. His statement of support for Humphrey has been relatively bland. I wouldn't go so far as to call it a *mariage de convenance*, but I'd compare the President and Dick Nixon to a couple of fighting roosters, circling each other, with knives attached to the spurs. Nothing will happen, mind you, unless one makes the first move.

"So there you have the two of them," Harlow said, switching metaphors, "each waiting for the other to knock the chip off his shoulder. RN doesn't want to knock it off, because LBJ can be just as vindictive as hell, and who knows what he might pull off on an international scale?"

Nixon grew more and more certain that President Johnson planned to pull off a pre-election peace gimmick; he was being passed information to that effect through Harlow's man in the White House and Richard Allen, who had good intelligence contacts. Nixon also remembered Johnson's willingness in 1966 to undertake a foreign tour just before Election Day.

Finally, two weeks before the end of the campaign, Nixon was told there was certain to be a bombing halt—and he knew what that would do to the vote of many mothers who were now leaning toward him but who could be swayed by some dramatic gesture.

Nixon felt the only way to counter this was with a pre-emptive strike. First came a radio speech about a "security gap"—reminiscent about the old "missile gap" charge of the 1960 Kennedy campaign—designed to scare Southern conservatives. Then came this statement, drafted by Harlow, with the Candidate's writing all over it:

STATEMENT BY RICHARD M. NIXON

Throughout this campaign, the President has been even-handed and straightforward with the major Presidential contenders about Vietnam. I know he has been subjected to intense pressures to contrive a fake peace from influential quarters within and outside his party. It is to his credit and of great importance to our country that he has withstood these pressures. Word has now come to me about meetings of Administration leaders in the White House yesterday and the day before to arrange a bombing halt in the very near future. This I believe to be true.

It has also been represented to me that this activity is a cynical, last-minute move by the President to salvage the candidacy of Mr. Humphrey. This I cannot believe.

I have reason to know that President Johnson is profoundly concerned about our half-million servicemen, including his two sons-in-law, in Vietnam. He will not sell them out. He will not sell out South Vietnam. He will not be party to a camou-flaged surrender. He will not play politics with this war. I am convinced of this.

In foreign affairs the President must be our nation's only spokesman. The Paris negotiations are exceedingly delicate. The Presidential candidates should never weaken our diplomatic hand with irresponsible comments on the matters at issue. I have maintained this position throughout the campaign.

Three prerequisites for a bombing halt have been made

2

(A)

clear in Washington, Paris, ~~and~~ Saigon ~~and Hanoi~~   re-establishment
~~and from~~ the DMZ; ~~stopping the~~ *a halt to* mortar and rocket attacks
on ~~helpless urban areas~~ *the cities (S. V. Nam;* and proper recognition of the govern-
ment of South Vietnam~~so~~ *in the peace negotiation.*

    The President's insistence upon these three prerequisites
~~requires our~~ *deserves our* support. The protection of our fighting men, as
the President ~~emphatically~~ *in his speech at the Century began to write.* stated six weeks ago, demands it.
The stability of the government of South Vietnam compels it. *eloquently*

    Making progress toward a durable and honorable peace is
far more important than any political campaign could ever be.
I will continue to do nothing that would undercut the President's
pursuit of an agreement that will save American lives and lay
~~a . . . .~~ for stability and peace in Vietnam and throughout
~~Southeast Asia.~~

It was a shot across Johnson's bow—a message, couched in pious, I-just-can't-believe-it terms, that he had better not pull any fast ones on the weekend before election, or Nixon would label it "cynical." Johnson got the message, and sent his own broadside right back in a Waldorf-Astoria speech on October 27, 1968, cutting through our rumor-spreading circumlocution and denouncing "ugly and unfair charges that have been made about our security gap and the charges that have been made about our attempts to win peace in the world."

Humphrey was closing the gap in the polls and it looked like the campaign of '68 would be another cliffhanger. In 1960, Nixon had blown his lead to Kennedy, but then came back to nearly even in the final week; in 1968, he was defending his lead against a closing challenger. And the long, long road back could all be for nought, we all thought, on the basis of a phony, grandstand maneuver by Lyndon Johnson that everybody would see through—after the election.

In an address to the nation on October 31, LBJ dropped his political bomb—the bombing halt, with the appearance that the National Liberation Front and the South Vietnamese would also enter the negotiations. I listened that Hallowe'en night, and heard the goblins of defeat echoing LBJ's words; with the "war over," the nation wouldn't need Nixon to bring peace, and could turn to the Democrats on pocketbook issues.

Speechwriters have a habit of reading speeches by the opposition writers like editors, making little corrections, noting nice turns of phrase, cluck-clucking over clichés. An odd phrase caught my eye in reading President

Johnson's text the next day. The impression was left that the South Vietnamese would be there at the peace table, but for some reason the President had not said so outright. Moreover, a correction had been made in a
New York *Times* subhead between its city edition and late city edition,
changing "will" to "can"—somebody there, too, had reread the speech and
caught the slight deception. I sent the following memo to the Candidate
right away:

RN FROM SAFIRE

    Strange curve in LBJ's speech last night:

    "A regular session of the Paris talks is going to take
place on Next Wednesday, Nov 6, at which the representatives
of the Government of South Vietnam <u>are free</u> to participate."

    Does not say they will be there. If it were all set,
the natural word to use would be "will" participate.

    The next sentence gives the <u>impression</u> that South Vietnam
will be there: "We are informed by the representatives of the
Hanoi government that the representatives of the National
Liberation Front will <u>also</u> be present."

    The "also" <u>seems</u> to refer back to the South Vietnamese,
but actually refers to Hanoi.

    This seems like nit-picking, but it gains credence when you
compare the early and late editions of the NY Times subhead:
Early: "Saigon and NLF Will Join in the Enlarged Paris Discussions."
Late: "Saigon and NLF <u>Can</u> Join in the Enlarged Paris Discussions."

    All of which could mean that LBJ did not have all his
ducks in a row; that political considerations at home did
indeed force him to halt the bombing before he had South
Vietnam's acceptance of terms.

The check mark was Nixon's; I was told to draft a statement fast that
would point out the lack of guarantees of mutual de-escalation, provide a
reason for President Thieu's refusal to come to Paris, and still not make
us look dog-in-the-manger about peace.

My rationale for Thieu's delaying action was this: by saying our allies
were "free to come," LBJ was in effect saying "come or else" because he
had already agreed for the Viet Cong to be there. Not surprising, then,
when a nation with a million men under arms and fighting for national
survival is told "take it or leave it," the likelihood is that they will leave it
and hope for a better American President in a few days. Nixon read the
statement I drafted and was worried about issuing it personally—to criticize

a "step toward peace," even a phony step, would be bad because the step did not seem phony to mothers living on hope. He gave it to Robert Finch, who sat down next to Dan Rapoport of United Press on the campaign plane, and gave him a story deploring the fact that LBJ did not have "his ducks in a row."

The pollsters told us afterward that there was a surge for Humphrey just after the President's speech, but twenty-four hours later, when Thieu balked and it became apparent there would be no instant peace, the support ebbed. That could have made the difference.

When people later wondered why Nixon thought so highly of President Thieu, they did not recall that Nixon probably would not be President were it not for Thieu. Nixon remembered.

The Dragon Lady

The great mystery of the 1968 campaign centers around Anna Chennault, Chinese-born widow of World War II hero General Claire Chennault, whose good looks and proclivity for diplomatic intrigue earned her the sobriquet "Dragon Lady," after the Milton Caniff cartoon character of that name. But Mrs. Chennault was not playing *Terry and the Pirates* —she was an outspoken hawk on the war, a friend of South Vietnamese politicians, and a Nixon fund-raiser.

The question is: Did Anna Chennault act as an agent of Candidate Nixon to urge South Vietnam's leaders to refuse to come to the Paris peace table under the terms offered by President Johnson just before Election Day?

Dammit, the answer appears to be yes and no. I cannot positively assert that she did so, or if she did, that it was at the direction of Mr. Nixon or his aides. Let me present the evidence I have been able to gather and let the reader decide.

On June 24 she wrote, on the stationery of her Flying Tiger Lines, about her friendship with "Vietnam Ambassador to the United States, Ambassador Bui Diem who is also the South Vietnam representative to the Paris conference. A newspaperman by profession and my close friend, he travels constantly between Saigon, Washington and Paris every month . . . I would like very much to suggest you meet him and talk with him if arrangements can be made. I myself will be leaving for Southeast Asia around July 15th but I could bring him to you either before July 15th or after the convention."

She wrote again on June 28, reminding Nixon that her prediction about the American withdrawal from Khesanh had come true, urging him to meet with President Thieu when he came to the United States, and saying, "I had a long talk with Ambassador Robert Hill . . ." She was also meeting with Senator John Tower, head of Nixon's "Key Issues Committee" and an old friend of hers, which indicates she was still in the category of those being handled tactfully.

On July 3, 1968, Nixon was sent a memo by Richard Allen, who was his substantive foreign policy adviser at the time—a kind of pre-Kissinger, whose rendezvous with Kissinger at the Fontainebleau Hotel during the convention is recounted earlier. Allen had been the target of a clumsy CIA probe that summer. A San Francisco banker was visited by an investigator asking about Allen who left a card that was easily traced to a CIA front. Allen rarely used his own telephone, hinting darkly that it was tapped, and it was true that if you called him you could hardly hear him, but we were sure he was trying to make himself more important with the cloak and dagger stuff.

Here is the memo in full:

3 July 68

To: DC

From: Dick Allen

Re: Possible meeting with South Vietnam Ambassador

Talked with Mrs. Chennault, who is long-time friend of Saigon's Ambassador to US, Biu Diem. He is now in Paris, designated official observer and representative of SVN government to the peace talks. He is due back in here (washington) next week some time.

Mrs. Chennault has apparently asked him if he would talk to DC. I explained schedule tight, but possible to check on available time.

Meeting would have to be absolute top secret, etc.

Initiative is ours—if DC can see him, I am to contact Mrs. Chennault, she will arrange.

I stressed that it is virtually certain that such a meeting would have to be here in NYC.

This would be a good opportunity to get filled in on events in Paris and other developments.

RN's notation was in scribble, and, referring to the words "top secret," reads:

Should be but I don't see how—with the S.S. [Secret Service] If it can be (secret) RN would like to see—if not—could Allen see for RN?

Allen says he thought about it a lot but decided a meeting would be a mistake. He stayed in touch with Mrs. Chennault, whose letters to Nixon now began cosily "Dear Dick," and on August 19 said, "The Vietnamese Ambassador, Mr. Bui Diem has just returned from Paris last night. John Tower and I had a long talk with him last night. I am sure John will have a chance to report to you personally in regard to our meeting."

On October 15, she sent a note to Nixon, who was then in Kansas City, saying she was still in touch with Tower's Key Issues committee (and thus somewhere out in left field), attaching a memo warning that a bombing pause was a fake issue—that once the North Vietnamese were not being bombed, they would tell the Americans to deal with the National Liberation Front, as they continued to support the Viet Cong from sanctuaries in the North.

The indications are that the Dragon Lady had been operating in what she was certain were South Vietnam's interests, and had not been restrained by the Nixon campaign, but had not been able to reach anybody at the top in the crucial last days—which meant the Candidate and his top staff were keeping hands off, leaving only Allen as a "listener."

Lyndon Baines Johnson knew of Mrs. Chennault's comings and goings; J. Edgar Hoover later told President-elect Richard Nixon that the FBI had been tapping her throughout the campaign, and Nixon told this to several aides. Ramsey Clark has written to me saying he never authorized any such tap—without the signature of the then-Attorney General, or a court order, the tap was clearly illegal. The CIA was watching Allen, and watching the South Vietnamese Embassy, and following Bui Diem. President Johnson, in his telephone conversations with Richard Nixon, let it be known he had information that some Nixon supporters were meddling in areas that were out of bounds.

In fact, Mrs. Chennault had every right as an American citizen to urge other nations to do whatever she wanted them to do, which is why her surveillance was illegal; had she been breaking the law that forbids U.S. nationals from negotiating with foreign powers, the surveillance would be admitted by now and action against her would have been taken. The pattern of tapping by several agencies of government, confirmed to Nixon by Hoover later, set up a "tolerance" of this type of activity that had disastrous ramifications later.

In sum, Anna Chennault was in close and frequent touch with the Nixon campaign and in close touch with the South Vietnamese Ambassador; she was not able to reach the top of the campaign for authorization to my knowledge, though it is possible she talked with Mitchell or Haldeman; she was not discouraged from her efforts, but she was frustrated in not being able to reach anybody other than Hill, Tower, and Allen at the crucial moments at the end.

Perhaps there is more to that story that would make a clear-cut answer possible; in all likelihood, it was a fuzzy situation and will remain so for years. Did Nixon direct an agent of his to get the South Vietnamese to hang back? No evidence of that; he only did not discourage her. Would Thieu have done what he did without Mrs. Chennault's intercession? Probably. Was this all going on in the context of a political campaign, with American negotiators in Paris frantically trying to get action before the U.S. Election Day? Certainly. Should Democrats be proud of the manipulation of foreign policy for political ends against a political deadline, and should Republicans be proud of letting supporters, once removed from the campaign itself, seek to frustrate those manipulations? No. It was not one of American politics' finest hours.

November 3, Los Angeles

We had given Pat Buchanan a birthday party the night before in the Century Plaza Hotel; now, in our suite on the eighteenth floor, we came together to prepare the questions and answers for the telethon scheduled for the next night, election eve.

There were about six big balloons, and a couple of dozen smaller balloons gently nuzzling each other in the corner of the room, left over from the party, the gift of John Nidecker, who did not think a rally was a rally without a balloon drop.

Not only were we all physically exhausted, we had begun to show the signs of mental strain. Humphrey had caught up in the polls; Lou Harris was predicting a Humphrey victory. Keogh, Anderson, Gavin, Price, Buchanan, and I sat there in the staff lounge, oppressed by the thought that the long comeback had been in vain.

Keogh started the discussion about the most likely questions to come up during the four-hour telethon. We were worried about questions about Agnew, and why he was not on television with Nixon; on the competing Humphrey telethon, Senator Muskie was sure to play an important part, and the Boss's decision to go without his Vice Presidential candidate invited comparison. Nixon's biggest mistake in the campaign, which he recognized now, was to lay off Muskie, directing all his fire at Humphrey. Muskie was vulnerable, reporter Clark Mollenhoff kept telling us, as "the Senator from TFX," a reference to an ill-fated aircraft that he had sponsored; there were some unsubstantiated accusations floating around about FHA scandals and Billy Sol Estes that could have been blown out of all proportion the way Agnew's record had been; and we had heard that Muskie would blow up under pressure—but the orders from Nixon were to ignore him, and as a result he came out of the campaign looking like Abe Lincoln.

Talking about this, Anderson—a serious author and academic—absently pushed a balloon that was on the floor over toward Gavin, who lightly kicked it back, only it went toward Keogh, the oldest and most dignified of the group, who kicked it back hard. Before we knew it the six of us were in a furious, glorious balloon fight—thirty balloons, large and small, were flying around the room, propelled by a half-dozen wild men who were laughing hysterically, kicking, punching, and butting balloons; Anderson lurched toward the door and slammed it shut lest any others in the campaign were to see the research and writing group gone bonkers. It lasted five minutes and stopped as suddenly as it started; Keogh pushed the balloons into the bathroom and, breathing heavily but feeling better, we went to work on the Q and A.

November 4

Talk about *déjà vu*—eight years ago, I had worked on an election-eve telethon we called "Dial Dick Nixon." Then, I had been sorting out questions about Quemoy and Matsu in the back of the TV studio, passing them to the celebrity interviewers; now somebody else was doing that, passing the questions to football coach Bud Wilkinson, and an older and steadier Nixon was going on and on and on into the night, straining, as he had done before, to get every last vote he could—so that he could not look back later and say, "If only I had not let up at the very end . . ."

Late at night, too late for it to really matter, he slipped and said, "Now let's get down to the nut-cutting . . ." He meant to say "brass tacks" or "short strokes," but instead used the vernacular based on castration that was so often used in political backrooms. A couple of reporters looked at me and said: "Did he say 'nut-cutting'? You wrote the political dictionary, Safire—what did he mean?" I mumbled something about a reference to the thriftiness of squirrels and stumbled to bed.

November 5, Election Day

We flew back across country on the day when it all goes out of your hands and lands in the laps of the citizens of the Republic who care to vote—a curious day always, when you keep wondering if there is not something else you should be doing.

Up front, Nixon was preparing his daughters for not winning. "Actually," said Dwight Chapin, "that's the way he prepares himself."

Buchanan and I had been switched out of our regular first-class seats to the middle of the plane, indicative of what was to follow, but RN called everybody up front in small groups to express his appreciation and to shoot the breeze. Keogh, Price, Buchanan, and I spent about a half hour with RN and Haldeman.

"Where are the excerpts for next week?" he asked as we filed in. "You know, we put out a hell of a volume of stuff. And they had to give it space, because it came out of my mouth—a nationwide radio speech, not just a position paper."

"Some of it made sense," I offered.

"You intellectuals."

Haldeman smiled. "Sure made the press work hard, writing those stories on the long speeches at the last minute. Kept 'em out of mischief."

"You fellows did a helluva job," said RN. "Curious, the double standard. Humphrey didn't do a thing on the issues, just one crime statement. If we had tried to get away with that, the press would have killed us."

Haldeman said that Humphrey on his telethon had changed his position on the surtax and on busing. Nixon nodded, understanding: "He had to wait until the end on that. Otherwise the whole liberal establishment would have landed on his head.

"I tell you, though," Nixon said, hand-slicing the air, "if we win, it's the end of Lou Harris. That's one luxury I'm going to indulge. I'll do to him what Truman did to Kaltenborn."

What caused the Humphrey rush at the end? "The bombing halt, no doubt about that. But who knows, it may not cut all one way. On that telethon, I talked about peace so much I thought I'd—ah, who can tell?" He looked out the window.

I was interested in a crucial phone call Nixon had made to President Johnson. Bryce Harlow told me he had received a call late Friday night from Everett Dirksen, who said he had just been speaking with President Johnson and something had to be done in a hurry to cool him off. Johnson, according to the Senate Minority Leader who had worked closely with the President on many matters, was ready to blow his stack—and blow the whistle on the Nixon campaign's attempt to defeat his peace efforts by getting President Thieu to hold back. Anna Chennault's name was mentioned. Harlow then went to Haldeman to get Nixon to call Johnson immediately, but Haldeman said RN had retired for the night. Harlow said to get him up, this was that important, and Nixon made the call.

I asked Nixon if the President really said, "Who's this guy Fink?" in referring to Finch's ducks-in-a-row interview. "Oh, sure." Nixon smiled. "'That guy Fink really took out after me,' he said. I said, 'What about your advisers and a few of the things they pulled?' I didn't let him get away with that."

Pat Buchanan said, "That 'nut-cutting' remark of yours on TV last night almost killed us all."

Nixon leaned back and smiled. "You fellows ever eat 'lamb fries'? I did, twenty years ago. Helping some Congressman in Missouri. We all ordered 'em—tasted like veal, breaded, you know? Then I asked what they were. They told me we'd been eating sheep's nuts, that the farmers 'bite 'em off.' When this is over, we'll go out and have a mess of them."

Everybody looked suitably horrified and we were laughing as we left. I sat at a typewriter in the staff section and wrote out a concession statement, in case we lost, and then some suggested remarks for a victory statement, drawing on that "Bring Us Together" observation of Dick Moore's which the Candidate had used so well in the Garden rally but didn't get covered. I gave it to Herb Klein, figuring he'd be near Nixon before going out to give in or get started.

"I saw many signs in this campaign," said Richard Nixon on the morning after he had been elected President. "Some of them were not friendly and some were very friendly. But the one that touched me the most was one that I saw in Deshler, Ohio, at the end of a long day of whistle-stopping, a little town, I suppose five times the population was there in the dusk, almost impossible to see—but a teenager held up a sign, 'Bring Us Together.' And that will be the great objective of this Administration at the outset, to bring the American people together. This will be an open

Administration, open to new ideas, open to men and women of both parties, open to the critics as well as those who support us. We want to bridge the generation gap. We want to bridge the gap between the races. We want to bring America together."

PART TWO

"IT SURE BEATS LOSING"

1. THE MAN AT THE WILSON DESK

Take a metaphoric leap: think of Nixon as a layer cake.

The icing, the public face or crust, is conservative, stern, dignified, proper—rather formal for a public man in our time, appealing to the elderly and the orderly, a sharp contrast to the two vividly personal Presidents who preceded him. He is aware of, and philosophic about, the other side of this coin, the other way this icing appears—as, literally, icing, cold and sugary, pious and stiffly obsequious, arrogant and aloof.

The first layer of Nixon underneath that icing is a progressive politician, willing and even eager to surprise with liberal ideas, delighted with the Disraeli comparison, surprisingly graceful in moments requiring diplomatic understanding or personal warmth, occasionally impulsive (the post-midnight trip to the Lincoln Memorial), often sentimental (one of the few items on his desk was a china Irish setter that was the first present he gave his wife, thanking her for taking care of his dog in 1941)—in this layer, a veritable Mr. Nice Guy.

Underneath *that* is an unnecessarily pugnacious man who had to scrape for everything he has in life and don't you forget it; self-made, self-pitying, but not self-centered; who regularly gets furious with what he considers to be loafers and bums who expect the world on a platter and think nothing of living off the sweat of hard-working people. This layer identifies with "the kind of good people who built this nation, not those snobs who are trying to tear it down," the square peg in the Oval Office who is the enemy of the "social planners" trying to push around his friends, the middle Americans.

The next layer is the poker player with a long record of winning, the politician with a long record of losing, then winning, then losing again, but not quitting until he absolutely had to quit—the spectator sportsman, the decision-maker with the guts to go all the way and take all the flak, the negotiator who will wait out the most patient or nervy opponent.

Under that is the hater, the impugner of motives, the man who claims he is not angry with the press because he cannot be angry with somebody he does not respect; this is the contemptuous, contemptible layer that stimulated him to engage "plumbers" to plug news leaks and to trample on civil liberties in what he saw as a higher cause. Nixon's Dr. Jekyll worried about Nixon's Mr. Hyde, and usually tried to suppress him, but mostly only tried to conceal him.

Another layer is the realist, the man who understands the motivation of nations and power groups, who senses weaknesses and opportunities in political alignments and international affairs, knows the internal pressures on other statesmen more sensitively than any adviser or agent, and who could summon up the confidence to impose his presence and much of his idea of order on the rest of the world.

Under that is the observer-participant, who is applauding or criticizing what he is doing while he is doing it, who edits his remarks as he makes them, who gains a long-headed perspective from a sense of history as well as an embarrassing self-consciousness from too great a concern about how his actions will appear to historians.

Then there is the man of extraordinary courage, the calculating risk-taker whose refusal to bend to pressure on matters of foreign policy led to "peace with honor," diplomacy triangulated and linked, and summit triumphs unprecedented for an American President that Churchill himself would have applauded. This is the layer that told a couple of visiting labor leaders "being on the side of the right is more important than winning" and sending for a copy of Whittaker Chambers' *Witness* to bear witness to that, sincerely believing what he said—and yet, to be on the safe side, this courageous man would force Maurice Stans to leave the Cabinet and raise the kind of money that would ensure financial overkill in winning an election.

Underneath that is the loner, who identifies with "the people" but hates to deal with more than a very few persons; the intellectual who prefers the hard study of written briefs to the liveliness of a spoken briefing, and who prefers the company of athletes to intellectuals, who dares to take the time to think things through alone, then wastes some of that precious time merely brooding; the Gaullist who sees the need for a mysterious, aloof mystique of leadership and uses that as a reinforcement for his natural inclination to avoid out-of-step counsel, who dreams above all else that he is the one thrust into the times uniquely equipped to be the peacemaker, and who, in personal isolation and withdrawal, comes to the conclusion that America cannot indulge in isolation and must withdraw with care from unwise commitments.

My cake metaphor is getting stale. Which layer do you like? Which layer do you hate? Is he the Norman Rockwell portrait or the Herblock cartoon —the strong Nixon of *Six Crises* or the weak Nixon of the Watergate transcripts?

That's the trouble with most perceptions of Nixon. One layer or another is chosen as "real" and the perceiver roots for that one layer's success. But the whole cake is the "real" Nixon, including some layers I have not mentioned because I do not know. When you take a bite of the cake that is Nixon, you must get a mouthful of all the layers; nibbling along one level is not permitted.

But in real life nobody gulps down a whole cake with all the layers. If our judgment is generally favorable, we tend to deny the unfavorable elements, and if we come down on the side that says, "I never could trust that guy," we will attribute the good layers to mischievous motives, lest cognitive dissonance scramble the neat patterns of our prejudices.

Insiders, of course, are the least likely to see or accept the whole man. The negative characteristics that are thrust at them need to be shunted on to somebody else, away from the President, because it is painful to dedicate oneself to someone less than one's ideal. Enter "The Black Hat"—Murray Chotiner or Bob Haldeman, or Chuck Colson, or anybody in a no-man or tough-guy category—to become the insiders' scapegoat for the sins of the top man. "If the Boss only knew what Haldeman was up to . . ." "If the President only knew what acts are carried out in his name by zealots . . ." To some insiders, the "real" Nixon is the man who placed his trust in Good Guys, white hats, like Shultz and Burns and Garment; to others, the white hats—white helmets, really—were worn by Ehrlichman, Connally, or Mitchell. The cliques had a confusing way of flowing into one another, but the tendency is always there to choose up sides at any given moment and attribute the reality of the President's personality and policy to the men around him who most closely approximate what one hopes that reality to be.

In the Presidency, a President should—and does—keep all kinds of company necessary to govern. Bob Haldeman, followed by Al Haig, thought like Nixon in many respects, but Nixon's greatest need for them was not as sounding boards but as organizers of the Nixon schedule, which Nixon was no good at. George Shultz shared some qualities of tenacity and free-market philosophy judgment with his boss, but was repeatedly placed in the center of the action for the economic acumen and personal integrity that did not duplicate Nixon's. "When two men always agree, one of them is unnecessary" may not be original, but it was Nixon's way most of the time. A leader needs good managers, and managers need a leader, but the last thing either needs is another of the same.

The temptation to judge which Nixon is the "real" Nixon in terms of a palace guard should be resisted; they are usually his tools, not his reflections. In succumbing to the temptation to so judge, as we all do, it is best to draw the circle wide enough to include the men of conflicting characters around the President. They do not always agree with each other, but Nixon does not always agree with himself.

To cite an example close to home: From 1966 through the middle of 1973, Nixon had three senior writers working on his speeches, messages, and remarks: Raymond K. Price, Jr., now forty-four, Patrick J. Buchanan, thirty-five, and myself, forty-four. On the old political spectrum, Price was the liberal, Buchanan the conservative, Safire the centrist; Price a

WASP, Buchanan a Catholic, Safire a Jew. Price's style is lyrical, Buchanan's is hard-hitting, mine is the way it is in this book. Price is introverted, I'm extroverted, Buchanan in between. It's fair to say we're different.

Nixon never wanted us to work in committee, not only because of his abhorrence of watered-down committee writing, but he wanted to cast his speeches according to the "tilt," as he put it, of his writers. He would sometimes give a Price draft to Buchanan for toughening, or a Buchanan draft to Price for softening, or a draft of either to me for making more quotable, but he kept his writers distinct; we knew he wanted us for what we were, and not for what we might think he thought his "perfect" writer would be.

There could be no perfect writer for Nixon because of the layer cake principle. When Nixon wanted to take a shot at somebody, he turned to Buchanan, who could do so with relish, and who could also provide concise, hard-hitting suggested answers in a press conference briefing book. When Nixon wanted a vision of the Nation's future, or wanted to express his compassion for the dependent, or to deal with urban matters, he turned to Price, and later to the staff Ray headed. When he wanted to deal with the work ethic or economic matters, political philosophy or a touch of humor, he worked with me. We all worked on foreign affairs speeches—with Price considered relatively dovish, Buchanan certainly hawkish (after his 1970 Cambodia effort), and me in the middle—but the President, Kissinger, and the NSC's Winston Lord had a hand in every line.

Within this neat layering of writing aides, there was a further Nixon-like complexity. Even when Buchanan was lambasting the "social planners" who decreed busing or defended abortion, that young man was sensitive to ethnic slurs or impolitic positions. Even when Price was "lowering our voices" in early 1969, that passionately anonymous man was taking a tougher line on Vietnam than Henry Kissinger was at the time. Thus, in the crosshatching of the cast of characters in his writing staff, Nixon illustrated a pattern of the way his mind worked. He would be good at playing three-dimensional chess, unless he had to sacrifice some favored pieces.

Did any of us have a relationship with Nixon that Samuel Rosenman had with FDR or Ted Sorensen with Kennedy? No. When he was at his most Presidential, Ray Price was the writer Nixon preferred; when he was at his most elemental, it was Pat Buchanan, for whom he also had a personal affection; and when he wanted the complicated made simple, or a line to be quoted, myself. There were other writers as well—Lee Huebner, who worked the hardest and received the least recognition, and John Andrews, who gave the President closest to what he asked for. Each of us represented a part of Nixon, but even taken together, we did not represent the whole Nixon.

We faced a "which Nixon?" problem in the 1968 campaign. After years of being center stage, Nixon spent years entirely offstage; when he reentered politics, he was a different man. He could not pretend to be the same as voters had remembered him, not only because it was not true but for the practical reason that a majority had showed twice it did not prefer him; at the same time, we could not trumpet his striking change because a "new Nixon" was an admission of opportunism.

For a time in the New Hampshire campaign, he tried to handle the frequently asked "have you really changed" question in an oblique way, to the effect that he was still himself, but that times change and there was a need to change with them. I told him that was an unsatisfying, weaseling-sounding answer and he agreed. We found the solution in the way the question was being asked: never in an overtly unfriendly fashion, often apologetically, and usually in a roundabout way, as if the questioner hated to probe too personally about his old reputation. The "new Nixon" was never a part of the questioner's phraseology, though that was the thrust of the query.

Whenever the question was asked afterward—and it never failed to be asked—Nixon would sharpen it by saying the words the questioner was reluctant to say: "Essentially, what you are asking is, 'Is there a new Nixon?'" The questioner would nod, as would the audience, admiring Nixon's courage in facing the hard question directly. Then the Candidate would win points for frankness: "The answer is yes—of course there's a 'new Nixon.' I've changed, just as America has changed, just as we've all changed over a course of years. But on the basic things—on matters of character, of conscience—that has not changed." In this way, Nixon left the impression of freshness and candor, just the opposite of what the attack phrase "the new Nixon" intended; by accepting it cheerfully, he turned a negative to a positive, and showed he could step up to a question that most men would have run away from. In truth, it was more skillful than gutsy, but it seemed more gutsy than skillful; the introspective Nixon knew all this, and the political Nixon had the ability to make points with it. And, to use a phrase that Henry Kissinger repeated often later, "it had the added advantage of being true." Both calculated and honest, at once intellectually sound and emotionally satisfying, it was hard to detect which layer of Nixon was on top.

The same jarring juxtaposition can be seen with a couple of other Nixon layers. There is the suspicious Nixon, distrustful of being trapped, not wanting to be lobbied in person, cautious about making a decision before he has to, secretive not only to a fault but to a brink. Right there, separated by the thinnest smear of filling, is the "big play" or "leapfrog" Nixon, heir to the grand Roosevelt style, which deserves a closer look.

"We're not going to do this halfway," Nixon told his economic advisers in July 1971, amid calls for wage-price guidelines and jawbones. "If and when we do it, we're gonna leapfrog 'em all."

A favorite criticism of Nixon is that he was infuriatingly inconsistent: opportunism, flip-flop, expediency are the words used to describe the willingness of the politician to "rise above principle." Liberals find a perverse pleasure in complaining about his pre-emption of some of their positions, as if accomplishment counts only if preceded by long-held views or deep-seated urges, and lack of personal commitment somehow sullies specific progress. Yet on the big decisions, Nixon was remarkably consistent in the way he made up his mind; the "big play," as he called it, was usually an end-around or a reversal of field. A handful of his common denominators:

1. When circumstances change, change your policy.

2. When the moment comes to jump—leapfrog over the position immediately ahead.

3. Resolve impasses on narrow issues by raising the level to a comprehensive approach so that dickering can take place along a broad front.

4. Never apologize or look back.*

Nixon would apply these rules in making the decisions most often cited as evidence of his inconsistency:

Welfare Reform: He could not place a minimum income floor under all welfare recipients without undermining the work ethic of working poor. The Nixon-Shultz solution was to leapfrog the Moynihan-Burns impasse —to add two million working poor to the welfare rolls, to accept four billion dollars more in "start-up costs" so that incentives to work could be built into a new system.

China: He could not leave eight hundred million Chinese "in angry isolation," nor was he inclined to extend *de facto* recognition little by little, allowing Soviet countermeasures to be taken abroad or a right-wing furor to build at home. Nixon looked forward to a sudden announcement of summit in Peking, ripping off a national blindfold with daring and panache, dumbfounding critics by leapfrogging what seekers of drip-by-drip détente might have tried.

Arms Limitation: The arms-control record was stuck in the worn-out groove of Soviet insistence on "total" disarmament and the rigid U.S. call for on-site inspection. The Nixon approach was to fractionalize the problem, in effect complicating it immensely, so that small "building blocks" could be used to construct a comprehensive balance of power during a moment of relative parity.

Wage-Price Policy: Nixon resisted half measures, while economic pressure and public impatience combined to make controls popular and practicable; when Nixon moved, he would move all the way to a freeze, combining that step with an even more drastic slamming-shut of the "gold window" and a border tax to make U.S. products competitive abroad. The whole of the New Economic Policy made more effective each of its parts. Three years later, he was vigorously denouncing his own "discredited patent medicine of wage and price controls."

Cambodia: Let Nixon explicate "the big play" in his own words. In early 1971 he was seeking Nelson Rockefeller's support for a limited beginning to revenue sharing. The New York Governor wanted Nixon to

---

* Presidential counsel Leonard Garment, paraphrasing a simpering saying of the day, characterized this heel-digging as: "Being President is never having to say you're sorry."

go much further in distributing revenues to states than planned. Nixon fully understood Rockefeller's point—the need to move surprisingly strongly—and reassured him in these terms:

"You are right on this point—if we are going to go, we should go for the big play. That's what happened with Cambodia. I sat right here with two Cabinet officers and my national security adviser and I asked what we needed to do. The recommendation of the Department of Defense was the most pusillanimous, little nit-picker I ever saw. 'Just bite off Parrot's Beak.'" That was a strip of land jutting toward Saigon. "I said you would have a hell of an uproar at home if you bite off the Beak. If you are going to take the heat, go for all the marbles. I said, 'How many sanctuaries are there, really?' And Defense said, 'Eight others.' I said, 'Since we're going to get unshirted hell for doing this at all, let's go after all the sanctuaries.'

"I have made some bad decisions, but a good one was this: When you bite the bullet, bite it hard—go for the big play. On revenue sharing, it might not be your play, Nelson, but it will be a big play."

Nixon's heroes are Presidents who went for the big play with gusto. True, he put up Eisenhower's portrait in the Cabinet Room but that was because he thought he should try to absorb some of Eisenhower's popularity by playing on their association, which was not really that close—Eisenhower was not Nixon's idea of what a President in these times should be. Nor was Woodrow Wilson, whose portrait Nixon also hung in the Cabinet Room; Nixon liked to quote Wilson in speeches, because Wilson is revered for his idealism, having tried to make the world safe for democracy. Eisenhower had the firmness and Wilson had the vision, but neither of them, in Nixon's eyes, had both—and both is what he was determined to have.

The Roosevelts, though, had both ideals and strength. When Nixon moved into the White House, he changed the name of the conference room across the hall from his Oval Office. What had been the Fish Room (named after Hamilton Fish, Secretary of State under President U. S. Grant) became the Roosevelt Room, decorated with plaques of Theodore Roosevelt and of Franklin D. Roosevelt. The slogan under the plaque of TR is a quotation from his works: "Aggressive fighting for the right is the noblest sport the world affords," and under FDR is a line from the Latin poet Seneca: "I shall hold my rudder true." A bust of TR sits on the mantel over the fireplace; scenes of the Rough Riders charging up San Juan Hill and Frederick Remington paintings of westerners shooting at Indians usually decorate the walls (and are discreetly removed when delegations of Indian leaders come to call). The Roosevelt Room is warm, not only from the constantly burning fire, but from the decor of browns and oranges and leather and dark wood.

Throughout Nixon's first term, every weekday morning at eight-fifteen, the senior staff would gather in the Roosevelt Room with Haldeman at the head of the table. In times of crisis or when it was otherwise important to present a united front, about thirty people were packed in to hear the President and then Haldeman or Kissinger exhort us to hang tough.*

A different, non-layer-cake way of looking at Nixon is as an amalgam of the two often-contradictory men memorialized in that Roosevelt Room. Like Teddy, Nixon believed in the virtues of hard work and self-reliance; like Franklin, he took pleasure in using devious methods to reach worthy goals. Like Teddy, he was ready to provide for the comforts of the press (TR brought the White House correspondents in out of the rain to a press room, and Nixon remade FDR's swimming pool into a lush press area); like Franklin, he was convinced the press, by and large, was against him. (FDR liked reporters and despised publishers, and Nixon was the other way around.) Like Teddy, Nixon wanted to offer a "square deal" of fairness to those who want to work and, like Franklin, he liked the idea of a new deal of bold surprises and grand designs. Like TR, he considered the Republican Party more of a tool than a home, and, like FDR, was looking for ways to construct a new majority. Like both Roosevelts, Nixon sought the solitude of the outdoors, on remote beaches and in the Shangri-la of Camp David; like both, he worked hard and long on his language, looking for the phrase or word picture (mollycoddle, pussyfooter, forgotten man) that would rally or inflame. Like Teddy, he surrounded himself with vigorous young men; like Franklin, he liked to upset organizational charts by assigning more than one man to the same job; like both Roosevelts, Nixon had a strong sense of national destiny and saw himself as the instrument and embodiment thereof. In preparing his second Inaugural Address, Nixon sent his writers only two previous Inaugurals for our study: TR in 1904, FDR in 1936.

The analogy ultimately breaks down. TR exuded straightforwardness and FDR was identified with compassion, neither Nixon's strong suit, and both Roosevelts were more dramatic innovators in domestic affairs. But the kinship in foreign affairs is there, from the big stick to the battle against isolationism.

In a burst of triviality, let us use a minor episode to take a large bite of the cake and see what all the layers taste like together.

When Richard Nixon was Vice President, he was proud to have in his office the historic "Wilson desk," a massive piece of furniture redolent with Presidential and idealistic associations. When he became President, he requested that the Wilson desk be placed in the Oval Office; it was there throughout his occupancy of that office, shown off to visitors and mentioned by guides with reverence. Nixon has used it hundreds of times to get into points about idealism, about how Presidents can be misunderstood, how peaceful men find themselves with need to do battle, how the distinction between men of thought and men of action can no longer be drawn, etc. It was used to trigger an emotional reference in his November

---

* The locution "hang tough," a Nixon Administration favorite, was derived from "hang loose," a taboo reference to relaxed testes; the slogan "hang tough" was popularized by a narcotics treatment center in California in the early Sixties.

3, 1969, "silent majority" speech to disclaim an ambition to conduct a "war to end wars."

The trouble was, the Wilson of the "Wilson desk" was not Woodrow Wilson, as Richard Nixon and everybody else had always assumed. It was Henry Wilson, Vice President during the Administration of Ulysses S. Grant. The bearer of this unwelcome information was Cecilia Bellinger, chief researcher of Jim Keogh's research and writing operation, who had been given it by an overly assiduous assistant curator at the White House. Since I was the most frequent Wilson-quoter on the writing staff, she brought it to me.

It seemed as if Hamilton Fish, a friend of Henry Wilson's in President Grant's Cabinet, were reaching from his grave to exact vengeance for the renaming of the Fish Room. My first inclination was to cover it up—what the President didn't know wouldn't hurt him—but once these things started to be bruited about, the odds were that some columnist would embarrass him with it soon.

I wrote the President a memo extolling the virtues of one Henry Wilson, an early abolitionist and one of the founders of the Republican Party and, incidentally, the man who had the good taste to select the desk at which President Nixon was now sitting. Not Woodrow Wilson, Henry Wilson—but still, "the Wilson desk." Perhaps the President could use this fact, I suggested, to illustrate a point on how dedicated we all are about historical accuracy, how you mustn't take anything for granted.

Silence from the Oval Office. From a variety of sources, I have been able to piece together some of the thoughts that probably went through the President's mind, which serve to illustrate the complexity of his reaction:

I'm certainly glad to know the truth about the desk . . .

Always knew Safire was a smart-ass . . .

How can they be sure Woodrow Wilson never sat at this desk?

This is an elitist plot to embarrass me.

The desk must have been made at the time of the Civil War; I want to know more about Grant's Vice President.

Think of all the people I told it belonged to Woodrow Wilson over the years.

Why couldn't we just leave it as the "Wilson desk" and let people think what they want?

It's good to know I have people who will stand up to me on this . . .

What's the best way to put out the truth without admitting error?

Why do they bother me with this insignificant stuff?

There goes a good item for speeches in New Jersey . . .

Wilson left so little behind; it's sad that even this symbol should turn out to be somebody else's . . .

New information keeps turning up—it could be this information is wrong and the desk really is Woodrow Wilson's . . .

I won't talk about it. Hell with it. Let 'em fix it in a footnote somewhere if they have to.

And so on page 909 of the 1969 edition of *Public Papers of the Presidents* this petulantly accurate footnote appears at the end of the historic "silent majority" speech:

[1] Later research indicated that the desk had not been President Woodrow Wilson's as had long been assumed but was used by Vice President Henry Wilson during President Grant's administration.

The man at the Wilson desk may not be the man at the real Wilson desk, but he is a real man nonetheless: not a lovable leader but not a collage of cruel cartoons, either. The thirty-sixth human being to serve as President of the United States, the second to stir the caldron of impeachment, and the first to be forced to resign in disgrace, should offer a challenge for study, not only a flag to rally 'round or fly upside down. One good place to begin is the first time he set foot on *Air Force One*, tentatively trying on the trappings of power he came to enjoy a little too much.

2. INTERREGNUM

President Johnson told President-elect Nixon he would be provided with a government aircraft to fly down to Key Biscayne on November 28, 1968. We showed up at the airfield to discover the number 26000 on the tail: not a back-up aircraft, but *Air Force One* itself, the identical plane in which Lyndon Johnson had taken the oath of office that day in Dallas five years before.

Nixon called his writers up front to the President's airborne office to chew the fat and to inspect the new diggings. He swiveled around in the President's easy chair, pushed a button that elevated the coffee table into a desk, put his feet up and grinned: "It sure beats losing."

We talked a little about the election campaign: "The papers underplayed the meaning of the bombing halt," Nixon insisted. "It meant three or four percentage points for sure. Johnson's timing was just a little bit off. We were in real danger on Saturday—if they had waited one more day, they would have had the election in the bag." A delay would have meant that President Thieu's negative reaction from Saigon, turning down the invitation to the Paris talks, would not have had a chance to sink in: the election would have been held amid a "peace scare"—the bombing halt's euphoria. Nixon evidently considered President Thieu's reluctance to have been crucial.

On George Wallace: "He's finished, like Goldwater in '64. He got nine million votes, but what did he win?" There was the comparison to Kennedy: "We didn't do badly. Kennedy lost thirty seats in 1960." (Actually, the Democrats lost twenty seats in the House, two in the Senate in 1960; Republicans gained four House and five Senate seats in 1968.)

The talk quickly came around to Cabinet posts: "I don't want anybody in the Cabinet older than I am," he said flatly, then promptly backed off. "Romney, maybe." Pat Buchanan, who always referred to Nixon as "the Old Man," said in wonderment, "You mean—you really want to *be* 'the Old Man'?" Ray Price put in a pitch for Daniel P. Moynihan, the urbanologist and sub-Cabinet member in the Kennedy-Johnson Administration. I added that we had already referred to Moynihan as the antibureaucratic "new liberal" who would be welcome in the "new alignment." Nixon cocked his head: "But could we count on him to be loyal? I don't mean Republican. I mean—you know—one of us."

On the beach at Key Biscayne, Nixon cruelly took his time before making staff announcements, but was anxious to move quickly on his Cabinet. Kennedy had pulled a public relations coup with his Cabinet appointments—all announcements made outdoors, in the sunshine of Palm Beach or wind of Hyannisport, Massachusetts, giving the TV cameras a sense of freshness and exuberance—and Nixon wanted to do something dramatic too. Frank Shakespeare came up with the idea of a television spectacular, announcing the Cabinet all at once and giving some of the reasons for the choices. Nixon went for it.

When he made his choices, the President-elect dictated some notes for us to work into the outline script. Dated December 9, 1968, referring to himself in the third person as RN, they show what he was thinking about his future Cabinet members.

Next to Bob Finch's name, he wrote "youth, imagination and firsthand experience in dealing with these problems in the nation's most populous state." Nixon did not remember George Shultz's first name, or how to spell his last, so he wrote: "Dr _____ Schultz has earned the respect of management and labor as one of the nation's outstanding mediators . . . like Finch, Hardin and Blount, he is in the younger age group." Maury Stans at Commerce: "because of his years of success in business on the fastest track in the world—Wall Street." David Kennedy at Treasury: "at 63, the oldest man in the Cabinet, but he brings vigor, imagination and drive . . . It is interesting to note that both Kennedy and Johnson had him on their list for this position." Attorney General John Mitchell: "the strong man in the campaign team and its leader, not because he was named as such but because he earned that place due to his immense competence . . . he will provide leadership far beyond the technical problems of his department . . ." Mel Laird at Defense: "the youngest Defense Secretary in history . . . A businessman in the Defense Department—like McNamara or Wilson—would employ many fine management techniques but might not be able to provide the insight . . . There was considerable pressure to keep Clark Clifford, but RN thought it would be a mistake to go forward with one who helped to shape the policies which RN has been criticizing." Rogers at State: "[Nelson] Rockefeller and [William] Scranton ruled themselves out. [Douglas] Dillon was strongly supported, but RN did not want to go to a man with a previous administration; also RN felt the party was against him* . . . considerable support for [Cyrus] Vance, but RN felt for this position he had to have his own man, not one who is basically a Johnson man . . . Bill Rogers was selected not primarily because of his ex-

* Dillon, a Republican, served as Secretary of the Treasury in the Kennedy and Johnson Administrations.

perience in foreign affairs, but because he had the intellect, negotiating skill and the judgment to meet the Russian, Chinese and North Vietnamese, or any other potential antagonist on an equal ground. In addition, he is an expert on handling the congress and the press—problems which have stumped most Secretaries of State in years past."

In his memo Nixon pointed to the nice geographical balance and again stressed the youth angle—"Rogers is the youngest Secretary of State and Laird is the youngest Secretary of Defense"—then turned to a crucial matter: "One difference in the selection of this Cabinet from the Kennedy Cabinet is that RN named the Cabinet before making any Sub-cabinet appointments . . . which means that Sub-cabinet appointees will not be imposed on the members of the Cabinet, although they will, of course, consult RN in making their selection." Nixon was determined to give his Cabinet members—whom he would describe as having "an extra dimension" on the TV show—much more of a say in running the government. He was sincere in this; it fit neatly into his basic idea of command structure, with decentralized authority. (Viewing it from six years in the future, the idea was set aside too soon. That was a pity; the "easy way" is to bring authority into the White House, which is what Nixon did, until he was forced to change his pattern somewhat in 1973 to conform to some of his '68 precepts.)

Bob Haldeman, avidly reading Patrick Anderson's *The President's Men*, and the book he thought taught most about the Presidential staff function,* Samuel I. Rosenman's *Working with Roosevelt*, studied the recommendations of management consultants and agreed that staff-power decentralization should be the theme. Since Arthur Burns, who was to be a powerful Counselor to the President to help get things started, had been promised the Federal Reserve Chairmanship as soon as William McChesney Martin's term ended, it followed that the power would flow away from the center—at least, within reason. This was an article of faith with Nixon, whose generation of Republicans were brought up to denounce the swollen White House staffs of the FDR days—the "janissariat"—and who matured in the staff system of the Eisenhower years, with Treasury Secretary George Humphrey effectively running the country and Secretary of State John Foster Dulles running the "free world."

After the Cabinet selection, the President called the writers into his suite at the Pierre Hotel. We trooped in past John Mitchell, who was just leaving, and who called out cheerily, "Here comes the Brain Trust!" to which Appointments Secretary Dwight Chapin cheerily added, "And Buchanan too." The President-elect had his feet up against a glass-topped coffee table, and as he talked to us about the Inaugural Address, the glass slowly began to slide. We watched, the way one watches a man unconcerned with a lengthening ash on his cigarette, with morbid fascination. James Keogh broke first and pushed the glass back.

* In 1974, Patrick Anderson was the writer chosen by Jeb Magruder to ghostwrite his book, *An American Life*.

Nixon began: "Anybody read Polk's Inaugural?" (Now that was a hell of a thing for the President-elect to say. You work for years to help him on his way, knock yourself out in an election campaign, go through all the tensions and jockeying-around of an interregnum, and the first question he asks you in your new capacity as Special Assistant to the President is a one-upper, to which you could not possibly have the answer, but he does.) I would be damned if I would admit having been absent the day my history class took up Polk's Inaugural, so I came back aggressively with one of the only two facts I could remember about Polk: "He was the only Speaker of the House ever to be elected President, you know," I said, as if in answer to Nixon's question. Sure enough, it worked; Nixon looked at me with new respect. In dealing with a President-elect, the important thing is to have an answer, if not to his question, to a related question.* Turning to Jim Keogh, who had nothing at all to offer about Polk's Inaugural, Nixon said he had also been reading all the others, and especially liked FDR's, Teddy Roosevelt's, Lincoln's, Kennedy's, and Jefferson's first. "Herbert Hoover's was the best of the long ones," he added. "Polk's was short. Read it. Kennedy's was an example of words being enough—in twenty-five years, maybe Johnson will look better than Kennedy. Johnson tortures himself with that.

"I don't know if it can be done," he said, "but I'd like to use an anecdote. You know, like something around what James Buchanan said: 'All my friends are dead, and all my enemies are now my friends.' Not that, but something like it." (That was a fascinating line for Nixon to be remembering. I checked out its authenticity to find, sadly, it is an apocryphal sharpening of a fuzzier line by the seventy-six-year-old President Buchanan. I only hope future generations give that kind of assist to fuzzy lines I worked on with Richard Nixon.)

He did call for Americans to "lower our voices" and in general made a fine beginning. Nixon's First Inaugural Address was to be infinitely better than his Second, just as his first acceptance speeches in 1960 and 1968 were better than his last in 1972. "We cannot learn from one another until we stop shouting at one another—until we speak quietly enough so that our words can be heard as well as our voices." Ray Price worked with him most closely on that speech, but standing in the cold on the wooden benches behind the Capitol, anybody who had a hand in the speech nudged his wife, or the girl he was with, whenever one of "his" lines came up. After it was over, the new President gave us a memento of an Inaugural medal in lucite with these words from the Inaugural on its stand: "I ask you to join in a high adventure—one as rich as humanity itself, and exciting as the times we live in."

Nixon sounded like Wilson that day, and made us all proud. Especially

---

* The other thing I knew about Polk was the use made of his name by Franklin Pierce in a slogan for his campaign: "We Polk'd you in 1844, we shall Pierce you in 1852!" Easy to groan, but Pierce won.

hopeful—in the light of that disturbing question he had asked about Moynihan, "Would he be 'one of us'?"—was the answer he had given in choosing Moynihan to be his adviser on urban affairs, and the best of all was the message we found in Polk's Inaugural, which boded well for the spirit of creative and civil controversy, discussed with lowered voices, spoken March 4, 1845:

"Although in our country the Chief Magistrate must almost of necessity be chosen by a party and stand pledged to its principles and measures, yet in his official action he should not be the President of a part alone, but of the whole people of the United States. While he executes the laws with an impartial hand, shrinks from no proper responsibility, and faithfully carries out in the executive department of the government the principles and policy of those who have chosen him, he should not be unmindful that our fellow citizens who have differed with him in opinion are entitled to the full and free exercise of their opinions and judgments, and that the right of all are entitled to respect and regard."

3. NO END RUNS

Harry Robbins ("Bob") Haldeman was the way his name appeared in news accounts, when it did appear—and any time it appeared was too often for a man with a genuine detestation for personal publicity. The President-elect referred to him in notes as "H", which he adopted as his own signature in memos because HRH was too readily spoofed as "His Royal Highness."

He would sit on the porch of Villa 41 at the Key Biscayne Hotel stretched out on a beach chair, sopping up the sun, head cocked to hold the telephone against his shoulder, making notes on the long yellow pad that would become one of the symbols of the Administration.

Haldeman studied the various methods used by other staff chiefs to organize the White House, and pored over the procedural recommendations made by management consultants, but his main problem then, and later, was the physical presence of the Man, Numero Uno, the Boss, You-Know-Who, the Highest Level—and all the other phrases we conjured up to refer to Nixon after he had been elected and before he became the President.

"What do we do with him?" Haldeman asked rhetorically one day in December 1968, rubbing his pencil back and forth across his crew cut and squinting into the sun. "He knows he needs to relax, so he comes down to Florida. He likes to swim, so he swims for ten minutes. Then that's over. He doesn't paint, he doesn't horseback-ride, he doesn't have a hobby. His best relaxation is talking shop, but he knows he should not be doing that, because that doesn't seem to be relaxing. So what do we do with him? It's a problem."

That never stopped being Haldeman's problem. Nixon is a restless man, to whom relaxation is often a planned and necessary part of a program. In Haldeman's eyes, if left to his own devices the President might act impulsively and get into trouble. Nixon distrusted his own impulsiveness as well, and placed Haldeman between himself and the rest of the world as a safety catch on a trigger. Knowing he was under that welcome restraint, Nixon could issue commands and otherwise finger the trigger, knowing full well the damn gun would not immediately go off. This was one of the subtleties in the relationship between the two men that befuddled observers who thought that Haldeman was building a wall around Nixon, when Nixon was building a wall of his own, with sandbag #1 named Haldeman.

In the interregnum, both men felt it was necessary to establish a new relationship with the people who had worked on the campaign, including the Old Nixon Hands. For that reason, the announcements of the White House staff were delayed for long weeks—nobody was to be assured they had a job because of long service, everybody was to sweat a little—until finally it was announced that Rose Woods and Bryce Harlow were to be with the President-elect when he moved into the White House, and then the staff announcements began to flow.

In building his wall, Nixon had to consider what to do about Rose, who had been with him since the Fifties, who knew where all the bodies were buried, who knew which contributor was also a friend and which was not, who loved, idolized, and mother-henned him, and whose brother Joe, Sheriff of Cook County, had made certain that Mayor Daley did not duplicate his alleged 1960 feat and steal the Illinois electoral votes. (Joe, in close touch with Rose all of 1968's election night, held back the filing of the returns in many districts, so that Daley's men did not know how many "extra" votes were needed to be cast in their own special way. Finally, Daley had to guess, and guessed short; that was one reason why Illinois, with its up-to-date voting machines, was so late in reporting on election night, and why Nixon carried the state.) Rose Woods was important to Nixon in many ways, and had a call on him now that the generation-long road to the White House had been traveled.

However, if Nixon were to have an effective barricade, he had to have only one point of entry. Haldeman was to be the sole doorkeeper. Haldeman had spoken to several Eisenhower intimates and had learned of the difficulties chief of staff Sherman Adams experienced with Eisenhower's personal secretary, Ann Whitman. A strong, intelligent woman with close ties to the Dewey camp, Mrs. Whitman was an alternate route to the President's attention when Sherman Adams performed his function as "abominable no-man." Haldeman would not permit that. Rose Woods could not be located in the office next door to the President's Oval Office, as personal secretaries to Presidents had been since Teddy Roosevelt had the West Wing built.

Nixon had to break this Haldeman-first news to Rose personally, a task he hated, and she reacted with the grief-stricken fury one might have expected of a loyal woman scorned. Rose and Nixon rode down in the Pierre Hotel elevator afterward, and the President-elect spoke to her twice; she would not speak to him; Bryce Harlow, the only other person in that confined space, refers to it as "the longest elevator ride ever taken by a man who had recently been elected President of the United States." But Nixon did not change his mind; although Rose was respected, honored, and even given some power as custodian of the lists of who would be invited to

White House functions, she did not have the genuine power of immediate proximity, and she hated Haldeman for that until the day, four years later, he was forced to leave, at which time she hated him for serving Nixon badly.

There was a purpose in Haldeman's choice of Rose Woods as the first person with whom to do battle. If he could interpose himself between the President and Rose, he could do damn near anything. Similarly, Haldeman made sure that everybody who wanted to continue working for Nixon as he went to the White House knew that they were applying for a job and were not receiving some position they had earned by dint of years of service. When I talked with him, he said, "I'd like you to come down—we're all too stiff. But would any troubles with Governor Kirk stick to you?" I had represented Florida's tourism and industrial development; he was referring to potential stories about scandal in the state government, which turned out not to be scandalous at all. When I said no, he asked, "Are you a veteran?" That seemed odd; I was a ten-year veteran with Nixon. "The Boss has a thing about people who ducked the service," he said. I said I had spent my two years in the Army, and a couple of weeks later Haldeman called me to say cheerily, "You may be nuts to do it, but the President would like you to come down as a Special Assistant. Twenty-eight thou." I took it.

Haldeman called the new appointees together at 9:30 A.M., December 19, 1968, in a large meeting room of the Hotel Pierre in New York—the Sapphire Room, a happy augury, I thought. Haldeman had already established himself in everyone's mind as the center of operations in the new Administration, but he wanted help in this first briefing from three men who had served other Presidents: Bryce Harlow, the soft-spoken voice of experience from the Eisenhower days; Henry Kissinger, an adviser to Rockefeller who had done some work in the Kennedy and Johnson Administrations; and Daniel Patrick Moynihan, a Kennedy Assistant Secretary of Labor. The three now ranked, with Haldeman and John Ehrlichman, as the senior aides: Harlow as legislative liaison, Kissinger for national security, Moynihan for urban affairs, though nobody knew quite how Moynihan was positioned against Ehrlichman or Arthur Burns, who was given Cabinet rank with the stratospheric title of "counselor."

"This is a political staff," said Harlow, surveying the room, "and many of you know many more Congressmen than I. These Congressmen will call you at the White House, and when it becomes apparent that you cannot help them, they will call me to complain about you." This drew a modest laugh; we thought he was kidding.

"Just because of your location at 1600 Pennsylvania Avenue," the diminutive old pro went on, "you are exceedingly important. As a result, you will be sought after. One technique we will see often is this: a Congressman will call us, expecting us to say no, since we are the professional mattresses, or soft barrier. Then they will call all the other assistants and go through the same catechism. Do not be taken in.

"Now that you are in the White House, you are talking with the voice of Jove. You cannot say something like 'I am confident that this will be done' anymore, because that is a canard.

"About calls originating from you," Bryce went on, coming to the point that had shaken the last President he had served, "you cannot make a 'private call.' The operator says, 'This is the White House calling,' and the person on the other end snaps to attention. Every call you make is a White House call. To independent agencies, make no calls at all. Sherman Adams made a call just to check on the status of something having to do with Mr. Goldfine—not, as he later pointed out, to influence the decision. He was asked acidly later, 'You don't mean to say that a White House call does not have influence?' "

Harlow's object was to put the fear of power in the new staffers and to block intrusions into his own area of responsibility. Kissinger spoke next, more to introduce himself and his ideas of orderliness to a group that knew the President-elect better than he did:

"I saw something of the early days of the Kennedy Administration," said this serious-miened, humorous-looking man with the wavy hair and the German accent. "At that time, the people on the White House staff wondered what they would do in the last two years of the President's term, when all the problems had all been solved." That was a low-key sitter-upper; here was somebody who knew how to address a class. He spoke of the cable traffic that flowed through diplomatic channels to the President: "We should not make policy on the basis of cables, but shape our cables on the basis of previously thought-out policies."

Dr. Kissinger echoed Harlow's caution: "The Departments cannot distinguish between the personal views of the White House staffer and the official views of the President. And they cannot call the President to find out. That is why I suggest we operate from a very low posture.

"Any responsible point of view," he assured us, "will be presented in some option presented to the President. There will be no roadblock. I will not hold up papers that come from the responsible department. They will know the status of each paper, and will be able to complain about that status. Some years ago, I watched the multilateral force decision in the making. It was managed by a group of five people who made it impossible to know who was deciding what at any given point. That is not the procedure I envision. I want to present to the President the views of the relevant departments, presented individually but together. Today, the only central form is an informal lunch once a week, without an agenda, without a follow-up. We can do better than that."

Moynihan, the Democrat, iconoclast and provocateur, with hair longer than any man's present, bow tie twinkling above his striped shirt, came on strong: "All the arguments you have heard for coordination ultimately fail. They have a half life of eighteen months, and they can get a lot of work done, but if you cannot do what you set out to do in the first couple of years, forget it."

"We have been through a period of tremendous activity. Three hundred ninety new programs have been started in the past four years. Two ideas a week is a lot. Now we're going to try to bring some level of coherence to specific problematic areas.

"It's like looking through water," said Moynihan, "and trying to figure out what's at the bottom. What happens at the local level is obscured.

"You can't pick up the morning paper without dealing with urban affairs, and for that reason there is a tendency for everybody to want to fiddle around with it. Everyone knows that foreign affairs can blow up in your face—but in urban problems, no matter what you do nothing much seems to change, so the attitude is 'let's try something—anything.' But if you do that, I'll be unhappy. I need your friendship and love—absent it, we're not going to be able to do what the President wants.

"Remember this," Moynihan concluded, "we are the only people in Washington who work only for the President."

Haldeman stopped being the emcee and took center stage himself. "Our job is not to do the work of government, but to get the work out to where it belongs—out to the Departments." (This was not a view that prevailed, but it was not a matter of being two-faced—Nixon and Haldeman honestly thought in the beginning that was the way it could and should be done.) "Don't let the work pile up on your desk—get rid of it, get it out to the Departments, but just be damn sure that what you do or say is right. Watch every little nuance.

"Assume everything you put on paper is a public document," Haldeman went on. "The privilege of private communication is no longer yours.

"Nothing goes to the President that is not completely staffed out first, for accuracy and form, for lateral coordination, checked for related material, reviewed by competent staff concerned with that area—and all that is essential for Presidential attention.

"Now about end-running. That is the principal occupation of 98 per cent of the people in the bureaucracy. Do not permit anybody to end-run you or any of the rest of us." Ominously he added: "Don't become a source of end-running yourself, or we'll miss you at the White House.

"The key staff can always communicate with and see the President when necessary. The priorities will be weighed on the basis of what visit will accomplish most. We've got to preserve his time for the things that matter. Now, that does not mean that everything will be reduced for him by the staff to the lowest common denominator. The President wants to make decisions himself, not to preside over decisions made by the staff. How we decide what is major and what is minor is the key to whether this is a good White House staff or a lousy one.

"We'll go gradually in systematizing because we've got to feel our way into this process and to make sure we don't put in something that screws itself up in formalities." That went over well with the Old Nixon Hands, worried about barriers. Haldeman continued:

"On procedure: there has always got to be a written agenda. Nobody goes in without a piece of paper on what he's going to talk about, because maybe somebody else should be there.

"He will also have meetings without staff members present. We'll develop a procedure to follow up these meetings by the right staff people.

"No request for Presidential time goes direct to the President. If you go to him and say, 'I need an hour,' he will say, 'Sure, come in tomorrow at five,' and seventeen people will be there tomorrow at five.

"If you bring a visitor in, and he wants to ask RN to go to the Boy Scout Jamboree, turn that off beforehand. Don't let them take paperwork in to him. It goes right to the bottom of his briefcase and never gets seen again, or it gets signed and becomes an order. All paper has to go into my office, and it will get to him after it has been staffed. National security affairs will go to Kissinger, personal matters to Rose Woods, political stuff to the National Committee, Congressional to Harlow. On mail that comes in to you, refer it to where it belongs. Remember—*don't let end runs happen.*"

Haldeman closed by reading from the Brownlow Commission report to FDR in 1936 about the qualities of a White House aide:

> ". . . would have no power to make decisions or issue instructions in [his] own right . . . would not be interposed between the President and the heads of his Departments . . . would not be assistant President in any sense . . . would remain in the background, issue no orders, make no decisions, emit no public statements . . . should be possessed of a high competence, great physical vigor and a passion for anonymity."

Using Louis Brownlow's criteria, a good handicapper might have assumed that Harlow would have stayed the longest (he left first, returning to help for a while after Watergate); Haldeman would have come a cropper on the interposition of himself between the Departments and the President (the policy changed); Moynihan would make his mark and depart at midterm (he did, returning toward the end to a diplomatic post ten thousand miles from Washington); and Kissinger would plod along closest to the job description, never quite achieving the notoriety of a Walt Rostow (his passion did not run in the direction of anonymity and his sensitivity to end runs was destined to exceed Haldeman's).

We milled around a bit after the meeting saying hello to each other, wondering to ourselves if this bunch of guys would be the group that would really run the country for the next four years. Haldeman kidded me about being the only one who saw the need to take notes, and suggested that if I came to the next meeting on time, I could thereby get the whole thing. He had an eye for history, which was good; later, he would come up with a method of preserving everything the President said, which was no good.

PART THREE

BONE IN THE THROAT

As Nixon took office, the bone in the nation's throat was the war in Vietnam: 550,000 U.S. troops were there, 300 men per week were being killed in action, and all—as Nixon had hammered away in the 1968 campaign—"with no end in sight."

His first approach to solving the dilemma—"with honor" was always in his plan—was to do what he had discussed with his writers more than a year before: to raise the diplomatic ante, to make a Vietnam settlement part of a global transaction. Therefore, the new President's first move was to visit the European capitals, probing De Gaulle on the possibilities of an opening to Red China, establishing his Presidential legitimacy at home as well. The first approaches to North Vietnam were conciliatory, talking in terms of withdrawal, which pleased even the most dovish members of the newly created National Security Council staff. When Nixon met with Premier Nguyen Van Thieu of South Vietnam on Midway Island, to announce the withdrawal of the first 25,000 Americans, he preceded this dovish move with a vigorous blast at "the new isolationists" at home: Nixon's foreign policy required an attempt at conciliation without having it interpreted as a show of weakness, to the Soviets, the Chinese, or the North Vietnamese. In private conversation with Thieu before the joint announcement at Midway, Nixon said, "I would not like to be breaking the umbilical cord to your people," and Thieu replied: "No, we have been saying for years we were getting stronger. And if that is the case, then we have to be willing to see some Americans leave."

In Nixon's eyes, the American "spirit"—as exemplified by the Apollo mission to the moon—was the most important psychological weapon that could be used in building the generation of peace. The way in which the war in Vietnam would be concluded would be another, more serious expression of that spirit, setting the tone for U.S. relations with its allies and adversaries in the years to come. "A reasonable chance to survive" was a line I wrote into a draft on Vietnam that became a kind of no man's land between doves and hawks in the United States, with each side interpreting how much of a chance was "reasonable."

As conciliation toward the North Vietnamese showed the first signs of failing, Nixon applied military pressure and did not, as many had hoped, step up the pace of withdrawal appreciably; the antiwar movement marshaled its forces and marched on Washington; Nixon marshaled his own forces with the "silent majority" speech and bought six more months. Then, in the spring of 1970, in the first crisis of his Presidency, an event took place that had not been expected by the United States or the North Vietnamese. A neutralist government in Cambodia, which had supinely permitted both warring nations to use its territory (one to resupply, the other to bomb the supply lines) was overturned by a pro-Western group. The North Vietnamese moved in; the United States countered the invasion with its own "incursion"; the U.S. campuses erupted; Kent State and Jackson State became household words; and Nixon spent a traumatic night visiting the Lincoln Memorial.

The Cambodian decision, which Nixon saw as absolutely necessary to prevent the victory of the Communist forces in Southeast Asia, temporarily stopped his secret opening to China, though it did not slow down the march toward an arms limitation agreement with the Soviet Union. The first period of Nixon foreign policy, from January 1969 to July 1970, was directed to getting out of a morass in a way that would impress the Soviets and Chinese with the U.S. resolve to "remain a great nation." During this time, connective tissue was slowly created that would become important in the next stage, when summitry was to bedazzle the public and help dislodge the bone in the throat.

1. HELLO, EUROPE

Air Force One was ready to head across the Atlantic. Members of the official party had boarded the plane and were awaiting takeoff. The President of the United States, who had held that title for thirty-three days, sat waiting with hands folded, staring out the window.

Bob Haldeman was the man who bore the responsibility for the logistics and arrangements of the first trip abroad of Richard Nixon as President. That morning, of all mornings, Haldeman had overslept. When his absence was noted, a helicopter was sent to fetch him. "Here comes our slightly fallible drill sergeant," said a smiling Henry Kissinger, Nixon's prize acquisition from Nelson Rockefeller. The President, not smiling, growled, "Good morning," and everyone who witnessed the baleful look directed at the Chief of Staff thought to himself, "Better him than me."

Despite the inauspicious start, the trip was useful both to our foreign policy and to the public perception of Nixon in Europe and at home. The purposes were properly modest: not a State visit or series of negotiations, but a start to the process of getting acquainted with European leaders who felt, with some justification, that American attention had been focused too long on Southeast Asia.

The February 1969 trip's attainable goals meant that the new President was playing it safe. In contrast with the 1972 Moscow trip, which included a major negotiating gamble, the first voyage of Nixon as President seems smooth indeed. But a misstep or misstatement would have been widely reported; the possibility of a blunder was always present and worried his advisers. Nixon's calm demeanor and frequent references to earlier trips made as Vice President reminded those around him that he was an old hand at diplomatic travel, and when he called us into his cabin between stops, it was more to settle us down and get us working together than to get advice.

Seating arrangements were rigidly organizational. Haldeman sat with Ehrlichman; Kissinger sat with his deputy, Lawrence Eagleburger; and William Rogers sat with Martin Hillenbrand, Assistant Secretary of State for European Affairs. Throughout the trip, the inexperienced Rogers' closest adviser was State Department Counselor Richard F. Pedersen.* There was little mingling.

Nixon spent the seven hours of the crossing in his maroon sports jacket studying all the statements that had been prepared for him—first by State, then by Kissinger's staff, then by Jim Keogh's writing staff with a final okay by Henry. On his arrival in Brussels, first stop of the tour, he exhibited his ability to improvise.

The President had a folder labeled "Statements: Brussels" that contained the arrival statement, the speech to the NATO council, and the departure statement. He stepped on the red carpet, shook hands with His Majesty, King Baudouin I, stepped up to the podium in front of the assembled bands and cameras, listened attentively to the welcome from the King, and then proceeded, as my heart sank, to read his arrival remarks from the departure statement.

The horrible thought crossed my mind that the President would get to the bottom of the page, thank the Belgians for their kind hospitality, and wish them a fond farewell, to the consternation of all. This did not come to pass, nor was the President's selection from the departure statement an error. He did not like the main portion of the arrival statement, so he substituted the departure material, ad-libbing a gracious close. This little episode shook up Kissinger, his staff, and me, showing us that the President would not be "programmed" but had the confidence in his own taste that enabled him to depart from texts. This could prove mildly troublesome, but it could be—and often was—most impressive to the audience, the traveling press, and to us.

Ad-libbing is fine when it comes on top of a statement a President is satisfied with, but it should not be the crutch for the staff to rely upon. I started rewriting statements and sending them into Dr. Kissinger late at night through Lawrence Eagleburger.† Two nights running, the changes were not read by Kissinger, much less okayed; Henry said he was "too damn bushed to bother with it." I said to hell with that; I had been on a campaign plane long enough the year before to know that what came out of the top man's mouth counted heavily. Henry came over to me on *Air Force One* and apologized: "We aren't going to do a trip this way again. These statements should be done two or three weeks in advance, cleared and set." On the rest of that trip, suggested changes were either made or turned down with good reason; on subsequent trips, Henry was true to his word—we were all set and cleared before we left. But in those early days and later, the frenetic pace of Kissinger's staff never let up. As we watched

---

* Several months later, Pedersen's name appeared on the list supplied by Kissinger of those to be tapped by the FBI. In effect, it was a tap on Rogers.

† Eagleburger threw up his hands after a few months and asked to be transferred to a job that human beings are accustomed to, returning for more punishment with Kissinger in 1973. His name always struck me as tragic; I thought of a great bird with a soaring spirit going through a meat grinder, feathers and all, and being turned into eagleburgers.

one of his secretaries blazing away at a typewriter in a hotel suite in Rome, seated on a suitcase, with her hair in curlers, Henry said proudly: "Working for me is like being in the Marines. After six months, either you go crazy or you think that's the only way to live." The campaign-hardened President was used to this pace; as Nixon put it, "You can do anything for a week."

To the NATO council in Brussels, the President began by saying the right thing: "I have come for work, not for ceremony; to inquire, not to insist; to consult, not to convince; to listen and learn and to begin what I hope will be a continuing interchange of ideas and insights." As he came to the body of his speech, he dropped the alliteration, and his tone changed from deferential (new President from the New World) to realistic (Commander-in-Chief of the common nuclear umbrella).

"We must . . . ask ourselves some hard questions. NATO was brought into being by the threat of the Soviet Union. What is the nature of that threat today? When NATO was founded, Europe's economies were still shattered by war. Now they are flourishing. How should this be reflected by changed relationships among the NATO partners?" It was not Nixon's purpose to offer answers yet, or to present an instant grand design; it was his purpose to show Europeans that he knew what the essential questions were, and to show a willingness to listen to allies in the development of answers.

Kissinger, of course, was in his element; he was one of the few members of the official party with foreign affairs negotiating experience. An incident at the NATO council illustrates both his self-confidence and innate playfulness.

Ron Ziegler had received permission to sit in on the council meeting at the enormous round table. Ron was then thirty, fresh from his job as an account executive at J. Walter Thompson, and patronizingly described (to his annoyance) as a lovable puppy dog by unfriendly columnists. During the meeting of the Council of Ministers, Kissinger passed a note to Ziegler, who was sitting on the other side of the table. All eyes followed the passing of the folded note from hand to hand around the table. The U.S. press secretary received it, read it poker-faced, nodded, and put it in his pocket. Afterward, I found out what Henry had written: "They are calling on people alphabetically. Don't worry, Ziegler—your turn will come."

To Ziegler's credit, he did not embrace diplomatic jargon on his first diplomatic journey. "Candid and sincere" were the words he used to characterize most of the talks, carefully eschewing the "fruitful exchange" cliché. I had told him, as a mnemonic, that when a participant in a meeting threw a tomato at another head of state, that was a fruitful exchange.

"Special relationship" was the operative phrase on the next stop, the United Kingdom—a phrase Winston Churchill coined to label the English-speaking Atlantic partnership. It was in the U.S. interest to make a point of this "special relationship"; it was in Prime Minister Harold Wilson's interest, as he headed then toward a union with Europe that he later opposed, to separate himself just a little from the U.S. embrace. As Wilson put it at the airport, after Nixon had special-relationshipped him, "Our special relationship is by no means exclusive."

A small diplomatic problem, but a potentially embarrassing one, had to do with the new British Ambassador to the United States. Wilson, expecting Lyndon Johnson to run and be re-elected, had appointed John Freeman, editor of the leftish *New Statesman* weekly magazine, who over the years had vilified Nixon. Now Freeman was headed to Washington, to the derision of the British press. Nixon, at a small stag dinner at 10 Downing Street, defused the situation with a graceful turn of phrase: "They say there's a new Nixon. And they wonder if there's a new Freeman. Let me set aside all possibility of embarrassment because our roles have changed. He's the new diplomat and I'm the 'new statesman.'" The assembled diplomats thumped the table in approval; Freeman, who had a tendency to perspire profusely, stopped sweating about his next couple of years in Washington. The line was originally written as a gag, a lighthearted play on the words of the magazine title; Nixon changed the tone, gave it seriousness and dignity, and used it to serve a diplomatic purpose. Back on the plane, the President showed me a note Harold Wilson had written on the back of the dinner menu: "That was one of the kindest and most generous acts I have known in a quarter century in politics. Just proves my point. You can't guarantee being born a Lord. It is possible—you've shown it—to be born a gentleman. H."

In England, they notice the little social things, and Nixon was aware of it. Ordinarily, when Nixon shakes hands with ladies, he makes an awkward little bow; he must have reminded himself about this, because when he shook hands with Queen Elizabeth, he did so without the bow—properly, as one Head of State to another.

We tried something different and refreshing in London: a meeting with twenty-five private citizens, off the record, no questions barred. The British men and women were opinion leaders, and some of their questions were precise and difficult. ("Is the American nuclear capability credible? Does NATO have the capacity for flexible response?") Nixon handled those in one-two-three fashion, but as the meeting wore on, the questions became more thought-provoking and his answers more philosophical. "In the U.S. today," he told the group of Britons, "there's a growing isolationism, a trend toward protectionism growing out of our experience in the Vietnam war. Tied into the trauma of our race problem, this has tended to make some people lash out. But it would be a mistake to assess the U.S. today only by the scenes of violence you may see on television . . ." On the Soviets: "My own view is that the Soviet Union is concerned about Asia, about what happens in Vietnam, but they—and we—consider Europe the blue chip. They have a concern about China, a concern about internal pressures from consumers, and a concern about the overall threat of nuclear confrontation. We are in a period when Soviet policy will not be as adventuresome. Partly, of course, this is because of the change in the times—because they now know what could happen, and what they could lose." On what came to be called linkage: "The purpose of having an agreement with the Soviets limiting arms is, of course, because an arms race could lead to war. There's a selfish reason, too—to ease up on arms expenditures. But we could freeze the arms level at where they are and still have a hell of a war—that's why I say that now is the time to move forward on several fronts. Arms agreements create trust toward the political settlements. But put it the other way around, too—political settlements could lead to arms agreements."

Scribbling notes in an anteroom, I liked the way a young man in the group took an expression from nuclear jargon and applied it to a social problem: "Don't you think, Mr. President, that society needs a more flexible response toward youth?" Nixon became more animated: "As I look at the 'student revolution' in the U.S.—back in the Thirties, the student rebel had a cause, a belief, a religion. Today, the revolt doesn't have that form—it's more negative, against the Establishment. But on the plus side, the student generation is infinitely more knowledgeable about the world than my own generation—and in a way, even more idealistic than we ever were. When a nation is at war, you fight to stay alive; in a depression you fight to make a living. But in a time of peace, we have to provide a way to help young people make the world a better place—to provide an outlet for a missionary spirit."

By the meeting's end, a roomful of influential Britons were ready to pass along the word that the new American President was not at all like the caricatures they had been sold over the years—he could grasp ideas, he spoke well and listened intently. (Being listened to by an intent Nixon can be an intellectually draining experience.) Moreover, the meeting gave Nixon something fresh and topical to talk about all over Europe: "You know, in talking things over with some private citizens in Britain," he said a half-dozen times, "I was struck by something one of the young people said about the new needs of students today . . ."

The trip to Berlin did not electrify the city the way Kennedy's visit did, but times had changed. The German names around Nixon were prominently mentioned in the German press: Haldeman, Ehrlichman, Ziegler, Hillenbrand, Sonnenfeldt, Mosbacher and Eagleburger made up quite a *Gesellschaft*. Haldeman watched the snappy German honor guard perform at the airport arrival and asked me, "How long do you think it will be before I get the White House staff shaped up like that?" He was probably kidding. Nixon picked up the soccer chant shouted by Berliners: "Ha-ho-hey!", spotted a sign that read "Ha-ho-hey, Nixon is OK," and responded to the audience gathered in the Seimans plant with "Ha-ho-hey, Berliners are OK." This did not go over all that well with the press corps, but it brought a delighted roar from the crowd.

Back in the plane, after presenting a picture of himself to the Mayor, Nixon was irritated. "I will not present my own picture to anybody ever again. It's pretentious. 'Here's a picture of me—' Nope, never."

Rose Woods said, "But it's probably been set up in Rome and Paris—"

"Knock it off." The President permitted himself to build up a head of steam on this minor point of protocol. "I don't care what they decided. I don't hand out pictures of myself. That's an order." He brooded out the window for a while. "I don't care if they stamp their feet and get all red in the face about it. The next State Department type who hands me a picture of myself to hand to somebody else, I'll—I'll wrap it around his neck." We didn't say anything. A few moments passed. Then we saw the President take an imaginary picture frame in his hands and pantomime the act of crashing it over the head of a pompous official, leaving his imaginary target with a kind of Elizabethan collar framing his neck. Nixon enjoyed the mental picture.

Highlight of the trip, both in substance and color, was Nixon's reunion with De Gaulle in Paris. An awkward flap had developed between the British and French on the eve of the President's trip: De Gaulle had made an indiscreet remark about expanding the Common Market to include the Scandinavians and British, and a British diplomat indiscreetly leaked it to the press. But Nixon sailed above it all. Nixon wanted to show De Gaulle that "Asia first" was not the U.S. policy, and at the same time asked him how best to approach Red China. He assured him there was no cause to worry about U.S. domination of Europe; in addition, he wanted to see what help he could count on from De Gaulle in the Middle East. On his side, De Gaulle felt the time ripe for an improvement in climate, especially with a U. S. President he respected and who he knew admired him.

As we landed at Orly, Nixon observed that De Gaulle was coatless; off went the Nixon topcoat. He had the arrival statement in his pocket, and the text was being given out; he would read it or ad-lib it depending on what De Gaulle did. (De Gaulle had memorized his, so Nixon spoke without notes as well.) Some reporters wondered why certain passages of the prepared statement were omitted, reading hidden meaning where none existed. It was hard to get them to believe the lines were left out because Nixon couldn't remember the whole thing.

Deplaning from *Air Force One* in those early days, the President had to pass through the length of the plane as he came from his cabin in the back. (Haldeman soon had the interior redesigned so that the President's cabin was in front.) The aisle would be cleared at every stop, and RN would zip through with some cheery comment, as he did when campaigning. At the bottom of the arrival statement I had written, "In case De Gaulle says, 'Vive les États-Unis,' you should say, 'Vive la France.'" Sweeping down the aisle, Nixon called out, "Here we go—Vive la France!"

In his arrival statement, in the public toasts and private conversations that followed, Nixon played what *Paris Presse* accurately called "imposing homage to de Gaulle." And he did it De Gaulle style—apparently ad lib. I rode in from the airport with Henry Kissinger, who was enjoying himself; when we came to the Champs Élysées, which had been cleared of all vehicles for the official cars, Henry murmured, "They shouldn't do this for me—they should know how it embarrasses me." The national security adviser was excited about the way the President had handled the trip so far: "He started out B-plus. But now he's got the ground under him. He's really got it. God, to stand up there without notes and to say the right thing —do you have any idea what that takes?"

At the State Dinner given by France in the ornate dining room of the Élysées Palace—all glittering chandeliers and candelabra, with medieval tapestries of Biblical scenes providing the backdrop (whispered sailing champion Emil "Bus" Mosbacher, our chief of protocol: "You know, these Frenchmen wrote the book on State Dinners.")—interpreters were seated behind and between guests who needed them. The interpreters did not eat: "I would love to give you half of my paté," the wife of Philippe de Gaulle, seated next to me, said over her shoulder, "but my husband would lose his job."

General de Gaulle rose to give his toast before the waiters had poured the champagne; those waiters scrambled to get those glasses full like SAC pilots in a Red Alert. It was an extraordinarily gracious toast, topping Nixon's effusive arrival statement. Nixon's response to the toast was more restrained, focusing on three points—De Gaulle's courage, his ability to convince, and his vision. The time to lay it on more substantially, Nixon knew, was at the return dinner at the U. S. Embassy the following night. He did.

Earlier that day the Nixon staff had met De Gaulle, and I suspect the general's champagne gambit with the waiters at dinner was deliberate because he had similar fun with Clem Conger, then deputy chief of protocol (later White House curator). Conger is both a born worrier and a stickler for doing things "right"—by protocol's book. When De Gaulle surprised us by sending word he would receive the touring Nixon staff, Clem desperately began lining us up in protocol order—Haldeman at one end, on down to me and then Ziegler at the lowest-ranking end. De Gaulle observed these goings on from across the room, waited until Conger was finished, and then deliberately went to the wrong end of the line to start the handshaking with the then-unimportant Ziegler. Conger closed his eyes in horror.

The general looked piercingly at each one of us—not a perfunctory hello, but a long, hard look at the men Nixon brought with him, through very thick glasses that explained why he did not want ever to read his prepared remarks. After De Gaulle had left, Haldeman came over to me, stuck out his hand and said, "Enchanté."

When the State Dinner drew to its stately end, I found myself in the small reception room talking to the general and his interpreter. I complimented him on being able to speak at length without notes, not the kind of remark that would get me or my country into trouble, and De Gaulle said: "I write it down, commit it to memory, then throw the paper away. Churchill used to do the same thing, but he never admitted it."

"Not many people do that anymore," I volunteered. De Gaulle leaned back, searched the room for Nixon, then pointed to him: "Ah, but what about him? What about him? That's just what he does." We talked for a while about speechmaking and he made an observation that I knew Nixon agreed with totally: "I think you should either read a speech or not read it, one or the other. I do not believe in looking down, looking up at the audience or the camera, looking down at the speech again—trying to seem as if you know it when you do not."*

I turned my new-found friend over to John Ehrlichman and accepted a glass of orange juice from one of the waiters. Whenever I visited the home of a French friend, the appearance of the orange juice meant that it was proper to think about going home—a nice hint that American hostesses could learn from. But RN was enjoying himself and told Ambassador Sargent Shriver he would stay ten minutes more. A couple of minutes later, the lights in the chandelier flickered; Bill Rogers went to Don Hughes, the President's military aide, and told him to get the President moving, the party was over. Nixon finally got the message: De Gaulle wanted to go to bed.

Late that night, Kissinger passed along to us a couple of moments in his talks with De Gaulle:

"If there were a United Europe," Henry said he asked the French President, "how would you prevent the Germans from dominating everything if they decided to?"

De Gaulle shrugged: "By war." That answer, with its sinister humor, fascinated Kissinger—to be able to say that, even kidding around, took him back to the days of Metternich, Castlereagh, and Talleyrand. Then, he reported, it was De Gaulle's turn to ask a question:

"Why don't you get out of Vietnam?"

Kissinger said he replied, "The credibility of the United States is important not only to us, but to our allies. We keep our commitments."

"Where else, besides Vietnam, is it so important?" De Gaulle asked.

"The Middle East, for example," Henry said.

De Gaulle shook his head and gave the American national security adviser an insight about Soviet power: "In the Middle East, it is your enemies who have the credibility problem, not you."

On the long flight home, the President called us into his cabin again to chew the fat.

Ehrlichman: "One blunder on this trip and it would have reverberated all around the world."

Kissinger (to the President): "You started out with the Berlin

---

* In the age of the teleprompter, the written script has a more sophisticated use. Walter Cronkite, who reads the news off a teleprompter near the TV camera's eye, holds a script and often looks down at it, to give the viewer the impression he is reading the papers in his hand, because no man could ad-lib the news. In ancient times, a reader looked up from a script to establish eye contact; today, he looks down at it to establish credibility.

crisis growing, with that Soames dispute between the British and the French, and you had nothing to offer but rhetoric."

Safire (looking up from note-taking): "You didn't like the rhetoric?"

Nixon: "These trips are not important for the rhetoric. They're important for what follows a year from now."

Kissinger: "You now have a platform for a policy. And specifically, you have an excellent chance for a three-year offset from the Germans."

Ehrlichman: "Interesting how you handled that, by delaying the discussion of it."

Kissinger: "Good progress on this trip. The Germans didn't know you, now they do. De Gaulle already admired you, but Wilson did not. The trip enabled the anti-Communist forces in Germany and Italy to get together without polarizing into pro-French and pro-American factions."

As it always did, the conversation turned to politics:

Nixon: "The intellectuals say, 'Be President of all the people and don't be controversial—say nothing.' De Gaulle tried that and lost; in the second round, he campaigned as a candidate, not as an above-the-battle President."

Haldeman (to Kissinger): "How does our resident intellectual feel about that?"

Kissinger: "I have nothing whatever to say about political campaigns. I am the only one I know who went to Miami last summer expecting Rockefeller to win. You won't get political advice from me."

Haldeman (to Safire): "Write that down. We want to remember that in 1972."

The President could not resist getting a pet prejudice off his chest.

Nixon: "The trouble with too many Foreign Service officers is that their first loyalty is to the Foreign Service. Always playing it safe. Incredible."

Time and again he returned to le général.

Nixon: "Why do you suppose there was so much press coverage of De Gaulle's being ready to come to the U.S.?"

Kissinger: "This is the first time in six years that there is a good probability of his coming."

Nixon: "Remember that great reception of Kennedy in France?"

Kissinger: "But De Gaulle cooled toward Kennedy right after the

Vienna trip and the deal in Nassau without consultation. That was a real slap in the face."

Nixon: "And after that, it was over."

Kissinger: "Yes. De Gaulle slammed the door to England in the Common Market, and we had no leverage."

Haldeman: "Then why did De Gaulle come to the Kennedy funeral?"

Nixon: "He's a gentleman."

Ehrlichman: "I was told he has left standing orders to be ready to leave for the U.S. within hours of the announcement of Eisenhower's funeral."

Nixon: "He'll go to funerals. He's a gentleman. I see that a lot of people are saying now that they supported De Gaulle all along on his decision not to revalue the franc. The hell with that, they're trying to rewrite what happened. I got out the clips of those days—they were all predicting devaluation and saying it was a necessary thing. That was a bad day at the National Security Council. They lied about the facts. Henry, isn't that so?"

Kissinger (cautiously): "It would certainly appear—"

Nixon: "Dammit, Henry, they lied!"

Haldeman (looking over the news summary that the telegraph operator had sent in): "I see where Bob Finch was in Israel."

Nixon: "I'm not going to Israel. Ireland, maybe. Not Israel. I've been there twice. Great people, doing a hell of a job. Lots of Moxie. You been there? Amazing. But a visit there is pure domestic U.S. politics, and I've got all the votes I'm ever going to get from there. (To a steward): Let's get some more hot chocolate. (To me, as if I were urging him to go): I'm not going to Israel!"

Haldeman (still flipping through news summary): "You know, the press on all this has been good back in the States."

Nixon (waving it off): "All first Presidential trips get good press."

The President was getting weary. Haldeman gave us the high-sign, and we left. Three hours later, refreshed and showered, Nixon appeared next to my seat to tell me how he had changed my draft of the Washington arrival remarks. The nap was all he needed for what seemed to be a rejuvenation—he was raring to go again.

Nixon's "good press" on his first trip to Europe as President reminded Americans that there was more to foreign policy than Vietnam, and informed Europeans that the new U. S. President was determined to be a force on the world scene. Historian Sir Denis Brogan wrote from London: "It is more than a century since [American Ambassador] James Russell Lowell complained of 'a certain condescension in foreigners.' At that time the condescension was not unnatural. The United States was a raw, new, ill-organized and in some ways repulsive society . . . There is no doubt that the visit of President Nixon was at first received here with a good deal of condescension. But the adroitness he displayed during the trip itself created a favorable impression and reversed the charges that he wished to impose American leadership. His modesty and attitude smoothed the ruffled feathers of Europe."

The word "adroit" was apt. Nixon moved with dexterity on his first trip abroad, more often smoothing than digging, reassuring Europeans who did not know him that he was not a throwback to the Fifties, and assuring European leaders who did know him that he knew the "blue chips" were more West than East. At the same time, he positioned himself Presidentially at home; there is an awkward period early in any Presidency when the title and the name do not seem to fit together, but the sight of foreign crowds cheering on nightly television helped most Americans accept "President Nixon." He knew a debate on the antiballistic missile was in the works, which he viewed as the first test of his foreign-defense policy leadership, and the European trip augmented his credentials. Above all, he wanted to get his toe in the water beyond the "water's edge," since his idea from the start was that the answer to dissent at home and the unending war in Vietnam could be found in a total reshuffling of the foreign affairs deck. There was the human element, too: Nixon liked to play his strong suit, and this first trip gave him the appearance of movement and the sense of power he needed.

Meat-and-potatoes accompanied the pageantry and color. When Nixon returned to Washington, he gathered the legislative leaders in the Cabinet Room to report on the purposes and results of his trip.

He told them his intent had been to show the Europeans he wanted their support for American policies, and—by consulting them beforehand —"to reduce their criticism if we could not get their support." He had created "a climate which can settle the close ones." He wanted Europeans to understand that he understood that "while the alliance was brought together out of fear, that fear no longer exists to the extent it once did." With the "fear quotient" receding, "a new cement" was needed for the Western alliance. Finally, he wanted to find out how strong the forces were for European unity: "The dream of European unity is not dead," the President reported, "but the steam has gone out of it." De Gaulle's nationalism was not the only nationalism on the continent.

NATO was coming up toward its twentieth anniversary, Nixon told the Congressmen, and he had pointed out to the Europeans that "they need NATO more than we do." He said the Europeans were now under no incentive to do more for themselves, because they feared "if they did more, we do less. I told them that the reverse is true. As others helped themselves, we would be willing to help more." While in Europe, he made sure the U.S. allies knew that the Soviets had made great strides in closing the strategic gap, and have widened their lead in conventional weaponry.

The old strategy that John Foster Dulles called "massive retaliatory power" was no longer tenable; Nixon rejected the theory that any conflict in Europe would result in a nuclear war between superpowers, and thus all that would be needed in the way of American forces there would be a "trip wire" of a few battalions. "Let's assume the Soviets moved in to occupy Berlin," the President assumed. He wanted a flexible response, to use strategic jargon—several choices as to what to do between nuclear war and nothing. He told that to the Europeans, Nixon reported, along with a "hard fact" that the American military commitment of nearly six divisions could not stay forever. He had used Majority Leader Mike Mansfield's resolutions calling for bringing the U.S. forces home as a good lever. "What we did in Europe," Nixon told Mansfield, "was impress upon them that the presence of American troops there was more in their interest than ours, that in the event of their withdrawal we could take care of ourselves but Europe would be subject to blackmail from the East."

Ticking off the other results of the trip, the President said we were ready for Four Power talks on the Middle East: "We know where the cards are, and where the chips are, and who has the chips." We were also ready for arms limitation talks with the Soviets—at least, we had Europe's understanding that we intended to move forward. And in the monetary and trade fields, with the British problem with the pound acute, Nixon said that everyone agreed that the wrong approach would be a monetary summit—an overhaul of the system was needed, but nobody wanted to have it until they all knew beforehand what could come out of it. Bankers in Europe, Nixon found, were less concerned with U.S. inflation and U.S. payments deficits than they were about the impact on them of a recession.

What about Vietnam? That was the bone in Nixon's throat: the Europeans knew it, the leadership of the U. S. Congress knew it. In the war critics' eyes, the Vietnam entanglement was keeping the United States from détente and a fresh approach to foreign policy; in Nixon's eyes, the way he would get out of Vietnam would be the single most determining factor in fashioning a stable peace in the world.

"This is a tightrope act," Nixon told Mansfield, Scott, Albert, Ford, and other Congressional leaders at this early stage of his Administration. The bombing halt was still in effect: "We want to avoid taking any military steps that would give them a pretext for breaking off talks." Our problem, he said, sounding more dovish in private than in public, was in trying to find a settlement with the North that would not be interpreted as a dishonoring of our commitments to South Vietnam, a settlement that would provide "some opportunity" for the South to have a chance "for some period of time." That is what he had told the Europeans, many of whom had understood, and some—not De Gaulle, of course—privately told him he had no other honorable alternative.

Months later, De Gaulle chose to put his power in jeopardy on a matter of constitutional principle and, when he lost, resigned. Helmut Sonnenfeldt, who was to become Kissinger's Kissinger, put his head in my office to say, "You know where this leaves us? We have a solution without a problem."

2. THE NEW ISOLATIONISTS

In the early summer of 1969, Richard Nixon realized he was in mortal danger of being perceived as a liberal. Worse, he felt this false perception could lead to a weakening of America's national will.

After a conciliatory Inaugural Address, he went through a lowered-voice period and press honeymoon, with his only legislative battle on the anti-ballistic missile, and even on that many Establishment liberals of the Cold War period, like Paul Douglas, were outspokenly on his side.

On Welfare, George Shultz was working out a humanistic synthesis of Pat Moynihan's floor under income and Arthur Burns's concern about the working poor, which would result in a stunningly compassionate family assistance proposal; on top of that, Shultz was working on his own "Philadelphia plan" to increase jobs for blacks in the construction unions. Tax reform had sailed through taking nine million poor people off the tax rolls on Nixon's initiative; and he put up no real fight to stop the cut in the oil depletion allowance.

Abroad, he had begun Vietnam troop withdrawals, changing the tenor of the division in U.S. society from which-way to how-fast, and had begun secret probes in the direction of China. Many of his public moves at home and abroad were interpreted, correctly so, as progressive; this was making him few friends on the left and building much resentment on the right. Nixon felt keenly the alienation of his natural constituency, even as he understood that his constituency never accurately pegged him. He had been perceived as staunchly conservative because of his lifelong, hard-line anti-Communism and because he was the target of the hatred of the people he proved wrong about Alger Hiss; in fact, his voting record on everything from civil rights to Medicare had been fairly progressive, certainly to the left of the Republican center.

Instinctively a conservative, bred to the value of self-reliance, Nixon adopted progressive views on social legislation after rational analysis and political education. His heart was on the right, and his head was, with FDR, "slightly left of center." Herblockian attacks on him over the years, however, caused conservatives to come to his defense. Nixon felt a kinship with them that transcended doctrinal differences, and usually *felt guilty about betraying their misconception of his positions.*

Being tagged as a liberal in domestic affairs was bad enough—he could live with that in the furtherance of centrist social policies, and if hard times threatened to grip the economy at election time, he was ready to become an activist in economic affairs—but what Nixon could not abide was an association with post-Vietnam liberalism's soft underbelly, which he considered to be a foolish despair about American values and a debilitating and dangerous boredom with world responsibility.

On May 14, 1969, he made his first speech to the American people about Vietnam, calling for mutual withdrawal, creation of an international body to supervise a cease-fire, internationally supervised free elections, and an agreement to abide by the 1954 Geneva and 1962 Laos accords. The tone was conciliatory; he was to follow this up with the first troop withdrawal announcement on June 8: twenty-five thousand American combat troops to come home by the end of August.

During that interval, as he prepared to reverse the course of American participation in that war, Nixon felt the need to reaffirm his belief in some old defense and foreign policy virtues. He did not want his act of beginning to withdraw to be misinterpreted by new-found friends and old adversaries. He felt he needed to show that Richard Nixon was not going soft. Troop withdrawal, a part of orderly Vietnamization, must not be taken as "cut and run" and, as he had shown in the ABM Senate fight, he was convinced that only tough-minded men with power to command could achieve arms control or a peace in Vietnam that guaranteed self-determination. He sensed that this was the time for a tough speech, for a reassertion of pride and confidence that would appall many liberals and unilateral disarmers and assorted weakeners of the national resolve. The forum Nixon chose was the Air Force Academy's graduating class, and the time, four days before the first withdrawal announcement.

Nixon told Kissinger he wanted Pat Buchanan to do the writing, which meant he wanted straight-ahead, no-nonsense prose crafted by a conservative true believer. On May 24, Kissinger briefed Buchanan, who made notes of what Henry told him and then returned a draft speech the next day.

With his new deputy and alter ego Colonel Al Haig, Henry selected paragraphs from Buchanan's draft, larded in a heavy argument for the "Safeguard" ABM system, and—at the President's direction—gave it to me for rewrite. That was not unusual; from time to time, speech drafts of mine were given to Buchanan for verbal toughening or ideological laundering, and turnabout was no insult.

But when Kissinger's version of Buchanan's draft based on Kissinger's transmission of the President's thoughts hit my desk, I had not been privy to any of this background. All I saw was a slam-bang hearkening-back to the Nixon of 1966, which—though it contained some anti-elitist points that I thought were long overdue—was far from the substance or style of anything we had submitted in recent years. So I scrapped most of what had been sent me and wrote a totally different speech, stressing the need for young airmen to take pride in their chosen profession, reinterpreting Eisenhower's comment about the "military-industrial complex," doing a simplified job on the ABM, and taking a middle position on defense cuts—against waste, not against muscle. I summarized the blast in the previous draft in a couple of paragraphs, giving the villain a name—"the new isolationists"—but it was not the focus of the draft I submitted.

The only thing the President liked about my draft was the "new isolationist" tag and the boiled-down version of the ABM argument. His purpose and thrust were lost, and he let Henry Kissinger know it. I was called to Henry's home on a Sunday morning, a little house facing Rock Creek Park, at which he rarely did business. I started to kid him about the ashtrays from "NAR"—his former boss, Nelson Rockefeller—but Dr. Kissinger was in no kidding mood. He told me what to write; I resisted; he changed his approach and proceeded to negotiate.

That may seem odd or improper. A speechwriter, one might think, is no policy setter, only an articulation aide whose highest duty is to reflect the desires of the President and his expert adviser. Not so. Nixon knew the predilections and biases of his writers, as well as their respective styles, and if he moved from right to center in writers, he knew what he was doing. Now, however, I saw what Nixon was getting at. As Henry put it, seated at his kitchen table after taking a call from Mel Laird, "One elusive thing on which the North Vietnamese will play is America's infinite sense of guilt. The President must counter that."

Next day, the President began to make changes in the text and by that time the speech was shaped roughly the way he wanted: the affirmative, patriotic thrust up front, then a statement of the fundamental differences in approach to defense policy, followed by a throwing down of the gauntlet to the new isolationists. A recapture of Eisenhower from the seekers of slashes in the defense budget began the second half of the speech, which crested with a moderate credo for young officers that urged them to fight waste in defense spending and to defend against an unwanted militarism.

As this speech of June 4, 1969, was crucial in the development of Nixon's defense stance, and is a perfect example of his political judgment, let me go into both substance and style.

This was what Kissinger and Haig originally passed on to Buchanan:

". . . The military services have come under unprecedented attack. There is a great deal of talk about reversing national priorities. Various aspects of our military programs have come under systematic, organized attack. In some circles, it has become justifiable to sneer at patriotism or attempts at greatness. As your Commander-in-Chief, I want to put some of my reflections on these subjects before you."

Pat sharpened it and added a bright hunter's metaphor; after I had deleted the whole thing, the President came to its rescue and gave it a little extra zing by changing "practice" to "fetish":

It is open season on the armed forces. Military programs
are ridiculed as needless if not deliberate waste. The military
profession is derided in some of the "best circles." Patriotism
is considered by some to be a backward "unfashionable" ~~practice~~ *fetish*
of the uneducated and unsophisticated. Nationalism is hailed and
applauded as a panacea for the ills of every nation -- except the
United States.

That paragraph, as the President knew, would go over well with the
cadets and churn up the ire of liberal columnists and editorial writers.
They would charge Nixon with using the strawman technique—nobody
was attacking "the armed forces," they later pointed out, only attacking
waste, mismanagement, and an unnecessarily high level of expenditures
that could better be used on urgent domestic concerns. The mythical fair-
minded observer might say that Nixon overdramatized, but in fact war
weariness had pushed the pendulum far over in the direction of anti-
militarism, anti-misleading-generals in Vietnam, anti-spending all that
money, and, to some people, anti-"armed forces." Draft evaders were
hardly considered slackers anymore, and there were no returning heroes.
The President disdained consensus and drew the battle line clearly:

> This paradox of military power is a symptom of something far
> deeper that is stirring in our body politic. It goes beyond the dissent
> about the war in Vietnam. It goes behind the fear of the "military-
> industrial complex."
>
> The underlying questions are really these:
>
> What is America's role in the world? What are the responsibilities
> of a great nation toward protecting freedom beyond its shores? Can
> we ever be *left* in peace if we do not actively assume the burden of
> *keeping* the peace?
>
> When great questions are posed, fundamental differences of opin-
> ion come into focus. It serves no purpose to gloss over these differ-
> ences, or to try to pretend they are mere matters of degree.

Nixon's purpose in that passage was to drive a wedge between a growing
majority of Americans who were fed up with the war in Vietnam and a
minority following the Fulbrights who took that disenchantment a long
step further, condemning America's "arrogance of power" and transfigur-
ing U.S. policy into unilateral disarmament, fast retrenchment everywhere, and an inward concern that invites the term of—pejorative though
it may be—"isolationism."

At that point in the speech, the President had written in the margin:

"As Dr. Stanley Hoffman wrote recently, there are those who insist that America's presence in the world is the only cause of the world's ills, and that our removal from it would insure both the world's salvation and the solution of all our own domestic problems." On second thought, Nixon crossed out the mention of Dr. Hoffman of Harvard—Henry would have curled up his toes and died on the spot at the reference to an intellectual rival—and wrote a direction to me to "paraphrase." That line became "America's powerful military presence on the world scene, they believe, makes peace abroad improbable and peace at home impossible." The next few paragraphs are in near-final form:

We should never underestimate the appeal of the isolationist school of thought. Their slogans are simplistic and powerful: "Charity begins at home." "Let's first solve our own problems and then we can deal with the problems of the world."

This simple formula touches a responsive chord with many an over-burdened taxpayer. It would be easy to buy some popularity by going along with the new isolationists. But it would be disastrous for our nation and the world.

I hold a totally different view of the world, and I come to a different conclusion about the direction America must take.

The danger to us has changed, but it has not vanished. We must revitalize our alliances, not abandon them.

We must rule out unilateral disarmament. In the real world that simply will not work. If we pursue arms control as an end in itself we will not achieve our end. The adversaries in the world today are not in conflict because they are armed. They are armed because they are in conflict and have not yet learned peaceful ways to resolve their conflicting national interests.

Across the top of the page, the President had written: "America has its faults, but if we ever took America out of the world, the rest of the free world would be living in terror."

I added "slavery" to "terror," but that was excessive. As Henry handed that back to me, he said, "The President said: 'Tell Safire I knocked out his slavery line, we liberals don't go for that right-wing language.' I thought that was very funny, don't you? Now let's be serious."

The next paragraphs were dead serious, expressing the President's fundamental approach to foreign policy as it affects domestic policy and the national spirit. Time and again throughout his Presidency, he would return to this theme, drawn from Teddy Roosevelt, Churchill, De Gaulle, and the wellspring of his own character:

> The aggressors of this world are not going to give the United States a period of grace in which to put our domestic house in order—just as the crises within our society cannot be put on a back burner until we resolve the problem of Vietnam.

There is no advancement for Americans at home in a retreat from the problems of the world. America has a vital national interest in world stability, and no other nation can uphold that interest for us.

Programs solving our domestic problems will be meaningless if we are not around to enjoy them. Nor can we conduct a successful policy of peace abroad if our society is at war with itself at home.

We stand at a crossroad in our history. We shall reaffirm our aspiration to greatness or we shall choose instead to withdraw into ourselves. The choice will affect far more than our foreign policy; it will determine the quality of our lives.

A nation needs many qualities, but it needs faith and confidence above all. Skeptics do not build societies; the idealists are the builders. Only societies that believe in themselves can rise to their challenges. Let us not, then, pose a false choice between meeting our responsibilities abroad and meeting the needs of our people at home. We shall meet both or we shall meet neither.

Now that I look back at it, I notice that the President wrote in, then crossed out, a line that ought to have stayed in: "A nation must mean something to itself before it can mean something to the world." That's Nixon, all right—I wonder why he chose not to say it then?

For those interested in the development of a line, let me include this rundown:

1. President to Kissinger to Buchanan: "If we are not able to do well both at home and abroad, we will not succeed in each of these areas separately."

2. Buchanan to Kissinger: "We shall rise to the challenges that history has placed before us both in the world and at home; we shall do both—or we shall do neither."

3. Kissinger to Safire: "We do not have the choice between global leadership and domestic needs. We shall do both or we shall do neither."

4. My change, and final Nixon fix: "Let us not, then, pose a false choice between meeting our responsibilities abroad and meeting the needs of our people at home. We shall meet both or we shall meet neither."

The reaction to the President's Air Force Academy speech was at once infuriated and perceptive. Here are excerpts from the President's News Summary the following week:

Charles Bartlett dismissed those who saw the address as the "old Nixon" and said that "in fairness, the hard-nosed character of the speech seems to be no more than an effort to keep a balance in the popular mood . . . The President is risking the ire of the liberals to evoke the counterweight of conservatives against the momentum of a mood that threatens to get out of hand." . . . James Deakin (St. Louis *Post-Dispatch*) says no Nixon speech since Jan. 20 "has caused more controversy or puzzlement and the White House has done little to clear the confusion." Max Frankel of the N.Y. *Times* says the critics feel "vastly stronger" as a result of the President's decision to confront them and that they will exhibit a "generally more hostile position" on all legislative matters. Frankel predicts if the President "conforms to earlier patterns of his Presidency, he will retreat from his harsh tone and perhaps even beg not to be misunderstood." . . . Max Lerner said, "Nixon's tactic is to get away from arguing about the war to arguing about patriotism and nationalism. It is an old tactic, and LBJ played with it a few times, but he never gave it all his ammunition as Nixon did." . . . Anthony Day (Phil. *Bulletin*) said the "speech looks like the first big mistake of his Presidency. And a gratuitous, foolish speech at that." . . . Joseph Kraft's visceral reaction was surprising and savage . . . "For my money, the President has been showing his worst side—the side that earned him the name Tricky Dicky." . . . Judd Arnett (Detroit *Free Press*) writes that "the cries of outrage from the left will increase in the days to come—but don't you think Mr. Nixon knew that before he went to Colorado Springs?"

President Nixon accomplished his purpose; he put his war critics on notice that he was ready to strike back, and that they were vulnerable to a charge of isolationism that could put them on the defensive. In a few months, after more troop withdrawals were announced, and he took the "spirit of Apollo" trip around the world, the Air Force Academy speech was viewed by many as an aberration, a throwback to the Old Nixon. They were kidding themselves. That was Nixon balancing his ship and firing a shot across the bow of his enemy. He made it plain that he was not interested in the approbation of much of the media—a calculated provocation too outrageous for writers to accept as anything but a governance gaffe—and he staked out a realistic, responsible attitude that was to be formalized in a few months as "The Nixon Doctrine."

The day after the "new isolationist" speech in Colorado Springs, the President met with the writers and Haldeman and Ehrlichman in Villa "A" of the Newporter Inn near his new home in San Clemente, and discussed the reaction to his speech in the light of his purpose:

"Put yourselves in the Russians' position. All they hear in the U.S. is 'no' to the ABM and MIRV; 'cut the defense budget by fifteen billion'; 'pull out of Vietnam'; 'the arrogance of power.' That's what they read in the papers and see on the television. Now, if all they were to hear from this Administration is comments from me about how we really want peace, then they'd be likely to interpret it as weakness. We can't let that happen."

I asked the President if he weren't worried about scaring the American public, and he replied sharply, "Turn that around—I don't want to scare our allies." We discussed intelligence data about a triangular pattern of missiles which, Henry Kissinger told us, "fit nothing in the world but our Minutemen missiles." Richard Whalen (who had served in early 1968 as a speechwriter and then stormed out) recently had submitted a disturbing speech on defense policy that was not going to be used, but as the President put it, "Even Whalen's speech isn't scary enough." Nixon did not want to make an alarmist ABM speech—he had cut the long passage in the Air Force Academy speech arguing for the Safeguard system—and asked us, "Is that the best way to get those few votes in the Senate? The most powerful argument on Safeguard is this: that the nation that is behind won't have the luxury of time to catch up. Next time, maybe twenty minutes.

"There would be a painful, jolting reaction if some of those guys in the Senate really understood what happened to our defenses." Nixon then had a few things to say about Senator Fulbright that it would serve no purpose to record, adding, "Mansfield is different, of course. The fact is, the lines have crossed in several areas, and ever since the Cuban missile crisis, the Russians are determined not to be humiliated again." That reminded him of President Kennedy and his mind slipped into political gear, thinking ahead to a campaign in which he would once again have to face a Kennedy: "Teddy may be barking up the wrong tree."

3. TALE OF TWO BRIDGES

The first extraterrestrial problem to face Earthling speechwriters was in the editing of the copy on the plaque that was going to mark man's first landing on the moon.

Here was the layout submitted to the White House by the National Aeronautics and Space Agency in May of 1969:

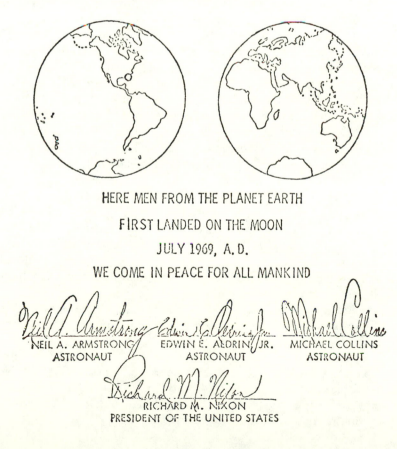

HERE MEN FROM THE PLANET EARTH

FIRST LANDED ON THE MOON

JULY 1969, A.D.

WE COME IN PEACE FOR ALL MANKIND

NEIL A. ARMSTRONG   EDWIN E. ALDRIN, JR.   MICHAEL COLLINS
ASTRONAUT   ASTRONAUT   ASTRONAUT

RICHARD M. NIXON
PRESIDENT OF THE UNITED STATES

Peter Flanigan was the Presidential assistant chosen to "honcho" (a Japanese word much in favor at the White House, meaning in its verb form "to follow through on") the President's participation in the first landing of man on the moon. Flanigan called Jim Keogh, Ray Price, Pat Buchanan, and me to his office on the second floor of the White House West Wing to look over the proposed plaque, and we picked a few nits:

"Landed" on the moon was all wrong, Buchanan pointed out. " 'Set foot' would be better," he said, "since other vehicles have in effect made soft landings on the moon." We agreed with that but would not go for his other suggestion: "Here, *two Americans*, Men from Planet Earth . . ." That was too chauvinistic, it was felt, if we want to stress the "all mankind" idea—besides, NASA was planning to place an American flag up there anyway.

"We come in peace" bothered me—sounded like a stereotyped salute from white settlers to Hollywood Indians. At least let's change the tense, I suggested, so that it would not seem to be directed to moon inhabitants, but to the people from Earth who take moon shuttles later on, and read the plaque to fellow space tourists. And the absence of any reference to God was troubling—the Founding Fathers had amended Mr. Jefferson's declaration to include a thank-you to Divine Providence, and I did not think it unduly pious to suggest that this first penetration of the heavens invoke some recognition of the Deity. The problem about God was, again, "mankind"—if we were to represent "all mankind," we couldn't just plug the Americans, and we could not talk about God, since hundreds of millions of Earth's inhabitants were represented by what John Foster Dulles used to call "godless Communism."

But the NASA draftsmen had found a way out. "A.D.," which stands for Anno Domini (Latin for "In the Year of Our Lord") could be the unarguable evidence that mankind—at least some of it—believed in God. Buchanan thought Anno Domini should be spelled out, rather than abbreviated, but the rest of us demurred—A.D. would do.

The date was in the copy solely for the A.D., because there was no way of making and affixing the plaque onto the launching device to be left on the moon with the exact date—NASA did not know far enough in advance what the specific date would be. Ordinarily, the vague date—"July 1969" —would have been left off, perhaps for amendment a couple of decades later by a plaque under the plaque, but since the date served a Godly purpose, it was put on in that monthly way.

We scrapped about other words. I wanted to change "the" moon to "its" moon, since hundreds of other moons would be explored in the next century, and I hated to see Earthlings of 1969 seem parochial. Flanigan pondered the arguments and solemnly sent the final version to the President, with alternative last lines: "A New Dawn for the Human Spirit," "A New Dawn of Peace for All Mankind," both in lieu of "We Come in Peace for All Mankind." The President liked the original last line, and we went with the wording that sits on the moon today.

The one item we did not bother to discuss was the signature of the President underneath the copy. Since the President, whoever he is, always signs a new Federal bridge or post office, we took it for granted he would sign his name to the moon project below the names of the astronauts. We were insensitive to the sensitivity of old Kennedy hands. This was later criticized as evidence of Nixon trying to horn in on a Kennedy project, and the criticism itself was revealing of the unnecessary us-against-them provocation of the Nixon-haters. The Washington *Post* tut-tutted; the Washington *Star* editorially blasted back, and the *Post* riposte, headlined "Flaque About a Pique About a Plaque," went this way:

> What we said was that many men, including two Presidents, have played major roles in our effort to reach the moon but that Mr. Nixon was not one of them; that this was a national effort, so defined by President Kennedy when he committed the Nation to it and that it therefore ought not to be treated like the kind of run-of-the-mill public works project which could be expected, by political tradition, to bear the name of the incumbent President; and that the inscription on the plaque—"We came in peace for all mankind"—struck us as just the right note, generous, large-minded, free of narrow chauvinism. And so we concluded that the signatures of the three astronauts would be enough. We did so on the assumption that the phrase "we came" referred to those who actually went along, and on the further assumption that although Mr. Nixon was elected President, as the *Star* correctly reports, and therefore "stands for all of us," as the *Star* quite properly points out, he was not, insofar as we understand the procedures last November, elected President of all mankind.

The President had decided that the moon landing was (a) a necessary shot in the arm to the American body politic, (b) a lift to the spirit of a war-weary people, (c) a boost for technology that was being unfairly derided by environmentalists—and (d), (e), and (f)—that he was going to be an enthusiastic part of it. Although Mr. Nixon was genuinely excited by the prospect of America's being first to the moon, he had a diplomatic thought in mind: that the "spirit of Apollo" could generate a wave of international prestige that would help him launch new initiatives toward China.

In a June meeting with Bob Haldeman, Len Garment, Peter Flanigan, and the writing staff in the Newporter Hotel in Newport Beach, California, Nixon listened to the alternative plans of how to handle the launch, the moon landing, and the splashdown, and the release of the astronauts from quarantine. I wanted to shoot the works—declare "Space Day," have the President fly to the carrier, accompanied by all the living pioneers of aviation, and give a Gettysburg address. Others were more conservative, perhaps sensitive to the criticism about "horning in" on the publicity. "Hold on, Safire," Flanigan said, "the President would have to fly halfway around the world."

"That's the whole idea," Nixon mused. "It's not convenient, it's halfway around the world—that would be a measure of the respect we show it." The men in the room explored the pros and cons of the President's going, and the reasons advanced were all cogent, but what was going through the President's mind had nothing to do with the reasons advanced by his advisers. He wanted to go to Romania to see Nicolae Ceausescu, who had exhibited some independence from Moscow and had sent signals that he could be a help in an approach to Chou En-Lai. Nixon wanted an excuse to go, and he wanted a note of triumph to set the tone for his initiative. The trip to the far Pacific was a perfect answer.

A gamble was involved. What if the moon shot turned out to be a disaster? Americans had become accustomed to happy endings on space flights, and so had I. But on June 13, Frank Borman—an astronaut the President liked and whom NASA had assigned to be our liaison—called me to say, "You want to be thinking of some alternative posture for the President in the event of mishaps on Apollo XI." When I didn't react promptly, Borman moved off the formal language: "—like what to do for the widows." The potential for tragedy was underscored by the nature of the failure that was most possible: inability to get the moon vehicle up off the moon, into lunar orbit where it would join the command capsule. Disaster would not come in the form of a sudden explosion—it would mean the men would be stranded on the moon, in communication with Mission Control as they slowly starved to death, or deliberately "closed down communication," the euphemism for suicide. I took Borman's caution to heart and prepared some appropriate remarks for the President about men who went to the moon to explore in peace, staying to rest in peace, and did not submit it, but Haldeman knew we were ready if tragedy were in store.

Borman was a good man to work with. Compact, efficient, with the confidence of having been out in space and come back, he was part of what is commonly called a "new breed" (he looked like Ross Perot, the billionaire computer manufacturer who hung around the White House). The astronaut would rocket around memos with timetables and "action responsibilities" that moved things along. Here is a fragment from a meeting in Flanigan's office with Borman, Dwight Chapin, and myself, going down the checklist on June 24, 1969:

> Flanigan: "Okay to add a Vatican message? Maybe with the other flags."
>
> Safire: "All right with me, but are we taking a Bible? I don't want to sound like a stiff, but—"
>
> Borman: "Maybe there'll be a Bible, if one of the guys takes a personal one."
>
> Safire: "Hell with that. Make it official—a Bible goes to the moon. Both Testaments."

Borman: "Check. I agree."

Flanigan: "All set with the plaque?"

Borman: "Yes, the guys agree that 'set foot' is better than 'landed.' The Russians may have put something there already."

Safire: "In the timetable here, who's this girl you're throwing out of the capsule?"

Chapin: "He means the line that says, 'Egress for EVA,' Frank."

Borman: "That means Armstrong leaves the capsule for Extra Vehicular Activity."

Borman was the kind of well-organized, highly motivated, intelligent serviceman Nixon admired, the product of a mission the President identified with. Us-against-them entered into it, since courageous astronauts were more the idols of the square young people than the antiwar demonstrators, and the spacemen exemplified what were called the old-fashioned virtues, what the President thought of as the American Character, the willingness, in his frequently used phrase, "to lay it all on the line." William Irwin Thompson, author of *At the Edge of History,* caught this subtle confrontation in a piece he did later about the Apollo project:

"Through an imaginative expansion of the spirit beyond the clever ironies and sophistications of the New York intelligentsia, the Southern and Midwestern hicks and the West Coast freaks have brought technology down to size. While the intellectuals complained about the dehumanization brought on by machines and sought out of love for their afflictions to make psychotherapy into a way of life, the religious hicks pricked the sky with a rocket, letting the hot air out and all the heavenly vibrations in."

That may be stretching it a bit, but us-against-them was present even in this reach into space. The only effort to add a note of culture to the moon landing, for example, met with a rebuff. Archibald MacLeish, the poet who had been Librarian of Congress and Assistant Secretary of State under FDR, had written a poem quoted by the President in his Inaugural address, using the phrase "riders on the Earth together," looking at the world from outer space. I thought it would be a good idea for the President to commission MacLeish to write a poem commemorating the first steps of man on the moon; the President agreed, said Elmo Roper was a friend of MacLeish's, and could be the "broker." I called Roper, who contacted MacLeish, who agreed; the President then wrote a formal note to the poet: "It is important that this be viewed not only as a great adventure, but in the perspective of a search for truth and a quest for peace. Nothing man has done more significantly dramatizes the need for an understanding of the common goals of the human race." But MacLeish, after eliciting the offer in writing, thought twice about doing anything with Nixon connected with it, and called Henry Kissinger to say he couldn't write to a deadline and would prefer to duck the assignment. In fact, he did write the poem, but not for President Nixon; it appeared in the New York *Times* on the day of the moon landing (not an especially inspired effort, but nobody scores every time he shoots the moon). This slap in the face did not go unnoticed, and was an episode to recall and mutter about when we were criticized for not considering the spiritual meaning of the moon landing.

Julian Scheer, NASA's Assistant Administrator for Public Affairs, sent me a memo on July 14 spelling out the proposal that the President have a telephone conversation with the astronauts on the lunar surface. He included a list of possible questions for the President to ask Armstrong and Aldrin ("Can you see any stars? Is the sky black? What color is the soil?"). I cut the list down to size, but the President decided not to make a long interview out of it. He wanted to express his appreciation on behalf of the American people, wish them Godspeed on the way home, and end it there: as Borman relayed to me the President's wishes, "just a what-hath-God-wrought kind of thing."

The idea of a Presidential telephone call offended an editorial writer at the New York *Times*. Just as the Washington *Post* writers had deplored the Nixon signature on the plaque, the *Times* saw this as "Nixoning the Moon," and blasted his plan to "share the stage with the three brave men on Apollo 11." Presidents Kennedy and Johnson launched and encouraged the program, the editorial said, and just because Nixon was President "by accident of the calendar" when the shot took place, he was engaging in "a publicity stunt of the type Khrushchev used to indulge in" which was "unworthy of a President of the United States."

This struck us all as a classic case of refusal to recognize Nixon's legitimacy by people who hated to see Nixon—even as President—sully a "Kennedy project" with his presence at its fruition. But with his personal enthusiasm high, and with his foreign policy fish to fry, Nixon prepared to represent all the people even if some of them resented it.

July 20, 1969, was the day that man approached the earth's satellite after a perfect flight, and also the day Senator Edward Kennedy approached the Edgartown, Massachusetts, police station after an eventful night at Chappaquiddick.

Pat Buchanan and I were in the office that Sunday, watching the tickers and TV for moon flight information, updating the information for the President's phone call, when the first news came through of an accident involving the Senator and a passenger at a small bridge. Pat looked at the yellow bulletin for a while, and said quietly to one of the staff working on the President's news summary, "See if the passenger was a girl." I was curious too, but certain the Kennedy clan could handle it without great political effect; besides, the incident would be muffled in the attention given the historic moment of man's first contact with a body in outer space.

That night, watching the moon walks of Armstrong and Aldrin—some seven hours after "The Eagle has landed!"—I experienced more than ever before, or since, that special exhilaration of being an aide to the President of the United States. It was nearly midnight in Washington, and I was periodically shaking my five-year-old son, Mark, to keep him awake so he could tell his own children he had seen it. The landing site was in the Mare Tranquilitatis; on CBS, Walter Cronkite had picked up the words "tranquillity base" from the astronauts and was making much of them. I said to my wife, "That's the point for the President to make, don't you think? To pick up the tranquillity theme?" She said yes, dear, and patted my hand; there was something inherently ridiculous about me, one of the tens of millions of viewers around the world, acting as if I were some kind of participant.

I reached for the phone and called the duty officer at the White House. That night it was Tod Hullin, a young aide of Ehrlichman's, and I asked him to pass along to the President the thought that tranquillity should be his keynote. A few minutes later, as I shook my son awake again, the President came on the screen with the telephone call to the men on the moon; it was brief, but the central point spoken by the President was: "As you talk to us from the Sea of Tranquillity, it inspires us to redouble our efforts to bring peace and tranquillity to Earth." My message had gone a quarter-million miles; I got the creepiest feeling, and my wife looked at me in wild surmise, first at our phone at home, then at the pictures on television from the moon.

Seventeen minutes after midnight, the President called me: "Well, I got in your tranquillity line. I held it down to about forty seconds, though— that was all it should have been. At a time when everybody's out to say historic things, I thought it would be best to keep it simple. The tranquillity point was important especially in view of the Romanian trip."

He was all excited: "Isn't it amazing? We'll have other days like this, Mars for example, but there's only one first time." As usual, he was considerate of his writers' feelings: "Both you and Ray gave me good things to say on space—I didn't use much, I know, but I'll use more at the splashdown. 'If men can reach the moon, men can reach agreement' I like—that's exactly what I want to get across.

"Frank Borman was sore as hell at that *Times* editorial," the President added. "He's a real patriot, that guy." I pointed out that the rocket had taken off from Cape Kennedy, and would splash down near Johnson Island, and they begrudged Nixon a phone call, and he laughed, then stopped laughing abruptly.

"You know, this is quite a day on another front, too." Nixon was referring to the Chappaquiddick incident. "It'll be hard to hush this one up; too many reporters want to win a Pulitzer Prize." He paused, and I could imagine him shaking his head in wonderment as he breathed, "In the back seat!" I suggested that the news of Kennedy's accident might be lost in the tumult of the moon landing, but the President saw it differently: "No, the fact that it happened this day could make it even more significant, especially the way they're trying to make this a Kennedy day. Strange . . ."

(Though I never knew him to "personally indulge," as they say, Nixon was never prudish about others' extramarital sex. He once told his staff assembled in the White House theater, "If you ever have to say you were working late, I'll cover for you," only half in jest. But what he could never fathom was a Presidential candidate taking unnecessary chances with women. In early 1968, when the press corps was deliciously buzzing about an affair between a Republican candidate and a member of his campaign staff, Nixon was thunderstruck, not at adultery, but at the gamble the candidate was taking: "Doesn't he know they know? Doesn't he give a damn?")

Shooting the moon, then, was instructive of what had gone before and what was to crop up again more bitterly: an active resentment of Nixon's "taking the credit" for what others, particularly Kennedy, had done; a stick-it-to-'em reaction by the Nixon men to that resentment; in turn, this resulted in a tendency to rub salt in wounds, ours as well as theirs, and to figure that the "enemies" would never recognize Nixon's legitimacy, no matter what he did. No quarter given, none expected. A few days after the moon landing, the White House distributed to staffers a photocopy of a Richmond *Times-Dispatch* editorial:

> As unhappy as it makes the New York *Times*, the fact is that Richard Nixon is now President of the United States. It was entirely fitting for him, as the representative of all the people of his nation, to commend the astronauts on their great achievement and to express to the largest worldwide television audience in history America's hope that this epochal achievement will inspire man on earth to redouble his efforts to achieve lasting peace . . . Only a bad case of Nixonphobia would lead anyone to view the President's phone call, as the *Times* did, as nothing more than "a publicity stunt . . ."

After the moon landing, a what-have-you-done-for-me-lately attitude took hold about space exploration; space became a popular budget item to cut, almost as popular a target for savings as foreign aid, and when the budget crunches came, Nixon went along with the demand to cut back NASA. He considered that a political necessity, but he did not make that cut, as he did others, with a budgeteer's zest; on the contrary, a Haldeman aide sent the following note to Henry Kissinger and Peter Flanigan on December 17, 1969:

December 17, 1969

MEMORANDUM FOR DR. KISSINGER
                            PETER FLANIGAN

The December 5 issue of the *C. S. Monitor* contained an article by Peter Stuart noting that most adults probably think the younger generations are star struck because of the space program, but the reaction of a large number of US students is "a wide yawn and not a little displeasure." During the Apollo 12 flight a New York disc jockey with a "mainstream" audience requested opinions on the space program. "Not one teenager called to defend the program." A typical reaction was that the money should be spent on Earth.

The President noted that this is counter to what we would hope were the case.

JOHN R. BROWN III

As for me, I have always felt a little guilty about my minor fiddling with our space program. The euphoria of my secondhand connection with the telephone call to men on the moon soon wore off, especially when the plaque I worked on received the following two comments.

The first, from CBS president Frank Stanton in a note to Frank Shakespeare, head of the United States Information Agency, on July 21, 1969:

FRANK STANTON   51 West 52 Street, New York 10019

July 21, 1969

Dear Frank:

There's nothing to be done about it, but I was distressed when I saw the graphics on the plaque for the moon. On critical pieces that will get worldwide display for centuries, is there no one in the Administration to whom the President can turn? Here we are on the cutting edge of space exploration with a third rate sign.

Too bad. But I had to get it off my chest.

Best,
Frank

A "third rate sign" was bad enough, but the crusher came in a letter to the Los Angeles *Times* from a reader named Rockwell Schnabel:

"Notwithstanding the phenomenal precision of the scientists concerned with the moon shot, a little mistake was overlooked. The inscription engraved on the plaque to be left on the moon reads 'Here men from the planet Earth first set foot Upon the Moon July 1969 AD.'

"This should, of .course, read 'July, AD 1969.' BC follows the year, whereas AD precedes it. How odd, that in spite of man's superhuman achievements, this error—a grammatical one—has occurred in the first printed words in outer space . . ."

4. THE KENNEDY CRITERION

"This is quite a day on another front, too," Nixon had said as men first walked on the moon. Kennedy. The name was a memory, a challenge, and a danger to Nixon men: a reminder of the 1960 defeat, a constant criterion held unfairly to today's President by people who liked to compare him with a myth, and a genuine threat to his re-election.

Nixon rarely measured himself against Lyndon Johnson; publicly never, and privately only to show how spending time with unfriendly journalists, as LBJ did, profited nought.

Nixon's standard as a modern President, conscious or not, was John F. Kennedy. The Kennedy "myth" appealed as it appalled; how, the Nixon men asked each other, could so much legend be made out of so little accomplishment?

Along with that envy for the way the Kennedys enthralled and bedazzled so much of the press went a genuine admiration for the way the Kennedys played the political game: with zest and calculation, with professionalism, with a high regard for personal loyalty and disregard of traditional obstacles. Kennedys would come to play and play to win, and when you beat a Kennedy you beat the best. (The trouble was, nobody ever did.)

Memory fuses great opponents, and men who had little in common are two sides of a common coin: Napoleon and Wellington, Dempsey and Firpo, Truman and Dewey, and Kennedy and Nixon. The 1960 race has been variously described as a classic, a watershed, a turning point; at least there can be no exaggeration in calling it heartbreakingly close. The experience is seared into the souls of the Nixon family and the Nixon men of 1960 who stayed around (Finch, Flanigan, Haldeman, Ehrlichman, John Whitaker, Pat Gray, myself, and the person who remembers best, Rose Mary Woods). The hackles of all still rise when Kennedy's reputed put-down after the '60 campaign is recalled: "No class." Nixon's finest pre-Presidential hour came soon after when he refused to challenge the election results in Illinois and Texas, when "we wuz robbed" had never been a more legitimate claim. The loser felt the effort—urged on him by Len Hall

—would diminish the legitimacy of Presidential leadership. Nixon said no, as good an example of "class" as has ever been shown by any man who had a Presidency stolen from him.

On his first visit to Berlin as President, Nixon avoided any direct mention of Kennedy, whose "Ich bin ein Berliner" was both thrilling and, as it turned out, somewhat excessive. ("Kennedy got the Berliners all excited," Nixon observed, "then let them down.") In the draft of his London arrival statement, there was a reference to Nixon as Vice President accompanying Queen Elizabeth to the dedication of the American Chapel in St. Paul's Cathedral and recalling the playing of the "Battle Hymn of the Republic" there. With the memory of Robert Kennedy's funeral train in his mind, he killed the paragraph, telling Kissinger "that's a Kennedy song." (The admonition did not carry into his second term. At a White House worship service on the day after his Second Inaugural, the Mormon Tabernacle Choir sang the "Battle Hymn" at the President's request.)

Nixon opened the White House to public visitors more than ever before, and put on some glittering "evenings" of entertainment, noting dryly later that it was as well handled as anything the Kennedys had done but that was not the word that would get out. He was never prouder of Mrs. Nixon than in watching the way she handled, with graciousness and warmth, the first visit back to the White House of Jacqueline Kennedy Onassis and her children.

As the Nixon Administration began to come under fire for rising unemployment, I sent in figures about the Kennedy years that the President put to frequent use. Kennedy had inherited a relatively high unemployment from Eisenhower (that mini-recession in 1960, among other things, caused Nixon's defeat), but unemployment went from 6.7 per cent in 1961 to 5.5 in 1962 and then back up to 5.7 in 1963; it took the Vietnam build-up in the mid-Sixties to push the rate down to 5.2 in 1964 under Johnson and then to its low of 3.5 in 1969. Nixon would not mention either President by name in this connection, but he frequently used "the eight Democratic years of the Sixties" until he decided he didn't want to use "Democratic years" either; he then focused on the "average unemployment in the early Sixties, before the war build-up began, is greater than the rate today." It was a legitimate political-economic point, and it was one Nixon made with special relish.

Ironically, the cold war rhetoric of portions of the Kennedy Inaugural ("we shall pay any price," etc.) came under attack years later by Democratic doves, never by Nixon; though the Nixon Doctrine moved U.S. policy away from the containment policy espoused by Kennedy, Nixon had a sentimental attachment to both the old policy and the brave rhetoric that went with it. And when the space program, given impetus by Kennedy, fell into disrepute among many liberals, Nixon found himself quoting Kennedy to shore up support for the kind of venture he felt was ennobling to America. (One of the few times Nixon quoted Kennedy directly came in a visit to a space installation, when I sent in "America has tossed its cap over the wall of space." Nixon could not resist muttering, "His guys gave him some great word-pictures.")

Nixon did not go to the opening of Kennedy Center, an occasion when his natural instincts coincided with good taste—that was an evening for Kennedys unalloyed with the presence of any other President—but he did go to the opening of the Eisenhower Theater in the Kennedy Center.

The most curious incident in the respectful, begrudgingly admiring attitude toward the Kennedy myth came just after the incident at the Chappaquiddick Bridge. Senator Ted Kennedy, career seemingly shattered but putting up a brave front, came to the White House with a group of other Senators some weeks afterward on an innocuous formal visit; Nixon took Kennedy away from the group, walked across the room far out of earshot of anyone else, and the two men had a talk that lasted about ten minutes. Nixon, who had experienced premature political burial himself, was talking gently and reassuringly, and Kennedy was listening. Only the two of them know what was said, but I have a hunch in tone and substance it was exactly right. My only hard evidence is a note the President scribbled to himself while preparing for a news conference, in the event he should be asked whether Kennedy's later defeat as majority whip meant the end of the Senator's career:

Defeat - doesn't
finish a man -
quit - does -
A man is not finished
when he's defeated.
He's finished
when he
quits.

5. HENRY THE K

"That was not a jingoistic speech," said the President after his blast at "the new isolationists" at the Air Force Academy, "but now they know we're not going to paint our tails white and run with the antelopes."

"They," of course, were the critics who wanted to stick their heads in the sand that Richard Nixon was destined to leave his footprints in. The President was euphoric after giving his critics that unexpected shot and enjoyed reading the reaction, but, typically, Henry Kissinger was having second thoughts about the uproar that the speech was causing among his old associates.

"Do you have the impression that was a jingoistic speech?" Henry asked me on the way to the Western White House one day, with a pained expression of which he was a master. "Not a bit, by jingo," I replied, figuring he had to be kidding. Henry had been with the President all the way in setting forth those hard-line positions, putting a ramrod in any prose of mine that seemed in the least bit conciliatory. He had to have known that the attack on new isolationism would not set well with his Harvard friends, but to my surprise Henry was not kidding—either because he was naïve, or two-faced, or torn by the need to use tough means to gain peaceful ends—and seemed genuinely anguished by the reaction to words he wanted in the speech.

In his rise from adviser to celebrity, to superstar, and ultimately to an overtly friendly nemesis, Henry Kissinger never lost that ability to project childlike anguish at the reaction of others to actions he had recommended with cold precision, and there were many times when it must have been sincere. I came to know him fairly well in 1969, to respect and admire him, and this might be a good place to take a closer look at him.

The first thing Henry Kissinger wanted his new associates to know about him was that he could take a kidding about the "Dr. Strangelove" image of the professor with the thick glasses and thicker accent.

About a week after the Inauguration, at a meeting in the Situation Room near the National Security adviser's basement office, Kissinger was fumbling through a mass of papers about the President's forthcoming European trip. John Ehrlichman, who had run the Presidential campaign tour with crackling efficiency, observed, "It's a little unnerving to see somebody this disorganized running the National Security Council." Kissinger exaggerated his German accent and mimicked actor Peter Sellers' portrayal of Strangelove: "You shoot off ze missiles, you never know where zey hit, but zey hit somsing."

Going over every word in a NATO speech I had drafted, he changed "world strategy" to "world view." "Ah," said I, "your *Weltanschauung*." He looked up, mock-startled: "How did you know I was Cherman?"

There was a playful quality to Henry that was endearing; not everyone was good-humored enough or secure enough to let himself be the butt of jokes. And he was strikingly different from the rest of the inner circle. When he saw how Haldeman, Ehrlichman, Chapin, and Ziegler were taken up with their walkie-talkie communications equipment, keeping them in touch with each other in separate cars in motorcades, Kissinger feigned distrust of all gadgetry. His radio code name was Woodcutter, but he identified himself on the air as Woodchopper, and after Bus Mosbacher called him Woodchuck, and I called him Woodpecker, he stopped identifying himself by code name at all, hoping his accent would do the trick, which it did. (Ehrlichman was Wisdom; Haldeman was Watchdog, but he gave that to Chapin; Ziegler was Whaleboat, and he dubbed me Multplug, the name of the device that channels microphones into a single outlet on a podium.) Kissinger, climbing into a car, would say to Ehrlichman in mock helplessness, "Would you work that movie gobbledegook to let them know where I am?"

As we came to know him, we could see how he categorized his associates and reacted to them differently. To the President, he was more deferential than any of us; we excused this on the grounds that he was the newcomer to the group, had never called Nixon by his first name or been made to feel needed by a man struggling to come back. (Moynihan hadn't either, but he had a saucier, less deferential style.) When the President came into the cabin at Camp David one day and announced, "I shot 126," Kissinger, the perfect courtier, said, "Your golf game is improving, Mr. President," and the Boss growled, "I was bowling, Henry." Yet Henry told others that kind of story about himself, in a self-deprecating way, and you had to like him for it.

In the same way, Henry was always respectful of Johnson, but his Teutonic accent imitating Johnson's Texas accent had his White House colleagues in stitches. On his first trip to the Pedernales to brief LBJ, Kissinger was given a tour that led him to believe the former President had him confused with West German Chancellor Kurt Kiesinger. "This was Comanche territory," LBJ told him. "You know, you Germans were great Indian fighters." Passing some picnic tables, LBJ pointed out that he had them installed along the roadside instead of hot dog stands "because you Germans love picnics." Referring to his instructions to his Secretary of

State, he said, "Ah tol' Dean Rusk—'Git on yo' horse!' That means 'high priority,' Professor!" Kissinger was especially shaken by President Johnson's habit of calling him "Professor Schlesinger."

"Lady Bird Johnson drove me back to the airstrip," Henry recounted, "and she asked me how I thought President Johnson seemed these days. I mumbled something about 'serenity in retirement' and she almost drove off the road. I suppose flattery has to be related to reality, however vaguely."

To his colleagues on the senior staff he would show the respect of a faculty member to other professors with tenure. After dictating some changes in a toast to General de Gaulle, he turned to Ray Price, who had drafted the original, to say diplomatically, "But what do you think, Ray? You've had more experience than I with this sort of thing. Is this a graceful toast?"

When Ray and the other writers began to bridle at the liberties he would take with the Presidential prose style, he would disclaim any interest in anything but substance: "You mustn't take my scribblings as gospel. There was a review of one of my books in London that said, 'I don't know if Kissinger writes well, but if the reader wants to understand him, the reader has to read well.'"

To his subordinates, he was a slave driver. To those few who could stand the gaff over a period of time, he built an admirable loyalty, but he also produced a well-strewn wayside with those who could not, or who were shocked to discover that his policy position was more hard-line Nixonian than they had expected. Watching Kissinger with his staff made one add a note of caution to an assessment: He was endearing only when he wanted to be and caused even those who were most attracted to him to wonder whether he was more respectful of position than personality.

One quality he displayed in those early days served as a good example to us all. When he goofed, he admitted it and moved to make amends, making the person who objected to a slight like him all the more at the end. To illustrate: He had accepted an invitation to a small dinner party for Washington *Post* publisher Katharine Graham at the Georgetown home of the Joseph Alsops, but had to work late, so he had his secretary telephone his regrets at 8 P.M. Joe Alsop, in a Churchillian rage, sent Henry a note the next day saying that it was always understandable to be on call for the President, but the idea of having a secretary offer apologies was intolerably rude: "For God's sake, call the hostess yourself." Kissinger promptly sent a gracious handwritten note to Susan Mary Alsop, one of the great ladies of Washington, not only apologizing, but thanking the Alsops for their patience in teaching him manners. Susan Mary was enchanted; Joe became his closest journalistic friend.

In the meantime, much to our delighted surprise, he was acquiring a reputation as a swinger. He took me aside from time to time to ask if this odd turn of events was a useful thing: "Do you suppose people will think the President's national security adviser is gaga?" I said Americans would sleep better every night knowing their national security was in the hands of a red-blooded American boy, but he should stop saying "gaga," which went out with the Charleston. Barbara Howar, a good-looking, acid-tongued Washington divorcée, dated him a few times and let the world know all about it; then he was photographed at a party next to Gloria Steinem and that became an "item." The President kidded him about his lovelife in an approving way, so Henry permitted himself to strut a bit. When Steinem, three years later, coldly testified, "I am not and have never been a girl friend of Henry Kissinger," he brought the house down at a correspondents' dinner with the perfect delivery of a line of Dick Moore's: "But she did not say that if elected, she would not serve." In an Administration not noted for its glamour, the idea of a swinging professor took hold. Was Henry really a Lothario? Women whose opinion I respect say he is an attractive, if shy, dinner partner; and he earned the devotion of a remarkable woman, Nancy Maginnis, a tall, Rockefeller researcher who was his number one, and often only, through all the publicity, until their marriage in 1974. One criterion in judging a man is the woman he chooses, and here Henry comes off very well.

In that pre-celebrity stage, the reputation as womanizer helped Henry get a nonfrightening renown. In this regard, his genuine interest in professional football came in handy, and I would pass along anecdotes to Hugh Sidey of Time-Life or Henry Hubbard of *Newsweek* of Kissinger at Washington Redskins' games:

—on a pass interference call against the Redskins' cornerback, owner Ed Williams would holler, "Bad call!"; former Chief Justice Earl Warren, in the next seat, would shake his head and say, "Poor judgment," and Henry would shake his fist at the referee and yell, "On vot theory?"

—after a call for some doctor came over the public address system, Henry turned to me and mused, "You know how we could empty out this stadium in one minute? Have the loudspeaker say, 'Dr. Kissinger, call your office—urgent!' "

—since pro football is a combination of power and strategy, it is natural for Henry to understand its complexities. He once analyzed the pattern of a quarterback's play calls, and predicted the next play and its failure. When this took place just as he had called it, I asked him what he would do if he were the quarterback; he replied, "Pass on first down deep in my own territory." When the quarterback did that later in the game, the ball was intercepted and run in for a touchdown, making Kissinger's quarterbacking look bad. He shrugged and brazened it out: "This only proves my point—never listen to the experts on the sidelines."

The experts on the sidelines were bothering him in 1969, far more than they did Nixon. In October in Key Biscayne, I came up to him sunning himself in front of his villa and told him he looked like a lobster. "In order to break women's hearts," he said automatically, "I am willing to risk sunstroke." But when we got to talking, he was depressed: "If only the guys who got us into this would give us the chance to get out of it. I wasn't second-guessing Vance and Harriman in 1965 when I told them privately we couldn't win the war—instead, I asked them how I could help. All we needed was for the criticism to hold off for another few months. If you were in Hanoi, and you were one of those who wanted to settle, would you get to first base with all these demonstrations in the U.S.?" I asked if we were getting anywhere with the negotiations. "You want my official or my private opinion?" Private—he shook his head no, using a word I had not heard up to then: "They're stonewalling." He picked up a long memo I had written about Federalism under the pen name "Publius" and said, "We're very much in the position of Rome. People there kept getting pulled into wars they didn't want."

Kissinger's primary source of power, then and later, was in his tuning-fork relationship with the President on the matters that mattered to them most. In the Situation Room, in the Roosevelt Room, in his basement office, and later in the grand corner office built for him a few steps down the hall from the Oval Office, he hammered home points to his colleagues that he could not say in public:

—on a cease-fire in Vietnam: "The doves call for a stand-pat cease-fire. The fact is that we have said cease-fire ten times, publicly; all Hanoi has to say is, 'What do you mean?' That's the way negotiation goes. But if we came in with a concrete plan, before any expression of interest on their part, we would be negotiating with ourselves again, and that's our biggest problem."

—on progress in Paris negotiations: "Hanoi has a real dilemma. We have plenty of dilemmas too, but they must deny all hope to the U.S. If they even pretend that progress is being made, then progress will be made. That's why they must flatly refuse to admit of any progress."

—on President Thieu: "We are not there for Thieu. We are there for self-determination, and what's so terrible about Americans being for self-determination? You can find it in Jefferson and Wilson. And what is amazing is the way the doves here say that Thieu should get rid of Ky. Thieu would *love* to get rid of Ky . . ."

—on the accusation that our diplomats had somehow missed a signal from the other side that might have led to peace: "We never have any trouble getting messages from North Vietnam. Harriman's idea that they are tender flowers who send signals that we can't read is not the case at all. They are tough cookies, and when they have a theme to get across, they get it across loud and clear."

—on the question of whether the ABM would be a deterrent if we could never test it to prove its efficacy: "We cannot know, but the Russians can't know either. For God's sake, it could have talcum powder inside, but if they don't know that, it would be a deterrent."

—on the possibility of a détente with the Soviets: "Nixon is the first President in a decade that has the Russians coming to him. He didn't get in that position by being a bleeding heart."

In public he couched these sentiments in scholarly, sometimes wryly humorous terms and was able to make the same points with greater effect in private talks with journalists, changing his emphasis but never his basic line. This scored points with both the press and with Nixon, the equivalent of making a spare in bowling by knocking over the sevenpin and tenpin.

And Henry was "meticulous," his favorite word in 1969. (His favorite word in 1970 was "concrete," in 1971 "normalize," in 1972 "precise," in 1973 "compassion," and in 1974 "honor.") In May he changed the word "negotiate" to "mediate," so that the United States could be in the position of being the peacemaker; when "cease-fire" was first used, he insisted on making it plural, so that it would apply to Laos and Cambodia. Nothing bypassed him on its way to the President, and the President appreciated that scrupulous attention to detail; when one of Haldeman's staff laid the President's schedule on the desk one morning, and it read "Meeting—AMB" instead of ABM, it was Haldeman who caught hell. Kissinger proofread all of his staff's work before it went to the President.

By the end of '69—the first phase in his career in Washington—Henry had become fairly well Nixonized. That is, he was thoroughly disenchanted with most members of the liberal and Ivy League academic communities, though he did not say so publicly; he had reached a modus vivendi with the Joint Chiefs and with Melvin Laird at Defense, and worked out ways to keep State out of as many major decisions as he could. Most important, he had a master plan—he called it a conceptual framework—and a unity of immediate purpose with his client, the most powerful man in the world. Henry was changing, gaining confidence, feeling his oats, expanding his authority, stepping on toes. Richard Nixon observed all this, shook his head admiringly, and said, "Henry plays the game hard, all right."

To be able to play the game hard, you often have to sell the game soft. Nixon had the feeling that Kissinger was too much the academic to understand public relations, and directed him to sit down with the men within the Administration who most often talked to the press to give them the word. By disclaiming any public relations sense, Kissinger was of course taking the best route of all, and his colleagues were drawn into the process of helping this man of substance who was not supposed to know anything about style.

We were disabused of that in a meeting on December 1, 1969, in the Situation Room, an ordinary conference room with a map on the wall that is adjacent to a communications room, but has a nice sense of drama because that is where the crisis-handlers assemble in times of crisis to handle crises. "We have a problem of style," Henry announced.

All three speechwriters were there, along with Flanigan, Moynihan, and Harlow, and a couple of new men in the information area: Charles Colson, a lawyer, and Jeb Magruder, a marketing man Bob Haldeman had brought in to give him control of Herb Klein's operation. Jeb perked up at Kissinger's announcement of a style problem, because the man whose experience was mainly in cosmetics marketing had been worried that all he would hear that day would be heavy foreign affairs stuff.

"We don't make a point of what we do," said Henry. "Take Okinawa." Earlier that year, President Nixon had decided that long-term relations with Japan were more important than the U.S. base on the island of Okinawa, which we had maintained there since the bloody battle of World War II. After working out alternative sites for nuclear weapons, the President went to old Mendel Rivers, chairman of the House Armed Services Committee, and John Stennis, chairman of the Senate committee of the same name, and told them he wanted to improve relations with Japan by returning Okinawa—would the Congress hold still for it? Because these two crusty old gentlemen trusted Richard Nixon on security matters, they went along, and as Henry put it, "When we acted we did so not grudgingly but generously. My point about style is that Nixon can do things that would have been unthinkable in a Democratic Administration. On Okinawa, we did not insist on getting our extra pound of flesh in a formal document. We need an ally, not a clause that could be overturned when the chips were down. If JFK had tried to make this deal, there would have been howls from Congress and the Pentagon." With some satisfaction, Henry added that the State Department had been kept completely in the dark about the whole transaction, until ten days before the end.

Pat Moynihan, who had worked in the Kennedy Administration, verified the point Henry had made: "It's the same on the domestic side. A liberal Administration would be hailed for what we have done."

Encouraged, Henry gave another example, on the use of chemical and biological warfare, which Nixon had recently renounced. People who had worked for Kennedy and Johnson told Kissinger that they had tried to get those Presidents to scrap the gas and kill the germs for years. (I had written the President's message on this, and asked an expert on germ warfare how disposal was to be carried out. "Easy," he replied, "we'll just stop feedin' 'em.") "Cy Vance and Averell Harriman thought I had won some saga of conflict," Henry recounted. "That's because they see policy issues as a morality play, where humiliating the military is part of shaping policy. We operate differently. We try to narrow the area of controversy." Kissinger explained how germ warfare was re-examined not on the basis of humanism vs. militarism, but on straight strategic theory: "The National Security Council found that germs could only be used effectively in a first strike, because of their long incubation period. In germ warfare, D-Day is when an epidemic breaks out, you don't know where it came from, and your enemy's population is immunized." This was the first time anybody in the room had even thought of germ warfare, and Henry's example was having a hypnotic effect. "Now, we had no thought of first use of such a weapon," Dr. Kissinger reassured us, "so our only interest in a germ warfare striking capacity was in retaliation. But the long incubation period makes that impractical—if we were ever hit with germs, we would use other means of immediate retaliation. By the time this practical argument went to the Joint Chiefs, no blood was shed in the meeting. The discussion in the NSC with the Joint Chiefs was not as heated as a seminar at Harvard, which would have started with the conclusion, of course."

The irony of this was that the academic community, which fortunately keeps an eye on such matters, was now crediting Kissinger for his courage in "facing up" to the Joint Chiefs—when what he had done was finesse the Joint Chiefs' position, reason them out of it in terms of military effectiveness rather than expostulate with them about unfair methods of fighting and the horrors of war. Even more important was the central point: Nixon's word was what had been needed to get this past the security-conscious committee chairmen in Congress.

What Kissinger was leading up to in these examples was something we would remember years later at a summit conference in Moscow: the effect of Nixon's tough reputation on the progress of Strategic Arms Limitation Talks (SALT). "On SALT," Henry lectured, "the first thing to remember is that there has been no conceptual breakthrough since 1961. Back then, the arms controllers were in a hostile environment. The only way they could win was to roll over the Joint Chiefs. Now, the dopesters say the arms controllers don't have White House support anymore. But the fact is we're not talking about one weapon like MIRV anymore. We're talking about weapons systems of tremendous technical complexity. Out of the arms control talks we want a codification of parity. This requires very careful preparation. We came up with seven different proposals. We said, 'Let's analyze what it is we want to limit, then figure out how much cheating could go on—under this hypothesis two hundred missiles could be hidden. What risk is involved in these two hundred missiles?' People come to me and say, 'Use us as a counterweight to the Joint Chiefs.' Well, the hell with that. I don't need it.

"Laird made a statement about SS-9; at the time I felt it was exaggerated. He turned out to be wrong—it was even worse than he said. The fact is that Laird *was* exaggerating on the data he had, but he hadn't analyzed the data.

"We have eight different building blocks for SALT, to meet their proposals. This is the first rational, comprehensive study of alternatives. The Soviets have adopted the same serious approach—no propaganda here. If we had gone the way the liberal community wanted us to, we would be dead in Helsinki today. We would have been frozen into one position. Our approach is not spectacular—but we have done more real work on arms control than the two previous administrations combined."

Pat Moynihan said: "You have to figure out a way to make this interesting. I came up with the Disraeli conversation with the President to help sell welfare reform—you know, progress coming fastest under 'Tory men with Liberal principles'—and told it to every press man I know, and it helped get the point across about only Nixon being able to do all this."

Kissinger wracked his brain for an anecdote. "There was one musing incident," he offered. "The Finns were a little taken aback at our selection of Helsinki as the site of the SALT talks. They needed us in their capital like a hole in the head. Somebody who is Finnish said, 'We only suggested Helsinki as the site for the SALT talks to show our neutrality, not to have you in Helsinki.'" Henry waited for the laugh; when it didn't come, he shrugged: "You guys don't think that's funny, but it kills diplomats."

Most of the men in the Situation Room that day were thinking not so much about getting out the point about Nixon style that Kissinger raised, but about the Kissinger style. What did this man, whom we thought we knew but hardly knew at all, have that fused him so closely to Nixon? Being "different" was not the question—so was Moynihan "different"—but what would this fusion do to Nixon and do to Kissinger?

They needed each other. The mutual need most often commented upon was Kissinger's for power backing and Nixon's for intellectual backing, but that only analyzed the obvious. At first, Kissinger may have seen Nixon as a vehicle for the realization of his own world view, but he soon came to appreciate the older, more experienced man's understanding of the political and personal motivations of foreign leaders, and his grasp of significant detail that can inspire and illuminate policy.

Kissinger had always been intellectually gutsy, but there was a vast difference between mental fortitude and actually behaving in a gutsy way: the courage to recommend a daring action pales before the courage to take the action. The knowledge that courageous advice is likely to be acted upon often profoundly affects the adviser, and it gave Kissinger pause; this knowledge made Kissinger more careful but did not make his advice more cautious, and that distinction was not lost on President Nixon.

Kissinger's reputation as a professor obscured his ability as a student, and there was nothing he learned more quickly, nor put into use more effectively, than Nixon's concept of the "big play." In Kissingerese, this idea would turgidly emerge as "bold stroke" or "new initiative," but the potential of occasional "fierceness" was a reality in itself, he soon learned, permeating and assisting all other patient and orderly "normalizations." Just as Kissinger's power derived from Nixon, so his intellectual expansion in his White House years was largely due to his association with a man who was willing to use power. The "exercise of power" is an apt metaphor. Without exercise, the sinews of power atrophy, and Kissinger was to increase his respect for Nixon's willingness to keep his power in readiness.

Nixon's need for Kissinger was closer to his need for Haldeman than his need for Moynihan. Haldeman provided the President a sense of organization and orderliness. Nixon candidly recognized this as a weakness in himself and compensated by vesting in Haldeman at least as much power as anyone else in government. Moynihan, on the other hand, provided intellectual stimulation, provocation, and much-needed irreverent good humor. Those who saw him as liberal-intellectual window dressing missed the point, because Nixon would hardly spend long hours of his own time, in private, on window dressing.

In the first year, Kissinger was more organizer and codifier than stimulant to Nixon, because a sense of bringing order out of chaos was what the President needed most. Nixon trusted neither State nor Defense Departments and wanted to make his decisions himself rather than rely on "option three"—the way a staff has of presenting a range of choices that forces the apparent decision-maker to choose the middle of a spectrum of five. Kissinger made a great point of his neutral, disciplined staff role. This was destined to change, less because Henry's personality changed than because the President's needs changed.

Working between the two men on a speech in the President's EOB office late in the year, I came up short on some fact about withdrawal numbers. Al Haig was sent for, came in with the answer typed neatly on a piece of paper, handed it to Henry, who dismissed him with a nod. The President said to Haig: "No, stay while we're doing this," and added to me in an aside, "Thought and action."

The phrase was a code message referring to a speech we had worked on in early 1966, based on a distinction Woodrow Wilson had drawn between two "men of thought and men of action." Nixon's speech line had read: "The man of thought who will not act is ineffective; the man of action who will not think is dangerous." As the reader may recall, Nixon had spent an inordinate amount of time fiddling with that line; now I knew why. In this particular context, he was applying it to a lieutenant colonel on Kissinger's staff who, the President knew, was both a brave combat soldier and a brilliant staff officer, whose morale would be boosted by being treated not as a messenger but as an adviser. Nixon probably considered that line good advice for a Kissinger, and certainly thought it a good prescription for a President. Nixon was already a good example of the amalgam of man of thought and man of action, and he could see the amalgamation taking place in his adviser for national security affairs. And the President—unbeknown to Kissinger—saw that combination in Al Haig, who was destined to wind up delicately engineering Nixon's resignation.

But in 1969, Kissinger resisted any move by any member of his own staff to deal directly with the President. On the first trip to Europe, when the President accepted an off-the-cuff invitation to address some German legislators, Hal Sonnenfeldt wrote some suggested remarks in longhand, passing them to Henry, who passed them to Nixon. When Sonnenfeldt apologized to the President later for his handwriting, Henry flared up, and the adviser's adviser did not soon again presume to talk directly to his superior's superior.

Kissinger's Haig was a military staff man who would lay out options for a commander, offer his opinion when asked for it, and then put his complete loyalty and penchant for orderliness behind whatever decision his superior made. This was never more vividly illustrated than in the episode that blighted the early stage of the Nixon-Kissinger relationship: the illegal use of the FBI to tap four newsmen and thirteen government officials under the guise of "national security."

In April 1969, the President, John Mitchell, and J. Edgar Hoover got to rubbing salt in each other's old wounds about "leaks," though no serious national security leaks had taken place in the new Administration. Henry Kissinger, who had put a few men into the National Security Council that Hoover was suspicious of, was anxious to show that he was one of the boys —that is, he would be more militantly security-conscious and leak-worried than even the President. He supplied the names of likely suspects, knowing they would be tapped, and probably assumed (as he later assured me time and again) that the taps were legal. Hoover, after all, had carried out FBI surveillance of this sort before, when Lyndon Johnson aide Marvin Watson asked for certain reporters to be watched.*

"I was new, I didn't know these guys, I went along with them," Henry told me in 1973, when I demanded to know why I was included on his list of taps, and he added that he had not known of my tap at all. Henry later inveigled the Senate Foreign Relations Committee to certify that Kissinger had not "initiated" the taps, and he swore that he was a reluctant participant in the distasteful program, but in fact the national security adviser was telling Director Hoover in 1969 that "we will destroy" the leakers and called him repeatedly to put on taps when a suspected leak occurred.

That was in May, when a New York *Times* story by William Beecher about the U.S. bombing of Communist lines in Cambodia drove Henry up his basement-office wall. Cambodia's Prince Norodom Sihanouk had tacitly approved the bombing of trails in Cambodian territory held and used by the North Vietnamese and Viet Cong, but it was felt that public admission of the U.S. bombing would require that the Cambodian leader demand that we desist. This suspected leak (it turned out to be no leak at all, but information from a correspondent on the scene in Cambodia) was followed by a different story revealing our Strategic Arms Limitation position, probably from a U.S. source that did not like the direction of the negotiations. These stories infuriated Henry, who was quite capable of a towering rage when it came to anything he construed as obstruction of his attempt to work out a peace. Later, he would point to them as justification for the beginning of the wiretap program, but this was untrue—the tapping had been decided upon, with his sycophantic and enthusiastic concurrence, well before the important suspected leaks.

As it was explained to me later by an embarrassed and worried Kissinger and Haig, the tapping procedure was this: The President, FBI Director J. Edgar Hoover, and Kissinger discussed the need for wiretaps in April 1969. The arrangement was made for Kissinger to supply the names to the Director, the conduit being Al Haig to William Sullivan of the FBI. Hoover required that each authorization be signed by John Mitchell, which he

---

* White House aides have been tapped before. A former high official of the FBI, who had something to do with my wiretap, told me of one he had worked on a generation before. Donald M. Nelson, a Sears Roebuck executive who served as chairman of the War Production Board, aroused President Roosevelt's suspicions in 1944. At FDR's request, the FBI followed Nelson everywhere and tapped both his office and home telephone.

thought would make the taps lawful (although the Supreme Court later decided that such taps were unlawful).

In the tapping of most of the government officials—particularly those members of Kissinger's National Security Council staff—some sort of case might be made that they had possession of the information that was leaked, and although eavesdropping was an intrusion on their civil liberty, that was the kind of thing workers for the NSC had to expect. Illegal and wrong, but in the minds of a national-security-conscious President and his chief aides, justifiable.

Then the fun began. Henry Kissinger was hardly averse to knowing what Defense Secretary Mel Laird and Secretary of State William Rogers were up to, and what they said before they went in to NSC meetings. This was indicated to him by taps on the phones of their closest aides—Lieutenant General Robert Pursley, senior military assistant to Laird, and Richard F. Pedersen, State Department counselor—neither man in the remotest sense a security risk, and neither one known to associate with reporters. The reason given for the Pursley and Pedersen taps was their possession of SALT information—actually, it enabled Kissinger to preview the opinions of their bosses, Laird and Rogers. This gave Henry a bureaucratic advantage, to say the least.

The tap that was placed on John Sears, a lawyer who used to be in the Nixon, Mudge firm, an early Nixon hand, and somebody John Mitchell did not like, was added—by Nixon and Mitchell—for purely political reasons. Both the tap on Sears and the one on me were said to have been triggered automatically by calls to us by newsman Henry Brandon, who was being tapped—as if Director Hoover could or would place wiretaps on the home and office telephones of White House aides (who might be talking to the President from time to time) without specific clearance from Kissinger.

The tap on my home telephone was of special interest because it was the only one of the taps requested by Colonel Haig that did not have a national security justification. The Sears tap was a John Mitchell special, but what troubled Henry and Al later was a letter from J. Edgar Hoover to John Mitchell saying that Colonel Haig had asked for surveillance of Safire. At first, both Henry and Al denied all knowledge of my tap; when the Hoover letter surfaced, all Haig could say was that the FBI was "covering its ass," taking his name in vain. I spoke to the FBI's William Sullivan at Haig's suggestion years later, and he told me—and later put in writing— that Haig was only the messenger, but it was Haig speaking "on White House request of the highest authority" who requested my phone be tapped.

Especially after testifying under oath in 1973 that he had been "astonished" at learning of my tap, Henry could never admit he ordered it or knew of it. Since he could not hang Haig with coming up with the idea on his own, the two old associates concocted a story that makes a liar out of FBI man Sullivan, whom I believe to be telling the truth. In addition, a convicted former Assistant to the President told me: "Your wife was British, Henry Brandon was British, Henry and Al learned the two of you were talking, so you were tapped." According to Sullivan, "It was the least productive tap of all, that's why it got taken off so fast, six weeks is nothing." But it bothers me, obviously, and colors what I write about Kissinger; I hope it is not personal pique that changed my view of his role in the Nixon years, but a certain understanding that comes when one is lied to by men who are convinced that consistent lying can be the right thing for the country.

Kissinger's reaction to the entire tapping episode, when questioned about it, is un-Kissinger-like. He gets visibly upset; he lies in an unstudied, amateurish way that can be found out; he is not himself. Kissinger tries to put the entire sordid story out of his mind, since it cannot be defended on any grounds, and since it leads, he knows, into non-FBI clandestine operations that could be more than embarrassing, operations Haig dismisses with "there were some dry runs made, but that was garbage." This is a reference to the kind of illegal espionage undertaken by White House agents to burglarize and tap the home of columnist Joseph Kraft, a Kissinger critic; the FBI also followed this newsman and induced the French Government to watch him while he was reporting in Paris.

The Kissinger defense is that he was the new member of the Nixon family in 1969; he was told by John Mitchell that wiretapping for national security was legal; that he does not know about taps other than the ones he should know about; and besides, since Kissinger was the only one who had the guts to go out in public and talk to the Georgetown "enemy" he did not want to be the one Nixon staffer who did not show due concern about leaks. But Kissinger, who takes the lion's share of credit for the Nixon foreign policy successes, cannot avoid at least a lamb's share of blame for some of these illegal doings, and the stricken look that crosses his face when the subject is brought up is far more real than the anguish he used to display to delegations of stop-the-bombing professors.

In 1970, about the time of the Cambodian incursion, Kissinger stepped out of the line of fire of wiretap information; in 1973 he must have been chilled when Special Prosecutor Archibald Cox, in his farewell press conference, said "the Ellsberg-Fielding break-in was described as matters affecting the national defense, and the tapping of William Safire's and John Sears's telephones was apparently treated as a national security matter. Those certainly raise very serious questions as to whether criminal wrongdoing was not involved."

When I asked Haig about this, the four-star general hinted that his orders to tap me had come from the President himself. To this day, Haig says the taps "don't give me gas pains," and thinks I am "battin' gnats."*

---

* Winston Lord was one of the Kissinger aides whose home telephone was tapped over a long period, but with a wrinkle that shows the ludicrous nature of some of our security procedures. Lord's wife, Betty, is Chinese-born and a gourmet cook; every morning, she calls her mother and they discuss intricate recipes in Chinese. Every day, this was recorded, taken to a translator, then turned over to the cryptographic service. Had there

The reason why it is logical to assume that the wiretap program had Dr. Kissinger's enthusiastic support, and why his subsequent protestation of distaste rings false, is the operation of his "dead key." All telephone calls to Henry Kissinger, except those few from girl friends, were monitored by a relay of stenographers in his outer office. President Nixon knew his calls were being taken down verbatim whenever he spoke to his national security adviser, and it is a good idea for a record of such calls to exist: when both men know they are being recorded, no moral problem arises. But not many other people who called Dr. Kissinger, and discussed matters in confidence, knew their words were being taken down and in some cases circulated. George Shultz, when Director of the Office of Management and Budget, was startled to learn from an NSC staffer of the details of a private call he had made earlier that day with Henry. After that, Shultz was guarded in whatever he said to Kissinger on the phone.

Henry would use the surreptitious "telecon" transcripts to prove his loyalty to the President. Complaining to a correspondent about the perfidy of his archrival, Secretary of State Rogers, Henry then edited the transcript, changing words to reflect stronger support of the President by Kissinger, and sent the revised version along to Haldeman—an act of dishonor to the unsuspecting reporter and an act of disloyalty to the President. A man who could do this was capable of eavesdropping on his associates without scruple, and was capable of getting a special thrill out of working most closely with those he spied upon most.

This tolerance of eavesdropping was the first step down the Watergate road. It led to eavesdropping by the plumbers, to attempted eavesdropping on the Democratic National Committee, and to the ultimately maniacal eavesdropping by the President, on the President, for the President, completing the circle and ensuring retribution. Eavesdropping to protect Presidential confidentiality led to the greatest hemorrhage of confidentiality in American history, and to the ruination of many good men. Henry Kissinger was deft in beguiling the Senate Foreign Relations Committee, but he cannot escape history's judgment of the way he watered the roots of Watergate.

In 1969 and 1970, however, Henry Kissinger was not troubled with the morality of the taps, because, for all practical purposes, they were precedented (he thought), legal (he assumed), and would never be discovered (of that he was certain). The mind of Henry the K had comprehensive ability almost equal to Richard Nixon's—that is, it could range the entire horizon, from the creation of grand geopolitical concepts to the manipulation of minute bargaining levers, and then go vertically with the same breath-taking sweep, from niggling little bureaucratic intrigues and tricks to a profound concern for "moral authority," stopping along the way at the pessimistic realism of Oswald Spengler (the author of *The Decline of*

---

been a code, it would surely have been broken, but all the computer ever ground out was Moo Goo Gai Pan.

the West, a book written in World War I that Kissinger urged Nixon to read).

Henry and I put in a hard day in mid-February 1970, working on the first "state of the world" message. The State Department had prepared its own foreign policy paper and refused to let the NSC staff look at it—"As if to say, 'You'll crib' " was the way Henry described State's lack of cooperation. But when State officials saw the Kissinger-NSC 40,000-word white paper, they decided to join their own effort to this quality product, assigning two of State's best policy planners, William Cargo and Miriam Camps, to work with us in Key Biscayne on the final draft. They proceeded with a line-by-line negotiation with Kissinger. One draft line read: "We *cannot* withdraw from the world." The woman from State, with a sharp editor's eye, said, "We can if we want to. It's not a question of our ability to withdraw, but of our intent not to." Kissinger, nodding, wrote in, "We have *no intention of* withdrawing from the world."

Nixon, who knew what kind of grinding work the preparation of this document was, would send over his fixes on individual chapters with encouraging calls. He phoned me on February 16 to say, "I want to be there at the announcement of this to give Henry a send-off. This is really the culmination of a career for him—it's a historic document, people will realize it more and more as time goes on." Almost as an afterthought, he went on, "A good theme to get across is that nobody else could have done this. Germ warfare, Okinawa, China—soon we'll do the genocide convention, and I'll get it through the Congress. But nobody else could." He added a pat on the back for the writing, which was less mine than Anthony Lake's and Winston Lord's.

Late that night, Henry and I took a walk around and around the pitch-and-putt golf course of the Key Biscayne Hotel. The night was balmy, the moon illuminated the silly little golf course, and we felt that warm feeling that comes from working well on a project that gave shape and meaning to what the President had done and what he hoped to do. We talked first of the report. "This could never have been done by a bureaucracy," Kissinger said, "without coming out like Pablum. It required a conceptual brain and a small group working on it." He ribbed me a little: "You helped too, Bill. The President says how pleased he is with your work. I liked the little comment you put next to one of my formulations, in the margin, 'This is how my little grandmother in Brooklyn would have expressed it.' I thought that was very funny. Everybody else thought it made you look like a smart-ass, but I told them it was very funny."

Soon we came to the inevitable subject, the likelihood of his survival in a battle with Bill Rogers. He was fairly pessimistic, and it made one feel almost protective toward him. "It's like the Arabs and the Israelis," Henry said, walking along the well-manicured greens. "I'll win all the battles, and he'll win the war. He only has to beat me once."

6. SILENT MAJORITY

"They" hounded Lyndon Johnson out of office. "They" made it impossible for Hubert Humphrey to be heard. In October 1969, after a long-enough interval to make Vietnam Nixon's War, "they" set their sights on Richard Nixon.

Columnist David Broder of the Washington *Post*, in one of the most perceptive and prescient newspaper pieces written in the Sixties, summed up the mood this way: ". . . the men and the movement that broke Lyndon Johnson's authority in 1968 are out to break Richard M. Nixon in 1969. The likelihood is great that they will succeed again, for breaking a President is, like most feats, easier to accomplish the second time around . . .

"First, the breakers arrogate to themselves a position of moral superiority. For that reason, a war that is unpopular, expensive and very probably unwise is labeled as immoral, indecent and intolerable." Broder concluded "The Breaking of the President" with: "The orators who remind us that Mr. Nixon has been in office for 9 months should remind themselves that he will remain there for 39 more months—unless, of course, they are willing to put their convictions to the test by moving to impeach him. Is that not, really, the proper course, rather than destroying his capacity to lead while leaving him in office, rather than leaving the nation with a broken President at its head for three years?" (This was written in 1969, not 1973.)

From Nixon's point of view, the breakers—"they"—fell into three groups. First were the people of all ages and all political persuasions who were sincerely motivated by their loathing of the Vietnam war—the McCarthy followers of 1968, joined by a widening circle of the war-weary in 1969. Second were the political figures who misread this group as a majority and, with a varying mixture of sincerity and opportunism, ran out ahead of the antiwar parade. The third were the nuts and kooks—the anarchists and yippies, deadbeats and acidheads, haters and burners to whom Vietnam was nothing more than a handy issue to help infuriate the Establishment, trigger right-wing repression, and pick up the marbles in the ensuing chaos. This final group was to meet Nixon face to face in San Jose at the end of 1970, and its stridency and violence did more than anything to help Nixon crystallize his new majority.

Theodore White, whose *Making of the President* books led to Broder's play on his title, had looked back on the 1968 election and told the columnist: "Never have America's leading cultural media, its university thinkers, its influence-makers been more intrigued by experiment and change; but in no election have the mute masses more completely separated themselves from such leadership and thinking. Mr. Nixon's problem is to interpret what the silent people think, and govern the country against the grain of what its more important thinkers think."

That fall, the Nixon Administration braced itself first for the nonviolent demonstrators of the nationwide "Moratorium" (they picked a word that Nixon used to wall off Vietnam comment throughout 1968, and would use again regarding busing in 1972); later, we prepared for the disruptive tactics of the New Mobilization Committee to End the War, who had threatened to bring Washington to a standstill. Jack Valenti, a former Johnson aide, told us with sympathy: "Now you guys will see how it feels to be prisoners in the White House."

The President announced he planned a major Vietnam address for November 3, 1969, which fell directly between the dates set for the two antiwar demonstrations. He scheduled his talk long in advance so as not to appear to be answering the demonstrations, but this bit of news management fooled nobody and only helped build interest in both the speech and the demonstrations. None of us knew what tone the President would use. In his first Vietnam address in May he had been conciliatory, and in his Air Force Academy speech in June he had been deliberately abrasive. I had worked with him on both of those but did not draw the November 3 assignment. After checking with Jim Keogh, I found that the President was treating this with the seriousness of an Inaugural or an acceptance address, doing it all himself.

It was one of those moments when public opinion awaits some event before moving in one direction or another. Nixon knew that. "I don't know if the country can be led here," he told Kissinger, "but we've got to try."

The President had put out word during the October Moratorium that he was watching a football game on television as the Moratorium marchers were circling the White House, a gesture of what he liked to call "cool contempt." That was a mistake, as it was aimed at the nonviolent group who were able to seize upon the slight as an example of Nixon callousness. But it indicated the direction of his thinking. When he was making the final changes in his November 3 speech, he wanted to draw the battle lines between us and them—of the folks versus the elitists, of the "mute masses," in White's alliterative phrase, against the noisy minority.

Henry Kissinger, Congressional liaison assistant Bryce Harlow, several other staffers, and I went up to the Hill for a briefing to Congressional leaders on the content and significance of the speech at 5:30 P.M. in room

202 of the Capitol, in advance of the President's 9 P.M. talk to the nation.

"There is nothing the President has thought more deeply about," Henry began, "or reflected on with greater anguish, than what he is about to say tonight. Night after night, he has worked until two or three in the morning, producing draft after draft. The war in Vietnam will be fully explained to the American people, with unprecedented candor—the good and the bad—leaving secret only a possible few overtures. I know that many of you have told him, 'Don't let Vietnam become Nixon's War,' but his only criterion is in making a peace with which we can live."

The Senators and Representatives in the room were seated around a long table with Kissinger at the head, listening in silence as he went through the President's speech, point by point, which need not be covered here, but some of the Kissinger interpretations are worth reviewing: "After tonight, nobody will be able to say we have not fully explained our policy . . . He answers Harriman's question, of why no initiative early in the Administration, by releasing the exchange of correspondence with Ho Chi Minh, which got nowhere . . . As a matter of fact, we have had a more intense negotiation with Averell Harriman than with Hanoi . . . If the President were to give the timetable for the complete troop withdrawal, he would lose whatever leverage he has . . . The practical meaning of the well-meaning pull-out proposal is that it gives Hanoi the incentive to delay. We cannot and will not go beyond a certain point in negotiation—that is unprecedented in Hanoi's experience. If support for the President is demonstrated, that will also be unprecedented to Hanoi. Their script is based on their French experience. You must remember, they are not waiting for some magic formula, they are waiting for the U.S. collapse."

After Kissinger finished his résumé of the speech, Senator Hugh Scott asked: "The TV people will ask me, 'What's new in it?' What's the answer?"

Henry shot back: "The answer is not what's new but what's right—" Harlow registered surprised alarm; Kissinger instantly saw that it was not the function of the President's national security adviser to deliver ripostes to the Minority Leader of the United States Senate, however well phrased, and he quickly tacked: "—but what's new is our commitment to end the war through Vietnamization. We have two choices, Senator: to get high grades for ingenuity, or for candor. In this case, we have chosen the latter, and the President says to the American people, 'Here is what we have to do.' We don't want to give the impression that we are pulling a rabbit out of a hat."

Harlow added, "The press is right outside this room, Senator. You might tell them that they will be briefed at 8 P.M." He did not have to add that he hoped nothing would be said by the Congressional leaders until after the President spoke. "What about Acheson and Humphrey?" Scott asked. "Acheson will give this his full support," Kissinger replied, "but it's best not to ask him to do it. We called Senator Humphrey and asked him what he would have liked to have said—and a number of key points he would make, we are making, especially the point that it would be irresponsible to tie yourself to a firm withdrawal timetable." This was delicately put and the political men in the room knew exactly why Henry was treading carefully. It was not for an Administration source to predict the reaction of the recently defeated Democratic candidate, but it was for him to show that he had been consulted.

House Minority Leader Jerry Ford asked, "Why now? What's the significance of the timing of the speech?" Kissinger insisted, "It is not the fact that demonstrations are scheduled next week. We wanted to do it on the first anniversary of the bombing halt, which was November 1, but it was too close to the speech he made on October 31 about Latin America." This sounded phony even as he said it, and he quickly moved off the subject; Ford would have to work out the real answer for himself, but at least he knew the Nixon line.

"A personal word," Henry added. It was apparent to his White House colleagues that he felt he had not done what he had come to do—to convey the magnitude of the need for outspoken support of the President at this time, without appearing to strain in pleading for that support. "I've been as close to this as anyone. I conducted a secret initiative for Johnson. I know the leaders in Hanoi have completely overestimated dissent in America. They have to maneuver between Peking and Moscow and their own hawks. They cannot be less hawkish than our responsible elements encourage them to be, which," he concluded unhappily, "is what gives this war its particular poignancy." Then he added: "The President told me: 'I don't know if this country can be led here—but we must try.'"

From the rundown of the speech, especially with its lack of a fresh initiative after a long build-up, and bracketed with demonstrations in the past week and scheduled for the next week, the impression in that room on the part of Scott, Ford, and the mostly friendly Congressmen—as well as the White House aides—was that the President was only going to shout into a storm. He had nothing to offer but a less palatable version of Churchill's blood, sweat, and tears, and we all knew that the American people did not elect a new President for that. We went back to the White House feeling uneasy.

I received a copy of the President's final text at 8:30 P.M., a half hour before the time for delivery. The President was down the hall in his EOB office, alone, practicing the speech. I skimmed the text quickly; it was long (thirty minutes, longer than any other prepared TV speech of his Presidency up to then); detailed, building a case as a lawyer would; as Kissinger had warned us, it was hard to find a "lead"; tough-sounding in places ("If I conclude that increased enemy action jeopardizes our remaining forces in Vietnam, I shall not hesitate to take strong and effective measures to deal with that situation. This is not a threat . . ." but of course it was a threat, which he carried out six months later in Cambodia) and conciliatory in places to dissenters: "I respect your idealism. I share your concern for peace. I want peace as much as you do." That was good—his tone was firm but not abrasive. I was pleased to see he paraphrased a Lincoln line I had sent in not long before about "ten angels swearing I was right" making no difference, as "I have chosen a plan for peace. I believe it will succeed . . . if it does succeed, what the critics say now won't matter. If it does succeed, anything I say then won't matter."* Then I had to shake my head at a stilted passage that began:

> I know it may not be fashionable to speak of patriotism or national destiny these days . . .
>
> Two hundred years ago this nation was weak and poor. But even then, America was the hope of millions in the world. Today we have become the strongest and richest nation in the world. The wheel of destiny has turned so that any hope the world has for the survival of peace and freedom will be determined by whether the American people have the moral stamina and the courage to meet the challenge of free world leadership.
>
> Let historians not record that when America was the most powerful nation in the world we passed on the other side of the road and allowed the last hopes for peace and freedom of millions of people to be suffocated by the forces of totalitarianism.
>
> And so tonight—to you, the great silent majority of my fellow Americans—I ask for your support.
>
> I pledged in my campaign for the Presidency to end the war in a way that we could win the peace. I have initiated a plan of action which will enable me to keep that pledge.
>
> The more support I can have from the American people, the sooner that pledge can be redeemed; for the more divided we are at home, the less likely the enemy is to negotiate at Paris.

That "silent majority" phrase did not grab me. We had used a similar construction early in the 1968 campaign—the "silent center," and "the new majority"; and then, frequently, candidate Nixon would exhort the "quiet Americans" and the "quiet majority." In May 1969, Vice President Agnew used "silent majority" several times in a speech—"it is time for America's silent majority to stand up for its rights"—and it had never taken hold. No catch phrase, I thought, but no harm done. Later, when the phrase was taken up with fervor as the rallying description for "us" as against "them," I asked the President about it, and he shrugged—if he had thought it would be picked up, he said, he would have capitalized it in the speech text.

So I breezed past the significance of what was to become known as "the President's historic, tide-turning 'silent majority' speech" and focused on the peroration—which had a minor mistake in it:

---

* He used that quotation again in 1974, as the conclusion of the speech releasing transcripts of his taped conversations.

Fifty years ago in this very room and at this very desk, President Woodrow Wilson wrote words which caught the imagination of a war-weary world during World War I. He said: "This is the war to end wars." His dream for peace after that war was shattered on the hard realities of great power politics, and Wilson died a broken man.

Tonight I do not tell you that the war in Vietnam is the war to end wars.

I do say that I have initiated a plan which will end this war in a way that will bring us closer to that great goal of a just and lasting peace to which Woodrow Wilson and every President in our history has been dedicated.

As President I hold the responsibility for choosing the best path to that goal and then for leading our nation along it.

I pledge to you tonight that I will meet this responsibility with all of the strength and wisdom I can command in accordance with your hopes, mindful of your concerns, sustained by your prayers.

Woodrow Wilson never actually wrote the phrase "war to end wars." Years before, researching my book about the origins of political phrases, I had dug out the coiner: H. G. Wells, in a 1914 book entitled *The War That Will End War*. President Wilson was associated with the phrase (at first idealistically and later cynically) and very likely had said it several times, but he had never written it down anywhere or used it in prepared speeches. Minor, nitpicking detail? Of course. Probably just to express my pique at not seeing the text more in advance, I called Bob Haldeman and told him about the mistake. (There was a second error that I did not catch at the time, about the "Wilson desk.")

"I hate to bother him just before he's ready to go on," Haldeman said. Then he made a decision: "If it's wrong, we ought to catch it."

"You're right," said I. "Go in and make the change on his reading copy."

"He's right down the hall from you," Haldeman said evenly, "you go ahead in. Better hurry."

I went through the anteroom in the President's EOB office and knocked on the door. He buzzed and I entered. The President was made up for television, dressed in his blue smoking jacket, and he did not want to be disturbed. My errand seemed to me now less of a good idea, but I had come too far to go back.

"Hate to bother you with a nitpick, but Wilson never wrote the words 'war to end wars.'"

The President looked at me as if I were crazy. "That was his big slogan. You sure of your facts?"

I explained that the phrase was closely associated with Wilson, that indeed he probably used it in speaking, but he never wrote it, that was H. G. Wells and I was sorry about that, Mr. President, but my facts were straight. It was now fifteen minutes before airtime, the President was supposed to go across the street to the Oval Office to talk to sixty million

Americans in the most important speech of his Presidency on the most divisive issue of our time, and here I was getting him upset about a lousy detail that nobody else in the country would be likely to notice.

"Has the text been handed out yet?" I said yes, but nothing counted as official until he said it. He shook his head, annoyed. "Not many people are as close a student of Wilson as you are. Leave it in. Let somebody prove he never wrote it."

I returned to my office, leaving the President standing at his desk, reading portions of the speech aloud. Ten minutes later, just before airtime, the President called back to say, "I intend to change the word 'wrote' to 'spoke.' Tell the boys to change it in the written copy to 'spoke'—say it was a hypo, or typo, or whatever the hell."

With his conscience satisfied about the ghost of Woodrow Wilson, the President went before the people with his "silent majority" speech—sensible, straightforward, down the middle, saying in essence, "Stick with me and I'll get out of it honorably." The peace movement's intensity was undoubtedly turned down; the New Mobe demonstrations later in the month only sealed the national resolve that was summoned that night by the President.

The day after the speech, the President called me to chew it over: "My object was to go over the heads of the columnists in this speech. We have been getting the reaction from across the country, and it's been pretty good. We've got to hold American public opinion with us for three or four months and then we can work this Vietnam thing out."

I told him I hoped he didn't intend to become a full-time speechwriter, and he gave a short chuckle: "No, thanks. I did write this one all by myself, you know, but that's the last one I'm going to do alone for a long time." He had something else to say, which was the reason for his call; after a while working for Nixon, you learned to let him come at it in his own good time:

"Did I clean up Wilson enough for you?" I laughed and apologized for buzzing around his head before he went on the air, and he said, "No, no, when you catch one like that, always tell me. I may not look like I appreciate it, but I do."

Sure enough, a few days later I received a letter from a historical-phrase buff, Richard Hanser of Larchmont, New York: "Like the reviewer for *Field and Stream* who concentrated on the gamekeeping passages in *Lady Chatterley's Lover*, I read the President's Vietnam speech from my own nutty viewpoint. I was most interested in the fifth paragraph from the end in which he attributed the phrase about 'war to end wars' to Wilson . . ."

In wistful triumph, I forwarded it to the President as proof that somebody out there cared about historical detail.

In retrospect, the "silent majority" speech was the most important of his first term, not so much for what the President said but for what the speech did. A bona fide event, a studied counterpunch to the events staged by a minority bidding to become dominant, the speech moved the country in the direction the President wanted it moved and most of the country wanted to be moved. "Pluralistic ignorance" is how behaviorists describe a situation in which the members of a majority are unaware they are in the majority, and it is a wrongheaded state for a democracy to be in; on November 3, 1969, Nixon dispelled pluralistic ignorance and gave the majority both its identity and a new confidence. When television commentators came on right after his speech not to recap but to rebut, the President reacted angrily, and later Vice President Agnew, using a phrase of Pat Buchanan's, was to denounce the "instant analysis." Many of us felt strongly that no unelected personality clothed in the garb of network objectivity should be interposed between the elected leader in the "bully pulpit" and the people. Television officials later saw the light or felt the heat, and the trend toward commentators' immediate rebuttal soon slowed.

What nobody at the time discussed, in the media or in the White House, was what the President had done in terms of his political philosophy. Three years later, in a radio campaign speech as remarkable as it was unremarked, Nixon reviewed the "silent majority" episode in the light of his view of leadership:

A leader must be willing to take unpopular stands when they are necessary. But a leader who insists on imposing on the people his own ideas of how they should live their lives—when those ideas go directly contrary to the values of the people themselves—does not understand the role of a leader in a democracy. And when he does find it necessary to take an unpopular stand, he has an obligation to explain it to the people, solicit their support, and win their approval.

Let me cite an example: In every Presidency there are moments when success or failure seems to hang in the balance, when an expression of confidence by the American people is vitally important.

One of those moments came toward the end of my first year in office. I had declared that we were going to end our involvement in the war in Vietnam with honor. I had made it plain that we fully understood the difference between settlement and surrender. As you may recall, the organized wrath of thousands of vocal demonstrators who opposed that policy descended on Washington. Commentators and columnists wondered whether we would witness what they referred to as "the breaking of the President."

On November 3, 1969, I came before my fellow Americans on radio and television to review our responsibilities and to summon up the strength of our national character.

The great silent majority of Americans—good people with good judgment who stand ready to do what they believe to be right—immediately responded. The response was powerful, nonpartisan, and unmistakable. The majority gave its consent, and the expressed will of the people made it possible for the Government to govern successfully.

I have seen the will of the majority in action, responding to a call to responsibility, to honor and to sacrifice. That is why I cannot ally myself with those who habitually scorn the will of the majority . . .

Nixon saw his Silent Majority as his main strength to negotiate with an opposition Congress and to check an increasingly critical press. In a memo Nixon wrote to Haldeman on December 9, 1969, he asked for an analysis of his strengths and weaknesses as perceived by the public. Referring to himself in the third person (maybe there was a third person), Nixon suggested some of the strengths: "The fact that after all the talking about weakness on television that he has made effective use of the medium, the effectiveness of the TV press conferences, the fact that no President in this century has had more opposition in the press and among the TV commentators and that in spite of that opposition has been able to maintain majority support."

The Silent Majority was with him despite the press. The President went on with his request to Haldeman: "I am sure that when you get together, other thoughts will occur to you as to where we have succeeded, where we have failed, and what our goals should be during the next year. Safire will be a good one, incidentally, to put his analysis to work on this subject." I appreciated that when a copy of the memo came my way but was struck by a departure from Nixon's mode of the past few years in the conclusion: "What I would like would be not a large collection of individual views, but one concise statement reflecting the varying viewpoints. My guess is that there will be considerable unanimity provided you stay away from programs."

Maybe there would have been and maybe there wouldn't, but when the assignment came to me, I wasn't going to make a survey, I was going to tell the President what I thought. "One concise statement reflecting the varying viewpoints" was a sign of over-organization; on a matter like strengths, weaknesses, and goals, a one-page list of options would hardly do. So I sent in my anticommittee product, which he read closely enough to ask me for a follow-up in a few months, because what I wrote about the Silent Majority intrigued him: "Positive themes that have come through: Identity with Middle America. Nixon is obviously President of most of the people; they think he understands what they are and what they want. The Silent Majority phrase crystallized and dramatized this identification . . . Negative themes: . . . We resent criticism. This is the other side of the coin of the crystallization of the Silent Majority; attacks on a biased press and sinister eastern establishment solidify some support, but in the long run, unless tempered, run the danger of appearing thin-skinned and whining."

Whenever any of his aides resisted the request for a tidy summary and gave him their points of view without Pablum, Nixon sat up and took notice. He read what they wrote and surprised them later by remembering it and occasionally zinging it back at them. But the perception Nixon had of the rise of the Silent Majority (which had been duly reported and even exaggerated in Nixon's favor by the press) reinforced his certainty that the press was the enemy and he could "maintain majority support" despite media opposition—indeed, using its opposition.

If the job of a leader is to lead, Nixon did his job on November 3, 1969. Five months before, he had righted his ship with a "new isolationists" speech, informing Hanoi that his withdrawals were not a sign of weakness and signaling the Soviets that his extrication from Vietnam could not be viewed as any softening of Nixon's position regarding strategic arms limitation. Six months later, he would make a strident and abrasive speech announcing his incursion into Cambodia—the "pitiful, helpless giant" speech—which would be as badly received as his "silent majority" speech was well received. Seen in sequence, the Nixon who spoke in June 1969 of the need to reject the "new isolationists" was being firm with a strategic purpose in mind; the Nixon who evoked the support of the "silent majority" in November 1969 was still firm, but this time coupled it with a solid and thoughtful emotional appeal, betting that the people of the nation were attuned to him; the Nixon who would lay it on with a spatula in May 1970 was tough, not firm, a President no longer tentative about his support but cocky about it, and who would let his deep-seated scorn for "them" spill out all over the air.

Throughout his first term, whenever Nixon was challenged, he usually responded well; when he won, he responded badly. Near the end of his first year, the reborn peace movement and the stubborn North Vietnamese were both challenging him; he responded with the powerful, insightful "silent majority" speech, and won his appeal. In mid-1970, he was on top, and what he would ultimately call the "expected excesses" of demonstrators became his reason for a harsh, self-pitying, and superpatriotic speech about his Cambodian decision. He lost that appeal.

7. THE CAMBODIAN DECISION

"It's amazing how fast Spring comes and goes," said the President to Haldeman, looking out the window of the Oval Office at the Rose Garden on the morning of May 1, 1970. "I hope the photographers got the pictures."

The night before, he had gone before the American people on television to announce the most momentous decision so far in his Presidency: the "incursion" into Cambodia by American and South Vietnamese troops, for the purpose of destroying what had been enemy supply sanctuaries. Nixon was certain he did what was necessary to lift the threat of a decisive North Vietnamese attack on Saigon in the coming year, while U.S. ground combat troops were being withdrawn.

The President felt fine. "He's experienced in this field," Haldeman told a couple of us later that day. "He knew he was grappling with a monumental problem, and he likes to rise to a major challenge. Our posture is hard, tough—no give. Don't talk about negotiations, and pass that to the rest of the people on the staff. The essence of the whole operation was secrecy, surprise. It has been a 100 per cent success, a military and diplomatic surprise, and the President feels right about it."

Nixon had spent a long, thoughtful ten days leading up to this "seventh crisis." He traveled to the mid-Pacific to greet the astronauts of Apollo 13 after their difficult and abortive voyage, then had breakfast in Honolulu with Admiral John McCain, who tried to sell him a plan to "clean out the sanctuaries" so as to protect remaining U.S. troops. McCain, a wiry and plain-spoken naval person, thought it might be a good way to keep from losing the war, and perhaps even to win. Nixon had already heard this preemptive strike option from Defense Secretary Laird, not long after the ruler of Cambodia, Prince Norodom Sihanouk, had been deposed by Lon Nol, his palindromic* Prime Minister, who was far less neutralist and far more pro-Western.

* Other recent leaders whose names form a palindrome are Burma's U Nu and France's Laval.

At the Western White House on April 20, the President gave a "progress report" on Vietnam: casualties down, 150,000 troops to be withdrawn in the coming year, but no progress on the negotiating front. He told the doves that he had done everything they had asked him to do, to no avail. Then, with an eye on reports of increased activity in Cambodia, where the Communists had reacted to Sihanouk's overthrow with a troop build-up, he added, "If I conclude increased enemy action jeopardizes our remaining forces in Vietnam, I shall not hesitate to take strong and effective measures . . ."

We were in an odd fix. Sihanouk had been a master opportunist, making a deal with the North Vietnamese that permitted them to use his territory for supply trails and for logistical supply areas within striking distance of Saigon, and making another deal with the Americans to permit them to bomb and otherwise harass the North Vietnamese using Cambodian territory. He demanded secrecy—otherwise, the cagey Cambodian would have to protest that his nation's neutrality was being violated by the side that blabbed. Both sides played his game, with the United States figuring that the status quo was not bad, as the North Vietnamese could not build up too heavily in Cambodia without offending Sihanouk or losing heavily to U.S. bombers. From the start, Nixon viewed the war in Southeast Asia as one war, with Laos and Cambodia used as active Communist staging and supply areas, and the U. S. President had the responsibility to protect a half million troops from potential disaster inflicted during a systematic withdrawal.

Then, without CIA involvement, Cambodia's Lon Nol upset Prince Sihanouk. An unforeseen, indigenous political development took place where both warring powers thought they had a stable military situation. The equation was upset. Nixon thought he could warn off the North Vietnamese, but they understandably viewed the overthrow of neutralist Sihanouk by a pro-Western leader as a military setback that could cost them the war.

By April 23 it was clear that the North Vietnamese were on the move to take over Cambodia, and that U.S. shipments of arms to Lon Nol's government would not stop them. Kissinger set up his executive committee, called WSAG (Washington Special Action Group), to recommend a strike of South Vietnamese forces into "Parrot's Beak," a strip of Cambodia pointing at Saigon. That night, the President's log shows a call placed at 6:30 P.M. to Senate Foreign Relations Committee Chairman J. William Fulbright, followed by a talk with Kissinger at Fulbright's home. There were ten calls to Kissinger between that time and 11 P.M. that night.

The next morning, the President met early—from 7:20 to 9:02 A.M.—with Director of Central Intelligence Richard Helms and his deputy, Lieutenant General Robert E. Cushman, who had been a former commander of I Corps in Vietnam, and Admiral Thomas H. Moore, chairman of the Joint Chiefs of Staff, along with Kissinger, to tell them he was ready to move ahead on Parrot's Beak, but he also wanted to discuss "The Fish-hook"—base areas 352 and 353—where the Communist central office for Vietnam, "COSVN," was thought to be headquartered. As the President told us later, "If we were going to take the flak for doing it at all, we might as well do it right."

He went up to Camp David with Bebe Rebozo, watched a movie—*The Cincinnati Kid*—and the next night choppered to the Navy Yard and sailed down the Potomac in the *Sequoia* with Bebe and John Mitchell. After the four-hour cruise, they returned to the White House and watched *Patton*, a movie that the President liked inordinately, which portrayed the World War II general to be—depending on the viewpoint of the viewer— either a patriot misunderstood by carping critics, or a passionate chauvinist incapable of understanding the sensitivities of his troops or the public. Nixon saw Patton as the former and relished the general's ability to move troops swiftly to a decisive conclusion.

On Sunday, April 26, there was a worship service in the White House. That afternoon, in a three-hour meeting with Mitchell and Kissinger, Nixon moved toward the decision. Nixon took dinner alone in the Lincoln sitting room, and the next morning, Monday, April 27, told Rogers and Laird of his decision to go all the way. He couldn't turn off the rest of the Presidency, however; he spent the rest of the day meeting Congressmen, Eskimo students, and a group of economists who had a lively debate in the Oval Office. (Activist Pierre Rinfret and conservative Milton Friedman nearly came to blows, but the President asked me not to take notes of those fireworks.)

Monday night, in his EOB office, Nixon talked briefly with John Mitchell. The two former law partners were joined by Henry Kissinger for a two-hour session that broke up at nine o'clock. The next morning he spoke to the Vice President for half an hour, to Haldeman and Kissinger most of the day; went downstairs to get a haircut from the White House barber, Milton Pitts—who was giving him a modern, "fuller" look—and finally spent an hour in the wicker chairs in the Rose Garden with John Ehrlichman, talking about the concerns John conveyed to him of how young people would react. (A couple of weeks before, Ehrlichman had protested to Haldeman that we were presenting a stony Carswell-Mitchell face to young people, which he felt was all wrong.)

Nixon went through eight drafts of the speech, about the normal amount, working with Pat Buchanan. This was not the time, the President was sure, for Ray Price's uplift or my tightrope walking. The speech gave it to the people "with the bark on," as Nixon liked to say—patriotic, angry, stick-with-me-or-else, alternately pious and strident—and he would soon be criticized for heightening and harshening the crisis with his pitch. But he undoubtedly felt that honesty in this case was the best policy, that if he was going to take a strong step he was not going to pretend it was anything less. Besides, the people who were going to criticize him for it would not be swayed by soothing words. He was convinced by the reaction to his

November 3 "silent majority" speech that he knew best how to carry it off. He was quickly disabused.

After the speech, Chief Justice Warren Burger dropped by the White House in his car to leave a letter for the President—it probably accompanied a draft speech by John Mitchell that Nixon had sent the Chief Justice to show that the Executive Branch was seeking no confrontation with the courts. Nixon asked Burger to stay awhile; the men talked for two hours.

Thus, in the rarefied atmosphere of the top, the air was calm. Nixon was doing his job, knew he was doing it the way he wanted to, and was actually enjoying it—he was a man trained to be President putting his experience and talents into play. The system he had created had worked well for him; the NSC had shown him what all the alternatives were and listed possible consequences; he had sat down with his yellow pad and put the pros and cons down in his own way, including a top line that read "time running out"; and, based on the best information and his best judgment, he had acted.

Nixon made one big mistake in his own demeanor, however; the morning after the speech, not realizing that the strain of the past week had taken its toll, he allowed himself to make a rambling, slurred statement to Pentagon employees that included the word "bums" in connection with some college demonstrators. Two days before, on April 28, Nixon had written to Professor M. N. Srinivas, a visiting scholar from India working at Stanford, a social anthropologist whose files had been destroyed by a fire bomb tossed by an angry student:

THE WHITE HOUSE
WASHINGTON

April 28, 1970

Dear Professor Srinivas:

As did countless other Americans, I responded with disbelief at the news that your study at the Center for Advanced Studies in the Behavioral Sciences had been firebombed, and that much of the work of a lifetime had been destroyed.

It can be small consolation for you to know that the overwhelming proportion of the American people, and of the American academic community, utterly reject the tactics of the person or persons who did this. To say that they are deranged, does not excuse them. To say, what is more probably the case, that they are simply evil, does not make them go away.

I hope that the great insights of social anthropology that you have brought to your studies might serve in this moment to help you understand this tragedy. Please at all events know that you are an honored and welcome guest, whose work is appreciated and valued in this nation as indeed throughout the world.

Sincerely,

Richard Nixon

Nixon was referring to students like those fire-bombers when he said "bums," but, especially in the post-Cambodia atmosphere, the word's use was a gaffe, and the press then put his feet to the fire unfairly. Soon it became a "fact" that Nixon had called all students or dissidents "bums," peaceful or otherwise, and this helped fuel the feeling of estrangement felt on campuses by dissenters convinced that Nixon had just expanded the war, and by antiwar leaders who saw this as a chance to revitalize their dying movement.

The night of the speech, Haldeman called the White House senior staff together in the Roosevelt Room, handing out an NSC paper for us to study, the first page of which gave us the picture:

THE WHITE HOUSE
WASHINGTON

POINTS ON THE CAMBODIA MILITARY ACTION

For the past ten days the enemy has enormously increased its activities in the "Cambodia pocket" that borders on South Vietnam.

These actions have been not defensive, but provocative; they cannot be ignored.

To ignore them would:

Jeopardize the entire South Vietnamese operation.
Affect our ability to continue our withdrawal.
Present an open American flank to the enemy.

This is not a long-term "quicksand" operation that would lead to a new "Vietnam situation" in Cambodia. It is a strike operation that is an integral part of our operations in Vietnam. It is not in reply to any of Lon Nol's requests for aid to Cambodia.

It must be remembered that:

Saigon is only 35 miles from Cambodia.

> Viet Cong and North Vietnamese troops until now have had
> an absolute sanctuary in Cambodia.
> They have been able to attack and then flee back across the
> border without danger of pursuit.

> This effort to clean out the enemy will result in a savings of
> American lives.

> Only the President has all the facts on this situation. He must act
> in what he considers to be the best interests of our country and
> our troops.

> The President will talk about the Cambodia situation tonight
> on national television.

Henry Kissinger briefed us on "this necessary action. With an open sea route and untrammeled use of the port of Sihanoukville, there would be no need for the Communists to move supplies down the Ho Chi Minh trail—that presents us with an intolerable prospect." Henry said that the purpose of the President's speech was to "bring home the fact that if they don't settle, things could get out of hand." Then he added, with emphasis added by understatement, "It would be undesirable for the White House staff to go around saying we don't really mean it." Many of the aides in the Roosevelt Room, he knew, would see this as a turning away from the steady effort to "wind down" the war, and Henry was crisp and tense: "We're trying to shock the Soviets into calling a conference, and we can't promote this by appearing to be weak. We're not pleading for a thing—this is a very tough speech."

The questions came at him: Isn't this expanding the war? "Look, we're not interested in Cambodia, we're only interested in it not being used as a base." Why don't the Thais help? "They hate the Cambodians, but we can't say that." Won't the doves land on our backs? "We'll get paid off if we end the war, not if we get the doves off our backs. The point is, we won't play the game on the Communists' rules. Anyone who wants to negotiate a peace must hang tough. If we get through this, we should have a negotiation by July or August."

Don Rumsfeld, then running OEO and destined to be Ambassador to NATO, shook his head: "We shouldn't say this is not an expansion, that's not credible." Irritated, Henry snapped back: "That is what makes me personally as well as institutionally impatient. Here the North Vietnamese have forty thousand troops marching on the capital of Cambodia, and a lousy fifty U.S. advisers go in last night, and you hear Senators say—we're the ones who are escalating!"

The tone of our questioning shook Kissinger—this was only the White House staff, and two tougher briefings lay ahead. "I have to brief my own staff now; I can't have them running loose saying what they think. Anything else?" I asked: "Doesn't this fly in the face of the Nixon Doctrine?" Henry exploded: "We wrote the goddam Doctrine, we can change it!" This was probably intended half in jest, and received half a laugh, which helped calm everybody a little. "We never said U.S. troops would never be used," Kissinger explained. "This doesn't apply to a situation where 425,000 Americans were already involved." As Kissinger left, Haldeman gave me a hard look—some of the nastier questions had been mine—and said, "The thing to remember is that this is the best way to end the war, and this is the best way to save U.S. lives." Al Haig, Henry's deputy, got up and—in an uncharacteristically loud voice—barked: "The basic substance of all this is, we have to be tough!" He seemed embarrassed at the loud sound of his soft voice, and concluded his presentation quickly.

We picked up our papers to go and listen to the President on television. Ehrlichman, worried more than most about campus reaction, put on a mock German accent to say, "Tomorrow, right here, a briefink on der operations around New Hafen." There were a few nervous titters—John was referring to a police roundup of Black Panther members in Connecticut—but he also believed this could blow the lid off campuses from Yale to Berkeley. We all felt the President had the strong majority of the people with him, though—and "saving lives of U.S. servicemen" would be a powerful rationale.

The President, in his April 30 speech, hit it very hard. "If when the chips are down, the U.S. acts like a pitiful helpless giant, the forces of totalitarianism and anarchy will threaten free nations and free institutions throughout the world." At the last minute, he changed "U.S." to "the world's most powerful nation" to add contrast to "pitiful helpless giant" which, for some reason of Mr. Nixon's own, did not have a comma between the adjectives. He outlined a few of the options open to him, which helped his audience in seeing the scope of the decision, and rallied support with "we will not be humiliated, we will not be defeated. We will not allow American men by the thousands to be killed by an enemy from privileged sanctuaries."

Then he took a slap at "them," referring to how the great decisions of Wilson, FDR, Eisenhower, and Kennedy had received the support of the nation: "In those decisions, the American people were not assailed by counsels of doubt and defeat from some of the most widely known opinion leaders of the nation." Many of his aides watching on television began to worry at that point if he would take the plunge into self-pity, which he certainly did. "I would rather be a one-term President," he added here, "and do what I believe is right than to be a two-term President at the cost of seeing America become a second-rate power and to see this nation accept the first defeat in its proud 190-year history."

Nixon had done what only Nixon could do—made a courageous decision and wrapped it in a pious and divisive speech. In retrospect, the Cambodian decision was the turning point of the war in Vietnam, making possible "peace with honor," not an altogether unworthy goal. Con-

trary to the fears of many doves, this move was part of the steady Vietnamization of the war—not an escalation of the war. Given his long-range plan,
Nixon made his best decision at the crucial moment; the "incursion" was
daring, surprising, successful in the short run and successful in the long
run. But Nixon acting as a leader came across to all too many people as a
belligerent con man.

Just as the President made a meaningful move in a mean-spirited way,
his staff began to sell the "making of the decision."

Colson, Buchanan, and some others began to organize the blazing-back
at the infuriated doves. I lent a willing hand in that but spent more time at
a project that had never been given a green light before: getting out the
details about how this President made a decision. Haldeman was unusually
cooperative. When I asked for the logs that are the basis for the opening
pages of this chapter, he told Chapin to lay it all out for me. With help
from Herb Klein, this led to "tick-tocks" in magazines—day-by-day detail-
ings of the amorphous thing called the decision-making process. Though
it turned out later that John Mitchell's participation was minimized, that
new openness was a good thing, we proceeded to make too much out of
a good thing. In no time, we were involved in a game plan to sell
the making of a decision, and in a meeting with Haldeman on May 1 we
were handed a poop sheet with items like these: "He did not move as LBJ
would have. It was not impulsive. He conferred and worked closely with
advisers. Decision made not under pressure but with reason." And: "As
is the President's style, he did it in a cool, calm, rational, and very Nixon-
like way. It takes all options into account and is in the best interest of the
country."

This all happened to be true, and if we did not try to point it out, who
would? Yet it occurred to some of the older pros in the room—Chotiner,
Klein, Keogh—that in trying to make a science of an art, it is possible to
over-organize things. Chuck Colson offered a mild criticism: "Wall Street
loves us for the President saying, 'Buy stocks,' just before going into Cambodia." Haldeman cut off the negative thinking with "Let me assure you,
he's weighed all the minuses."

The next day, before a meeting with legislative leaders, the Cabinet
came together and Secretary Rogers made a brief talk about the main
theme of the situation: that there could be no equivocating when it came
to a command decision, what the President had done took great courage,
and the reason for no consultation was the necessary element of surprise.
The President needed their support, Rogers concluded—both "moral and
verbal." Haldeman's deputy, Alex Butterfield, who was there, told me
about this, adding, "Rogers was not as forceful as he might have been." He
added that Attorney General Mitchell came in afterward with a simpler,
more direct "May I suggest you tell anybody who asks you that the main
point is to save American lives."

The next morning, Sunday, May 3, Haldeman brought all the people who
talked with people into the Roosevelt Room: Bryce Harlow, Eugene

Cowan, Bill Timmons, Lyn Nofziger, Murray Chotiner, Ken Belieu, Harry Dent, Jeb Magruder, Jim Keogh, Herb Klein, Pat Buchanan, Ron Ziegler, Dwight Chapin, and Chuck Colson. For a surprise, Haldeman was complimentary: "We moved to execute a plan well. A week ago, none of us thought we'd be at this point today. The President is pleased. Do not back off any strong moves, our overall plan is to move forward on all fronts. No waffling. Here's some good news—Gallup will show a 51 per cent approval rating, up from the previous 49 per cent."

We had overemphasized COSVN—people expected American troops to find a miniature Pentagon in the jungle—and had begun to get some heat on that, with critics wondering where the central headquarters of the Viet Cong was, and why we had not captured it, documents and all. Nor was there heavy fighting; had there been, Nixon felt with some irony, he would have been attacked for the heavy casualties, but as it was, he was being attacked for making much ado about nothing. The answer could not be the subtle line that Henry Kissinger had tentatively offered at one meeting—that once violated, the Cambodian border was no longer sacrosanct, and Viet Cong units would always have to use rear areas for their supply caches. "Cache" became a vogue word for about a month—Len Garment left me a note one night wondering whether Kissinger had been able to "check a cache"—and we started to stress what a lot of supplies we were capturing.

To our surprise, the President walked into the Roosevelt Room and proceeded to give us a ten-minute briefing and pep talk.

"Keep in mind," he said, standing, his hands on the back of a chair (it wasn't his meeting, just an impromptu drop-in), "once a decision is made, it's made. It's important for all of us to have confidence for the next three weeks. It's all going according to plan, successfully. We're getting plenty of flak, but there's going to be an awful lot of egg on a lot of politicians' faces if they go in the wrong direction.

"The purpose of the operation from the beginning was not the destruction of enemy personnel, but matériel. We were doing this to buy the time we need for Vietnamization. We've bought a lot of time already. By the end of the operation, we'll have bought enough time.

"More important than enemy killed"—Nixon felt it was important that we get this straight, the absence of enemy casualties—"is the destruction of their potential to attack. It takes ten months to build up this complex, and we're tearing the living bejeesus out of it. Anything that walked is gone after that barrage, and the B-52 raids. Of course, you need pictures of the supplies captured, but first they have to be careful about booby traps.

"Remember," Nixon said, looking as if the strain was beginning to tell, but his voice was firm, "I have great confidence in the rightness of our decision. It will shorten the war and allow the Vietnamization program to continue on schedule.

"Don't be defensive. Don't say it will be limited to this long, or that area. It is not limited in its effect on the infiltration of troops and supplies. The diplomatic point is the most important of all: they have to decide whether they want to take us on all over again. In terms of that pressure on them to negotiate, this was essential, but we'll know more in two months.

"People say, 'This will be a great success or a great failure.' But it cannot be a failure, because we don't expect capitulation. We planned this so well, that we have now reached the point where the withdrawal program can go forward in safety. Frankly, we anticipated many more casualties." Now he came to the point of why he had Haldeman bring us in, and why he wanted to tell us himself of the posture he expected from the White House staff.

"Don't play a soft line—I don't want to see any aid and comfort to anybody here. The big game is to pull this off. It's a bold move, imaginative, and it's no more of this screwing around—say that and it will go better with Congressmen you talk to. It's important that some of our Congressmen say that not supporting the President is sticking a knife in the back of U.S. troops, and attacking us on this is giving aid and comfort to the enemy—use that phrase, because that's what it really is." He had a few rough things to say about certain Congressmen, and when he could see that several members of his staff were looking more and more forlorn, he said in a curiously mild way, "Don't worry about divisiveness. Having drawn the sword, don't take it out—stick it in hard, because for people to go squealing around while a combat operation is under way, undercutting the very purpose of the action where good men are losing their lives—that's beyond the pale. Hit 'em in the gut. No defensiveness."

That was a rough charge to his own troops, and he knew it. He pushed the chair forward and in what we took to be a reference to his "bums" slip when he had been exhausted, said, "Get some sleep tonight. It sometimes helps," and walked out.

Al Haig, Kissinger's deputy, who had emerged as an important fellow in this crisis, gulped, "That's a tough act to follow," and proceeded to brief for about fifteen minutes on both the tactics and strategy of the operation. He switched back and forth between what we could use publicly and what we could not, which annoyed Haldeman, and when Haig pointed out that confidential cables said that U.S. troop morale was up, Haldeman cut in: "It doesn't mean tiddle-de-shit for you to read that in your secret cables, Al, when nobody knows it. We can't have these damned confused briefings," said Haldeman, with no concern for Haig's feelings, "with some stuff you can use and some you cannot, because nobody can remember what's usable and what's not." The President's appearance had obviously soured the mood of his chief assistant; when Lyn Nofziger suggested, "Let's not have Dave Packard brief," a point about the Deputy Defense Secretary he had made before, Haldeman snapped, "Let's get the hell off that. If there's a negative, make it once and drop it, and hit the positives." Eugene Cowan of the Congressional relations staff said that it would not hurt for the President to meet with the Senate Foreign Relations Committee, since he was meeting with other committees. Haldeman shook his head: "It's been decided that he won't meet with them alone. Let's move on."

The next day, May 4, there was a demonstration at Kent State University in Ohio at which four students—two girls and two boys—were shot to death, and eight other students wounded, by National Guard troops, reportedly after they had been fired upon by a sniper.

I watched the television report of the Kent State killings with George Shultz in his office at the Labor Department. The network played the tape of the tragic moment twice; the first time, Shultz, a former Marine, said of the sound of gunfire from the National Guard, "Did that sound like a salvo to you?" After the rerun, with great sadness, Shultz answered his question: "That was a salvo." The government, in an organized fashion, had executed some demonstrators on a command. Never mind that the Guardsmen were "kids" nearly as frightened and inexperienced as the students they faced; whatever the provocation, the Guardsmen represented the government and the victims were not doing anything for which they deserved summary execution. Shultz seemed actually groggy after the second running of the news film; he had been a Marine, but he had also been Dean of the College of Business Administration at the University of Chicago.

The President, who had received wide public support for his praise of the Chicago police after the 1968 Democratic Convention, put out a statement as ill-conceived as it was well-phrased: "This should remind us all once again that when dissent turns to violence it invites tragedy." Taken together with the "bums" remark, many young people on campus thought they had an enemy in the White House. The "siege mentality" gripped them, as their own frequently evoked nightmares of repression suddenly seemed real. The attacks on the President in the press and in the Congress became savage, and what had been anticipated as an expectable and answerable reaction against the President by doves suddenly was transformed into a national sense of revulsion at the gunfire that the Cambodian action had triggered in a Midwestern college.

Unprepared for this kind of reaction—Kent State could not have been foreseen—the White House "hung tough" when it should have been more quickly responsive. Nixon and Haldeman clung to the original game plan when the nature of the game had been altered, a "freeze" that persisted about seventy-two hours, against the urging of Shultz, Ehrlichman, Garment, and other "white hats."

Henry Kissinger, who had urged the President to undertake the Cambodian incursion, did not freeze at Kent State's horror. With infinite patience, he held long debates with his staff members, letting many of the angriest fully dump their arguments and emotions on him. Anthony Lake, who had been closest to him when the first "state of the world" was written only a few months before, resigned and later went to work for George McGovern; but for years afterward, even after he learned to his disgust that his home phone had been tapped by the FBI and the reports read by Kissinger, he remained ambivalent toward his former mentor. Slave driver and self-proclaimed megalomaniac (mere egomaniac wouldn't do) in normal times, Kissinger was sympathetic to the point of anguish toward his "students" under stress. He continued to keep up his contacts with Averell Harriman and others despised by other Nixon men as "the Georgetown set," and could even point to results that had to impress the President.

Henry told me that Robert McNamara, Johnson's Defense Secretary, now World Bank president, came into Kissinger's office at the peak of the furor and put on his desk a list of ten prominent Americans, saying quietly, "You pick five, and I'll call the other five, to get their support." (Henry did not forget; years later, he arranged for McNamara's reappointment.)

But Henry's attitude of concern contrasted sharply with Haldeman's; in fact, the Kissinger anguish—an emotion dramatized by the man's ability to let suffering show in facial expressions and body movements—came to be regarded by the President as a sign of weakness. Haldeman told me later that Henry's unfortunate tendency to look back after a decision had been made, and to agonize again over it, was a drawback the President noticed; according to Haldeman, the President told Kissinger, "Remember Lot's wife," in one of Nixon's infrequent Biblical references. (Two years later, in Moscow, Kissinger did indeed turn into a pillar of SALT.)

Henry's angst did not reflect overt disloyalty; however, the example set by Secretary of the Interior Walter Hickel on May 6 was another matter. Nixon, convinced the West deserved representation in the Cabinet, had chosen Hickel, then Governor of Alaska, over Rogers Morton of Maryland (who wanted the job, deserved it, and later got it). The Hickel appointment was denounced by environmentalists as a sellout to big-business developers, but Nixon stuck by him through the delay in Senate confirmation, saying, "And the last shall be first." (Come to think of it, Nixon used Biblical quotations more than we realized.) Hickel swung the other way quickly, winning friends in the District of Columbia and losing them in the White House. In the midst of the Kent State reaction, he wrote a letter to the President urging Nixon to open up his lines of communication to young people and, while he was at it, "consider meeting, on an individual and conversational basis, with members of your Cabinet." The sentiment was sincere, and the point about young people well taken, but the letter was leaked to the Press before the President saw it, always an insult to a politician; coming at such a crucial moment, it was viewed as disloyalty under fire. Although Hickel's complaint about his own isolation from the President fit well into the charges of "one-man rule" being made by critical editorialists, insiders knew why Hickel rarely got to see Nixon: because the President neither liked nor respected him. For the same reason in reverse, George Shultz did get to see Nixon whenever he wanted to, not because Labor was more important than Interior, nor because

Shultz was hard or soft on demonstrations, but because the President considered Shultz *"un homme sérieux."*

Nixon wanted to fire Hickel outright (though not face-to-face, he hated that), but Ted Stevens—an Old Nixon Hand from the 1960 campaign, now a Senator from Alaska—prevailed on Haldeman to hold off until after the November '70 election. Stevens didn't want an ousted Hickel campaigning against him, which was reasonable, so, as Haldeman told us, "The decision is made, but the execution of it is deferred."

The President was sent reports of editorial reaction overseas as well as at home. The *Times* of London said "the extension of the war into Cambodia and the further demonstration at Kent State University of the vicious incompetence of some sections of the American National Guard have . . . caused a great shock in Europe . . . There is the conviction that President Nixon is pushing inexorably down a road which leads to disaster." Contrariwise, the London *Sunday Telegraph* wrote: "For a second President to allow his foreign policy to be shaped by campus pressure would turn America into a kindergarten state . . . can the Anglo-American liberal establishment not realize that the man now in the White House is a formidable figure, who has to be taken seriously—a President who believes in his cause just as passionately as they believe in theirs?"

Still in a hang-tough mood on May 6, Nixon met with the Senate Foreign Relations Committee, but on his terms—in conjunction with the House Foreign Affairs Committee. When a distressed Senator Jacob Javits asked how Congress could "properly manifest our will," the President said, "The cleanest way is to declare war, but that would be a great mistake." He added that the Congress, through the appropriation process, could always control what the President could do, but "I don't see what purpose another declaration or resolution would serve." With some heat, Nixon told Javits: "I will protect our men in Vietnam unless Congress hamstrings me. If it does that, then you will have to take the responsibility for American lives." Senator Albert Gore was next up. "You base your action on the principle that the end justifies the means," Gore charged, calling the "incursion," as we liked to call it, "a violation of the border of a sovereign nation." The President shot back: "The sanctuaries are enemy-occupied territory; they are controlled by an enemy that is attacking American forces."

Senator Claiborne Pell of Rhode Island then made a short speech about the effect of the President's action on the nation, and concluded with: "I object to your characterization of student radicals as 'bums.'" The President, in concluding his reply, said: "About my reference to bums. I had just received a pathetic letter from a Stanford scholar. A student radical had burned his notes, the work of twenty years. The fellow who threw that firebomb was a bum."

That tense meeting had only one lighter moment, when a Congressman complained that the name "Operation Total Victory" was out of place. The President said that the code name for the American activities is "Rock

Crusher," that the South Vietnamese call their action "Total Victory." Kissinger, at the President's side, explained that the South Vietnamese always used "Total Victory" as a code name. "This is Operation Total Victory number forty-three."

The next day, under Alexander Butterfield's name, the President sent a memo to every member of his Cabinet, which included this central point:

PERSONAL
— To make some fairly hard-hitting points, you can say very bluntly:

— "Look, you can vote against the war in Vietnam and vote against the war in Cambodia, but there are 450,000 American men there, so don't tie the hands of our Commander-in-Chief. If you do, then *you* must assume responsibility for their lives . . . rather than leaving such responsibility, and the decisions connected with it, to him.

— "Don't stab our men in the back while *they are fighting for this country* in Vietnam.

— "Don't take any actions on the floor of Congress which will give aid and comfort to the enemy and encourage that enemy to launch more offensives and kill more Americans."

In this electric atmosphere, the President scheduled a press conference for Friday night, May 8. On the basis of the foregoing information, I had every expectation that the President would do the wrong thing—"hit 'em in the gut," clobber his critics as they were clobbering him, and hang as tough as he was urging the White House staff to do.

But in this situation, as in many others, what the President said privately, what he urged his associates to do, he would not do himself. On the contrary, after venting his political spleen privately, he would then go out publicly and conduct himself as befits a President. That is what he did at that press conference, at the end of a week in which the nation seemed to tear itself apart. To the question "What do you think the students are trying to say?" Nixon replied sensibly: "They are trying to say that they want peace. They are trying to say that they want to stop the killing. They are trying to say that they want to end the draft. They are trying to say that we ought to get out of Vietnam. I agree with everything they are trying to accomplish . . ." He went on to say later, "When the action is hot, keep the rhetoric cool." Most of the press corps had come in a hostile mood; he was cool, calm, precise, above the battle, Daniel in the lion's den, Nixon at his most effective—a boss who made his staff proud, because he did not follow the wrongheaded advice he had been giving us.

In the next chapter, I will go into detail on the rest of that night, which turned out to be the most traumatic and most uplifting of his first term, but let us now take the Cambodian action to its conclusion. For a subsequent press conference later that summer, Nixon worked over the briefing book prepared for him by Pat Buchanan and, on this question, by Henry Kissinger. Nixon's assessment of Cambodia in July 1970:

Yes   get out.
want   troop withdrawal
reduce casualties
a lasting peace

(This contributed to all)

At the same time, preparing for a question about the Hatfield-McGovern Amendment which would have fixed a withdrawal schedule, he wrote of his fondest hope:

For these reasons, I trust the Senate will reject this ill-advised Amendment by a visible and unmistakable margin.

The President's handwritten comment can be seen in Plate 6 following page 200, and is translated here:

How we end the war—determines how long lasting the peace will be. [If] It is—cut and run—accept defeat—would lose the peace we now have a chance to win.

"We now have a chance to win" was how Nixon felt after Cambodia. The word "win" was taboo, of course—"end" was the verb to be used in connection with the war. But the possibility of a U.S. victory must have crossed North Vietnamese minds, for their own "chance to win" had been effectively blocked. Not until after this thought sank in, over two years later, did the secret talks in Paris begin their trek toward a conclusion.

Henry Kissinger saw his own chance to win on another front: the battle between his National Security Council and William Rogers' State Department. Kissinger had been strongly in favor of the move into Cambodia, Rogers strongly against; afterward, columnists had a field day writing about the difference of opinion between the two "principal advisers" on the effect of the incursion on the Paris negotiations. Kissinger told his White House compatriots that the foreign service establishment was taking advantage of Rogers' vanity by putting out the line that Rogers was being overruled in his efforts to be reasonable in negotiations with the North Vietnamese. "It's all right to have a heavy and a nice guy," Henry grumbled, "like Eisenhower and Dulles, when it's all part of a strategy. The President should be the nice guy—not Rogers. This is not strategy, and it's no way to conduct foreign policy. If this kind of thing keeps up, I'll have to quit."

Henry was pacing around his new ground-level corner office as he said this—he had made the move upstairs, breaking free of the "White House basement" atmosphere of his predecessors—and he saw Bob Haldeman and his assistant, Larry Higby, through the picture window. They came up to the window and mashed their noses against it, peering in at all his secret documents, looking grotesquely funny. Kissinger stopped knocking the Secretary of State long enough to make a face back and say, "I got to get some curtains."

In this book, we will return to the subject of Vietnam as the "high adventure" of summitry began, and examine a thesis that, after Cambodia, Nixon stopped treating Vietnam as a proving-ground necessary for the successful negotiation with Russia and China and began using his negotiations with the Soviet and Chinese Communists to exert intolerable pressure on the North Vietnamese.

At the time of the Cambodian incursion, I drafted speeches and wrote memoranda urging a hard line throughout the Administration; we were all accused of attempting "orchestration," which was exactly what we were doing. On May 5, David Young, Henry Kissinger's personal aide (who later went on to "plumbers" fame), called me to ask a question about a word, since he had been told I had written a dictionary of political slang: "What does the word 'flack' mean?"

Since the young aide of Dr. Kissinger was determined not to give me anything in the way of context, I applied the first law of bureaucratic maneuver and gave him nothing back. "The word 'flak,'" I explained accurately but misleadingly, "is an acronym for the German words *Fleiger*— aircraft, *Abwehr*—defense, *Kanonen*—gunfire. It's a World War II coinage for antiaircraft fire, and has come to mean any heavy criticism." He thanked me and hung up. A moment later, he called back: "Dr. Kissinger says he doesn't need you to teach him German, but a columnist—Joe Kraft—just called him 'an Administration flack' and he wants to know whether he should take offense." With that, I passed along the current definition of "flack"—an apologist or paid proponent—but, to cheer Henry up, added he should not take offense since our relationship with the press was important. When next I saw Henry, he gloomily said, "I better take offense."

We all pursued our flackery for the wisdom of the President's Cambodian decision in our own ways, and I think in a useful cause. My opinions were expressed in an answer to an angry letter from Robert S. Shriver, a student at Phillips Exeter Academy whose uncle was John F. Kennedy, and whose father was destined to be on the ticket against Nixon and Agnew in 1972:

September 2, 1970

Dear Mr. Shriver:

This is a belated response to your letter to the President of May 12. The volume of mail has been quite heavy and we are doing our best to catch up.

Your letter was written in the heat of one of the nation's most difficult moments, and perhaps events over the summer have modified some of your opinions. But let me answer the specific challenges you posed:

1. "What is the point for which you so nonchalantly risked the lives of hundreds of young Americans?"

Cambodia had been invaded by the North Vietnamese. There was only one logical reason for their invasion: they wanted to use that nation as a staging ground for an offensive in the spring of 1971, when most American combat troops would have been withdrawn. The lives of the remaining American support troops would have been vulnerable, along with the civilian population of Saigon, about 30 miles from the frontier.

The point of our Cambodian action was to deny this military advantage to the North Vietnamese, which was done; to capture weapons and supplies that would have been used against us throughout 1970, which was done; and to make it possible for us to continue our program of troop withdrawals without endangering the lives of our men still there, which is what is happening right now.

As the President said when the action began, the point was to save lives. You may consider that statement Orwellian, but the steadily dropping casualty figures since that time prove the point valid. Its ultimate test will come next spring; we believe the remaining U.S. troops in the process of replacement by South Vietnamese will be adequately protected.

We believe it would have been nonchalant to the point of recklessness to have left our men exposed to attack from a close-in flank.

You probably differ. But consider the consequences of the President or your being wrong. If the President were wrong, he would have lowered casualties only slightly in the long run at a cost of considerable angry division at home. If you had the decision to make and were wrong, you would have had to accept responsibility for not thwarting an attack that might well have cost many thousands of American lives. Your "downside risk" was far greater.

2. "Are you not yet convinced that a military victory in the Vietnamese war is impossible?"

If we were seeking a military solution, we would be the first nation in history to be doing so by steadily withdrawing its troops. Since President Nixon took office, the pattern of escalation has been reversed. 165,000 troops will have been brought home by next month, with an additional 100,000 scheduled by mid-April, and reduction of U.S. troop strength in other Asian nations is in process. These are not the actions of a nation going all-out for victory in the field. These are the actions of a nation ready and willing to negotiate, while turning the defense of South Vietnam back to the South Vietnamese.

A military solution is not in the cards; our Cambodian action was taken to make sure that the North Vietnamese did not achieve a military solution of their own.

3. "You did not consult with the Congress, which is the body that actually represents the American people."

This presupposes that the Cambodian action was a change in the national policy, toward—rather than away from—a greater involvement in Southeast Asia. But the past three months have shown that Cambodia was a military action taken to further the stated policy of the Administration, which was the overwhelming support of the Congress: to turn the war, and hopefully the peace, over to the people of South Vietnam. The action was limited in time and space; our troops got in and got out; the element of surprise helped to make it a success; the President acted within his authority as Commander in Chief.

The limits of Presidential power should always be a subject of debate. Personally, I think Lincoln overstepped the bounds by suspending habeas corpus, and FDR reached too far in trying to pack the Supreme Court. In this case, it is my own opinion that the President acted well within the limits of his power, and with ample precedent.

I hope, however, that you are not raising a Constitutional point to justify another cause. What if, to take an extreme example, some future Congress declared war over a President's protests? Would you then support the prerogatives of the Commander in Chief, and hold that he "actually" represents the people? I am not raising this unlikely possibility to be argumentative, but to challenge the basis of your position. As a Constitutional question, however, I assume the constant tension among the three branches of Government was intentionally built into our system by its framers. If only Congress were intended to represent the people, we would have a Prime Minister and not go through the process of electing Presidents.

Your primary point, I think, is that the people are not represented in decisions of this kind. Since a majority of the people did support the President in this decision, I take it that you mean a minority did not get fair representation. That's an interesting point: is a minority "represented" when its views are not followed? I believe it can be, if you take representation to mean a voice commensurate with the size of a constituency.

Your voice is not only articulated, but it is heard; it is not only heard, but it is listened to. An elected leadership owes that voice both respect and attention, but if the leadership felt constrained to follow it we would invite a tyranny of the minority. Government "by consent of the governed" can never be taken to mean "by assent of 100 per cent of the governed," or we would be paralyzed by 200 million potential vetoes.

One reason for the Heard Report and the Scranton Commission was to make certain that a minority viewpoint—in this case that of many of those on campus—was publicly aired, and carefully considered in the highest councils of Government. In addition, the President has had meetings with student leaders; younger members of his own staff have been visiting campuses; and White House staffers have been meeting here with student groups. No other group representing 4 per cent of the public has had greater access to decision-makers, and it has been good for all of us.

5. "Sure you want to get re-elected in 1972 but I don't think it is your God-given right to risk the lives of members of my generation to further your political aims."

I like to think you were only letting off steam on this point. Do you really believe that this President, or any President, would deliberately prolong a war, or enter a war, or fail to end a war as speedily as humanly possible—just to stay in office? Do you buy Kenneth O'Donnell's theory that President Kennedy refrained from withdrawing American troops from Vietnam in 1963 because he was afraid of the political repercussions, and planned to withdraw them only after he was re-elected? I don't think it is right to libel the motives of any President, dead or alive, in order to let off steam or to gain publicity or for any other reason. Sure you have the right to do so—the Constitution-given right—but does it do you, or the President, or the nation any good for you to do it?

How do you feel when students who oppose the draft are accused of cowardice? That's hitting below the belt, right? How is that sort of low blow any different from attributing a decision that affects men's lives to a lust for votes? Certainly a man in public life has to expect more savage attacks than a man on campus, but how high do you want to fly the double standard?

One practical note: this President is pledged to end the war, and has announced that he expects to be held accountable at the polls if he does not. The path of political expediency would be to cop out, not cop in.

6. "I hoped for a president who would show what we call *guts*. My uncle wrote a book called *Profiles in Courage*. I was hoping you would follow this example."

A few of us here, too, have read that book, and commend to you this central passage:

> "The voters selected us, in short, because they had confidence in our judgment and our ability to exercise that judgment from a position where we could determine what were their own best interests, as a part of the nation's interests. This may mean that we must on occasion lead, inform, correct and sometimes even ignore constituent opinion, if we are to exercise fully that judgment for which we were elected. But acting without selfish motive or private bias, those who follow the dictates of an intelligent conscience are not aristocrats, demagogues, eccentrics or callous politicians insensitive to the feelings of the public. They expect—and not without considerable trepidation—their constituents to be the final judges of the wisdom of their course; but they have the faith that those constituents—today, tomorrow or even in another generation—will at least respect the principles that motivated their independent stand."

The President appreciates your writing to him, and in another

8-8-69

PLATE 5. An Elliot Richardson doodle.

PLATE 6. In the briefing book for a press conference held May 8, 1970, President Nixon wrote these notes in anticipation of a question about the McGovern-Hatfield "amendment to end the war."

For these reasons, I trust the Senate will reject this

ill-advised Amendment by a visible and unmistakable margin.

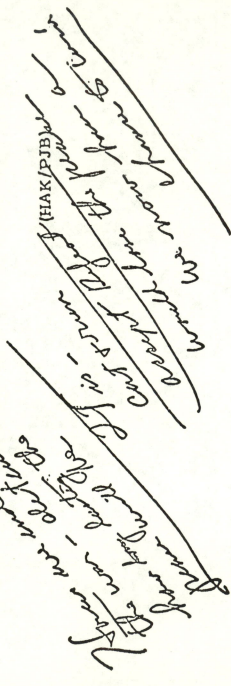

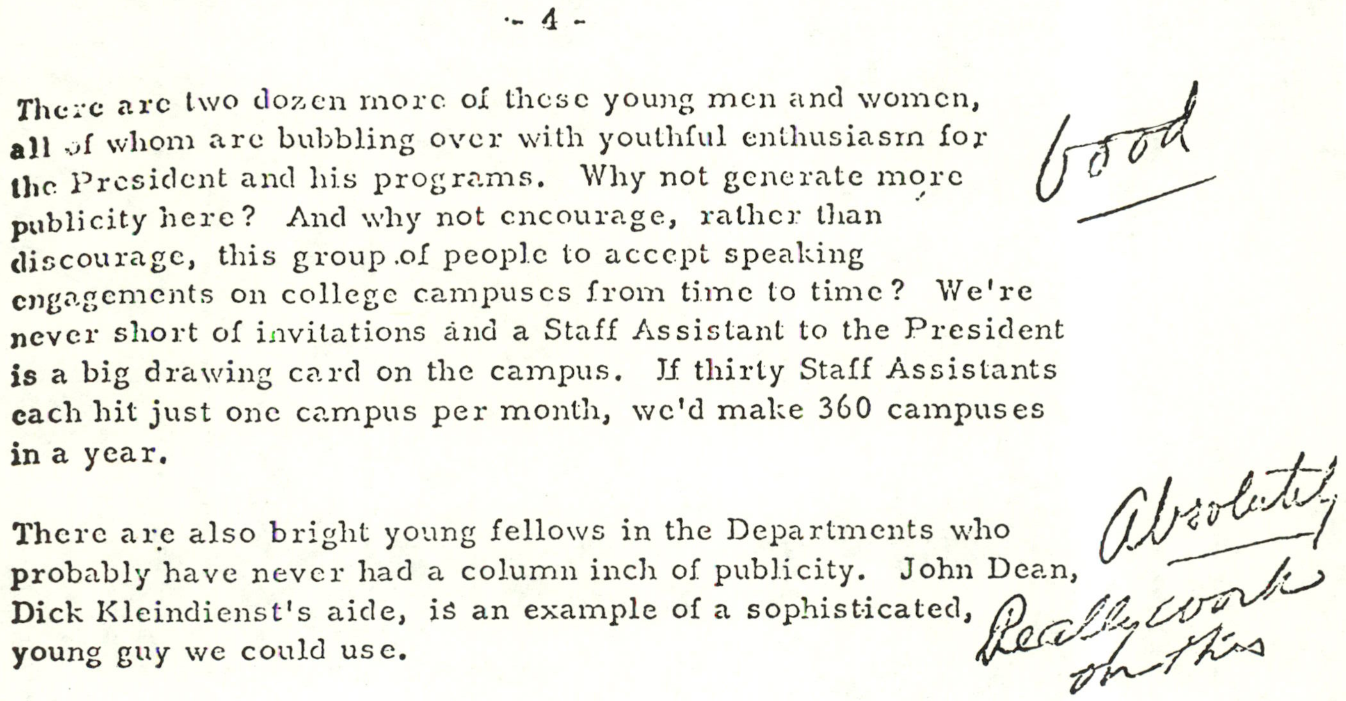

There are two dozen more of these young men and women, all of whom are bubbling over with youthful enthusiasm for the President and his programs. Why not generate more publicity here? And why not encourage, rather than discourage, this group of people to accept speaking engagements on college campuses from time to time? We're never short of invitations and a Staff Assistant to the President is a big drawing card on the campus. If thirty Staff Assistants each hit just one campus per month, we'd make 360 campuses in a year.

There are also bright young fellows in the Departments who probably have never had a column inch of publicity. John Dean, Dick Kleindienst's aide, is an example of a sophisticated, young guy we could use.

Good ___

Absolutely ___
Really work on this

PLATE 7. H. R. Haldeman writes his answer on a memo to him from Jeb Magruder — and signs his political death warrant.

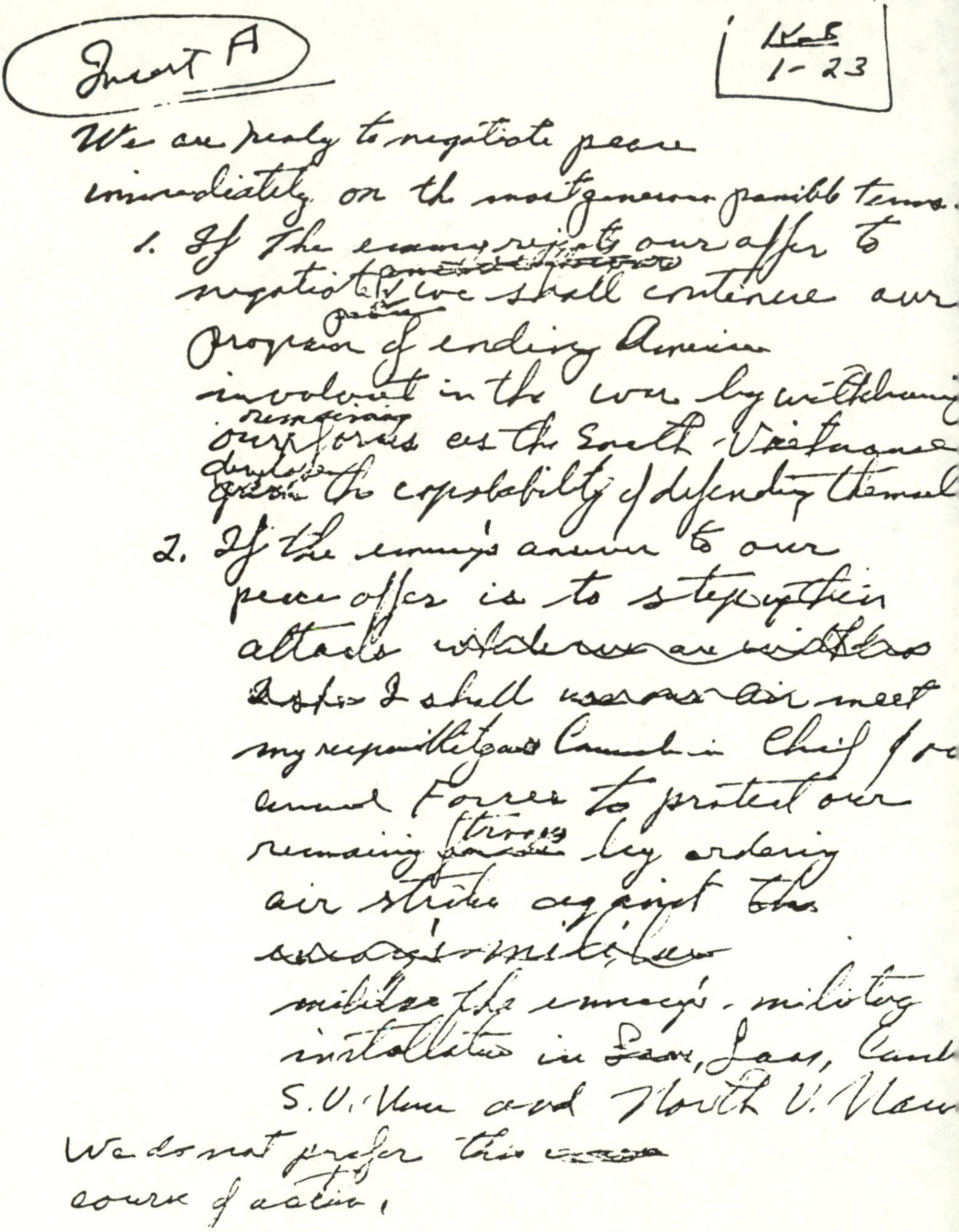

Insert A

LKE
1-23

We are ready to negotiate peace immediately on the most generous possible terms.

1. If the enemy rejects our offer to negotiate, we shall continue our program of ending American involvement in the war by withdrawing our forces as the South Vietnamese given the capability of defending themselves

2. If the enemy's answer to our peace offer is to step up their attacks wherever an withdraws after I shall meet my responsibility as Commander in Chief of our armed forces to protect our remaining forces by ordering air strikes against the enemy's military installations in Laos, and S. Vietnam and North Vietnam

We do not prefer this course of action.

PLATE 8. President Nixon's tentative insert in a Vietnam speech, January 25, 1972.

sense, appreciates your point of view. I have gone on at length here, with no patronizing thoughts of pulled punches, and hope you will read this in the constructive and responsive spirit in which it was written. I hope to hear from you again.

Sincerely,

William L. Safire
Special Assistant to
The President

8. THE NIGHT AT THE LINCOLN MEMORIAL

The strangest, most impulsive, and perhaps most revealing night of Nixon's Presidency took place May 9, 1970.

That week, it seemed, the country was going through an unprecedented agony in the aftermath of the decision to "clean out the sanctuaries" in Cambodia.

The decision presented difficulty enough in rallying public opinion, but, as we have seen, the speech that announced the move appeared to fling down a gauntlet, containing rhetoric that enabled critics to claim that the clock had been turned back to the mid-Sixties. There was also a note sure to infuriate Nixon's natural anti-constituency ("This may make me a one-term President"). Though it was a speech written by Nixon (and Patrick Buchanan), it was not a typical Nixon speech. No hope was offered opponents, no ambiguous language was there that could be used in moderating interpretation.

Then came the unforeseeable tragedy at Kent State where National Guardsmen (frightened kids with guns) shot and killed four students (angry kids without guns) and the silent scream of the girl in the photograph bending over a crumpled body could be felt across the land.

I had been watching the President's low-keyed, calming press conference in a hotel room in Atlanta. Nixon had been scheduled to dedicate the Stone Mountain Memorial the next day but had sent Vice President Agnew in his place. The monument is a huge sculpture carved into the granite face of a mountain, similar to Mount Rushmore, but celebrating Confederate heroes: Robert E. Lee, Jefferson Davis, and Stonewall Jackson. The President and I had worked on his speech for the occasion; he liked the result and only reluctantly turned it over to the VP; I went along to watch.

In those days, relatively few staffers thought to call up the President after a television appearance. I called the White House about 11 P.M., left word, and received a call back in a few minutes. The President was in an odd mood—like the night of the Miami acceptance speech—keyed up and relaxed at the same time, too exhausted to sleep, rambling in his remarks, and prone to take you into his confidence. When he so obviously felt like talking, I was under no pressure to make my point succinctly; it was like talking to a different man in a different job.

"All this business up here, it'll work out okay," the President said. "If the crazies try anything, we'll clobber them—relax, whenever I say anything like that, it drives people up the wall, I know. The country's been through a terrible experience this week. We've got to do the right thing, and we will.

"In Cambodia, we had to give an important answer to an important challenge. Oh, it's easy to flyspeck it, and they will, but you've got to do the right thing. We're trying all we can to bring this war to an end, but what's right is right. What are you doing in Atlanta?"

When I reminded him, he said, "You know, my father's grandfather is buried down there. My father's father was born after his father was killed in the Civil War.

"That's a good speech Agnew is giving down there," he said. "I wrote it myself." Puzzled, I looked into the phone. The President chuckled, "You helped. You know, I believe in all this—my mother's grandfather ran an underground railroad. When I was a kid, it was easy to hate Robert E. Lee and Davis and Jackson. For 115 years, most Americans have been taught that all those guys down South were sons of bitches. But Robert E. Lee was the greatest general we ever had, and Jackson the greatest division commander. Davis was not to be compared to Lincoln, but he was a good man.

"In this speech I was trying to show how we are one people. I'm the goddamndest desegregationist there is, but it has to be done the right way. We mustn't ever give any indication that we don't care about the South, about their feelings. We've got to care.

"This Southern Strategy stuff—all we're doing is treating the South with the same respect as the North. But your friends in New York won't see it that way."

This last dig at the liberal establishment was delivered in good humor, without rancor. He went on easily about a variety of subjects ("I had to make a tough statement for Israel myself, the State Department would never do it") and I had the impression he was walking around a point that was worrying him.

"On the Agnew speech tomorrow," he said finally, "I hope to hell he doesn't hit the students." I assured him the Vice President would not. "Thank God. You're a nice guy, Safire, now get to work, goddammit."

He continued talking on the telephone for about an hour to people who had called in. The telephone log for that night makes interesting reading:

TELEPHONE LOG
NIGHT OF MAY 8–9, 1970

9:22 P.M.	Dr. Henry Kissinger
10:35 P.M.	Rose Mary Woods
10:35 P.M.	Tricia Nixon
10:35 P.M.	Secy. William Rogers
10:37 P.M.	Dr. Henry Kissinger
10:37 P.M.	H. R. Haldeman
10:39 P.M.	Mrs. Nixon
10:50 P.M.	Dr. Norman Vincent Peale
10:56 P.M.	Secy. John Volpe
10:59 P.M.	Cong. L. H. Fountain
11:00 P.M.	Hobart Lewis
11:00 P.M.	William Safire
11:07 P.M.	Secy. George Shultz
11:11 P.M.	Secy. Melvin Laird
11:11 P.M.	Dr. Henry Kissinger
11:12 P.M.	The Rev. Billy Graham
11:21 P.M.	John Ehrlichman
11:26 P.M.	H. R. Haldeman
11:28 P.M.	Secy. Walter Hickel
11:31 P.M.	Rose Mary Woods
11:31 P.M.	B. Rebozo
11:38 P.M.	Dr. Daniel P. Moynihan
11:40 P.M.	Cong. Jos. Monaghan
11:47 P.M.	H. R. Haldeman
11:50 P.M.	Cliff Miller
12:03 A.M.	Rose Mary Woods
12:18 A.M.	H. R. Haldeman
12:20 A.M.	H. R. Haldeman
12:24 A.M.	Dr. Henry Kissinger
12:29 A.M.	U. Secy. V. Alexis Johnson
12:33 A.M.	Dr. Henry Kissinger
12:46 A.M.	H. R. Haldeman
12:47 A.M.	Ron Ziegler
12:48 A.M.	Patrick Buchanan
12:48 A.M.	Dr. Henry Kissinger
12:58 A.M.	Gov. Nelson Rockefeller
1:07 A.M.	Herb Klein
1:13 A.M.	Nancy Dickerson
1:15 A.M.	Ron Ziegler
1:22 A.M.	Helen Thomas, UPI
1:26 A.M.	B. Rebozo
1:29 A.M.	Atty. Gen. John Mitchell
1:31 A.M.	Gov. Thomas Dewey
1:41 A.M.	H. R. Haldeman
1:51 A.M.	Rose Mary Woods
1:55 A.M.	Dr. Henry Kissinger
3:24 A.M.	Paul Keyes
3:38 A.M.	Dr. Henry Kissinger
3:47 A.M.	Ron Ziegler
3:50 A.M.	Helen Thomas
4:22 A.M.	Manolo Sanchez

He finished on the telephone at two-fifteen and went to bed. He "slept soundly until shortly after four o'clock," as he later put it—actually, it was three-fifteen—and went into the Lincoln Sitting Room off his bedroom. He put a record on the turntable: Rachmaninoff's First Piano Concerto, Eugene Ormandy conducting the Philadelphia Orchestra, Philippe Entremont soloist. Manolo Sanchez, his valet, heard the music and soon appeared in a bathrobe to ask if the President wanted anything.

The President, standing at the window looking at the small groups of students beginning to gather on the grounds of the Washington Monument said no. Then he asked, "Have you ever been to the Lincoln Memorial at night?"

Sanchez said no. "Get your clothes on, we'll go." They dressed; at four thirty-five they went out on the South Lawn of the White House, facing the Ellipse and Washington Monument.

Egil ("Bud") Krogh, who worked for the Domestic Council on matters affecting the Department of Justice, was at a Secret Service Command Post in the Peace Corps' building when he heard the loudspeaker squawk: "Searchlight is on the lawn." Moments later: "Searchlight has asked for a car." Krogh asked the Signal operator to awaken John Ehrlichman at home, then told his boss that the President was about to go out. Ehrlichman suggested Krogh go over to the White House lawn, introduce himself, and ask if he could be of assistance. Krogh arrived too late at the lawn and followed the President to the Lincoln Memorial.

The President, who dictated a diary note later that he had never seen the Secret Service so "petrified with apprehension," had insisted when he ordered the car that nobody on his staff or in the press be informed of his plans. When Krogh, and later Ron Ziegler, showed up at the Lincoln Memorial, Nixon assumed with some irritation that they had disobeyed his instructions. In fact, they had not; Krogh had overheard the flash.

The President and Manolo got out of the car and walked up the long flight of steps toward the Memorial. Along with the inscription over the Tomb of the Unknown Soldier, the President said in his diary the next day, the inscription on the Lincoln Memorial is the most unforgettable: "In this temple, as in the hearts of the people for whom he saved the Union, the memory of Abraham Lincoln is enshrined forever."

After looking at the Gettysburg and Second Inaugural words on the walls, the President walked over to a group of about eight students, all men, half from upstate New York. He asked the usual questions about where they were from and how old they were, what they were studying, and said he hoped they would take in some of the other memorials while they were in Washington, though this was his favorite. He said he hadn't been at the Lincoln Memorial at night for ten years, but he'd woken up early after his press conference and wanted Manolo to see it.

The group grew to about twenty-five. A Krogh memo for the President's file described the scene: "It was very quiet, even hushed, and the President was speaking in a very low, conversational tone to the students, really in with them, not out in front talking to them. He asked one girl where she was from and she replied, Los Altos, California. He then gestured about the hills around the town and indicated that he knew about it. The students were all very quiet, dressed in old blue jeans, some army jackets with wild, outlandish hairdos. I asked one of the girls if any of them had had some sleep and she said no. Many of them indicated that they had just come to town and didn't know where they could sleep.

"I turned around," wrote Krogh, "and looked out from the Memorial and saw that the Washington Monument was picking up a soft shade of pink. There was a haziness about the morning, and the profound quiet of the Lincoln Memorial blended beautifully with the changing morning colors."

One of the students told the President they had not been able to hear the press conference because they had been driving to Washington for the demonstration. The President said he was sorry they missed it, because he had tried to explain that his goals in Vietnam were the same as their own —to stop the killing and end the war. Not to get into Cambodia, but to get out of Vietnam. This was met with silence.

The President said he realized that most of them would not agree but that he hoped that they would not allow disagreement on that issue to lead them to fail to give him a hearing on other issues. He particularly hoped that their hatred of the war would not turn into a hatred of our whole system. "I know that probably most of you think I'm an S.O.B., but I want you to know that I understand just how you feel."

He recalled that when he left law school, just before he was married, how excited he was when he listened on the radio to Neville Chamberlain's return from Munich with "peace in our time."

"I had so little in those days," the President recalled he told the group of students, "that the prospect of going into the service was almost unbearable, and I felt the United States' staying out of any kind of a conflict was worth paying any price whatever." As a Quaker, he was close at the time to being a pacifist, and when he read Winston's all-out criticism of Chamberlain, "I thought Churchill was a madman." In retrospect, he said, he knew he was wrong. Chamberlain was a good man, but Churchill was a wiser one, even though there was a time when Churchill was extremely unpopular because of his "antipeace" stand.

Nixon then tried to move the conversation into areas where he could draw the students out. Travel was a good subject to start with. When one of the young men said he couldn't afford to travel, the President said that's what he thought when he was young, but that he borrowed the money and took a trip to Mexico and to Central America with his wife. "If you wait until you can afford it, you'll be too old to enjoy it." He urged them to start with the United States, particularly the West, and that got him talking about Indians. "What we have done with the American Indians is in its way just as bad as what we imposed on Negroes. We took a proud and independent race and virtually destroyed them. We have to find ways to bring them back into decent lives in this country."

The President expressed concern to the students—all white—about the way that blacks are separating from whites on college campuses. "You must find a way to communicate with the blacks in your universities."

Talking to the girl from Los Altos, California, he moved the conversation to the environment. Right below where he lived in California, he recounted, there was a fine surfing beach, denied to public use because it was Marine Corps property. He had turned this into a public beach—one example of his campaign to put Government property to better uses than military. Most of the group nodded in approval.

He then said that it was one of his great hopes that during his Administration "the great mainland of China would be opened up so that we could know the seven hundred million people who live in China and who are one of the most remarkable people on earth." Another nod of approval. He surveyed India, "terribly poor, but with a history and philosophical background and a mystique which we should try to understand, Malaysia, you're right, we do have a Peace Corps there," and the Soviet Union.

When a girl asked what Moscow was like, the President replied, "Gray. If you really want to know Russia, its exciting variety and history, you must go to Leningrad." The people were really more outgoing there, he said, since they were not so much under the domination of the central government. While talking about cities, he commended to them Prague and Warsaw; to an architectural student he suggested Novosibirsk, a raw, new city in the heart of Siberia, and Samarkand, where the people were Asians. One of the students wanted to know if she could get a visa to such cities; the President said he was sure they could and if they contacted his office he would help out. That got a quick chuckle.

What really mattered, said the President, coming to the point he wanted to leave with them, was not so much the architecture of the cities, or the air pollution, or other material concerns. Travel, he felt, brought them in contact with the character of a people. The Haitians, for example, while poor, had a dignity and grace that he found moving enough to want to return. The people are the important thing, he said, and it is important that the students should not become alienated from the people of their own country, with their great variety and character.

The group had grown and now included some older and less awe-struck members. One said, "I hope you realize that we are willing to die for what we believe in."

"Certainly, I realize that," the President said. "Do you realize that many of us, when we were your age, were also willing to die for what we believed in, and are willing to do so today? The point is that we are trying to build a world in which you will not have to die for what you believe in." This got across, but when he began to point out how strategic arms limitation talks were progressing, he could see he was losing their attention. A girl, in a kind of delayed reaction to what had been said earlier, said that she was not interested in what Prague looked like, that she was more interested in what kind of life we build in the United States.

Nixon countered by pointing out that the purpose of discussing Prague and other places was not to discuss places but people. In the next twenty-five years, with the world getting smaller, he said, it was important that Americans know and understand people all over the world, beginning with the people in our own country.

He tried again to make his central point: "I know the great emphasis that is currently being put on the environment—the necessity to have clear air, clean water, clean streets." The President quickly reviewed his commitment to environmental programs. "But you must remember that something that is completely clean can also be completely sterile and without spirit. What we must all think about is why we are here, what are those elements of the spirit that really matter. Honestly, I don't have the answer, but I know that young people today are searching for the answer just as I was searching forty years ago. But I want to be sure all of you realize that ending the war and cleaning up the streets and air and water is not going to solve the spiritual hunger that all of us have—which has been the great mystery of life from the beginning of time."

Through the last twenty minutes of conversation, Manolo had come up several times to murmur that the President had a telephone call in his car; as the crowd began to mount, the Secret Service were getting even more concerned, and were especially worried about the rally leadership getting wind of the visit. The President shook hands, said he had to go, and walked down the steps into the dawn.

Krogh, in his memo for the President's record, picks up the story: "As we walked down the steps from the Memorial, a young man with wild, shaggy hair and a red beard darted down the steps to our left taking pictures of the President as we proceeded down. When we got to the bottom of the steps, the President motioned him over, and he came rather happily not knowing quite what to expect. The President asked him to hand his camera to Dr. Walter Tkach, which he did, and Dr. Tkach took a picture of the President and the young man on the third or fourth step up from the bottom by the street. The President then spent some time talking to the man, and you could see by the proximity of the President to each person that he talked to that there was a deep effort to reach out and into the young people he was seeing. Another small group formed about him at the base of the Memorial. A row of young girls ranging from 21 to 24, a couple from Syracuse University, were approached by him. He asked each one where she was from, and to one of the girls when she said she was 24, the President said, 'That's Tricia's age.' He said this with a smile and she smiled back at him. When one of them answered that she was from Syracuse University, the President responded that he had been there once. He talked briefly about the Syracuse football team."

The photographer with the red beard "seemed to be quite delighted," the President noted later, "it was, in fact, the broadest smile that I saw on the entire visit." Hoping he would pass the word along, the President reprised his main theme. "I know you came a long way for this event. I know you are terribly frustrated and angry about our policy and opposed to it.

But I just hope your opposition doesn't turn into a blind hatred of the country. This is a great country, with all of its faults, and if you have any doubt about it, go down to the passport office. You won't see many people lining up to get out of the country—but abroad, you will see a number lining up to get in."

In the car, the President asked Sanchez if he had ever visited the Capitol. He had not. (If he had, the President would have said "but never at dawn.") As they headed up Constitution Avenue, a couple of demonstrators in a white Volvo tried to keep pace, zooming alongside the car following the Presidential automobile and causing more Secret Service consternation.

They went into the Senate through the entrance under the steps. The President, with Sanchez, took the elevator to the Senate Chamber. The door was locked, which was not surprising at that early hour; the President and Manolo, accompanied by Dr. Tkach, Krogh, and the Secret Service agents walked toward the House side of the Capitol, looking at the statues in the Rotunda under the Capitol dome. The President tried another door—to the office he had used as Vice President in the Fifties—but it too was locked. A cleaning woman was sweeping up in the Rotunda; the President asked her what time she had to begin working, listened to her answer, shook his head, and commented that it seemed awfully early. Then a Secret Service agent, Robert Taylor, asked her if she had any keys, which she did not; shaking her head, she watched the group move on.

In the House section of the Capitol, they ran into a custodian named Frazer, who got over his surprise in a hurry and informed the President that he and Nixon had come to the Congress the same year, 1947, when Frazer joined up as a page for Charles Halleck. Agent Taylor asked if the custodian could go and find a key to the House chamber. For five minutes everybody stood around, and Frazer came back to let them in.

President Nixon showed Manolo Sanchez the empty House chamber in some detail, including the bullet holes caused a generation ago by Puerto Rican zealots. The President found the place where he had sat as a House member in the Forties, and tried it for size. He was pleased he still fit in the chair. He took Sanchez down front and brought him up to the Speaker's Chair, sat him down in it. The President went down to the first row, sat down, told Manolo to go ahead and make a speech. Manolo made a few appropriate remarks about being proud to be an American citizen; the President, his party, and the cleaning women applauded.

They left to look for a place to have breakfast but nothing was open in the House. Three Negro cleaning women, all of whom had met the President when he was Vice President, came up to say farewell. One, Mrs. Carrie Moore, asked him to sign her Bible. She was a striking woman, aged and dignified; the President signed it, saying he was glad to see that she carried her Bible with her, but "the trouble is that most of us these days don't read it enough." She replied solemnly, "Mr. President, I read it all the time." The President stood there a moment, holding her hand, reminded of something, and then was impelled to say, "You know, my mother was a saint. She died two years ago. She was a saint." There was a long pause. With a lump in his throat, the President squeezed her hand. "You be a saint too." "I'll try, Mr. President."

On the way out, the President said to the head of the Secret Service detail that he'd like to eat breakfast at a restaurant on Connecticut Avenue. At 6:40 A.M. he was still unwilling to re-enter the White House routine. Outside the Capitol, they were joined by Bob Haldeman, Ron Ziegler, and Dwight Chapin and went to the Rib Room of the Mayflower Hotel, where the President ordered corned beef hash with a poached egg on it, the first time he'd had that in five years. ("The last time I had this was on a train.") It was also the first time since he had been President that he went to a Washington restaurant. After breakfast, he wanted to walk back to the White House, but the Secret Service dissuaded him. "As we drove away from the restaurant," the President noted later, "eight to ten of the waitresses all stood at the door, outside on the street, and waved goodbye." He waved back.

The President re-entered the White House at 7:30 A.M.—the foray had been about three hours—and was still keyed up. Ron Ziegler had begun to brief the first of the reporters to arrive, Garrett Horner of the Washington *Star*, but the President came into the press secretary's office to tell Horner about the night's activities himself. "I said to them, 'Sure, you came here to demonstrate and shout your slogans on the Ellipse. That's all right. Just keep it peaceful. Remember,' I said, 'I feel just as deeply about this as you do.'" When Horner asked if he planned to have student leaders come into the White House, he replied, "The one thing I don't want is to bring them in here and exploit them. I think this has been far more useful. There were no TV cameras, no press. They did not feel the awesome power of the White House. I was trying to relate to them in a way they could feel that I understood their problems."

Later that morning Ziegler and Horner briefed the rest of the White House press corps on what was termed "the sunrise visit." Because Horner and Ziegler had to report secondhand on what the President reported to them about the visit, it was a disjointed and inadequate briefing. From the reporters' point of view, it was hard to get a handle on the story: Was the President pulling some kind of stunt? Wasn't this kind of out of character for him? Why wasn't the visit open for full press coverage?

Of course, reporters went out looking for students who had been there. The one most frequently quoted was a Syracuse University sophomore, one of the girls the President had talked to briefly on his way to the car: "I hope it was because he was tired," the girl was quoted as saying, "but most of what he was saying was absurd. Here we had come from a university that's completely uptight—on strike—and when we told him where we were from, he talked about the football team."

The girl was being truthful enough—she had not been at the extended talk inside the Memorial, and she felt the few words she had heard were patronizing. The reporters were not deliberately slanting the reaction story —she happened to be the one they found who was around the scene, and all the others had scattered. But the result—especially after these reactions were reported on the evening television news programs—was that the President, a few days after calling some students who set fire to campuses "bums," had compounded his error by talking condescendingly about trivial matters like football or visiting foreign cities with students who had come in seriousness to protest about the war.

From a public relations point of view, then, the visit to the Lincoln Memorial was a flop. Had the visit been planned with public relations in mind, it might have been a success.

As the President pointed out to Haldeman later, he could have made sure some cameras were there, and engaged in a spirited dialogue with the students about why we were in Cambodia, why we have not ended the war sooner, the morality of the war, a subject and a format that would have had him at a distinct advantage and one that certainly would have made more news.

But he had not preplanned the visit. He had the impulse to get out and mingle with some young people who were frightened and worried about their country. When he got to them, most of them seemed the kind of lower-middle-class kids he had grown up with, and it occurred to him that this was probably the only time any of them would talk to a President of the United States. They could see him on television as often as they liked discussing the subjects that brought them to Washington, but here was a chance, as he put it, "to try to lift them a bit out of the miserable intellectual wasteland in which they now wander aimlessly around."

So he veered away from making debating points, and instead of using the twenty-five or thirty students there in the Memorial as a device for talking to all students across the United States, he talked only to the students who were there. To a few individuals, he tried to get across something of what a President should mean to people, as expressed in the inscription on the Lincoln Memorial.

He didn't have a gimmick. He did not stage a "confrontation" with full coverage and the result never in doubt. He was their President, he was there with them, he did not have horns, he treated them with respect, he was not going to destroy their freedom or their country. His presence there was not going to reassure millions of students or influence a single commentator, but there was something to be said for his being there, with a few people, at that moment. It was good for him, good for them, good for the nation.

Was there an ulterior motive? If there had been one, it would have gone this way: (1) The press pressure was on for the President to meet with a delegation of the students, to contrast his attitude of concern in 1970 to his attitude of studied indifference in 1969, when he pointedly watched television football during the demonstrations. (2) If he were to meet with students, the only thing the leaders could do to satisfy their constituencies would be to denounce him to his face and then use the White House press room as a TV forum to tell the nation how they told off the President. (3) Therefore, the smartest thing the President could do in that situation would be to go over the heads of the rally leaders, go out and see the average protester on hallowed ground like the Lincoln Memorial, and be able to avert subsequent confrontations with publicity-hip demonstrators by saying he met the students already. He could even take the highhanded position of not wanting to exploit the young people by putting them on display.

Frankly, that makes a good "game plan"—I wish I'd recommended it. But the fact is, nobody did. If that had been in the President's mind, it would have been given some modicum of planning to ensure proper coverage. And certainly Haldeman would have known about it—there were no secrets from him. No, there is no explaining away Nixon's night at the Memorial as a devious plot. On the contrary, it was an impetuous act of compassion that—ironically—lack of planning made appear unconvincing.

After the visit was treated by the papers as an example of Nixon's condescension and insensitivity, he was asked by Haldeman if it would not have been better to have centered a televised discussion on what his Administration was doing to meet student concerns on the draft, on the war, on the environment. "I really wonder, in the long run," Haldeman says the President replied, "if this is all the legacy we want to leave. If it is, then perhaps we should do our job as expeditiously as we can, and get out. If the news gimmicks are all that count, if the big promises are the only thing that means anything anymore, then maybe we should leave the responsibilities of the government to the true materialists, the socialists and totalitarians, who talk idealism but rule ruthlessly without any regard to individual considerations—the respect for personality that I tried to emphasize in my dialogue with the students."

All in all, it was one strange night for Richard Nixon. He broke out of the cocoon that separates the President from the rest of humanity for three hours, enjoyed a taste of real life and the bitter aftertaste. He spoke to a small and unrepresentative sampling of today's youth, revisited the scene of his own political youth in the House chamber, reacted poignantly to a memory of his early youth and a Bible-carrying mother, and let his natural impulses carry him along in the aftermath of crisis.

In so doing, Nixon deeply inspired a young man who had never seen him up close before—"Bud" Krogh—who, as head of a special investigating unit that called itself "the plumbers," followed orders in a way that led him to the break-in of Daniel Ellsberg's psychiatrist's office. From his close observation of Nixon on his visit to the Lincoln Memorial, Krogh regarded the President as a compassionate and profoundly misunderstood man, harboring no ill will to peaceful demonstrators. The thirty-year-old aide to John Ehrlichman would then have done practically anything the President asked him to do.

PART FOUR

LOWERED VOICES

Pat Moynihan had it right at the first meeting of the staff, back at the Pierre Hotel during the interregnum: "If you cannot do what you set out to do in the first couple of years, forget it."

With Dr. Arthur Burns as the first and best counselor to the President in the White House, taking a careful approach to policy issues, reminding the rest of the staff of the promises that had been made throughout the campaign, trying to protect the President from the effects of sloppy staff work; with Moynihan, Bob Finch, and Donald Rumsfeld pushing for new ideas and progressive goals; and with George Shultz emerging as the creative synthesizer, the man who could conjure up a surprisingly different way to an agreed-upon objective; with a couple of anonymous men, Haldeman and Ehrlichman, getting better known as doers who took as their mission—as Nixon said—"to break all the china in the White House if you have to," the domestic side of the Nixon Administration was more exciting than its conservative, gray visage showed.

Certain targets of opportunity presented themselves, from tax reform to environmental control, where cresting public opinion and Congressional willingness made "bold new initiatives" easy. With all rhetorical zeal, John Mitchell—the "new Attorney General" which Nixon had promised during the campaign—scowled at evildoers, proposed new immunity statutes to make it easier for prosecutors to "get at the higher-ups," toughened up the antitrust enforcement (traditional in Republican Administrations), and recommended "strict constructionist" judges, not all good choices. The economy would not be a problem in the first year of the first term, because the big cutbacks in Vietnam spending and the return from the armed forces of a couple million employables were off in the future; the President's decision was to introduce a note of fiscal responsibility and try to hold down inflation.

All this, in a sense, was housekeeping. Important enough, but the kind of action taken by most Administrations, and not what the President and some of his more ambitious advisers had in mind. "Nobody is going to remember us," Nixon liked to tell his aides, "for managing things 10 per cent better."

The great idea—the "New Federalism" as it was called, with a thud—was to reverse the flow of power, which had been steadily (and for a long time properly) moving from the states and localities to the Federal Government in Washington, and to sort out the level of government that could most efficiently respond. Revenue sharing, an old but untried idea, was the centerpiece of this concept, and it would get its start while the Nixon men were fresh and confident.

The other approach to the same idea, less imaginative and "bold" but more immediately important, was to stop the surge in the percentage of the Gross National Product that was dependent on government spending. Every year, the government services grew faster than did the rest of the country's institutions. Though there could be no stopping the growth of government, Nixon felt there could be a slowing of its alarming rate of increase, and ultimately a lessening of the danger of its domination of the private sector. Moreover, the portion of wages that went to taxes on all levels had increased from one fourth a generation ago to one third today, and there seemed nothing to stop the trend toward one half tomorrow. That would be the redistribution of wealth on a grand scale, and old-time liberals could make a case for its advisability, but that was not what the Nixon men saw themselves elected for. On the contrary, the President felt, the only way for individual freedom to flourish and the pervasive feeling of powerlessness to be dispelled was for elected leaders to get the government under control. In dollars-and-cents terms, that meant putting the power to spend discretionary income in the hands of the person who earned it, and not—in Nixon rhetoric—in the hands of the bureaucrats in Washington.

Controlling the government's habit of just getting bigger was a herculean task; special-interest constituencies were everywhere, with good access to the Congress and the press, ready to turn every "downhold" of expenses into an assault on free milk for poor babies. In so many cases, the special-interest cause was good; only in its totality was the cause of Federal care antilibertarian.

In essence, the New Federalism, as we saw it—or the Old Stinginess, as critics saw it—was an attempt to return power: by taking less of the paycheck in taxes, by sharing the revenue decisions with localities, and by slowing Federal dominance of individual lives. It was also the resistance to an opposition Congress that spoke darkly of White House power grabs but was all too anxious to thrust on the President dictatorial powers to control the economy in peacetime.

Nixon was too politic to say it, but he was trying to put personal liberty ahead of social security (we called it putting self-reliance ahead of dependency); but while this was going on, Nixon was secretly putting national security too far ahead of personal liberty. That was one wrenching anomaly, never understood by the men—Haldeman, Mitchell—who were the most powerful voices on the domestic scene at the beginning.

In its heyday of reform, when restoration and renewal were the bywords, the Nixon Administration did much that was original and far-reaching. The "lowered voices" Nixon promised in his Inaugural were necessary after the tumult of the Sixties; the Nixon dignity contrasted well with the Johnson stridency; desegregation went forward more smoothly without the symbolic Appomattoxes that would have stirred resentment; the controversy was there, but more rational, less passionate.

A sharing of power with states and localities began; that was good. The voices were lowered: that, too, was good. Some of the voices were in whispers, however, about ways to keep secrets, and that turned out to be very, very bad, clouding domestic policy's brightest moments in the Nixon years.

1. THE NEW FEDERALISM

Four months into the new Administration, the President sent a number of its members a heavy sheaf of papers with this covering note: "John Gardner's Godkin Lectures express better than anything I have yet read what I hope will serve as the basic philosophy of this Administration. I commend them for your weekend reading."

I didn't wait until the weekend, needing as I did a look at Nixon's basic philosophy like an addict's long-postponed fix. Early in the 1968 campaign, I had taken a crack at some elements of the Nixon political philosophy: a greater emphasis on personal freedom, the decentralization of Federal power, changeover from specific categorical grants to more string-free bloc grants, all answering the new needs of the "new alignment." These were no more than gropings toward some central theme; Nixon had deliberately let it remain fuzzy because a political philosophy often tends to lose votes when articulated.

During the 1968–69 interregnum, Leonard Garment and Ray Price studied a thoughtful memorandum by Richard Goodwin, who had been a Kennedy, Johnson, and McCarthy speechwriter, which later appeared as an article in *The New Yorker* entitled, "Sources of the Public Unhappiness." Goodwin held that all political movements were attempts at the redistribution of power, and pointed to Jefferson's statement: "It is not by the consolidation, or concentration of powers, but by their distribution, that good government is effected." Goodwin urged that "the first task of a new Administration should be to construct institutions with authority and jurisdiction adapted to the policies they are to administer, and to concern itself with reallocating responsibility within the Federal system"—rather than proceed with minor modifications in the programs that existed. "Public unhappiness" was caused by the explosive extension of government and the accompanying growth of an individual's sense of powerlessness.

Gardner, who had been John Kennedy's Secretary of Health, Education and Welfare, attracted Nixon's attention with his welcome warning that nobody had a monopoly on morality: "One of the most corrosive of social delusions," Gardner wrote in his Godkin Lectures, "is the conviction on the part of the individual that he and his kind of people are uniquely faithful to the true American morality but that others who are morally less worthy are bringing the nation down." Like Goodwin, Gardner saw nothing wrong with approaching political philosophy on a problem-solving basis: "The machinery of the society is not working in a fashion that will permit us to solve any of our problems effectively. That reality is supremely boring to most social critics . . . their unwillingness to grapple with these processes defeats them."

Nixon, comfortable with problem-solving and reliant on self-reliance, read Gardner's thesis that "contemporary demoralization stems from a breakdown in the relationship of the individual to society," and was impressed by his emphasis on pluralism; "this means, in practical terms, a concern for the vitality of local leadership, for the strength and autonomy of State and local government, for the vigor and creativity of the private sector."

It was good to see Nixon reading Gardner, subscribing to his ideas enough to circulate them to Cabinet and White House staff with his unqualified endorsement, and not shying away from Gardner's ringing defense of nonviolent dissent. Nixon was undoubtedly influenced by Gardner's "voluntarist" conclusion, not putting all the burden on Washington: "We have recently inaugurated a new President. No matter how gifted he may prove to be, he cannot save us from ourselves." That was the spirit, Nixon thought: self-reliant, affirmative, reformist.

But the new Administration needed more than a spirit or an attitude: Moynihan, Burns, and Shultz were coming up with an array of ideas that often seemed to pull in different directions, solving problems in a way that gave the impression of a zigzag philosophy, or no philosophy at all. Oddly, however, the speechwriters could guess about 85 per cent of the time which way the President would decide on any major domestic decision. That was a clue that his thinking had a pattern, and posed a challenge to explore and express it.

The assignment fell to me:

October 2, 1969

MEMORANDUM FOR BILL SAFIRE

The President noted in the News Summary of September 30 remarks made by Eric Severeid* of CBS from the night before. Severeid, among other things, pointed out that the President's personality and philosophy is beginning to undergo a sharp analysis in Washington—just like what happened to our last President. Few seem aware of the Nixon political philosophy, or

---

* When James Reston saw this years later, his comment was "Don't they know how to spell the names on their own 'enemies list'?" Sev*a*reid is the name.

his vision of America—outside of his hope for domestic tranquility. Severeid noted that Hugh Sidey described policies leaning to the left and appointments leaning to the right, but asked Eric, what will predominate in the end. The President feels that this general subject area of what the President's philosophy is would be worth some work and effort by our PR group. Would you please follow up?

H. R. HALDEMAN

The "PR group"—I could never get the President to stop using that name—was not as Madison Avenue as its name implied. Ray Price, Pat Buchanan, Jim Keogh, Len Garment, Herb Klein, and I were the permanent members in Nixon's first year or so, with others floating casually in and out that year, and we would get together once or twice a week to try to think about issues and projects that did not require a daily deadline.

Haldeman routed the memo to me because I had been struggling with a "New Federalist Paper" ever since the President announced "The New Federalism" (Pat Buchanan's phrase) to a Governors' conference the month before. All I had come up with was a somnolent analysis of "selective decentralization," which was too narrow and programmatic. Strange, fitting a philosophy to the set of deeds, but sometimes that is what has to be done.

The reason why political power had been centralizing all our lives was that local government had been unable to meet the crisis of depression and unwilling to adapt to the revolution in civil rights. And the reason why the opposite trend—decentralization—was now becoming popular was that the central government had shown itself to be notoriously inefficient, even infuriating, in some of its widely advertised programs. Conservatives stood for decentralization out of habit, since it dispersed the loci of power; liberals now embraced it out of desperation, since the big-government way was not getting local problems solved and was bringing liberal goals into disrepute. As a result, the conservative ideology of local control meshed with the liberal desire for a bigger social bang for the buck. But centralization or decentralization was not the main point at all. These were only methods of meeting public needs. Substance—social justice and personal freedom—was more important than form—"the direction of the flow of power."

This much we knew: Power should be permitted to seek the level where the problem can most fairly and expeditiously be handled. "Power to the People" was a slambang slogan; local control and "participatory democracy" were fashionable ideas after forty years of the accretion of power to the central government; and decentralization was certainly the direction Nixon had in mind—most of the time. *But not always.* In the understanding of that "but," the reason for major exceptions, is the idea of the New Federalism.

What, for example, do you do when Daniel P. Moynihan makes the case for cash (intellectually dressed up as an "income strategy")? He held that poor people would have more dignity and freedom if given money from a central source, rather than social services from a local source. To accept the thesis, as Nixon routinely did, that society had to take care of people who were genuinely dependent, is to accept the duty of taking care of them in a way that most respects their personal freedom. That means government must find a way to dispense with welfare snoopers (that's how we characterized a wide variety of well-meaning patronizations) and instead provide poor people with cold cash, or, taking one step backward, at least with stamps that enable them to buy food. And the most efficient and fairest way to do this was the way ol' centralized Social Security did it: with the Federal Government mailing out checks of the same amount to people in the same circumstances.

The result of that kind of welfare reform was more fairness, more personal freedom—but hardly decentralization. It could be conservatized with "work registration" requirements and festooned with anti-cheating strictures, but no matter how you tried to sell it, the heart of the matter was that the best way to solve the welfare mess was to wrench much of it out of state and local hands and provide a national minimum "floor" (which all but Moynihan grimly refused to acknowledge as a "guaranteed minimum income" because it was not guaranteed to the able-bodied). If that be centralization, we murmured defiantly, make the most of it.

The New Federalism, in retrospect, was a necessary sorting-out of Federal aid programs with an eye to tailoring the solution to fit the problem, rather than to a doctrinaire espousal of either a pejorative "Washington knows best" or its opposite, the appealing "all problems should be solved at the grass roots."

In situations where conditions vary locally, and where face-to-face contact between government and public is important, the object was to decentralize: manpower training, urban and rural development, and schooling were the types of action that now needed less of the dead hand of the far-removed Federal bureaucrat. Result: variety, diversity, innovation, local control, hot arguments in the mayor's office, less alienation and less of a feeling of personal powerlessness by the citizen who could not otherwise find the man accountable for his fate.

But in situations that cried out for nationwide action—environmental regulations, health research, welfare payments—that was more than ever the job for central government. We boiled it all down to two sentences in the 1971 State of the Union message: "Whenever it makes the best sense for us to act as a whole nation, the Federal government should and will lead the way. But where State or local governments can better do what needs to be done, let us see that they have the resources to do it there."

So far, so simple—and hard to argue with. But what if a program is best applied locally, and the locality—out of orneriness, prejudice, or nobility —says to hell with it? Or applies it unfairly? Rita Hauser, a New York attorney, commented on my first attempts to write a doctrine without being doctrinaire: "I am not sure you deal adequately with the cliché that government which is closest to the people is the best. Blacks in the South never have felt this, and indeed, have a morbid fear that this Administration intends to return power there to the detriment of blacks." Mrs. Hauser gave an illustration: "Trailers were recently distributed by HUD to victims of the hurricane Camille. Distribution was made locally. The Lawyers Committee for Civil Rights, of which I am on the Executive Group, learned from our local office that no black victims received any trailers. Intervention from Washington alone remedied the situation."

I tried to resolve this in a paper for the President, entitled "New Federalist Paper #1," signing it "Publius." (That was the pseudonym of founding fathers Hamilton, Jay, and Madison for their Federalist Papers, as these revered publicists put out what might now be referred to as "an orchestrated propaganda line" to sell the American Constitution.) It was commented on first by Moynihan and then the President, fixes made, and circulated around the Administration or to anybody outside who asked for a copy. A vigorous rebuttal came from the right by lawyer Tom Charles Huston, writing as "Cato," and the disagreement that bubbled within the Administration on its emerging domestic philosophy may enliven what otherwise would be an especially soporific chapter.

The Publius paper's essence is this: Our purpose is to come to grips with a paradox, which is a need both for national unity and local diversity; a need to establish equality and fairness at the national level and uniqueness and innovation at the local level. Sounds easy, but the conflict built into the paradox has exploded in riots and built unresponsive bureaucracies.

Step one in coming to grips with the unity-diversity paradox is to begin to decentralize administration: to say that barriers previously used to stymie social progress—the former obstacle of "states' rights"—have now become "rights of first refusal." Local authority will now regain the capacity to meet local needs itself, and gain an additional right to Federal financial help—but it has given up the right it once held to neglect the needs of its citizens. Result: "national localism," not much more local power in deciding *what* to do, but considerably more power in deciding *how* to do it so as to fit their differing needs of different communities.

Step two is to decentralize only selectively, remembering that power seeks its own level. The Federal Government has shown itself to be best at collecting and distributing cash and worst at enlisting and distributing services. Local government works best the other way around. On the theory that the ship only exists for the sake of the passengers, decisions about where power should flow must be made on a basis of how best government service can be tailored to individual needs.

Step three is to figure out a way of identifying and resolving basic disputes between the nation as a whole and the individual as a person. There is such a thing as "the national conscience"—what a growing majority of the people think is "only fair"—and this national conscience, on any issue, will probably clash with local conscience somewhere. In the way this clash of conscience is resolved is the test of the New Federalism.

Here we come to the heart of it: If the national conscience ("Dammit, I guess blacks deserve an equal break" or "Dammit, we've got to do something about the smog") rides roughshod over the *local* conscience ("Dammit, that smoggy plant provides jobs for our people"), if it allows no room for adjustment and gradual acceptance, hatred is bred, as the rights and traditions of a local majority are ignored. But if that national conscience knuckles under to local conscience so as to allow the law to be bent out of shape, or national policy to be permanently warped, hatred is also bred, as the rights of a minority are denied.

Today, most Americans assume that fairness in principle still lies in Federal standards and minimums, but that fairness in administration usually lies closest to home. Kennedy was right when he said, "Life is unfair," but there must be ways to keep lessening inequity to make life more fair. The New Federalism seeks to fuse two elements: a greater respect for national conscience by individuals, and more respect for local concerns in the application of that conscience.

Examples were plentiful from welfare (should be centralized for more fairness) to unemployment insurance (best operated at the state level, but states should be pushed into wider coverage and greater benefits) to manpower training (Federal Government should turn administration over to the states as they develop capacity to administer the program).

Revenue sharing, of course, is the most obvious and often cited example of the New Federalist approach, taking the "categorical" grants, which had been doled out by Washington and mother-henned all the way by central government, and changing them to "bloc" grants, dropping specific guidelines so as to let local government direct the money and accept responsibility for its decisions. (Richard Nathan, then of the Budget Bureau and now of Brookings Institution, who understood and developed the New Federalism more clearly and profoundly than anybody else in the Nixon Administration, facetiously proposed calling bloc grants "General Grants" —but quickly withdrew that because it recalled a too-Republican and too-corrupt Administration.) As it turned out, the "general grants"—to the tune of six billion dollars a year—was the most important legislative achievement of the Nixon Administration in terms of New Federal philosophy. In its fairly prosaic way, revenue sharing—the baby of Democrats Walter Heller and Joseph Pechman—represented a genuine revolution in the way decisions are made about the allocation of resources.

Bob Haldeman, stunned at receiving a 10,000-word document on this subject only a couple of days after he asked for it, passed it to John Ehrlichman and Pat Moynihan for their review. Ehrlichman penciled in his changes and Moynihan sent this memo, which not only contains good sense but shows the way he thought and wrote, and why other White House aides found it a pleasure to be in contact with him:

THE WHITE HOUSE
WASHINGTON

October 6, 1969

MEMORANDUM FOR

"PUBLIUS"

You are not only a Patriot, Sir, but a wise Patriot. Who but such a man would have the wit to conceal his identity when addressing himself to the Public Interest.

I am much persuaded, much impressed by National Localism. I very much hope you will get this out, and start the discussion.

I have but two general comments.

First, you cannot avoid the issue of race. You and I may see the New Federalism in the terms you describe, but in the black and/or liberal community—the people who will read the essay— it is seen as a fairly straightforward device to remand the South- ern Negro to the custody of Bull Connor, more or less thereby re- instituting the system of caste oppression which only finally began to break up under the poundings of Federal edicts in the 1960's.

There are answers to this, but you must present them, having first raised the issue. The principal answer, I would think, is that we are striving to overcome the terrible class oppression of the Southern black—and poor white—as an integral part of the New Localism. The Family Assistance Program has the potential to dismantle Southern rural feudalism once and for all—and to do so in a matter of years. (Interesting note: Steve Hess went up to New York to speak to a bunch of telephone executives last week. I asked how it went. He replied they seemed mainly to be trying to gauge the demand for telephones in the black homes of the south once FAP payments start flowing.) Revenue sharing will probably have a somewhat similar effect.

Another point, that probably should be raised, is that we are probably going to have to be more candid with ourselves as to the real effect of the 1960's legislation. Did it transform the South, or did it drive it out of the two party system? I.e. how much effect have we really had on local attitudes? Are they worse now than ever?

My problem here is that I don't really know what "the adminis- tration" thinks about all this. Mostly it doesn't think at all.

Second, I think you should touch on the desirability of maintaining local responsibility for social problems that no one understands. Education is a good example. Almost nothing is known about education. This is a recent discovery, but a fairly solid one. In particular, almost nothing is known about the process whereby children of the poor and disadvantaged can be brought, as a group, to the level of achievement of the non-poor, non-disadvantaged. When problems like this come along, they tend to be pushed upwards in the government hierarchy. (Crime is a similar problem. So far as I can tell, no one in the Department of Justice knows anything much about preventing crime. So far as I know, no one does.) When the higher level of government, having taken on the assignment, predictably fails to perform, all manner of mass paranoia ensues. This is now much in evidence with respect to schools. They are not delivering on their promises. They don't know how. But the public that was promised does not know this. It can only assume deliberate default. Result: as I say, paranoia all round.

You have a genius for formulating such principles. Something to the effect that in the absence of confident knowledge that can be applied nationally, problems should be dealt with on a local basis of instinct and judgment on grounds that the resulting failures are not extrapolated into a default of the social system itself, and also in the hope that the resulting variety of effort might produce that random set of monkeys typing *The Merchant of Venice*. Whereupon it might prove replicable.

Let us by all means talk about this.

Daniel P. Moynihan

I incorporated some of Moynihan's ideas in a new draft and sent the turgid essay in to the President. The "Publius" paper may have been liberal social philosophy dressed in popular conservative clothes regarding delivery systems, but that was Nixon's lifelong domestic policy. He had always been fairly progressive, "modern" Republican, had a good voting record for education and social concerns. As a Vice President, he backed up a junior HEW official, Elliot Richardson, in an education fight in an Eisenhower Cabinet meeting, which Richardson never forgot.* Always considered a man of the political right, Nixon's conservative coloration (particularly its anti-Communist hue) had enabled him to be progressive with relative impunity to his hard-core constituency, often to the surprise of his advisers. When John Ehrlichman, with some trepidation, put forth a liberal view on Washington, D.C., home rule, Nixon looked at him as if

---

* In the end, Richardson forgot.

he were crazy: "Hell, I've been for home rule in the District since I came to this town twenty-five years ago."

About a month later, back came the Publius essay from the President with notation that showed his desire to be seen as "bold" rather than conservative, and to try out a slogan:

It is not the middle of an old road. It is a New Road —

Federalist approach to governing might ultimately be considered a useful

new development in American politics -- and what has been assumed to

be simple pragmatism may reveal an ideological subtlety.

On substance, however, his comment was to knock out the Moynihan addition about the Negro poor to be helped by the Family Assistance Plan, the Nixon welfare reform proposal.

Excellent —but   { *A major change is needed on page 21 & 22.*

New Federalist Paper #1   *The entire*   6th Draft: 11/22/69 - Safire

By Publius   *emphasis is on Negro poor - Bring out fact that all poor are helped by Family assistance*

We like the blessings of strong central government: a clear direction

toward social goals, a willingness to counteract economic freezings and

overheatings, a single voice in world affairs. But we are repelled by

centralization's side effects: ineffective administration that breeds

resentment, inflexible bureaucracy that breeds alienation.

We also like the blessings of decentralization or "home rule," with

its respect for diversity, its ready response to local demands, its

personality tailored to its constituents. But we are repelled, ~~most of~~

by frequent local unwillingness or inability to meet human needs.

Do we have to choose one way or the other -- centralization or

decentralization -- taking the bitter with whatever we consider the

sweet? Many think not, and have been experimenting with a synthesis of the most desirable in both central government and local control. It

has been called "the new Federalism. "

For a time, the synthesis is likely to be praised or dismissed as

"middle of the road, " and the ready acceptance of this label by the men

espousing it may be a safe posture. Sooner or later, however, both

critics and supporters will discover something more afoot. This New

The President's comments on my sixth draft read:

> Excellent but a major change is needed on page 21 & 22. The entire emphasis is on *Negro* poor—bring out the fact that *all* poor are helped by Family Assistance.

Pat Buchanan, the President's speechwriter of the right, read the essay with dismay and passed it to Tom Charles Huston, who was then on his staff, for reply. The cadaverous Huston was the former head of Young Americans for Freedom, as strict a constructionist as one could find, and he wrote a sharp reply titled "The Pretensions of New Publius Exposed" and signed it with the pseudonym of Cato, an eighteenth-century English essayist:

"To the extent that the substantive thesis may be isolated from the glittering phrases, New Publius appears to be making these points: (1) centralized government lends itself well to defining goals and establishing priorities, but tends to be administratively inefficient; (2) decentralized government is responsive to the needs and desires of the people at the local level, but permits an element of discretion which may thwart national objectives and policies; (3) a new approach, one in which the respective advantages of centralization and decentralization are synthesized into a comprehensive system of government, is both desirable and possible. This approach he calls 'national localism' . . .

"If, for example," continued "Cato" Huston, "New Publius is simply saying that within the scope of legitimate Federal authority Congress may choose to give the States first option on the administration of a Federal program, such a statement is unobjectionable. If, however, New Publius is saying that once the Federal Government determines that a problem—any problem—exists and decides that something should be done about it, the States have the first option to take action and if they refuse the Federal Government may rightly act on its own—if this be his argument, then not only is it objectionable, it is revolutionary.

"Throughout the essay by New Publius one catches glimpses of the heavy hand and iron fist. He envisages a New Federalism in which national authority says to local authority, 'Do it your way, but do it.' Such a political scheme is necessarily authoritarian in implication, if not in practice; it denies discretion and thus denies freedom, for no man is free who lacks the power to say No."

After making his point defending the rights of states against Federal encroachment, Huston turned to my evocation of a "national conscience" or sense of fairness:

"New Publius makes this astounding statement: 'To the New Federalists, morality in a nation is determined not by government policy, church degree, or social leadership—what is moral is what most people who think about morality at all think is moral at a given time.'

"The morality of New Publius is a politicized morality, a pervasive, nationalized, super-guideline in conformity with which individuals are required to live. It is political expediency masquerading as morality, formulated by politicians and administered by bureaucrats, having the sustaining power of the latest Gallup Poll.

"If the Government in Washington is free to determine the national conscience, it is free to force adherence to it. In the name of 'national conscience' (which has a striking similarity to 'the general will') it can ignore state lines and private rights, extending its power into every corner of the land and imposing it directly on every individual. It thus becomes a total government, bound by no restraints other than those voluntarily assumed by the men temporarily in command."

Good stuff; makes you think, especially that last line; if I were to write my essay again, I would be more careful about the extension of Federal power, and more defensive about moral relativism.

Some of these arguments have been made moot by the legal extension of equality by the Supreme Court. The equal opportunity extended in the desegregation decisions, the one-man-one-vote equality guaranteed in *Baker v. Carr*, followed by a California decision voiding the property tax as the method of perpetuating inequality in education—all these have made decentralization less of a danger to the "national conscience," since discrimination is no longer a local option in handling Federal funds.

With these new guarantees now the law of the land, the "do-it-your-way" message to the localities requires less administrative control from Washington because the "fairness" is built into law that applies at the local level. In that sense, court decisions extending equity into individual voting, schooling and other civil rights ultimately gathers power to the national government. Law Professor Alexander Bickel told a New Federalist gathering in 1973: "Every decision that expands Constitutional rights, that construes the Constitution so as to make it cover more, protect more, do more than it did before, is a decision that centralizes power."

To the question "Did the Nixon Administration have any political philosophy to call its own?" the answer has to be yes, sort of—inarticulately expressed, jerry-built after the fact, but for all that, fairly sound and right for its time. Moynihan's comment "I don't really know what 'the Administration' thinks about all this. Mostly it doesn't think at all" was the comment, after all, of a thinker who spent many hours thinking aloud with the Top Man.

George Shultz, who gave much serious attention to the New Federalism, made one of the rare, good speeches about it in 1970, calling for "a society more pluralistic in its operation and more equal in its opportunity." He surprised his University of Chicago audience by complaining that "the Nixon Administration is not being well enough criticized. I didn't say not enough; I said not *well* enough." Revenue sharing at a time of Federal budget deficits had been attacked as "having no revenue to share" which was not only demagogic but stupid, and the attention of most commentators concentrated on whether revenue sharing funds would be "new money" or just "old money" (previous categorial grants redirected in lump sums), ignoring the meaning of the change in power direction inherent in the plan. Perhaps the New Federalists had marbles in their mouths, but they did not have the benefit of very much intelligent, constructive criticism. Henry Steele Commager's remark was indicative of the profundity of the comment: "It's not new and it's not Federalism."

The greatest strengths of the New Federalism have been (a) its practicability in applying power at its proper level—centralized when that is fairest and most efficient, localized when those advantages accrue in local dealings, (b) its ability to alleviate a malaise caused by the breakdown of the Great Society expectations without overreacting and shutting off aid entirely, (c) its revitalizing effect in churning up local government arguments (many of its most vigorous critics turned out to be local bureaucrats who did not want the responsibility of deciding local priorities), and (d) its seriousness of purpose. By 1974 revenue sharing was running at the rate of over five billion dollars a year, hardly a pilot program, and will grow.

The greatest weakness predicted for the New Federalism—venality of officials at the local level, and the revulsion that graft and corruption would generate—turned out, in the light of the exposure of Federal-level venality in Watergate, to be not such a striking problem. There has been anger when local areas decided to use revenue sharing funds for tennis courts and golf courses rather than more traditional, socially called-for expenditures, but that is part of "trusting the people"; so is the frequent use of the money for property tax relief, which critics say uses funds to alleviate tax pressure on the affluent, but is again the price liberals have to pay for liberally letting local citizens decide their own destiny as much as possible.

Those New Federalist weaknesses, which are usually attacked from the political left, are especially vulnerable to criticism from the right: that any system which severs the power-to-spend from the responsibility-to-tax encourages local officialdom to spend too much. I do not have a satisfying answer to that, other than to mumble that the New Federalism has allowed room for the participation of future generations in its improvement.

To another question, "Did the Nixonites have in mind a form of despotism, ruling from the White House untrammeled by Constitution or precedent?" the practice of the New Federalism provides a welcome and surprising answer:

The whole idea of Federalism, old and new, is to disperse power, not to concentrate power. Nixon, so frequently blasted for a "power grab"—with his impoundment of funds, his evocation of executive privilege, his desire for secrecy in foreign affairs—succeeded, with his revenue-sharing achievements, in forcing the first major decentralization and diffusion of governmental power in more than forty years. The people in Congress and in the Federal bureaucracy who most frequently condemned his power-grabbiness were concerned not that the power being grabbed was going to the President, which that particular power was not, but away from them, which it certainly was.

When Nixon saw nothing wrong in revenues returned to localities being used for property tax reduction, this was interpreted as pandering to the people's worst instincts, but it fit a philosophy that held that the individual, and not the government, should decide how "discretionary" money was to be spent.

A dollar not taxed and used "for the public good" was not a dollar that went into a mattress. It was a dollar spent by a free American to buy what he wanted, which generated economic activities and jobs, most often more efficiently than stimulation by government. This was not a fat cat's rationale for stinginess, not tightwaddism, but a long-considered, rational decision by a President to transfer power, and he was fully aware of the consequences of his actions to bolster the "private sector." In Nixon's mind, however, the loss of power in "Washington" was equated with the diminishing of Congressional, not Presidential power.

For nearly two centuries, the history of the nation has been the history of centralization: from Hamilton and Jackson and FDR in economics, to Jefferson and Polk and "manifest destiny," to John Marshall and Earl Warren in the nationalization of "fairness," to what historian Daniel J. Boorstin has called "consumer communities" established by national brands. "Mere size is no sin," 300-lb. William Howard Taft told Louis Brandeis, but he was wrong. The small negatives in concentration's great advantages steadily built up into a loud popular "no," affecting Big Government no less than Big Industry. "I know we can't go back to mom-and-pop grocery stores," Nixon wistfully told his Cabinet Committee on Economic Policy in 1969, "but does everything have to be sold in a supermarket?"

President Nixon, in basic instincts, in his fuzzily espoused "New Federalism," and specifically in his revenue sharing, succeeded in cutting down the power of "Washington" in the nation's life, or, to use a favored term, at least in decreasing Federal power's rate of increase. And there was the rub: the old Congressional power had built-in "federalist" safeguards, but the relatively new and faster-growing Presidential power did not. For all the willingness of the "New Federalism" to come to grips with the paradox caused by a desire for both national fairness and local diversity, it could not overcome the paradox in its leader's sense of mission. In order to return "power to the people," Nixon first had to wrench it out of the hands of the satraps that had controlled it for generations, and they naturally charged him with seeking all their power for himself.

That charge, I submit, was false; but the lessening of Congressional power, as envisaged by the New Federalism, without a concomitant lessening of Executive power, meant a relative increase in the power of the President as against the Congress. In hindsight, this might have called for a soft line, rather than a bold approach, but against an opposition Congress, no such soft line would have caused any change at all. That was Nixon's dilemma in the New Federalism: to bring about a diffusion of Washington's power without the remaining Washington power lopsidedly lodged in the White House.

He did not bring it off. But he brought about far more change in a direction of selective decentralization than has met the eye. Were it not for his eavesdropping mania and vindictiveness in victory, he might well be remembered as a President who sensed the danger of muscle-bound central government, who tried—with more success than he was credited with—to make the right philosophic correction in the nation's course, at the right moment, helping to preserve our diversity while satisfying our conscience.

To flash forward a moment, I recall going to the Eisenhower Theater in the Kennedy Center with George Shultz in the spring of 1974. At intermission, we were standing on the balcony overlooking the bust of Eisenhower, under whose banner both George and I had entered politics. Shultz was then Treasury Secretary, the longest-lived member of the Nixon Cabinet; he had resigned, and because he had not interfered with the Internal Revenue Service's report on the President's taxes, Nixon had not tried to prevail upon Shultz—the best man left in the battered Administration—to stay. George could not have felt badly about leaving the dank atmosphere of the White House of those days to take a lucrative job in industry, but he was depressed about what had become of the New Federalism's opportunity: "What a waste. In the first term we discovered where the levers were, how to actually change the direction of power away from Washington. And then we had to go through the price control business and that was out of our system. Here was a new term, a real mandate, a chance to put some good ideas into action. Now it's all gone up in smoke. We had it in our hands to do such great, sound things, in the way that was right for the country. We had it right in our hands . . ."

But in its early days, the greatest test of the New Federalism was on the issue in American life that had long pitted "fairness" against "local control" —school desegregation. Let us now examine how the New Federalists handled desegregation before the issue became completely identified with busing.

2. THE WAYWARD BUS

"The Court was right on *Brown* and wrong on *Green,*" Richard Nixon told a few of us in June 1968. That fundamental attitude toward two landmark cases in the field of education persisted throughout his Presidency. He felt strongly that school desegregation was right; more desegregation was accomplished during his first term than in the fourteen years since the *Brown v. Board of Education* decisions of 1954. Nixon felt equally strongly that compulsory integration of schools was wrong, especially when achieved by the technique of busing pupils long distances away from their homes, a requirement some lower courts drew from the *Green v. New Kent County* decision of 1968.

Nixon's instinctive reaction was in the direction of getting government out of the social decisions of the people. Just as government should not enforce the beliefs of those who felt the races should be separated, it should not enforce the beliefs of those who felt the races should not be separated. For generations, government had wrongly intervened to segregate, and now it had the responsibility to make certain that desegregation took place wherever racial separation had come about by law. That, to Nixon, was not only fair, it was the indisputable law of the land, and he was determined to carry it out with the least possible racial friction. At the same time, even in the *Green* decision rejecting freedom-of-choice evasions and demanding plans that work "now," he did not believe that the pendulum had swung all the way over to the kind of integration exemplified by the involuntary busing of school children. That, he was convinced, was not only unfair, but disrupted good education and inflamed racial hatred—"a bad means to a good end." By carrying out desegregation much more quickly than had taken place under Eisenhower, Kennedy, and Johnson, Nixon felt he could avoid a confrontation with the courts, which had grown understandably impatient with all the foot-dragging. He was concerned that if *de jure* segregation was not ended (as had been ordered in 1954), the courts would step up the pressure by moving to end *de facto* segregation (caused by housing patterns and economic pressures rather than official action) and then the roof would blow off.

Through the election year of 1968 and the focus on Vietnam in the year of 1969, the issue that became known as "forced busing" was not on the front burner of public attention. But as the problem moved north, the intensity of opposition began to make itself felt. The President appointed a Cabinet committee to help smooth and speed desegregation, with Vice President Agnew as chairman (a symbol of conservatism) and Secretary of Labor George Shultz, vice chairman (a relentless mediator with liberal credentials). The name of the game was to enlist the support of local committees in the holdout Southern communities, to join with them in damning the intrusive, abrasive tacts of the bureaucrats from up north, and to get them to do what they would not do under the previous form of pressure.

Nixon's policy of make-it-happen, but don't make it seem like Appomattox, was moving along in its low-keyed, inarticulate way, when it was sharply challenged within the Administration from the conservative wing. Professor Alexander Bickel had written a warning of the dangers of reading desegregation as integration in the *New Republic*; the New York *Times* front-paged a piece on rising violence in racially mixed schools; and on February 12, 1970 (Lincoln's birthday), Pat Buchanan, who had scored a few months earlier with a speech on the media in Des Moines for the Vice President (and almost followed that with a ripsnorter on Mylai until it was shot down by cooler heads) sent a memo to the President enclosing a draft of a speech for the Vice President:

Finally, the national mood among blacks and white *alike* is toward black separatism and white separatism. Where the Court in 1954 ruled at the crest of a national tide; their current rulings go against the grain of rising and angry public opinion . . . Let me say candidly that for the foreseeable future, it is all over for compulsory social integration in the USA; because that body of public approval which must be present for a social change of this magnitude is not there; indeed, a hard opposite opinion is building . . . I am deeply concerned that Wallace will in the immediate future force the President to carry out a court ruling whether with marshals or troops—which would make the little demagogue invincible in areas and end our chances of destroying him by 1972 . . . The second era of Re-Construction is over; the ship of Integration is going down; it is not our ship; it belongs to national liberalism—and we cannot salvage it; and we ought not to be aboard. For the first time since 1954, the national civil rights community is going to sustain an up-and-down defeat. It may come now; it may come hard; it may be disguised and dragged out—but it can no longer be avoided . . . The Vice President might be able to deliver a thought-out address, all cheer lines out, moving to the Right of the President and giving RN time to move the distance we have to move which is essentially to a qualified freedom of choice posture . . .

Both Buchanan's memo and his draft speech were impassioned, hard-hitting, and a sharp departure with Nixon policy. The first two paragraphs of the draft speech are indicative:

> The other day, one of the President's Assistants phoned a friend in Charleston, South Carolina to inquire how the Administration was faring in the South—after the latest court rulings ordering immediate integration of the public schools.
>
> His South Carolinian friend paused a moment and said, "I am looking out my window right now at old Ford Sumter out there in the harbor; and if the Federal Government didn't have the atomic bomb, we'd be firing on it."

The President circulated it to the members of his Cabinet committee on education for comment, and received enough shocked responses to tell Buchanan on February 17 to scrap the draft speech, that he was going to "continue along the current road." The young conservative promptly wrote him an appeal, suggesting a moratorium on court orders (an idea that Nixon rejected at the time but did not forget) and concluding ". . . in implementing these decisions, as they are handed down . . . we will lay down our political life for our enemies, like Bayh and the others who will, as you said, 'hold our feet to the fire.' Certainly, greater love hath no man."

The same day, Vice President Agnew sent Buchanan a cautious and nearly formal reply:

> . . . There is little disagreement with the logic of your argument and the conclusion that recent court decisions are destructive of quality education in the United States.
>
> Although I share your concern about compulsory, artificially imposed integration, I do feel that your conclusion that "integration appears to damage rather than advance both the cause of education and the cause of racial harmony" is too broad. Integration itself, where it is brought about by congenial interests and by the desire of the parties involved, can only advance social tranquility. Our problem arises because social acceptance does not come about naturally, but is being legally demanded by courts and legislative bodies. Unless we make this distinction clear, we are vulnerable to legitimate attack.
>
> Obviously, the President's charge to me in his directive creating the Cabinet level committee to assist in the desegregation of Southern schools would not allow me to give the suggested speech as it now appears. Nevertheless, the political situation in my judgment demands that we move to some extent in the direction of indicating disfavor with the apparent consequences of recent court decisions. I am strongly of the opinion that if we wait too long the opposition party will seize the initiative and will use this issue to fragment our new-

found credibility in the South and, in fact, to erode our strong position among the middle class silent majority throughout the country. It therefore remains for us to stake out a defensible position that is practical and sensible and to promptly articulate same . . .

Buchanan took note of the moderated tone and wrote a calmer speech that hardly budged off his original position. The President assigned Leonard Garment, his former law partner who was his special consultant on civil rights,* to work with Buchanan on another draft. Both Buchanan and Garment are civil, fairly soft-spoken gentlemen; but they worked all night long in Buchanan's office, shouting at each other, pounding tables, producing a document by 8 A.M. that neither man liked.

Even as Garment was fighting Buchanan on every line of the speech, he sent a memo suggesting to the President that the speech not be given by the Vice President at all. Garment knew that the President would permit Agnew considerable leeway on the right, since a Vice Presidential utterance did not commit the Administration, but that whatever Agnew said would be interpreted by the civil rights community as Nixon gospel and ignite vigorous protest. If the speech could be taken away from the Vice President and turned into a Presidential statement, it would perforce be more moderate; what's more, time could be taken to do a thorough, thoughtful job. So Garment filibustered in this memo to the President of February 19, 1970:

> I believe the speech should be the President's. The subject—particularly at this moment—is of surpassing constitutional, social and political importance. The concepts presently under discussion are philosophically and pragmatically sound, but careful work is needed to articulate the principles clearly and with sympathy to the different principles and interests involved. The issue, I believe, is one that should be explored with the nation, by the President, via television, not in Atlanta by the Vice President in a speech assembled under great time pressure. Great care must be taken to avoid inflaming an already difficult situation and in the process making it impossible to achieve goals the Administration has set for itself. Too much is at stake to risk any but the most prudent course . . . an essential goal must be to avoid prematurely polarizing the executive and the judiciary. I am convinced the courts *will* give unless backed up against the wall. The consequences then become murky.
>
> I annex some comments on this issue by Ray Price that articulate my own sentiments better than I myself can.

By inserting Price into the situation, the Nixon-wise Garment enabled the President to see a sample of the kind of writing which would be done

* Garment's best line years later: "Stonewalling doth not misprision make . . ."

on a document from the highest level. A couple of samples from speechwriter Price's early approach:

> We want to achieve a set of conditions in which neither the laws
> nor the institutions supported by law any longer draw an invidious
> distinction based on race; and going one step further, we seek to re-
> pair the human damage wrought by past segregation, and to give the
> black child, as nearly as possible, that equal place at the starting line
> that his parents were denied—and with it, the pride, the dignity, the
> self-respect, that are the birthright of a free American.
>
> We can do no less and still be true either to our conscience or to
> our Constitution. And most Southerners today, I think, would accept
> this as their duty . . .
>
> We also have to recognize that in a free society, there are limits to
> the amount of coercion that can reasonably be used; that profound
> social changes take time to accomplish; that we cannot afford to sacri-
> fice the education of an entire generation on the altar of an abstract
> ideal, no matter how desirable; and that children themselves are
> highly sensitive to conflict, and highly vulnerable to lasting psychic
> injury.

Garment concluded with a point he knew would be especially telling
with Nixon: that the opportunity was present to "lead" the Supreme Court
by mobilizing public opinion behind desegregation, so that the Court
would not have to plunge into integration. He "should not throw down
the gauntlet to the Court," wrote Garment, by forcing the Court to go
further and bringing on a Constitutional crisis.

The next afternoon, Jim Keogh had scheduled a meeting of the writing
staff with the President in the Oval Office. Price, Buchanan and I were
there, with Lee Huebner and Bill Gavin, and Haldeman and Harlow. The
talk centered around schools and race, and Nixon let us know quickly how
he had decided to handle the Agnew speech:

"I want to do something on this myself—what's today's date, the
twentieth?—by the first of March. I need at least ten days to think it
through, but leadership has to be exerted in this area. I'm getting ready,
so should all of you. Anybody has ideas, I want them. But no speech before a live audience—just a statement in writing."

Nixon had decided to do it himself, and the Agnew Atlanta speech was
aborted. "I may go on TV. If something could be written that was very
brief," Nixon mused, "possibly even eloquent . . ." Then he shook his
head—TV required too clear a direction—and came down again for a careful, written statement: "The busing thing is complicated as hell. Look—
'quality education' is a code word, can you imagine? Javits says that integration is working, but the stories in the New York *Times* say differently."

Nixon chewed on one tip of his glasses for a moment. "I will probably have to separate myself from the traditional civil rights groups on the recent court decisions. If the Supreme Court goes as far as *de facto* racial balance, all hell will break loose. I'll have to speak in a sound way, on that fine line, representing the decent body of opinion, rejecting extremism on both sides. You know"—the President leaned forward and made the point to us that Garment had made to him in his memo that morning—"it could influence the next Court decision."

I suggested that if he wanted to mobilize public opinion, he dramatize his statement with a visit to a schoolroom. Price said no, and the President agreed that he would do best to stay away from any kind of emotional setting. Harlow, in a voice we had to lean forward to hear, used the kind of word-picture that was his trademark: "You ought to keep a hand in the back of the American people, pushing for desegregation, using television the way you did on November third." That was a reference to the "silent majority" speech.

"The Nation is at an historic moment," the President said. (That looks pretentious in cold type; the President did not intone it sonorously, he said it matter of factly, so that it did not sound like the President of the United States announcing that the Nation was at an historic moment, but more as an interested observer who might get involved in the action.) "I want to hit this in a way that will affect the Court, before the California [Serrano] case comes up.

"If the Court comes down on the wrong side, we're caught. My bent is quite conservative on this, maybe too much so. I'm interested in what will work for education—*Brown* was right, it was concerned with better education, but *Green* and the others were more concerned with race. If the Court had written Green in a way where freedom of choice was permitted when it was honest, breaking down the dual system, and not permitted when it was used as a subterfuge, then it would be okay—we'd all be better off."

Nixon swiveled around in his chair and looked out the Oval Office window. "You're not going to solve this race problem for a hundred years. Intermarriage and all that, assimilation, it will happen, but not in our time. Desegregation, though, that has to happen now.

"That's why we have to hit this minority enterprise thing so hard—sure, they laugh at it—but better jobs, better housing, that's the only way Negroes are going to be able to move to Scarsdale." He pointed at Haldeman, a fellow Californian: "Bob, that's the only way they're going to get into Palisades High and Whittier High."

I asked how the President intended to make the case that desegregation was good and integration was not. He winced to indicate the difficulty of popularizing a complex position, and put it this way: "I'll be speaking out against extreme decisions that bus children across town, so that people, as they reluctantly carry out the law to desegregate, will not line up overwhelmingly against integration.

"Forget the polls, people don't tell the truth to pollsters in this. I think the majority of people are against integration. The majority are scared to death of the black militants, and of the white militants as well. Let's start out by saying (Nixon adopted a speech voice), 'We are against segregation because it leads to inferior education. Now, what is the responsible way to have equality of opportunity? To end segregated education, we must use methods that impair education to the least extent possible. The goal is not integration, it is desegregation, and the overriding concern must be better education.'" He stopped sketching a speech. "This is a profound argument, and it could be debated, but the reason behind the *Brown* decision was not race but better education. If, in carrying out that decision, we destroy education, we defeat its goal.

"The subsequent decisions about quotas and racial balance are wrong—you'll delight the racists when you say that, but so what, it's true."

We talked about the politics of the situation for a while, and the President saw nothing but harm in it: "There is no mileage in doing the right thing here, there's only mileage for demagogues. Put it this way: There's mileage for anybody who wants to be Governor, no mileage for somebody who has to be President." Looking at me taking notes, he smiled and added: "That is not to say that Governors are demagogues.

"Reagan, Kirk down in Florida, they can emphasize the negatives—all the failures of integration. Seventy-five per cent of the people, black and white, will agree—I know this country. But it's not right—maybe it's okay for a candidate, not for a President.

"You see, at the time of the Brown decision in 1954, sentiment for integration was much higher than it is now. Bob was telling me about Stanford—at first, the blacks integrated, but after a few months, they grouped up by themselves, that's the way it is. The nation has a different attitude now. A hell of a lot of classrooms are jungles, dangerous as hell. With that quotient in there, a statement on this subject that is interpreted as being on one side or the other—well, you might stir up a reaction detrimental to the country. I could do a speech about the failure of integration—most of the country would agree—but then you'd have the Court coming out against us, and we would have a Constitutional crisis.

"You have to remember," Nixon said, coming back to the idea that intrigued him most, "that somewhere down the road I may have to carry out this law. I can't throw down the gauntlet to the Court. I have to move the Court now, before the decision, by mobilizing public opinion."

Harlow, who was having his problems as Nixon's aide dealing with the Senate, said the President would be pressed for his stand on the Stennis amendment, a maneuver which sought to slow down desegregation in the South by demanding it first be speeded up in the North. The President saw comment on that amendment as a trap and, mocking an old story, showed how he was going to handle it: "There are two different versions of that amendment; John's for both, and I'm for Old John." Haldeman added wryly what Ziegler had been putting out: "We were against the Stennis amendment, though we were for it in concept."

The President shrugged: "This is the perfect example of one of those cases where leadership is not good politics, but you have to do it."

At a reception later, Haldeman came over to Garment and said, "You won." The President had decided to make his desegregation statement not as a speech but as a Presidential paper. Garment and Price and Bryce Harlow were to work on it, but John Ehrlichman was to be the point of contact and would get whatever other opinions he saw fit, including Robert Mardian at HEW and Stanley Pottinger at Justice, as well as significant outside contributions from Alexander Bickel of Yale and James Coleman of Johns Hopkins. Before a speech draft or statement, however, the President first wanted to study an option paper—in this case, including thorough memoranda of law, with necessary back-up material. He did not want a consensus, with arguments fuzzed over; he was willing to permit an internal Donnybrook so as to decide for himself. He did not view the advocates of differing positions as heroes or villains, as bleeding hearts or bigots; on the contrary, the special function of Ehrlichman in this process was to depersonalize advocacy, so that the President would not let irritation with (or affection for) any individual sway his judgment. John would channel in arguments and funnel out directions, making certain not to "lobby" the President from his privileged position, and providing a knowledgeable sounding board for the President in long conversations on the subject.

The choices wrenching in different directions were fairly clear. To let the situation drift, which hardly seemed desirable; to amend the Constitution, a last resort that would take too long; to redirect desegregation by legislation, an approach suggested by Bickel, who was being helpful in exploring alternatives; or a Presidential position, using the "bully pulpit" to lead the courts and public opinion.

On March 5, Garment submitted a book of about two hundred pages to Ehrlichman containing his recommendations, suggestions from HEW and Justice, a lengthy submission from Shultz and an analysis by Bickel, along with preliminary draft statements from Keogh and Price. The President took it with him to Key Biscayne.

Down there, he discussed it with Administration conservatives, especially Bryce Harlow, who, with Buchanan, became the primary critic of the draft statement, with Robert Mardian adding some legal demurrers. But, as White House staffers soon come to know, "control" of a document is in the hands of the group or person the President designates—in this case Price was the writer, and he resisted revision with a ferocity uncharacteristic of him. Price wrote Ehrlichman:

> Whatever editing is done over there, I think it's vital that I get a final crack at it *afterwards*—and that I have the *last* crack at it before it's finally approved by you or the President. I'm afraid that otherwise we risk something that would make the flap over "benign neglect" seem positively benign . . . I'm quite serious about this. As you know, the whole subject is a mine-field of code words, subtleties and

sensitivities, and I'm really concerned that the Southern Strategists or Court-Confrontationists might make seemingly minor changes that would have devastating impact in print—or else that would have the effect, *perhaps* even inadvertently, of gutting the whole statement.

Garment backed Price up as the liberals stayed on the offensive:

> Word, sentence and organizational changes *now* can dangerously upset the meaning, even the validity of the document, each part of which was worked over with *enormous* care by Ray. As you noted the other day, it will be scrutinized carefully and critically by the press, bar, judiciary, Congress, etc. Each sentence has been weighed with this in mind.

The President would transmit his thoughts through Ehrlichman, and the tide ran in the liberals' favor: caution to make certain the rhetoric did not offend conservatives or Southerners, but directing substantial amounts of money to help desegregating schools. The following distinction over the use of the word "wrong" was typical:

MEMORANDUM

THE WHITE HOUSE
WASHINGTON

March 16, 1970

FOR RAY PRICE
    LEN GARMENT

The President does not want the desegregation issue in the statement grounded on "moral wrong". If we must disagree with segregation, it is not because Southerners are morally wrong but rather because they are legally wrong and therefore we should only say that they are "wrong".

The President also notes that white northern liberals frequently condemn the south and yet send their own children to private schools. They are just as wrong as intractible southerners and the President suggests that we say so in the statement.

He would like to announce in the statement that we will make available $500 million in FY '71 and a billion dollars in FY '72 to upgrade educational facilities, teaching, equipment, etc. in racially impacted areas.

John D. Ehrlichman

As the statement came down to the wire, Garment won Mardian over on several legal points, and Harlow tried what only a skillful speechwriter can do in such circumstances. He wrote a completely fresh version of the statement, providing the President with a literate and unified alternative.

I found out about this from a grim-faced Price on March 20, as he was hurrying down the hall to the President's EOB office: "The Southern Caucus is trying a play," was the way Ray put it. "Dent, Harlow, Mardian and Buchanan have come up with their own draft. Much softer. It'll be on the President's desk at 5 p.m." That sounded to me as if he had been forewarned by Haldeman or the President himself, an indication that the "play" would not succeed. True to form, the President considered the Harlow draft carefully, then set it aside. Then, with Harlow, he went over the Price draft line by line, word by word. Harlow was the consummate Presidential staffer; satisfied that the President had given careful thought to all the alternatives, he pitched in to improve the draft the President wanted. "On no other document in the years I was there," Harlow told me later, "did the President deliberate more than on this one. When it was finished, it said just exactly what he wanted to say."

In the statement issued March 24 the President reviewed what the Supreme Court had said, and then recent lower court rulings. He outlined the difference between *de jure* and *de facto* segregation, and listed the basic points most of the courts presently agreed upon, and touched on some of the complex problems: "Racial balance has been discovered to be neither a static nor a finite condition; in many cases it has turned out to be only a way station on the road to resegregation." "Good faith" was explored, the "rule of reason" explained, and local initiative encouraged, but the determination to enforce was not fudged: "Deliberate racial segregation of pupils by official action is unlawful, wherever it exists. In the words of the Supreme Court, it must be eliminated 'root and branch'—and it must be eliminated at once."

The President proposed to spend $1.5 billion on disadvantaged schools on an emergency basis (a proposal, like welfare reform, which failed because liberals did not consider it to be enough, and inner-city schools wound up with no extra aid) and, at my suggestion, made clear he was offending both extremes:

> I am aware that there are many sincere Americans who believe deeply in instant solutions and who will say that my approach does not go far enough fast enough. They feel that the only way to bring about justice is to integrate all schools now, everywhere, no matter what the cost in the disruption of education.
>
> I am aware, too, that there are many equally sincere citizens—North and South, black and white—who believe that racial separation is right, and wish the clock of progress would stop or be turned back to 1953. They will be disappointed, too.

Looking far past the moment, he examined the meaning of segregation-integration in the context of personal freedom:

> In speaking of "desegregation" or "integration," we often lose sight of what these mean within the context of a free, open, pluralistic society. We cannot be free, and at the same time be required to fit our lives into prescribed places on a racial grid—whether segregated or integrated, and whether by some mathematical formula or by automatic assignment. Neither can we be free, and at the same time be denied—because of race—the right to associate with our fellow citizens on a basis of human equality.

The message concluded, as I had hoped, with a reference to the "national conscience," a central tenet of the New Federalism:

> I am confident that we can preserve and improve our schools, carry out the mandate of our Constitution, and be true to our national conscience.

Buchanan was not happy about it. "A golden opportunity missed," he said, because the President had not taken the leadership against judges ordering desegregation. The President was satisfied that he had done the right thing, though he glared at Garment whenever a lower court made what Nixon considered an irresponsible decision—the central idea of the President's desegregation message had been to lead the courts, to reassure them that extreme decisions were not needed to get reasonable action. In that regard, the message failed, but in retrospect, it was a worthwhile effort by a centrist President who wanted steady progress without rising resentment.

As the new school term approached, long-time conservative supporters of the President felt the pressure of desegregation and demanded to make their case directly to Nixon. On August 6, 1970, the President and Attorney General John Mitchell met for three hours with Southern conservatives who were unhappy with school desegregation plans. Mitchell passed the word to a few of us later that RN handled Senator Strom Thurmond perfectly. Strom, his dander up, came in with a folder full of grievances. Nixon called on everyone else first, being infinitely patient, letting them cover points in Thurmond's case. The Senator—who had done so much to get Nixon the Republican nomination two years before—kept crossing points off his list until his turn came, and by that time he wasn't so angry anymore. Afterward, Mitchell and RN and Haldeman went out on the yacht *Sequoia*; Mitchell said he expected the President to explode. No; Nixon was glad it was over with, and glad he had been able to stay in the center.

But the center was in the process of shifting. And the next time the President faced the situation, in March 1972, several courts had raised the

hackles of the Silent Majority with decisions considered extreme, and
George Wallace was teaching the assembled Democratic establishment in
a Florida primary the political meaning of "forced busing." In their 1970
bid to avert judicial excess, the moderates in the Nixon Administration
had made their case successfully to the President; two years later the conservatives' time would come.

During one of the meetings, I picked up a doodle by John Ehrlichman,
drawn in the Roosevelt Room:

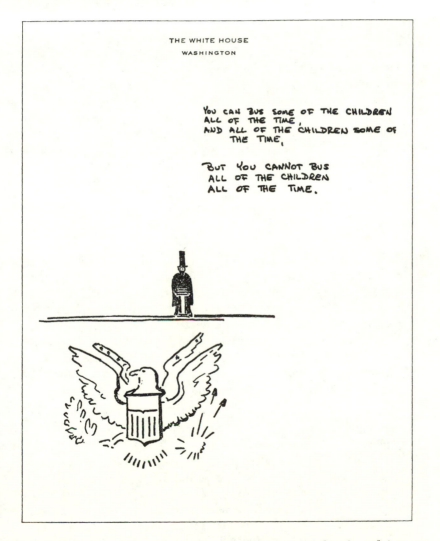

Relations between the races, when they do not involve forced integration or the necessary enforcement of rights, are usually regarded as matters
for courts to work out or sociologists to discuss. The original argument for
segregation—that intermingling in education would lead to intermarriage

—was usually a scare tactic. Yet to some families "race relations" has come to have a different meaning—blood relations of a different race—and a remote end of the Nixon family is included.

I came across a couple of letters written by Nixon to the family of Philip Timberlake, of Newport Beach, California, a distant cousin of Nixon's. One, in 1966, was a condolence note to Timberlake's wife, Frances, when one of their sons died after an overdose of LSD. The other was in response to a letter from one of the daughters in 1973, married now to a Negro. She had written the President: "My husband and I wanted to attend your inauguration since I was invited but because my husband happens to be of the Negro race, my father didn't want him or our baby to go . . . I really made a big mistake by letting my father's racist opinion keep us from going . . . there never has been a Negro person directly involved in the inauguration in which he was a relative of the President of the United States. I would appreciate it very much if you could give me some type of moral support . . ."

The month of March 1973 was a worrisome time for Nixon, but he sent the kind of letter back to his young relation, Mrs. David Jackson of Santa Ana, California, that reflected his general attitude on the subject:

March 30, 1973

Dear Mary:

I am sorry that you missed the Inaugural, and I can understand your feeling upset about it. The ceremonies went smoothly, and it was a grand day. Pat and I felt the parade was the best we'd ever seen. But, of course, these "occasions" which we all participate in from time to time are not the important part of life. What gives life its real meaning is how we realize ourselves on a day-to-day basis. I think you would be making a mistake to allow this sense of bitterness toward your father to spoil the happiness you can now have as a wife and mother.

You mentioned civil rights in your letter. This is a complicated area; in a sense we deal here with two separate problems. The problem of discrimination because of race is being corrected by law. We no longer allow people in this country to be denied jobs or homes or services of one kind or another because of the color of their skin. But the problem of prejudice, which involves people's emotions, is impossible to legislate away. The only thing that can change deeply-ingrained human attitudes is the passage of time. I have seen great changes in this during my life—you will see even more in yours.

Your father is not a young man. It is unfortunately true that as we get older we find it very hard to change our ways. This is true the world over, and has always been true. It may be that you will have to accept the fact that you cannot alter your father's feelings. Accept it, and don't brood over it. It is not anyone's fault.

I am happy that your husband is obtaining such a fine education. This is a very sound thing for him to do. I advise you to help him and encourage him in every way you can so that he may realize his career ambitions. This will ensure a truly bright future for both of you in the years ahead.

I have asked a member of my staff to send you some mementos from the Inaugural. I think your daughter will enjoy looking at them when she is older.

With every best wish for your happiness,

Sincerely,
Richard Nixon

3. "DAMNGOVERNMENT"

Defending President Andrew Jackson's appointment of Martin Van Buren in 1832 as Ambassador to England from an attack by Henry Clay, New York Senator William Marcy said: "It may be, sir, that the politicians of New York are not as fastidious as some gentlemen are as to disclosing the principles on which they act. They boldly preach what they practice . . . If they are successful, they claim, as a matter of right, the advantages of success. They see nothing wrong in the rule, that to the victor belong the spoils of the enemy."

Marcy's candor besmirched his reputation; he is remembered today not as a Senator, Governor, or Secretary of State, but as the defender of the nefarious "spoils system" which has been replaced by the Civil Service's merit system, over which a halo circles.

And yet, Civil Service's necessary reform, which was designed to protect the public payroll from political hacks, hangers-on, and brothers-in-law, has become encrusted with barnacles of its own. Not counting the military, three million people now work for Uncle Sam, five times as many as in 1932. As hiring gets easier and firing more difficult, as more government officials surround themselves with more protection, the strong trend runs toward taking government away from accountability, out of the people's reach. The "insolence of office" grows with the number of offices; I recall giving a reporter a brush-off on a busy day, and my gorge rose when she snapped, "I'm paying your salary, you know," but she was right. (Fortunately, she was Elizabeth Drew, who was then with public television, and I was able to put on my own taxpayer's hat and snap back, "And I'm paying yours.") No longer do much of the spoils belong to the victor; all too often, in F. Scott Fitzgerald's phrase, the victor belongs to the spoils.

To Richard Nixon, government was half a word—the whole word was "damngovernment," and the people who ran it contrary to his policies were the "damnbureaucrats."

This political stance was at once curious, anomalous, and entirely sensible. Instead of allying himself with the lethargic behemoth that was the public image of the Federal Government, the President stood alongside the people most resentful of it. In his State of the Union address in 1971, Nixon articulated the frustration of every citizen who had been waltzed around by powerful paper-pushers when, complete with hand gesture to his throat, he told the assembled Congress: "Let's face it. Most Americans today are simply fed up with government at all levels." Neither phrase nor gesture had been written in the early drafts of the speech—"fed up" was quintessential Nixon.

The antibureaucratic tilt to the President's operational philosophy was no pose struck for cameramen. Woodrow Wilson had temporarily turned on his political sponsors when he took office, and New York Mayor Robert Wagner was re-elected in 1962 by campaigning against the "bosses" who originally put him in power, but never had a political figure refused to become in the least associated with his permanent governmental colleagues. Nixon had spent eight months as a bureaucrat in 1942, working for the Office of Price Administration, and there learned to despise price control and bureaucracy in general. He was the outsider who refused to become an insider; on top of the heap, he rejected the heap.

In the eight years as Eisenhower's Vice President, Nixon saw the effects of the little red tape machine and was aware of Harry Truman's observation about his newly elected successor: "He'll sit right here, and he'll say do this, do that! And nothing will happen. Poor Ike. It won't be a bit like the Army. He'll find it very frustrating."

A President's ability to govern depends partially on his equity in public opinion, partially on his relations with Congress, and largely on his willingness to impose his will on his own Executive Branch. In reality, the Executive Branch has dug its own roots in the fertile soil of the Civil Service system; the so-called Chief Executive can tug and haul all day and never rip up the bureaucracy. The reform of the spoils system threatens to become a spoiler system, capable of frustrating the initiatives of the newly elected, smothering fresh ideas in interminable studies, diffusing responsibility, and, above all, capable of protecting itself. "Any change is resisted," President Nixon told aide Peter Flanigan in 1969, "because bureaucrats have a vested interest in the chaos in which they exist."

Nixon-like, I should piously add that there are many dedicated men and women who have devoted their lives to making the process of democracy work. They are called public servants. (If you want to be neutral about a government employee, call him a civil servant. If you want to heap abuse on him, call him a bureaucrat. If you want to defend him, call him a "career official" or say with Alben Barkley: "A bureaucrat is a Democrat who holds a job a Republican wants.") Self-respecting bureaucrats will admit that the government moves only when it is whipped or teased, and of the new Nixon men only Moynihan and Kissinger had any skill in the manipulation of the bureaucracy. As others learned the tricks of leak, threat, transfer, appointment, browbeating, and lavish praise, the Administration won a few and lost a few. The President, spotting evidence of churlish bureaucratic behavior in his news summary, would fire off demands to his aides, then complain to the teams working on reorganization, "It's easy to know what's being done, but it's hard to know what's *not* being done."

Flanigan, when accused of butting into some independent agency's business, would take a tattered clipping out of his wallet and pass it to his accuser. It was a letter dated May 27, 1944, from Prime Minister Churchill to his Minister of Fuel and Power, triggered by a report in the *Yorkshire Post* of a householder who was fined three guineas for having borrowed coal from a neighbor: "I hope you will put a stop to nonsense like this. Nothing makes departments so unpopular as these acts of petty bureaucratic folly which come to light from time to time and are, I fear, only typical of a vast amount of silly wrongdoing by small officials or committees. You should make an example of the people concerned with this."

In all likelihood, Churchill's minister sided with his bureaucracy and only went through the motions of reprimand. The reason is the first law of bureaucratic survival: Seduce the Boss. Department heads become representatives of empires, measuring their success by the scope of their responsibility, the growth of their staffs, and the burgeoning of their budgets.

George Romney, with his private-enterprise credentials as a manager who ran a fairly tight ship as Governor of Michigan,* was thoroughly sold —one could cruelly say brainwashed—by the experts at the Department of Housing and Urban Development on the wisdom of expanding many Great Society programs. Nixon, who had campaigned against "more of the same" in 1968, listened to Romney make a presentation to the Cabinet calling for the continuation of the Model Cities program in early 1969 and called Pat Moynihan into the Oval Office immediately afterward. "Fold up Model Cities," the President told his urban affairs adviser. "That project is going to be a failure and a waste of money and you know it." Moynihan replied, "Give me twenty-four hours," which as far as Moynihan knew the President took to mean that was all the time needed to fold it up, but the next day Pat was back with a recommended reprieve. Model Cities could not be folded, he insisted, not because it would be a success, but because it had been made a symbol of Administration commitment to cities. Not only would most of the media automatically come down on top of this decision as evidence of urban desertion, but a backdown would demoralize HUD and—this was the clincher—would understandably infuriate Negro leaders who had been promised Federal aid. Nixon agreed that a change of Administration and philosophy was no cause for breaking the government's word. As a result, the program went on for four more years, finally folding in 1973. The same $2.3 billion could have been better spent through revenue sharing in cities, but obeisance had to be paid to bureaucratic momentum and the expectations induced by expansive promises.

The pitiless white light of publicity as often tends to protect bureaucracy

---

* Romney's enthusiastic piety caused critics of his Presidential effort in 1968 to say he only wanted the Presidency as a steppingstone.

as to shake it up. While newspaper exposés of pettiness or corruption some-time result in bureaucratic embarrassment or even prosecution, the press has been frequently used by the bureaucracy to build its protective shell. An adept bureaucrat, his domain threatened by a cutoff of funds, is able to alert those interest groups about to be adversely affected and to zero them in on the appropriate newsmen. A judicious leak, a horrendous prediction of the homelessness, starvation, or pestilence the cutback would cause, a follow-up reaction story about the interest group, a letter campaign by them to interested Congressmen, a severe editorial or two, and the public interest gives way to the bureaucracy's focused interest.

(One bureaucrat's reluctance to be eased out of his job brought forth the most convoluted pun of the Nixon Administration. The man's name was Lawrence Lapin, and when he refused to budge, aide Leonard Garment was heard to muse, "Lapins make lousy leavers." This was an arcane reference to a magazine article of a generation ago, "Latins Make Lousy Lovers," and went past all the young men in the room.)

Sounding off to Secretary of State Rogers along these lines one after-noon in early 1973, I was cautioned not to let my rhetoric turn my head. "It's the interplay between elected officials and the bureaucracy that makes this town work," said Rogers. "Businessmen in particular have a hard time seeing this. When a new idea comes along, a Foreign Service Officer will tend to look at it in the light of all his experience, to insist that it be thought through carefully because it's hard to correct a mistake in di-plomacy. I've seen the President talking to a foreign service officer, and I knew exactly what was going through the President's head: 'This guy is against me.' Well, he's not, nor is he against new initiatives—he just wants to be careful. Lots of times that comes out negative-sounding, and it's a problem I have, but there are subtleties to the business of the relationship between the bureaucracy and the elected officials."

True enough. Bill Rogers knew better than most how it was to defend a President to a bureaucracy and vice versa. And the resistance of some ca-reer officials, particularly in IRS with George Shultz's backing, prevented zealots like John Dean from turning government power into a political weapon. But a recognition of the need for a bureaucracy's experience, sense of continuity, and caution does not require an executive to tolerate its innate reluctance to rock the boat, and the President usually indulged his prejudices against bureaucratic inertia to good effect. (A notable excep-tion: J. Edgar Hoover's objection to the Huston burglary plan.)

Publicity can sometimes be used to shame the bureaucracy into at least a token move toward modernization. Preparing a message to Congress early in 1970 on economy in government, I spotted a tiny item in a long list of program termination recommendations: the Board of Tea-Tasters, an archaic little item that could be used as a symbol of waste and inertia. This is how the President's message spotted it:

"As an extreme example, the government since 1897 has had a special

Board of Tea-Tasters. At one time in the dim past, there may have been good reason to single out tea for such special taste tests, but that reason no longer exists. Nevertheless, a separate Tea-Tasting Board has gone right along, at the taxpayer's expense, because nobody up to now took the trouble to take a hard look at why it was in existence. The general attitude was: It did not cost much, it provided a few jobs, so why upset the teacart?

"That attitude should have no place in this government. The taxpayer's dollar deserves to be treated with more respect."

This was only wasting about $125,000 a year, a drop in the slop-bowl, but there was a jocular, lifted-pinky sound to "Tea-Taster," and it was sure to be picked up by television newscasters. (David Brinkley, not ordinarily a Nixon Administration enthusiast, went for this with gusto.) As an object lesson in waste, with the scorn of commentators and columnists heaped upon them and the pressure of the Executive Branch demanding their removal, one might have thought the Tea-Tasters had had it. Enter some friendly Congressmen, solicitous of the views of some important tea importers, to point out that the board served a useful function in maintaining the quality of imported tea. That's nonsense. The standard Food and Drug Administration spot-check system used on all other imported foods is all that is needed, but the old board had tradition and tea industry pride going for it, plus influence on the House Ways and Means Committee. Specific legislation was needed from this committee to fold up the board, and it was not forthcoming. The President, under the threat of a writ of mandamus from the courts, had to reappoint the Tea-Tasting Board. There they sit today, a delightful anachronism, thumbing their noses at President and press, sipping their tea from the public trough, too small a boondoggle to raise an editorialist's ire, their longevity a testament to bureaucratic *chutzpah*.

But one fight did send a shiver through the bureaucracy, giving credibility to Presidential ukases on waste and inertia: the project for the demolition of Department of Defense buildings N and W, the Munitions Building and the Main Navy Building, familiarly known to the White House staff as the "Mall Clearance Project" and referred to by the President of the United States as "knocking down those goddam eyesores on the Mall." In this case political spoils were not involved, but the personal habits and comforts of long-time government employees were, and the details here will serve to represent the details of a thousand other skirmishes.

The battle of the bureaucracy began in August 1969, when the newly elected President was on his way to Camp David in *Marine One*, the Presidential helicopter. Looking out the window at the Lincoln Memorial, with its reflecting pool and long Mall stretching toward the Washington Monument, the classic design of Pierre L'Enfant marred only by a group of "temporary" World War I buildings on the Mall, the President remarked: "Are those old buildings still there? I was stationed there during the war for a while. Look at the way they louse up the Mall—why are they still up?"

John Ehrlichman pointed out the obvious: "Nobody ever said to pull 'em down." Nixon looked sharply at him: "Well, I'm telling you—knock 'em down." He looked at Colonel Don Hughes, his Air Force aide, and just to be sure added, "I'm telling you too."

A week later, in a wide-ranging meeting in his Western White House office in San Clemente, I heard him change a subject and interject this thought to Ehrlichman: "What about those temporary Navy buildings on the Mall, by the way? Tear 'em down, kick the Navy the hell out!"

Previous Presidents, conservationists, architects, editorialists, and letter writers had all denounced the buildings as eyesores, but for some reason their protests were in vain; nobody ever stood up for the building complex, nobody suggested that they not be torn down one day, but just—not now. Unverifiable rumor had it that Franklin Roosevelt, who ordered the complex built when he was Assistant Secretary of the Navy in 1918, chose the Mall as the site because he was certain public opinion would not tolerate their continuance after World War I. During his own Presidency, a generation later, he did not press the matter of demolition, instead adding some prefabs to the complex. So there they stood, aesthetically indefensible, publicly undefended, but, like a reformer's Mount Everest, "there"— untouched by the wrecker's ball.

A formal memo from Ehrlichman to Colonel Hughes started the ball rolling:

August 8, 1969

TO: COLONEL HUGHES

FROM: JOHN EHRLICHMAN

There are a number of old Navy buildings on the north side of the Mall between the White House and the Lincoln Memorial.

The President has decided that they should be removed according to a plan which will ensure that all have disappeared by 1972.

Would you please check and advise me of the feasibility of this decision, providing a timetable for their clearance?

If you have questions, I'll be very glad to talk with you about this.

The ball rolled a little way and then stopped. The Navy explained to the military aide that a few of the buildings were coming down now, that some would come down in a few years, but the biggest one, where top brass officers were located, should stand forever. Hughes went along with the foot-dragging in the following memo:

August 28, 1969

MEMORANDUM FOR THE PRESIDENT

SUBJECT: Removal of Defense buildings on the Mall

You expressed a desire to have Department of Defense buildings
located on the Mall between the White House and the Lincoln
Memorial removed by 1972. The structures in question are tem-
porary buildings N and W, the Munitions Building and the
Main Navy Building. All of these structures belong to GSA with
Defense as tenants.

The GSA has, at present, plans and programmed funds to remove
temporary buildings N and W and the Munitions Building by
approximately the end of 1970. The Main Navy Building was
scheduled to be demolished to coincide with the construction of
a Defense office building at Bolling Air Force Base, but not earlier
than Fiscal Year 1975. The Bolling Air Force Base construction
is encountering Congressional problems.

A contract for demolition of temporary buildings N and W was
awarded on August 1, and presently demolition of temporary
building N is underway. These buildings will be eliminated by
the end of February, 1970. Therefore, we can legitimately make a
White House release to the effect that this clean-up program is
underway.

If we are to vacate and demolish the Main Navy Building in
accordance with your original instructions, the one time costs
would be $3,280,000, with continuing annual rental costs approxi-
mately $6.5 million (reduced by $1.6 million—present mainte-
nance and operations for Main Navy Building.)

The Main Navy Building, although old, is not a temporary structure, and its appearance is not as unsightly as those which will
be demolished. Therefore, principally in the interest of economy
but also to avoid relocating Navy personnel in separate rental
facilities, I recommend that you accept this program in its present form.

APPROVE——   DISAPPROVE——   SEE ME——

COLONEL JAMES D. HUGHES

The President wasn't having any of this. Every time he drove to the
Presidential yacht *Sequoia*, he passed those buildings; indeed, he told his

Secret Service driver to pass the "temporary" buildings whenever possible so he could see how demolition was coming along. His feeling was apparent in this memo from Haldeman to Ehrlichman:

THE WHITE HOUSE
WASHINGTON

September 30, 1969

MEMORANDUM FOR: MR. EHRLICHMAN

As I recall, you were handling the project of demolition of the temporary buildings in D.C. The President feels that only one little building is being taken down and the main complex has not been touched. He wants all of this underway in the next day or so, and we should get a report to him.

If this is not your project, please let me know who is handling it.

H. R. HALDEMAN

The Navy sent a memo to Hughes, who sent a memo to Ehrlichman, who sent a memo to the President reporting that the destruction of some of the buildings was coming along fine but the big one—Main Navy— would take a little while:

". . . The destruction of Main Navy is scheduled to coincide with the construction of a Defense Office Building on Bolling Air Force Base. The Defense Department estimates that the Bolling office space will be available sometime in 1975 . . ."

In effect, the Department of Defense was telling the President that his order would be put into effect sometime toward the end of his second term, maybe, if there were a second term and if he didn't forget about it. Nixon, who had walked down those very corridors, knew that the Navy attitude was "wear 'em down—we've been through this battle before." Never say no, but never say when; informally, the word was passed to the Navy personnel in the building that this too would pass—nobody was going to send twelve thousand people away from the District to work in Virginia or Maryland.

The President had a little talk with Ehrlichman, and the next memo kept various feet to the fire:

October 27, 1969

TO: COLONEL HUGHES

FROM: JOHN EHRLICHMAN

RE: DEFENSE BUILDINGS ON THE MALL

The President has decided that he wants all the temporary government buildings on the Mall razed. He would like this done as soon as possible, including the Main Navy Building where heretofore had been deferred until approximately 1975.

The present schedules call for the Munitions Building, Building N and Building W to be down approximately by the end of 1970. Would you please initiate the appropriate action to see that the Main Navy Building is demolished by the end of 1970 also?

At that point, the Navy realized this was no passing Presidential fancy. A twenty-man briefing was set up to show the White House how serious and costly a blow our ill-considered demolition would be to naval efficiency —a "dog and pony show" complete with maps and charts. The invitations to this meeting were sent out by Colonel Hughes; and the following memo *to* Ehrlichman, in which the President's Air Force aide says, "John Ehrlichman has asked me to invite you to attend this meeting," is shown here to illustrate that bureaucratic error was rife among antibureaucrats too, the difference being that the White House nonsense was unintentional:

THE WHITE HOUSE
WASHINGTON

November 17, 1969

MEMORANDUM FOR: Mr. John Ehrlichman—

The study of the project to vacate and demolish all temporary buildings including Munitions and Main Navy Building on the Mall by the end of calendar year 1970 is ready for presentation to the senior White House staff. There are significant considerations and side effects in many areas which should be discussed before this final proposal is presented to the President.

GSA and the Department of Defense will present a briefing on this project at 4:00 p.m. on Friday, November 21 in the Roosevelt Room. John Ehrlichman has asked me to invite you to attend this meeting. This is a major project of great importance to the administration and I strongly urge that you personally attend.

COLONEL JAMES D. HUGHES

At the dog and pony show, one chart dealt with the dire consequences of the "fragmentation" of the Naval Matériel Command if they were moved to other locations:

FRAGMENTATION OF NMC

- SEPARATION INTO TWO AREAS — 4 LOCATIONS — TEN BUILDINGS
- PERMANENCY OF FRAGMENTATION — 10 TO 20 YEAR LEASE
- REAL ESTATE LOBBY WILL OPPOSE VACATING LEASEHOLDS
- LOSS OF DAILY INTERFACE WITHIN NMC AND RELATED NAVY OFFICES
- MOVEMENT OF 12,000 PERSONNEL AND MATERIALS AMONG TEN BUILDINGS
- REVERSAL OF EFFORTS TO CONSOLIDATE NMC
- ADDITIONAL COSTS OF ADMINISTRATION AND SECURITY RUNS COUNTER TO AUSTERITY PROGRAM
- DIFFICULTY OF PUBLIC CONTACT BECAUSE OF TEN LOCATIONS

As if that were not bad enough, the demolition plans were uneconomic:

DEMOLITION SCHEDULE

- PAST EXPERIENCE MAKES 30 JUNE 1970 DEMOLITION OF MUNITIONS DOUBTFUL
- TELEPHONE CO. ADVISES THAT REQUIRED TELEPHONE SERVICE ON ROUTE 1 CORRIDOR CANNOT BE PROVIDED BEFORE SPRING 1971
- CRASH EFFORT vs. PLANNED EFFORT TO VACATE MAIN NAVY-MUNITIONS WILL BE COSTLY

I will not wear the reader down with all the charts, as the presentation was intended to do, but it is worth looking at the way one chart showed how the Navy flexed its political muscle with Congress:

POLITICAL REACTION

ARMED SERVICES COMMITTEES

- DEFERRAL OR ABANDONMENT OF DEFENSE OFFICE BUILDING AT BOLLING AFTER EXPENDITURE OF APPROXIMATELY $4 MILLION ON PLANS
- INTEREST IN USE OF BOLLING-ANACOSTIA TRACT TO MEET DOD ADMINISTRATIVE SPACE REQUIRE-MENTS
- REVERSAL OF DOD'S NCR MASTER PLANNING
- LEASE ACQUISITION CLEARANCE UNDER TITLE 10 USC

APPROPRIATION COMMITTEES

- ADDITIONAL LEASE COSTS
- INCREASED ADMINISTRATIVE COSTS
- ADDITIONAL ONE TIME MOVE AND CONSTRUCTION COSTS

EXPANSION OF NATIONAL AIRPORT

MARYLAND CONGRESSIONAL DELEGATION

- RELOCATION OF APPROXIMATELY 12,000 EMPLOYEES FROM D.C. TO VIRGINIA WITH NONE GOING TO MARYLAND

REAL ESTATE INTERESTS

- PRESSURE FROM MARYLAND INTERESTS AS WELL AS THOSE IN ALEXANDRIA, FAIRFAX, AND FALLS CHURCH

Robert Kunzig, a Pennsylvania political ally of Minority Leader Hugh Scott, and who had been made head of the General Services Administration, felt that the President had a right to expect an order to be carried out. After listening to presentations like these, usually held in the bomb-shelter conference room in the East Wing, Kunzig made a wistful comment: "You know, I always feel that if a bomb dropped on Washington, the good ol' U. S. Navy could be expected to fight on, wherever it was, till victory. It seems to me, from what you're saying, that if we tear down these old buildings near the White House the whole goddam U. S. Navy will cease to function!"

Soon afterward, John Ehrlichman found out what the Army-Navy game was for. Most Americans fondly believe that the Army-Navy game is a morale-building test of skill and athletic prowess between two of the great armed forces academies. In truth, it does two other things: First, it provides a potential aggressor the perfect moment to attack the United States, as the command structure of the nation's armed forces is otherwise occupied; second, it provides the focal point and forum for the most intensive lobbying effort of Army and Navy "legislative liaison." Ehrlichman had delightedly accepted the Navy's invitation to the game. On the train to Philadelphia on November 29, the reason he had been selected for this largesse became apparent. A stream of Admirals slipped into the seat next to him in the club car to chip away, one by one, at the idea of destroying the Navy's historic Mall buildings and scattering a unified command to the four winds. Each admiral had a separate piece of the argument; each had been programmed to know whom he followed and whom he preceded; and in this way, the target was subjected to ninety minutes of sustained offshore shelling.

Next, newspaper stories began to appear, mainly in the Civil Service columns of the Washington *Daily News*, to the effect that the removal of "Main Navy" would mean the loss of thousands of jobs to the District's blacks and cause traffic problems going to Virginia. Kunzig, who with the rest of GSA and the White House staff became "The Enemy" to Navy men in this project, was able to counter this by discovering that over half the people working in those buildings at the time lived in Virginia—a move would be beneficial to a majority of workers and would subtract from, not add to, traffic on the bridges. Navy Secretary John Chafee wrote to Secretary of Defense Melvin Laird on November 22: "These dates do not provide time for a planned and orderly move. Adherence to them will prove to be disruptive and expensive." Laird asked that this letter be sent in to the President.

Once again, Richard Nixon, President of the United States, Commander-in-Chief of its armed forces, Most Powerful Leader of the Free World, huffed and puffed and tried to blow the houses down:

December 1, 1969

MEMORANDUM FOR: Honorable Melvin R. Laird
Secretary of Defense

Honorable R. L. Kunzig
Administrator of General Services

SUBJECT: Mall Clearance Project

The President has directed the removal of all of the temporary buildings on the Mall, including Main Navy and the Munitions

Building by the end of 1970. In making this decision, he considered all of the alternatives submitted by the Department of Defense. This memorandum constitutes authority to proceed with the necessary plans and actions to complete the project by the end of calendar year 1970.

JAMES D. HUGHES
Colonel, United States Air Force
Military Assistant to the President

cc: Mr. Ehrlichman

About this time, an item appeared in the same newspaper column that was the usual recipient of Navy leaks: "The President has told his aides that there is a Navy admiral who will soon be an ensign if those buildings on the Mall are not torn down."

The next day, Kunzig received a friendly call: "I'm that admiral who soon may be an ensign. You know—maybe you and I ought to have lunch." The logjam began to break up. But Nixon was not taking the assurances he read in memos at face value. He kept driving past those buildings, asking, "When are we going to see grass growing there?"

Don Hughes took him literally, as well he should have, in this memo of January 26, 1970:

". . . The present schedule will result in the demolition of the Munitions Building in July or August and the Main Navy Building in November. This will accomplish your wish to have the Mall cleared by the end of this year. However, it should be pointed out that while the buildings will be removed by the end of December 1970, *the landscaping will not be completed until a later date.*"

Ehrlichman, meanwhile, had to make sure the Navy personnel would have someplace else to work; whenever an obstacle arose, the reluctant movers in Navy would seize upon it as an opportunity for delay. A request for a widening of streets in the chosen location in Virginia was turned down, and some Naval officer happily threw up his hands—no wider streets, no move, no demolition of Main Navy. Ehrlichman called Linwood Holton, newly elected Governor of Virginia: "Lin, we're putting a big payroll into your State; we'd sure appreciate your help on widening some streets." The President's assistant, head of the Domestic Council, kept knocking down excuses for delay, stung by the President's philosophical taunt: "You know, they'll just horse you around a few years, thinking we'll forget about it. It'll never happen."

It did. On July 15, 1970, Hughes sent the President a memo that few thought would ever be written:

July 15, 1970

MEMORANDUM FOR THE PRESIDENT

SUBJECT: Mall Clearance Project

Today Bob Kunzig, the Administrator of GSA, presided over a demolition ceremony for the Main Navy/Munitions Building complex on the Mall. This is a significant milestone in the Mall Clearance Project and is precisely the date that has been scheduled from the outset for the demolition of these buildings to begin.

At the present time, the entire project is on time and on track, and there are no foreseen difficulties which would preclude completion of this project by 31 December 1970.

BRIGADIER GENERAL JAMES D. HUGHES

cc: Mr. Ehrlichman
    Mr. Ziegler

Main Navy died hard. This may be apocryphal, but on the final weekend before its demolition, GSA officials say they received a call from Admiral Hyman Rickover announcing that since his new office was not yet fully ready, he refused to vacate his premises. When news of this reached the White House, a smile of grudging admiration crossed the lips of the men pressing the demolition project at the picture of this crusty old naval officer going down with his office. The Admiral, himself a heroic foe of Navy establishmentarianism, was informed that if he wanted a confrontation, he would be provided same. We had visions of him being carried out of his office, arms grimly folded like Sewell Avery of Montgomery Ward defying FDR in 1944, the greatest symbol of bureaucratic resistance that could be staged. The same thought might have crossed Rickover's mind and he backed down and moved out.

GSA's Kunzig took photographers and a sledgehammer to the historic moment of demolition. One wall had been specially weakened to provide a satisfying collapse upon impact; Kunzig swung the sledgehammer and, as he ruefully told us later, "nothing happened—not only did the wall not collapse, but not a speck of plaster had the decency to fall off the wall."

Because the President of the United States took a continuing interest, because at least two of his aides were made to feel that its success was a crucial test of their ability, and because the President kept prodding, prodding, issuing orders, refusing to be "reasonable," a few miserable buildings were finally knocked down and their occupants reassigned. An elephant gun should not be used to kill a rabbit, the saying goes, but on some

matters affecting entrenched bureaucratic elephants, only elephant guns
will do. Combining pride, relief, and wonderment, the President called
Ehrlichman and then Hughes to say, "We have finally gotten something
done."

Why have I taken the reader down Bureaucracy Lane, the path of most
resistance? I am not anti-Navy; the battle would have been the same if the
old buildings had been occupied by the Postal Service or the Bureau of
Indian Affairs. Nor have I ever believed that Presidential fiats should go
unchallenged—the objections of courageous staffers or bureaucrats (public
servants in this case) are, as we have seen, a necessary check on the reign.

The point here is that Nixon learned by the middle of his first term what
could be done and what could not be done within the Executive Branch,
and the degree of difficulty in making the monster of government move
confirmed his worst suspicions. He called in a management expert, Roy
Ash of Litton Industries, who worked closely with Haldeman in developing a plan for a more efficient way to manage the Executive Branch, coming to grips with the duplication, overlaps, and spaces between stools that
the present system displayed, and essentially making possible policy direction from the man elected to make policy. Ash presented his proposals in
December 1970 to a frigid Cabinet, each member worried about losing
access to the President. At the last minute, former Texas Governor John
Connally, a member of Ash's council, stood up and in ten minutes woke
everybody up to the plan's potential (and his own).

"We're going to do some big things with the Cabinet," the President told
me one night in 1970. I reminded him how we came in determined to let
the Cabinet run their own departments. He shrugged and referred to his
State of the Union address before the joint session of Congress in early
1970: "You notice the way, when I got to the reorganization part, I gave a
long look down the line of Cabinet members? I wanted them to know I
mean business."

I suggested that if he meant to make government reorganization his
Great Crusade, he would put the whole country to sleep. "I know it has
no sex appeal," Nixon agreed. "And we're not going to get it this year or
next from the Congress—maybe the natural resources part, but certainly
not the rest; it'll upset too many apple carts. But it's a start, and it fits in
with the whole approach. You know, Bill, people have really had it up to
here with government."

Nixon, if he wanted to change the direction of government, was presented with Hobson's choice—that is, no choice at all. He could try to let
the departments run themselves, which would result in the bureaucracy's
managing the managers, frustrating his reforms, and continuing to grow
along the lines of Parkinson's Law; or he could try to take all control inside the White House, re-creating the government that existed fifty years
ago and plunking it down on top of the current enterprise. Neither alternative was appetizing. In the back of his mind a third route was being
mapped: infiltration of the departments with Nixon men, trained by Hal-

deman and Ehrlichman in the first term to take command of the substruc-
ture in the second term. This was later viewed as almost a subversion of our
democratic way of life, but it hardly seemed venal at the time.

"How long a half life does a White House operative have?" asked Moynihan in a burst of prescience toward the end of his tenure. The use of the
word from physics was apt: "half life" is the time it takes for half the
atoms in a substance to disintegrate; in government, it is the time it takes
for a White House staffer to lose his perspective, his central overview, and
his sense of commitment to the President's goals when he has been dispatched to work in one of the outlying departments of the Executive
Branch.

Take John Whitaker, for example. I first met John in 1960, when he was
an advance man in the Nixon campaign; he stayed in touch through the
Sixties while working as a geologist, and headed the advance men in 1968,
joining the White House staff after the election to become the liaison with
Interior, where he is now Undersecretary. I kidded him about his half-life
expectancy. "Listen," he insisted, at the beginning of 1973, before disil-
lusionment set in, "it'll last all the way through, you'll see. When you're
out here, and you know the White House ropes, you can make things happen. Look, I won't send in a long proposal for the President to dedicate
some dam—I'll call the appointments secretary and say, 'On the next dull
news day, when you're looking for a place to go, this can be set up anytime
in October,' and it'll have a chance." Whitaker, a strong environmentalist
admired by many of Nixon's adversaries, believed in the infiltration system
in his time of transition: "There was a dispute over here in Interior, and
I said to the guys, 'Here's what the President's philosophy is about this
kind of thing,' and the guys looked at me with their eyes popping. Nobody
ever attached anything they did to the President's philosophy before. It's
our fault if we don't get it through; the bureaucracy can't be expected to
read our minds."

Nixon knew that the bureaucracy was similar to the Supreme Court. If
he could change its makeup, he could affect the generation beyond his
own occupancy of the White House. If men from the Roosevelt and Truman Administrations now dominated much of the upper middle level of
the government machinery, perhaps men imbued with the Nixon outlook
could permeate the bureaucracy of future Administrations. If you can't
lick it, join it. At any rate, in a private meeting with Nelson Rockefeller
as 1971 began, Nixon told him, "We're going to reorganize the government
come hell or high water. That's why we have Connally—not for Texas
politics but for national politics. He'll be pitching those Congressmen
hard as hell and sitting on top of Treasury he'll be able to pitch pretty
hard. Now we're down to the nut-cutting."

It was never easy, but the bureaucracy knew they had a President in
town. Over the years of Nixon's first term, the bureaucracy's defender
became—of all people—the liberals, who are supposed to espouse change,
but who wound up helping the bureaucracy do what it does best—resist

change—because the change was in the direction away from Washington.

At the time, the Nixon men were perceived as the Good Guys, scraping off the barnacles, making the government more responsive to the will of the people. In time, as the Nixon men came to be seen as the Bad Guys, the entire recalcitrant bureaucracy gained a heroic stature it did not deserve. Certainly the few bureaucrats who rebelled against peremptory, foolish, or invidious orders from the White House were heroes, but the wrongheaded orders were hardly the rule. New brooms will sweep anew, and the bureaucracy will resist again, emboldened by a legend they will perpetrate of brave men who dragged a foot for democracy. But at least they won't do it from Main Navy and the prefabs on the Mall.

Of all the words of tongue or pen, goes the poem, the saddest are these: "It might have been." Even sadder, perhaps, are words the President scribbled at the bottom of a memo telling him some pet project could never get off the ground. The elected leader of two hundred million Americans wrote in frustration:

4. THE RISE OF JOHN MITCHELL

Picture a natural athlete, who in his youth moonlighted by playing semipro ice hockey, the roughest, fastest sport of all; who, in later years, maintained a golf game that enabled him to spot his puffing opponents ten and twenty strokes.

Picture the same man in World War II, a born leader, a Navy Commander, choosing a command in the highest-risk, most daring and exciting branch of the Navy, patrol torpedo boats (and one of whose lieutenants later became a President).

Picture him in middle age, still the hopeless romantic, choosing to marry an unstable, glamorous Southern belle, and as she cracked under the tension of the attention she called upon herself, resolutely sticking by her against all prudence until she left him because, as he kept putting it to cynical questioners, "I love her."

That combination of certain characteristics common to Jim Thorpe, John Kennedy, and Rhett Butler was none other than the dour, pipe-sucking, bloodhound-visaged "heavy" of the Nixon Administration, "the second most powerful man in America," Nixon's first Attorney General, John Newton Mitchell.

In 1973 he lost it all: his wife, his reputation for integrity, his cool, his money, his future, retaining only—and in heightened form—his public image as an unfeeling, heavy-lidded villain dedicated only to the success of Richard Nixon.

John Mitchell was the rock upon which Nixon built his church, and when that rock began to crumble, Nixon was not able to shore up his foundations quickly enough.

"I've found the heavyweight," Nixon told me in 1967. He had been worried about filling the job of campaign manager with a man who had what politicians call "heft," the kind of authority, presence and stature that enables a man to dominate a roomful of ambitious and suspicious politicians. In 1960 Nixon would call nobody his "manager." Former Republican National Chairman Leonard Hall had been Nixon's campaign "chairman," because Nixon did not fully trust anyone with the whole job of managing his most important campaign. Robert Finch was placed in tandem with Hall with the title of campaign "director," a fuzzing of responsibility which —combined with Nixon's dabbling in details—provided a lesson in mismanagement he was not to forget. Hall, a recognized heavyweight in politics, finished the campaign furious at Nixon for undercutting him and blowing an election that should have been won, though he was too good a soldier to say anything publicly.

In Nixon's eyes, Mitchell combined the heft and decisiveness of Hall with the perceptive, Hamlet-like analysis of Finch. Mitchell was a successful New York lawyer, a front runner on what Nixon liked to call "the fastest track of all"; moreover, Mitchell was intimately familiar with state politics. Though "municipal bond lawyer" sounded far removed from politics, it was politics nearly unalloyed. Mitchell had to know, and keep the confidence of, hundreds of politicians across the country who controlled the law business on their local bond issues and who needed Mitchell's banking and Wall Street clout.* In the midst of the abortive push by Nelson Rockefeller just before the Republican Convention of 1968, Mitchell proudly showed me evidence of business he had brought into the Nixon, Mudge law firm—a prospectus on a New York State housing bond issue, freshly issued by the state that had the most anti-Nixon delegation of all.

Nixon saw in John Mitchell a man who was accustomed to making $200,000 a year; who did not need the job of campaign manager or any job it might lead to, because he elaborately gave the impression of being above ego needs; and who, in age, self-confidence, and sense of authority, was at least Nixon's equal. Easy to rely on, hard to get, untrammeled by past defeat and with no commitments to other candidates on the national scene, Mitchell became Nixon's most sought-after trophy. And unlike most of the men Nixon had been attracting in 1966 and 1967, Mitchell was tough. Ellsworth, Finch, Flanigan, Price, and I helped Nixon bridge into essentially liberal areas with a light touch. The other men from the Nixon, Mudge law firm—Len Garment, John Sears, and Tom Evans—were smooth rather than abrasive, but as delegate hunting began to supersede "imagery" in the comeback, more politically calloused hands were called for. In came Kleindienst, Haldeman, and, above all, Mitchell.

It was Mitchell whom Nixon men went to for answers; he had a way of getting to the nub of the problem and then laying out alternative routes to the solution, proposing his recommendation, and then—this is where he left many politicians behind—picking up the telephone and making something happen. After a while, the reputation he earned for being a decision-maker put pressure on him to make decisions too quickly.

When the '68 campaign ended, he did not want to come to Washington. Nixon told me why on the telephone: "He's worried about his wife, Martha. You know, she's had this problem for years, but I told him the hell

* "Clout," which originated in Chicago politics, means "influence"; it is often used interchangeably with "stroke," which in Nixon usage as a noun is more closely synonymous with "power."

with it, come down and she'll be all right, or at least no worse than she was in Rye." Martha Mitchell had what was once known as a screw loose—no drinking problem, but an overblown yen for attention and a habit of pouring her heart out to strangers on the telephone late at night. As the wife of a municipal bond lawyer, that was only a matter for Westchester gossip; as the Attorney General's lady, it could create problems. Mitchell was amused by her, proud of her, defensive about her, and obviously attached to her. He knew he was taking a big chance in coming to Washington, a place that held no special charms for him, but he acquiesced. Many men strike a pose of reluctance about high-level government service; in Mitchell's case, he meant it. Nixon had offered the Attorney General's post to Bob Finch, assuming correctly he would turn it down. "I'm no cop," Finch told me he had told the President-elect, which was true, adding wistfully, "Still, we've come so far, for so long, I'd hate to miss all of it now," and he chose to leave the Lieutenant-Governorship of California for the dead end of HEW. Then Nixon gave the law-and-order job to a man just the opposite of Finch in many ways. Finch and Mitchell later came to cordially despise each other (Mitchell okayed an illegal FBI wiretap on Finch's former aide, James McLane, in 1970) but kept their feelings under wraps in Cabinet meetings. Mitchell felt about Finch the way Kissinger felt about Rogers: pleasing personality, loyal, but incompetent. With Mitchell, Nixon could tell the voters he kept his promise: to appoint a "new Attorney General"—something new Presidents have a habit of doing—but, as promised, an AG in sharp contrast with LBJ's civil libertarian Ramsey Clark. The Mitchell appointment was mostly criticized by people who worried that Nixon might actually have meant his law-and-order rhetoric, and a few isolated voices who thought that the tradition of appointing a campaign manager to be AG should be discarded.

In fact, Mitchell knew the relationship of rhetoric to reality better than most and, in his most remembered public statement, said: "You'd be better informed if, instead of listening to what we say, you watch what we do." This was greeted as evidence of two-facedness, but was an honest—and hopeful—statement from a politician who knew his Southern constituency needed constant respect and attention, but who also knew the trend of law had to be in a direction of desegregation. When Nixon opened a Cabinet meeting on February 18, 1970, he was concerned about the Stennis Amendment, a Southern turning of the tables on the North, calling for a cutoff of all Federal funds to school districts which failed to integrate, even based on *de facto*, rather than *de jure*, segregation. The President looked around and said, "Mr. Attorney General, are you here?" "I think so," Mitchell mumbled, slung low in his Cabinet table chair to the right of the Vice President. "I thought you were out with Finch working on that Stennis Amendment," the President said. "Which side are you on?" Mitchell said that he was on the right side: "Right in the middle." George Shultz said: "Don't you know that old proverb, 'He who walks in the middle of the road gets hit from both sides'?" Mitchell only grunted;

he was known as the architect and exponent of a "Southern strategy," when in reality he was a supporter of a "battleground state" strategy in politics. He saw the need to lean right when you were moving left, taking as many conservative friends with you as possible when you had to go in a progressive direction.

Mitchell reminded Nixon often that he was down in Washington because Nixon needed him, not because he sought the job. At a 1969 Cabinet meeting, the President introduced Lawrence Walsh, a member of the U.S. peace delegation to Paris. Mitchell remarked that he and Walsh used to see each other at the Wall Street Club. The President shot in an unlikely question: "You didn't say that with any nostalgia, did you, John?" Mitchell shrugged: "It varies."

Mitchell was not variable after making a commitment, however. When Labor Secretary George Shultz won him over to the Philadelphia Plan, the most startling, gutsy race-relations effort undertaken by the Administration (putting pressure on white-dominated labor unions to admit black members for good jobs in government contract work, something Democratic Administrations dependent on organized Labor's political support could not do), Mitchell never wavered in the face of labor, conservative, or racist reaction. He grasped Shultz's aim, to show blacks that the Administration would help them gain the opportunity for economic advancement, now far more important than new laws or more welfare, the thrust of which was consistent with a spirit of self-reliance. "When Mitchell's with you," Shultz told me in some wonderment then, "he's like a rock." This lasted for a couple of years, until Charles Colson's appeal to labor as a bloc in the "new majority" took these matters out of Mitchell's hands.

I saw Mitchell as a rock firsthand, when William Casey, a New York lawyer, author, and venture capitalist, was nominated to be Chairman of the Securities and Exchange Commission. Casey—an OSS, veteran law partner of Len Hall's and an energetic, brilliant man—had been sued several times in stockholder actions, settling some and fighting others, as most active businessmen have done. John Dean III, an ambitious young protégé of Mitchell's at the Justice Department, who had been named White House Counsel after John Ehrlichman moved up and Mitchell adversary John Sears had been forced out, was assigned to monitor conflict-of-interest matters. Dean was a purist about conflict-of-interest ethics; his job would have been easier if eunuchs were appointed to jobs, because no conflict charges could then be made. Such a policy, if adopted by any President, would mean that a great many good, activist executives and men with the scars of experience could not work in Washington, because they had previously led careers "in the arena." Dean, Commerce Secretary Maurice Stans, Presidential Assistant Peter Flanigan, and I—along both as a friend of Casey's and as the so-called public opinion expert—went to Mitchell's cluttered office at the Department of Justice to talk it over. Dean made the case against Casey—presenting everything that might look bad or make a headline—and indicated, without making a firm recommendation, that it would be simpler to ask Casey to withdraw his name, rather than take the chance of a Senate turndown.

Mitchell asked a few detailed questions, then to Dean: "Did Casey ever lie to you?" "No, sir," replied Dean.

"Is he prepared to fight?" "Yes."

"Then," said Mitchell, taking the pipe out of his mouth, "the man is entitled to his day in court," and that was that. Mitchell was, as Shultz described him, like a rock. Casey's nomination sailed through without much Senate resistance, and he turned out to be a superb appointment, reinvigorating a moribund SEC. (Years later, Mitchell and Stans were to be indicted for having set up an appointment with Casey and financier Robert Vesco, allegedly in return for a campaign contribution. The SEC chairman did the proper thing: turned the man over to the SEC's general counsel, exerting no pressure. Since no fix had been put in, the prosecution case was weak, probably motivated by a desire in the New York U. S. Attorney's office to take a ride on Watergate publicity. Mitchell and Stans were acquitted.)

In the spring of 1970, Mitchell was at his peak as a Nixon intimate. He had recommended a respected, sitting Federal appellate judge, Clement F. Haynsworth, Jr., for the Supreme Court; but when Nixon nominated him, the accumulated resentment of Washington liberals at the forced retirement of Justice Abe Fortas for conflict of interest made itself felt. Haynsworth was unfairly pilloried for conflict of interest charges which, strictly applied, might have been grounds for the impeachment of Justice William O. Douglas. But Haynsworth had an impediment in his speech—he stuttered—and he could not properly defend himself in the court of public opinion. A fine jurist, he returned to the appellate bench and distinguished himself there in later years. His politically inspired rejection was not one of the Senate liberals' finest hours.

Mitchell, still looking for a strict constructionist Southerner who was a Republican, then came up with G. Harrold Carswell. Nixon, angry at his Haynsworth defeat and trusting his AG's judgment, nominated him. The selection of Carswell, almost out of spite, was one of the most ill-advised public acts of the early Nixon Presidency. Carswell was just another guy. Senator Roman Hruska, in Carswell's defense, put forth a thesis that mediocrity deserved representation, which—though it might have been given consideration at Democratic Convention reform proceedings—was hardly appropriate for a nomination to the nation's highest court. Nixon, embittered at the Haynsworth rejection, supported Carswell like a man biting down on a toothache. I ran into Haldeman one afternoon in late March of 1970, who told me, "Kleindienst spent a nasty forty-five minutes in the President's office—he has the job of getting Carswell confirmed."

When Carswell was deservedly rejected by the Senate, Nixon's reaction was to close ranks with Mitchell against "them." Aboard the *Sequoia* the night of April 8, Nixon talked over the affair with Haldeman and Mitchell. They were convinced that the Senate liberals, and the liberal press, were out to block the expressed will of the people on "strict construction"; the President did a slow burn; the next morning, he called Pat Buchanan. "In that indifferent voice he uses when he is really pissed off," Pat told me later, the President ordered a statement: "Get up a statement on law and order," Nixon told Buchanan, "blasting the Senate on holding back the crime bills. Should take about three minutes for you to knock out—get it here by three o'clock." Bryce Harlow and Len Garment heard about what was afoot and suggested a different reaction: for the President to invite the Senators who had voted for the two nominations to a White House reception and thank-you. The President said no; he wanted to issue a blast.

With some misgivings—the House of Representatives, not the Senate, was responsible for bottling up the crime bills—Buchanan started this oblique blasting-back at the Senate for the Carswell rejection, but was interrupted at 2 P.M. by Haldeman, who passed along the President's change of mind: hit the Senate directly about Carswell. Buchanan's typewriter smoked, but not enough. An hour later the President personally added an intemperate blast at the Senate's "hypocrisy" and "regional discrimination" for the "vicious" and "malicious" character assassination of his two nominees, with Mitchell nodding as the "red meat" went in. Nixon read the statement for television cameras, blatantly whipping up Southern resentment, bitterly defending his "power of appointment," turned and stalked out, Mitchell behind him. Was the display of anger cool and calculated— "only be angry when your real anger has passed" he often told us—or was this a genuine fit of pique? I think Nixon did a slow burn, fanned by Mitchell's anxious defense of his own bad advice, and the blow-up was as real as it was demeaning.

From Nixon's point of view, however, there was cause for resentment. The previous Haynsworth turndown proved to him that his Senate enemies were hypocritical in their concentration on Carswell's intellectual inadequacy. Besides, when Harry Truman appointed mediocre Sherman Minton, there was no hullaballoo raised about scholarly achievements. The Senate, he felt, was applying new and higher standards of probity (re Haynsworth) and background (Carswell's generation-ago aid to a country club's black exclusion policy, hardly comparable to Justice Black's Ku Klux Klan membership), only for one reason—to deny the President his right to influence the direction of the Supreme Court by the nature of his nominations. The people had spoken, Nixon held, and liberal Senators were trumping up charges to block the will of the people. The appointment power was not to be snatched from this President by a newly militant Senate.

Nixon and Mitchell were right, in a sense, but they were more wrong. They confused (with Colson's help) the word "nominate" with "appoint." The President had the power to nominate but shared the power to appoint with the Senate. Had Nixon followed up the nomination of Haynsworth—a good judge and a conservative—with another of the same stripe (like Harry Blackmun, who was later confirmed), he would have made the ideological impact on the Court he had sought. The Senate could not keep finding reasons to turn down qualified conservatives; but in Carswell, Mitchell provided Nixon with a man the Senate had not only the reason but the obligation to turn down. Times had changed since Harry Truman's day. Nixon, if he was going to change the direction of the Court, would have to do it with unassailable men.

Mitchell, the finder of Carswell, buttressed Nixon's feelings of Senate persecution to defend his own position. But it was all a bad business, and Nixon—when he stopped focusing on the Senate—knew Mitchell was at fault.

The reverberations to the Carswell rejection extended into the old "impeach Earl Warren" crowd, and surfaced in an unlikely place. Jerry Ford, the usually sensible House Minority Leader, threatened to lead an "impeach William Douglas" movement on grounds of conflict of interest. First Fortas, then Haynsworth, then Douglas on conflict of interest—where would it all lead? The matter threatened to get out of hand. Leonard Garment urged John Mitchell to call off the counterattack, and independently wrote the President a memo on it. The President knew he was better off outlasting Douglas, who was aging, than condoning an ouster effort. Nixon telephoned Mitchell, rather than Ford directly, and told Mitchell to tell Ford, with whom he had frequent contact, to "turn it off." Mitchell did not want to discuss this with Ford, and pleaded "separation of powers," holding that it might be improper for the Executive to tell the Legislative to lay off the Judiciary. He told Nixon he would get the lay-off-the-Court message across in a Law Day address the following week.

Mitchell, who could stand like a rock, could also whip around like a swivel chair. Jack Landau, his departing speechwriter, wrote a swan song that did not sound at all like John Mitchell. The New York *Times* headlined, "Mitchell Warns of Danger in Attacks on High Court," adding with understatement in a subhead, "Speech a Departure from Usual Tone." Mitchell, who had been called "the Iron Chancellor," "El Supremo," and "Mr. Tough," called for "an end to irresponsible and malicious criticism which will not only damage the Court but will undermine all of our courts and our respect for our system of laws," adding with particular reference to Douglas, "the Justices of the Supreme Court live alone with their consciences, that their sincerity, scholarship and devotion to this generation and to future generations is beyond reproach." While he was at it, Mitchell endorsed the *Miranda* decision: "that all criminal defendants must be treated equally regardless of their financial status"; Nixon had, for years, lumped *Miranda* in with those "permissive" decisions that led to the imbalance between "the peace forces and the criminal forces."

When pushed, Mitchell had gone all the way. Perhaps he compensated for some extreme positions taken in the 1968 campaign, perhaps he was trying to forestall an exodus from the Justice Department of some of its best young talent, who had a tendency to listen to "what we say." These were part of the mix. An added ingredient was subtle pressure on the

President, transmitted to Mitchell, from Chief Justice Warren Burger, that the time had come to stop tearing down the reputation of the Court.

The nature of that pressure had to do with the other, more traumatic, event that had been shaping up that month of April, 1970. John Mitchell, as a member of the National Security Council, and as one of the President's more tough-minded confidants, was at the center of the decision to launch an incursion into the sanctuaries being used by Communists in Cambodia.

Mitchell, more than Defense Secretary Laird and far more than Secretary of State Rogers, counseled for the more extensive action. As we have seen, it was Mitchell and Kissinger that the President saw most as the decision point was reached.

On April 30, the night the President made his speech to the nation about Cambodia, the Chief Justice dropped by the White House to pay an unannounced visit after the speech. The next day a cryptic explanation was given that he came by to "deliver a letter." Burger, in denying it had anything to do with Cambodia, simply said it was "judicial business" that required personal delivery since he "couldn't reach the President all day by telephone." The Chief Justice's business, of course, was the Mitchell speech, scheduled to be given the next day to the Washington chapter of the Bar Association. Nixon had asked Burger to look it over and give him his comments before delivery, which was as flattering to the Chief Justice as the speech was reassuring to the Court. The two men spent two hours together that night. Next day, John Mitchell gave the Supreme Court of the United States a clean bill of health. (The Burger visit was unusual but not improper; on another occasion, working on the President's address to the judicial conference in Williamsburg in 1971 on judicial reform, I checked out the speech with both Mitchell and the Chief Justice. Mitchell's comments were cursory, Burger's detailed and to the point, though the Chief Justice refrained from writing on the draft, making verbal suggestions to me in his chambers until he was sure I had it exactly right.)

Soon after the Kent State and Jackson State tragedies, the two lines of Mitchell activity—adviser on foreign affairs and enforcer of domestic security—converged. The idea went to the President for the "coordination" of intelligence activities, as Tom Charles Huston made his bid for a modified police state, and for five days the damnable "Huston" plan was in effect. When J. Edgar Hoover belatedly objected, Mitchell backed up the FBI and the plan was shelved.

Between the Carswell fiasco, the reaction to Cambodia, and the Mitchell backing-off at Nixon's desired "coordination" of foreign intelligence activity, including burglary, the relationship between Nixon and his Attorney General began to cool. As Julie Eisenhower told me, "After 1970 we didn't see the Mitchells much for dinner." Mitchell was fallible. Ehrlichman and a new force, Charles Colson, let it be known that the Justice Department was really not so well run, which was true—Mitchell was no administrator. (If we had lost the 1968 campaign—that is, if ½ of

1 per cent of the votes had switched—Mitchell would have been assailed as a terrible administrator. His talent was to "ride herd" and advise, not to organize and run.) Haldeman wanted no part of Mitchell in the 1970 campaign, and largely ignored him in its planning. When that midterm effort did not go so well, Mitchell jibed that Haldeman's campaign had made the President look like "a candidate for sheriff," and Nixon began to plan his 1972 campaign staff along the lines of 1960, rather than 1968—with Mitchell in the Len Hall role as symbol.

In retrospect, Mitchell looked a lot tougher than he was, and was usually a moderating influence on the let's-crack-'em school. When the President proposed to invite Judge Julius Hoffman, the "Chicago 7" trial judge, to the White House, Mitchell put the kibosh on it with an amazed "I understand the law and order bit, but Jesus Christ!"

He was overrated as an executive. He was susceptible to good advice. When communications executive Richard Moore, an old Nixon friend, came into the Nixon Administration in 1970, he was assigned to improving Mitchell's relations with the press, a job thought to be akin to Augeanstable cleaning, but Moore found his "client" receptive. At a Gridiron Club dinner, Mitchell told the correspondents, "If you quit bugging me, I'll quit bugging you." That was a funny line, and well delivered; many a false word is said in jest.

One reason why Mitchell was ambivalent about the press was the curious treatment given his wife, Martha. From the start, Martha Mitchell was vulnerable to press attack; but if the dreaded "media" traveled in a pack, at least in this case they ran toward her with tails wagging. She was outspoken, colorful, talkative, defiant—seemingly untouched by public relations soothing syrup, and they lapped up what she had to offer. The press, in a kindness rarely extended celebrities, protected her—as if journalists who might slam her for being neurotic or exhibitionistic were, by virtue of attacking somebody so clearly not in the Administration mold, thereby pro-colorlessness. Martha got away with murder. If there were any press "conspiracy," it was in the way the press corps gentled Martha along, treating ner as a source of amusement. As a result, she became a heroine to Republican fund-raisers, outdrawing even Spiro Agnew at the top of his rousing form. She was nervous, but cunning; a native shrewdness kept her out of the deep trouble her need for attention might have gotten her into. Her husbanq, who had been prepared for the worst, was delighted with the best press of anybody in the Administration. His wife was happy to be a celebrity, which made Mitchell happy, and it even moderated his animus toward the press.

John Mitchell was the man who played the "heavy," who most insiders were sure was really *not* a heavy, but who really *was* a heavy—not out of greed or power-lust or venality, but out of inexperience in government operations, overconfidence, and a confusion in his own mind about the balance between national security and individual liberty.

With luck, Mitchell could have gotten by. We will examine his fall from grace later in the book, when he ran out of luck.

5. LONERS STICK TOGETHER

The Nixon men prodding the bureaucracy—with some success—found themselves building a bureaucracy of their own, and toward the end of the first year began to enjoy what most they criticized.

The White House staff was shaking down. As Pat Moynihan had predicted, John Ehrlichman was finding out where the Bureau of the Budget was and Bob Haldeman had published his telephone directory, and they had taken charge. The idea of putting all that executive power out there in the boondocks of the Cabinet departments produced too many delays and overlaps; to White House staffers in a hurry it seemed much more efficient to do it the centralized way. Except for George Shultz's Labor Department, which was known to be on the ball, the administrative power began to flow in toward the West Wing of the White House.

A deliberate pointing to enemies, real or imagined; a new attitude of solidarity around the Man. As these forces took shape, the lower-the-voices theme began to get lost. (President James Polk, whose President-of-all-the-People Inaugural Nixon had admired, would have understood the problem: after his unifying beginning, Polk induced a war with Mexico and won the California territory, getting all the abolitionists furious at him for seeming to extend slavery.)

The change of attitude and direction of administrative power has been simplistically denounced as a "power grab" isolating the President behind a "Berlin Wall" and contributing to a paranoia at the top and a siege mentality. Some of that is true; a lot of it is not.

Nixon, Bob Haldeman, and Al Haig were loners; in a superficially gregarious way, so was Henry Kissinger. The word is not pejorative—great men, for example, must be loners—but the loner-liness of Nixon and his closest aides explains something about the us-against-them superpartisanship that so affected his Presidency.

Two criticisms offered by scholars at the kind of organization Nixon brought to the White House are useful to study now. One, Irving Janis' "groupthink," has to do with the dangers of over-organization; the other,

Richard Hofstadter's "paranoid style," has to do with the methods used by that kind of organization.

Irving Janis, psychology professor at Yale, described "groupthink," which he (and much of the academic group) thinks led to Johnson's escalation of the Vietnam war, Kennedy's Bay of Pigs, Truman's invasion of North Korea, FDR's failure to be prepared for Pearl Harbor, and Nixon's failure to cope with Watergate. Groupthink is defined by Janis as "the concurrence-seeking tendency, which fosters over-optimism, lack of vigilance and sloganistic thinking about the weakness and immorality of outgroups."

Let's look at some of the symptoms he lists and see how each applies to Richard Nixon and his group:

"An illusion of invulnerability . . . which creates excessive optimism and encourages taking extreme risks."

No. If anything, the Nixon men were afflicted by an illusion of vulnerability: at the head of a minority party, looking for ways to broaden support; living in an island of hostility, which was Washington, D.C., or so most of the Nixon men felt; winners by an eyelash in 1968, just as we lost by an eyelash in 1960, and thought during the first term we would likely win or lose by an eyelash in 1972. The wide swings of the public mood (inflation fears, to recession fears, to renewed inflation fears, honeymoon, to Cambodia–Kent State, to Peking and Moscow, to dismay at Christmas bombing, to the relief of peace) never gave the Nixonians excessive optimism over any sustained length of time. Starting a secret negotiation with Peking was risky, not starting a "plumbers" unit to protect secrecy. Calculated risks for peace were carefully weighed, never the unseen risks of letting an antiscoundrel force turn into a personal secret police.

"An inherent belief in the group's inherent morality, inclining the members to ignore the ethical or moral consequences of their decisions."

Yes, but. The Nixon men saw themselves as from the suburban heartland, where morality is supposed to be bred in the bone, revered and honored, not afflicted with the relativism of the big cities and swinging elitists. The Nixon men didn't run their country down, didn't go in for permissiveness, abortion, or pornography, and rejected the criminal-coddling talk that looked for "root causes" and blamed society for the wrongdoing of individuals.

Such self-righteousness mirrored the self-righteous vocabulary of the antiwar movement, studded with "indecent," "immoral," "obscene"—as if turning an ally over to what we were sure would be a bloodbath, with hundreds of thousands of Asians slaughtered as at Hue, were the moral thing to do. The self-righteousness of the Ins is more dangerous than the same trait in the Outs, but because both sides had their zealots, the belief in inherent morality on both sides was disastrously intensified.

"Direct pressure on any member who expresses strong arguments against any of the group's stereotypes, illusions or commitments, making

clear that this type of dissent is contrary to what is expected of all loyal members."

Yes. When I objected to the torrent of interviews given by the President in early 1971, arguing that it made him look like a sudden convert to publicity, I was ostracized for three months. Nor did Commerce Secretary Peter Peterson's flirtation with "the Georgetown cocktail party set" endear him to the President.

On the other hand, to use a favored phrase, the Nixon Administration prided itself in not moving in lockstep nearly as much as the Johnson Administration. Pat Moynihan and Arthur Burns, for example, were permitted to broadcast their conflicting views on welfare. Wherever domestic policy was being decided the President permitted wide latitude in discussion, in return expecting "good soldiering" when the final decision was made. Secretary Shultz, who fought for a rational oil import policy, was rebuffed publicly and fell into line ("Not every difference of opinion is a difference of principle"—Jefferson). He stayed to see his policy adopted years later. Trial balloons, leaks of appointments, disagreements on domestic legislation—in fact, the "open" Nixon Administration of 1969 was unzippered, and was criticized for "lack of direction," a euphemism for not enough internal authoritarianism.

"Self-censorship of deviations from the apparent group consensus, reflecting each member's inclination to minimize to himself the importance of his doubts and counter arguments."

Janis has an insight here, better described as the "Am I crazy?" syndrome. When you are in a meeting in the Roosevelt Room across from the Oval Office in the White House, and men of power and experience around you accept certain "givens"—like media hostility or the impossibility of reconciliation with liberal Republicans—you ask yourself, less out of fear of being turned down than out of fear of being an ass, whether you can continue to have any of your opinions respected if you challenge assumptions that the group agreed upon long ago.

One subtlety here that political psychologists may not be aware of: certain members of the Nixon group, their loyalty proved over the years, were indulged as iconoclasts, encouraged to have their own nongroup set of assumptions in certain areas, and were expected to present their objections at meetings so that the devil would not be denied an advocate. In these cases—Len Garment on civil rights, myself on loosening up the reverential atmosphere, Herb Klein on press conferences—the house oddballs were expected to speak up. None of us felt constricted by the am-I-crazy syndrome, since that sort of against-the-grain thinking was expected. Oddly, Buchanan—the conservative true believer—was also considered an iconoclast.

But the self-censorship did take place in areas outside of one's iconoclastic "specialties"; when I volunteered a suggestion in a Vietnam speech draft that no more draftees be sent to fight, I was promptly taken off the speech entirely, and was less inclined to do that again.

Janis has more to tell us, but his slant on the Nixon staff structure opens up some of the central questions about Nixon the person. Did he insist on groupthink? Was he the victim of it? What pressure did he exert, and what did he receive, to conform to certain stereotypes?

For some help in those areas, we move from Yale's Professor Janis to Columbia's late Professor Richard Hofstadter, author of *Anti-Intellectualism in American Life* and especially the essay "The Paranoid Style in American Politics."

Paranoid is a strong word to use in connection with a President of the United States. Nixon's critics had used it frequently to describe him. One of the obvious themes of this book, that an excess of "us-against-them" partisanship has pernicious results, is natural ammunition to supply anyone who wants to think the American people twice elected a paranoid nut. But Hofstadter used the word to describe a style, not a man. "No other word," he wrote, "adequately evokes the qualities of heated exaggeration, suspiciousness, and conspiratorial fantasy that I have in mind." And he carefully added: "Nothing entirely prevents a sound program or a sound issue from being advocated in the paranoid style . . ." Environmentalists use it against combination of companies out to despoil the land; Zionists see a conspiratorial connection between Arabs, oil companies, and the Department of State; Ralph Nader has the paranoid style of the trust busters of the past; and populist orators old and new have inveighed against real or fancied conspiracies of banks, railroads, Big Government bureaucracies, and pointy-headed professors ganging up on "the little man." The paranoid style is almost invariably the style of the political reformer.

The central fact about the paranoid style, as we apply it to Nixon, is this: *Here is the first time in Presidential politics that the paranoid style has been used by a leader of the majority*. Ordinarily, this style is used by movements that see themselves beset by, and surrounded by, enemies vastly more numerous and well financed than themselves. But Nixon had proclaimed the Silent Majority, and firmly believed himself to be a Gulliver beset by Lilliputians not nearly so powerful as he and his supporters were.

Why? If you have the majority with you, why blaze away at the offensive minority with Eastern Establishment conspiracies, Washington–New York axes, *Times-Post*-CBS mental monopolies, and academic-foundation-Government bureaucracy alliances?

Here's why. First, it worked. Just as the NATO alliance was created by the fear of the Soviet power along its border, so did the Silent Majority identify itself by the presence of the noisy minority.

Second, the paranoid style of the new majority comes out of the fact that it had long ago grown accustomed to being the permanent minority. Right-wingers had been "out" since 1932, and not until Vietnam, the failure of Great Society programs to deliver services well, and the civil rights backlash did conservatives find themselves in the saddle. They do not quickly change their style; it is not in the nature of conservatives to do so.

Nixon began as a Communist-hunter, a man aware of a vast conspiracy, calling his constituents to combat it. He could change his policies and his outlook much faster than he could change his style. He blithely told Republican Congressmen who blanched at budget deficits: "It will take you a little while to get used to fighting *for* what you've been fighting *against* all your lives."

Third, the picture of the White House in 1969 ringed by the peace-now forces is a good symbol of a majority "surrounded" by a minority. More pervasively later, there was the feeling of ostracism and begrudgement of legitimacy Nixon and many of his men felt about their physical environment—liberal, Democratic Washington, D.C.

Nixon, safely on the inside, remained the perennial Outsider; when he talked about the Establishment (which some of his critics considered him the boss of) he was talking about all those other guys. He was the duly elected, anti-Establishment President of what he called the "damngovernment," a bureaucratic monster beyond any man's control, and he was not in place for long—most Nixon men, like most Republicans who come to Washington, generally plan to go home soon. Home was not on the Potomac.

Loners, transients, men without roots—all that is frequently attributed to the Californians, usually by people who have not put down roots in California—but political restlessness is undeniably Nixon's mark, and kept him on the road even as President. "Get out of Washington," he told his writers, "go talk to real people." When he traveled outside Washington, he didn't talk to "people"—he likes to deal with as few individuals as possible, and thinks of the people in the aggregate—but when he bounced from Washington to San Clemente to Key Biscayne to Camp David, he was not only fulfilling a need to move around, he was consciously saying that he was not a man of the East, of the Establishment; he wanted to show there is no law that says the country must be governed constantly from the District of Columbia. (The New York *Times* in late 1973 decided to stop calling San Clemente's compound "The Western White House." Nixon would say, "You see? We got to them.") The need to stick together is the mark of the out-group, which puts a higher premium on loyalty—and it must not be forgotten that an in-group that perceives itself as the out-group continues to act like the out-group.

Why, Nixon wondered, did "those people" hate him so? Why did they criticize him one day for failing to lead, and then when he did, criticize him for polarizing our society? He knew what he wanted for America—a renaissance of the self-confident American spirit, a new sturdiness to the American character, equal opportunity, free markets and free men, and "what we have not had since the Eisenhower years, prosperity without inflation and without war." Those were, he insisted, "great goals." He declared them in public and he shared those thoughts with his associates in private. With noble motives like that, he figured, anybody who opposed him must have had ignoble motives of their own—such as an oligarchical lust for power, or a deep-seated antipathy against him as a person, or a perverse refusal to accept democratic mandates.

Bob Haldeman, the extension of Nixon used to reinforce this style, was —paradoxically—the man usually most alert to the dangers of groupthink. Most of the time, Haldeman saw his role not as Al Capone's Frank Nitti, "The Enforcer," but as a guardian of open options, making certain the President never received only one view on an issue. Nixon told Haldeman, and Kissinger as well, that he wanted to see all the alternatives and the likely consequences of each and not the kind of committee product Sherman Adams used to feed Eisenhower. Accordingly, Nixon was *not* fed "groupthink," and rarely chose the insipid "option three" of five possibilities, nor did he seek to impose it on his staff—that is, not about *issues*. Where the inner circle's groupthink and paranoid style did reinforce each other disastrously was on *attitudes*, but nobody thought to guard against that.

The attitude that fire had to be fought with fire, "leaks" with "plumbers," political opponents with the full range of Government pressures, that threats were of such magnitude that they called up the most severe response—unfortunately, this was never "staffed out," to use Haldeman's favorite phrase, and there is where the programmers needed "input" above all.

6. NIXON'S HALDEMAN

"He doesn't want to organize," Bob Haldeman said of the President, "he wants to *be* organized." The former head of the J. Walter Thompson advertising agency in Los Angeles, UCLA campus politician, hard-working and well-regarded member of the California Board of Regents, teetotaling Christian Scientist, manager of the 1962 Nixon campaign for California Governor, Haldeman proceeded to do the job Nixon wanted.

Haldeman saw to it that everything was organized.

He organized reactions. After the President's Silent Majority speech, one of Haldeman's quiet, polite young men (they kept wearing out, like sub-Steinmetzes, and being replaced) contacted financier Ross Perot who had an idea for running ads, getting a mail pull from coupons in them, and bringing mail in the truckloads to the White House from dozens of different cities. In a meeting with Alex Butterfield and Ron Ziegler, Haldeman called for a report on the Silent Majority reaction. Butterfield said Perot reported he was carefully holding on to all the letters he received in the various cities in which ads had been run. Where were the letters being held? In banks. "You mean," said Ziegler, "when reporters ask me, 'Where is the Silent Majority,' I can say we have them locked up in bank vaults all over the country?" Butterfield deadpanned yes, and added another piece of the organized plan: "It's all part of 'One Nation Under God' month."

Haldeman organized ideas. I had thought that it would be nice for somebody (me, for example) to hang around the meetings the President had with people where no press was present. Not the formal meetings, but the offbeat and colorful sessions that few people knew Nixon took the time for, from medal presentations to delegations of orange blossom queens. The President was remarkably kind and generous at these sessions, sometimes funny, and with Haldeman the only man looking in, whatever of human interest transpired was soon lost. "I cannot remember anything funny that happens," Bob readily admitted. "It's a failing of mine. Even when I was an advertising salesman and I needed jokes, I couldn't remember one." Not only the President, but his staff had some color to offer at these uncovered moments. When Al Haig was getting his second star pinned on by the President, Haldeman snapped, "Stop smiling, look hawkish," and Haig allowed as how, working for Henry, "It's been a race between a second star and a cardiac."

To my dismay, Haldeman launched a "project"—"color reporters" jobs were assigned to a dozen aides, forms were drawn up to be filled out, and another group of disseminators were assigned to pump out the color. Big waste of time. An idea which might have been useful in telling the truth about an unseen facet of the President—if handled with a light touch— was crunched into a superorganized pulp.

Haldeman organized the staff. And reorganized it. He liked charts. When in late 1969 Bryce Harlow and Pat Moynihan were pushed upstairs out of operational assignments to counselors' jobs, Haldeman asked me to write the press release describing the new power structure and I asked him to draw a picture of it. This is how it looked:

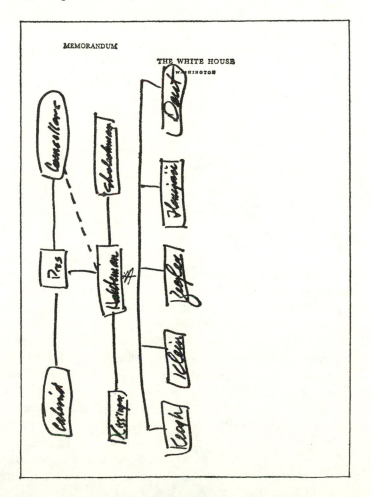

John Ehrlichman didn't like that—it had the President dealing direct with the Cabinet—and suggested another, which put the Ehrlichman Domestic Council more in the forefront. Haldeman grunted and drew this caricature of the Ehrlichman plan:

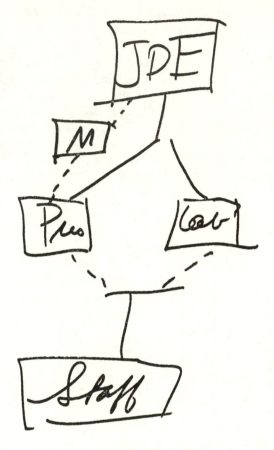

In organizing more substantive ideas, Haldeman knew his stuff. Since his mental set was almost identical with the President's, and he would not be adding anything to the President's understanding of a situation, he refrained from offering his own opinion on most substantive matters. He made certain, however, that every memorandum that went to the President was "staffed out"—that is, had concurring or objecting views from any other staffer or department the memo-writer's idea affected. And better than most summarizers, Haldeman could effectively put forth an absent or inarticulate aide's point of view. Each of us, telling Haldeman what we thought about a given matter, would be certain that our point of view would get to the Old Man "with the bark off," reduced to essentials, and put persuasively—without the tone of voice or added comment that would undercut it in transmission. That was Haldeman's greatest talent, his most important contribution, and should be taken into consideration in any assessment of him or of Nixon's use of him.

In organizing the presentation of ideas, Haldeman had to step on toes. Dwight Chapin, an extension of Haldeman's extension of Nixon, but with a cheerier soul and more outgoing demeanor, explained to me why Haldeman in mid-1969 had moved to cut down private access to the President of even the closest aides: "Arthur Burns came into the President's office with three things, one day, said it was urgent. One was to get a picture signed for his doctor; another was to get something signed adding to Burns's staff, which the President should never have even seen, and the third was something that could have waited a week. Since then, we have a note-taker in everybody's meetings with the Boss, to make sure nothing gets signed." In taking this action, and in Chapin's well-intended explanation of it, a weakness is apparent. No harm could have come from Dr. Burns taking care of some minor personal matters with the President, but great harm could come from denying the President the private counsel of a man with the independence of mind, experience, and judgment of a Burns. Whether "something could have waited a week" or not was arguable; perhaps Burns thought it was wise to head a problem off before it became a crisis.

At any rate, the decision was made by Nixon to "have a note-taker present," ostensibly to protect the President from signing papers blindly, or (a better reason) to take action on commitments the President made. That not only effectively told the staff that Haldeman spoke for the President but made him the target for resentment from people who formerly could sit down and talk with Nixon without a note-taker present. Such resentment of Haldeman was misdirected: the man who wanted it that way was the President, and Haldeman was his tool. Nixon did not like to see many people, and wanted to see still fewer privately, a truth that took a long while to dawn on aides who thought that Haldeman and Ehrlichman were building a "Berlin Wall" around an unsuspecting leader.

Haldeman organized the President's time. When a supporter of perennial candidate William Jennings Bryan bragged that his candidate had made nineteen speeches in a single day, an opponent asked, "When does he think?" Time to think was what Nixon wanted—alone, or just noodling out loud with Haldeman, Ehrlichman, Kissinger, or Ziegler, using them as sounding boards—and time to think is what Haldeman gave him. There will always be two sides to this coin. One side is the overinvolved, hyperactive President (like LBJ) getting everybody on the phone at all hours of the day and night, running a war with one hand and a Great Society with another, manipulating the Congress with a free foot—who has no time to think about the great issues and fundamental directions a President must understand and get others to act upon. Flip the coin, to the President on the mountaintop who grasps the great trends of the times, who looks far ahead to shape events, and who delegates so much authority for day-to-day

decision-making that he loses contact with reality and abdicates responsibility he cannot delegate for "running the country." Obviously, some
balance must be struck, but each President operates in his own way, which
means he will stress the great points of the side he leans to, while his critics
will issue blasts at his "obsession with detail, the mark of a poor executive"
or his "isolation, the mark of a poor executive."

The man whose life Haldeman scheduled had some strong ideas of his
own about whom he should see and what he should be doing. "I'll do fewer
state visits than any President in history," I once heard Nixon tell Haldeman. "Most of them are a waste of time. I saw your list of visits coming
up, with the President of Bongo on it. I crossed it off, we have two other
African Presidents coming up. And we do too many of the charity pictures,
the way Johnson did. We have to develop our own style; we've been too
much on the Johnson kick."

Haldeman's doorkeeper function was a recognition of his power and was
the cause of the President's first wrenching decision about staff. (The
reaction of Rose Mary Woods to the news that she was not to be permitted
the use of the office next to the President is recounted earlier.) It was also
the cause of some spoofing. When the President told the Cabinet that
George Shultz had been elevated to head the Office of Management and
Budget, and would have vast and vague powers that would extend the
former Labor Secretary's arm into every cranny of government, Nixon
turned and left after he finished his remarks. Shultz started to respond,
then stopped, looking a little sheepish, when he saw the President was
gone. Moynihan turned to the man who had just been introduced as the
most powerful man in the Cabinet and said, "If you want to thank the
President, you'll have to see Haldeman."

Haldeman's only real rival—for Nixon's time, and in the decision-
making process—was Charles Colson, whom Nixon used for political
hatchetwork. Whenever the President called Colson, Haldeman instantly
knew about it. One day, as Colson went barreling out of his office to answer a Presidential summons, Joan Hall, Colson's secretary, went to the
window overlooking the street between the EOB and the White House
and told me: "In one minute, you'll see Bob Haldeman come out of that
West Basement exit and run up these steps." She was right; either Haldeman saw the Colson button light up on his copy of the President's call
director, or had arranged to be tipped off another way, but he was determined not to let Colson end-run him with the Old Man.

Suggestions for Presidential appointments were "staffed out." That was
a verb intended by Haldeman to mean "studied by the staff," but too often
meant "responsibility irretrievably spread." I was frequently on the staffing-
out list, along with Dick Moore and Pat Buchanan, on suggestions for
people who might be colorful. Here is how it looked when an offbeat one
was treated with the usual, organized formality, along with my response:

THE WHITE HOUSE

WASHINGTON

January 4, 1971

MEMORANDUM FOR   Pat Buchanan
                        Henry Kissinger
                        Herb Klein
                    √ Bill Safire

FROM: Hugh Sloan

RE: Mayor of Limerick, Ireland

Do you recommend an appointment with the President for the
Mayor and his wife?

                    yes___√___   no_____

My handwritten comment was:

> *When the Mayor of Limerick arrives,*
> *We could take him to all the dives—*
> *But the Mayor and spouse*
> *Should see the White House*
> *Which they'll remember all of their lives.*

The ultimate decision which Hugh Sloan brought down from his boss,
Haldeman, was not to bring the Mayor of Limerick in to see the President. Pity.

At Nixon's direction, Haldeman "stole Wednesday"—that is, took the
day in the middle of the week out of the flow of activity requiring the
President's attendance. No meetings, no pictures, no events were customarily set for Wednesday, giving the President time to think. As he wished,
he had been organized.

Haldeman organized the dissemination of the President's thinking.
How is the President's "point of view," or at least the direction of the
President's thinking, communicated to a staff grown so large that it sees
its leader only when they are turned out for the arrival of his helicopter

on the lawn? Haldeman would make notes of what the President was thinking, organize a group of disseminators to tell it to. This group would then pass it along, or organize another group of operators, who would keep it to themselves but act upon it. Example: To the disseminators, Haldeman would say, at the end of 1969: "The President doesn't want us to be talking in terms of unemployment, but in terms of 100 million jobs. Be positive." Or: "The President thinks that 1970 will be the worst of the years we'll be here. There'll be inflation, unemployment, no visible turnaround on crime, the war still going on, a midterm election coming up, and we've been in office long enough for everything to be blamed on us. After 1970 he thinks there'll be an upturn, the merits of our case will be seen, and we'll be in damn good position in 1972. But he thinks we have to build up the mystique about him now, before things get worse in 1970, so we'll be able to ride it out. Here's exactly what he said. I wrote it down." Haldeman consulted his yellow pad. "Here it is: '*No leader survives simply by doing well. A leader survives when people have confidence in him when he's not doing well.*' That's why we have to get out the word about his personal attributes, the way he exercises power, the way he handles the workload—he knows, quite cold-bloodedly, that this will aid his ability to lead when times are tough. That's why we have to build equity now—Ike did it. John Kennedy did it, better than anybody. So should Nixon."

Here is an example of Haldeman passing the word to the staff on the direction of the President's thinking in early 1971, not for dissemination, but for internal guidance: "The President wants greater emphasis on goals, not programs. He thinks everybody in this Administration is thinking, 'How can we do it better?' instead of from the citizen's angle, 'What's in it for me?'" (That was a result of Colson's urging that Nixon try to assemble bloc votes for the coming campaign.) "He thinks the reason nobody cares about the New American Revolution is 'people don't care as much about the government running better as much as the government running cheaper.' And look, when you start your work on the State of the Union for next year, stick to goals, not programs. The budget will be the platform. He told Ehrlichman 'that's what I wanted to do this year, but you dragged me down with programs.' The President is concerned that he is going to be remembered for nothing in domestic affairs, and he wants more visible and memorable programs, but he wants them directed to his goals."

Haldeman to the PR group: "The point the President makes is to stay on top of the press to right the wrongs—when they make a mistake, point it out. Considering the opposition of the newspapers like the *Times*, and magazines like *Life* and *Look*, it's something of a miracle that he survived so well. The secret is, he has not made an effort to cater to the press, he ignored them and talked directly to the country without using the press as a filter. Meanwhile, we have kept the press serviced, not using him, which is the way we want it. A senior reporter wrote to him that 15 per cent of the press was friendly to Nixon, 20 per cent was objective, and 65 per cent negative. That last 65 per cent cannot be won over—the better RN does, the more frustrated they are. They're sore now because he's doing better than they predicted. They'll throw us a bone now and then, but never forget they want to bring us down. The only time they give us a good break is when they need to rebuild their reputation for credibility to hit us next time.

"Remember how they were all writing that 'Nixon's in Trouble' last October? All the Administration advisers"—he looked at me—"you guys included, were saying to cave in a little. He went the opposite way from the way you and the press was demanding with his November third speech, he stood firm, called up the 'silent majority' and reversed public opinion in one hour. If he had gone the other way, we would be in the soup today, because anything we would have given them would have been inadequate, and only by giving them nothing did he turn the situation around. The editorials in the *Times* and *Post* and *Life* won't affect him pro or con, so don't be influenced by their criticism or overjoyed when they say we do something right. He doesn't want to hear about them."

As Haldeman passed along these comments, some for our private edification and some to get across to the public, he invited objection and received it, which he duly passed on to the President. At the conclusion of one of his meetings, Haldeman said, "And the President wants it known that he intends to cut the White House staff." I asked, "Then why are you telling us all this?" and Lyn Nofziger, a political aide, put in: "To help the guys who are being fired with their memoirs." Haldeman, who liked to laugh, broke up.

Haldeman organized the execution of the President's orders. (The reader will note certain heavyhandedness in the organization of this chapter, which is the proper mood to be in when reading or writing about Haldeman.) When the President asked for information, and a request went out, it was up to Haldeman to see to it that the request did not disappear in the abyss of some government agency. Deadlines for response were included with every request, which was annoying at times, but necessary. And when the President made a decision, Haldeman saw to it that the decision was "implemented," in the favorite word of the bureaucracy, presumably more official-sounding than "carried out."

To me, more interesting and revealing of Nixon than the story of how decisions were carried out was the fact that Haldeman also had *the responsibility not to carry out orders* he felt were ill-conceived or badly put. To pose the question:

When a candidate for President, or the President himself, gives a subordinate a command, adding, "That's an order!" for emphasis, does a conscientious aide carry it out then and there?

The answer is no. The aide is not placed close to the center of power to transmit thunderbolts. The President, or candidate, has him there—and trusts him—to avert mistakes.

In William Manchester's worshipful book about John F. Kennedy, the author wrote about a day dawning "as cool and crisp as a Kennedy order," causing reviewer Tom Wicker to observe, "This may be an allowable descriptive, but not to those who tried to decipher a large part of the Kennedy syntax as recorded at many news conferences."

Orders are not always orders, even when they are couched in command nomenclature and issued with the crackle of authority. Sometimes they are ways of unwinding or of stimulating suggestions, and occasionally they are merely thoughts spoken aloud.

A man in power must have men around him whom his awesome power does not intimidate. For Nixon, above all others, it was Haldeman.

The President was reluctant to bark, "That's an order," at other aides because (1) they might think he was a martinet, (2) he did not want them to think he wanted to be surrounded with yes-men, and (3) they might actually carry out the orders without warning him of the consequences. I once saw the President make a 180-degree turn in midflight as he was giving a direction to Ron Ziegler: "That's an order, Ron—no discussion. Unless, of course, you disagree." On trifling matters involving personal pique, Haldeman felt free to ignore or countermand the President. After a soup-spilling episode, the President decreed: "There will be no more soup served at State Dinners." (They're still serving soup.) On more important matters, such as his irritation with Jewish militants who demonstrated against French President Georges Pompidou, Haldeman delayed carrying out orders until Nixon had cooled off, and changed his mind. Long-time intimacy with the Man gave aides like Haldeman the right—and the obligation—to resist orders. Secretary Rogers was another who knew how to roll with a punchy order. When Nixon sent him a note telling him to "fire everybody in Laos" for not carrying out his commands in 1971, Rogers let it go by, happened to mention that he didn't do it in a conversation with the President a few weeks later, and the President wondered what the Secretary of State was talking about: "You said to 'fire everybody in Laos,' remember?" Rogers said. "Oh hell, Bill," the President smiled, "you know me better than that."

Lesser aides used other methods when the President's demands were unreasonable (and they were rarely so—Nixon was exceptionally considerate to his personal aides and secretaries, leaving Haldeman as the only one he "beat-up on"). After a speech at a fund-raising dinner in Detroit, the President was scheduled to greet the fattest of the fat cats in his suite. He was tired and wanted to go to bed, but the guests were not yet assembled to come and meet the President. "Get 'em in here," Nixon growled to aide Steve Bull, who picked up his walkie-talkie and said to an advance man, "Duval, Duval, get 'em in here!" Mike Duval replied, "They're all over the place, I can't yet," and when Bull relayed this to the Chief Executive, the response was "*Now.*" When that relayed word hit Duval like a missile, the resourceful young man walked into another reception room where some gentlemen from the Culligan Water Company were meeting —nothing to do with the fund-raising event—and told them the President of the United States would like to shake their hands. Advance man Duval and Bull ushered them, dumbfounded, in to see Nixon, who thanked them graciously for their support and shook their hands. The real fat cats were told later that the President couldn't see them, some important matters had come up. Nixon never knew.

More subtle than ignoring an order you know to be impulsive, or carrying it out in a harmless way, is to interpret and carry out an order that is imprecisely phrased. Here is a somewhat offbeat illustration of the alter-ego relationship between the President and Haldeman involving a "direct order."

In the '68 campaign, a standard feature was the airport rally—an excellent way to make a brief appearance, get regional TV coverage, fire up the local troops, "work the fence" in a fairly controlled situation. The Nixon advance men had the airport rally down to a science—a classic of organization.

Once, in Cleveland, they goofed. The crowd at the airport consisted of two busloads of bewildered ten-year-old kids. No signs, no cheers, no decent platform to speak from, and the PA system was on the blink. Bad day. The traveling press, bored with the efficient clockwork of Nixon rallies, would have a field day writing about a "significant lack of turnout" in Ohio.

The Candidate was exhausted, he was angry, but he was determined not to blow his stack. Nixon sat in silence in his forward compartment as the *Tricia* gained altitude, and then said in a tightly controlled voice to Haldeman, "*There will be no more landing at airports!*"

Haldeman jotted that down on his yellow pad. A look of consternation crossed his face, as the significance of the order sank in. The logistical problem was immense—if no landing at airports, where? Highways? Open fields? Skydive in? Haldeman shook his head and ran a line through what he had written.

Obviously, what the Candidate meant was: "There will be no more *rallies* at airports." But the Candidate was wrong about that. Just because one airport rally was a disaster was no reason to condemn the technique; the local evening TV shows needed the film. Haldeman knew that Nixon knew that too and was only indulging in some understandable pique. Haldeman's final interpretation of Nixon's words, later conveyed chillingly to advance men, was: "There will be no more *unsuccessful* airport rallies." And *that* was an order.

I have been having some fun here, writing about the bright sides of Haldeman, always with the exception of his feelings about the press, because he is not the man of the caricatures: the Prussian, martinet, crew-cutted ("Bob, why don't you let your hair grow?" "Who'd know me?"*), humorless, intense, unquestioning. He had some good times, he had a good appreciation of humor, and a feel for the more ridiculous manifestations of power. When the President's silly request for fancy dress for the White House police brought a reaction of derision, the President actually wanted to hang tough and go through with it. "Pompidou is coming," Haldeman told me on the porch of his villa in Key Biscayne in February 1970. "What do we do about the uniforms of the White House police? President says the hell with the criticism, but I dunno . . ." I told him the primary complaint had to do with the Graustarkian helmets, which made the cops look like refugees from a road company of a Sigmund Romberg operetta. Haldeman changed the helmets, telling Ziegler to say for once we backed off; he gave the news to the President with a different slant: the helmets had to be changed to more sensible caps at the request of the police, but the white summer uniforms would remain and the hell with the press. A confrontation was averted, and somewhere in the Nixon archives there are scores of only slightly used helmets.

There was a darker side to Haldeman, reflective of Nixon's darker side.

He could hate. He hated obscenity-shouting demonstrators with a vengeance, and occasionally wreaked it: at the Long Island sports arena in the '72 campaign, a small knot of demonstrators started to mar what was an otherwise beautiful rally. Haldeman leaped to his feet, roared, "Throw 'em out!" the cords standing out on his reddened neck, drawing worried looks from Fred Malek and other aides in his own box; the demonstrators were thrown out, as they would have been anyway. Demonstrators upset Nixon, and Haldeman, observing from afar, was right up on the rostrum being tortured too; Nixon pretended to ignore them, but his rhythm was always off when they were around, and he tended to shorten his speeches so he could get out of there.

Haldeman would see any admission of error as an intolerable sign of weakness. Often it is good to support a loyal staffer or Congressman who has put his foot in his mouth; public figures too prone to walk away from loyalists in trouble find themselves with no loyalists left. I have had the benefit of Haldeman's protection and have also seen the Haldeman ire flare: when I submitted a suggested answer for a Presidential press conference about the peremptory way Fred Malek had dismissed some of Walter Hickel's staff at Interior, this angry note came back, written in red:

* In 1973, after he left the White House, Haldeman let his hair grow. He was right—nobody knew him.

CONFIDENTIAL

Safire

December 10, 1970.

You could not possibly be more wrong. With whom was this checked? H

MEMORANDUM FOR THE PRESIDENT

FROM: BILL SAFIRE

SUBJECT: One-Liners for Press Conference

Lithuanian defector: When a man chooses freedom, he should be able to expect that free men will choose to defend him.

POWs: These men willingly risked their lives for their country, and this country is willing to take some risks for them.

Hickel: Two years ago tonight, I said I wanted Cabinet members with an extra dimension, but his extra dimension was not the one I had in mind.

Interior Staffers: The abrupt manner in which the staffers were fired was a mistake, and it was promptly rectified.

Not true   *no rectification took place*

My Lai: Whatever the outcome of the trials, the fact that the accused were brough to trial says a great deal about the character of this nation.

Press conferences: I enjoy press conferences, but a President can't spend too much of his time doing the things he enjoys.

Rail strike: I will resist the temptation to say to Congress 'I told you so' -- instead, I'll say 'let's see to it that it will not happen again.'

The President's ramrod was criticized often enough for refusing to admit a mistake—no signs of weakness allowed—but there was another side to that coin. In protecting Malek in this instance, he was letting all White House staffers know that in a tight spot they would not be abandoned. Even when wrong, if they were acting out of loyalty and good in-

tentions, they would be protected, and all the more if they were taking a
rap for someone higher up. Most often, in routine government operations,
a functionary's mistakes are magnified and he is acutely embarrassed; then
it is a comforting and occasionally inspiring thing to have a chief of staff
who helps stand the gaff, bawling you out in private but defending you in
public. "Covering up," it is called. A staff chief who is too ready to blow
the whistle on his subordinates is considered weak and self-protective;
there is a certain band on the strata of executive offenses in which
"cover-up" can be good management and even good government. The difficulty begins when covering up gets to be a habit, automatically applied in
all situations, as everyone was to discover later. By that time, any example
of "hanging tough" for any reason was denounced as venal, which is
foolish.

Equally foolish was Haldeman's sanctification of plumbing: the eleva-
tion of leak-plugging (the normal type, not the clandestine kind practiced
by the Krogh-Young operation) into a standard operating procedure. For
example, I could not get an advance copy of the printed version of the
1971 Budget because Haldeman had me on a list of likely "leakers"; although dozens of copies were made available to the press forty-eight hours
before the official release, I was denied access because I was on Haldeman's
little list. The Budget Bureau's press officer, who had just given a copy to
Tass, the Soviet news agency, felt awkward about turning me down. "The
order from Haldeman seemed a little nutty," he told me later, "since you
wrote the goddam message that year and you'd been working with all the
drafts for months." Since I associated with known Democrats and newsmen of my own free will, I was suspect, and once on Haldeman's list as a
leaker, there was no getting off.

One problem that Haldeman caused was professional. His job as chief
of staff also included chief of public relations, keeper of the myth, expert
on how to influence public opinion. He understood public relations to be
the use of techniques to badger, bully, bribe, entice, and persuade people
to your "side," which could be accomplished only by organizing and orchestrating and hammering away. The President agreed, indeed had great
faith in the "PR types" getting together and "putting out the line," building the mystique, always thinking of the Kennedy model as the perfect
PR operation. I wrote memos by the score on how to identify and get
across positive themes; leadership in a democracy requires persuasion.

But the hard sell was not "PR." Public relations (usually pronounced
with a sneer by politicians who wish theirs was better, and by some journalists who envy the salaries of the people in it) is a process of understanding what your goals are, what your public's needs are, and
engaging in a constant two-way communication, adjusting the one to fit
the other as much as possible without losing sight of your principle. Public
relations persuades and is persuaded; it causes movement as it adjusts; it
buys as it sells; it never loses contact. Herb Klein had a good idea of this,
but Nixon and Haldeman did not want him in charge of "public relations"

from the start; Jeb Magruder, Haldeman's man, was placed in Klein's shop as the Deputy Director of Communications (when Haldeman wanted to be sure he had control of the 1972 campaign, he put his man Magruder there as Mitchell's deputy). Haldeman, and later Charles Colson, ran a brand of news management they called public relations, and the President called "PR," but it tried to reduce an art to a science, which does not work. Nixon liked to say that "politics is poetry, not prose"; he did not understand that it can be the same with public relations. As a professional PR man, Haldeman was merely a good adman.

Haldeman's detestation of the press ran deeper than Buchanan's and nearly as deep as Nixon's, which paralleled the Mindanao Deep, but that need not be belabored here. We shall come to "the press is the enemy" later. But Haldeman did not often help to restrain the President's natural inclination to overreact to press criticism, which Bob should have done, even if he agreed with his boss. Haldeman let his feelings show too intensely in interviews; on television, he used the phrase "knowingly aid and abet our enemies" about the doves opposing the President, which is exactly what the President told him to say; this was escalated by commentators to "practically a charge of treason," and then Haldeman was hit for charging the President's opponents with treason. (My reaction was anger at the unfair escalation of Haldeman's remark until he told me that the escalation was fine with him.) We all thought Haldeman was not very good on television; in the end, he fooled us all with a performance before a Senate committee of a young man whose restraint, respect, and decorum were unassailable, a man of intelligence and sincerity who obviously could not be the man who struck terror in so many politicians' hearts.

That was the worst part of the Haldeman story. It is one thing to be a President's professional sonofabitch, the "abominable no-man" as they used to call Sherman Adams, who draws upon himself the resentment that would otherwise be directed at his boss. But just as he enjoyed too much the luxurious trappings of office on a Presidential trip—the advance men first worked out where Haldeman would stay, and then the President, because they worked for Haldeman—he enjoyed the play of power too much. Like the man who put him at the center, Haldeman thought that the response to his orders would fall short to some degree, so he compensated by ordering too much. When a businessman friend told me, after Haldeman's fall, that he had always tape-recorded his conversations with the President's aide, and I told my friend he ought to be ashamed of himself, the businessman replied that when he had publicly criticized the President, "Haldeman called to say it was well within their power to destroy me." I could see Haldeman, coldly angry, indulging in some harsh hyperbole that a man with such power must scrupulously guard against.

Haldeman was also a good-time Charlie with the public's money, an unconscionable lapse in a man who should have been conscious of the way things look. He knew the Kennedys and the Johnsons had spent millions on facilities near their homes. Nixon, he figured, deserved no less, and with inflation, such necessities and frills cost more. In the White House, which is a national museum, a case could be made for building a needed new entrance at the West Wing, and no reporters complained about the snazzy new press facility over the swimming pool, but all the offices were redone with more elegance than was seemly; the interior of *Air Force One* was rebuilt twice—at great cost—to make it more private and comfortable; Camp David was transformed from a rustic hideaway into a mountain mansion, and nobody ever asked how much it would cost, much less how it would appear as an example of an Administration dedicated to saving the taxpayers' dollars. At Key Biscayne and San Clemente, Haldeman made no visible effort to protect the President from the charge of simple graft, of fancying up his house at the public expense. The General Services Administration would automatically okay any Secret Service request, and there was no apparent exercise of control—what the hell, Haldeman figured, Nixon planned to leave San Clemente to the public in his will—but the mistake was in the appearance of undue lavishness, and the appearance of unconcern that was the mistake of the man who was in charge of appearances.

Such mistakes—in treating an art as a science, in getting trapped in the trappings of power, and in peopling the White House with bootlicking Magruders—are overshadowed by the greatest single disservice any Presidential aide ever performed for his chief: installing a voice-activated, indiscriminate recording system.

Haldeman was certain that liberal historians of the future would cheat Nixon out of his due. To thwart their anticipated plot to demean his boss, he made possible the ruination of the Nixon Administration. In 1974 the President told a friend that he had mentioned to Haldeman in 1972 that it would be a good idea to get started "cleaning up" the tapes, and Haldeman had said no, there was plenty of time. In the decision to eavesdrop on everybody, and in his brushoff of the suggestion to begin the editing process, the keeper of the flame made it possible to pull down the temple.

What hurts Haldeman most today is surely that realization. Because he would stop at nothing to prove the greatness of his client-friend-leader, he made possible the proof that Nixon in a duty-versus-loyalty crisis could be considerably less than great. To Haldeman, charges that the Nixon men wanted to set up a police state are ridiculously overblown; charges that they tried to show their boss off to his best advantage are cheerfully dismissed; charges that Haldeman tried to permeate the Federal establishment with Nixon men are true enough, and so what; but the charge that Haldeman not only failed his boss but caused his downfall undoubtedly smarts.

Haldeman was incensed by leaks out of a noble motive: to protect a series of moves that would help his boss secure the world from war. He was obsessed by a desire to provide history with its raw material so as to ultimately serve the cause of truth, and prevent the denigration of a peacemaker. In this, Haldeman was motivated as a patriot, not a power-seeker, as faithful Horatio and not as guileful Guildenstern, as a man who wanted his President remembered for all the good he did and not lessened by professional demeanors.

Yet Haldeman the leak-plugger turned out to be the Ultimate Leaker, the source of the most excruciating revelations, the means by which Nixon was drained of his power. As protector of the President's privacy, he undermined the confidentiality of the Presidency as nobody ever has. As builder of the "myth" that helps leaders govern in hard times, he made possible the besplattering of an honest reputation. By his own terms—of results counting, never mind the motive, and spare me the explanations—this man who never tried to take the credit deserves a great deal of the blame.

Haldeman was where he was because he knew Nixon better than anybody, and he should have known that Nixon instincts needed more restraint. In hindsight, we can say that the man with the privilege of not following orders should have exercised that privilege in reducing Nixon's misplaced passion to plug leaks. Instead, he brought to his staff a young man named Tom Charles Huston, who was far more intelligent than any of Haldeman's other helpers, and who placed the knife on the table in the first act of the play.

7. LOOMINGS

Where did Watergate begin? When did Nixon, in his hurry to be great, become—in Wilson's word—"heedless"?

What came to be regarded as an arrogant abuse of power grew in the Petri jar of mutual distrust: on one side, a "silent majority" tired of being manipulated and experimented with, and on the other, an articulate minority frustrated at being unable to stop the war it hated and unable to cure poverty and racial unrest with the standard remedies. Richard Nixon was, in his way, a superb unifier—but a unifier of a great faction, and the focuser and unifier of the antifaction. There might have been nothing wrong with this realignment of forces but for the virulence of the strain of controversy that resulted.

Nixon underestimated the intensity of the opposition, which may be surprising in light of Nixon's understanding of "the intensity factor" in polls. Perhaps that was because Nixon came into office vaguely allied with the Impassioned Aginners, who hated Johnson and could not hate as heartily the man who opposed Johnson's partner, Humphrey. But in a relatively short time, Nixon succeeded in focusing the organized hate of the Sixties on himself, thereby adding new legions to the aging but still influential group that had distrusted him for a generation. Through the comeback years, and the campaign of 1968, Nixon held his contempt for the press in careful check, but his gut feeling never abated, and after becoming President he naturally interpreted the normal adversary relationship between press and President—on the upswing during the Sixties—as particularly directed at him. And when, as he always suspected it would, the press in 1969 appeared to put the desire to embarrass Nixon ahead of what he considered the requirements of loyalty to the nation—"selling out your country to sell newspapers"—he overreacted incredibly.

The explosion may have occurred because the room was filled with Nixonian gas, but the match that set him off was struck by the enterprising reporters who wrote stories that would never have been filed a generation ago. Nixon seethed at leaks. Not only did they make him the only world leader who could not deal in secret on foreign affairs, he was the first American President to take office with such scrutiny commonplace, and on the rise.

But he felt that many of the important things he had to do could only be done in secret—or, to use the preferred euphemisms, in private or in confidence. Arms limitation was one; America's positions in the past, stuck on the point of on-site inspection, could now be changed thanks to new technology, but little could be accomplished with the Soviets if they suspected Nixon's approach to be based on propaganda. To the leadership of a closed society, leaks looked like propaganda, since totalitarians could not conceive of a major power unable to hold its national security cards close to its vest. In one way, the leaks helped the Soviets, by revealing our prepared positions; in another way, they troubled Soviet Ambassador Anatoly Dobrynin, who "made representations" because it appeared to reveal bad faith.

The negotiations to settle the war in Vietnam was another vast area of necessary secrecy. Nixon was certain the only serious negotiations were those to be held in secret, and he turned out to be as right in this as he had been on SALT. Finally, the need for secrecy, which was so easily labeled an obsession later, was an important element of his opening to China.

These were great reasons for secrecy. No President could have had more noble motives than to end the arms race that imperiled the human race; to end the war that had bled and dispirited the United States in the past decade; and to begin the intricate, triangular diplomacy that would create a balance of power and perhaps a stable world order for the next generation.

With reasons and motives like those, and the opportunity he felt was unique to this generation to stop the self-slaughter that had become habitual with mankind, Nixon indulged himself in despising reporters who —unwittingly or not—undercut his efforts for peace just to get a hot story, or officials who betrayed the nation's trust just to curry favor with some reporter. "You're not impressing them, you know, when you leak a story," he told his senior staff one day. "They're using you, and they have only contempt for the leakers. They'll flatter you, and invite you to all the parties in Georgetown, but they know who's weak and who's not."

When millions of human lives are at stake; when the success of a negotiation could be jeopardized by a premature publication, and more men killed in the prolongation of a war; when the most daring gamble in this generation's diplomacy requires absolute confidence between former adversaries in order to succeed—what would be wrong, Nixon wondered, legally or morally, in using the forces of law to discover the leakers and to stop them before they ruined chances for success? And if the FBI is muscle-bound or its great old man of the past is inadequate to the stormy present, what is wrong with assigning a special unit to the job of riding herd on the counterintelligence fiefdoms or, when necessary, taking over for them?

What was wrong, of course, was just about everything, on sober second thought; and no pointing to hitherto-secret precedents or emphasizing the gravity of all that hung in the balance justifies the degree to which the individual's Fourth Amendment right to privacy was raped. But this has been abundantly pointed out; perhaps it will be helpful in explaining the context of the moves that later became known as Watergate to suggest that there was a gray area, hard to define at the time, between heroism and villainy. Civil liberty and national security often conflict, but are mutually dependent; Nixon could point to Lincoln's choice of security over habeas corpus liberty although the 1970 demonstrations were no Civil War. In examining great mistakes, it is unfair to ascribe only mean motives—or only noble motives. Not only were motives mixed, but the men at the center had different mixes of mix.

Tom Charles Huston is a good example. For two and a half years he was, in the words of the song, "the boy next door"—his office was room 123 and mine 125 of the old Executive Office Building. Huston was a gaunt, melancholy young man, twenty-eight in 1969, who looked like John Carradine when that movie villain was shooting Jesse James in the back. He proudly displayed a portrait of John C. Calhoun on his office wall, and nullification, in one sense, was Huston's business, too—to keep tabs on the radical terrorist groups who, as he later put it, might trigger a wave of repression and thus imperil democracy. I was writing speeches making that point at the time, too, and still believe that official repression was the hope of the violent demonstrators who hoped to thrive in the ensuing upheaval. Many demonstration leaders wanted nothing more than "police riots" in front of TV cameras to cause revulsion at such repression and thus radicalize the moderates. But it was Huston who came up with the actual plan for repression.

Huston is a man of thought and a fairly good writer—a selection of his work appears in an earlier chapter on the New Federalism, since he challenged my theories on the subject rather sharply on Constitutional grounds. He prowled through secondhand bookstore collections of old books, a hobby of mine as well, and we used to compare notes and give each other tips on stores and book sales.

He started at the White House working for Pat Buchanan on the news summary. Word got around that the people in that shop were strongly on the right, and once the President twitted Buchanan on the far-right reputation of his staff, quickly adding, "No, Pat, I know how hard everybody tries to cover it right down the middle, and of course that's what I need." Toward the end of 1969, Huston stopped working on the news summary and began doing odd jobs for Bob Haldeman, and in a few months was out of Buchanan's orbit entirely, though he remained in the office next to mine along "writers row." By mid-1970, Huston had convinced Haldeman of his need for a secretary who was totally secure, and received one from

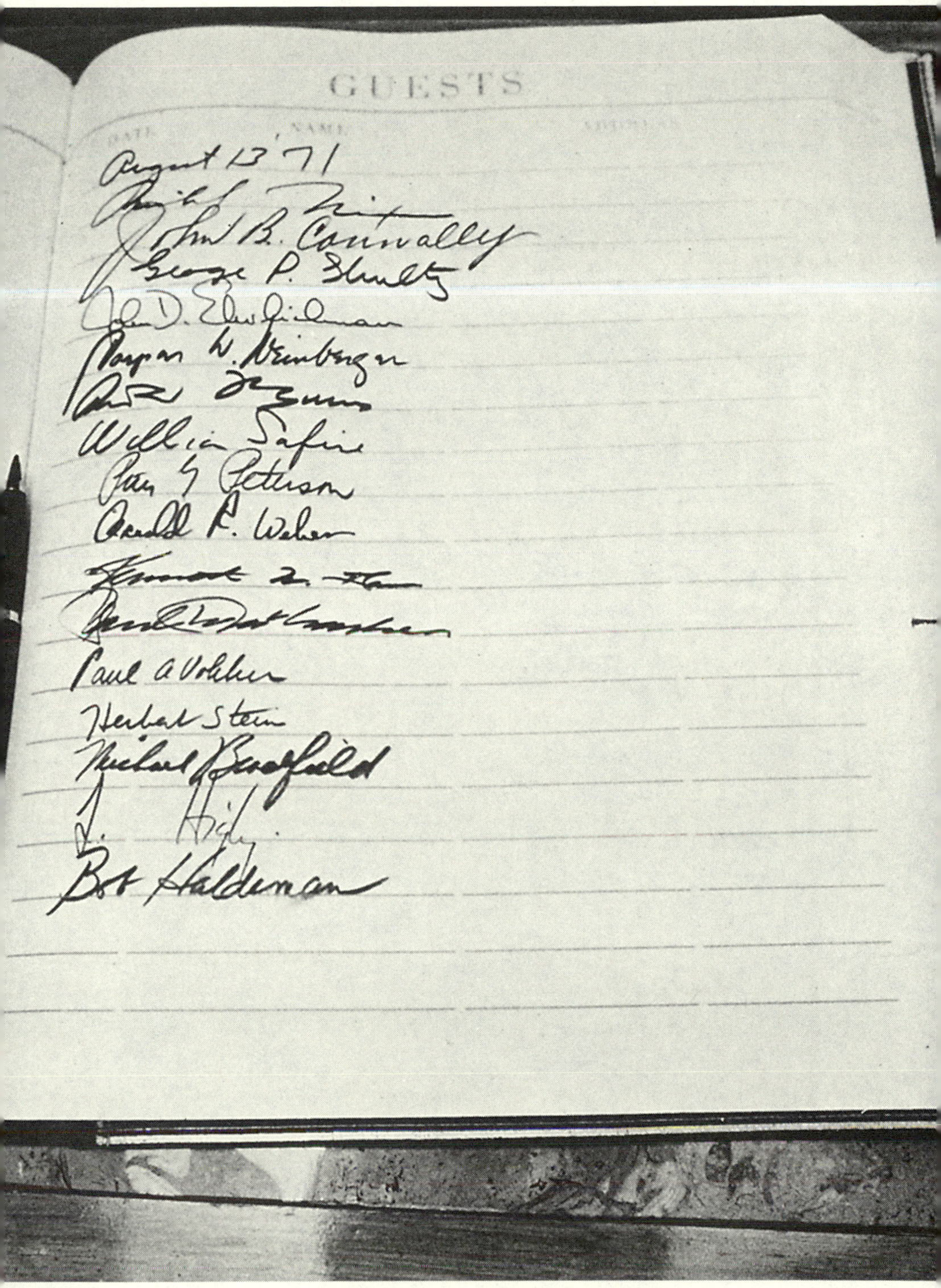

PLATE 9. Camp David Guest Book, August 13, 1971.

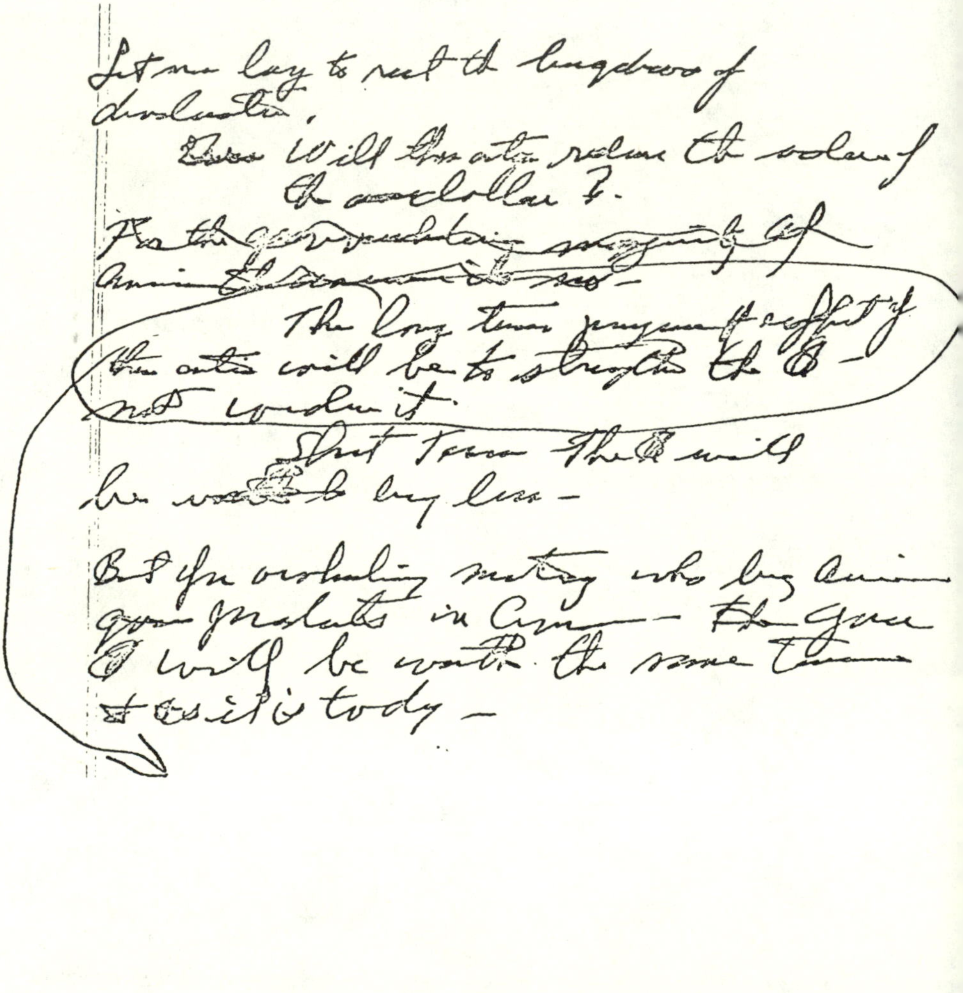

PLATE 10. On a yellow pad, President Nixon writes out his explanation for the devaluation of the dollar. The President's notes for his speech of August 15, 1971, begin "Let me lay to rest the bugaboo of devaluation . . ."

PLATE 11. With Federal Reserve Chairman Arthur Burns.

PLATE 12. The President gives his blessing to John Connally, his Treasury Secretary.

the FBI. Huston sliced off a corner of his own spacious office and had a wall built, giving her privacy, and had special locks installed. But this secretiveness was alloyed by a certain wryness. He circulated a memo to all members of Writers Row that March 18 was the birthday of his hero, John C. Calhoun, and he hoped it would be observed appropriately. As a past president of Young Americans for Freedom, bastion of stanch young conservatism, he welcomed a current president of that group to his office, and was thunderstruck when a kid in jeans, a dirty T-shirt, and long hair sauntered in.

What I most admired Huston for was his uncanny ability to scrounge furniture. He had one of those cavernous offices that ate up a lot of chairs and tables and desks and bookcases; he would keep a hawk-eye out for people leaving the EOB and, late at night, pounce on their leavings. In this way, he came by the best-looking set of black leather chairs in the EOB, which would otherwise have taken a year's wait in the normal course of requisition. Huston was resourceful.

How could this young man, a studious Constitutionalist, an advocate of states' rights against the intrusion of the Federal Government, turn out to be the architect who preceded the "plumbers" and the philosopher behind the abuse of power?

Because he was convinced, as Daniel Ellsberg was convinced, that there is a "higher order of patriotism" than most of us live by; that the forces of evil and totalitarianism stalk the land, threaten our institutions as never before, and require extraordinary and even extralegal means to counter them—to fight their fire with fire, to infiltrate their organizations, and, if necessary, surreptitiously enter and rifle their files. "We're in a state of siege," Huston would say frequently. It sounds foolish enough now, but when you drove to work on a fine summer day in Washington, and there were guardsmen with bayonets every fifty yards on the Rock Creek Parkway, and the White House was ringed by an impenetrable wall of buses, "siege" did not seem like such an excessive word.

None of us thought Huston was any more than a liaison man with the gumshoes. My secretary, Sally Cutting, who occasionally took his calls when his secretary was out, gaily referred to Huston as "X-5" as she jotted down messages to call various intelligence alphabet agencies. Yet he turned out to be the proponent of unlimited police power—the man who wrote the 1970 memo that was signed by all the agency heads, approved by the President, and which for five days institutionalized burglary as a tool of law enforcement. Go-it-alone J. Edgar Hoover soon had second thoughts —perhaps not so much concern for civil liberty as a worry about bureaucratic encroachment on his FBI and (a touch of irony) the coming on duty of the Executive Protective Service as security for embassies, making "bag jobs" more difficult.

Huston came to despise Chuck Colson, whose rise began in mid-1970, after Huston's hopes for a central role in subversive-hunting had gone a-glimmering. Colson represented bloc politics, special interest appeals, pressure group cultivation, all the things the Democrats did in the cities and the Republicans were not good at.

Colson was later to become generally known as a villain, the man in charge of "dirty tricks," but he did adjust Nixon's programs more to segments of the electorate's wishes. Nothing could be more infuriating to a True Believer who operates on principle and is not concerned with public opinion. "Few people in the White House," Huston wrote bitterly later, "were concerned with issues of substance and those who were became overwhelmed by people who had nothing to do but put out crap, by public relations people and by special interest group people."

Huston says he quit because the men like him who had firm ideological principles, both liberal and conservative, were replaced by technocrats and pragmatists; the heady battles of Moynihan v. Burns in 1969 were reduced to budget arguments and what Huston felt were unconscionable compromises in the "New Federalism" in 1971. I suppose Huston is convinced that centrists are devoid of principle, and only True Believers of the left or right are to be believed; carried to its logical extreme, that burning zealotry is what nourished the seeds of Watergate.

Huston really left because he couldn't get through to Haldeman after the heyday of his intelligence coordination memos ended. Huston was Haldeman's hostile-demonstrations man, in a sense; when a columnist asked me about plans of the 1970 March on Washington, I forwarded the request to Haldeman and was told that Huston would give me a dossier for transmission to the reporter. He did, and I told the columnist I would meet him across the street—on the corner of 17th and F Streets—to hand over some background on the "New Mobe." I did, and the columnist wrote a fairly well-informed piece on the subject, based on material that had never been classified as secret. (Years later, Haldeman surveillance man Jack Caulfield told me that I was under suspicion as a leaker because I had been seen handing over some documents to a columnist on the corner of 17th and F. The right hand never knew what the left hand was doing.)

By 1971 the demonstration business was falling off. Deputy Counsel Fred Fielding sent his boss, John Dean, a memo on January 26 pointing out that "the total number of major disturbances in RN's first two years is less than the total for 1968 alone (22–17)." Civil disturbances had decreased in cities, though they had increased on campuses—but after the post-Cambodia reaction, even student riots diminished in size and frequency. Haldeman, who was always willing to use demonstrations against Nixon to the President's advantage, was quite prepared to use the decline of demonstrations to his advantage, too, and sent me that information to include in future speeches by the Vice President. For Huston, calm in the streets meant a dull period of make-work.

One of the tasks then assigned to Huston by Haldeman was to analyze the mail on Lieutenant William Calley and Mylai. Huston thought a plain count was a mail clerk's job, so he wrote an analysis with his recommendation that the President should not intervene on Calley's behalf. Larry

Higby sent back a message from *Air Force One*—was this the letter-writers' reaction or Huston's? That depressed Tom, and then came a final indignity: a request from Haldeman to compile a list of newsmen "who wrote Nixon off in the past" with quotations from them, dating back ten years, that Nixon was through. This was a periodic exercise based on grumbles from the Oval Office about newsmen who had always underestimated him, and most of us knew that the best thing to do about such requests was to ignore them. Huston mentioned his dissatisfaction with this assignment to Buchanan, who was amazed that this foolish scab-flicking was still going on, and suggested Huston send in a memo with one quotation on it, of a man underestimating Nixon's future: "This is my last press conference, and you guys won't have Nixon to kick around anymore." (On the subject of press bias, my friend Buchanan may have been a little crazy, but he was never stupid.)

The proposal Huston made to give the government the right—denied to the King of England under common law—to break and enter a citizen's home without a warrant, which became a short-lived Presidential policy, was in his mind a "principled decision"—that is, one based upon the principle that the threat to domestic security is of such gravity that it is necessary to suspend our rights in order to preserve them. Huston would argue that he espoused no such "right"—that he gave it the clear label of illegality—but that sometimes it was necessary to break the law to preserve the law, that it had been done in the past, and that pious protestations of horror were hypocritical.

Huston was contemptuous of the conciliatory approach to dissent, as expressed by Ray Price in the "lower our voices" line in the Inaugural. In a top-secret memo that John Dean later released, Huston wrote on August 5, 1970: "Perhaps lowered voices and peace in Vietnam will defuse the tense situation we face, but I wouldn't want to rely on it exclusively." He quoted an anticipated objection from J. Edgar Hoover: " 'The risks are too great; these folks are going to get the President in trouble and RN had better listen to me.' The answer is that we have considered the risks, we believe they are acceptable and justified under the circumstances . . . the Director of the FBI is paid to take risks where the security of the country is at stake." The risks were, to say the least, poorly calculated. Huston argued that the FBI Director could authorize burglaries without written orders from above: "He has his authority from the President and he doesn't need a written memo from the AG. To maintain security," he added, "we should avoid written communications in this area." That's why Huston needed to write the memo.

Huston's certainty that he was doing the right thing in protecting the nation; his impatience with bureaucratic wrangling that stood in the way of his break-in policy, which he was certain was right because it had been done before and nobody had been caught; his arrogance that equated opposition to his proposals as the embodiment of evil (my own efforts to define the New Federalism he blasted not as inept or confused, which they

might have been, but an example of "moral relativism," to be abhorred)—
all this was tragic enough in a young man exposed too much to the face
of hatred in demonstrations, but when his ideas were accepted and approved by the President of the United States—even for five days, until
Hoover and Mitchell had a chance to shoot them down—that was the
President's tragedy, and the nation's.

Huston, the True Believer, Nixon's ideological Ellsberg, was destined
to be dissatisfied with Nixon from the start; yet there was that streak in
Nixon that admired the steel in the backbone of men like Huston, the
militant patriotism, the contempt for the draft evaders and runners-down
of America. Once in a while, Nixon would make a decision that pleased
the True Believers of either side. He endowed the arts and humanities in a
way that amazed and pleased the liberals, and, on a far more significant
scale, he delighted the hardest of hard-liners with what Huston would consider a "principled decision" on domestic security, heedless of the ends-
justify-means morality because he was sure it would never be discovered,
leading to a train of events that wound up in the wreckage of his Administration.

The seeds of scandal, then, began with the seventeen wiretaps undertaken on national security grounds to get at the source of leaks to reporters, begun in 1969 and continuing into 1971; then, the plumbers operation that was put into effect after Huston's grand plan was aborted by
Hoover's recalcitrance; then, and concurrently, the Caulfield-Ulasewicz
operation to dig up dirt on political figures. With all this going on, it was
not surprising for one of the operatives, a man named G. Gordon Liddy, to
look up at the Democratic headquarters at 2600 Virginia Avenue, NW, in
early 1972, and wonder what it would be like to know exactly what was
going on in there.

8. A SWEARING-IN

One of the fringe benefits of working at the White House is that you can ask people in big jobs for little favors. When my wife, Helene, who was born in England, was set to become an American citizen, I asked Dwight Chapin to ask the President if we could hold the swearing-in in his office. After checking, Dwight suggested I ask the Vice President.

Spiro Agnew agreed to stand up for her, and William O'Brien at the Immigration and Naturalization Service said he would bring the Federal judge needed to administer the oath. This seemed like an imposition on the judge, but O'Brien assured me he would bring a Republican appointee who would get a kick out of meeting Agnew and who could make the standard citizenship pitch.

Sure enough, the Immigration men showed up at the Vice President's office with a perfect choice: a cornball-patriotic, square little guy who handled the proceedings with dignity and warmth, a Nixon-Agnew kind of judge who advised us to go to the Honor America Day festivities the following week (a counter-demonstration Chuck Colson had a hand in cooking up). But for all his squareness, and his shy pride at meeting the Vice President, he was right for the kind of occasion, which was, and should have been, unabashedly patriotic and self-consciously solemn.

With Agnew's permission, I plunked a tape recorder on top of his desk to record my wife's oath of citizenship, which was fortunate since it also picked up the off-the-cuff remarks made by the judge and the Vice President. See Plate 3 following page 56 for a visual recording of the event.

After administering the oath, the judge spoke gently to Helene, who was swallowing hard, and to our two children, who tried to pay attention, about the meaning of citizenship.

"You know," he began, "when I preside over Naturalization proceedings, Mr. and Mrs. Safire, Mr. Vice President, we usually have about eighty-five or ninety people, and one of the most enjoyable parts of my job is this occasion.

"Even though I don't have a prepared talk or anything like that, I just can't resist the opportunity to say something I feel very deeply about, sort of ad-libbing, as you know, so if I mispronounce a word here or there or my grammar or English isn't correct or anything, I hope you'll forgive me.

"But as I look over the faces of these people taking the oath, they're from various countries, from all over the world, and they have Italian names, Irish names, Greek names, Lithuanian, Slavs, everything, I often ask myself, 'What does citizenship mean to these people?' And I preface my remarks something like this. Wouldn't it be a much greater country, Mr. Vice President, wouldn't we be a greater, more unified country if after a person has received his citizenship, every one of them—I hope you will remember this—if you are ever asked what you are, do not say, 'I'm Italian, I'm Greek, Irish, English,' anything like that—you must proudly say, 'I'm an American.'

"You must proudly say you're an American," the judge repeated. "Suppose that everybody in this country, all the different minorities, were to do that—you know what it would do? It would make us a stronger and more united and greater country." He went on: "I feel deeply about this because it strikes home to me as I know it does to the Vice President. I remember the days in Waterbury, Connecticut, where I was born, where my dad, who was an immigrant, came here from Italy. Came here when he was seven years old, didn't have any friends to amount to anything, had a stepfather. He used to tell me about the rough days he had makin' fifteen and sixteen dollars a week as a barber, trying to support a family. And they talk about 'living in the ghetto'—really, this amuses me, because we've seen that kind of a life, I know I have, and I'm sure the Vice President has. But we had a wonderful family—we had a wonderful family life.

"We didn't have all this crime that's going on now. And all these things that we are confronted with. My father used to tell me about the days it was so hard to get a job and the people of Italian extraction, first, second, and third generation, had to remove or strike a vowel at the end of their name. Instead of having a name like Morano, they'd say Moran. It would be easier to get a job. Just think how far we've come from those days. They used to have signs at the factories, he told me, 'No Irish need apply,' for a job. Things like that.

"A little while ago, when we met, the Vice President said to me, 'What is your heritage?'—he could tell I had an Italian name, I suppose. But when anybody asks me what I am, I say, 'I'm an American.' It's true, I'm proud of my heritage, proud of what this country did for my mother and father, that gave me an opportunity to become a Federal judge, which I love, incidentally. You're now just as much an American as the Vice President is, or the President of the United States. Thank you very much."

We all clapped. The judge smiled proudly, turned to the Vice President and asked if he wanted to add a few words. He did—the straight I-am-an-American approach, it seemed to him, was slightly out of date.

"First of all," the Vice President said, "I've been very moved by your remarks, and I want to congratulate Mr. Safire's family for having another citizen in the family. Bill has done a little moonlighting with me, even though his primary assignment is on a loftier level than mine.

"One of the reasons Bill writes for me is because of some things you've said, Judge. He understands the feelings I have which are not quite similar to the ones you have. You and I come from fathers who emigrated to this country, and both of us have seen those fathers struggle to become identified with our systems. And both of us have seen our fathers able to educate their sons and achieve for them through their dedication, a higher station than both fathers were able to.

"Notwithstanding that, I don't think that I'm one whit more 'American' than my father was, and I've never seen a man who was more dedicated to this country and its free system than he was. He was naturalized in Schenectady, New York. He came here when he was about twenty-one or -two years old. He had no friends—similar to your father," he said to the judge, "and oddly enough he turned to barbering, too. I guess that's one thing they thought they could get away with doing fairly badly while they were learning. He didn't know much about barbering, but he learned enough to work his way into business for himself and into a fairly affluent life. He was wiped out in the Depression and dragged himself back into the economic picture huckstering vegetables on a truck, which I really admired in him.

"My father left me with one thing. He left me with the idea that no matter how bad things got, a person in the United States who *wanted* to make a living, *could* make a living. And this made me willing to live a more high-risk kind of life. I was never afraid to leave a secure position to venture further because I knew that if failure overtook me while struggling for a higher station, and taking the risks that the world carried, that I'd always be able to feed my family because I knew I'd never face the economic hardship that my father faced. And if he could do it, I could do it.

"Another point I want to make," the Vice President said, "naturalization has a particularly emotional tinge for me. When I was active in my Kiwanis Club in the neighborhood, a very active one, I was chairman of a public affairs welcoming committee. One of the things that I did was to begin bringing newly naturalized citizens to the Kiwanis meetings—the first time that had ever been done in the Kiwanis Club. We'd invite them and honor them at the Club and welcome them into the United States community. It was a tremendously emotional thing, both for our Club members and for the people we brought.

"Which brings me to the last point. The judge said, and he emphasized several times, to remember that 'we are all Americans.' But the danger, Judge, doesn't come today from the points that used to be dangerous. We don't need to forget that we are Italians, or Greeks, or English, or French, or German, or whatever the case may be, because these are not the points of division anymore. National heritage is a wonderful thing, something to be proud of and remember, and not to try to hide or erase.

"The dangers of division today come from too much emphasis on designating and separating the minority groups which make up America. The media, sometimes in their efforts to promote causes, will say 'the young, the black, the poor.' Well, these people are all Americans, 'the young, the

black, the poor' are Americans. And I think it's the height of oversimplifi-
cation to suppose that 'the young' are an amorphous mass that think alike,
that 'the black' people think alike, or 'the poor' think alike.

"Our country is being divided," Agnew continued, "in many cases by the
people who are screaming loudest about divisions. It's those people, those
who say that the President and I are dividing the country, as we attempt
to rally people who believe in this country. We don't visualize America as
a loose amalgam of minority interests. We can't have a great country if we
look at ourselves in that way. I'm terribly concerned about the emphasis
on minority grouping, or the emphasis on the identities of interest of the
various small social groupings, turning one American against the other in
very subtle ways. And this is being done by the very people who are calling
for unity.

"America is cohesive," Agnew concluded. "We should all have pride in
our ethnic backgrounds and our heritage. But we still must consider ourselves free to think and develop our political opinions as we wish to, not
because we are members of one physically identifiable or ethnically identifiable group or the other. I didn't mean to make a long speech but I think
it's very important."

The judge was impressed, as were all of us. The Vice President was
right, I think, to point out that the old divisions of nationality were no
longer dangerous—indeed, were useful to remember in showing our diversity—but that the present danger came from a false assumption that
groupings based on race, age, and income would conform to standards of
alienation set forth by self-appointed spokesmen.

Agnew was on the threshold of a campaign that would use him as lightning rod in the protection of a structure beginning to house a new majority. In a way that would be attacked as demagogic, he was girding for
an assault on oversimplifiers. He was a man of ideas and articulation, who
—because he was assigned the role the President called "the cutting edge,"
and performed it with zest—would be portrayed as a boob and a mud-
slinger. But he had a way of touching chords in people, as he did with those
in his office that day, that made them respect his good sense and his willingness to say what was on his mind. I hoped, as I left, he would ask me
to work on some more speeches with him someday.

On the way out of the Vice President's office, the District Court judge
motioned me aside. He had noticed that I had a photographer present,
and he wondered if he might possibly have taken a picture of him with the
Vice President. I said, with less condescension than usual at one of these
requests, that it was the least I could do to make up for the imposition on
his time, and set up the shot, promising to send him an autographed
photograph taken with the Vice President of the United States. A Federal
judge is an important person, but he is no celebrity, and he was delighted
at the prospect of this memento for his office wall.

"How do you spell the name, Judge?" I asked, pulling out a pencil and
paper.

"Sirica," he said, and spelled it out for me. "S-I-R-I-C-A."

PART FIVE

SEEDS OF DESTRUCTION

1. "US" AGAINST "THEM"

The 1969 renovation of Lafayette Park, across Pennsylvania Avenue from the White House, seemed to take forever. The contractor wasn't doing all that much—just repaving the walks in the block-square park, and adding a fountain, doing some fresh planting around the statues of Von Steuben, Kosciusko, Rochambeau, and Lafayette (all foreigners who had helped George Washington) and Andrew Jackson (an afterthought), and shining up the plaque on the Bernard M. Baruch Bench of Inspiration, where I often went to speculate—but the park was fenced around in plywood, and contests were held to see which elementary school class could paint the fence most creatively. Nobody complained about how slowly the work was going.

The renovation job took eighteen months because the White House did not want Lafayette Park used for demonstrations. Hard to believe, now, but quite plausible in the context of the times. The park was a perfect spot for sit-ins and lie-ins, statues perfect for chaining oneself to, with the floodlighted White House offering an unparalleled backdrop for photographers.

Paranoia? A sly forerunner to the repression later characterized by wiretaps, special investigation units, a break-in at a psychiatrist's office, and the like? Before leaping to this conclusion, it is useful to recall a beautiful spring morning in 1970, driving to work at the White House through Rock Creek Park, which winds its way through Northwest Washington. That park is less manicured than the small urban park in front of the White House, and a real creek rages through there when the Potomac shows signs of flooding. On that fragrant June morning I had my convertible top down and the radio on loud.

The news on the radio was about the demonstrations planned to bring the government to a halt, and the impossible possibility was given reality by the presence, every fifty yards or so, of a soldier in full field uniform, pack on his back, bayonet at the ready.

Soldiers strung out all the way to work is a curious phenomenon. Near the White House, the men in khaki were backed up with blue-helmeted police, and the buses—always the buses—parked flat snout to flat back, ringing the White House and environs with a barrier more formidable and less grim than barbed wire. As in the nineteenth century, wagons in a circle were the best defense. Local newsmen rarely spoke at the time of "repression" or warned of police brutality, since the Government of the United States was under actual threat of siege by a few thousand of its citizens. The nation's ninth largest city was in danger of being closed down, and local residents, including editorial writers, were concerned less about the rights of dissenters than their personal safety.

In looking back on those days, some people recall wonderful young people marching silently and peacefully, carrying candles for peace; others recall the garbage-throwers and tire-slashers, vandals roaming the streets, bawling obscenities, terrorizing residents. Both kinds were there; seldom in the same time and place, but retrospect has a way of telescoping perceptions of time and place. The demonstrations could be viewed as democratic dissent being freely expressed by free people, with an unfortunate few spoiling things for the vast majority of dissenters—or as an outpouring of delighted rage by kooks and cowards and professional revolutionaries, with a few nice people duped by them into thinking this was a peaceful demonstration. The very different points of view illustrate the difference between "us" and "them." As the gap widened, the danger grew. The real danger was not what the contemptible action of the violent could do to us, but what the contemptuous reaction of the powerful could do to them. And to us.

The election of 1968, and the reaction to the events of the first half of Nixon's first term, confirmed in the minds of the President and his most trusted advisers that:

1. "We" would never have an appeal to "them," and it was a waste of time trying to win them over or appease them.

2. "They" could be useful to "us," as the villain, the object against which all of our supporters, as well as those who might become our supporters, could be rallied.

3. Our forum was the Presidency, and their forum was the Eastern Establishment press, and since they "managed" the news we would be better off discrediting the news media.

4. "We" were on the side of the right, representing the will of the people in a democracy, and majoritarians had the duty to identify and overcome the anti-democratic elitists.

There was disagreement within the Administration about all of these theses, particularly about the intensity with which we should fight the press, but there was little dissent on the assumption that lay beneath all of them: that it was "them" against "us" on nearly everything.

The China initiative was coming to fruition and the relationship with the Soviet Union was changing dramatically; with great breakthroughs in the works in the world and with a rightward swing evident in the country, Richard Nixon decided—more by osmosis and momentum than by analysis and decision—that the best political course was to make vivid and take more advantage of the difference between "us" and "them."

This was one of those amorphous nondecisions that decided much of the character of the Administration. For years, it had been assumed that there were more of "them" than there were of "us," whether this was true or not. Nixon could hope and guess that the Wallace vote of 1968 was mostly a Nixon vote in the absence of Wallace, but he could not be sure, nor could he be sure that Wallace would not run again—the Governor sent messages through his fellow Alabamian, Postmaster General Winton Blount, that if he ran, his third-party candidacy would be helpful to Nixon, and Nixon sent back word that said, in effect, thanks but we would prefer it if Governor Wallace did not run.

With the Silent Majority gaining an identity, however, first in the reaction to the President's speech of November 3, 1969, and then with the hard-hat march in mid-1970 reacting against the reaction to the Cambodian decision, the President's dream of a "new majority" began to take shape. Nixon always had a feeling that "folks" were with him and were the majority, but he always felt the necessity of winning over the swing voter, the sophisticated folks or folksily sophisticated. The realization that the old Nixon "enemies" and the new, all lumped together, did not pose a great threat to Nixon's majority, but might even help solidify it, caused a sea-change in the Nixon mood, from an analytical how-do-we-run-against-them to a satisfied run-'em-out-of-town.

The Administration would not be partisan in the old sense, because Republicans were still the minority; nor would it be bipartisan or nonpartisan, since neither would provide the magnetic field necessary for disparate forces to coalesce. It would be superpartisan—that is, aggressively majoritarian, building a new coalition by playing off the unpopularity of the minority.

Again, it is important to stress that this was not arrived at in a "decision-making process." It evolved; some was planned, some was fortuitous, some came as gifts to the new majority from the masochism of the new minority. "Bring us together," never the Nixon watchword, was used to bring "us" together—the like-minded, the forgotten Americans, the "good, decent, taxpaying, law-abiding people"—and the best way to do that was to frequently point to the difference between the quiet movers and the noisy "movement."

Who were "they," anyway?

Nixon and his men came at that two ways, because by defining "them" we could identify ourselves.

Just as a paranoid has some real enemies, the Nixon people had some real thematic villains. *Elitism* was one, combining social snobbery, the arrogance of wealth, and—most important—the Hamiltonian idea that some were privileged by birth and education to rule.

Welfarism was another, which the "work ethic" was designed to confront; because the shorthand was simplistic, the substance of the difference ought not to be dismissed as unreal. In the welfarism target area were the "social planners" (a favorite phrase of Buchanan's) who were forcing schoolchildren to be bused, bringing slums to suburbs, and labeling as a bigot anybody who stood in their way.

Another villain was the *new isolationism* and unilateral disarmament, a penchant for weakness which would, in Nixon's view, bring the nation to the ultimate choice of war or surrender of freedom. Timing was important here: the usual elitists—the Eastern Establishment, loosely called—used to be vigorously, responsibly opposed to the redneck isolationists of the South and Midwest. The Vietnam guilt complex flopped their usual position.

"Permissiveness" was almost as wide-ranging a form of villainy as elitism, rooted deep into America's malaise. The most obvious target was the Judiciary, especially Supreme Court decisions that seemed to protect the accused to an extent that overlooked the victim; in local terms, judges who made a revolving door out of the back end of the paddy wagon were objects of resentment. A tough judge like "Maximum John" Sirica was more to the Nixon taste. (Pity that Nixon missed that chance to get to know Sirica.) But permissiveness to criminals was only part of the story. The general breakdown in respect for tradition by young people—which, when you think about it, is traditional—accompanied by a world-owes-me-a-living attitude by many, and the frightening rise in the use of drugs gave credence to Vice President Agnew's charge that this had become a "Spock-marked generation," featuring "demand feeding up to the age of thirty." But the philosophical route was not the only way of defining "them" and thereby identifying "us"; there were groups who probably held most of the above beliefs but who had a distinction all their own in the Nixon tartarus of villainy.

One of the groups was the *Washington Establishment*, a kind of permanent, floating crap game of power. The dolls are chic hostesses and smart writers, the guys are dynamic lawyers and reporters, the food is delicious, the wine the right temperature at the Georgetown dinner parties (more dens of inequity than iniquity); the connections run two generations deep in the government bureaucracy, and Nixonian newcomers had the impression they were regarded as hard-to-tolerate transients.

I recall an evening in 1971 at the Georgetown home of Polly Wisner. The friendly and urbane Mrs. Wisner, widow of a high CIA official in that agency's salad days, puts together a diverse and lively group, and I found myself after dinner arguing Vietnam policy with Clark Clifford. I had just worked on a Presidential Vietnam speech, and Clifford had just blasted it publicly at length. In the dining room, the superlawyer—a former Truman speechwriter—left-handedly complimented my "artfulness," and I admired how he made an essentially specious case with great skill. Clayton Fritchie, a columnist who had been Adlai Stevenson's speechwriter, egged Clifford on from a dovish point of view. Stewart Alsop (who always had a wild, secret desire to be a speechwriter) provided the counterbalance, as he was still fairly hawkish at the time. (Alsop, along with Charlie Bartlett, had invented the hawk-dove metaphor in an article on the Cuban missile crisis and the gifted Stew—who later described himself as the "rabbi" in my conversion to journalism—was an adept second in any duel.) Nobody gave an inch; nobody got excited; we got to know each other's positions a little better; and we enjoyed ourselves.

I recounted the episode to Haldeman the next day and the mention of Clifford's name was like waving a red bull in front of an angry flag. Clifford was the very personification of "them": he had helped mire the United States in Vietnam, and now that Nixon was extricating the nation from the result of the folly of men like Clifford, he had the gall to tell us that the only way out was abject surrender. Beyond that, he was a certified Nixon-hater, a new hero of the Movement, and a frequent writer in the best of the worst media. Any form of association with the likes of Clifford—even in argument—was, in Haldeman's view, only a way of encouraging him to clobber us. My travels in Washington Establishment land were frowned upon, as were Pete Peterson's; only Henry Kissinger had the franchise.

Another villain was the old-fashioned, *knee-jerk Nixon-hater*, who reacted to Nixon like Pavlov's dog salivating at the bell. Middle-aged now, not in the Movement, not sure of his position on the left anymore, but fixing on one star in the firmament—hating that s.o.b. from the Fifties who was another Joe McCarthy but too smart to get caught. Nixon did not forget his old nemesis, either: when I was assigned to work on Agnew speeches in the 1970 campaign, I suggested that the Vice President ridicule as "Johnnies-come-lately" some of the Democratic candidates who had flip-flopped dramatically on the "law and order" issue. Pat Buchanan, after speaking with the President, sent me a note: ". . . we should abandon the 'Johnny-Come-Lately' approach since the average voter does not mind a fellow changing his mind. Just as the President is still being tarred for comments in the Hiss case, and the Helen Gahagan Douglas race—so these radical liberals should be forced to live down forever the quotes they have made."

Another part of "them" was the *Kennedy apparat*. The use of a spy-novel word added a nicely sinister note to their description. They had whipped us in 1960, and in so doing taught the Nixonians a good deal about how to win at all costs. An article of faith in the Nixon countermyth is how the Kennedyites outspent Nixon, defrauded him, and "stole the election" in Missouri, Texas, and Illinois, with nobody to so much as wag a finger at them. The public shoving of Mrs. Lyndon Johnson, wife of the Vice Presidential candidate, the outraged reaction to which helped "steal" Texas in 1960 for Kennedy–Johnson, is viewed as an induced incident. "If anybody pushes your wife, tell her to fall down" is an admonition Nixon passed on to Agnew as a result of it.

In the polarized view, the Kennedyites got us into the right war but in such a way as to make it impossible to win. They called fifteen thousand troops "advisers," got away with it, and have been complaining about every other President's "credibility" ever since; they tried to redistribute income in a way that sapped personal initiative; and, although nominally out of power, the old royalty permeates the Washington atmosphere with the potential of the Restoration. The Nixonites envied JFK for the way he was able to manipulate the media, and profoundly respected the Kennedy *apparatchiks* for the ruthless way they play the game.

The quintessential "them," of course, is the *establishment media*—the New York *Times,* the Washington *Post,* the "leers and sneers" from television commentators on CBS and NBC, the needling columnists. "The press is the enemy," the President would say, and that subject receives a separate chapter herein.

Alone with the President one day, I mentioned that columnist Mary McGrory had been to a dinner party at my home. The next day, Haldeman pointedly told me that there was not a chance that I could ever persuade Miss McGrory to ever be fair about anything to do with Nixon, and to invite "them" into our homes was hopeless. "I pay no attention to them," Nixon insisted, but he paid a great deal of attention to them, and whenever—in the New York *Times*—a William Shannon called him "an unprincipled adventurer" or an Anthony Lewis flirted with "war criminal" and Nixon in the same paragraph, the President would seethe. "They" never attributed a good motive to him, nor he to them, and both suspected that anybody who strolled out into no-man's-land was a fool to be scorned or a knave to be watched.

I have been misusing a word all along—the *movement* is too fluid to have real political meaning. It was originally the labor Movement, then the civil rights Movement, then the antiwar Movement, then—or simultaneously—the counterculture, touting adversarianism as a philosophy, espoused by articulate dissenters as well as in the grunted "y'knows" of dropouts and depressionaries.

To "us" the most useful part of "them" were the Impassioned Aginners: people with a contrary point of view, people who reacted against any point of view, but above all people whose pervasive belief was "those who are in authority must be wrong." (In my first month in Washington with the new Nixon Administration, I complained to a columnist about some unfair comment about Nixon; his reply was, "Never forget that we were just as unfair to Lyndon Johnson.")

The young, long-haired shock troops of the Impassioned Aginners, their loose leadership frustrated primarily by Nixon's refusal to terminate the war by simply pulling out, were ready to go beyond what had been the limits of dissent: violence was necessary, desertion was good, lawbreaking in a cause higher than the established order's murderous causes was to be praised.

Even before that kind of provocation, which was stimulated by what the Aginners felt was the most unprecedented decade of official deception, a feeling had grown in the minds of the President and his closest advisers that "something had to be done" to answer the new threat. Lawlessness sanctioned by the counterestablishment had to be met with "extreme measures" by the government, which, the President could persuade himself, had been done before.

Was planned polarization a good idea? In some ways, it could have been. The acknowledgment of disagreement is often useful and realistic: there had been no "bipartisan foreign policy" for years, and the "water's edge" was the place where most politics began, not ended. Unity is a fine and noble thing to be for, like freedom, but the only way freedom can exist is in the acknowledgment of the limitations of freedom; in the same way, we can have a "national unity" only if we leave it loose and general, and recognize the diversity and difference that are inherent in, or endemic to, democracy. The 1820 Era of Good Feeling was a time of stagnation and petty bickering, and the nation was fortunate it was quickly replaced by Jacksonian two-party partisanship; one hundred and fifty years later, "consensus" was tried again and soon became a dirty word.

In this spirit of creative controversy, the President and his men began to define and to articulate real policy differences with "them," especially in the direction of the flow of power: "they" thought the localities could not handle power, and would be unfair to the poor and the weak; "we" felt that Washington domination had had its day, and had caused the present alienation.

So "us versus them" might well have been a good idea philosophically, since it invited debate on issues; it was surely a good idea politically, since there were now more of "us" than "them"; it seemed a good idea morally, since it was never doubted that "we" were right and "they" were wrong.

The trouble was, it all got out of hand. The most passionate of the Aginners particularly succeeded in provoking "us" into the reaction they feared or hoped "we" were capable of. This led to the genuine—not rhetorical— "repression" they had been talking about, in the encroachments on civil liberties by tappers, plumbers, and the like. When the evidence of repression came to light, "they" proclaimed they had been right all along, demanded a political bloodletting, which is why some Nixon men now quote the words of cartoonist Walt Kelly's Pogo: "We have seen the enemy and they is us."

During the Nixon first term, of course, measures taken to counter "them" did not in the least seem "out of hand." Indeed, if democracy is government responsive to the will of the people, the judgment the people made overwhelmingly in 1972 was that the President was on the side of the most responsive. But in the development of *esprit* within both groups —the Ellsbergs on one hand and the Kroghs, Liddys, Hunts, and even Colsons on the other, both with passionate convictions of "higher moral laws"—politics was reduced to a form of savagery previously unknown in this country. Did this mean the handwringing tut-tutting about "polarization" was right, and the hard-nosed, pragmatic denunciations of "consensus" was wrong? I doubt it, but something happened in the development into a rampage of "us against them" that never happened before, and should never happen again.

In 1968 "they" were split on Humphrey, rallying to his cause too late, but after Nixon's election and honeymoon, "they" began coming together —in the minds of Nixon men, with a vengeance, led by old Nixon-haters in the press. A natural choosing-up of sides had begun, which is not unhealthy as long as there is some connective tissue. Unhappily, the connective tissue did not develop. On Nixon's side, if you were not for us, you were against us; on the extreme anti-Nixon side, if you were for him, you were a wrongo; on the pro-Nixon zealot's side, a wrongo had no rights.

Here is where a complexity enters. Nixon, the Number One "us," felt in his heart all the fears, hates, and resentments of us-against-them, and yet in many ways *he was one of "them"*: that is, he was intellectual, prone to examine a problem in all its facets, appreciative of subtlety; he was an inward and private man; and he enjoyed all too much the trappings of luxury and power. For a generation, he had been one of the power elite, familiar with world affairs and at ease with world leaders, and despite a conservative image earned by his hard-line anti-Communism and Hiss days, generally came down on the progressive side of the Republican Party's policy. In one breath, Nixon would dismiss a politician with "he's not 'folks,' he'll never understand," but in the next breath he could be one of them, telling a speechwriter who was getting too verbose "we sophisticates can listen to a speech for a half hour, but after ten minutes, the average guy wants a beer."

Does this mean that the sophisticated, worldly, "real" Nixon put on a folksy mask, stuck a hayseed in his mouth, and talked in pious simplicity to an electorate he knew was a majority and from which he had sprung, but whom he had long ago outgrown? Was he Huey Long dishing out the cornpone, the smart pol being very smart by not seeming too damn smart? Not usually: Nixon was proud of being "folks," and considered it quite consistent for one man to combine a complex understanding of arms limitation negotiations with a generalized feel for what's best. When he was forced to stop saying, "We must balance the Federal budget so that the American housewife can balance the family budget," Nixon felt a real loss.

Nixon knew his natural constituency to be the more conservative, the worried, the rattled yearning to breathe easy, the older and not as well educated, the disciplined and the satisfied, the sensible and the managerial —the "Middle American" as against Eric Goldman's "Metroamerican." They could see Nixon as a hero and not be misled. Though Nixon was the epitome of "us," because Nixon was also possessed of some of the smarter attributes of "them," he could cut into his opposition's traditional support.

That would help explain his inroads into Labor, into the Democratic Catholic vote and the liberal Jewish vote, at the same time he was holding onto his natural constituency; the fact that the Democrats would ultimately choose a candidate that deliciously exemplified "them" certainly magnified all this, but the realignment was taking place on Nixon's initiative as well.

Nixon's approach to what used to be considered "blocs" in building his new majority was new and different to American politics. Instead of appealing to their direct interests, he originally found the common denominators of their interests and used that as the key to let the blocs in the kitchen door. Later, he was to revert to more traditional wooing of special interests. His triumph was in isolating the opposition, identifying the villain; his tragedy was in letting the gulf between "us" and "them" grow to the extent when some of "us" thought the most extreme measures were needed to curb "them."

Where, then, was the source of the excess of zeal that led to Watergate? Roots could be found in the bitter political education of 1960, where the "Nixon deed"—the deed to Nixon's Washington home, which, like all similar deeds in that area at the time, contained a restrictive covenant—was used by Kennedy campaigners to inflame blacks against him; in his conviction that "they" were leaking away our national security, which led to the wiretapping started in May 1969, a first step down the eavesdropping road; in the miscalculations of Haldeman, who discounted excessive counterattacks in his certainty that "we're not that good," figuring 80 per cent of all planning was pure talk, but some men down the line tried all too hard to be that good; in the natural reaction to the face of hatred we would see in a crowd at San Jose, and the sardonic reaction to the press "coverup" of San Jose; in "Don't bother the Boss with this" to "Don't let this touch the Boss" to "Don't try to pin this on me."

When John Mitchell sent Assistant Attorney General Robert Mardian to argue the Keith case before the Supreme Court in 1971 (Solicitor General Griswold would not sign his name to the brief) the government held that it needed no court warrant to wiretap for "domestic security." In rejecting this national security-above-civil-liberties argument, Justice Lewis F. Powell, Jr.—a strict-constructionist Nixon appointee from the South, writing for a unanimous Court—held: "History abundantly documents the tendency of government—however benevolent and benign its motives—to view with suspicion those who most fervently dispute its policies. Fourth Amendment protections become the more necessary when the targets of official surveillance may be those suspected of unorthodoxy in their political beliefs."

When Nixon later spoke of the "expected excesses" of others as the reason for the excesses of "us," he put his finger on the political philosophy of the pre-emptive strike, which is rooted in an attitude of "us against them," a golden rule turned by perverse political alchemists to read: Do it unto others before they do it unto you.

2. THE '70 CAMPAIGN BEGINS

"There's a realignment going on," the President told us at the start of the 1970 midterm election campaign. "Agnew can be a realigner . . . What we do in this campaign will have enormous effect on 1972."

Conventional wisdom has it that Nixon and Agnew conducted a slashing, hard-driving campaign in the off-year of 1970, alienated a large segment of the public in so doing, and the result in terms of a change in Congressional seats was not worth the effort.

Mistakes were made in the campaign, the most glaring one directly attributable to this writer, and Vice President Agnew did get roughed up in the press as he blazed away at the "radic-libs." But sociological battle lines were drawn that changed our "law and order" issue of 1968 to the more diffuse "permissiveness" issue in 1972, and a political trap was laid that forced many Democratic candidates to choose between rejecting or embracing the Far Left, encouraging the intraparty wounds of 1968 to fester and making unity all the harder for Democrats in 1972.

The first discussion of the midterm elections that I can recall took place at a meeting of Republican legislative leaders and their wives, sitting around a squared table in the State Dining Room decorated with red and white carnations three days before Christmas, 1969. "Thanks for inviting wives," said Jerry Ford to the President, "it's nice to be together some few hours during the holidays."

Nixon wanted to stress the theme in the coming year of the hard time a Congress of one party gave an Administration of another party. Ford agreed, and put his finger on the issue: "My greatest disappointment is this: languishing unpassed are eighteen crime bills in five different committees. Not one reported out." The President encouraged him: "That's a great theme for Lincoln Day speeches." The House Minority Leader continued: "On another front, 139 House Republicans reversed their old traditions and voted for an increase in the national debt. Frankly," he added, "we hope everybody but you forgets this. But look at the record—sixty major reforms and requests, and next to no action." Turning to the wives,

Ford asked, "How would you ladies like it if you sent your husbands to the market with a long list and all they came home with was razor blades and booze?"

At that meeting, Labor Secretary George Shultz and black Assistant Secretary Art Fletcher made an eloquent pitch for the Administration's "Philadelphia Plan," opening up the construction trades to blacks. Nixon showed his pride at this liberal side of his Administration. "The Democrats are token-oriented," he pointed out, "we're job-oriented."

But as the midterm elections approached, Nixon fixed his sights on the issue that led the polls: law and order, and began planning to use his fast-developing Vice President as his "cutting edge."

Bryce Harlow is a man with a lot of experience, a conservative outlook, and a polite demeanor. Like Pat Moynihan, he is an Oklahoman; both men are good writers and both managed to preserve their independence and integrity. But Bryce is unlike Pat in many other respects. He was an Eisenhower speechwriter, a Nixon man toward the end of the wilderness years, and was the second person Nixon appointed to the White House staff (after Rose Mary Woods). The five-foot-two Harlow once described an argument with tall Rogers Morton as "an eyeball-to-kneecap confrontation," and was the Nixon staff man that Vice President Agnew trusted most. Harlow's job as Assistant for Congressional Affairs was coming to an end in late 1970 because he wanted to return to the lucrative caldrons of Proctor & Gamble, and besides, the President felt he was too soft on Congress. When the Vice President was chosen to be the instrument of Nixon's 1970 campaign, the President sweetened the deal by offering Agnew the short-term services of Bryce.

Harlow then reached out for three other Nixon aides: Pat Buchanan, Martin Anderson, and me. His recruitment was skillful.

"Brother Safire, I have always considered you *primus inter pares* of the speechwriters," he began, using the Latin for "first among equals."

"I appreciate that, Counselor, but that's what Buchanan says you just told him."

"I consider you both *primus inter pares*," Harlow replied evenly. "Yours is the opportunity to volunteer for a refreshing and one might even say exhilarating political experience," spoofing his offer even as he made it, "that of assisting our Vice President as he carries the banner of truth to the far reaches of the land, which the President cannot do because he is burdened by the affairs of state. Let me emphasize it would be entirely voluntary. You may, if you prefer, continue along your humdrum path."

I asked to be dealt in, but pointed out that Buchanan and I often clashed on ideology, and a campaign plane is no place for such struggles. "That's another reason why the Presi—why the Vice President wanted you along, to tilt back toward the middle," Harlow replied. "When necessary, I will serve as arbiter."

"You'll be the straw boss, then?"

"I would consider myself *primus inter pares*," Harlow said.

The presence of four Nixon aides on the Agnew campaign plane was signal enough to reporters that the enterprise had more than the normal blessing of the White House, though Ron Ziegler doggedly maintained a slight separation: "The Vice President, as always, speaks for himself, and has the confidence of the President" was the ambiguous line adhered to, which drove reporters up the wall; they wanted an unequivocal statement that the Vice President spoke for the President, which of course they would never get.

On September 9, 1970, from ten-fifteen till noon, the four aides on temporary duty were given a sometimes-pointed, sometimes-rambling political briefing by the President in the Oval Office. The Vice President was not present, for reasons of Nixon's own. Other political operatives were there: Bob Finch, Bob Haldeman, Don Rumsfeld, Harry Dent, Murray Chotiner, and Harlow's aide, Dick Burress.

Harlow opened with brief remarks about the Vice President's schedule: Illinois, Wyoming, California, Nevada, New Mexico, and Michigan on the first swing.

Nixon: "Will you have TV along? Don't let Agnew spend time with the network specials. Play the wires and local TV. When he was abroad—and I watched this pretty carefully—the only time he got adequate coverage was when he concentrated on the wires and TV. Forget the columnists."

The President was animated and decisive, dominating the discussion for two hours. "One thing to be concerned about is this: Agnew comes in and attacks this or that person. I'm afraid it would be 'Agnew attacks Stevenson. Agnew attacks Tunney. Agnew attacks whoever.' That makes him seem like a common scold—if he's considered as an outsider, attacking a local man, that is too high a price to pay. Instead, put 'em all in a bag. Say the local man is 'typical' of a group. You can put all the Democratic candidates in a bag except Gale McGee. We can't in good conscience go after him that way.

"Another thing—we are not out for a Republican Senate," the President said. "We are out to get rid of the radicals. The point is that the only Republican coming up who is a radical is Goodell. Now about him—I'll give you the line: Both major party candidates in New York oppose the President. The only candidate who doesn't is Buckley. The President's usual rule of endorsing all Republican candidates is being revoked in this case. We are dropping Goodell over the side. Everyone knows it. Also, before I forget, we are not supporting the Republican candidate against Byrd in Virginia.

"Have you all read the Scammon-Wattenberg book?* All the Democrats are reading it. That's why Humphrey, Moss, Cannon, all say they are 'men of the center.' Hang their past quotes on them. All Democrats are trying

* *The Real Majority*, by Richard M. Scammon and Ben J. Wattenberg (New York: Coward, McCann & Geoghegan, 1970).

to blur their image; they are petrified about permissiveness being hung on them—toward crime, toward students. The reason why the votes on Haynsworth and Carswell are significant is because they were votes against the confirmation of judges who would rectify the imbalance in the courts.

"What's the reason for doing this now?" the President asked rhetorically. "We have to provide a counterploy to what the other side is doing. This strategy is not for after the '70 election. It is for before the election. The Administration thrust is centrist. But now even a way-out type like McGovern is racing toward the center. We have to force them to repudiate the left, which loses them votes, or else to take the left—which gives us the center.

"That's the way this campaign has to be fought. The Democrats are trying to move over to the center, keeping us on the defensive on the economic issue. On inflation: don't go into the drawn-out business about the trade-off about price stability and unemployment. Just say this is what happens when you go from war to peace. We should hit them hard on the Vietnam issue. But on the left-right business, get them on the defensive: 'I don't question his sincerity—he deeply believes this radical philosophy.' Then they'll be saying, 'Gee, I'm not a radical.'

"Permissiveness," Nixon punched home, "is the key theme."

Bob Finch pointed out that Rockefeller wanted Agnew in Syracuse. The President smiled. Harlow said that some upstaters in New York were blaming Rockefeller for keeping Agnew out.

Nixon said mildly, "We want Rocky to win."

Finch: "Rocky himself wants Agnew to come."

The President shook his head in wonderment, probably recalling the delicate way Rockefeller had used Nixon in his 1966 campaign for New York Governor. "Isn't that something! They're really reading the tea leaves, aren't they? I may want to do New York myself. Delay an answer. God, I can't believe it."

Harlow said that Senator Charles Percy had asked to come along on the Agnew trip to Illinois.

The President: "Sure, take Percy. Of course, if I thought Goodell had a chance of winning, we would be for him. Since he doesn't, we drop him over the side. This is a signal for others to stick with us in the future. Let's be tough. What's the matter, Buchanan, you don't like that?" Of course, Pat Buchanan did like that—he was a True Believer in the two-ideology system.

"Turning to speeches, as I said, lump all radicals together but leave McGee out." Senator Gale McGee, Democrat of Wyoming, was an outspoken hawk on Vietnam. "Moss, Montoya, Hart, Hartke, Gore, Burdick, and Symington—don't talk about them individually or personally—say, 'My wife likes them,' or something. But we need a phrase like 'little group of willful men' showing they are peas in a pod." Here Nixon pretended to go on the stump to show what he meant: "Nine times out of ten, in a choice between a strong bill and a weak one, they will be for the weak one.

Nine times out of ten, in a choice between a strong U.S. and a weak U.S., they'll say, 'Trust the Russians.' We need strong political leaders."

Chotiner suggested it might be a good idea to hit Congressman Gene Tunney, running against Republican Senator George Murphy, with a charge of absenteeism.

The President: "That is for Murphy to decide, not for Agnew. For the Vice President to come in and take a guy on personally would make him a martyr."

Haldeman asked about the campaign in Tennessee of Congressman William Brock, a Republican, against Democratic Senator Albert Gore. "Brock's problem is not in getting the Agnew vote," Haldeman pointed out, "it's in getting the liberals."

The President, nodding: "Brock has voted against everything—Social Security, Appalachia, everything. While Family Assistance is not a good issue generally, it may be good for Brock. Let him be *for* something. On the economic issue, he has got to prove he isn't an encrusted old type. In 1950—Murray remembers this—Helen Gahagan talked about the economic issue while I talked foreign policy. We never really clashed. And I won." Chotiner, sitting there like the Ghost of Christmas Past, nodded.

The President had another thought: "Don't blame labor for inflation. Don't get an antilabor tag on any of our candidates. Here's the line: 'Let's understand once and for all the candidates who say they are Democrats are not basically Democrats. They have broken away from the Democratic Party. These issues are bigger than Democrat or Republican. Vote against those who have deserted the principles of the Democratic Party.'

"The object is to make it comfortable, fashionable for Democrats to vote against their party. Do a speech on this being a contest between conservatives and ultra-radicals. Conservative is a good word. This is dangerous, but the polls show that as Republican strength has gone down, conservative strength has gone up. Seventy-eight per cent of the American people think the courts have gone too far toward permissiveness."

Rumsfeld, a former Congressman from Illinois who was not enamored of Agnew, wondered whether people knew what the word "permissiveness" meant.

The President: "Good point, do a fast check. Now in Michigan, we are not going to win. We are just going in for the ducks of it. Take the Democratic platform and run against that. That stuff about amnesty for draft dodgers. I've developed a quote: 'Young men have to make a choice; fifty thousand American men died for their choice and two hundred draft dodgers will have to live with their choice.' Call upon the Democrats in Michigan to repudiate their platform.

"I have asked for a list of quotes. If we were Democrats," the President said, glaring at Haldeman, "we would have had them a month ago." Haldeman said they were coming. (Somebody's tailfeathers would soon be singed.) "Call on our opponents to repudiate these quotes. If they don't, you have an issue. If they do, it won't help them any.

"Remember this, the heartland of the Democratic Party is on the left. The heartland of the Republican Party is on the right. Remember '62 in California? The Democrats made us repudiate the right; that was clever. Let's make them do the same thing now with the left.

"Now, about Agnew himself. Not many people have the energy for the kind of grueling campaign you remember in '68. Don't work him too hard. Give him a chance to look good and feel good. Work the fence only if the candidate is there with him. There is no need to work the fence alone." In political lingo, when a candidate breaks away from his protected cocoon to greet a crowd behind a barrier, that is called "working the fence."

"About the press. You will hear them say, 'Joe here will write a bad story if you don't see him.' The hell with that. We are the only ones who read the columns; the voters don't read them."

Chotiner said that Conservative James Buckley's supporters in New York needed a signal that their man would get the White House nod over Republican, but leftish, Charles Goodell.

The President mused aloud: "Maybe we should drop Goodell in the Illinois speech. 'We're taking a hands-off policy because he has deserted us.' No. Do it this way: (1) We don't endorse Goodell; (2) we do not yet endorse Buckley; (3) when we put them in a bag, we don't say the bag holds only Democrats. Along about the first of October, put him in the bag with the others. But be careful—don't talk about Senators—talk about candidates. We want a few others not running this year to have a chance to come home. Any time you talk Democrats v. Republicans, we lose. Any time you talk radicals v. responsibles, we win.

"At a fund-raiser, get away from the party. Say, 'I am proud of my party but this issue is bigger than the party.' The National Committee has been organizing better and better fewer and fewer people.

"On second thought, it's too early to break it off with Goodell. Let's say for now, 'Let New Yorkers decide who can best support the President.'" Nixon often switched back and forth in the same meeting; only the final instruction counted.

"All through the farm belt states, remember that people might not approve too quickly what you say, but they remember it longer. In New York they will holler for you like mad and then go vote for the other guy.

"Please, Bill"—the President leaned forward and tapped my knee— "don't try to please the press by saying something new all the time. Keep saying what works. Tom Dewey told me you have to tell people something at least four times before they remember it. We all have 'the' speech. Lincoln made the House Divided speech at least a hundred times before Cooper Union. Bryant made the Cross of Gold speech two hundred and fifty times before the convention. We make a mistake on this. If you get a good line for Agnew, get him to repeat it. Use it again. Every good line must become part of the American memory.

"There's a realignment taking place," the President said with emphasis. "Agnew can be a realigner. If he can appeal to one-third of the Democrats, we'll win two-thirds of the races. In all your preparing you are talking to the swing vote, the independent voter. That's 5 per cent of the people. What we do in this campaign will have an enormous effect on 1972.

"Don't use the expression 'thinking Democrats.' The ivory-tower types go for Galbraith. Find ways to talk of the dignity of work and pay respects to our Catholic friends. We could have had a mass at the Labor Dinner and 80 per cent of the people would have hit the rail.

"On abortion—get off it." Buchanan pointed out that Agnew might have taken a position on this earlier.

"Well, just say it's a state matter and get off it. And stay off Israel. Not a vote in it. We are doing the right thing there. And you can tell your Jewish friends privately that we're doing all the right things, which is true, but the country is three to one against us on it. The country doesn't want to get into a war in the Middle East.

"Show how the local incumbent sits in conferences with the President. That has a big effect. 'There is no man the President counts on more . . .' —that kind of thing. Generally, stay off local issues, give them a little flip but don't promise any dams. Don't mention state legislative candidates— 'good old Joe Doaks who served the party for thirty-five years'—that bores everybody.

"There's a very good gimmick for Congressional candidates. Bring them all up together after the speech and stand with them, all waving your arms. Work it out with the advance man.

"Spend time with the TV cameramen and only those special columnists who are your friends. Pick the guys that count. At other times you can waste a lot of time talking, but in a campaign you shoot at targets that count. I wouldn't spend any time with the newsweeklies, they don't affect local elections at all. But cover the local press. See to it the local commentator meets the Vice President—it's a big deal for him. And these men will have infinitely greater effect than the national press on the election. In press conferences call on the local reporters. The AP and UPI and the three networks should get to ask some questions, but two-thirds of them should come from the local press.

"And at the end of a day, bring in the local Mr. Big in the news media and give him an exclusive. Play your friends. It has enormous effect."

On the way out of the Oval Office political seminar, the President cautioned us: "Make no predictions, lay the groundwork for afterward; the average loss in an off-year is thirty-five seats. Say we're going to do better. And in the Senate the party in power makes no gains at all. Say we'll do better."

These notes were not the whole of the Nixon political sermon. He ranged from the philosophic to the nitty-gritty, and we staggered out of there looking as if we had been watching a two-hour display of political pyrotechnics. In April the President had decided he would not abandon his economic game plan, though he understood at that time it meant that the 1970 campaign would be conducted amid bad economic news. Now we were coming into those distressing figures: inflation at the rate of 5 per cent and rising, unemployment up to 5 per cent and rising, the "worst of both worlds"—perhaps necessary in the long run, but politically costly in the short run—and here was the President taking the offensive. The aphorism of Marshal Foch came to mind: "My center is giving way, my right is in retreat; situation excellent. I shall attack."

Would Agnew be able to capture and hold the attention of the media for a solid month, until the President returned from Europe and began discreet campaigning himself? Would the Democratic candidates see through our strategy, which was fairly obvious, and refuse to take the defensive on the social issue? Would they ignore the Vice President, denying him the conflict necessary for newsmaking, and focus instead on bad economic news, pressing their traditional strength with workingmen and consumers?

Fat chance, most of us thought. But it might work for a while, and it was worth a try.

And the damndest thing was, in a short-term political sense, it *did* work. Democratic candidates, with the Agnew steamroller on the way, spent most of their time getting pictures taken climbing in and out of police cars, awkwardly assuming hard-nosed positions on crime, and making altogether illiberal sounds.

Into the lists sailed Spiro T. Agnew, the most modern version of the Happy Warrior, to test Nixon's theory that the best economic defense was a "social issue" offense. To provide a traveling press corps with color, we announced that we would be the only campaign in history with an unabridged dictionary (the Merriam-Webster Second Edition, not the permissive Third) and Buchanan tried out a little of his alliteration, calling his targets "pusillanimous pussyfooters"; I added with "vicars of vacillation"; George McGovern got into the alliteration act by denouncing Agnew's "foaming fusillades." Agnew relished every moment of this. He came up with "he mounted the moment with the relish of a randy rogue," but we talked him out of that. To add spice to a San Diego speech, he asked us to come up with an updated version of Adlai Stevenson's "prophets of gloom and doom" with which to flay the perennial pessimists. I went overboard, suggesting a choice between "hopeless, hysterical hypochondriacs of history" and "nattering nabobs of negativism," and the Vice President laughed and said, "Hell, let's use both." Tongue in cheek, that is what he did, drawing an appreciative laugh from his audience and a pleased smile from the national press corps traveling along, unaccustomed to fresh leads at every stop from a Republican politician.

The Agnew attack, delivered with a merry bravado, was not received in good humor; "radic-lib," a coinage of the Vice President's own, sounded ominously like the "comsymp" of the John Birchers to some liberal commentators, and the man Nixon said would be his "cutting edge" became the lightning rod for a delayed counterattack. Besides, Agnew was hitting home: permissiveness, elitism, and a generalized tolerance for political and social immorality were new themes for the political stump, where one usually spoke of inflation, taxes, and war. Only thirty seconds of a speech would be reported on national television, giving the impression he was speaking only Nixon-style punchlines, but that was not a fair impression: the speeches were often long, original, controversial, and thoughtful. To his writers, Agnew was a delight. He provided us with an eleven-page, single-spaced memo of his ideas for speeches, would scribble all over his drafts with new thoughts, and would kick the gong around afterward not to see "what went over" but to analyze what points belonged in the argument. "At last I feel surrounded by an atmosphere of creativity," he said. Quite a campaigner.

The President had a lot of advice for his Vice President. In a meeting in the Oval Office with Agnew, Harlow, and myself on September 24, 1970, after Agnew had given Nixon his assessment of the Senate races he had observed so far, the President peppered him with ideas:

"Don't let the Secret Service get in the way of the photo car—if anybody is going to shoot you, he'll shoot you." I blinked; Agnew did not. "Stop the motorcade, break up the schedule, walk out into a crowd. Just take a walk. Any time you can get on TV with a warm thing like that, it's worth while. It's true you are the cutting edge, but also let them see the warm, human man.

"The fund-raising audiences are the flattest of all. Most of the people who come are okay, but the TV boys will focus on those sodden-looking old bastards." Here the President slumped in his chair, dropped his jaw, and rolled his eyes up at the ceiling, perfectly imitating a sodden-looking old bastard. Straightening up, he added, "Walter Judd used to say, 'You have got to make love to the people.' It's always been a very difficult thing for me to do, but you must plunge into the crowds. You have to show you care, and of course," he added, "you must care."

The Vice President wondered if it was a good idea to speak to union leaders. After Bryce Harlow voiced a reservation, the President said: "Rank and file is always more important than fat cats. Walk into a plant one day. Be late for a meeting. And just for the ducks of it, you might pop onto a campus—completely unplanned. Be unpredictable. Go for the color in the next two weeks and then the hard substance the last three weeks to Election Day. Remember, the airport fence is no longer a new picture— go to a department store, the salesgirls will go right up the wall.

"Be prepared to blast hell out of the Scranton Commission Report," said Nixon, who had asked the former Pennsylvania Governor to prepare the report. "They are at least four months out of tune—78 per cent of the people think that college administrators are too soft. Hit the faculties, never the students. Force the Democrats to defend the Scranton Report, be uncompromising and tough, because we're right—we've resisted the overly tough stuff. I worked out myself a much more specific approach: anybody who bombs or burns a Federally assisted institution faces Federal prosecution."

A certain irony has to be pointed out here. The President, who was programming his Vice President to blast "permissiveness," had just a few
months before okayed a plan that would have permitted the government
to go into the burglary business on a systematic basis, for what he considered proper national security reasons—the Vice President would have been
stunned if he had known of that. Meanwhile, the Vice President was allegedly accepting cash pay-offs in his office from Maryland contractors to
whom he had steered state business, and his refrigerator was being stocked
free by a friendly supermarket chain—: the President would have been
appalled to learn of this petty graft.

(Soon afterward, I wrote a piece for the New York *Times*'s op-ed page,
and asked John Dean, the President's new counsel, if it was all right to
keep the $150 they had sent; he ruled that it might be considered a conflict
of interest, and I had to return the check. That was a good idea, I thought:
it was good that we had men like Dean around to make sure nobody did
anything criticizable. It was those little niggling things that brought down
the wrath of the simon-pure in previous Administrations: deep freezes in
Truman's day, vicuña coats in Eisenhower's. No such conflicts of interest
marred the Nixon Administration.)

Harlow, Buchanan, and I were accustomed to working for Nixon, with
his tightly controlled methods and speeches based on crowd-stirring one-
liners. Agnew was easier-going, far less intense personally, friendlier, lazier,
and more interested in teaching than exhorting. He didn't like to brood
alone, but would play cards with his secretary, or talk things over with his
staff. Formal in his appearance, always combed and well turned out ("I'm
on the best-dressed list and the President is off, what do we do now?"),
Agnew could be warmly informal with the men he worked with. I will not
soon forget the sight of the tired Vice President of the United States,
two o'clock in the morning after a long day's campaigning, swapping dirty
jokes with Bob Hope over the telephone and laughing until tears rolled
down his cheeks.

But Agnew was serious about his message. His attacks were felt and resented. Agnew knew that as the "cutting edge" he would be harming his
own political chances, but he had been given an assignment and he carried it forward with zest.

As October began, I was snatched off the Vice President's plane and
sent to Ireland to meet the President's *Spirit of '76* to work on a Vietnam cease-fire proposal, which I will deal with in a later chapter. When he
returned, Nixon planned to replace the Vice President as the center attraction of the '70 campaign, conducting himself as a world leader requesting
support in the Congress. This was good politics, and it made sense in the
President's overall strategy to build the support he needed in the Congress
for "strong" defense and foreign policies, which would help him negotiate
an honorable peace in the Far East and a stable arms agreement with the
Soviets.

The plan was to switch the spotlight from the "hot" Agnew, now becoming the belated bull's-eye of the distracted Democrats (the alliteration habit is hard to kick), to the "cool" Nixon, above the battle, just returned from Europe to carry the message of the generation of peace. If beatnik demonstrators threw rocks at him, so much the worse for them in the public eye.

That was the plan. But they came at Nixon harder than he thought possible, and he slammed back in a way that made him seem harsher than he wanted to appear. We went out to California and said hello to hatred.

3. THE WAY TO SAN JOSE

Do you know the way to San Jose?
I've been away so long, I may go wrong and lose my way.
Do you know the way to San Jose?
I'm going back to find some peace of mind in San Jose.
  L.A. is a great big freeway, put a hundred down and
  buy a car. In a week, maybe two, they'll make you a
  star. Weeks turn into years, how quick they pass,
And all the stars that never were are parking cars and
pumping gas . . .

(copyright Hal David, Burt Bacharach)

The thousand people who came to San Jose, California, to greet the President of the United States on October 29, 1970, were not "parking cars and pumping gas"—they were throwing rocks and screaming obscenities in the most serious mob attack on a national leader in American history.

The story of the San Jose riot, the strangely contradictory and begrudging coverage of it, the reaction of Nixon at the time and after second thought, and the decisions and blunders of his staff in its aftermath, exposed Richard Nixon to proofs of some of his worst prejudices about protesters and reporters, sealing dislike and suspicion more deeply in his mind and enlarging the gulf between "us" and "them." Campaign tactics for the 1972 election were determined that weekend, too, in overreaction to the lessons drawn from the mistakes of 1970.

The motorcade rolled into San Jose with the advance car of photographers shooting back at the President's limousine (a car built more like a tank, but with an innocently civilian appearance) followed by the Greyhound buses filled with press and White House staff. I was in the next to last bus and could hardly believe what I saw.

Obscene signs were nothing new, and the chant of "One, two, three, four, we don't want your fuckin' war" had long since lost its shock value; demonstrators had plagued both parties since the late Sixties and were beginning to seem more a drag than a dread. Ordinarily, they worked their disruptive *schtick* in groups of twenty or thirty, popping up in an otherwise friendly crowd, but that night in San Jose was different.

Slowing down as we approached the civic auditorium, we were treated to the screams, howls, and roars of the representatives of the outer fringes of the counterculture. A screamer would look in our windows, lock onto one person's gaze, yell an oath, and make a gesture with arm or middle finger. Hundreds upon hundreds of them, faces contorted, worked up into a froth of hatred, doing everything a body can do with voice and gesture to express loathing and disgust. This was a lynch mob, no cause or ideology involved, only an orgy of generalized hate. One girl, about fifteen, long blond hair streaming down her back, sat astride the shoulders of an older man with head hidden by his own hair and beard, proudly waving a sign she felt gave a new double meaning to the name "Dick," all the while bawling a series of unrelated obscenities. She gave it all she had.

Their plan was to throw only epithets on our way in; a more serious onslaught was reserved for later. Inside the hall, five thousand tense and worried supporters made up the auditorium "rally"; Senator George Murphy and Governor Ronald Reagan spoke to warm them up, but even before the President came on, the sound of a battering ram was heard. The hall was actually, not figuratively, besieged; the demonstrators outside envisioned it as a drum to beat upon; the staff, after a few nervous self-assurances that this kind of thing only helped our cause, began to worry about getting out safely with the President. The people in that hall, ourselves included, were at once defiant and fearful, a state which is at the least a tribute to the success of the mob's intended intimidation. The Secret Service men, who always had seemed too numerous and too officious before, now seemed to us like a too-small band of too-mortal men.

Let the President describe the scene, from the reading copy of the speech he gave on the subject a few days later (Rose Mary Woods, in preparing the reading copy, breaks up the paragraphs into an e. e. cummings poem):

THE PRESIDENT'S READING COPY

Phoenix, Arizona

October 31, 1970

Thursday night in San Jose, I spoke to a crowd of 5,000 fine Americans.

1. They were exercising their right to assemble peaceably, to listen to political speakers, to weigh the issues in the campaign of 1970.

Outside the hall, a mob of about a thousand haters gathered.

1. We could see the hate in their faces as we drove into the hall, and in the obscene signs they waved.

2. We could hear the hate in their voices as they chanted their obscenities.

3. Inside the hall, we could hear them pounding on the doors as if they could not bear the thought of people listening respectfully to the Governor of the State of California, the Senior Senator from California, and the President of the United States.

4. Along the campaign trail we have seen and heard demonstrators.

   (1) But never before in this campaign was there such an atmosphere of hatred.

       1. As we came out of the hall and entered the motorcade, the haters surged past the barricades and began throwing rocks.

          (1) Not small stones—large rocks, heavy enough to smash windows.

          (2) And not just directed at me, though some hit the Presidential car—most of the rocks hit the buses carrying the Press and my staff, as well as the police vehicles.

What of the reaction of the people who came, peacefully to the rally?

1. Many who brought their children were terrified;

   (1) others were incensed at the insult to their elected leaders;

   (2) all were repelled by the atmosphere of violence and hatred that marred the event.

2. They thought to themselves: Is this America?

   (1) Is this the land where reason and peaceful discussion is the hallmark of a free society?

Some say that the violent dissent is caused by the war in Vietnam.

1. It is about time we branded this line of thinking—this alibi for violence, for what it is—pure nonsense.

(1)   There is no greater hypocrisy than a man carrying a
banner that says "peace" in one hand while hurling a
rock or a bomb with the other hand.

On Plate 16, following page 392, you can see how the President sharpened up that last line in his own hand to read: "Those who carry a peace
sign in one hand and throw a bomb or brick with another are the super
hypocrites of our time."

The San Jose police had driven the demonstrators away from the doors
of the auditorium and out of the official parking place. The motorcade was
parked in a circle, much like that of a wagon train under siege, with the
inside of the circle secured by motorcycle cavalry and the outside left to
the savages. After the rally, I boarded my bus and could see the scene inside the circle—about 150 Nixon supporters near his limousine at the auditorium entrance, well lit by television lights as cameramen awaited his exit
and greeting to the small crowd around his car. The President came out
and did his usual thing—climbed atop the car and wiggled the V sign to
his cheering supporters and the cameras behind them.

The Nixon people ringing the car (supporters, reporters, cameramen,
aides, and Secret Service, which would make up a crowd for a television
news backdrop in the middle of a desert) were not the only ones who hol-
lered at his signal. A reaction of fury and spleen was heard from outside
the ring of buses in the parking lot. One reporter, Martin Schram of Newsday, said he heard the candidate "in a low, angry voice to a nearby confidant" say, "That's what they hate to see." This murmured remark,
overheard by one reporter and by no other reporter or aide there at the
time, amid shouts and jeering and cheering, became the basis of a point of
view of many of those covering the event: that the President taunted the
demonstrators into violence. The responsibility for the attack, under that
theory, was not so much the antiwar militants', but that of the President,
who led them into rock-throwing in order to cast himself in a sympathetic
role, and to focus public anger on the youthful dissidents.

The motorcade moved out of the parking lot and ran a gauntlet of curs-
ing demonstrators. As Time reported: "The eggs began to fly even before
the motorcade moved out . . . Dozens of rocks were thrown, some the size
of a potato. They bounced off the President's well-armored car, and they
smashed windows in the press and staff buses trailing behind . . ." I
was in the staff bus with Rose Woods, the President's secretary, when the
rocks began to hit the steel sides. She said, "Just like Caracas"—she had
previous experience along these lines when Nixon, then Vice President,
was stoned in Venezuela—and she hit the deck in the aisle, shouting to the
rest of us to do the same. I, like a jerk, kept looking out the window. When
a rock slammed into the window on the opposite side of the bus, I was
showered with glass splinters, but with my face turned away, I was unhurt
and hastened to join my colleagues on the floor. In a minute, it was over
and the buses were roaring toward the airport. By the time we got aboard

Air Force One, I had a draft of a statement prepared for the Boss. In the office aboard the plane, he was icy quiet, his mind ticking over the alternatives; he wanted to react but not overreact, and he wanted to dissociate the violent mob from the "good people" of San Jose. He toned the statement down, and by the time it was handed out it was primarily a teaser for his speech the next night:

FOR IMMEDIATE RELEASE   October 29, 1970

Office of the White House Press Secretary
(El Toro MCAS, El Toro, California)

STATEMENT BY THE PRESIDENT

The stoning at San Jose is an example of the viciousness of the lawless elements in our society.

This was no outburst by a single individual. This was the action of an unruly mob that represents the worst in America. I have been careful to point out that these are the actions of a violent few.

It is important that all Americans keep this perspective. But the time has come to take the gloves off and speak to this kind of behavior in a forthright way. Freedom of speech and freedom of assembly cannot exist when people who peacefully attend rallies are attacked with flying rocks.

Tomorrow night at Anaheim I will discuss what America must do to end the wave of violence and terrorism by the radical anti-democratic elements in our society.

At the Marine terminal near San Clemente, I talked with the traveling press corps. Senator George Murphy was talking to television cameras about the attack, and several of the reporters for newspapers were getting sore about "the way you guys are trying to exploit this." I mumbled something about it all being a figment of our imagination, tilted my head and shook some glass splinters out at them. But the media pulling-away continued; most reports clearly stated the fact of the riot and the rock-throwing, but in the "overnights" and follow-ups one could feel the need for "balance," which would come from the so-called Presidential taunting of the crowd, and then for the way we sought to overemphasize the attack. The San Jose police chief was quoted as saying, "The barrage on President Nixon was verbal. It was not physical. This so-called riot has been exaggerated." That was a good example of a man covering up for some lapses in police protection, but his words were treated as evidence that perhaps the whole thing was a pseudo-event. When two skeptical reporters demanded a close look at the President's limousine, the Secret Service complied at Ron Ziegler's direction. This accommodation to reporters' demands for evidence was turned topsy-turvy by *Life* magazine as an unprecedented example of our efforts to extract the most sympathy from the attack.

This troubled the Nixon men. We had been accused before of importing dissidents to rallies so that the President could be vilified, and thereupon denounce the shouters. As the *Columbia Journalism Review* was to ask later, "Was the Presidential campaign party a target of mass violence the weekend before the Election, or were the media 'used' to create this impression?" The reviewer's conclusion was "it was not a proud day for the Presidency, for the police, or, unhappily, for the press"—only because some of the press had passed along the story of a real riot. Revisionists, at work almost at once, said that no rocks were found at the scene. They didn't say anything about eggs. (It's a funny thing about eggs—they are not lying there by the side of the road to be picked up by a group of Our Children when driven to understandable frenzy by Presidential finger-wiggling. Eggs require malice aforethought—they have to be brought to a riot. They have to be brought by people who have in mind the intent to throw them.)

The traveling press did not distort the story of what happened in San Jose that night. But in many cases the story was resisted; it was certainly resented; it was played down with hard looks at any description of what happened that seemed to be playing it up. Most of the reporters felt the riot helped Nixon by making villains out of his enemies, and were determined not to join in—the word was so often used—"exploitation." Such reluctance to be used is laudatory, but would have been better received by the Nixon men had there been some evidence of more than perfunctory press disapproval of the rioters. For, in fact, if one of the wayward activists had killed somebody with one of those rocks, it would have been murder; they had gone past demonstrating, they were engaged in a criminal attack; they were not suddenly incensed, they came with their missiles in their hands. A little passion in the commentary about their conduct might not have been misplaced, but it could not come from us and not much came from the men and women covering the story. They were motivated by a sense of duty; the President noticed and noted a certain lack of a sense of outrage.

A mob attack upon a U. S. President—unique in our history, and a serious matter for thoughtful students of behavior in our society—was thus being trivialized, swept under the rug (more, to the reporters' credit, in the questioning aimed at us than in the stories actually filed). To Nixon and his men, the attack was more proof, if any more were needed, of the deep-seatedness of the hatred of Nixon by the lunatic fringe. The apparent willingness of much of the media to minimize this contributed to the isolation of the men around the President more than most of us realized at the time.

The President, through Haldeman, asked me to do a speech, "tough, but calm," in a hurry. I had one in shape by noon the next day, in time for his Anaheim appearance that night, which was scheduled for live nation-wide telecast on the Friday before the following Tuesday's election. Had the President gone with that speech that night, allowing some of his honest emotion to show, and followed with a low-key, thoughtful speech on Election Eve, the election outcome might have been different—certainly the interpretation of it would have changed—but Nixon wanted to be cautious. He put my draft about the San Jose riot in his pocket and went on nation-wide TV from Anaheim that night with "the" speech—the one he had been giving all around the country in the past few weeks. Concerned about overreacting, he did not react at all. The next day, in Phoenix, at an airport hangar in the morning, he delivered his hard-hitting speech about San Jose. The audience loved it. He enjoyed giving it. He went back to California and thought about how the San Jose incident was so quickly forgotten.

One point in the Phoenix speech he had been especially anxious to make had to do with his personal mobility as President. Lyndon Johnson, it had been noted, was a virtual prisoner in the White House, his outside appearances largely limited to military installations, and Nixon was determined to break away from that constraint. His addition to this passage came from the heart:

1. As long as I am President, no band of violent

   thugs is going to keep me from going out and

   speaking with the American people wherever they

   want to hear me and wherever I want to go.

   (1) This is a free country, and I fully intend ~American~

   to share that freedom with my fellow ~citizens~.

   This President is not cooped up in W.H.

He delivered "This President is not going to be cooped up in the White House" with body English. On the plane back to California, he talked with us about how the episode at San Jose had been quickly forgotten, as he had anticipated, then went back to his use of the words "cooped up" in this way: "You know, that's the kind of word-picture my mother would have used back in Indiana. You can just feel the chicken coop, with the wires pressing down on the chickens all jammed together in the pen." Here the President hunched down, emulating the action of a cooped-up chicken. "Folks know what that means. That's the kind of word you can feel."

The essence of the speech was in these lines:

"The answer to bluster is not more bluster; the answer to bluster is firmness. The answer to a wave of violence is not a wave of repression—that is exactly what the violent few want, so they can enlist the sympathies of the moderates. The answer to violence is the strong application of fair American justice.

"And the answer to violent dissent is not an oppression of legitimate dissent. The great danger to dissent today comes not from the forces of law, but from the organized tyranny of some dissenters.

" 'Law and order' are not code words for racism or repression. 'Law and order' are code words for freedom from fear in America. This new attitude means that parents must exercise their responsibility for moral guidance. It means that college administrators and college faculties must stop caving in to the demands of a radical few. It means that moderate students must take a position that says to the violent: 'Hit the books or hit the road.'

"If we do not act now to protect our freedom, we will lose our freedom.

"If we do not choose the tough-minded approach to violence, we will allow violence to gain a terrible momentum. If a man chooses to dress differently, or wear his hair differently—if he has any—or to talk in a way that repels decent people—that's his business. But when he picks up a rock, then it becomes your business and my business to stop him. That's, you see, what American freedom is all about.

"When a man cannot bring his child . . . to a political rally for fear the person in the next seat will start yelling some filthy obscenity, when a man can't bring his wife to a rally for fear she is going to be pushed around by an unruly mob, and when any American faces the risk of a rock being thrown at him when he tries to speak—then I say appeasement has gone too far, and it's time to draw the line."

The next day, Sunday, I was called into the Western White House office of Bob Haldeman and handed a large package containing a black-and-white videotape of the Phoenix speech. "Take this into L.A., to the Soandso Studios on Eleventh Street, and ask for a man named Carruthers. Edit it so it would fit a half hour, or fifteen minutes. If it's any good, we'll go with it on Election Eve."

I told Haldeman he sounded like an old British movie about Scotland Yard—"This is a job for Carruthers." I was a little surprised we were not going with the standard format on Election Eve—"Now that all the campaigning is over, my friends, I just wanted to talk to you quietly tonight about some of the great questions that you, in the privacy of the voting booth, are going to decide about the future of this nation, etc., etc." But I did not object—the speech in the can he handed me was one I believed in and one that had had no exposure at all; pride of authorship, the excitement and fatigue that come toward the end of a long campaign, the resentment that the mob in San Jose had done its thing and gone unanswered, all combined to cloud a judgment that was not being asked for but would have been listened to if volunteered. I lugged the tape to the studio in Los Angeles, murmuring melodramatically to the girl at the desk, "I'm from the White House, and I'm here to see a man named Carruthers."

4. A GOOD HONEST APPRAISAL

Bill Carruthers was an independent television producer, located in Los Angeles, whom Haldeman was considering as a replacement for Roger Ailes, a flamboyant, modish talent. The job at hand was simply to edit a tape, but I was also to give my assessment to Haldeman on the new man as a possible producer of more ambitious White House television projects.

We looked at the 25-minute tape, and it was terrible: grainy black and white, with the audio barely audible. A local Phoenix station had broadcast the speech, and this was the copy; weeks later, we discovered that a high-quality color film had also been made, with perfect sound, but nobody planning or producing the show knew about that at the time. "We'll have to put it through an equalizer," said Carruthers calmly. "That will improve the audio somewhat. It will never be good quality, but maybe it will sound like newsfilm." I went to a nearby phone to pass this along to Haldeman at the Western White House: It would look and sound like a scratchy documentary rather than a well-produced political broadcast, which might add to its credibility. While I was waiting for a Haldeman aide to check this out, I overheard a conversation between a girl helping edit the tape and Carruthers:

"They gotta be crazy to want to broadcast this," the girl said.

"Look, you don't understand," Carruthers whispered. "These are the people who run the country. They know what they're doing."

"Sure makes him look like the old Tricky Dick to me."

"I don't want to hear another word like that out of you," Carruthers said urgently, looking furtively to see if I had overheard. "They run the country, they know what's good political television."

I could see that Carruthers was going to be one of us. His little show biz assistant, what did she know except her own political prejudices mixed with an automatic demand for technical slickness? Dopey little dame, I thought.

To fill a half hour for those stations who would carry that much, we padded the speech subtly and skillfully, tacking crowd shots on over long titles, adding a breath here and there that the President did not take. To cut the speech to fifteen minutes for the networks—it seemed that the Democrats had been willing to buy the other fifteen minutes, and were preparing something with Senator Muskie—we tightened applause, snipped unnecessary lines, sped up the pace. We worked all night, and by morning we could each recite every line of the speech, having heard it a hundred times. Because we knew it by heart, we could hear it clearly.

Frank Stanton, president of CBS, saw it before broadcast and called his old friend Frank Shakespeare, head of USIA, to suggest the tape quality was so poor as to be unbroadcastable. Shakespeare knew how impossible it would be to pass that through to the point of decision and did not. Jeb Magruder, a gung-ho Haldeman assistant handling the purchase of air time, called me from back East to report a general feeling by network officials that the tape was not good quality. I said I knew that, and everybody knew that, and the network officials were hardly on our side, and what else was new? Magruder offered tentatively, "Maybe we should scrub the whole thing?" At that point, I had had it. I was scruffy and exhausted, I had done what they told me to do, and all I heard from one of our own top people was a replay of the reaction of that dopey little dame: "They gotta be crazy to want to broadcast this."

I told Magruder to stiffen his upper lip and to tell the networks we knew what we were doing. When he kept complaining, I asked him if he wanted to take responsibility for killing it. Magruder was then, and still is, a man of mirrors; he backed off.

It only cost us a couple of hundred thousand dollars and two or three Senate seats, as all the experts pointed out later. Nixon's election eve show was "hot"—hard-driving, angry, and too political—while Muskie's speech was "cool"—written by Richard Goodwin with a nice sense of place and contrast. Evans and Novak: "The unfortunate 15-minute segment was a caricature of the President's frenetic campaigning style." Tom Wicker in the New York *Times*: "The goof that allowed Nixon to appear on television Monday night in an ill-made and high-pitched campaign film with a bad sound track is in glaring contrast to the quietly impressive appearance of Senator Muskie . . ."

The day after the program—Election Day—the President called me into his San Clemente office. Haldeman was there and had briefed him on the reaction to the show, including a call from Dean Burch, chairman of the Federal Communications Commission, who wondered whether we put on a tape of such low audio quality "on purpose"—it seems that the FCC switchboard was flooded with calls from irate Republicans who insisted that the networks were sabotaging the President by rendering him inaudible.

The President sipped a Dubonnet and contemplated the plate of cottage cheese and peaches on his desk. He did not deal with what he knew for me must have been Topic A; instead, he told me with great satisfaction of the votes cast by Manolo and Fina Sanchez, his long-time domestic servants whom he had vouched for in citizenship ceremonies: "It was their first vote, and Manolo said he had never been so proud in his life. He said he couldn't understand those people who had the right to vote and didn't bother to. I got a kick out of that; they're the kind of citizens this country can use." As an afterthought, he said, "It was the first time I voted in person in a long time. Since '62, here in California.

"Remember a couple of years ago on this day? God, it's different to be rooting for your fellows when you aren't on the ballot yourself. Anyway, it'll probably come out a wash."

I was more pessimistic, particularly in view of the way his election eve broadcast had deposited a large egg on the American doorstep, and suggested we come up with a bold new initiative of some kind to get us off the defensive.

"No," the President said, slicing the air with his left hand, "that will just look like we were disappointed. I'm not a believer in raising a fuss to camouflage bad news, it doesn't work. No matter what happens today, get out this line: compared to the usual off-year losses—twenty seats if you take one average, forty, if you take another—we did well. One month ago, I decided to make the effort in twenty-one states—you were there, Bill, you know this to be true—despite the fact that in only one state did the RNC polls show the Republican ahead. That was Tennessee, of course, and I'm only talking about the key races. If Buckley beats Goodell, that's picking up a seat for us despite the fact that it will not show up in the numbers. Same thing with Bentsen over Yarborough, even if he beats Bush—the move is to the right, whatever the party labels."

Nixon looked at his untouched cottage cheese as if it were a losing candidate he had gamely supported against his better judgment. Pulling it toward him, he poked a listless fork into it and said, "Don't say the people who lost weren't good candidates. God knows in most cases that's true, but it's no alibi for us, and you don't kick anybody when they're down. Let 'em blame it on me, or the economy, or whatever they like.

"Incidentally"—here it comes, I thought—"I was surprised at the negative nature of the Muskie rebuttal last night. He wasted a lot of precious time defending the Democrats on law and order, and he hardly hit us on the economy at all. That's the mistake they've been making all along —do you suppose they like to be on the defensive?"

I said I thought that Richard Goodwin, writing for Muskie, had set the scene brilliantly—beginning with the glories of Maine and evocations of a simpler and seemingly happier past. "At least," I added glumly, "you could hear him."

The President was philosophical about that: "We did the best with what we had. Let 'em holler."

After the rest of the reviews were in, I waited for the sky to fall. It did not. Haldeman did not permit anyone to make me the scapegoat; as usual when somebody goofed, the chief of staff passed the word to hang tough. (A year later, Evans and Novak wrote that Magruder was more at fault than he was in this episode; Jeb automatically assumed that I had knifed him, which I had not, but in the Magruder view of life, such buck-passing and back-stabbing was standard procedure.) The President, in an oblique and tactful way, suggested I send him a memo with my observations about the election eve program.

I did not avoid responsibility (not so brave—I couldn't have), particularly for not aborting the program after technical objections were raised, thereby absolving Carruthers of blame; he went on to become our producer, not only good at his job but much more outspoken with his opinions—he learned the hard way that night in 1970 the need to challenge "expert" judgment. In my memo, I could not help adding this:

> Our mistake was ironic. We decided *not* to exploit the incident on the Friday night telecast, but to handle the matter in a released text speech Saturday. Our decision was to *downplay* at first; then we decided to go to national TV on Monday with the Saturday speech.
>
> If we had gone with the "tough" speech Friday, there would have been no Muskie counter that night; we could then have gone with a more general, lower-key effort on election night. In retrospect, that would have been the best approach . . .
>
> Lessons for the future:
>
> 1. The final show of a campaign should be thoughtful and low-key.
>
> 2. Never trust a local station to do a remote; whenever there is the slight possibility of later use, invest in a professional production.
>
> 3. We should not be scared off all hard-hitting speeches by the reaction to this: There is a time and place for a tough speech in a campaign, just not at the very end.
>
> 4. On the technical side, always check Signal for audio comparison; always investigate other tapes and film for video comparison.
>
> A final thought: If the final show had been a remote of a unifying, warmhearted discussion with young people or something similar, poor tape quality would have been overlooked by commentators. The resentment at the strategy and content did much to add to the gleeful derision of the technical side of this program.

The President reviewed my memo carefully and returned it to me with these words written across the top:

Good honest
appraisal

That was sensitive management on his part. Nixon wanted to make sure I understood what had gone amiss but knew I did not need additional abuse for my sins.

The President, who rarely went out of his way to admit a mistake publicly, did so two months later during a television interview with Eric Sevareid of CBS and Howard K. Smith of ABC:

> Mr. Sevareid: "Do you regret the rebroadcast of the Phoenix speech about the San Jose incident?"
>
> The President: "Yes. I think that was a mistake. As a matter of fact, we apparently felt at that time, that the speech said some things that needed to be said, but having it rebroadcast the night before election is not something that I would have perhaps planned had I been, shall we say, running the campaign. Incidentally, when I am the candidate, I run the campaign."
>
> Mr. Smith: "It was a technically bad tape, too. You could hardly hear you on it."
>
> The President: "Yes, it was technically bad, and I do not think it was the right speech to make the night before election. I would have preferred to go on, as you know I usually do, in a quiet studio type of program, talking quietly to the American people about the choice and then letting them make the choice, and if I am in another campaign, that is the way it will be the night before election. We won't run that kind of tape again."

Loyal Nixon men who had not worked on the 1970 campaign, from John Mitchell to Ray Price, focused on the election eve show as the symbol of all a Nixon campaign should not be. Their message sunk in, as deeply as they might have wished, and resulted in the decisions in 1972 to conduct "the campaign that never was" by surrogate, posturing the President as almost too busy to run. On Election Eve, 1972, the President would make a taped, five-minute, low-keyed appeal which could have satisfied the ear of the most demanding stereo or quadraphonic buff.

In terms of immediate results, Republicans gained two Senate seats and lost eight House seats, fairly good for the party in power in an off-year election, although the GOP took a severe beating in the governorships. More ominously, Nixon showed his first inclinations to determine his support on ideological rather than party grounds—Buckley defeated Goodell with Agnew's help—and that trend was to continue into Nixon's second term.

The central point of the '70 campaign was not apparent to our critics or to us at the time of immediate post-mortem. True, the Social Issue kept the economic downturn from clobbering us; the use of the V.P. as "cutting edge" hurt him later; the numbers of candidates helped or saved will never be known, but the good campaigners locally were the ones who won. Something else, more profound and less perceptible, took hold that autumn: "elitism" and "permissiveness," which had been sociologists' terms, became household words. Radical chic, national guilt, self-hate became more suspect. A backlash against demonstrators, part of a general self-identification of Middle America, gained momentum, strengthening Nixon's hand and presaging his easy domination of McGovern two years later. Considerable comment at the time held Agnew discredited and the President hurt by the campaign, but opinion shifts had begun, resentments took deeper hold, support for the President (if not his party) began to broaden. A responsive chord had been touched, its greater significance not in the image on TV of a divisive President in a fighting mood in Phoenix, but in the revulsion of a growing new majority to the kind of event that took place that bad night in San Jose.

5. "THE PRESS IS THE ENEMY"

Was there a conspiracy, as Walter Cronkite of CBS once solemnly charged, on the part of the Nixon Administration to discredit and malign the press?

Was this so-called "anti-media campaign" encouraged, directed, and urged on by the President himself?

Did this alleged campaign to defame and intimidate Nixon-hating newsmen succeed, isolating and weakening them politically? And did it contribute to the us-against-them divisions that then cracked back at Nixon after his election victory?

The above questions are slanted so as to elicit a ringing response of "Nonsense!" But the answer to all those questions is, sadly, yes.

In all the world of "us against them," the press was the quintessential "them," the fount and the succor of other "thems." In terms of power, the academic "them" was insignificant; the social-cultural elitist "them" was useful as a foil that would help attract workingmen to a Nixon coalition; the liberal, political "them" was in the process of destroying itself by narrowing its base along severe ideological-faddist lines; but the journalistic "them" was formidable and infuriating, a force to be feared in its own right, but even more important, a magnifying glass and public address system that gave strength and attention to all the other "thems."

Adlai Stevenson had the same feeling of being persecuted by what he called "the one-party press" in 1952, and put it this way: ". . . the overwhelming majority of the press is just against Democrats. And it is against Democrats, so far as I can see, not after a sober and considered review of the alternatives, but automatically, as dogs are against cats. As soon as a newspaper—I speak of the great majority, not the enlightened ten per cent —sees a Democratic candidate, it is filled with an unconquerable yen to chase him up an alley . . ."

Nixon's reaction was not to run up the alley. When the press (speaking throughout this chapter of the influential, opinion-making "Eastern Establishment" media, not the enlightened 90 per cent) came after him, Nixon's reaction was to arch his back and flash his claws directly at the attacker's eyes.

I must have heard Richard Nixon say "the press is the enemy" a dozen times; and there was no doubt that his instincts were to do battle with what he was certain was an ideological bias against nonliberals combined with a personal bias against him. But he always left open an escape hatch to those aides who wanted to believe his views about the media were battle-scarred but sensible, and would allow them to win an occasional battle for accessibility or candor.

For example, Nixon was civil and sometimes even friendly to individual journalists. There were many instances of personal thoughtfulness that few people except the individual reporter concerned ever learned about, which is as it should be. When ABC television reporter John Scali narrated a documentary about Red China in 1966, the sponsor—the 3M Company—received a barrage of letters from Chiang Kai-shek supporters in the United States, and the company was not happy about having been involved in something "controversial." At the request of an ABC network executive, lawyer Dick Nixon wrote a letter to the sponsor's chairman, an old friend, to say he liked the show and to offhandedly attest to the long-time anti-Communism of Scali, a reporter who had accompanied him on some of his foreign travels. The sponsor heat came off; Scali was not aware of it until I mentioned it to him in 1973, as he left the White House staff to become the U. S. Ambassador to the UN. Another instance of thoughtfulness was a handwritten condolence note to Murray Kempton, the columnist and author, at a sad time in his life; the letter, from an admiring adversary in the Oval Office, which I spotted on Rose Woods's desk, was tasteful and private. I have no way of knowing how often this kind of thing was done but it probably was more often than one would suspect, since Nixon knew that public knowledge of a nice gesture from him might compromise the journalist.

Nixon showed his respect for the power of the press in other ways. He did his homework for press conferences, keeping his cool under the most savage questioning (as after Cambodia); he gave White House officials and Cabinet members far more leeway than had his predecessors in debating undecided domestic policy matters in public; he paid attention to what the press was saying in an unprecedented way, with daily fifty-page news summaries that displayed the entire range of coverage and opinion in the big networks and little magazines, supplementing them with his own grim reading of the Los Angeles *Times*, the New York *Times*, the Washington *Post* and the Washington *Star*. (This kind of attention can be considered the most sincere compliment, but was viewed by suspicious newsmen as a sinister "monitoring" of the press, on the theory that the only thing worse than not being read was being carefully read.)

The news summary, compiled by former schoolteacher Mort Allin and a band of midnight gnomes, became a way of checking on problems that would not otherwise have come to his attention, a trigger for ideas. Nixon would scribble notes on the margins, or dictate them to Alex Butterfield, who sometimes sat with the President while he was going through the summary, took notes of comments and passed them on. Sometimes they were as short as a man's initials followed by a question mark or exclamation mark; occasionally they caused a lengthy memo to Haldeman or Ehrlichman. It was a good way to give somebody a jab, or a pat on the back, as the plates following page 392 show.

Nobody on the Nixon staff could be called "pro-press," of course, since to be "for" the press was taken to be against the press's adversary, the incumbent Administration; but one did not have to be "anti-press," either. Herb Klein was expected to represent the press constituency; others— Moynihan, Garment, McGregor, all the writers—were not apparently challenged about their press friendships, or asked to "clear" interviews with a central authority, and this freedom to move around was salutory. I had spent twelve years as a professional press agent before entering the speechwriting field, and saw the press as an occasionally biased, usually reasonable channel of communication. Reporters provided more an opportunity for, than an obstacle to, good public relations, a phrase that held no pejorative horrors for me. Between writing speeches, I stumbled around in the no-man's-land between media and government, making friends among ideological and institutional adversaries, strolling through the mine fields together, secure in the knowledge that I was a trusted Nixon man, and deserved that trust. I was convinced that the President—though he got hopping mad at the unfairness inflicted on him so often by a largely hostile press corps—was at bottom realistic about the adversary relationship, and appreciated the attempts of loyal aides to get out and proselytize.

I was wrong about that. Some reflection on what happened during my White House years, buttressed by subsequent revelations, has persuaded me that Nixon's attitude toward the press, though sometimes understandable, was neither justifiable nor defensible—especially when his hatred of the press carried him beyond the bounds of good sense.

When Nixon said, "The press is the enemy," he was not saying, as some of us had hoped, "Be careful, its interest in gathering information is not our interest of developing policy" or "There is an ideological bias as well as an institutional opposition in the attitude of the press" or even "They're a pain in the neck, and don't waste your time with 'em." He was saying exactly what he meant: "The press is the *enemy*" to be hated and beaten, and in that vein of vengeance that ran through his relationship with another power center, in his indulgence of his most combative and abrasive instincts against what he saw to be an unelected and unrepresentative elite, lay Nixon's greatest personal and political weakness and the cause of his downfall.

Nixon's hatred was not acquired suddenly or capriciously. Since Nixon had appeared on the national scene riding the tide of anti-Communism, he had been criticized and maligned by Washington commentators who generally were liberal in their political leanings. His Hiss case success, proving he was right and the liberals who refused to believe him were wrong, only reinforced the bitter resentments against him. His emotional "Checkers speech" defense saved his political life in 1952 but sickened Democratic partisans, who liked neither his pitch nor his piety. During the Eisenhower years, Nixon was the political warrior, and on the receiving end of the shots while Ike received the above-the-battle adulation. The liberal Republican media supported Rockefeller against him for the nomination in 1960, and most of the reporters on the 1960 campaign were noisily, snidely, and openly hostile to Nixon—even more so in the '62 campaign for Governor of California. "They" never let Nixon up; they applied a double standard to his actions, impugned his motives, derided his squareness, and gloried in his defeats. Nixon watched his wife and children cry when they saw some of the cartoons blackening his reputation; he seethed inside, always pretending to have a thick skin but never losing his hypersensitivity to criticism, taking a final satisfaction at blasting his tormentors at his "last press conference" in 1962. Nixon, who would ultimately be forced to resign for the abuse of power, all his life was on the receiving end of powerful abuse.

With the possible exceptions of Lincoln, Jackson, and FDR, never has an American politician been the recipient of so much vitriol, year in and year out; no man has been so publicly despised over a span of an entire generation, with the attack led by the press, which all too often put personality above principle, charisma ahead of character.

FDR had said of the economic royalists of his time: "They hate me— *and I welcome their hatred!*" That's how Nixon felt about the press, only much more so, and like FDR he could see a method in his own madness. Here was a villain, a target, the bearer of so many bad tidings during the Sixties, a runner-down of America. Eisenhower had touched a chord at the 1964 Republican Convention when he referred to "sensation-seeking columnists and commentators" which stirred an unexpected ovation. In putting down the press, Nixon could satisfy his own primal hatred and tell himself it was good politics as well, and, on top of that, slamming doors in its face was necessary to national security. Such combinations are hard to find.

During one period of his career, however, Nixon enjoyed a fairly good press: in 1965 to 1968, during the comeback in New York. At first, he was a muted, chastened long shot, and, strangely enough, a fresh face to many reporters who had not formed stereotypes of him in the Fifties. That's when I came to know Nixon, and my view of his view of the press was shaped by a common need to get his name, his views, and his possibilities in the newspaper. We sought out the press, rescheduled Nixon's flights when a reporter couldn't make it, and when he could sat him right next to Nixon for a long flight. (Later, this degenerated into the "ten-minute bounce": exactly ten minutes before a plane was to land, a columnist would be brought into the Candidate's or President's cabin, so that the interview would be terminated not by Nixon but by the landing.) In the comeback, Nixon knew his stuff. He needed the publicity; he liked talking politics; he made himself accessible. As a result, he had the first good press in his life, and since those were my formative years with him, I could believe that the pre-1962 wounds could be forgotten.

The first tactical mistake President Nixon made about the press was to adopt the old labor movement policy of "Reward your friends, punish your enemies." If done with a light hand—an occasional tip to an objective reporter, an exclusive interview to a columnist from time to time— the first half of that guidance is effective, and is common practice in politics. But Nixon personalized press criticism. He took everything critical as a personal blast at him; when he read a by-line, the writer came to life in his mind, grinning evilly at him—and his press relations were laid on with the heaviest of hands. Periodically, aides received notice that some reporter or publication was beyond the pale, never to be talked to, and the President was not kidding. In the summer of 1969, I paid attention to one of these fiats and did not return calls from *Newsweek* for a couple of weeks; to my dismay, *Newsweek* began "behaving itself" as a result of being shut off from all White House contact, but then it loosed a blast and several of us could say that the freeze policy was a failure. I never again paid any attention to instructions not to talk to a given reporter, convinced that the President's inclinations had been amplified out of all proportion by zealous aides, whose silly freezes could be challenged with impunity. Not until mid-1973 did I learn that these contacts with the press had caused my phone to be tapped in 1969 by the FBI at the direction of a suspicious President and national security adviser.

The freeze foolishness could be documented ad nauseam; here's one:

May 19, 1969

MEMORANDUM FOR: MR. HALDEMAN

On May 11th, Thomas Ottenad wrote in the *St. Louis Post-Dispatch* that a dispute had erupted among high Administration officials over the President's initial reaction to the recent shooting down of the EC-121. Ottenad said that a secondary area of disagreement existed over the President's alleged dissatisfaction with military intelligence operations, and that the in-house controversies had cast a cloud over "how Mr. Nixon wants to be viewed by foreign nations."

After reading the resume of the Ottenad news item, the President jotted a short note to you in which he said that he had told Ron Ziegler *not* to permit our people to talk to the *Post-Dispatch*, the *New York Times*, or the *Washington Post*. He directed that all contacts with these news agencies (no matter how slight or how infrequently) be terminated immediately.

ALEXANDER P. BUTTERFIELD

cc: Mr. Ehrlichman √
    Mr. Klein
    Mr. Ziegler

Fortunately, most of these strictures wore off after a while, or were eroded carefully and gradually by Klein, Ziegler, and especially Buchanan, who was so totally trusted to be anti-press that he could get away with fraternization. Buchanan's attitude was curious: he studied the press more carefully than anyone, felt the unfairness so often inflicted by the press more deeply, articulated his feeling in memos and draft speeches filled with thunder and hard argument, but he was not petty, bitchy, or mean. Buchanan enjoyed the company of the press: one night at my house, he talked with a liberal columnist all evening, fascinated and politely disagreeing on everything; the columnist might have been surprised at his civility and intelligence, but never let on.

Buchanan had a sense of humor about the press, too, which Nixon and Haldeman never had. Pat perpetrated an elaborate practical joke on Herb Klein, composing a phony memo from Klein to the President, and arranged to have Chapin or Ziegler mention the memo to Klein. When the startled Director of Communications asked, "What memo?" they were to show him the memo purportedly from Klein and say it was on the President's desk. (This phony memo, not from Klein, must be read in the knowledge that each item is opposite to the President's thinking about each individual.)

MEMORANDUM TO THE PRESIDENT

FROM HERB KLEIN

SEPTEMBER 22, 1969

Below is a list of commentators and writers who have sometimes criticized us in the past, but who should be included in the "ten-man" media meetings—because with them we can make some yardage; they are all influential, and all susceptible to the Presidential charm.

1. Jack Chancellor, Dan Schorr (only one of the two, and one at a time).

2. Marvin Kalb (the real heavyweight at CBS).

3. Max Frankel (a Times man who would benefit greatly from a private pipeline to the President, and who is likely to reciprocate).

4. Marty Nolan (a young guy at the Boston Globe who, in my judgment, offers us the best hope of progress there).

5. Dick Dudman, St. Louis Post-Dispatch. (You may not know Dudman, but he is the real comer at the P-D, and I can think of no better way to end run Mark Childs for a touchdown.)

6. Martin Agronsky. (He has his own show, and audience ratings are phenomenal.)

7. Stu Loory. (To keep our lines good to the LA Times and the West Coast).

8. Pete Lisagor. (He carries great weight with other writers; and his base in Chicago and the CDN service.)

9. Tom Braden (the Braden-Mankiewicz column is the hottest property in the business, and we have a better chance with Tom than with Frank, although this is a toss-up).

10. Bob Novak. (Rolly Evans is hopeless; and there is sharp competition between the two.)

Two other suggestions I would make along these lines of extending recognition that might yield surprising returns:

a. Sander Vanocur—an old Kennedy intimate, but a guy now looking for a new place to land.

b. Jack Anderson—with Drew Pearson dead, this guy also needs sources desperately to make a living, and his column is still the largest in the country.

Herb Klein

The above memo was *never written by Klein* nor delivered to the President (who might have taken it seriously and put Klein on the next rocket to the moon).*

Although the President frequently conveyed his uptight feelings about the press to his staff, he was more careful—even eminently philosophical—about press coverage in speaking to the Cabinet. At a Cabinet meeting on April 15, 1969, Transportation Secretary John Volpe complained that, contrary to press reports, the Nixon Administration had appointed more black people to high-level positions than had any previous Administration. "We are performing and we must let the country know that we are," the underrated Volpe insisted, and wanted the Cabinet and the world to know that the stories in the newspapers to the contrary "were erroneous." Nixon motioned at him to calm down. "Here's what our standard must be," the

---

* Nixon's passion about individual reporters occasionally turned him to flights of fancy. On the 1970 campaign trail, he asked Ziegler to name four of the most outspoken anti-Nixon reporters to the press pool assigned to ride back to Washington aboard *Air Force One* with the President. Ziegler was nonplussed; since his previous orders had been not to let these men near the President, even when their turn for the pool came up on rotation, he asked why. Grinned the President: "Put 'em on *Air Force One*, have it take off, and then I'll ride back on the press plane!" Nixon's imaginative plan was not carried out.

President said. "Let's do the right thing. Whenever the Federal Government is involved, we must be sure that we are absolutely fair and absolutely equal. But let's have no illusion about the reaction to our efforts. The professional protestors—and the press as well—will never be satisfied. The protestors need this issue and so they will do everything they can to keep it alive.

"For the press," the President continued with eminent good sense and dispassion, "progress is not news—trouble is news. They don't win Pulitzer Prizes for being *for* something. So don't get too excited when you read criticism in the papers. We have to do the right thing and then be strong about it, and decent enough to take the criticism and not be bitter about it. You have to learn to laugh it off."

If he had followed his own advice, much trouble could have been averted. Had he not been embittered, the press would not have become docile, or mended its ways, or ceased to abuse its privileges, or fallen in love with Richard Nixon; it would have continued to carp, growing even more strident when its carping was shrugged off. But Nixon only pretended to shrug it off; his elaborate unconcern was faked. "It doesn't affect me a bit" is only said by men pretending not to be affected. The press knew when its barbs drew blood, and went for more.

Nixon's "conversations" with TV commentators in '70 and '71 allowed some of the Nixon warmth to come through his customary brisk grasp of the subject matter, and Haldeman suggested that the blame for "why the President did not get along better with the press" be shifted. "Reverse the question," Haldeman directed, "and say that possibly the fault was not that of the President's but of the press. Perhaps it is time that a column be written as to why the press does not get along with the President rather than the subject being constantly on the basis of RN 'doesn't understand' the press and that somehow his press relations are responsible for the antagonism of the press." There was a plaintive note to Haldeman's hope, stimulated by the President himself, whose wish was not that he could reduce the "antagonism," but that his antagonist be blamed for it.

It was soon after this time—in March 1971—that I found myself embroiled in an angry disagreement with the President.

For about two years the proponents of greater accessibility of the President to the press on the White House staff would win some and then lose some battles, but would be encouraged by the President to keep the pressure on. Then, in the first two months of 1971, the dam happily burst; in and around the launching of the "New American Revolution," and coming back after what he was determined to characterize as a midterm election victory, the President granted a spate of private interviews: to Peregrine Worsthorne of the London *Telegraph*, Barbara Walters of NBC's "Today" show, to a group of women reporters, to C. L. Sulzberger of the New York *Times*, to Howard K. Smith on television—all good, and taken together (as they were by most commentators) a happy augury for a more open Administration and a less-isolated President.

In mid-March—Saint Patrick's Day—the President called me on a different subject, to ask when it was he told people to invest in the stock market. I remembered vividly—April 28, 1970—which disappointed him; he thought it was nearly the first anniversary of his advice and it would be a good way to remind everybody of the strength of the bull market. "You'd have to be pretty stupid," he said, "not to make money in a market that's up 40 per cent from its lows."

I then brought up the subject of all the calls I had been receiving from Nixon-watchers about "the new openness" and said I thought that was a refreshing spirit. The President, quickly irritated, cut me short: "It's not true. Don't get in that trap. They only want to show how isolated we were before. I saw Sulzberger twice before, you know, and Sidey." Could be, I said, but he was being much more open, and what was wrong with taking advantage of it and not being so defensive? I could feel him getting more annoyed. "Talk to Haldeman," he snapped finally. "He'll show you how many interviews I had last year. And I promised Barbara Walters to do her show a year ago. It is *not* true that we are any more 'open' now."

I wrote a memo to Haldeman and took it across the street to his office. "That was quite a boo-boo," Bob said as I came in. Obviously, the President had called him to tell him I had been snared by an Eastern liberal trap.

"You're not allowed to disagree?"

"That wasn't the boo-boo," Bob replied, "you didn't have your facts straight. He doesn't like that at all." He handed me a twenty-page report titled "The President and the Media" which was a tabulation of every press conference, individual meeting, and telephone call the President had held with "media people" from network presidents to college newspaper editors. It was one of those asinine documents prepared to enable the President to justify his feelings of being picked upon, listing names and dates that showed he was not "isolated" but had wasted a lot of his valuable time with an unappreciative press.

I analyzed the raw data that night and came back to Haldeman with proof that I was right about a new openness, based on his set of facts: news conferences, twelve in 1969, seven in 1970, two in the two months of 1971. Scheduled appointments with media people, 21 in 1969, 18 in 1970, 8 so far in 1971. Telephone calls (counting telephone calls seemed stretching it but the list for '70–'71 is interesting and is footnoted here*), 20 in

* 1970
January 21	Bailey Howard, Editor, Chicago *Sun-Times*
January 26	Paul Hume, Washington *Post*
March 21	Garnett Horner, Washington *Star*
	Robert Semple, N.Y. *Times*
	Herb Kaplow, NBC
March 31	William S. White, syndicated columnist
April 11	Mrs. Oveta Culp Hobby, Chairman of the Board/Editor, Houston *Post*
April 13	James Hagerty, ABC
April 19	Otis Chandler, Publisher, L.A. *Times*

1969, 23 in 1970, 10 in the two months of 1971. "The fact is," I concluded triumphantly, "the President has recently tripled his accessibility to the press. My point is that we should not try to dispute that fact, but to use it to our advantage."

A Pyrrhic victory. Haldeman looked it over, agreed I was right, showed it to the President, who reacted by promptly canceling his next news conference. He was only prepared to be more accessible if it did not *seem* as if he were being more accessible, and if it did not admit that he had been less accessible before. Nixon was extraordinarily sensitive to the charge that his new openness was "image-making," and, sure enough, when the press started calling it that, he clammed up as never before.

As for me, I was told by Haldeman that I had won the argument, that my facts were straight, but as it turned out, my argument had boomeranged, and I had lost the accessibility war. It was to apply personally as well. For three solid months I did not receive a speech assignment from the President, or a phone call, or a memo, or a nod in the hall as he was passing by. With Leonard Garment, another accessibility nut, I was stricken from the list of invitees to Tricia Nixon's wedding, and the New York *Times* society reporter duly noted that we were the only old-timers to be singled out in that way. Neither Grace Garment nor Helene Safire were pacified by explanations from their husbands about the necessary fluctuations in the popularity of loyal Presidential aides.* I answered my

April 21	Edwin Dale, Jr., New York *Times*
April 28	Joseph Alsop, syndicated columnist
May 3	Joseph Alsop, syndicated columnist
May 9	Nancy Dickerson, NBC
	Helen Thomas, UPI
May 29	George Hearst, Publisher, L.A. *Herald-Examiner*
	Victor Riesel, syndicated columnist
	George Hearst, L.A. *Herald-Examiner*
	Otis Chandler, Publisher, L.A. *Times*
July 31	Carl Greenberg, L.A. *Times*
October 11	Joseph Alsop, syndicated columnist
October 25	William F. Buckley, syndicated columnist
November 3	William F. Buckley, syndicated columnist
	James Copley, Publisher, San Diego *Union*
1971	
January 19	Eugene Pulliam, Publisher, Arizona *Republic*
February 4	Roscoe Drummond, syndicated columnist
February 5	Ben Bradlee, Editor, Washington *Post*
February 7	Joseph Alsop, syndicated columnist
February 9	George Putnam, Los Angeles television
March 3	William Gress, Des Moines television
March 5	Al Capp, cartoonist
March 6	Martin Hayden, Detroit *News*
March 6	Victor Riesel, syndicated columnist
March 7	Helen Thomas, UPI

* Garment and I, who remained on the burning deck long after most of the intimates had fled or been indicted, would ruefully remind each other of our pariah period with a cryptic "RTW," which stood for "Remember Tricia's Wedding."

mail, attended earnest, low-level meetings, learned about the operations of government, and otherwise occupied myself during this "freeze" until suddenly the President needed me for something and I was back in his and Haldeman's good graces as if nothing had happened. Interesting: I had exhibited terrible judgment editing the television tape at the end of the '70 campaign, had been forgiven readily and even "covered for"; but when I had been right about this "openness" and recognized as right, I was condemned to spend three months in Coventry. Nixon was very sensitive about the press.

In the Nixon White House, the press became "the media," because the word had a manipulative, Madison Avenue, all-encompassing connotation, and the press hated it. "Press" conferences became "news" conferences, ostensibly because the word "press" was usually applied to writing press and the conferences included electronic journalists, but really because he wanted to leave the impression that the conference was the *President's* conference to make news and not the *press's* conference with the President. At the start of the Administration, Nixon and Haldeman did not even want a press secretary, just a low-level spokesman, or assistant in matters dealing with the media, but Ziegler fought for the traditional title and was grudgingly given it; on the first European trip, Haldeman put the press secretary on the bottom of the protocol list to show the low estimation of the job, but Ron quickly climbed up despite his demeaning line of work.

A word here about Ziegler. In 1972 a network bureau chief in Washington, pledging me to darkest secrecy, said he thought Ziegler was the most effective Presidential press secretary since Jim Hagerty, and probably better at the care and feeding of the press on trips than Hagerty. His praise for Ziegler had to be anonymous because it would have seemed like snuggling up to the White House, a position no self-respecting journalist would ever allow himself to assume. Most of the press corps began by treating Ziegler like a puppy-dog front man, recognizing his advertising background and low rating in the inner circle to be the insult it really was; then, as he grew in stature in the White House inner circle, and his ability to fend off their questions gained some finesse, they began to see him as the symbol of their frustrations. Though journalists are quick to point out that "it is unfair to blame the messenger for the bad news," many angrily blamed messenger Ziegler for the lack of news or the manipulation of the news, often forgetting that his role was to be more the President's press secretary than the press's representative to the President.

Ron was a better reporter than some reporters. Before an 11 A.M. briefing, he would study the papers and the wires, and call around the White House and the agencies of government, not only to find out what he could say but what he could not say. Learning when to stop is a skill that was underestimated by most of his interlocutors. He has a necessary sense of humor (his imitation of comedian David Frye imitating the President, eyes rolling upward and fingers wiggling the "V" sign, is hilarious);

an unnecessary streak of cruelty that probably comes from contemptuous treatment by Haldeman at staff meetings as a mouth and not a mind; a blotter-like memory that can absorb a briefing and play it back in more coherent form; and an unfortunate inclination to use the language of the computer. "Programmed," "input," and "time frame" are pretentious and sententious, and deserved the derision they received. ("Inoperative" was a bum rap. The antonym to Ziegler's "operative" was first used in a question by reporter R. W. Apple of the New York *Times*, and Ziegler, not thinking, adopted it.)

The job he held for more than four years is harder than almost any other job in government: the fury with which the press corps sometimes goes after the press secretary dismays some of the White House regulars themselves. One Saturday morning, when there was no briefing, I was in the Health Unit, the combination sauna-shower-exercise room Haldeman had built in the basement of the EOB. Ziegler was showering; something went wrong with the plumbing, and the water turned first scalding hot and then freezing cold; Ziegler in his panic couldn't get the door to the shower stall open and took the full fury of the crazed plumbing. When he got out, the press secretary sat huddled in a towel for ten minutes, skin red and teeth chattering, and all he could say was, "Jesus, it was just like the daily briefing."

If there was any bring-us-together benefit to Mr. Nixon's animus toward the press, it was the cement provided to the President's relationship with his Vice President. Spiro Agnew too had been savaged in the media; in the '68 campaign, his reputation as a bumbler had been so built up in the press that the Democrats could run a television commercial that put his name on the screen and had behind it thirty seconds of hysterical laughter. It was the most distasteful, unfair, and audience-insulting commercial since LBJ's "daisy spot" against Goldwater.

After some television commentators rebutted and immediately dismissed Nixon's November 3, 1969, "silent majority" speech, and the press criticism of the President began to build up on the basis of the old stereotypes, Pat Buchanan turned away from his news summaries long enough to belt out a speech for the Vice President's Des Moines, Iowa, appearance on November 13. Agnew liked it. Buchanan went over the speech line by line with the President. Nixon read it all the way through without expression, as he does when he is excited, and Pat told me he commented: "This really flicks the scab off, doesn't it?" The President then added a few lines, toughening it up. Only three drafts were written—very few for a major address. It retained its white-heat vitality.

That was the opening gun—blasting the "instant analysis" of commentators and adversary-culture tilt of the television networks—of a campaign to belittle, discredit, and generally wear down the credibility of the burr under Nixon's saddle. Agnew's Des Moines speech, and his follow-up speech a week later in Montgomery, Alabama, ripping into the Washington *Post* and New York *Times*, contained material that was overdue (and much taken from the *Columbia Journalism Review*). Haldeman and Ziegler asked the President to get the V.P. to scrap his follow-up speech; Buchanan made the case for going ahead, and the President said to let 'er rip.

Publicly, most news executives responded by wrapping themselves in the First Amendment, just as Nixon was later to respond to criticism of his invasions of civil liberty by wrapping himself in the mantle of national security; privately, many reporters and defenders of press freedom admitted that Nixon, through Agnew, was hitting where the press was vulnerable in its excess of advocacy and loss of the value of objectivity in news columns. When "instant analysis" was first attacked, the networks stood firm on their right to comment immediately after a Presidential speech; but a sharp rebuttal of an elected leader by a presumably objective reporter, immediately after a President's effort to rally the nation, was a matter for legitimate debate. When the press was riding high after Watergate four years later, CBS took that opportunity to drop the practice and substitute a more equitable "equal time" approach.

Some self-anointed spokesmen of the press ("self-anointed" is a sneer word, more lip-curling than "so-called") challenged a government official's right to criticize broadcasting, which is sort of a regulated industry; intimidation, they charged, though nobody admitted to being intimidated. This was a shallow defense, as if any power center were immune from criticism by any other; but when the new White House Office of Telecommunications Policy began making noises at local stations to put heat on their networks to stop "ideological plugola," that was government intimidation plain and simple.

When members of the press took up the cause of objectivity or deplored the constant attack on basic institutions, it was a healthy sign—as if a Nixon Cabinet member had chosen to speak out against a set government policy (which nobody really did, not even Hickel). Columnist Robert Novak's indictment at Kenyon College of the knee-jerk press, often out of touch with and contemptuous of majority sentiment, was a courageous act by a man confident enough of the press's strength for it to withstand self-criticism. Chuck Colson tried to use it to buttress the elitist-media case, but the fact that a major columnist was blowing the whistle on his confrères actually undermined the "monolith" charge. (On September 13, 1969, the President read a summary of one of the Evans and Novak newsletters containing what the summarizer called "some of the most negative comment on the Administration to date." Nixon sent a written note to Herb Klein: "1. Get some tough letters to these guys from subscribers. 2. Be sure they are cut off." Klein did neither. His routine refusal to carry out these ukases was why Old Hand Klein was not in close, and why he emerged from the ruins with his reputation intact.)

Educator-writer Irving Kristol's metaphor was especially sonorous: "One does have a right to be worried about the fact that this new populism seems animated by a hostility, not to specific injustices or inequities, but to the institutions of the republic itself. The older populist journalism was always ready, when things went wrong, to shout: 'Shoot the piano-player!' The new demagogic journalism is constantly and no less shrilly suggesting: 'Shoot the piano.' "

Not all of us realized it at the time, but that is what Nixon was doing to the institution of the press: shooting down not the individual excesses, not exposing the injustices and hypocrisy of individual charges, but discrediting the press itself: shooting the piano.

Let us consider, for example, a mini-Watergate: the Dan Schorr episode. Schorr, a reporter for CBS television news, tries to be objective, and often gives the other side a break, but his reporting, in my view, reflects a liberal attitude. This does not cripple his reporting; on the contrary, he is a superb reporter, if you don't mind coming at a story from the liberal side. As Buchanan indicated in his spoofing "memo from Klein" quoted earlier, Schorr had earned a place over the years in the farrago of Nixon villains: as an expert on health and education matters, he was in the Administration's hair just in that area where it didn't need anybody in its hair.

I wrote a line in the 1971 State of the Union about seeking a cure for cancer; the original and much longer draft language from HEW contained "and sickle-cell anemia" which I couldn't include in my allotted twelve words about cancer because it required a seven-word explanation that sickle-cell anemia was a disease that mostly affected black children. Schorr practically ignored the 200-million-dollar commitment to curing cancer in his TV report, concentrating on the possible neglect of the sickle-cell anemia program. He was wrong—the program to seek a cure for sickle-cell anemia was in the program, if not the speech—but it was an example of sharp, aggressive reporting by a man with good contacts inside the government. Then, in March 1971, the President went out of his way to single Schorr out, challenging his accuracy on an ABM story.

The crowning touch came in mid-August of that year, with the Pentagon Papers decisions still on everybody's mind, when the President made a surprise commitment on aid to parochial schools to the Knights of Columbus (see page 561). The film of the President's pledge was followed by a dash of cold holy water from Schorr quoting both Administration and Catholic sources that there were no plans to deliver on that commitment. The President, who felt his sources within the Administration were even better than Schorr's, was more than moderately angry.

Within a few hours, Haldeman had requested an FBI report on Daniel Schorr. The request was immoral: nothing that could possibly be in the FBI file had any bearing on his right to report what he did. The last publicly known misuse of the FBI by the White House in relation to the press was the "rap in the night" on reporters' doors by the FBI when Attorney General Robert Kennedy asked for information about steel executives. In the Schorr episode, I think, the same stupid excess of zeal followed the original order to the FBI; Haldeman insists he only asked for the FBI file and did not intend to order a full field investigation; but the word was garbled in transmission, and before Haldeman knew it, FBI agents were talking to all Schorr's friends and employers. A story was then cooked up by Haldeman to cover the original mistake in asking for the FBI file: the cover was that Schorr was being considered for a government job. Fred Malek, at Haldeman's orders, took the rap for this, and admitted when nudged that some member of his recruitment band had indeed asked for the check. The cover story was not believable, but nobody could prove it wasn't so, and it was a fairly plausible excuse if you accepted the possible existence of a gibbering idiot in the White House recruitment operation. Having dealt with some of our recruiters, I believed the cover story completely.

The Washington *Post* broke this story several months after the episode had occurred (Ken Clawson, who was to become the successor to Herb Klein, was the enterprising reporter), intimating that Charles Colson was the fingerman, since Colson had complained to CBS executives about Schorr on another matter. A Presidential press conference was coming up, and I was working on the briefing book; assuming the question would arise, I went to Colson with a draft answer for the President. Colson, who got away with a lot of tough in-fighting, was sore about being unfairly accused of a dirty trick—like Jesse James, he was blamed for every train robbery in the territory. He really had nothing to do with what he was being blamed for (which Len Garment called "poetic injustice," since he got away with a lot of other stuff). Colson promptly okayed my draft answer, which contained a good idea, called Ehrlichman and cleared it with him, too.

I took it to the President. The draft answer read: "The only objection (to the FBI check) seems to be that he was not asked beforehand if he were interested in the job. That objection, it seems to me, makes sense— to avoid even the appearance of intimidation.

"Accordingly, I have ordered that whenever a member of the press is considered for a government job, he be informed beforehand why the customary FBI check is being made, and if he or she is not interested, then the matter will be dropped . . ." The President made only one change— from "a member of the press" to "anybody," which made the directive much more sweeping—and told me to give it to Ron Ziegler to issue in his own name after the press conference, because he was certain the question was not going to be asked. I thought Nixon was wrong about that, but he wasn't, and Ron put it out; after that, a major civil-liberties reform went into effect on the use of the FBI in checking into prospective government employees. I was happy about having had something to do with it, and relieved that the President acted so decisively and correctly when the matter was brought to his attention.

Then, during the Watergate hearings in 1973, it came out that the whole job-offer thing was a lie; that Haldeman might not have been out to intimidate Schorr with an open full-field investigation, but he did demand to see what was already in the Schorr file—for a purpose that can only be assumed went beyond idle curiosity.

The purpose for asking for the file was perforce venal; the implementation of the request was botched; the cover-up was effective for a while. That's why it all qualifies as a mini-Watergate. Moreover, somebody like me wandered around in the midst of it certain that it was low-level stupidity and not high-level deviousness, trumpeting this conclusion to others, never tipped off to the fact that the real story was otherwise and it might be a good idea to shut up. I am not ordinarily so easily duped; the secret of my self-delusion was a misplaced certainty that there was more stupidity at the bottom than villainy at the top, and that was what misled a lot of us a year later, after the Watergate break-in.

Why didn't the press exploit the Schorr episode? Why didn't it blow it up, as Nixon would have said, out of all proportion? That is what is hard to understand about the press: while it is hypersensitive to honest criticism by government officials, and while it clutches the First Amendment to its bosom at the expense of guarantees of fair trial and privacy, the press becomes curiously meek and self-conscious in the face of specific examples of unconscionable harassment. Dan Schorr did not want to make a cause célèbre out of himself because he is a working journalist and that would have dried up many of his sources or, worse, made his judgments on the air seem biased.

CBS, his news organization, is after all an association of government-licensed stations and none of them wants a vendetta; and his associates in the press figure if the reporter himself doesn't want to fight it out with lawsuits, then it is not for them to take the lead. This happened not only with the Schorr episode, but with the wiretapping of the telephones of four newsmen over a two-year span.

Here was the state of the President's mind in the summer of 1969 regarding the press, in a memorandum I discovered four years later:

June 10, 1969

PLEASE TREAT AS CONFIDENTIAL

MEMORANDUM FOR: MR. EHRLICHMAN

The President read in a recent news summary that many of his critics complain about the Administration's not being "as open as promised." His only comment, addressed to you, appears below:

"John—Tell Herb and Ron to ignore this kind of criticism. The fact of the matter is that we are far *too* open. If we treat the press with a little more contempt we'll probably get better treatment."

ALEXANDER P. BUTTERFIELD

cc: Mr. Klein
    Mr. Ziegler

During this time, a flaw in his own character—fervid hatred of the press —set in motion the eavesdropping process that was to flaw his Presidency.

A wiretapping program was begun, recounted earlier in the chapter about leak-wary Henry Kissinger. The fact that all this eavesdropping was going on, however, and the fact that William Beecher and Hedrick Smith of the New York *Times*, Henry Brandon of the London *Sunday Times*, and Marvin Kalb of CBS were being overheard, paved the way for decisions to send former New York Detective John Caulfield to columnist Joseph Kraft's home to see what he could find, and to send another team of second-story men into the office of a psychiatrist on another man's trail.

In 1971, with this anti-press, anti-leak operation under way, with the capacity for clandestine and illegal penetration "in place," the New York *Times* published the Pentagon Papers. Politically, the publication of old Johnson Administration secrets could only be helpful to Nixon, but he could not know what documents were going to be published, and he did know that the press was arrogating to itself the decision as to what would be a national security secret—which he found dangerous and intolerable. To Nixon, the publication of the Pentagon Papers was a challenge by the elite, unelected press to the primacy of power of the democratically elected government. A moral issue was at stake, and whatever political benefit might be gained by the discrediting of the Kennedy-Johnson Administrations and whatever restraint he might have felt in seeking a Constitutional challenge were set aside in this fundamental conflict he had all his life with the damned press thinking it was above the law.

I still think a good case can be made for opposing publication in the courts: The press should not have the power to decide what is a defense secret and what is not; we elect a government for that. At the time, I urged John Ehrlichman to parallel the court cases with some constructive legislative proposals. First, to speed the declassification process, since so much is unnecessarily stamped "secret," and second, to make clear what the penalties are for specific acts of lifting demonstrably secret material out of government files. No individual should have the right to walk off with classified national security documents, to publish them in support of his own cause or for his own profit. Not former Presidents, nor even former White House aides who go to work for great newspapers and write books like this one.

In retrospect, of course, publishing the Pentagon Papers was the right and proper thing for the newspapers to do: not for the reasons then advanced, but because President Nixon was defiling the government's right to file by the improper use of "national security" as the reason for illegal eavesdropping and burglary. There was never a right to tap reporters' telephones without a warrant, as the Supreme Court later held; there was no right for the government to eavesdrop on its own employees' conversations without a court warrant, and especially not those who had no access to secret data; there was no right to break into the home of a columnist or set the FBI on his trail to Paris. In the face of these offenses to press freedom, the publication of the Pentagon Papers now can be viewed as a necessary resistance to illegal harassment.

Well and good, in retrospect; but at the time, the President felt that what he was doing to restrain publication in court was needed for the orderly operation of government, and especially for the progress of its diplomacy. Fanning the flames of righteousness was the rumor flying around the White House that all forty-seven volumes of the papers had been delivered to the Soviet Embassy and had been shipped in the diplomatic pouch to Moscow. Finally, there was the problem of not knowing what the hell was in the papers anyway—it was too much to read too fast.

Nixon went to court and succeeded in establishing the principle of "prior restraint" in the government's relations with the press; although the press treated the ultimate publication of the Pentagon Papers as a great victory for press freedom, the Supreme Court's opinion that the government could seek restraint of publication of secrets beforehand—rather than seek to punish offenders after the fact—was a victory for "national security" and a setback for First Amendment protections.

Nixon could not abide even his limited victory over the press, especially since it was being interpreted by editorialists just the other way—as successful press defiance of his government's position. The press was the enemy, and he wanted total victory. The target became the man who did the leaking, Daniel Ellsberg. J. Edgar Hoover and the FBI were not up to the job, the President was told—Hoover was a racetrack buddy of Ellsberg's father-in-law—and so the job of finding out everything Ellsberg told his psychiatrist went to the Special Investigations Unit, the "plumbers," downstairs in Room 16 of the Old EOB.

When Nixon called Egil Krogh into the Oval Office and motivated him to get the goods on Ellsberg, he might not have been committing an illegal act himself, but he should have known that he wound up a man who worked for John Ehrlichman's old law firm in Seattle—a fine, "straight arrow," just turned thirty—who would then have done anything to save the country from subversives.

For the second time, a hatred of the press—a need to "stop the leaks" and to teach the leakers a lesson—caused Nixon to go over the brink, to lose all sense of balance, to defend his privacy at the expense of everyone else's right to privacy, and to create the climate that led to Watergate. Given the readiness to wiretap and burglarize in these other matters (and given the blessed amateurishness of the men in charge) it is hard to see how there would not have been a Watergate somewhere down the line.

In June 1972, about the time of the month that the final break-in at Democratic headquarters was being headlined modestly as a "caper," the President was getting ready for a press conference and got to thinking about what he might say about his relationship with the press. Here is the way his mind was running, treating his scribbled notes as a kind of poetry:

I used to worry about
how I was doing with Press
Now I only worry about
I am doing the job—
    If I do good job bad press won't hurt me
    If I do bad job good press won't save me—

Some say press is too hostile

I don't get many soft balls
and don't want any

the tougher the question
the better the answer

If I start characterizing your
questions—you will
start characterizing my answers
I guess you will anyway

I try to do my best
& you try to do your best
&
Pretty general knowledge
press is hostile to President

Doesn't help to have
President hostile to press
You will note I never
complain about you individual

"Novak—more and more
of D.C. press corps
share in total the
views taken by
dominant liberals
who control
Demo party."

On June 10, 1972, the President was talking about the political campaign ahead with Chuck Colson, who was spending much more time alone with the Boss than most of Haldeman's crowd liked. Nixon pointed to a story by Godfrey Sperling of the *Christian Science Monitor*, excerpted in the news summary, about the "love affair" George McGovern was having with the press—not so much what the press was saying about McGovern, but what it was leaving out. Colson reported that a conversation he had recently had with a reporter from a news magazine made the same point: that the tough scrutiny always given every Nixon act was not being applied to the man who had confounded the press by winning the Democratic nomination.

The President wrote an extraordinarily frank memo to Buchanan, copy to Colson, which—as the President put it—"lays it on the line."

"What we have here," the President wrote, "is a situation where the working press, because they really believe in their hearts exactly what McGovern believes in, are frantically doing everything they can to clean him up and make him a respectable candidate for the nomination. My guess is that if you were to interview the working press traveling with McGovern, you would find that 90% of them were agreed with his stand on amnesty, abortion, pot, surrender in Vietnam, confiscation of wealth, the $1,000 baby bonus for welfare recipients, etc. As realists they know that these positions, however, may sink him in the election. And typical of the left wing they are willing to use any means whatever to get their man nominated, even if it means covering up his real views during the period of the campaign so that he can win the election and then have the opportunity to put his views in practice through the power he acquired."

Nixon warmed to his theme, which he put in this nutshell:

"It is very important in terms of the final campaign that the media be effectively discredited." He would never say that to Klein, Ziegler, Dick Moore, or any of the people who believed in dealing with, or handling, or trying to make inroads into individual judgments among members of the press. After the media pilloried McGovern on the Eagleton affair, Frank Mankiewicz of the McGovern staff, debating with me on television, was bitter about press treatment, while I was saying it had been pretty fair.* The President would not have agreed, but he didn't censure me for it.

"What we have here is a situation," the President went on (he often used that opening to a topic), "where the Eastern Establishment media finally has a candidate who almost totally shares their views. Here again, if you consider the real ideological bent of the New York *Times*, the Washington *Post*, *Time*, *Newsweek*, and the three television networks, you will find overwhelmingly that their editorial bias comes down on the side of amnesty, pot, abortion, confiscation of wealth (unless it is theirs), massive increases in welfare, unilateral disarmament, reduction of their defenses, and surrender in Vietnam. Now they have a candidate within sight of the nomination who shares all these views. Now the country will find out whether what the media has been standing for during these last five years really represents the majority thinking of the country or is, in fact, a minority view. Incidentally, that piece by Father Greeley in the Washington *Star* recently may be somewhat prophetic in this respect. As you may recall, he entitled it, 'The Movement Has Had It.' I would put it somewhat broader: 'The Liberal Establishment Media May Have Had It.' "

Something strange, subtle, and not too believable happened at this point. With Nixon feeling and writing this way, one might imagine that a campaign of press intimidation was launched. Indeed, there was a series of events that made it appear that an anti-media campaign was under way.

---

* In the debate, the wry Mankiewicz objected to my characterization of his remarks as "complaining about the press." When I asked him to put the tone of his own remarks in a single word, he thought for a moment and replied, "I'd call it 'whining.' "

At the risk of blowing my credibility entirely, let me try to explain what really did happen.

Contrary to Nixon's expectations, the press did not go out to try and help McGovern "get well." Instead, the press—with no Nixon to kick around anymore, because he seldom appeared—stayed after McGovern, savaging him mercilessly, as if angry with him for making them look so foolish in the primaries. Nixon was flabbergasted at the way "they" had turned on "them."

At that time, most reporters believed that the President passed the word to lay off the press—to call off the program of intimidation that had been taking place in the summer of 1972. The President never called it off, but it came off, and here's the hard-to-believe part—he never did give the order to begin the intimidation that the press thought it saw going on. Come inside a meeting of the news management team.

I arrived late at the regular meeting of the Planning Group in the Roosevelt Room. The meeting convened every Monday, Wednesday, and Friday at 2:30 P.M., Chuck Colson in charge, with the men concerned with external relations present: Herb Klein or Ron Ziegler or one of their deputies (usually Bruce Whelihan or Ken Clawson); Dick Moore, John Scali, and occasionally Pat Buchanan; Dwight Chapin or David Parker to present the President's schedule; sometimes John Ehrlichman or Ken Cole from the Domestic Council. The purpose of the group was to plan the public activities of the President, and to see that Administration figures were lined up to make news in an orderly fashion—that is, no two major stories purposely broken on the same day, or if a bad story was due, to try and smother it with other news.

This could be darkly described as "managing the news," but it occurred in the White House long before we ever got there; there was a significance in holding the meetings in the room named for the two Roosevelts, since it was Teddy who delightedly "discovered Monday"—he found that news broken on Sunday received a big news play because little else happened for the Monday morning newspapers—and FDR has never been matched in the manipulation of the White House press.

The reason I arrived late was that I had finally caught on to the art of White House meetingsmanship. Nothing ever happened in the first fifteen minutes because not enough people were there, and Colson was on the phone to the President (of the United States or of a large union). Nothing really happened toward the end of the long session; the best time to be there was from two forty-five to three-fifteen, and your obviously harried-looking exit was taken to mean that the President was impatiently awaiting your presence. Colson put up with this since he and Haldeman considered me one of the "creative people."

They were going over the week's planned releases by the Cabinet members, never one of the meeting's highlights, and I decided to change the subject: "How come nobody ever informed me of our new kick-the-media-in-the-teeth strategy?"

Colson looked up, surprised. "Lots of things happen around here before and after you drop in on these meetings, Safire, but that isn't one of them. What new strategy?"

I said I had to take my hat off to the brilliant orchestration of media intimidation, and ticked off the events of the past couple of weeks:

—John Ehrlichman had made news by directly quoting the President as saying he didn't like press conferences because reporters ask "a lot of flabby and fairly dumb questions."

—Pat Buchanan, on a Liz Drew interview on public television, said he thought that media bias would lead citizens to demand antitrust action against the most powerful segments of the press.

—*Monday*, the sassy weekly publication of the Republican National Committee edited by John Lofton, had started a drumfire against the media in every edition. "CBS News Accentuates Negative, Distorts Facts in Reporting Vietnam Action" were headlines in both its May 15 and June 5 issues.

John Scali, listening to this litany of anti-media barbs, bristled. (Scali is a born bristler, bristling even when he is happy, but this time he was angry.) "Idiocy," he called it, "absolutely no need for this ever, and especially at this time."

Colson, a perceptive man, caught my point. "It does appear to be orchestrated," he said, "and a lot better orchestrated than the stuff we try to orchestrate."

We went over the events one by one: Ehrlichman just popped off in passing, and, as he put it to us, "I wanted to reach out and pull those words back as soon as I heard them coming out." Buchanan, who was not at this meeting (he hated meetings too), had told us he had no intention of mentioning antitrust action against media giants in his interview with Liz Drew; indeed, he had been embarrassed by the need for the Justice Department to issue a denial of any intent along those lines. And Colson, who turned *Monday* on to this subject, had simply forgotten to turn it off.

From time to time, the Administration at the President's request had placed a shot across the bow of the press with careful design and powerful effect, as in the Vice President's 1970 Des Moines speech; in mid-1972, however, no such "campaign" was envisaged. It had come about by a combination of mental set in the minds of some White House staffers and a string of unrelated episodes. Everyone at the news-management table that day agreed that the incidents were a mistake, and similar shots should be discouraged, what with press in full cry after McGovern. John Scali, who was headed out to San Clemente later that day, said he would pass the word to the people with the President at the Western White House.

A few days later, Robert Semple, then White House correspondent for the New York *Times*, returned from San Clemente and called Pat Buchanan to get his reaction to the "directive" that had been issued by the President that the Administration lay off the press.

I know exactly what flashed through Buchanan's mind: *Serves me right for cutting that class—I knew they'd do something at one of those damn two-thirty meetings, and I wouldn't find out about it until a reporter asked me. Hell, Semple is a straight-shooter, he wouldn't have a cockeyed story; it must be that I just never got the word from the President via Colson. So I'll have a temperate, middle-way, cooperative reaction.* Buchanan then confirmed the story, reserving the right to criticize the press again if it became unfair.

This confirmation of the rumored Presidential "directive" by Buchanan, one of the Administration's leading media critics, put the seal of accuracy on the *Times* story. The rest of the people concerned within the government believed it (including many who very much wanted to believe that the anti-media campaign was wrongheaded, and that the Boss would put a stop to it when it came to his attention), and they discussed it with Washington columnists as an inside fact, which was then re-echoed for a couple of weeks until it became a steel cable in the web of Accepted Truth.

But it never happened. Nixon had not yet put his "strategy" to intimidate into action; the anti-press statements were part of a pattern only viewed in retrospect and not in advance; and there was only a general meeting in which it was declared intelligent to try to cut that out, not a stern fiat from on high to switch from the previous nonstrategy to a new nonstrategy.

However, the perceived set of facts, and not the paradoxical truth, was what the press acted upon and the President reacted to. The anti-media campaign had been "dropped." Only Colson and Buchanan knew of the plan that had been in the back of Nixon's mind to stick it to the press, which he had not put into action when the press crossed him up by going after his opponent. The rest of us were relieved and vindicated; we always were loftily certain that Nixon's hatred of the press was an exaggeration perpetrated by the Nixon-haters.

Nixon felt abandoned, I think, by his combination tormentor-and-whipping-boy, during this period of phony peace. But after a few months, the Washington *Post* began to worry the Watergate story, to the President's irritation; when that newspaper began to headline the "dirty tricks" undertaken by Donald Segretti as acts of sabotage directly masterminded by Dwight Chapin and Bob Haldeman, the President saw that as a vicious personal attack on his "family"—and he was satisfied again that the press had shown its real colors, as "the enemy."

And after Nixon won in 1972, after the enemy, the press, had been not only trounced but humiliated in Nixon's only landslide victory; after the press came back in 1973 and blazed at him for the Christmas bombing of Hanoi, and then, when the bombing worked and forced a peace, refused to concede he had been right; after the angry President held the press's feet to the fire, glorying in his triumph and embittered at the refusal of recognition of his victory over what he saw to be the powerful apostles of weakness, the cracks began to appear in the base of his edifice. Judge Sirica, "maximum John," the kind of hanging judge civil libertarians worry most about, applied the awful pressure of lifetimes in jail for first offenses; first James McCord, then Jeb Magruder and Howard Hunt; the press, which had tried and failed to make Watergate the issue, came alive again, and came up off the bloody sand swinging a mace.

The same brand of hate, the same degree of hate, was now turned back on the President. At a garden party, of all places, at Easter-time in 1973, one editor of a powerful publication who hated Richard Nixon with the same blind devotion as he had worshipped John Kennedy, told me, "There's got to be a bloodletting."

Did the country really need a bloodletting? I wondered. "Damn right," he said, the look in his eye reminding me of Bob Haldeman when he caught sight of a group of noisy protesters at a rally in Long Island, "We've got to make sure nobody even thinks of doing anything like this again."

When I crossed the occupational street, returning to journalism after a generation in politics and public relations, I could see how a touch of fear lent an edge of viciousness to the counterattack by the press. Writers who wanted to "get" Nixon because they didn't trust him, or they despised him personally, now had an added incentive—that if they did not discredit and cripple him permanently, he had shown that he was capable of doing literally anything to ruin them. "If you would strike at a king," was Emerson's advice, "make sure you kill him." Nixon had shown he would give no quarter; a reporter doing a story about the misuse of the FBI by politicians, I discovered, may not admit it but worries about what the FBI —or some extralegal "plumbers"—can do to him and his family.

What had happened? The confrontation between Nixon and the press had come and gone in the early Sixties. Nixon bore a grudge, and after he became President, even during his press honeymoon, started changing the rules of the boxing match. He planted a microphone in the opposing fighter's corner, to learn his strategy, and encouraged the crowd to holler at the challenger to intimidate him; when the challenger slipped a roll of dimes into his glove, the champ slipped a roll of quarters into his own, and the fight became bloodier. Suddenly it wasn't a boxing match at all, nor a brawl, but a death struggle between gladiators in an arena, no rules, survival the only victory, death the only defeat, and suddenly Nixon's favorite quotation from Theodore Roosevelt gained a sinister meaning: "It is not the critic who counts . . . the credit belongs to the man who is actually in the arena, whose face is marred with sweat and dust and blood . . ."

Did it really happen here? Did it have to play to the bitter end? Couldn't good sense and a natural moderation have pulled the gladiators apart, back when they were only boxers? Did it have to come to "The liberal establishment media may have had it" and "There's got to be a bloodletting"?

I suppose it did. Nixon, who always knew he had a deep and dark rage within him, mastered his temper in just about every other area, but kept "flicking off the scab," in his skin-crawling metaphor, when it came to the quintessential "them," the press. He had contempt for them, as elitist, antidemocratic, lordly, arrogant lookers-down-their-noses at the elected representative of the folks, and he did everything he could get away with to destroy them—becoming, along the way, elitist, lordly, and dangerously arrogant.

The chapter about the press, which is more critical of President Nixon than others, might be snatched out of the context of this book by Nixon-haters who enjoy being "them" to shovel one more spadeful of guilt onto the mountain of evidence to show Nixon was the product of what Jefferson called "elective despotism." But judging Nixon only by his close-to-irrational animus to the press, or judging him only by the transcripts, is— like judging Achilles by his heel or Job by his challenge to God—misleading. There is more to this many-faceted man than his worst side. The press that Nixon hated has often overlooked the sympathetic and even noble sides to this President, for good reason—because it was faced with the most mean-spirited and ignoble side.

Nixon wanted the press, in his coldly analytical phrase, "effectively discredited." He nearly succeeded. In the month of February 1973, he had his foot on the "liberal establishment press's" neck; and he found no pleasure in that success because the only people whose good opinion he never had and always wanted were the people whose necks were under his foot. After Watergate, Nixon received all he expected to receive from the press triumphant, and what he got he deserved.

"The press brought Nixon down." It is tempting to say, the way one says, "Money is the root of all evil." In fact, the undoing of Nixon had as little to do with the press as money has to do with evil. It was the *love* of money that St. Paul held to be the root of all evil; it was his own *hatred* of the press that slowly, steadily, and then suddenly pulled Nixon down. But Nixon's penchant for secrecy, extreme though it was, has been too readily assumed to be an irrational quirk of a persecuted, conspiratorial mind; there can be good reasons for secrecy, and understandable worry about necessary security being violated unnecessarily.

Consider what was going on about the time the Pentagon Papers were published: the President was about to announce his trip to Peking, and Chou En-lai was disturbed about dealing with a government that could not keep a secret. Let us see how a series of events was combined with a philosophy of "the press is the enemy" to produce a passion that made some underlings feel there were no stops on what they could do.

6. TO PEKING IN SECRET

Richard Nixon always dreamed of going to China. A Californian, he fronted on the Pacific, and looked to Asia, rather than the Atlantic and Europe. He served in the Pacific during World War II. Korea and Vietnam focused his attention on the East in the Fifties and Sixties. And in 1965 he almost made it. His law client, John Shaheen, who was building an oil refinery in Newfoundland, had an idea to get the Premier of that province sent to China by the Prime Minister of Canada. As Shaheen put it to Nixon: "Let's see if Joey Smallwood can get assigned a mission to China by Mike Pearson and you go along as his lawyer." The trip was quickly arranged with the Canadians, and would have projected the long-forgotten Nixon back into the headlines, but President Johnson's State Department would not grant Nixon permission to go.

China fascinated Nixon then because of its mystery, its seeming impenetrability, and the political-diplomatic vistas it opened to him. As the man in the early Fifties who condemned "appeasers" in the State Department who "lost" China, and who called upon President Truman to bar all free world trade with the Communists there, Nixon saw himself as uniquely qualified to re-establish relations with that isolated quarter of the world. The irony of his policy flip-flop did not escape him, but his own changed view was natural and realistic after a generation of Communist legitimacy, and Nixon knew that he was the political figure best able to hold the conservatives in the United States in line in an opening to the East.

This theme—"Only Nixon Could Have"—permeates much of what Nixon accomplished, what he thought he could accomplish, and what he resented at not getting the credit for accomplishing. Kissinger and Pat Moynihan discussed the usefulness of the Nixon reputation for anti-Communism in his dealings with the security-conscious barons of the Congress, Chairmen Mendel Rivers and John Stennis of the House and Senate Armed Services Committees, on matters like the ending of germ warfare capability and the return of Okinawa to Japan. "Only Nixon Could Have" came up again in memos Nixon stimulated Haldeman to write, paving the way for dealings with the Soviets on SALT with a minimum of reaction from the far right, which might have presented a President of more liberal mein with a considerable problem. On the domestic side, too, "only Nixon" could have even proposed welfare reform like the Family Assistance Plan, Moynihan insisted, and though the President later abandoned "FAP," a far-reaching food stamp program was quietly put in place reaching fourteen million Americans. Nixon's ability to bring along the right-wing, grumbling but with "no place else to go," was seen to be one of his greatest strengths. We will never know if a liberal President could have done what Nixon did in relation to the Soviet Union, China, and welfare reform —perhaps the right-wing reaction was overly feared and would have curled up under pressure—but certainly Nixon's reputation for toughness helped him reduce U.S. commitments abroad in good and honorable order, and his hard-earned "reputation for fierceness," as Kissinger later called it, would eventually force an honorable peace in Vietnam.

In 1967, dictating notes and instructions for an article he was preparing for *Foreign Affairs* magazine on "Asia After Vietnam," Nixon said "pursuing a peaceful solution is not inconsistent with advocating a strong military line. On unifying the country, I suggest that it be made *crystal clear* that the basic problem is getting the North Vietnamese and Chinese to know that there will be no withdrawal and that *every responsible leader* in this country accepts this as a political and diplomatic reality" (italics his). At that time, China was in the grip of the Cultural Revolution, and nobody in the West knew quite what was going on in that bloody power play; this is what Nixon was thinking, though he certainly did not include it in his article: "The current nuttiness in Peking underlines the manipulative techniques of the Chinese and their dangerous delusions as to their own power and the flabbiness of the West. My old friend Marshal Lin is back in the news"—Lin Piao, Mao's designated successor, whom Nixon had said several times was an incipient Hitler and who later was killed attempting to unseat Mao, had been drawing renewed attention—"and while the argument is made that his [Lin's] fulminations are rhetoric which reveals weakness, it seems reasonable to take his threats at face value (particularly as he gets up in the world)." Nixon drafted some language to make that point: "We have been told by Marshal Lin Piao, the heir apparent to Mao Tse Tung, that a communist victory in Viet Nam will be followed by a succession of such 'people's wars of liberation' in Asia, Africa, and Latin America. Communist China has already announced support for a 'people's war' in Thailand. Will the free world again ignore a blueprint for aggression as it did in the tragic years before World War II?" Writing the subsequent article in *Foreign Affairs* helped Nixon think through the China problem; if the war in Vietnam were permitted to drag on for five years or longer, he figured, there would come about "the development of a sufficient nuclear delivery capability on China's part to affect the Asian power structure. It does seem crazy for the U.S. to play the 'stalemate' game—the problem is too dynamic for it to remain a stalemate very long." Nixon's idea was to sharply increase the bombing and naval blockading of the North Vietnamese, thereby forcing an early end to the war* and averting a confrontation with China when it could boast operational ICBMs. Nixon weighed every word in the article that was finally written in 1967. It was published in *Foreign Affairs*, and then Nixon got his friend Hobart Lewis to condense and print it in the *Reader's Digest*. In this article, Nixon decided to wave the olive branch: "Taking the long view, we simply cannot afford to leave China forever outside the family of nations, there to nurture its fantasies, cherish its hates and threaten its neighbors. There is no place on this small planet for a billion of its potentially most able people to live in angry isolation." We used this point strongly with liberal Republicans long leery of Nixon, as evidence that "only Nixon" could establish relations with China—Rockefeller couldn't and Reagan wouldn't —but the fact that Nixon's interest in China was politically useful did not mean that it was not sincere. (The end of that sentence is not deliberately Kissingeresque.)

Eleven days after he opened for business in the White House—January 31, 1969—the President read an intriguing intelligence report about China, mulled it over, and sent Henry Kissinger a short note the next day to "put out the line" that Nixon was exploring possibilities of rapprochement with the Red Chinese, and without making any governmental overtures, to see what private individuals could begin making connections.

National Security Study Memorandum 14 went out four days later: a directive to State, Defense, and CIA to begin a close look at U.S. policy toward China, the dangers and opportunities of alternative courses. (In a new preface to *Six Crises* in 1968, Nixon became enamored of a metaphor I lifted from James Reston's column, and he used it in speeches and private talks: "The Chinese have a symbol for the word 'crisis.' One brush stroke stands for danger. The other brush stroke stands for opportunity. We must recognize the danger, but we must seize the opportunity . . .")

On his first trip to Europe in February 1969, Nixon broached the subject with Charles de Gaulle, and wound up having a long talk with André Malraux, a writer who had spent years in China, was an old friend of Mao Tse-tung's, and had recently returned from talks with the Chinese leaders in Peking.

Nixon guardedly told the Congressional leaders about this chat when he returned to Washington. On March 4, 1969, after a good night's sleep

---

* In 1973, a week after the Vietnam cease-fire agreement, I asked Henry Kissinger what we should have done if we had the four years to live over. His reply: "We should have bombed the hell out of them the minute we got into office." More thoughtfully, he added: "The North Vietnamese started an offensive in February 1969. We should have responded strongly. We should have taken on the doves right then—start bombing and mining the harbors. The war would have been over in 1970."

and a sun lamp treatment, the President looked well rested after his grueling trip, and launched into an impressive fifty-minute *tour d'horizon* for the leaders in the Cabinet Room. Senator George Aiken of Vermont asked if the time had not come for some overtures to the Chinese Communists, and Nixon guardedly replied "now is not the time" to trade with them or bring them into the UN. Another questioner tried it from another angle: how about siding with the Soviets against the Chinese, then? "That might be good short-range policy," the President said, "but from the long-range point of view, it would be suicidal." There were "some people," Nixon added (our old friends, "those who," always wrong), who felt that the split between the Soviets and the Chinese was not deep or lasting, but he did not agree with them. "Fights between exponents of the same ideologies are usually more severe than fights between those of differing ideologies, and even religions." He reported how British Prime Minister Harold Wilson had told Secretary of State Bill Rogers and himself about how he had heard horrible insults between Arabs and Jew, but they were nothing compared to what Wilson had heard Alexei Kosygin say about his Chinese "allies."

Without mentioning his opening probes toward the Chinese, the President passed along to the Congressional leaders part of what he had learned from Malraux. Mao had said to the writer that the United States could never destroy China, but as Malraux reported to Nixon, it really never occurred to Mao that the United States might not *want* to destroy China. According to Nixon, Mao had told Malraux there was only one difference between the Soviets and the Americans: the Russians were "barbarians who come by land" to invade China and the Americans were "barbarians who come by sea." The President concluded that Malraux felt it was one of history's greatest tragedies that "the richest and most productive people in the world"—the Americans—were at odds with the Chinese, "the poorest and most populous nation in the world."

An economic move was Nixon's opening gambit. Five months after that visit in Paris, on July 21, 1969, the State Department modified U.S. travel controls so that tourists could buy up to $100 in Chinese goods, and U.S. citizens' passports were to be validated automatically in a variety of professions. Next day, the President flew to the Pacific to greet the returning moon men, kept on going to Pakistan (Yahyah Khan in Lahore was going to be useful in making secret arrangements), and then to Romania, where President Nicolae Ceausescu, in the outer reaches of the Soviet orbit, was to be helpful in making contacts with the Red Chinese. After his return to the United States, the President hosted a State Dinner for the astronauts in Los Angeles on August 13 and met with the National Security Council the next day on China policy at the Western White House.

"Let's look at what has actually been happening," Nixon told his advisers, as they examined some of the assumptions that had seemed so factual in the past. "Can we sustain our previous assumptions?" Nixon pretended to give consideration to the question of what kind of U.S. policy would best build a safer world—isolation or dialogue—but made apparent the direction of his thinking: "We must look at China on a long-term basis. We cannot let China stay permanently isolated."

On August 18, 1969, Nixon was chewing the fat about future plans with Keogh, Price, Buchanan, and myself in his office at the Coast Guard station in San Clemente, and he brought up the subject of why the liberals could never be won over. "They've been hollering for years, 'Recognize Red China,' but when we make a little move toward China via Romania, they go up the wall—they say we're antagonizing the Soviet Union." He shook his head. "That's what pulls the scab right off and lets you see the raw sore of their thinking. The worst thing that could happen for us would be for the Soviet Union to gobble up Red China. We can't let it happen. It gives us problems on the right." He looked at Buchanan. " 'Dealing with those Chinese bastards?' they'll say. We're not doing this because we love the Chinese. We just have to see to it that the U.S. plays both sides."

The President explained how an exploitation of the differences between China and the Soviet Union would give the Soviets more of an incentive to deal with us. Nixon had rejected some recent, suspicious-sounding "collective security" talk of Brezhnev's: "I went all over Asia shooting that down. If the U.S. and the Soviet Union joined in such a pact, it would not only mean whites versus nonwhites, it would mean giving respectability to the Communist parties in the European countries. It would pull the Soviet irons out of the fire. Why should we help them unless they help us? They haven't helped on Vietnam, on the Mideast, on the arms talks. We've got to give them a reason to help us."

Two months later, U. S. Ambassador Walter Stoessel was instructed to make contact with the Chinese Ambassador in Warsaw, which he did at a Yugoslav fashion show.

Another economic goody was tossed in the pot in December, eliminating most controls on the transactions of U.S.-owned firms abroad with the Chinese, and on January 8, 1970, soon after the U. S. Seventh Fleet called off its regular patrol in the Taiwan Strait, the United States and China agreed to reopen the Warsaw ambassadorial talks, which placed the contacts between the two nations on a more formal footing. My own first inkling that something serious about China was afoot came in this memo as I was trying to straighten out some of Henry Kissinger's convoluted bureaucratese in the first "State of the World" report:

MEMORANDUM

THE WHITE HOUSE
WASHINGTON

TOP SECRET/SENSITIVE   February 11, 1970

MEMORANDUM FOR BILL SAFIRE

FROM: Henry A. Kissinger

SUBJECT: The President's Annual Review of U.S. Foreign Policy

Attached is one section which was not included in the package this morning, "Communist China."

In addition, there is one changed page for the "Issues for the Future" portion of Section IV and two changed pages (pages 4 and 5) for the "Willingness to Negotiate" section.

Attachments

Through 1970, Nixon worked on the Chinese, applying the opposite of water torture: a bit-by-bit relaxation of economic restrictions, little flatteries, and probes through the Pakistanis and the Romanians. Meanwhile, the Soviets were pressing for a summit meeting; Nixon dragged a foot, hoping to bring the Chinese along so that he could make Soviet concern at Sino-American relations a wedge to get the Soviets to help arrange a cease-fire in Vietnam.

The President revealed a little of this at a Cabinet meeting on February 18, 1970: "It has been twenty-five years since World War II, and the United States' approach in foreign affairs hasn't changed much. Now there is change. We are adopting a policy that is relevant to today. And a key element of that change is the recognition that now the Communist world is split." In the first State of the World report, the President alluded to that division in a gingerly way; when Elliot Richardson, then at State, said, "It will be interesting to see what the press does with it"—meaning the whole updating of foreign policy—the President replied, "The press picks up only the hot news. Despite their claim to the contrary, the press is quite unsophisticated about this. They will miss the basic thrust."

The Chinese were in no hurry. In an interview with *Time* magazine editors, on October 5, 1970, the President permitted himself an earnest wish: "If there is anything I want to do before I die, it is to go to China. If I don't, I want my children to."

While Henry Kissinger was working on the next annual foreign policy report, it came to the President's attention that Mao had granted an interview to Edgar Snow on December 18, 1970, which was not published in *Life* magazine until April 30, 1971. (*Life*'s editors did not know what they had.) Snow reported that his old friend Mao was considering inviting Americans, including the President, to China: "He should be welcomed because, Mao explained, at present the problems between China and the U.S.A. would have to be solved with Nixon. Mao would be happy to talk with him, either as a tourist or as President."

The second "State of the World" report was issued in February 1971. The President pointedly used the official name for Red China—"the People's Republic of China"—which he had first done at a toast to Romanian Premier Ceausescu a few months before. Nixon noted that the Cultural Revolution's turmoil seemed to be over (now that he was President, he stopped referring to it as "nuttiness"), and said "there could be new opportunities" for normalization of relations.

In April the President was sent a handwritten note from a man who had served as one of the intermediaries between the United States and China. Kissinger looked at it first and knew he had something historic in hand. He called the President's military aide, told him not to let the President go to bed without seeing him—there was a stag dinner that night—and met the President in the Lincoln sitting room afterward. Kissinger read the message aloud and handed it to Nixon for examination; according to Henry, the President said, "It seems to me they want a very high-level contact—maybe even a summit meeting."

Around that time, the U.S. ping-pong team was invited to visit mainland China, accepted, and on April 14 Chou En-lai told them: "You have opened a new page in the relations of the Chinese and American people." That day, Nixon announced a series of stops easing controls on shipping, currency, and travel, and two days later told the American Society of Newspaper Editors of a conversation he had with his daughters about the possibility of going to China someday: "I hope they do. As a matter of fact, I hope sometime I do."

The President decided that Henry Kissinger was the man to send to Peking to set up the summit—and, with that decision, in effect declared Henry the winner in the jockeying between Kissinger and Secretary of State Rogers. In June the President was glad he had made that April decision choosing Kissinger, because Henry represented to him the essence of what could be done in secret, with powerful men working urgently behind the scenes and away from the prying eyes and obstacle-creating questions of reporters. That became important because the greatest fruit of Nixon secrecy was ripening as a great exposure of governmental secrecy was exploding on the front pages of the New York *Times*. On June 13 the *Times* began publication of "the Pentagon Papers," an exhaustive look into the origins of U.S. involvement in Indochina, which the government in its lethargy never declassified.

There was Nixon, with two intermediary nations expecting absolute secrecy as one condition of their aid; with China finally coming around, but absolutely insistent on secrecy and suspicious of any propaganda tricks; with the intelligence apparatus of the Soviet Union straining to find out what was going on between a friendly enemy and a hated ally; and, in Nixon's mind, with the fate of the world's peaceful future quite possibly hanging in the balance. There was the premier newspaper in the United States trumpeting top-secret documents about the Kennedy-Johnson years every day, and who knew what they would publish next. Nixon was beside himself at the press's arrogance at deciding for itself what was secret and what was not; worried that if the press got away with this, they would feel free to reveal any secret at all; and convinced that a supine acceptance of this stripping-away of the U. S. Government's ability to deal confidentially was harmful to his summit negotiations.

Under what he considered intolerable provocation, the power of the elected Presidency under challenge by the power of the elitist press, Nixon reacted strongly—directing John Mitchell to restrain publication in court —and then proceeded to overreact wildly, directing Egil Krogh to use the "plumbers" to find out what Daniel Ellsberg was up to, and thereby to teach the secret-leakers a lesson they would never forget.

Kissinger quietly slipped from Pakistan to Peking on July 9, and the President made his announcement of a Peking summit on July 15, 1971. As Nixon put it later in a private meeting, "Three hundred and eighty-six words, and I wrote every word myself; I said what needed to be said and not one word more."

Secrecy. The subject became a passion with Nixon and Kissinger, beginning with the Pentagon Papers publication and showing in that meeting with Congressional leaders after the announcement of the Peking trip. Everybody on the White House staff was impressed with the need for secrecy, and the writers and researchers were asked for quotations that would be appropriate. (My own contribution was from Dag Hammarskjöld: "The most dangerous of all moral dilemmas: when we are obliged to conceal truth in order to help the truth to be victorious.")

Meeting with Hugh Scott, Jerry Ford, and other Republican Congressional leaders that week, the President said he had no choice but to give the go-ahead to Mitchell to seek the prohibition of publication; otherwise, the precedent would be set that would enable every official who disagreed with Administration policy to steal secret papers and, in the hope of changing that policy, slip them to the press. (Precisely this was done subsequently in the case of the Administration's "tilt" toward Pakistan in its relations with India.)

"Sure, the Democrats look bad" in the papers being published, Nixon told the leaders, and certainly many of the same Democrats who plunged us into Vietnam were now doing all they could to thwart his efforts to pull us out of "the mess they created." Here the President thought he spotted the ulterior motive of the New York *Times* in publishing these documents now, although they had been in the newspaper's possession for some months: the Hatfield-McGovern amendment requiring the withdrawal of all American troops from Vietnam by the end of the year was coming to a vote on the Senate floor any day now. The Pentagon Papers furor would help the sponsors of that amendment, and if Hatfield-McGovern passed, Nixon warned the leaders, he would break off the Paris talks because Congress would have crippled his power to negotiate. "There is much more going on than any of you know," Nixon hinted, "don't underestimate the power of the President, don't underestimate what can be done." Hugh Scott, the Minority Leader of the Senate, predicted accurately that McGovern-Hatfield would be defeated when it came up the next day.

In the President's mind, and in Henry Kissinger's, the China initiative, the Pentagon Papers, and the "end-the-war" amendment were all wrapped up in the same package. The assault by the hostile press on the President's ability to conduct diplomatic negotiations, tied into and supporting the Senate's efforts along those lines, was harming our efforts to end the war in Vietnam in a way that would not sell out President Thieu and—unintentionally—harming our efforts to begin a dialogue with the mainland Chinese.

"We would like the enemy to negotiate with us and not with the Washington *Post*," said Kissinger in that GOP leadership meeting. "There is a school of thought which believes that the North Vietnamese conduct negotiations by dropping vague clues whose meaning we are supposed to guess . . . when we miss one of those clues, we are supposed to go out and flagellate ourselves . . . The history of negotiations with the North Vietnamese is that they will wring out of us every concession they can realize, and in return, promise us 'constructive talks.'" Then Kissinger told Ford and the others the meaning of the China announcement on the Vietnamese negotiations: "Hanoi's leaders are perplexed about the international situation. With their native Vietnamese suspiciousness and their Communist paranoia, they are deeply troubled about what is going on between the U.S. and China. There is nothing the Chinese can tell them that will convince Hanoi that no double-cross is in the offing. They have fought for twenty-five years, and now they see great things happening around them; great decisions are being made and they fear they may be left out."

The point could not be more plain: with all this delicate negotiation going on, with the subtleties of pressure being applied to end bloodshed in a way that would not invite more bloodshed, it was believed to be imperative that none of it be struck down by an influential portion of the press that was either ignorant of the consequences of its activities, or malicious in its intent to thwart the Administration and justify its own dovish line. That was why Nixon and Kissinger were convinced that the right to secrecy had to remain in the hands of elected officials and not be permitted to be arrogated to itself by the press.

Four days later, with the Hatfield-McGovern amendment defeated and the impact of the Peking visit giving the President a new sense of strength, Nixon met with the bipartisan leadership of the Senate and House, not just the Republicans.

Solemnly he thanked them for their responsible statements after his announcements, and continued: "The meeting that will eventually take place is a momentous change, not only in the relations between our two countries. The ramifications go far beyond the United States and China, and beyond next year." After that hint about Russia and assurance that he was not doing this to assure his own re-election, Nixon added that if this trip to Peking were not taken, then a number of items would go undiscussed: "With the Soviet Union, we have a number of channels, but with Mainland China, we have no channels. They must be opened at this level." He explained why the date had been chosen as before May 1972: "May would throw this right into the political season." (The Moscow summit took place May 23–29, 1972.)

The President, with Senate Majority Leader Mike Mansfield on his right and Speaker Carl Albert on his left, looked down the Cabinet table at Foreign Relations Committee Chairman J. William Fulbright, a man he cordially despised and distrusted, and said: "I will try to tell you as much as possible this morning. But without secrecy, there would be no meeting. Without secrecy, there will be no success . . . even among friendly nations, we can't negotiate in the newspapers, if we do, it's down the tube. And when you're negotiating with someone you don't know, that makes it doubly difficult. If we appear guarded today, it is not because of any lack of confidence in the leadership here, but we want to succeed."

Henry Kissinger began his briefing by saying how "the President was directly involved in conversations with the other world leaders—" The President interrupted to give Bill Rogers a plug: "Also the Secretary of State." Kissinger said deferentially, "Of course." Henry went on to describe his visit, the facts of which are public knowledge today, until the President again cut in to get across his point about secrecy: "Could I interrupt—we got three messages from them urging us to keep our side of the bargain, to keep this secret."

Kissinger concluded with: "Self-discipline on our part is essential. This is not an attempt to line up some countries against other countries."

Secretary Rogers took a less didactic tack: "We're traveling a promising road but a dangerous road. It will require self-discipline, because everybody will want to speculate, and we can't help it if they do. But we do not want the Chinese to feel we're exploiting them."

"Or," the President added in reference to Vietnam, "exploit the meeting to the disadvantage of another nation with whom they have dealings." (With Fulbright in the room, Nixon was not going to speak as frankly as he had a few days before.) Rogers nodded, continuing: "We don't have any secret agreement. We need the views of the members of Congress— but if publicly expressed, they would jeopardize the visit." Nixon picked up that cue: "We don't think we're the fount of all wisdom. Some of you will have ideas, and Bill will quarterback the way we get them, but we need your views on a private basis, not on a TV extravaganza."

Bill Rogers handled most of the questions from the Congressmen about the reaction of other nations—"the Soviets have been quiet, but Yugoslavia is ecstatic, and Romania too"—and the effect on Nationalist China in the UN. His was a conciliatory approach, and whenever the President wanted to slip an iron fist into Rogers' kid glove he would interject: "If the Chinese get the impression that we're using them to gig somebody else—the Soviet Union or Hanoi—or if it looks like we're getting ready to flush our friends down the tube—the talks will be compromised."

The Democratic leadership, on the spot, was uncomfortable. House Armed Services Chairman Edward Hebert, who had taken over the chairmanship when Mendel Rivers died, grumbled, "It won't be that simple. You're not trying to tie our tongues, I hope . . . we're gonna hear more stuff about 'secret agreements' than you ever saw."

The President backed off a little: "When we say, 'Say nothing,' we only mean say nothing about details. And don't say, 'The Administration position is . . .'" Speaker Albert volunteered, "I'm prepared to say, 'The Administration can speak for itself.'" Minority Leader Ford nodded approvingly. When Senator Carl Ellender asked if Kissinger had made an agreement about the President's forthcoming visit, the President said coolly, "A Presidential adviser does not make agreements," to which Kissinger assented solemnly.

The President wanted the nation to know that he had consulted the bipartisan leadership, but he did not want to tell them much, and he dwelt on the need for not doing so in this meeting with them. They were politicians too, well aware of this, and only went along so far. Senator Fulbright, for example, said, "You have no objection, I take it, if the Committee expresses itself, with no relation to the Administration's position. We're very sympathetic. We completely agree with what you're doing. But of course it is impossible to stifle the Committee's inquiries into the roots of our Asian policy." This reference to the Pentagon Papers revelations and the follow-ups was a direct and knowing caress of the President's temper trigger. Nixon said only, "I would appreciate it if you would have a talk with Bill. It might be a sensitive thing." Rogers came in with "Obviously we can't ask Congress to stop its hearings," and Nixon jabbed with "If you say, 'When the President goes to China, he ought to do this or that,' that would not be helpful . . . Look. If you have strong feelings, let me know privately. Put yourself in the mind of whoever has to sit at the conference table . . . The nature of totalitarian societies is conspiratorial. If it seems the U.S. did this not because we were seeking better relations with mainland China, but because we're frying other fish—then they'll feel differently."

Speaker Albert wanted to know what effect this would have on the war in Vietnam. Kissinger said flatly, "Any speculation on the effect on Vietnam would be counterproductive. It would defeat the by-products that could come from this." Taking his cue from the President, the National Security Adviser would not be as candid with the Democrats as he had been with Scott and Ford a few days before. But Secretary Rogers was more flexible: "We Americans can't stop ourselves from saying what we think." Senator Fulbright acted irritated with the earlier Kissinger response: "We just can't stand mute. We have to say something. We are going to have some historical hearings. I think that background we develop will support you, not interfere with you." Kissinger, who could see which way the wind was blowing, spun with it: "It may even help." The President stepped in: "But under no circumstances should you say that we say the trip to Peking will help in Vietnam. That's *verboten*, we're not saying it." Chairman John Stennis of Senate Armed Services relieved the tension with "I think you made a good move and I'm going to back you up. A lot of self-discipline is required of us."

The President took that opportunity to take them to the mountaintop. "Mike [Mansfield] made an interesting comment when he heard the statement: 'The secrecy was like the Manhattan Project.' Look at that Manhattan Project that built the atom bomb. Secrecy was necessary, and the project was successful. I know we're concerned about Vietnam. But the real question here is: Is there a chance for success far beyond Vietnam? The very fact of this meeting means there is a chance for peace. And when I say peace, I don't mean we're all going to lie down in the manger together." He mildly derided the comment of the ping-pong diplomats, that the President would "get to know the Chinese." With some sarcasm, Nixon said, "That's what I need to do, get to know 750 million people, that'll be quite a trip." He shook his head. "If there's anybody with a less euphoric attitude on summitry, and on the relations with Communist countries, it is myself.

"But look way down the road, get this in historic perspective. On SALT —maybe we can get an agreement. What does it mean, twenty years from now, with another nation outside the club? It is impossible to have peace with a great power totally isolated."

Old Ellender of Louisiana shook his head in admiration about another subject entirely: "This was the best kept secret of the Administration."

"I would go further," the President said grimly. "It was the only secret."

Majority Leader Mike Mansfield, who often spoke last at these meetings, and whose independent opinion was the most respected of all, spoke his mind: "On our side, we're walking on eggshells. On the other side, Chou is walking on eggshells. The attitude of this group, Mr. President, is one of understanding . . . If answers are to be given by any of us, they are to be prefaced with 'This is my own opinion, not the Administration's.' Because of the delicacy of the situation—and the promise of moving out of the old era into a new one—I will stop and think before I speak."

That was all the President could ask for. But on the way out, Nixon added to Fulbright, "Decline to speculate."

A couple of hours after his meeting with the bipartisan leaders, the

President assembled the senior White House staff in the Roosevelt Room and gave us the word on that subject bothering him most: ". . . the subject of secrecy. Without secrecy, there would have been no motivation for, or acceptance to this meeting (in Peking). Without secrecy, there can be no chance of success. In the critical early stages of this," the President said sternly, "only Henry and I knew. At the end, only some members of Henry's staff, and Secretary Rogers, knew. Nobody else in the United States knew."

The President had only been able to request restraint from the Congressional leadership. Now, with his staff, he could let more of his personal feelings show.

"On negotiations generally, take our good friends the British, they know there is a greater chance to succeed in negotiations if they are done privately. Oh, I know it makes a big hero out of the little boy who leaks it out"—there was more than an edge of sarcasm in the President's voice, he was letting himself get angry—"or who falls for the reporter who says, 'This is just for my own guidance.' Take the great newspapers, 'All the News That's Fit to Print.' Now *any* news is fit to print. .

"Oh, now and then you might find a reporter you can tell something" —here it comes, I thought, he always zagged a little like that before making his point—"but if one 'great' paper proceeds with the assumption that any news is fit to print, *don't give 'em any news!* Not unless it's fit to print." He was referring, of course, to the slogan next to the masthead of the New York *Times*. "The first element of trust is in dealing in confidence, but then some little jackass on the White House staff, or at State or Defense, torpedoes the whole thing. I cannot emphasize too strongly the obsession some people have to talk to the press." I had the feeling he was directing his remarks to me, but half the people in the room felt the same way about themselves. "The meeting in Peking will abort if there is not secrecy."

Nixon mimicked the jackasses: "They say, 'Why does it hurt to pass the word that this is going to drive the Russians up the wall?' Well, the way to make sure that won't happen, is to speculate about it. 'What can we say, then?' You can say, 'Gee, I don't know anything more.' And when people say, 'Aren't you dumb?' say, 'Yes, I am!' The people the press have the greatest contempt for are the babblers"—Nixon had said that on other occasions—"so don't leak. *Say nothing!* Don't guess! Don't claim it will help or hurt us politically."

A fair characterization of those remarks is a tirade. We had never heard Nixon lash into his senior staff that way; the Senate's amendment to end the war, the Peking visit, and the Pentagon Papers publication combined to affect him to an extent that he would let rage show beyond one or two close associates. A self-conscious man, Nixon could tell the effect he was having not just on us but on our estimation of him; consequently, he changed his tone of voice as he turned to more positive matters than the damnable press and the babblers who were out to torpedo the country.

Although it is easy now to talk of an obsession on Nixon's part about leaks, leading to crimes against Daniel Ellsberg, it might be remembered that the President saw himself playing for high stakes with the most noble motive: to set up a new structure of peace. It is not hard to imagine his pique at some staffer who wanted to look important to some reporter, or some reporter who considered an exclusive story to be more important than the nation's interest, to throw a monkey wrench into these delicate works. Nixon's worry about the Chinese concern for secrecy was probably not exaggerated—they probably "made representations" several times at evidences of bad faith that may have come from leaks—and to indulge the Chinese demand for privacy seemed so little for a President to ask of a responsible press and a loyal White House staff, when so much good could be done.

"This was a terribly difficult decision for the Chinese," Nixon explained, in a calmer voice. "For the leaders of the ideologically activist side of the Communist world to sit down with the head of the capitalist world— that's an enormous decision for them. Three months ago, these same Chinese were kicking Moscow for getting along with the capitalists on SALT.

"It's a great problem for us too, with Taiwan and the other nations. But the reason it has to be done: a fourth of the world's people live in Communist China. Today they're not a significant power, but twenty-five years from now they could be decisive. For the United States not to do what it can at this time, when it can, would lead to a situation of great danger. We could have total détente with the Soviet Union—but that would mean nothing if the Chinese are outside the international community." President Nixon was rolling now, his anger passed, and we could get a sense of his excitement.

"Will it mean we will have wonderful relations?" he asked rhetorically, and we all knew his answer to that: "Not at all. We will continue to have competition. They know, as we know, that the world is not going to be worth living in if we don't find some way to get these potentially explosive forces under control.

"The decision to meet was made not because we have illusions or because we're euphoric. Of all the men who have occupied this chair in the past"—this was in the Roosevelt Room, and he was flanked by plaques of Theodore and Franklin Roosevelt—"the least euphoric in regard to the attitudes of the Communist powers is myself. Not because I have any built-in hard-line propensities—you don't act like a barbarian—it is just that where vital interests are involved, great powers consult their vital interests. The reason we are meeting with the Chinese is that vital interests in some cases may coincide.

"This is traumatic for the Chinese and for us. But what we will have done is to make the world a little safer. More competitive—but safer, in terms of nuclear confrontation."

The President was silent for a moment, and then came back at his earlier point in a gentler way: "Our Chinese friends read everything of significance that comes out of the United States. That's why I say the stakes are too high to indulge in the luxury of seeming to be smart when you meet people."

The stakes could not have been higher, which is why the germinating seeds of destruction cannot be identified simplistically as a paranoid style, or an irrational impulse to strike back at "them," or an arrogance of power, or a natural combativeness. Nixon was a President who recognized the need for a diminution of the American presence all over the world, but who was determined not to permit a lessening of the American influence in the highest councils of the world. He wanted power to flow "back to the people" and away from Washington, but not in a way that diminished the power of the Presidency to act boldly when the situation demanded activism.

In seeking to achieve these complex goals, Nixon was faced with the real opposition of powerful groups and voices, and he joined the battle with them emotionally, culturally, politically, and intellectually. Fighting that "good fight," he made a couple of bad mistakes. First, he placed the need for secrecy and security far ahead of the need to protect civil liberty, and second, the President—in the most powerful position in the world—allowed himself the luxury of wanting to beat "them" as much as they wanted to beat him.

PART SIX

HIGH ADVENTURE

When you take a call on an aircraft, the Signal Corps operator is careful to warn, "This is an insecure communication"; the reaction of most mortals is to talk so cryptically as to become incomprehensible to the person on the other end of the line.

I was flying along and flailing away in the fall of 1970 with Vice President Agnew on the *Michelle Ann II* headed into Salt Lake City, when writing chief Jim Keogh called from the White House: "The President, who is now in Romania, would like you to meet him at Shannon Airport in Ireland day after tomorrow. Do you read?"

"I read, I read, I'm on my way. What's it all about—I mean, nature of assignment is what?"

"No further advice," said Keogh. "Be on the ramp when *Air Force One* lands."

That was the sort of "human drama" every aide has in mind when he signs up. Behind the Iron Curtain, the President of the United States looks around and—in a Thurberian voice like thin ice breaking—says, "Where's Safire?" His aides stammer, "He doesn't seem to be on the manifest," and the President barks, "I need him! Get hold of him, no matter what it takes, and have him meet me in Ireland to do The Big One."

I asked Bryce Harlow, my seatmate at the time, if that was the likely scenario, and Bryce said, "You've been at the White House all these years, and you still think you're Lanny Budd? Forget it. The Man wants you to come back with him on the trans-Atlantic leg of the trip. That's when they'll be discussing the President's participation in the Congressional campaigns. Be ready with your recommendations as to which states and candidates need help, and which are beyond redemption."

Harlow's estimate was drearily logical. That was also the conclusion several reporters leaped to when they spotted me on the airstrip in Shannon, Ireland, waiting for *Air Force One* to land and for the President to make his way to County Limerick for a sentimental journey to the land of his forebears. I pooh-poohed the suggestions of the White House press corps that I had been summoned for crass political reasons, pointing instead to my vast experience as a limerick writer.

The great silver-and-blue Presidential aircraft landed, jets screaming as it slowly approached the welcoming crowd, with *United States of America* emblazoned across the gleaming fuselage—the arrival of that plane was always an impressive and inspiring sight. Haldeman, as usual, marched off the plane with his home movie camera fixed in front of his face. I went up to him, making faces in the lens until he took it out of his eye, and asked him why the President had sent for me.

"Translation," he announced.

"Gaelic? I was absent the day we had Gaelic."

"You're here to translate one of Henry's speeches into English," Haldeman explained. "Cease-fire proposal. Some of Kissinger's staffers will get to you in your room."

Back at Dromoland Castle—a castle turned into a hotel, where I had been assigned a dungeon room, presumably for security reasons—there was a sign on my door from Robert Houdak, one of Henry Kissinger's assistants. "I have what you want," Houdak had written, adding, "Neither Good Looks, Girls, Nor Money."

The NSC speech draft I was handed on October 3, 1970, called for a "standstill cease-fire." That was the lead, responding to the demands being made by dovish Senators in the States for "peace now." The proposal was what Nixon would call "grandstanding" or "showboating," presented primarily for its political impact in the States, buying Nixon some more time, with little chance of its acceptance by the North Vietnamese, but with every chance of its embrace by editorial writers who wanted a dramatic offer which they thought would break the logjam in negotiations. Likely to be overlooked—and per instructions, to be written in a way that would ensure its being overlooked by laymen—was a proposal that the United States would withdraw all its troops twelve months after a settlement, a substantive idea that Nixon felt he could live with if he could negotiate a method of monitoring about half the North Vietnamese withdrawal.

Next to nearly every paragraph in the Kissinger draft speech was the Nixon notation "Boil down." The President said, "Make it short," when I had been helicopted over to Kilfrush House, the estate of millionaire supporter Jack Mulcahy, where Nixon, Kissinger, and Haldeman were staying. "Cut it to ten minutes," the President said. "Get rid of all the historical stuff—that way, the papers will run it all." I didn't like the phrase "standstill cease-fire"—that was what we were calling the situation in the Mideast, and it was the phrase the Vietnam doves were using—what was wrong with the word "armistice"? Kissinger blanched—that had a legal meaning he did not want to use. I then tried an archaic "cease-fire-in-place" which was accepted as our lead phrase. Neither the President nor Kissinger worried much about what it was called since it was not likely to be accepted.

Kissinger could tell I was concerned about the President's broadcasting a proposal that was popular at home but not possible at the negotiation table—that was not Nixon's way. "We want to get proposals judged on their merits," Henry told me, "not on whether they are acceptable. The problem we face is that according to many in the U.S., a proposal that is not 'new' is not 'good'—they say rigidity is bad and flexibility is good. But one-sided flexibility encourages rigidity." With the cease-fire-in-place, we were making a proposal that was not new to the North Vietnamese, but seemed new to the American public. "The big question is," Henry said, "does the other side want to settle for anything less than total victory? Their demands are absurd: they want us to withdraw and on the way out to overthrow the Saigon Government." He brooded about that a minute. "If we ever decide to withdraw, it'll be up to them to overthrow the Saigon Government—not us."

Since Kissinger was scheduled to take a detour down to London by himself that day, Haldeman told me to take Henry's room in Kilfrush House. It was cavernous—a thirty-by-twenty-foot bedroom, with a walk-in closet that was like a large locker room, and a bathroom marbled like Angus beef —a former stable that had been remodeled into a modern castle. General Don Hughes, the President's military aide, and I sat on the edge of the bed while Kissinger prepared to depart. I kept urging Henry to go, as I wanted the room to myself, and Hughes, deadpan, was explaining to Dr. Kissinger why he had been unable to provide him with an Air Force jet to take him to London, but had instead laid on an old bus, which would speed him to London in fourteen hours bumpily but in perfect safety. Kissinger, despite his qualms about the cease-fire-in-place gimmick, and with a lingering resentment about being pushed in his negotiations by Ambassador David Bruce's requests and the President's political requirements, was looking forward to his rendezvous in London. He deadpanned back to Hughes that he would be happy to go by slow bus, but he would be thinking all the way how American security no longer required an Air Force—and telling me to stop pushing him out of his room. "Now I know how the Palestinian Arabs feel."*

The kidding around, the hanging loose, the weighing of political considerations back home while probing for an opening with the "other side" (in Kissinger's adoption of Dean Rusk terminology) or "the enemy" (as Nixon insisted on calling the North Vietnamese), all accompanied a dread that infected anyone who came into contact with the Southeast Asian situation. What if the Communists wanted only to win, and were talking only while we had the troop-withdrawal lever to keep them at the negotiating table? Nixon was convinced at that time that the testing of the American will—his will, really—in Vietnam would determine the future of his dealings with the Soviets and the Chinese. He was confident that he

* Hughes, a well-disciplined officer who had been Nixon's aide in the Fifties, had a fey sense of humor. Standing at rigid attention at an arrival ceremony for Spanish Prince Juan Carlos, the general whispered to the man next to him, "The whole thing's off, the Prince just turned back into a frog."

could hold his majority at home for "peace with honor." Kissinger was less sure, especially when he saw Nixon say one thing and do another on minor items. For example, on the flight back to the States from Ireland, the President told Kissinger and myself about the speech: "I don't want to raise false hopes at the end, I want to end with a down." Then, in describing the forthcoming speech to reporters, the President called it "the most comprehensive report ever"—which raised hopes considerably. Kissinger was dismayed. "I saw him head out to the news conference," Henry said, with a medium-anguished look, "but I had no idea he'd say that." I had to reply, "That's just what Herb Klein said back in '62."

The recalcitrance—or, from their point of view, the dogged courage—of the North Vietnamese had a fundamental effect on Nixon's world view. From the start, he had seen Southeast Asia as a bone in the throat that had to be cleared before major-power peace construction could begin, and that the manner of its clearing would illustrate America's resolve and help lay the foundations for a stable, peaceful balance of power.

But Nixon did not have forever. The Chinese leaders were aging; the moment of Soviet power parity was at hand; Nixon's own first term was nearly half-finished. At about this time, in my view, Southeast Asia ceased to be a key to the dealings with the superpower, Russia, and the superpower-to-be, China; instead, the slowly developing dealings with Russia and China became Nixon's means of steadily pressuring the North Vietnamese. Vietnam would no longer be primarily a place of proving American resolve prior to engaging with superpowers; it became primarily a test of the Soviet Union and China's desire to deal with the United States.

Nixon understood this shift while it was going on. He had not planned it that way, but was enough of a poker player to take advantage of the cards as they came, and his statecraft made a plus out of a minus. There was a serenity about Nixon when he was dealing on the world scene. He had a sense of history, and, unlike Henry Kissinger, who urged the President to read Oswald Spengler's pessimistic *Decline of the West*, Nixon was confident not only of the rightness of his cause but of its ultimate success. To Jerry Ford at a Republican leadership meeting, Nixon said that he might need the Congress to give the President a little leeway in extending "most favored nation" status on certain Communist trading partners, "for reasons that are, let us say, conspiratorial in nature." Ford nodded, trying to look conspiratorial.

The conspiracy was to finesse the war in Southeast Asia: to end it by doing what Nixon had originally thought to do in the Sixties, and which was described by others as his "secret plan"—to raise the ante, to shift the focus, so that the bone would be dislodged not by the loud harrumphing that goes with clearing the throat, but by turning world power relationships upside down and shaking.

In his Inaugural Address, Nixon had invited his countrymen to join in "a high adventure." By this he meant the adventure of making peace, of shaping rather than reacting to events, an art form for which American

Presidents have not been especially noted. His October 7, 1970, speech about Vietnam was hailed by the dovish editorial page of the New York *Times*, which said the speech "fully warrants its advance description as a 'major new initiative for peace' . . . Hanoi can ask no more as an American opening bid." The doves were satisfied for a time; when Hanoi did not respond to the peace proposal, the doves in the United States came to the conclusion that there must have been something lacking in the proposal rather than anything dishonorable in the Communist intentions. The grandstanding did its delaying job; the really major initiatives, toward China, first, and then toward the Soviet Union, were foremost in the President's mind.

This section deals with those summits: Peking and Moscow, the springtime of content that was also the personal summit of the thirty-seventh American President. As he approached negotiation at the highest level, Nixon saw the summits as the crowning achievements of his first term, major steps toward a reordering of power structure in the world. Only a year later, after Watergate, he would look back on them as the salvation of his pre-election promises and the justification his Administration would find in the eyes of history.

1. STATE OF THE WORLD

Only Nixon could have done it. The Tory with the liberal principles, the internationalist with the hard-nosed reputation, the believer in free markets with the willingness, as he put it, to "leapfrog 'em all"—only Nixon, of all the men in the forefront of American public life, could have taken the steps he took in the eighteen-month period of 1971 and the first half of 1972.

The "only Nixon" theme, which was something he and Bob Haldeman were anxious to get across to a reluctant press, had—in Henry Kissinger's phrase—"the added advantage of being true." Not that any of it went smoothly. Early in 1971, I received this with a little red tag on it from Haldeman:

February 2, 1971

MEMORANDUM FOR: HENRY KISSINGER

FROM: H. R. HALDEMAN

Regarding the President's television activity in conjunction with the State of the World, he now feels that it is probably desirable to make some kind of a television appearance.

If he does, however, it must be an absolute maximum of 2000 words and he very much hopes it will be less. He is completely serious on this and personally I think he is right. He should not go on for a half hour address unless there is some major hard line lead in the report. As of now I understand there are none.

His present intention would be to use ten minutes at news time, probably 7:00 pm. The text for his use should be written with that in mind.

He would like Safire to do the draft for him on this and he would like to have it written now so he can start giving some thought to it and working on it.

cc: Mr. Safire √

Henry Kissinger's office suite was being ripped apart in a spirit of the purest panic when I went to see him in early February 1971 about the "State of the World" speech, a summary of a 60,000-word message to the Congress.

Ashen-faced aide David Young was rummaging through papers on a conference table. Long-legged Julie Pineau, composure shattered, was on her knees going through a wastepaper basket. Al Haig would not let himself appear rattled, but his self-control was being tested as he methodically leafed through papers on his desk.

"I'm here to see about the 'State of the World,'" I said to the reception-ist, like a handyman on a housecall. She rolled her eyes heavenward and motioned me into Dr. Kissinger's office.

"I am sorry to expose you to this," Henry said grimly, "but I cannot work with you now, or do anything else, until I find a piece of paper I had in my hand not five minutes ago. If we do not find it now, my vaunted staff will put it into a mill that distributes it all over the goddam bureaucracy."

"Relax, Henry," I said, being helpful, "it'll turn up."

He looked at me in wonderment. "I am the National Security Adviser to the President of the United States," he announced. "I have just mis-placed the most sensitive, the most top-secret piece of paper that exists in the entire government at this moment. Somehow I think a greater sense of urgency is required than to sprawl all over my sofa and say, 'It'll turn up.'"

Five frantic minutes later it was turned up by Haig in a batch of top-secret cables. A recommendation on how to break the impasse on the SALT talks was indeed a sensitive matter, and Henry could hardly be faulted for worrying about the idea being noised about.

With the shelling in Henry's suite over, people began moving about the bunker at a normally hectic pace, speaking in their customary murmurs.

"Get me Lord," he said to his secretary, and closed his office door. This was not an appeal for Divine assistance, but a call for Winston Lord, his chief assistant for drafting documents. When the aide did not appear in thirty seconds from his office one floor below, Henry went to the door and said to the receptionist: "Do you suppose you could prevail on Mr. Lord to share with me a few moments of his valuable time?"

Henry Kissinger must have been as impossible a man to work for as he was a pleasure to work with. He pounds assistants into the ground. "I don't need an intelligent, sensitive human being for an assistant," he once told me, "what I need is a good, smart robot." Then he smiled; he was only kidding.

Al Haig, his deputy, and Win Lord were far from robots; they were then and are still highly intelligent human beings—devoid of alter-egotism—who understood the man they worked under better than he understood himself. Unlike the fabled aides to Darryl F. Zanuck ("Don't say yes until I finish talking!"), these were no sycophants. They humored Henry, tolerated his rages, put up with abuse, and worked grueling hours because they knew they could say "no" on enterprises of great moment and Henry would stop and carefully consider their views. They were also emotionally selfless. "If it helps Henry think better to blow his stack at one of us," Lord once told me, "considering the pressure he is under and the enormity of the problems he is coping with—then who cares about his temper? It's within the family, it harms nobody—we can take it. So he's not an easy boss. But where do you get another one like him?" Unmentioned was another fact: If you could stand the gaff, a speedy rise to the top was possible.

Kissinger had several reasons to be edgy that day in February 1971. His second "State of the World" report was in its labor-pains stage, and everyone on the NSC staff was puffing as if in preparation for natural childbirth. The secret talks with Le Duc Tho had begun in Paris and anything said or written about Vietnam publicly had to be phrased so as not to harm the private negotiations. There was movement toward the visit to China. The behind-the-scenes clashes with the State Department were threatening to break out into open conflict. And the decision to support a strike at the Ho Chi Minh trail in Laos had recently convulsed the level of leadership just below the President.

On the night of February 3, Secretary Rogers, supported by Secretary Laird, advised the President not to move South Vietnamese troops into Laos. They felt that the reaction within the United States would be similar to the post-Cambodia agony, and this time he would lose the support of much of his Silent Majority. Kissinger's counsel, in favor of the strike, was relatively muted that night. The next morning Henry went to the President and said that in case he had not been forceful enough the night before, he wanted the President to know that he strongly urged the move into Laos. Nixon told him he had already decided to do it.

Kissinger had a right to think that neither the Cambodian nor the Laos operations would have taken place without his urging of that course on the President. Pacing around his corner office—his basement days were far behind—on February 15, he put it bluntly to me: "Laos would not have happened if I had not been here. It would not have happened if I had been here and somebody else was in the Oval Office, like Rockefeller, whom I respect, but who wouldn't have gone against both his Secretary of State and Secretary of Defense. But because the two of us are here, the President and myself, we have a chance of *winning* this thing." In Henry's mind, "only Nixon could have" was absolutely true, once modified to "only Nixon and Kissinger could have." Henry had come to the conclusion that because Nixon was where he was and Kissinger was where he was, not only was there a good chance that the Vietnam situation could be honorably salvaged, but a train of events would accompany its solution that would help to strike the necessary balance of world power for the next generation. Small wonder, then, that Henry saw his role in dramatic terms, that he was tense at that particular moment, and that he was especially sensitive to what was—in his mind—unconscionable sniping from State.

I tried to kid him along, suggesting State was doing a good job in the Middle East without his help, as in the Israeli-Egyptian cease-fire: "That damn cease-fire," he shot back, "brought us closer to World War III than anything since the Cuban missile crisis." Henry could banter better than most men in Washington—I liked the way he once looked around the room at an Italian dinner and remarked, "I must be the only man here whose name ends in a consonant"—but on the subject of the State Department, he was not joking.

"I'll resign," he said. "You guys think I'm kidding when I say this, but I'll resign. I don't have to put up with this."

"If you quit, Henry," I reminded him, "you'll never get a phone call from a beautiful woman again. The secret of your attraction is your proximity to power."

No matter how infuriated, Kissinger always had time to reflect upon an interesting observation. "You're right about that, Safire, it would be a tremendous sacrifice. But be serious. Come with me."

He marched me into Al Haig's office nearby and demanded: "Where is that cable that shows how State is stabbing me in the back?" Haig pulled open his righthand drawer and handed me the cable copy, asking, with his tight little smile, "You cleared for secret?" Henry pointed to a paragraph that showed how some foreign service officer cast a slur on Kissinger to an official of another nation. "Can you believe that?"

"What I can't believe," I said, "is how Al Haig can misplace the most secret piece of paper in the government, but when it comes to a cable knocking State, he can put his hand on it in two seconds." That broke Henry up, and we went to work on the "State of the World" address in good spirits.

The official title of these annual foreign policy reports varies, but they are referred to by many newsmen as "State of the World" reports and addresses, since they are delivered just after the President's State of the Union message. Since it would be presumptuous for any world leader to label his own address "the state of the world" (he does not, after all, run the world) he must stick to the universally ignored title, trusting to newsmen to continue to call it the "State of the World" in their irreverent way. (Henry's original title for the 1970 report was "A Strategy for Peace," subtitled "U. S. Foreign Policy in the '70s," which bothered me—I could have sworn

I'd heard "strategy for peace" before. The report was on the presses when it was discovered that "Strategy for Peace" was the title of a John F. Kennedy collection of speeches. In a flash, the title and the subtitle were transposed.)

Substantively, the purpose of Nixon's address—and of the lengthy report it summarized—was to lift the nation's eyes above preoccupation with Vietnam to see how our foreign policy was building peace throughout the world. It was important, too, to show how our actions in Vietnam were not an aberration of policy—that the "right way out" helped that policy elsewhere in the world.

Since the short speech, like the long report, was intended to be analytical rather than of immediate news interest, I urged that it be given on radio, not television. It is worth examining in some detail now, as a prism to separate the individual passions and thoughts of men near the decision center.

The first draft—a selection of paragraphs from the long message to Congress—was a nine-point MEGO on the Richter scale.*

After four drafts, Kissinger, Lord, and I had worked out an approach that could then be submitted to the President focused in this way:

"—how we are getting out of the war this Nation has been in for the past six years;

"—how we have created a new and different foreign policy approach for the United States in a greatly changed world;

"—and how we are applying that approach in working with others to build a lasting peace."

The situation in Vietnam; an explanation of our foreign policy generally; a report on its success. A sensible arrangement of topics, adhering to Nixon's organized style.

The refinements in thought and language as the speech moved from draft to draft illustrated some problems and opportunities at hand. In the matter of the Laos operation, I had refused to use the military word "interdiction," substituting "cutoff of much of the enemy's supplies"; Kissinger changed that to "disruption," less specific and more accurate. There was a line buried in the speech that Henry gave much thought to: "When the Government of the People's Republic of China is ready to resume talks with us in Warsaw, it will find us receptive to agreements that further the legitimate national interests of China and its neighbors." He drew a line through "resume talks with us in Warsaw" and substituted "engage in talks" without specifying where or limiting it to resumption on a lower level.

* That is news magazine lingo; a Richter scale measures the power of earthquakes, and a MEGO is an acronym coined by *Newsweek* staffers for "my eyes glaze over," to describe audience reaction to subjects that everyone agrees are important but are surefire soporifics. Latin American policy, Eurodollars, and manpower training are MEGOs. A speech on government reorganization, written and delivered in a monotone, can achieve the 10-point MEGO on the Richter scale, putting the entire audience to sleep.

SOVIET PRESENCE IN EGYPT

Q.   Mr. President: A high White House official has been quoted as saying this government's policy is to "expel" the Russians from the Middle East. That, coupled with your TV interview, has in the eyes of some undercut your Middle Eastern Peace initiatives. Can you tell us if it is indeed American policy to "expel" the Soviets -- and whether you think our peace efforts have been damaged by your television remarks?

A.   America's objective in the Middle East is peace.

All our efforts are directed toward making progress toward the kind of settlement that will bring a durable peace to that region.

Along with other top level officials of this Administration, I have spoken of the dangers inherent in the Mid-East Situation -- as part of the background of the new United States initiative. Those dangers are the strongest arguments I know for making that initiative successful.

As for Soviet combat forces in the UAR, we view their presence there with concern -- even though it is claimed they are there in a strictly defensive role. If that is indeed the reason for their presence -- then they can be withdrawn when there is a peace settlement. Again, it is that settlement toward which our efforts are being made today.

(PJB/HAK)

The word expel was used in that context -- and as all statements by White House spokesmen, fully reflected my views.   (HAK)

PLATE 13. In the President's briefing book, Henry A. Kissinger asks for Presidential support of his overly strong use of the word "expel" — which the President, in his notation, softened.

PLATE 14. Some examples of President Nixon's use of the Presidential news summary as a vehicle for sending messages to supporters and staff members. On this page Mr. Nixon wrote, "Good job, Ron!" to Governor Ronald Reagan.

2

<u>REAGAN</u>

Gov. Reagan says the fact that the California Legal Rural Assistance asked RN's cousin to make public the fact that he is on welfare merely reinforces his opinion of the relief organization. Reagan insisted at a news conference yesterday that CRLA "doesn't serve the poor, it uses them."...

Mrs. Milhous said she was asked by a CRLA official, whom she did not identify, to make their plight known to newsmen. "The very fact that CRLA got a hold of those unfortunate people and persuaded them to make themselves available to the press was just reinforcement for my opinion of CRLA," said Reagan.

TRADE

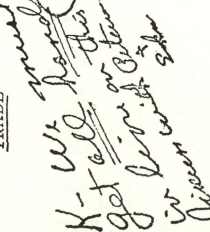

Secy Stans predicted a worsening in America's trade position in 1971 and called for expanded American trade with Russia and its European Allies. Stans said the U.S. now accounts for only 5/10 of East–West trade and could do better. "This is a market where American goods are needed and wanted, and one that we are ideally suited to satisfy," he said of the Soviet Union and Eastern European countries.

* * *

SPACE FUNDS

Former Interior Secy Udall and Milton Eisenhower said the Space program should be ended and the funds saved channeled into domestic social programs. Eisenhower said ending Space expenditures would free $3 billion for social programs.

* * * *

PLATE 15. A Presidential note on the news summary to Henry Kissinger: "K — we must get *all hands* in line on this. Discuss with Petersen and Ehrlichman." In the second instance, the instruction to Kissinger is merely a couple of exclamation marks.

Some say that the violent dissent is caused by the war in Vietnam.

1. It is about time we branded this line of thinking,

    this alibi for violence, for what it is -- pure nonsense.

    Those who carry a peace sign in one hand

    (1) There is no greater hypocrisy than a man carrying

    + there a limb or link with a smile

    a banner, that says "peace" in one hand, while hurling

    are the super hypocrite of our time

    a rock or a bomb with the other hand.

PLATE 16. In the reading copy of his Phoenix speech toward the end of the 1970 midterm campaign, President Nixon "punches up" a punch line.

On the evening of February 18, 1971, the President called me at home to say he enjoyed giving some remarks I had worked on at the Woodrow Wilson Center for scholars. About the "State of the World," Nixon asked, "Is there a lead in it? That's the one thing Henry doesn't understand." I said, "Maybe if you extended a hand to Red China—" and he cut me off sharply: "No—we have other fish to fry."

I had been more optimistic on SALT than Henry wished the President to be, and he changed "I have reason to believe that specific agreements will be reached this year to curb the arms race" to "I strongly hope" the agreements "can" be reached.

The President had in mind something more than a summary of a staff-prepared 60,000-word report. A speech differs from a "document." Something about the fact of the words passing Presidential lips gives it a different character. Nixon understood this and, without saying so, made clear that his purpose in speaking was not merely to call attention to the longer document: he wanted to use this occasion to show the connection between his Vietnam policy and his longer-range goals.

Saturday afternoon, February 20, I received a call at home from Bob Haldeman: "The TV speech is out, it's now for radio with clips for TV of the President delivering the radio speech. Give him a call at Camp David, he has a lot of changes."

The way you call a President is to dial 456-1414, identify yourself to the operator, and say, "The President, please." It is always a jolt when he comes right on the phone.

"I think you said the other day, Bill, that we should not oversell the foreign policy report since we don't have anything new to say. I agree. I want to do something for a thoughtful audience, not a massive TV audience. At night, if you go on television, you have to have a contest, or an announcement, or an event like the State of the Union. This would be right for radio. Get the figures on the best time, maybe when the commuters are driving home. All right, you have the speech draft in front of you? I've jotted down some ideas, let me give them to you."

Using his formal speech voice, he dictated: "What America does or does not do will ensure peace in the world. To end a war is easy, but to end it in a way that won't bring on another war is hard. If aggression is rewarded in South Vietnam, the danger of more aggression is ominously increased. If it fails, it is discouraged everywhere. We seek a peace in which both North Vietnam and South Vietnam would be freed of domination."

His voice changed its tone: "I have some more along those lines, but kick that around for a start. How's your day tomorrow?" I said I was available to join him at Camp David. "You sure you don't have family plans? Say so if you do." I felt like hollering, "I'll come, I'll come!" but held myself to a modest reassurance that I was not busy. He said, "See if you could make it up here about 11 A.M. I like to sleep late on Sundays."

Next morning, February 21, in a small office in Aspen cottage at Camp

David, the President talked in general terms about what he wanted to say: "To get out in a way that would vitiate the purpose of an effort that cost forty-five thousand American lives would be a great tragedy. It would gnaw at the conscience of the Nation for years to come. I'd like to say something in terms of looking back one day and saying, 'That was a fine hour for America,' but this is not the time to say that, it would send too many people up the wall.

"Our purpose," he wanted me to know, "only in a minuscule sense was saving South Vietnam. In its broadest sense, our purpose was to produce a better chance for peace in the Pacific and in the world."

In that sense, the President thought that the war was for a worthwhile purpose, despite the decade-long bungling of gradualism. At the same time, Nixon knew that it would be a mistake for him to take on the burden of that argument. "But I will never cast a speech as 'we're doing our best to slink out.' We are getting out in a way that saves Vietnam. Here's a line: 'Our purpose was not to conquer North Vietnam, but to give both North and South a right to live in peace without being dominated by the other.' "

He dictated a long passage, as he sometimes did with his writers, discussing alternative phrasing along the way. He was certain of how much time he wanted to devote to each of the parts of the world: "The length is about right for Africa, that's essentially a European area of influence, but I want to build up the section about Latin America. Now on the Mideast—go talk to Joe Sisco. Let's brag a little about the cease-fire. I know how Henry feels about this. He doesn't think it's going to work. He thinks we're selling out the Israelis, and let's face it, he's a little jealous that it's a State Department project."

I mentioned that a cease-fire might be helpful between the Rogers and Kissinger camps in the U. S. Government. "None of that comes from Bill or Henry, you know—they're both too big for that. It's that middle echelon trying to stir things up." I shrugged; if that was what he wanted me to think he thought, okay, but I could hear a furious Rogers once telling Henry, "I work for the President. I don't work for you." Nixon read my mind and added, "I know Henry plays the game hard, but Bill's been around a long time, he knows how to handle himself."

The President gave me careful instructions about how to navigate between State and the NSC in the clearance of the speech. He was most specific about who was to see what, and where copies of the speech were to be shown but not left behind—"I don't want this floating around channels."

Nixon added instructions on points in the speech. "I just don't like the stuff about 'partnership.' I know it's Henry's idea, but it's just not true. We're not partners, we have more freedom of action than that. Use the 'mutual respect' idea more. I want to see another draft on Wednesday. I'll work on it that afternoon and may give it that night from my EOB office."

He spent a lot of time on one line:

+ insured our withdrawal program

Just as last year's cutoff of supplies through Cambodia has
The purpose of
saved lives this year, this year's disruption of the Ho Chi Minh Trail *in Laos*
is to   + insure the contin... success of our
will save lives next year. *withdrawal program*

can't promise this

In the left margin, Kissinger had written: "We can't promise this"; his objection was met by the President's addition of "the purpose of."

In clearing a speech, a speechwriter is expected to protect his sources. He does not say to State "this line comes from Defense" and he resists saying to anyone, "This line the President wrote himself and underlined it," because that might inhibit criticism.

I took the new, fifth draft of the speech to Henry Kissinger, who hated it: "It is sure to offend every intellectual. A reference to 'winning the peace' is especially offensive," and "the part about aggression is pure Rusk."

I took it to Bill Rogers, who wondered if there was an unnecessary note in it about defending the basic purpose of the war. After all, he pointed out, we were getting out of Vietnam and had no need to explain why we got in originally.

In the Middle East portion, Rogers wrote in some language to show the Arabs we wanted to be friends with them too, and by telephone added a line of policy: "The U.S. is fully prepared to play a responsible and co-operative role in keeping the peace arrived at by negotiations between the parties."

I took it next to Secretary of Defense Melvin Laird, whom I did not know because I had not worked on the Cambodian-incursion speech. The President called me midafternoon on February 23 to say, "Take the defense portion of this over to Laird. Well, no, show him the whole thing, but don't leave it behind for the bureaucracy to go over."

About five-thirty, I waited in Laird's Pentagon anteroom with the speech under my arm. Al Haig reached me by telephone there; he said that Laird had called Kissinger to ask who this Safire was who was bringing him a speech. Henry had strongly objected to Haldeman about being bypassed, insisting that the speech be kept within NSC channels. Haldeman, knowing the President's wishes, shrugged it off and said maybe it would be a good idea next time to get Henry to call ahead to Laird.

The Defense Secretary had been through a grueling six-hour session before a Congressional committee and was feeling a little edgy. He said he would take the speech home with him and get it back to me in the morning. His suggestion was not unreasonable, but I had been directed otherwise by the President. I politely said no, that I would sit there with him while he went over it and then take it back with me.

"Then here," Laird said, "take it!" and threw it in my face. "How can I be expected to go over a speech line by line in a few minutes? I won't give it my approval that way!"

I picked the speech up off the floor and told the Defense Secretary he wasn't insulting me, he was insulting the President, which was okay with me but was that what he really wanted to do?

While Laird fumed, I handed him the speech back and he held on to it this time. "I went over the Cambodia speech for hours," he said. "I sent back detailed corrections. I cut out that part about COSVN, all that stuff that later got us into trouble. And what happened? Not a single suggestion of mine was taken—not one!"

I was tempted to reply that the White House staff was aware that he had made that very point to every columnist he could buttonhole—at a time when a united front was especially important—but my function was to get his okay on a speech and not to argue about past clearances. I also recalled a private assessment of Laird by Kissinger: "A devious man, but when cornered, a patriot." So I sat quietly while he read the speech.

He made a few minor changes and said, "I didn't know this was just a recap," by way of cooling off.

The next morning, Henry saw the President early, and word came to me that the next version had to have Henry's approval prior to submission to the President. Winston Lord rewrote my sixth draft, cutting out all the material the President had dictated. At that point, I had to show my cards. I said no, the President had added some portions himself and was entitled to see a draft with his own additions included. I would, however, put brackets around anything Henry objected to.

Since the President had asked to see me at eleven-thirty alone, Henry decided to go along with the bracketing procedure. As a skilled negotiator, he bracketed an entire passage and then double-bracketed lines within the passage he found especially objectionable—building a fallback position into the draft submission. I told Henry that the line he liked least also rubbed Bill Rogers the wrong way; he praised the good judgment of the Secretary of State, but I could tell that I had upset him in making mention of Rogers' review at all of sections other than the Middle East. Henry was concerned, he told me in a friendly way later, that State was creating an independent channel to the President through the speech-writing staff, and he was determined to counter any end runs.

The President looked at the bracketing on the sixth draft and smiled. He crossed out only the lines that were double-bracketed and left in the rest. "I understand his objections, and I'll go along part of the way. But there are some things I want to say."

The passage, as delivered, read:

> It matters very much how we end this war.
> To end a war is simple.

But to end a war in a way that will not bring on another war is far from simple.

In Southeast Asia today, aggression is failing—thanks to the determination of the South Vietnamese people and to the courage and sacrifice of America's fighting men.

That brings us to a point that we have been at several times before in this century: aggression turned back, a war ending.

We are at a critical moment in history: What America does—or fails to do—will determine whether peace and freedom can be won in the coming generation.

That is why the way in which we end this conflict is so crucial to our efforts to build a lasting peace in coming decades.

The right way out of Vietnam is crucial to our changing role in the world and to the peace in the world.

This passage was hardly the stuff of headlines; in retrospect, and in its modified form, it seems tame enough. But the idea of "rewarding aggression" was anathema to Nixon, and aggression was his definition of the central fact of Vietnam. Kissinger wanted to set the word aside as outmoded rhetoric unhelpful to progress; Nixon found it necessary to use to remind his supporters why we were there and to shore up their patience.

"Our going in was right," the President explained to me, "but the way we did it was wrong. Now the way we get out of it has to be right."

He called in Kissinger, who was on his way to a large press briefing on his lengthy document. We discussed the speech in general terms for a few moments, then Kissinger rose to go. The President said, "Tell the reporters you were late because you were working with me on the speech I'm making at eleven o'clock tomorrow morning on radio."

Henry promptly came back and sat down, to show that keeping reporters waiting was of no consequence compared to counseling the President, but that was not at all what the President had in mind: "No, no, Henry, go ahead—but be sure and tell 'em about my speech tomorrow."

The President said he would work over the speech a little while longer by himself, and as I was on the way out the door he wondered what I thought its impact would be.

"No news in it," I said. "Frankly, it's not going to set the world on fire."

"That's the whole object of our foreign policy," Nixon said, almost to himself, "not to set the world on fire."

2. SECRET NEGOTIATIONS, INSIDE AND OUT

Sitting in the warm sunshine on January 16, 1972, watching the Dallas Cowboys trounce the Miami Dolphins in the Super Bowl, I received a hard nudge from David Mahoney, an old friend with whom I had flown down to New Orleans to see the game. Assuming he wanted some peanuts, I passed over my bag, but Mahoney was pointing at a stadium public address speaker. The announcer was telling me to call my office.

That had never happened to me before and made me feel like a big shot or a doctor. When I called the White House, Bob Haldeman's aide, Larry Higby, came on and said furtively: "This has to be absolutely top secret, but get back here fast."

If it was so secret, I asked, why did he have me paged in a stadium packed with eighty thousand fans? When the well-mannered Higby goofed, he readily admitted it. "Worse than that," he said, "the public-address sound was picked up on television and carried to sixty million fans watching the game at home." We agreed that nobody would suspect I was being called back for a secret assignment because not even the Presidential staff of a banana republic would bumble like that.

When I returned to Washington, the smile was wiped off my face with an imposing-looking memo. Here is the first page, which can be published without blushing because the subject is not secret anymore:

TOP SECRET/SENSITIVE/EXCLUSIVELY EYES ONLY

Sunday—January 16, 1972

MEMORANDUM FOR BILL SAFIRE

FROM   THE PRESIDENT

After reading the proposed text of a Presidential TV Speech on Negotiation—which has been prepared by Henry's staff—I want you to read the memorandum that I am now dictating and then prepare the first draft of a television speech to be made on Tuesday, the 25th of January.

What I will dictate will be very sketchy. On the other hand, it will give you the general impression of what I am trying to get across and the structure of the speech.

The length is critical—2400 words, or in other words a maximum of twenty minutes is as much as I can possibly have. The Kissinger draft is around 3400 words as I recall. As you can tell from reading it, it has all the substance in it but there is too much turgid prose and too much complex discussion of eight points, seven points, nine points, etc., without getting to the heart of the matter that people are interested in—what we offered, what they turned down and what the hopes are for a negotiated settlement now.

The tone of the President's memo-draft was that of a man who had conceded as much at the negotiating table as he honorably could, and having been rejected, deserved the sympathy and understanding of his compatriots. On the last page of his memo-draft, this note appears in the use of "the extra mile":

TOP SECRET/SENSITIVE/EXCLUSIVELY EYES ONLY

a settlement which is fair to North Vietnam, to the people of South Vietnam and, above all, it deserves the united support of the American people.

This has been a long and agonizing struggle for our people but it is difficult to see how anyone, regardless of his position on the war, could now say that we have not gone the extra mile in offering a negotiated settlement which is fair to everybody concerned.

> (The conclusion, of course, is important and will be difficult to bring off—I would like for you to try your hand at it—after you read the entire record you may get some ideas that could fit it).

I did try my hand at it, and he used the theme in the paragraph before the ending, putting it in his own words:

Some of our citizens have become accustomed to thinking that whatever our government says must be false, and whatever our enemies say must be true, as far as this war is concerned. Well, the record I have revealed tonight proves the contrary. We can now demonstrate publicly what we have long been demonstrating privately—that America has taken the initiative not only to end our participation in this war, but to end the war itself for all concerned."

In the President's memo-draft, Nixon outlined the speech he wanted to give about the failure of the secret negotiations in Paris, spelling out many of the efforts that had been made in private negotiations and making public an offer to withdraw all U.S. troops six months from the signing of an agreement and a cease-fire.

This was a speech with tragic overtones. Fifteen months before, returning from his European trip, he had made an offer that the editorial writers were then calling for, of a "standstill cease-fire," which was meaningless grandstanding. Nixon knew it had little chance of acceptance but publicly made the gesture just before the midterm elections to show the American public which side was prepared to "stop the killing" right away. Now, however, the President was admitting that his fondest hopes for a secret peace deal had been dashed—that the frequent missions to Paris by Henry Kissinger had gone for nought. By bringing into the open the offer he had made in secret, Nixon answered the doves at home who were berating him for not having made the offer of a date certain for U.S. withdrawal in return for a cease-fire and a POW exchange. By getting out of that squeeze, he hoped to put a world-opinion squeeze on the North Vietnamese to break the impasse.

A substantive matter bothered all of us as the speech went through its drafts. The President was making public an offer he had previously made privately; it had been ignored, but not rejected; and, as Kissinger put it, "the North Vietnamese never leave a proposal on the table if they mean to throw it off. They complete the record brutally." The carrot of a fixed withdrawal date had not been nibbled at, and we wondered, would it help or harm the proposal to accompany it with a threat of increased air strikes?

Nixon wrote it in to see how it would sound:

> 1. If the enemy rejects our offer to negotiate, we shall continue our program of ending American involvement in the war by withdrawing our remaining forces as the South Vietnamese develop the capability of defending themselves.
>
> 2. If the enemy's answer to our peace offer is to step up our attacks, I shall meet my responsibilities as commander in chief of our armed forces to protect our remaining troops by ordering air strikes against the enemy's military installations in Laos, Cambodia, South Vietnam and North Vietnam. We do not prefer this course of action.

(Plate 8, following page 200, shows this in Nixon's own hand.)

Both Henry Kissinger and Bill Rogers counseled strongly against such a specific threat; instead, the paragraph was ended at "our remaining troops." When the speech was still in early draft form and a week away from delivery, I asked Kissinger why he had not wanted strong language if that was the President's intent. "The purpose of the speech is not only to show that we responded to their proposals privately," said Henry, "which they have been saying publicly we have not. The purpose is to give decent people a chance to come over to our side. We will be hit with a military offensive from the North in March or April, and it pays for us to be very conciliatory early. If we have to counterattack, then we'll be attacking a truculent enemy who chose to make war and not peace."

Weren't we betraying a diplomatic trust by telling the story of the secret negotiations? "Look, we kept it secret as long as the secret channel was in tandem with the public channel," Henry stated. "They gave us a nine-point secret proposal a week before they made their seven-point proposal; we asked which they wanted us to respond to, and they said the nine-point secret one. Even so, we responded to both." Kissinger was especially bitter about the way Hanoi had manipulated U.S. politicians who had taken the enemy's word that we had not responded. "For the first time, they've used the secret talks to create confusion, and we cannot permit that."

Working on the speech, it was not hard to see that several other negotiations were going on—triangular diplomacy—between the principals on the American side. The President had told me that all typing of this top-secret speech was to be done only by Rose Mary Woods; this was ostensibly to keep as small as possible the circle of those in the know of the revelation of the secret talks, but actually to keep an open channel between the President and his writer. Whatever Rose typed, she would ordinarily give the President directly, without going through Henry. In this way, the President could also cut in Secretary of State Rogers, who would then be contributing in tandem with the National Security Adviser rather than trying to force suggestions through him.

This was not a case of keeping the Secretary of State happy—the suggestions Rogers made were well-taken. We had been having trouble with calling the fixed-date withdrawal proposal "new," since it had previously been made secretly. Rogers put "made public" in the lead (which seems obvious enough now, but had us all breaking our heads at the time). Rogers also pointed out the first question to be raised by the proposal: did "all our forces" include air and sea as well? (It did not.) What irked Rogers most was a phrase that had been put in by Kissinger or his aide, Winston Lord: "On his way back from Peking, Dr. Kissinger—" Rogers said, "That's pretty strong linkage. If I were the Chinese, I'd get mad as hell." He was referring to a possibility that the President would be interpreted as saying the Chinese had been helpful in the secret talks, which was a point Henry agreed to, and the phrase was cut. Perhaps Bill was also concerned that there were too many references to the ubiquitous Dr. Kissinger in the speech.

The President thought so too. That was one reason why he specified that the NSC draft be cast aside completely, to be replaced by my extension of the draft he dictated to Rose. What Nixon termed the "turgid prose" was a good excuse; Henry was never insulted by that but reveled in it as evidence that he was scholarly and not demagogic. The President, with a good news sense, was aware that the feature story of Henry's series of clandestine meetings with Le Duc Tho would overshadow the news story of the niceties of who offered what and when. Nixon put it accurately in a phone call to me on January 17: "There's good cops and robbers stuff here." In the NSC draft the President wrote across the top: "I have marked passages which may be worth considering for inclusion in the final draft,"

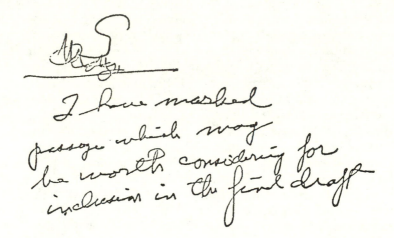

and alongside one paragraph "OK—but not too shrill" and changed "We" to "I" in several places, since he was the President and in charge. He occasionally made certain the draft reflected the fact that Kissinger worked for him. Wherever "I asked Dr. Kissinger" appeared, Nixon changed it to "I directed." Kissinger had overstepped a little; the President, with regard as much to the sensitivities of his Secretary of State as his own, by the simple bureaucratic technique of temporarily imposing a writer on the speech, put Henry down a little.

Exactly a year before, the President had been annoyed by a story by Terence Smith in the New York *Times*, first of a seven-part series about foreign policy, which headlined on the front page: "Decision Power Ebbing at the State Department." If any newspaper was very important in diplomatic circles, it was the *Times*, and the story stung Rogers. It certainly appeared to be a Kissinger-inspired piece, but for the fact that the writer was then the regular State Department man for the *Times* whose regular contacts were not at the White House. The lead was devastating: "The Department of State, once the proud and undisputed steward of foreign policy, has finally acknowledged what others have long been saying: that it is no longer in charge of the United States' foreign affairs and that it cannot reasonably expect to be so again."

Haldeman called me to say that the President was thinking of issuing a statement refuting the *Times* story, which was causing dismay at State. I said the flap did not seem worthy of a Presidential statement, and that Ziegler should handle it at the next day's press briefing. Haldeman said the President would probably go along with that, but that I should prepare some guidance for Ziegler.

I called Henry, who knew that something was afoot to rebut the *Times* piece; however, instead of being sheepish about one of his staff putting a torpedo into his rival on the front page of the *Times*, he was furious at what he regarded as a State Department plot to get him. According to Kissinger, who was convinced the source was not an NSC staffer, the whole thing was a State plant to force the President to support Rogers and undercut Kissinger. Henry knew I was working on the response and demanded to see me right away. That sounded like fireworks, so I trotted across the street to the West Wing.

"If Rogers doesn't knuckle under, I go!" That was the trumpet call that greeted me as I stepped across the Kissinger threshold. Al Haig motioned me in and closed the door. I always got a kick out of Henry in tantrum, and he knew it; I said that his pronouncement was pretty melodramatic, and did he have any more lines like that from Grade B movies?

He started to cool off, then decided against it. "You and Haldeman don't think I'm serious about this, but I mean it! I like this job, I am equipped for it, but I cannot stay under these circumstances."

Henry picked up the *Times*, looked at the offending front page, and dropped it back on the table. "I called Terence Smith in here and showed him how everything in his article was wrong—he said he got it from a senior official at State. Not from here, from State. This Ostpolitik thing goes beyond one man's vanity."

He was referring to the American attitude toward West Germany's policy of improving its relations with East Germany. The Timesman had written: "The official United States view, as outlined repeatedly in public by Mr. Rogers, is unqualified endorsement. But Mr. Kissinger and other members of the White House staff recently undercut that by disclosing personal reservations . . . the result was a furor in Bonn. The West German Government dispatched a high-level emissary to Washington to find out which view accurately reflected the American position. Significantly, the envoy went to the White House for his answer and emerged declaring himself satisfied that all was in order."

Henry spelled it out from his viewpoint. "Our Minister in Bonn—not the Ambassador, our man, but the State Department Minister—told an Assistant Secretary of State of West Germany that I was poisoning the President's mind about Ostpolitik. So the Germans sent a man here to talk to me. He showed me the report from the German official who talked to our Minister—do you read German?—here's the salient paragraph—" (As he started to translate, I looked over his shoulder at the document, and he was careful to translate accurately. Henry has always believed I read German, which I do not, because of a crack I made once about his *Weltanschauung*.) "—'Kissinger is taking a hard line for these reasons'—

and then it lists all the reasons—'and State Department recommends that Brandt come over to Washington quickly to set the President straight.' The last line is great: 'Kissinger won't come over to Germany because he will not leave the President's side for one day for fear he will lose his influence.'" Henry hit the page with his fist.

"Can you imagine that? That's what somebody in *our* State Department is telling somebody in a *foreign country* about the President's national security adviser!" I could see why he was angry. "That isn't all," he said, and went into a similar Middle Eastern situation that I will not recount. "For Crissake!" he cried, "we stopped the war in Jordan because of what a few hard, tough men did right here—and State was out of it." Kissinger went into detail on another instance of suspected duplicity, then: "Last week, the Secretary of State fired off a cable to Egypt without sending a copy to the President as a courtesy—not for clearance, mind you, not even as a courtesy."

Kissinger's voice broke a couple of times as he paced and talked, he was so worked up. Haig, standing in the corner, kept nodding in agreement or sympathy. "So," Henry concluded, addressing me as if I were a writer representing an alien power, "if you do anything that supports State at my expense, I've had it. I'm fed up with this sort of stuff. They're trying to get the President to undercut me, and I will not stand for it." He sat down.

"You feel better now?" I asked. "No!" Henry pronounced, bounding up again—this was good for him, getting it off his chest—"Look what they tried to do with the Cuban submarines. After the Russian tender was on its way back home, State gives a backgrounder to Max Frankel at the *Times* that said I overemphasized the crisis, that no senior official recognized it as such. Can you imagine what the Russians said to the guy who recommended they pull it back? 'You dumb cluck—you see, we never had to.' And then after it was all over, somebody in State turns around and claims in *Newsweek* they were the ones who did it after all." Henry's ire was running down. "At least that wasn't dangerous," he murmured, "—just sick."

I suggested that there always had to be tension between the State Department and the NSC—it was in the nature of the balance of powers within the Executive Branch, between elected leaders and ongoing bureaucracy—and, without being argumentative, ticked off several items supplied to me by Bill Rogers where Henry had unnecessarily slammed him up against the wall.

In one case, Henry had sent a letter to the Japanese Ambassador, concluding with "if you have any further questions, communicate with me directly"—an obvious attempt to circumvent the Secretary of State, who traditionally dealt with foreign embassies. Another item that irritated Rogers was the turndown of a request from State that the President see the Ambassador of Chile, followed by Kissinger telling the Ambassador, "Why didn't you come to see me in the first place?" Kissinger promptly arranged an appointment to see Nixon. (When I suggested to Rogers that his own staff was the source of a lot of the friction, the Secretary of State replied: "You tell me I should cool down my own staff here. I've tried. Personally, I've never said a word about what I've told you here to any reporter. But the staff sees what goes on, they read letters like this one before I do. How do you think they feel? And who can stop them from passing it on?")

Kissinger nodded, not in agreement but as if I had proven that I had been primed by his enemies to stick a knife in his back.

"Remember, Bill," he said slowly, not in anger anymore but with some deliberation, "—and I want you to know that I consider you a friend—if the President's reaction to this story undercuts me, I've had it. I had nothing to do with this *Times* story, nor did any of my people talk to Terence Smith. This is just State's way of getting the President to come out and say the Secretary of State is the principal adviser on foreign policy."

I told him, in seriousness, to watch out for rigid, so-called "moral stands," which made compromise impossible, and would serve the President badly. Back in my office, I wrote a guideline for Ron Ziegler, stressing that the thrust of the story came from a thorough self-critique by the State Department, which is not a sign of weakness but of strength, and suggesting he not get into a defense of the power of State in particular, but to mumble that "the President feels he has a strong Cabinet, including a strong State Department . . ." which is about what he did. Neither State nor Kissinger was pleased completely with that, nor was the press, so it seemed to be the right course.

In any event, this 1971 contretemps has been presented here in all its bombastic triviality to show that life was not bloodless and gray near the foreign-policy center of the Nixon Administration; that petty jealousies can affect men who are far from petty in the most serious undertakings; and that Richard Nixon had his hands full in handling the men who handled foreign affairs, staying above it but staying with it.

Late that afternoon of January 18, 1972, the President went over a draft with me in his EOB office. When he had finished writing in some changes, he felt like talking about the relationship between two men he liked: Rogers, a lifelong friend and trusted ally, with whom he was comfortable, and Kissinger, a strategic thinker snatched from the Rockefeller orbit, with whom he felt well served. The President also felt that it was important his writers never take sides in bureaucratic tuggings-and-haulings; we were his personal extensions in expressing himself, and could weave in and out as neutrals in his behalf between other, more important appointees. This was an accustomed and interesting role; he had used me before between George Shultz and Arthur Burns on economic policy. In these instances, top appointees know exactly how the President is using the lesser aides, and accept the middlemen's temporary importance because they know writers are no challenge to their continuing authority. But Henry would occasionally resist this, and sometimes win: "No end runs" was a phrase he had picked up from Haldeman.

The President got to talking about the battles on his staff. "I was reading about Disraeli and Melbourne last night"—he often said that—"God, did they have fights in their cabinets. I'm sorry about how Henry and Bill go at each other. It's really deep-seated. Henry thinks Bill isn't very deep, and Bill thinks Henry is power-crazy."

I said that wasn't the half of it—each thought the other was an egomaniac.

"And in a sense," the President responded cheerfully, "they're both right. Ego is something we all have, and either you grow out of it or it takes you over. I've grown out of it.

"It's really a compensation for an inferiority complex. Henry has that, of course—and Bill has it too in this area, because this isn't his original field, and he knows Henry knows more than he does about foreign policy.

"It's a pity, really. I have an affection for them both. I could always get along with anybody—Stassen, whoever, no matter what I thought of them. Not these two.

"Well," he said, walking me to the door, "you work your own smooth way between them. Tell Henry all the stuff he had in his draft is perfect for him to use in his on-the-record backgrounder afterward. Show this draft to Bill on Thursday; tell Henry you're going to sell it to him. Bill won't like even mentioning Henry in the speech but, what the hell, it's down to the minimum. Bill's a good tactician, not a strategist. He would have caved in on Cambodia and the riots, but afterward he was a good soldier." (I left to work my smooth way, but first went to a typewriter and wrote down the above. The meeting was tape-recorded, I imagine; some parts of the conversation I have still left out, but when this account is compared with the tape someday, it will hold up.)

Thirty-six hours later, I sent in another draft with this cover memo, flashing its importance across the top as if in neon:

TOP SECRET/SENSITIVE/EXCLUSIVELY EYES ONLY

January 20, 1972

MEMORANDUM FOR THE PRESIDENT

RE: TUESDAY SPEECH

FROM: BILL SAFIRE

This fourth draft is considerably cleaner than the version you looked at yesterday.

It reflects the changes Bill Rogers suggested this morning; those changes and my own have been approved by Henry.

It cuts down on the detail of some of the earlier meetings, and focuses more on the October proposal.

On tone, I think it is important that the message
not be "we flopped on the secret talks, but you have to give us
credit for trying," but "public disclosure at this point is needed
to put the pressure on the North Vietnamese to negotiate our
very good deal."

A copy of this has been sent to President Thieu
tonight (Thursday).

I'll be in touch with the switchboard all weekend.

Over the weekend, I received President Thieu's changes through Winston Lord at the NSC. The South Vietnamese leader suggested that the
President call the Viet Cong by their preferred name, the National Liberation Front (shades of Nixon and the "People's Republic" of China), and
added "with the full knowledge and approval of President Thieu" to the
beginning. John Connally was also consulted, and had a political jab to
add. Referring to Nixon's inherited war, he wrote: "the only thing that
had been settled in Paris was the shape of the conference table."

Henry wanted to send a signal to Le Duc Tho that would ameliorate
the unilateral revelation of the secret talks. In went a paragraph reiterating
a private proposal made in May 1971 that we stood ready to settle only
military issues and leave political matters to the Vietnamese alone. In addition, President Nixon advanced an idea that was accepted in Saigon
more quickly than he anticipated: for Thieu to offer to resign one month
before elections. Thieu was sufficiently confident of victory—or of a North
Vietnamese rejection of the whole plan—to agree, and Nixon delightedly
added it to his speech as evidence of reasonableness. "Now we're moving
beyond our offer," the President told me, "this puts the heat on them."
Then he cautioned: "Always use the term 'overthrow.' The North Vietnamese condition is that we 'overthrow' the Government of South Vietnam. And that we'll never do."

Having engineered a good agreement with Thieu, Kissinger turned once
again to the bureaucratic warfare going on in and around the White
House. As an answer to the President's display of pique, which he construed as a personal rebuke, and as a signal to Rogers to stop acting like
a Secretary of State, Henry took firm command of the speech. On January
24, I had sent a fifth draft over to Rose. The President told me he would
send it back in an hour so I could take it to Rogers. But a couple of hours
later I received a call from Henry. He had been with the President and reviewed the changes. Several lines that seemed to me fairly important were
out because "they would not translate well," and there would be no need
for me to show the final draft to the Secretary of State. "Isn't that for the
President to decide, Henry? I've already told Bill I'd be over there with it."
"I'm telling you what the President said," said Henry. I asked if I could
have a final copy to check for errors. He said no, he would do the checking.
I called Rogers and said most of his changes had been included and there

wasn't really any need for me to run over there on a cold day, was there? He got the message.

I wished then I had suggested to Ziegler a year before that he undertake a more forceful defense of the State Department, since Henry respected and would have responded well to the application of power, but it was too late, and I supposed the President knew what he was doing.

3. CHINA REPORT

"It's marvelous to have something to congratulate you for," future Commerce Secretary Peter Peterson said to Henry Kissinger when he returned from his secret trip to Peking, "other than your presumed sexual experiences." Henry put on a Groucho Marx leer: "Ah, but I'm a believer in the linkage theory."

Briefing his colleagues at that time—when the President was in the midst of a fury against the press for its publication of the Pentagon Papers, its timing, he thought, calculated to help pass the end-the-war amendments and threatening the secrecy vital to the China initiative—Kissinger had cautioned us against saying anything that might admit to linkage. "We should just shut up. Nothing will impress the Chinese more than quiet. The more we drop hints, the more we seem like sophomores. A lot of forces are at work; this could be a diplomatic revolution but it could be killed by talk. It took two and a half years to nurture it to this point, so let's not blow it by being clever."

Henry had set the complexity of the problem with this analogy: "Any argument we hear from Taiwan, they'll get from North Vietnam. Any argument we get from Japan, they'll get infinitely more from the Soviet Union. When we think of our right-wing reaction, think of their left-wing reaction."

Dr. Kissinger permitted a hushed, mystical quality to come into his voice when he spoke of the China trip: "This is not like dealing with the Russians, who'll fight you for a dime and lose a million in good will in the process. In this encounter, we're playing the big game, both of us are, and they need a strong American President for their game. The idea that they might have held out the invitation in order to cancel it is wrong, they have already paid the price by inviting us. They don't regain their virginity by canceling it."

All the Chinese leaders were in their seventies, all had gone through the mystical experience of a thirty-year revolution, and all would probably go at once—that was why this was the time to move. If this opportunity were missed, it might not soon return. While fundamental forces of history would ultimately prevail, the governments were of mortal men who could be replaced by other men, not so inclined to cap their careers with an opening to the West, or not so powerful as to be able to overcome internal opposition.

Just as the negotiations with the Soviet Union were timed to a moment of relative equality in power, and could not be unduly delayed, the opening to mainland China was timed to a moment of coinciding interests with old men in power. And the opportunity increased in geometric progression for the United States because it could deal with both "moments" at the same moment, and, as Henry Kissinger put it, "when dealing with two opponents, don't only deal with the stronger one."

I can write about President Nixon's journey to Peking with all the inside knowledge of somebody who didn't get to go on the trip, so I won't try to give a secondhand account of the days and nights in China. Read Pat Buchanan's book someday. Here, instead, are my minutes of the President's report to the Cabinet on his return, February 29, 1972—tired, happy, exhilarated, proud. See Plate 20, following page 488.

He began by distributing souvenirs, gifts he brought back for each of the Cabinet members: a studded box with a quilted interior (smelling of moth balls, I thought) and a covered teacup and saucer, filled with a strong Chinese tea. "Now you can say you drank from the cup Mao Tse-tung and Chou En-lai drank from." When somebody said he had been making a lot of news lately, the President smiled and nodded, "News is something that has mystery, and that's what this trip had."

He leaned forward and began to report to his Cabinet members about the trip he had been dreaming of for so many years. I wrote most of it down, sitting near Ehrlichman against the wall—he was doodling as he listened—and while the secretly recorded tapes will ultimately be the official record, these raw notes will be helpful in the meanwhile.

"Chou said to me, 'Our meeting will shake the world.'" The President began, "I said that it would change the world.

"I will talk in general terms this morning and then leave it to Bill and Henry to be more specific. I understand that none of the Cabinet could hear my speech last night because of the PA system. Read it; it's worthwhile.

"One point to be recognized is the naïve assumption, particularly among Americans, that problems evaporate when nations get to know one another. That's nonsense. The idea that either of us is going to be affected by mere personal visits is just baloney.

"It helps to be polite and to have communication. I don't believe in hot rhetoric. But we are not going to have instant peace. We have set up a process where common ground can gradually be expanded.

"Mao is an old"—the President checked himself—"Mao is approaching eighty. In terms of mental equipment, he is quick, earthy; he is one who does not get into tactics but who sees strategic concepts with great vision —a vision of course totally different from ours.

"Now let me tell you about Chou En-lai. We had twenty hours head-to-head. They don't conduct meetings as we do. With them, and this is true of Mao too, just the principals talk. Neither Henry nor his counterpart participated—99 per cent of the talking was Chou and myself. Chou has the vitality and mental vigor of a man of forty. He works eighteen hours a day, and he is as good at the end of a conversation as at the beginning. His mind moves quickly, and he never shows mental fatigue. I have met all the world leaders of this generation at their peak, except Churchill—Adenauer, De Gaulle, all of them. And there is no leader I have met who exceeds Chou En-lai's ability to conduct a conversation at the highest level.

"We both sat across the table without notes," Nixon continued to a rapt Cabinet. "He didn't read anything to me nor I to him. He had done his homework, as had Mao, about me—and of course I knew him. He had a remarkable knowledge, considering their closed society, as to what is going on in our society and in the rest of the world. And rather than seeing everything through Marxist eyeglasses, he has an objective historical perspective.

"This was an experience which perhaps will not be exceeded in my lifetime.

"You would think that he would be nit-picking on words in the communiqué. We did discuss this issue, that issue, but he began by looking at the whole world—he reasons from the general to the specific. That I liked, because I tend to do the same. Seeing the great forces first, you have a better understanding of the specifics.

"There was plenty of tough and straight talk. Tough, but elegant and courteous in terms of tone on both sides. But if in our private conversations we can discuss these great differences in a civilized tone—there is a chance you can find that glimmer of a hope of common ground.

"Chou is a totally dedicated Communist, believes deeply in his system, and he never for a moment let me forget that. I was a totally dedicated believer in the free enterprise system, and I never let him forget that. But we didn't let this distract us, or give a belligerent note to our communication.

"Another characteristic of his that is similar to mine: Whenever he said anything particularly tough, he became much cooler. When it was really down to extremely controversial issues, both of us spoke in a way that the interpreter couldn't quite hear. Of course, talking loudly tends to make you much less impressive.

"Most important, and the unsophisticated people in the press missed this, there is a new relationship now between the People's Republic and the U.S. We have renounced the threat of force and the use of force against each other as well as other nations; we agree that neither nation should dominate Asia. This they recognize as the heart of the communiqué. The other issues are all part of the mosaic but a new relationship has come about at this time—and nobody knows how long it will last—thanks to the fact that we have resolved not to settle our differences by war.

"A word about the future: The tendency will be, on our side, for us to pick up everything on the Peking radio that criticizes the U.S., and on their side to pick up every statement by a Senator or whoever here criticizing them. And then to say—'that ends the relationship.'

"Of course, at the UN there will be differences. But we must not assume these continued differences mean there will be a change in the new relationship. Part of the communiqué says that the differences will continue. The question is: Whether we shall live with them or whether we will die for them.

"One thing that characterized the meetings was this: I treated them with dignity and they treated me with dignity. Riding to the airport with their most hard-line military leader, age fifty-four, we passed a beautiful children's park. He said that twenty-five years ago that was a golf course, and a sign outside had said, 'No Chinese Allowed.' The great sin, far greater than commercial exploitation or military domination, was the affront to their dignity—treating them as inferiors.

"I say thank God we believe in our own system, especially after seeing their regimentation, but don't make the mistake of underestimating them. Whatever the failures of their system, there is in their leader class a spirit that makes them formidable either as adversaries or—not friends—as people with whom we have some understanding.

"Among the young there is a dedication to their system that is something to reckon with. There is a temptation just to say that because it takes the spirit out of people there is nothing for us to be concerned about.

"But they know what they want, they are determined to get it, and they are going all out for it.

"What we in America need is a sense of destiny," Nixon ruminated aloud. "The leader class in the U.S. sometimes lacks the backbone, the strength, that they have. History tells us that as nations become better educated they tend to soften. Now if they came here, they would be popeyed, as Khrushchev was. But as we look at the Soviet Union on the one side and China on the other—even though their systems are ones that we could never agree with, we must reckon with them in order to build a peaceful world.

"I put it best at the toast: 'What brings us together here? Not our common beliefs but our common interests.' Because these interests are there, we are together finding those areas that will serve our interests. But let us not think that those years of not being in communication, of not knowing each other, have now changed and that now we know each other, we can all get along. It goes deeper than that.

"I am confident that the chances for peace in the Pacific are better now than they were ten days ago."

If only Nixon's presentation to his Cabinet had been telecast, live, without him knowing it. The men in the room, old pros, most of them, were moved; the man at the middle of the table, flanked by the Secretaries of State and Defense, had just shown himself to be the kind of person one would hope to see as President of the United States. He turned to his right and said to Secretary Rogers, "Bill, how did you see it?"

Rogers had been humiliated on the trip to China; Kissinger had been invited to accompany the President to the meeting with Mao, not the Secretary of State, and it had hurt his pride, but he did not let any of this show in his talk to his fellow Cabinet members:

"I agree that the spirit of their leadership is such that we must revise our own spirit of leadership. One of the advantages of the trip will be to revive interest in our own system. They built that Great Hall of the People in ten months, and their discipline is unbelievable—when it snowed thousands of people turned out to clear the streets. But I don't think any American could visit there and not say, 'I'm lucky to be an American.'"

"The President gave us all flags to wear in our lapels," Rogers said. "In changing suits during the first couple of days I kind of forgot off and on, but after a few days—and not for any silly patriotic reason—I found myself wanting to put it on."

"They wore their Mao buttons," Nixon interjected, "so I thought we should wear the flag." He did not add that he always wore his everywhere.

Rogers continued: "A girl came up to Chou En-lai and handed him the galleys of the next day's newspapers, and there he was—rearranging the front page."

The President nodded, muttering, "I'd like to rearrange a front page now and then."

Rogers: "One day Chou appeared in my suite and started talking, with no fanfare. In my discussions with their Foreign Minister he wouldn't answer one question."

The President: "They only answer at the top—well, Gromyko could answer, but that's an exception."

Rogers: "They don't ask questions unless somebody tells them to."

The President: "When you took issue with them, they were not contentious—as distinguished from the Russians who come back sharply at you."

Rogers: "I would say the response from the international community has been very good with minor exceptions. Mrs. Nixon was great. All of us can take great pride in the visit."

The President: "Right now Bill and Henry and I ought to be in bed. If we are inarticulate, it's because we are talking in our sleep."

Kissinger: "I can talk inarticulately even when I am wide awake."

Rogers Morton: "But then it's deliberate."

The President signaled to Henry Kissinger to give his impressions. "There are three levels on which our trip will be judged," Kissinger said. "First, the newspaper reports—who won and who lost. Second, what does it do to the basic direction of U.S.-China policy. Third, what will the impact be of these two societies on the other.

"The contrast," Kissinger continued, "is this: We have dealt with the sluggish bureaucratic types of Eastern Europe—the second generation of revolutionaries. We have not dealt before with"—I will delete a few characterizations—"who are the first generation. These are the men of the Long March who could have no rational expectation of survival at that time but who were motivated by an almost religious conviction. They live in the future. We judge by different standards. We talk compromise; they talk principles; we exalt stability; they believe in struggle.

"To use a Biblical metaphor, 'In the beginning was the word.' For them the very fact of a joint communiqué is a startling event. We look at a communiqué as a legal document and with our infinite capacity for masochism pick out what is wrong in it. You hear some criticism today about how they published this outrageous position and we came back so mildly. Remember, this was published in every paper in every province in China. It would be foolish to engage in a slugging match.

"We shouldn't judge their rhetoric always by how it sounds." Henry cautioned, "Comparatively speaking, their own rhetoric has never been so mild.

"We are asked why we didn't affirm our commitment to Taiwan. An equally pertinent question would be why they did not denounce our commitment to Taiwan?" Henry appeared to be pressing here, on the defensive; maybe he had been shaken in the previous meeting with Congressional leaders.

"To put it in the document would have been too much. They let us go beyond the document in our press conference in Shanghai.

"There have been some substantial achievements—cultural and other exchanges, formalization of diplomatic contacts. Don't forget that ten months ago a long-haired ping-pong player meeting with Chou was big news.

"What will we do as a result of this communiqué that we do not do already? Terminating forces in Taiwan—we say we will do all that in the Nixon Doctrine. But the communiqué itself is not the important thing. The important thing is that we have begun to regulate our relationship.

"This dialogue could not have occurred at any lower level. Let me point out where the President scored his most notable success. Usually the idea in diplomatic discussions is to accentuate the positive, but the President began by saying, 'You have no reason to trust me because you don't know me.' That is not the usually recommended form. Then the President went into why we are staying in the Pacific rather than getting out."

Staring down at the table, hands folded, Kissinger tried to lift the meeting back up to where the President had left it.

"These are not trivial people. They have imposed on their society a tremendous wrench. They may be more worried about Soviet troops on their northern border than they are about U.S. troops in Japan. But they will be saying, 'All troops must get out.' A test of our maturity will be to recognize the difference in our position, despite their need not to differentiate in rhetoric.

"When you look at them, they are not well off. But they will challenge us in a moral way very powerfully. They have a sense of purpose and of direction. The President has set a major new direction. When the words of this communiqué are forgotten"—he still seemed to feel guilty about it—"this visit will be remembered. Just as they looked at the President to see if he knew where he was going—and we passed that test—now they will look at our society to see what they can get out of it.

"What flowed through this new channel exceeded my expectations."

The President took over again. "Their evaluation of us will be in two areas. Wealth will not impress; power will. Even more important is a sense of purpose. They look at our society and see our emphasis on material things as a weakness. What they look for is strength of character. As their willingness to sacrifice shows, they have this.

"We must show them," Nixon continued, "they are dealing with a nation that has the strength and the character to be a responsible power. That's why, when they say, 'Get out of the Pacific, take all your forces home'—and they will continue to say that—for the U.S. to fail to meet its responsibility would lead inevitably to their figuring that we don't have the strength. It would lower their respect and remove any chance for their affection.

"They speak very buoyantly of our revolution, of what we have accomplished. But they wonder if after two hundred years we have come too far from the soil and lost the guts and the steel that make a nation great. If we are responsible, they will respect us. If not—we just ain't going to matter."

HUD's George Romney said he was glad the Chinese met somebody who gave them the right idea about the United States; Transportation's John Volpe allowed as how the trip helped the New Hampshire primary; Defense's Mel Laird meticulously pointed out how we must interpret the communiqué in terms of the foreign policy report of 1971–72—all part of the Nixon Doctrine.

The President: "While it is true they will continue to say 'get out' of Vietnam, and while some will say our relations would be better with the People's Republic of China if we did get out, the opposite would be true."

Bill Rogers had a point to make that appeared to contradict Kissinger on the moral challenge. "I don't think that their kind of discipline will be successful in the long run. I don't care what kind of religious fervor motivates the leadership. I think the genius of the Chinese people that you see in Singapore and all over the world goes deeper than that."

The President didn't take sides. "But the most naïve comment," he said, "was Eric Sevareid's that there was more freedom in Moscow. I have been there and there is no more freedom in Moscow than in Peking. When I talked to Khrushchev, if anyone had said then that the Russians would be ahead of the U.S. in ICBMs, I would have said they were crazy. But when they concentrate they can be a hell of a military force."

The difference of opinion seemed to be about the Chinese sense of purpose and what it would lead to. Kissinger spoke of a powerful Communist sense of purpose; Rogers held that this was a superficial regimentation of a more fundamental traditional national trait; Nixon pointed to the power that regimentation could command. Those are three different slants that would be fascinating to explore, but the question was not pursued.

Pete Peterson, the new Secretary of Commerce, asked, "Why were they interested in meeting us?"

"Cold-blooded interest," the President replied. "I don't agree with Malraux, who thought they wanted aid. They look around and see themselves encircled. They need someone who is not antagonistic. They know the Soviets have more troops on their border than in Western Europe. There is Japan and India. What about the U.S.? (1) We are a long way off. (2) While they would never say publicly that Russia or Japan or India had any designs on them, they know that the U.S. has no designs on them. Why did this meeting take place? That's why—not to buy any computers."

4. THE GUNS OF APRIL

The spring of 1972 was the apex of Richard Nixon's career. John F. Kennedy chose these lines from Edmund Burke's eulogy of Charles James Fox as the keynote for his book, *Profiles in Courage:* "He may live long, he may do much. But here is the summit. He can never exceed what he does this day."

In a six-week span, Nixon rose to the final challenge of his Vietnam policy by a foe that never wanted to negotiate and always wanted to win; he reacted with the application of enough power to counter that bid for victory, but with enough coolness in its presentation to the American public to be accepted without another Kent State. He came back with enough restraint in his choice of weapons and targets to permit a summit conference to be held and with enough power so that his display of nerve helped achieve the kind of arms limitation agreement he wanted. High-stakes poker all the way, and Nixon took the pot.

In Hanoi, the response to the proposals made public in the President's January 25 speech revealing the impasse in the secret talks came fairly swiftly: silence on the negotiating front and the expected spring offensive on the battlefield. American troops in Vietnam were down to 95,000 in early April, less than 6,000 of them combat troops; now the defense was up to the South Vietnamese.

At two o'clock on the afternoon of April 8, 1972, Bob Haldeman called me from Key Biscayne to tell me the President wanted a speech drafted in a hurry, warning the Communists of the consequences of their actions in Vietnam. "President says to be sure to use the word 'enemy.'" At the same moment, the President was on the phone to Henry Kissinger, who, 'as always, had a secretary on his "dead key" extension taking verbatim notes. Here is the salient portion of that conversation as transcribed by Henry's secretary—a monologue by the President that shows what was going on in his mind:

TELCON
President/Mr. Kissinger
Middle of Conversation
4/8/72   2:00

RN: You can tell them:

1.   Call it a report on Vietnam
2.   Tone: Confidence and matter of fact that as you may have noticed, there has been a massive, violent invasion by North Vietnames in South Vietnam in violation of (and repeat this point) our agreements.

3.   What we are doing to meet this:
    a.   As far as this being met on the ground by the South Vietnamese forces—they are fighting to defend their homeland
    b.   there will be no ground forces there, of ours however, we are using our air power against those military installations both in South Vietnam and North Vietnam that will support this invasion (say with the most modern Soviet equipment)
    c.   And say these attacks are to continue until the invasion (I don't know if we should use this phrase) is stopped.

Make the point up to this that

1.   There is an invasion and they have broken their agreement
2.   South Vietnam will meet the ground demands
3.   U.S. is not committing ground forces but using air power and the South Vietnames are also effective in this area, and that is the situation.

Now for the diplomatic front and not defensively—on January 25 we made a peace proposal and 12 trips (and give the essence of the offer; total withdrawal of our forces and use ceasefire) and what has happened and been their answer:: a continuing build up of forces and we showed restraint and offered to negotiate in private and public channels and they refused and continued to build up. Say they were attacking us and that is why the talks halted—Amb. Porter has offered to go back on the 13th and is prepared to do so when they stop their invasion (we shouldn't use that word I don't think). The private thing—we must think about our real interest in having private negotiations and we should not say anything that that would really have an affect of torpedo-ing it—hint at it maybe—we are prepared to negotiate publicly or privately *but not at the point of a gun*. There are those who say that the US should _____ the North Vietnamese-

= just withdraw—this would be no negotiation at all—it would be a surrender and a turning over the country to the communists (use this and the word enemy often) and that the US is seeing the end of this long war and point out when I came into office how many forces there were (and how many I have there now) And say that some men who were silent are now critical (I don't know if the President meant this the other way around). and we ask for American support for the only honorable policy.

This has to be short and terse and tell the people the things they need to know. About 1500 words, 10 minutes. We can say that we have consistently agreed to see their terms but they have refused this and we will not support a surrender.

Let one of your guys work with Safire on it so he can pull together what he needs—I need the text by 8:00 Sunday night, because Monday I am tied up. We can always look at it Wednesday to see how the situation stands, but we must lay out the points soon.

With Win Lord's help, I had the draft done the next day (there was a sign in my office: "In by ten, out by five, specify if no starch") and transmitted it with a cover note:

THE WHITE HOUSE

WASHINGTON

April 9, 1972.

MEMORANDUM FOR: THE PRESIDENT

FROM: BILL SAFIRE

SUBJECT: Vietnam Speech

The attached draft, approved by Kissinger, covers the points relayed to me by Haldeman and adds:

1. an analysis of what the Communist objectives are in this military offensive. By setting their objectives high (cutting country in half, taking Saigon, driving deep down from North), we can better point to their lack of success. If we do not do this, the capture of a couple of cities will be heralded as the defeat of Vietnamization.

2. a map. Folks do not know what is going on; in a matter-of-fact report to the people on Vietnam, use of a map would be

helpful. *Note:* Henry wants to think over whether or not we spell
out how many Communist troops are attacking.

3. a downplay of the word "invasion." I use "offensive" and
"attack"—if you decide to go with invasion, the speech would be
tougher but might be slightly more worrisome.

cc: Henry Kissinger
    Ray Price

The President decided not to give the speech right away. Perhaps there
was something the Soviets could do to restrain the North Vietnamese,
since they had much invested in the forthcoming Moscow summit conference, and the tanks that were rolling across the DMZ into South Vietnam were made in the USSR. Anatoly Dobrynin, the fast-talking engineer
who was the well-connected Soviet Ambassador to Washington, spent a lot
of time with Henry Kissinger in the corner office of the West Wing, and
then the two men left secretly for Moscow. (Kissinger later said proudly
that it was the first time a Soviet Ambassador flew to Moscow in *Air Force
One.*)

The points Kissinger made to General Secretary Leonid Brezhnev are
reported in detail in the chapter that follows, but on the subject of Vietnam, this is what he went to Moscow carefully prepared to say: that we
had not anticipated the summit would coincide with renewed, intense
fighting there. We had to take account of the Soviets' help to the North
Vietnamese, and their ally's attempt to "win the war *and drive the President out of office.*" That dramatic way of putting it—blatantly improper
for a representative of a democracy—was understandable to the Soviet
leadership to whom survival in the place of power was the name of the
game. Henry went on to warn that not only the climate of the summit
would be affected by the North Vietnamese invasion, but the specific accomplishments expected to flow from it—which the Soviets took to mean
the trade agreements they were seeking. For that reason, said the President's representative, both parties had an interest in getting the fighting
stopped and negotiations resumed—and in the United States, the success
or failure of the summit would be seen by the Congress and the public
in the light of results in ending the war. Kissinger made it clear that while
SALT was of enormous long-range significance, the problem of Vietnam
"has to be uppermost in our mind and on our agenda."

Brezhnev understood and the Russians tried to respond. Before the end
of the month, the President announced that negotiations in Paris would
be resumed and he let it be known that he expected some favorable movement. The speech was updated and the President delivered it on April 26.
There was a no-nonsense tone to it this time, and there was no pussyfooting about the word "invasion" anymore:

"What we are witnessing here—what is being brutally inflicted on the

Republic of Vietnam—is a clear case of naked and unprovoked aggression across an international border. There is only one word for it—invasion." Nixon announced a continued but somewhat reduced withdrawal schedule of American troops, and said that Ambassador William Porter would return to the negotiating table the next day, "with the firm expectation that productive talks leading to rapid progress will follow through all available channels." He wasn't giving them a bombing halt in return for coming to the table. "They sold that package to the United States once before, in 1968, and we are not going to buy it again in 1972." (Nixon did not forget those hectic days before his election.)

Henry zipped over to Paris for a private talk with Le Duc Tho—the "all-available channel"—and returned a day later burning mad. He had been, to use the term gaining popularity, "stonewalled"—peace still lay across the river and in the trees, and the Soviet assurances had been largely wishful thinking.

Aboard the *Sequoia*, where he had sailed with John Mitchell mulling over a Cambodian incursion two years before, the President discussed the alternatives with Kissinger and Al Haig. Next day, May 3, the NSC started cranking out the option papers. For the rest of the week Nixon spoke mainly to Kissinger and to John Connally, who was planning to leave the Cabinet soon, but who had the kind of feel Nixon wanted for domestic reaction. Having burned himself once in the way he did what he was sure was the right thing, he was doubly careful. The President did not want to trigger another post-Cambodia reaction.

He flew to Camp David with Julie on Friday night, May 6, wrote a speech in rough outline on a notepad, and that night dictated a draft of his speech into a dictaphone. Next day writer Ray Price went up—I had done the last two Vietnam speeches and was beginning to sound like Henry Kissinger—only to discover that the dictating machine had gone on the blink (or the President pushed the wrong button) and a third of the speech had been lost. The President had a few harsh things to say to Ray about recording machines and dictated again, asking Price to turn the notes into "a very businesslike, very factual, short, hard-hitting speech cut down to the bare essentials." The writer was told not to show the early draft to Kissinger or Rogers.

Ray had a draft ready that night and watched with some astonishment as the President not only cut down Price's prose but cut into material he had drafted himself. Out went the "I could take the popular way" passage, and a cloying "It would be reprehensible to play politics with peace and I'm not going to do that"—remember Cambodia—and in went "Let us not slide back toward the dark shadows of a previous age," aimed at the Soviets.

The guts of the decision was put in flat, factual terms, no histrionics: "All entrances to North Vietnamese ports will be mined to prevent access to these ports and North Vietnamese naval operations from these ports." And in an oblique way—by omitting it from a list of conditions necessary to lift the blockade—the President made a concession nearly as dramatic as the act of mining the harbors: to permit North Vietnamese troops to remain in South Vietnam after a cease-fire. Nixon did not want to play up the concession in a speech taking punitive action, so Kissinger put out the word in backgrounders.

Sunday morning, Nixon called Rogers home from Europe to an NSC meeting the next day, and called Henry Kissinger to come up to Camp David and review the speech that day from the technical side. Next day, he informed the NSC—Rogers, Laird, Agnew, Helms, and others—of his decision. Laird opposed it, saying later he had only been playing devil's advocate. Nixon was not taking a vote. He went from the Cabinet Room to his EOB office for separate discussions with Connally and Kissinger, and from there sent the order that had U.S. aircraft carriers undertake the mission of mining the harbors.

Before making his speech, the President went to the Roosevelt Room to brief—not consult with—the Democratic and Republican leaders of the House and Senate. He was coolly correct, a President performing a Constitutional courtesy, and his attitude was summed up in the line "If you can give me your support, I would appreciate it. If you cannot, I will understand." Several of the Senators—including the usually laconic Mike Mansfield, Majority Leader—were incensed, and showed their strong reaction to the men the President left behind to take questions. That meeting was as tense a session as I attended in four years, and the unadorned minutes tell the story.

THE WHITE HOUSE

WASHINGTON

May 10, 1972.

MEMORANDUM FOR: THE PRESIDENT'S FILE
FROM: WILLIAM SAFIRE

Briefing of Bipartisan Leaders—Monday, May 8, 1972, 8 p.m.

Present: Albert, Boggs, Scott, Maillard, Morgan, Fulbright, Mansfield, Griffin, Stennis, Arends, Ford, Aiken, Laird, Rogers, Moorer, MacGregor, Haig, Timmons, Mahon, Safire and others.

The President entered the Roosevelt Room, cordially greeted a few of the Senators, hoped Mike Mansfield, recently returned from China, was "not too tired—I know how it is. You don't know when to go to the bathroom or when to get up."

The President, before he began, asked the leaders to mention to

Margaret Chase Smith that we had tried to get her here, but she was unavailable.

"Let me come directly to the point and tell you of a decision I have had to make. You can support it only if you know the options. After I indicate the reasons for my decisions, I'll call on Admiral Moorer and Mel Laird to brief and then Bill Rogers to follow that. I will leave, but any questions you want to ask me, ask them and I'll stand by their answers. We were all in a three-hour meeting together this morning.

"First, a word about where we are since April 26. It seems a long time ago. The North Vietnamese offensive has moved on. The South Vietnamese soldiers continue to fight bravely in some places, not so in others. However, the North Vietnamese offensive still has a considerable amount of potency. If it continues, and if South Vietnam can't contain it, then not only will we have the immediate problem of Hue, which is a symbolic place, but the North Vietnamese will have achieved their bigger objective of causing the acceptance of a defeated psychology. That is a danger we must weigh.

"The second point has to do with 700,000 refugees. Twenty thousand civilian casualties have occurred in cities shelled by the North Vietnamese. It has been a brutal assault on the civilian population. No American ground forces are involved.

"On the negotiating front, you know about the two public sessions. There has also been a private session. On May 2, Dr. Kissinger went to Paris and met with Le Duc Tho for an extended private meeting. Also in four days in Moscow, Vietnam was not only discussed by the Soviet leaders, they urged us to go back to the conference table, leading us to believe they would play a constructive role. Whether they did or not is unknown. But the results are clear. The North Vietnamese had the most insulting, intransigent attitude in five years of negotiation. Dr. Kissinger offered all the old proposals and some new ones, and they were rejected. It is quite obvious that North Vietnam, with their initial successes on the battlefield, are taking a harder line than ever. We have offered everything and more and have been turned down flat.

"Now we come to a value judgment and one I have to make: If the offensive continues at the present pace, there is substantial danger that South Vietnam would not be able to resist, which would endanger the lives of 69,000 US soldiers, particularly 10,000 in the Eye Corps area.

"To protect them, to prevent the success of aggression, to secure the release of our POWs, here are the options: One, we could continue to do what we are doing; when you don't make decisions, you don't get blamed. But the situation could worsen.

"Two, another way is to withdraw. There is substantial opinion for that. But an acceptance of defeat on those terms would be unacceptable; it would encourage aggression. What the North Vietnamese insist upon is that we get out and impose a Communist government. They insist that Thieu must go. I do not accept this.

"Three, the negotiation track we will continue to pursue. The Russians and the North Vietnamese are aware of this, and they can choose to use it.

"We have to do something to affect the situation, based on denying the weapons of war to those who would use them for aggression. That is why all harbors will be mined. All countries who have ships in them have been informed. Our military forces will have instructions to cut off supplies to the enemy in every way. In any event we will use both mining and the interdiction of supplies. Those are terms of art and Bill Rogers will explain what they mean.

"Our air strikes in North Vietnam will be directed primarily to the three railroads that lead to Vietnam.

"We have made a new offer on the peace side. I am indicating that we will continue this interdiction by sea and rail until the enemy releases our POWs and agrees to a cease-fire. Then all Americans will be out by four months.

"This is very strong medicine. It was a very difficult decision for me to make. I know it will be very difficult to support. But just to let this offensive go on is too great a risk. The negotiation path has been closed to us.

"This action is directed not at the destruction of the North, but at the cutting off of supplies. This is the cleanest, best, most direct way of ending the war.

"If you can give me your support, I would appreciate it. If you cannot, I will understand."

The President got up to leave and Admiral Moorer rose at the other end of the table and with his aide began setting up the maps.

Mike Mansfield, who was sitting near the President and who looked unusually pale, handed the President a manila envelope on the way out which was his written report on China.

After the President's departure, Admiral Moorer gave the details of the mining operation and was sharply questioned by Senators Mansfield and Fulbright. Both Secretary Laird and Secretary Rogers assisted in responding to these questions. At five minutes to nine, the briefing ended, and the leaders went downstairs to the White House Mess to watch the President's address.

Discussion After President's Departure from Roosevelt Room, Monday, May 8, 1972.

Moorer: "At most, 39 ships of foreign registry are in these ports, 35 of which are in Haiphong Harbor. This is about average. They process about 42 ships a month through the harbor."

Mansfield, his voice trembling, interrupted: "How long ago were these orders issued?"

Moorer (looking at Laird): "Today, this afternoon."

Mansfield: "What it means is that the war is enlarged. It appears to me that we are embarking on a dangerous course. We are courting danger here that could extend the war, increase the number of war prisoners and make peace more difficult to achieve."

Moorer, standing at the map, was nonplussed and Laird answered for the Pentagon: "As far as extension is concerned, Mike, it was extended by the enemy. It's not a fair charge to charge us with that responsibility."

Rogers (in an ameliatory tone): "Compared with bombing Haiphong, this is much more limited, wouldn't you say, Admiral Moorer?"

Moorer: "Yes. Mines are a passive weapon."

Rogers: "The enemy has used mines before in this conflict."

Mansfield: "What will the effect be on the dikes?"

Moorer: "None."

Mansfield: "They don't float?"

Moorer: "No. They sink to the bottom."

Rogers: "This is not a traditional blockade. We're not challenging ships on the high seas."

Scott: "As I see it, what we are saying to countries who are supplying the enemy is—they must stop. The most important feature of all this is that the President offers to withdraw all forces on two conditions: the release of prisoners and a cease-fire."

Ford: "How will the mines be distributed?"

Moorer: "Carrier aircraft. We can open the channel when the situation warrants."

Laird: "We shouldn't talk about that."

Mahon: "How high are these being dropped from?"

Moorer: "A couple of hundred feet."

Rogers: "We will notify the UN to show them this is not a blockade. This is a move to create a climate. It is quite clear the enemy has no interest in negotiating. Maybe they never will. They have created the impression that they will not and we will. There were other actions more extreme, against the civilian population. This is less extreme and I hope will be effective."

Scott: "When the President said all forces, did he mean all sea and air forces as well?"

Rogers: "Let's wait and see what he says."

Mansfield (firmly): "The President said 'all forces.'"

Albert: "Had any protest yet?"

Rogers: "No. Sir Alec Douglas Home said today that the US has done everything possible to bring the war to an end. NATO continues to support us in trying to prevent a total defeat. The President feels that this has some hope of success."

A Congressman (whose face I didn't recognize): "Without this, would the North Vietnamese just move in?"

Rogers: "We don't want to demoralize the South Vietnamese by admitting it."

Congressman: "Why can't we just pull them all out tonight? Just supposing the President decided to take them all out. I know we have to protect them—but if we wanted them out, could we move them out now? I am not arguing whether or not it is advisable; I just want to know whether we can get our 60,000 men out in a hurry."

Moorer didn't have an answer to this and looked to Laird, who replied, "If you were going to surrender, you could."

The Congressman: "I may thoroughly agree with you. I don't know. I just want to be sure there is no Dunkirk involved."

(This was a crucial part of the talk since with the Gulf of Tonkin Resolution being repealed, the President's main Constitutional right to remain in Vietnam was pegged to the protection of US troops there. That's why he always included the protection of the remaining troops as a reason for his action, even though he could pull those troops out quickly. The Congressman was attacking the President's justification for his action and Laird, in telling the truth, may have stepped into a trap.)

Fulbright, oddly, didn't pursue that line of questioning. Instead, he asked "what about those railroads he is going to bomb—the ones that come out of China?"

Rogers: "It is important to recognize that we are not going to bomb China."

Fulbright: "But the railroads *from* China . . ."

Rogers (refusing to accept Fulbright's definition of the railroads): "These railroads are in the north part of North Vietnam; they were bombed in 1968. We are bombing in North Vietnam."

Aiken: "How many refugees could we get out and where could they go? Especially the ones the North would like to get even with."

Laird: "It would be impossible to get them out."

Aiken: "If we gave up—couldn't something about the refugees be arranged?"

Rogers: "We couldn't get them out."

Laird: "And none are moving north; they're all moving south."

Rogers: "We will observe all the rules of war as far as mining is concerned. There will be no mining of the high seas. The key question of course is the one Mike raises—is this an escalation of the war? Or a response to the enemy's escalation?"

Ford: "You tried to go down the middle."

Fulbright: "Have you advised the Russians and Chinese, and have they found it acceptable?"

Rogers: "Come on, Bill, of course not. They would never agree to this."

Fulbright: "I agree with Mike. It seems like an enlargement of the war. There is no longer a Gulf of Tonkin Resolution, and I don't know your justification under the Constitution. You are going to the UN with legal justification of the mining—but what will you tell the American people?"

Rogers: "Let's listen to the President."

Fulbright: "How about giving us a legal justification?"

Rogers: "You know that, Bill. Let's listen to the President now."

I couldn't watch all three network reactions at the same time, so next morning I read the President's News Summary with more than the usual interest. PNS . . . Post-Speech Commentary:

> ABC Jarriel called the move a "slap in the face" to USSR; a move inviting "direct confrontation" between 2 superpowers as never seen before . . . HKSmith pointed out blockages are legal in wars, but the problem is whether this is a war . . . Koppel indicated the summit had to be affected in some way. NBC Chancellor led by saying the military decision was the "most significant decision in the history of US involvement in VN war." . . . And it means another naval confrontation with USSR as there was 10 years ago in Cuba. Chancellor said "We have a problem here"—"the USSR will have to react." Moscow correspondent Stevens said RN's moves "practically kill prospects of a summit." Valeriani . . . added USSR "can't sit still for this. How can they receive him now?" Chancellor summed up "We've agreed that the summit is certainly in jeopardy and a new phase of the war has begun." CBS Sevareid said it's a "very drastic action" . . . a "serious new initiative" said Rather. Kalb said RN was "directing a rather frontal challenge at USSR" . . . It puts summit "very, very much in jeopardy"—less than 50-50 RN is going anywhere but he doesn't want to call it off—he wants Soviets to have to do that.
>
> *Reaction:* Aiken was discouraged . . . "it is brinkmanship." Margaret Smith supported RN "wholeheartedly." Javits said "No one can foretell the consequences." McGovern called the blockade "a flirtation with World War III." Wallace wants to "think it through" . . . EMK labeled the decision "ominous" and said "I think it's folly . . . a futile military gesture taken in desperation."

The word around the White House in the days that followed was that there was no "fix" in with the Russians, but if you were scheduled to go on the Moscow trip and needed shots, to get the shots. Haldeman was gleeful that the President's critics could be shown up quickly and dramatically and made arrangements for the RNC's publication "Monday," as well as hawkish Senators, to hoot at some of the opposition's predictions when they turned out to be wrong.

I sent Haldeman a memo suggesting that the President's critics would quickly say (1) thank God the Russians were more responsible than our reckless President and (2) Nixon really had assurances all along from the Russians. Bob brooded about this awhile, but on May 15, when it became apparent that the summit would still take place, he read this statement by McGovern in the News Summary: McGovern was "delighted" by the Russian response. "It is remarkable indeed and they have to be commended for their restraint in the face of a highly provocative action."

Haldeman, who had been hoping against hope I would be proven wrong, went right up the flue. This is a portion of memo he fired to Colson:

THE WHITE HOUSE

WASHINGTON

May 15, 1972

CONFIDENTIAL/EYES ONLY

MEMORANDUM FOR: CHARLES COLSON

FROM: H. R. HALDEMAN

In evaluating the developments since the Monday speech, some pretty clear lines of direction come through as far as our PR is concerned.

We have the ironic situation that, after initially reacting to the Monday announcement with almost hysterical predictions that we had blown the Russian summit and our whole "Generation of Peace" foreign policy, the columnists and commentators—with a considerable amount of egg on their faces—now have the gall to say that the Monday decision was wrong and reckless but that the Soviet Union is showing great restraint in continuing the summit nevertheless.

This is again the most devastating proof of the fact that whatever we do and however it comes out, we are going to be torn to pieces by our liberal critics in the press and on television.

What really matters now, of course, is how it all comes out. We shall continue the military action that is necessary to bring about a negotiated settlement as soon as possible.

But, on the other hand, regardless of how it comes out—whether we succeed or fail—we at least deserve out of this whole rather difficult experience a recognition that the decision was a courageous one in which the President put his country above politics and was willing to risk his own personal future in order to do what he thought was right for the country, for our POWs, and for the Americans who were still in Vietnam, for the 17 million Vietnamese who do not want a Communist government, and, most important of all, for the preservation of the credibility of American foreign policy in the years ahead . . .

Looking back to the Kennedy years, fourteen months after the Cuban missile crisis—actually until the very day he died—there were columns, speeches, etc., referring to the courage he had displayed, the statesmanship, etc., etc., in handling that crisis. He had the advantage of a sympathetic press corps but on the other hand if you were to check his staff at that time, you would surely find that they had that as a prime PR objective.

We must double the effort that he had due to the fact that our problem is doubly as difficult because of the opposition of the press.

At least we have one thing going for us—what the President has done both on the China initiative and now again here—exceeds by light years in the impact it will have on the future of the world and of this country, anything that Kennedy did in the Cuban crisis. In other words, we have a much better case to sell. The question is whether we can do an adequate job of selling it.

Again, we have the recurrent comparison to Kennedy, the envy of the way JFK's men could "handle" the media, the grudging respect for his rhetoric. After Nixon's Haiphong speech, Senator Frank Church, a leading dove, quoted English orator Charles James Fox's attack in 1800 on a British Minister who had urged the continuance of the war against France: ". . . he is forced to acknowledge that, at the end of a 7-years conflict, we are come to a new era in the war, at which he thinks it necessary only to press all his former arguments to induce us to persevere . . . to carry it on upon principles which, if adopted, may make it eternal." When the Washington *Post* gave this striking parallel a play, the *Wall Street Journal* pointed out that the Peace of Amiens which followed two years later did not appease Napoleon, and England wound up having to fight a much stronger France all over again. The News Summary editor, Mort Allin, sent that in to the President, who enjoyed it. He knew when he was making history.

Nixon knew, too, he was taking the Soviet leaders, who were not without their own internal opposition on détente, to "a hard place in the road." In mining the Haiphong harbor and intensifying the bombing of the North, Nixon was doing more than "keeping his word" and maintaining his reputation for occasional "fierceness": the President was (a) admitting he had overestimated Saigon's capacity to resist a sustained attack, (b) demanding that Moscow begin to share his agony on Vietnam, by suffering —as America had long suffered—some loss of face in not going all-out to help an ally win a war.

Psychologically, the North Vietnamese spring offensive was a shock to Nixon that he was determined to pass along to the Soviets, hoping they would then pass the shock to the North Vietnamese. In electric terms, Nixon wanted to be a conductor rather than a ground. Nixon was signaling to the Soviets that superpowers must together lay bare superweaknesses: that if Vietnam were to be the scene of the loss of respect for American power, it could also be the scene of the embarrassment of Soviet power. For the Soviets to react to Nixon's harbor-mining by calling off the summit would be evidence of a basic motive by the Soviets to achieve superiority; for the Soviets to react by not reacting—and to let the summit go forward —would be a statement of an understanding of parity. Nixon's Haiphong decision, then, was not an expression of diplomatic *machismo*: it was his answer to a test first posed by a relatively "independent" North Vietnam to the U.S. policy of Vietnamization and to the Soviet policy of continuing pressure-by-proxy. Nixon transferred the pressure to the Soviets by the device of meeting the raised ante with the passive weapon of mines, simultaneously sending word through Dobrynin that it was not Nixon, but the Soviets' North Vietnamese allies, who had aggressively raised the ante.

The Soviets were infuriated by the tough reaction, as Nixon was to discover in Brezhnev's dacha, but they had—as Nixon liked to put it—"their own fish to fry." The limitations of superpower were now evident to both parties, and the Russians had revealed the extent of their need for a deal. Nixon was going to use that revelation at a crucial moment in Moscow.

"Strength means nothing," Nixon recounted to a Congressional reception some time later, "unless there is a will to use it . . .

"If, for example, when I went to Moscow, late in May, at that time we had had Soviet tanks run by the North Vietnamese rumbling through the streets of Hue, and Saigon being shelled, we would not have been able to deal with the Soviets on the basis of equal respect. We wouldn't have been worth talking to . . . in a sense, and they would have known it."

5. THE ROAD TO MOSCOW

Preparing our response to North Vietnam's all-out drive to win the war in the spring of 1972, the President and Henry Kissinger were also preparing for the summit conference in Moscow. "Linkage"—the tactic demanding that progress on one front must be related to, or linked with, progress elsewhere—was to be practiced by Nixon in a way that made a model of a DNA molecule look simple.

The President and his national security adviser planned the approach to the wide-ranging negotiations. Some agreements—oceanography, space cooperation—were important in themselves, but hardly the stuff of summits—yet they added to the "heft" of the conference. On Strategic Arms Limitation, last-minute work was needed at the top to resolve impasses, but even this could have been done through diplomatic channels, just as pressure to slow down arms shipments to the North Vietnamese might have been applied by withholding desired trade agreements. Yet taken together—the position of relative equality in military strength, the Sino-Soviet split, and the economic breakup of the "postwar world"—made the moment unique for a meeting at the summit that would punctuate the past and build some connective tissue for the future.

Nixon and Kissinger were determined that this not be a "spirit of" summit. The spirits of Camp David, Glassboro, and other get-acquainted or publicity-stunt summits would not be summoned from this vasty deep. Instead, they wanted this to be a summit of substance, "meticulously" (a favorite Kissinger word) prepared by serious men on both sides aware of the potential of the moment and the danger of letting the moment slip away.

Toughness of mind was the first requirement in any dealings with the Soviets, according to Nixon. They respected power, lived in an atmosphere of power, and philosophical subtleties could be explored at length only after the power lines were laid. When Ray Price and I asked Henry Kissinger for guidance on the tone of the remarks for the President (he had already given us the substance) he replied waspishly: "Tough. None of your goddam peacenik-y toasts. This is not like in China, swearing eternal friendship. Tough." Price, a man not ordinarily given to oral argument, snapped back: "We were writing hawkish speeches for Nixon when you were turning out dovish statements for Rockefeller, remember?" Both Henry and I looked at Ray with surprise and new respect; the shy former editorial writer reddened. With a diplomatic touch, Henry said that the tone of the toasts should be along Ray's tough-sounding lines, with a heavy overlay of reminders about comradeship and bravery in World War II.

Henry was working on a speech of his own, the most important of his life, to be given to the Soviet leaders at the preparatory meeting from April 18 to 22, a month before the summit. He wanted to get across what he liked to call his "conceptual framework." Nixon wanted him to communicate to the Soviet leadership an understanding of the kind of man Nixon was, which would strengthen the President's hand at the meeting of leaders. And both wanted Henry to make clear that everything had much to do with everything else—that linkage lived.

In his speech to the April 1971 Communist Party Congress, General Secretary Leonid Brezhnev had prepared the ground for a general détente. Ambassadors from Iron Curtain countries circulated around Washington dinner parties spreading the word that now was the moment, which if not seized might not soon come again. Ambassador to the United States Anatoly Dobrynin was not as heavy-handed as that, but made clear that the Soviets felt that summitry time was ripe, and Nixon's 1972 China journey had whetted their appetite even more; however, when it came to helping the United States on resolving the situation in Vietnam as evidence of good faith, the Soviets had never been prepared to go that far. Kissinger, in his prepared opening remarks nearly one year to the day after Brezhnev's public opening gambit, embraced the "seize the moment" idea, based as it was on the coincidence of equal strength.

Making some necessary diplomatic cuts, I will quote from the fourth and final draft of Kissinger's opening statement to the Soviet leaders. Henry later confirmed to me it is substantially what he actually said, so I will put it in quotes, though I was not present, because it is a useful study of what Kissinger thought the President wanted the other leaders to know before he met them. I take no delight in using classified material, but the Soviets heard it in early 1972 and it will do no harm for Americans to review it now:

> "You and we have many problems but we do have the advantage, at the present time, of being able to deal with each other from positions of essential equality. And that provides us with a unique moment in our histories to reach everlasting agreements. In fact, the opportunities for broad cooperation open to the leaders of our two countries at present have never been greater and may decline again if they are not grasped.
>
> "You have known President Nixon for more than a decade and

he is aware that you have raised questions about his attitudes, orientation and predictability. Some of your public statements have tried to analyze his behavior in terms of 'forces' influencing him. The President combines concern for long-term evolution with detailed interest in concrete day-to-day decisions. The evolution he sees—and wants to contribute to—is one of a world of several interacting major powers, competitive but respectful of each other's interests. Within this basic framework, he sees an opportunity for all countries to develop their own identity. This view of the world corresponds to the President's personal background and up-bringing.

"At the same time, he can be tough and even ruthless in dealing with specific problems. You probably recognize that the President is bound to see the present situation in Vietnam not only in its local context but as a renewed effort by outside powers to intervene in our domestic political processes. Moreover, *as President he is bound to be keenly sensitive to the fact that our last President was forced to vacate his office because of the effects of the Vietnam war. President Nixon will not permit three Presidents in a row to leave office under abnormal circumstances.* It may seem that what he is doing to prevent this from occurring is 'unpredictable'; it is in fact quite consistent with his fighting instincts when issues of principle and vital interest are at stake. His reaction should have been expected.

"But I have also found that once a matter is settled, the President is prepared to proceed with matters that are in the common interest with those who were on the opposite side in a dispute. This is true in his domestic as well as foreign policies. We would say that he 'does not bear grudges.' The President can look beyond the issues of the moment to the broader evolution and the wider interests. He is conciliatory because he recognizes that only those agreements are kept which nations wish to keep.

"Let me make this more specific and relate it directly to you. The President has a reputation from his past as an anti-Communist. You may think that this is a basic prejudice which sooner or later will assert itself. (Actually, I would not find such a view on your side surprising. I would have thought that you would only regard it as normal that a 'capitalist' should be anti-Communist and that you would not respect him if he were not.)

"But as a practical matter the President understands that whether he likes your system or not will not affect its existence; just as your likes and dislikes do not affect our existence. He will enter a contest with you when you challenge him and he will do and say things that you may regard as challenging you. But he will not lose sight of the special role that our two countries must play if there is to be peace in the world. That, rather than anti-

Communism, is the point that will again and again reassert itself
—whatever the turbulences of the moment.

"Of course, it is also characteristic of the President to be patient and tenacious. His political biography testifies to that. He
will accept a setback or a detour—and wait until he can rechart
his course. When he has done this, he has shown unusual consistency, even when he makes the most radical moves—which his
position enables him to do."

This was straight-from-the-shoulder talk; Kissinger's references to the
U.S. political scene were improper, of course, since continuance in office
should hardly be the reason for a U.S. leader's reaction to a foreign power's
military offensive, but presumably he felt he was representing Nixon and
not the nation.

Kissinger then went into a brief discussion of the American relationship
with China, which I will not quote directly because I want to leave him
something for his own book. The Soviets were most concerned, we knew,
with the timing of Nixon's actions toward China, coinciding as they did
with the deterioration of Soviet relations with Peking. Because that happened to be the case, Kissinger held, that was no cause to assume it was
the only basis of American-Chinese dealings, and in any event there could
not be any collusion against the Soviet Union by the Americans and Chinese in the world of today. He also assured the Soviets that we were only
at the beginning of a process with the Chinese, and major specific agreements were not likely soon.

Having modestly reminded the Soviets of the brilliant exploitation of
their weakness by American diplomacy, Kissinger then laid stress on the
provocative North Vietnamese invasion and urged that—in addition to
specific tasks both nations had in common·at the summit—some "rules of
conduct" be promulgated that might be the framework for future dealings. This idea was to be brought to fruition at the Moscow summit, and
generally overlooked at the time as campaign rhetoric, but Kissinger has
always felt that the "rules" were as important as any agreement signed in
Moscow. Then he began tying the knots of linkage:

"The viability of any agreement in so central an area as that of
strategic arms depends heavily on the general political relationship between us. The President strongly feels that arms control
agreements serve little purpose if existing arms are used for aggression or pressure . . .

"Bilateral relations and trade. Here we have broad long-term
opportunities to develop cooperative relations. We are currently
engaged in a whole series of negotiations ranging from trade issues, to scientific and outer space cooperation.

"Both of us stand to gain. But we must be realistic: a lasting
and productive set of relationships, with perhaps hundreds or

thousands of our people working with each other and perhaps billions of dollars of business activity, can only be achieved in a healthy political environment. The past history of our relations has clearly shown the connection between the political aspects and others, like the economic. The President wants to be candid with you: he cannot make commitments, say for credits or tariff concessions, if these measures do not command wide support among our public and in the Congress. And this depends critically on the state of our political relations. Moreover, we must make sure that once commitments have been entered into they will not soon be undermined by renewed crises and deterioration of our relations. I say this not because we want you to 'pay a price' for economic and other relations with us or because we expect you to sacrifice important political and security interests for the sake of trade relations. I say it as an objective fact of political life."

Kissinger's formal speech to Brezhnev was well received. On the subject of Vietnam, Henry had even more to offer. In the cease-fire-in-place speech made the previous October—the one neither the President nor Kissinger had any hopes of the North Vietnamese accepting—there had been a phrase of art that I had objected to at the time as too fuzzy, but Henry had insisted be left just as it was: that the armies of Indochina "must remain within their national frontiers." The North Vietnamese, who thought of all of Vietnam as one country, could interpret that as a hint that we could permit them to leave some of their army in South Vietnam. In Moscow, at the President's direction, Kissinger made the proposal more specifically, tying it in with a demand that the North Vietnamese drop their insistence for the overthrow of President Thieu. These were hardly nit-pickings; previously, we had always insisted on "mutual withdrawals," attaching as much importance to that as the Communists did to the removal of Thieu. Moscow, Nixon thought, would be the best place for this initiative; Soviet Ambassador Dobrynin thought he could deliver, tried, and failed. The North Vietnamese were doing too well at first in their big spring offensive, and the bombing of the North was too traumatic an experience later for negotiations to take hold. But the basic deal offered in Moscow—we let the troops stay south, they let Thieu stay as President—turned out to be the deal that was made six months later.

Kissinger reported back to the President not only on the substance of the Soviet remarks—Kosygin did not reveal how much wheat the Soviets ultimately wanted to buy, but as Dobrynin said privately later, that would not have been smart bargaining—and included some favorite Brezhnev folk stories for the President's use in speeches. The Soviet leader surprised Kissinger, Helmut Sonnenfeldt, and other NSC staffers with his American political habit of "pressing the flesh"—punching an arm, squeezing, back-patting—which he dropped for a more dignified pose when the American

President arrived. Nixon had been prepared for a back-slapper on the basis of his aides' reports, but Brezhnev was to cross him up, exhibiting a wit and dignity that was most impressive. When Henry brought along the entire contingent of NSC staffers to the final meeting, so that everybody could tell grandchildren they met the top man, Brezhnev took note of the increased size of the delegation, and deftly countered Henry's harping on U.S. troop withdrawals as evidence of our good faith in Southeast Asia: "For people who talk so much about your withdrawals," said the Soviet leader, "you bring your reinforcements up very quietly."

Kissinger's most important contribution to the Moscow summit, as well as to the China trip, was in laborious preparation. There never was a bilateral conference so well prepared for the turning of a page. With the major exception of the SALT negotiations, Kissinger's job was largely over as summit time neared, and Nixon's job intensified. As in the China experience, when the time drew near for departure, the President drew back into isolation and Kissinger felt brushed aside. In 1969, Henry would have assented to this Presidential prerogative without a pout; in 1972, however, he was a superstar in his own right and resented being shoved into the background.

I was writing the President's opening toast for the first night in Moscow at the end of the State dinner in Granovit Hall. Henry glanced at my four-page draft and said, "You need two more pages." I said, no, Haldeman told me one thousand words tops, and Kissinger exploded: "Foreign policy decided by flacks!" I glared at him, since I was not ashamed of my own public relations background, and Henry hastily added, "I don't mean you, Bill, I mean them." He pointed down the hall toward Haldeman, Chapin, and Ziegler. "The President was telling me just the other day," he added puckishly, "how much he liked your work." This was a staff joke about one-upmanship, a standard routine of Presidential aides, not meant to be taken seriously. He called Haldeman to get him to get the President to change to fifteen hundred words, because that was how long Dobrynin told him Podgorny would go; the fact that he had to deal with Haldeman and could not go direct to the President irritated him immensely. It was Nixon putting him down again. "A week ago," Henry said with passion, "he would have done anything I asked, he was on his *knees*—God! And now I have to talk to Haldeman."

I couldn't help wondering if power games like these were played about the General Secretary and the Politburo. We would be in the Kremlin soon enough, however, and once abroad, the President's men dropped their rivalries and served him better than any outside observer could imagine.

The pettiness of White House intrigue might not be expected to occupy a mind filled with grand designs, daring sweeps of intellect, and the most noble of motives—to end an arms race and get the world into the habit of peace—but Kissinger jockeyed for power around the President and used everyone he could to suit his ends, for two reasons: first, intrigue was second nature to him, an exercise he went through often without thinking;

second, Henry's power was an amalgam of the reach of his mind and the power bestowed upon him by the President, and to lose even the appearance of power, weakened his ability to perform. After his "foreign policy decided by flacks!" blast, he mollified me with a thought well directed to himself: "You are not ambitious to *be* something, you are ambitious to *do* something, and that makes all the difference in a man."*

The carryings-on of Henry Kissinger, the virtuoso of varying virtue, were tolerated by President Nixon because he too was a man who wanted to *do* something, and saw in Kissinger a unique tool to help him do it. Writing in the New York *Times* that week, James Reston, a man not given to exaggeration, sought to convey the crucial role of Kissinger at that state in history: "Henry Kissinger has got beyond the news . . . he is going to be left to the psychological novelists . . .

"To master the details and complexities of the President's agenda in Peking and Moscow, to keep the summit meetings alive while American troops are in Taiwan and American bombers are over North Vietnam, to keep the fundamental differences straight and still find areas for agreement and common interest—all this is hard enough. But Kissinger . . . has been loyal to the President without ignoring or evading the opposition or assuming bad faith on the part of those who oppose the war."

Kissinger's brilliant maneuvering in this period between the Peking and Moscow summits was played on the world stage in full view of his appreciative audience. The manipulation of Kissinger by the President, from care and feeding and periodic deflation of ego to the occasional stiffening of backbone, was totally hidden from public view. Nixon, who thought of himself not as he was but as he thought of himself, could use Kissinger as a marionette, and then place himself in his own marionette's hands because the President profoundly understood in his assistant the needs he refused to examine in himself. (Reston is right: perhaps all this is better left to the psychological novelists.)

On May 17 the President must have done something nice because Henry was in a much better mood as he went over some preparatory material with Ray Price, writer John Andrews (a new man, developing quickly into the President's favorite remarks-suggester and short-speech drafter) and myself. "We want to get away from hyperbole," said the greatest national security adviser since Creation. "The Chinese are beside themselves with the possibility of great power collusion. So say we have a common interest in making peace, and don't use the 'new era' stuff. Friendly, not sentimental . . ." Still a tough tone? "Look, for three years we tried to interest the Russians in Vietnam. The first time they showed any signs of interest was when their ships were threatened in Haiphong."

Henry was a happy man. "Taking Hanoi off the front page is like a military defeat for them. China did that last year. Russia this year. Now

---

* Two years later, after I had criticized his role in the wiretapping of the seventeen officials and newsmen, Henry told me: "God save us from men out to preserve their purity." He takes all criticism personally, and assumes it is all personally motivated.

Hanoi has been made to look like a parochial problem." Smiling, he shook his head in mock self-pity: "And all the President says is he wishes Gromyko was working for him."

He told us of the contrast between the ways the Russians and the Chinese prepared for their Nixon arrivals. Brezhnev had proudly shown Kissinger the Presidential quarters, something the Chinese would never do, Henry explained to us, since the Chinese have always felt culturally superior, the Russians culturally inferior. The Russians of a century ago hired Germans or Frenchmen to handle their foreign relations, and not until 1880 was there a foreign minister born in Russia; all the Russian Foreign Ministry archives before 1820 are written in French.

Brezhnev had shown Henry the antique urns on pedestals set up along the corridors of Nixon's Kremlin apartment. Only one was uncovered, beautifully polished—all the rest were covered with shrouds to keep off the dust. Brezhnev told Kissinger: "We will take off the shrouds two hours before President Nixon gets here." This amused Henry: "It reminded me of my grandmother," he told us. "The house had to be cleaned spic and span on Thursday, and everything covered up so it would be right for Friday night." He laughed again and then became serious. "But never forget," he said in a statement I never forgot, "that feelings of inferiority can lead to bluster and to arrogance."

6. THE MOSCOW SUMMIT

Lying on a beach in Puerto Rico, I was pleased to learn from this telegram that thirteen years after the "kitchen conference," I would be returning to Moscow with Richard Nixon:

> TRIED TO REACH YOU THIS MORNING FOR HALDEMAN TO
> CONFIRM PRESIDENT WANTS BOTH YOU AND PRICE TO
> ACCOMPANY HIM TO
> RUSSIA THOUGHT THIS MIGHT MAKE A GREAT
> VACATION EVEN BETTER REGARDS
> DWIGHT L CHAPIN
>
> COLL 36
>
> SNT OPTR 4 MARCH30/72 1617
>
> 385758CERROBEACH

Moscow in 1972 was a city with a mayor named Promislov, a perfect name for a politician and a happy augury for summiteers. The most popular tune in the Russian and Armenian restaurant-nightclubs was "Those Were the Days, My Friend" but we all knew that *these* were the days of high drama that would never be forgotten. Most of the American party was quartered in the huge new Rossiya Hotel. Its top-floor restaurant, overlooking the Kremlin and the American flag flying atop the President's apartment, was promptly dubbed the "Top O' the Marx." Huge cakes of soap were available in the bathrooms (the Russians had heard that the American party had been warned by its advance men that there might not be soap) and baskets of fresh cucumbers and tomatoes on every table to prove that there were no shortages of fresh cucumbers and tomatoes (we smuggled them out and gave them to resident correspondents and diplomats who could not buy them readily in Moscow). The stores were jammed, the people were healthy and ruddy, the cars were few but store windows on Red Square displayed new automobile tires, and the foreign-currency Berioska stores offered bargains in amber, alexandrite, and color-ful, wooden toy Kremlin towers.

Détente was in the air. People were under instructions to be naturally friendly, though there were some sour notes. When a Soviet Foreign Ministry official took me to lunch and asked why the American public was not universally behind the search for peace, I said I couldn't hear him for the sound of the Russian tanks rolling across the DMZ in Vietnam; he coolly replied that "we should really send them quieter tanks." Each American official had a Soviet driver and car assigned to him, but when a trip inside the Kremlin was called for, a different driver was needed. Instead of saying outright that the special drivers were required for inside-the-Kremlin work, an Orwellian excuse would be given: "Your regular driver is at the airport." The regular driver was leaning against the fender of the car not twenty feet away from the dispatcher, but the man stuck to his story.

Of greater concern, American journalists would pass on messages like this, addressed to Mrs. Nixon: "The tone of this letter will sound dissonant to the atmosphere that surrounds you here. There exist violations of rights. On Monday, May 21, early in the morning, four men broke into our house and dragged away my husband. The reason they gave for this was our 'intent' to violate public order during the visit of Mr. Nixon and you to Moscow." The letter told how the woman's husband, a scientist and a Jew, had been persecuted since he expressed a desire to go to Israel. He and his son were arrested a few days before and the wife was left with a younger son: "The two of us remain in this empty apartment, with the silent telephone which has been disconnected. And all this, just because we want to live together with our people in our homeland. Very respected Mrs. Nixon! I address you, your mother's heart, in the hopes of participation and help . . ." I passed it along to Henry Kissinger, and made sure Mrs. Nixon saw the original. There was no direct reply possible, but it was useful to remember we were still in the totalitarian USSR, détente or no.

I introduce those dissonances in an otherwise affirmative moment in modern world history because the President, Henry Kissinger, or anybody else in the American party could not honestly say they knew why the Soviets wanted a relaxation of the tensions that had existed since the end of World War II. While there were plenty of apparent reasons for détente —the moment of parity, the Soviet weakness in agricultural production and need for technology, the weakening of the Western alliance in the presence of a thaw—there was no proof that ultimate purpose of Soviet policy had changed from world domination to permanent equilibrium. Nixon was of a suspicious turn of mind; the attitudes he formed in his thirties and forties would not alter drastically as he neared sixty. Détente, he let his writers know, suited the Soviets at the moment, and was a tactic used by men who took the long view, but represented no basic change in purpose. Détente was peaceful, but it was not peace. Accordingly, he played off the Soviet's current desire for détente to get what he could be-fore the moment of hard dealing came. Nixon did more than "triangulate" with China; he exploited the division in the Communist world by building a three-dimensional chess set and making the first move in the game. He would take the Soviets' tactical need for détente now and use it to put in place relationships that would make it difficult to change the tactic away from détente tomorrow.

Nixon had been euphoric, filled with wonderment and the sense of history, at the prospect of going to China, but he was withdrawn and filled with a sense of caution in returning to Moscow. He was determined to accomplish in Moscow what he had been training to do all his life: to strike some bargains based on such self-interest that could not be easily overturned, and to so engage the other superpower in a complex of negotiations that their tactic of détente would fit itself into his strategy for peace.

In many ways, by this stage of the Nixon-Kissinger relationship, the two men had mentally merged, but there were differing fields of interest: Nixon had a sense of the crowd, the power forces that come from having to deal with the needs and whims of large numbers of people, giving spirit, emotion, and "moxie"—a favorite locution—to Kissinger's sense of the subtle balance of power alignments. Where Kissinger could operate in what he liked to call a "conceptual framework" with Ambassador Dobrynin, Nixon could get on the same wavelength as General Secretary Brezhnev: that came not from the men's stations but from their lives. Neither Nixon nor Kissinger was expert in economic affairs, but the President felt the pressure to discipline his interest to come to grips with events that affected consumers. The President would turn to his national security adviser for grasp of detail as well as grasp of strategy, but only Nixon could sense in a personal way just what the Russian leader was going through with Central Committee member Pyotr Shelest of the Ukraine, an active opponent of the tactic of détente. Only an elected leader could decide how hard to push for an agreement; a political sense was needed to be able to calibrate the degree of "give" in both sides' bureaucracies and public opinions.

Nixon had placed a political timing on his springtime of summits: close enough to the fall 1972 election campaign to be effective, far enough away not to be too blatantly political. Circumstance, and his own fell clutch on it, had given a twist to the President's timing, with the Soviets at a disadvantage after the mining of Haiphong harbor. But the ultimate timing was Nixon's own brand of statecraft. Not as enamored of summits as Churchill, not as suspicious of them as De Gaulle, he had a "long view" as dedicated as any Communist and a good sense of how to keep the heat on until time and fruit were ripe. And Nixon's ingrained suspicion of the State Department was not unprecedented. He was aware of this message from FDR to Churchill in 1942: "I know you will not mind my being brutally frank when I tell you that I think I can handle Stalin personally better than either your Foreign Office or my State Department."

In negotiating technique, Nixon and Kissinger put on a formidable display, like a two-man interrogation team where one man holds a truncheon and the other offers a cigarette.

Nixon's way was to appear rigid, sit tight for a long time, and then go for a "bold new approach" that can be considerably different from his original position. Kissinger, on the contrary, was willing to invest heavily —in money and, if necessary, in lives—to achieve bargaining credibility, that is, an understanding by his adversary that a Kissinger proposal has about five degrees of leeway in it and no more. "Have the other guy punch pillows," Henry explained to me, "never confront, but never yield." A proposal put forth by Kissinger on behalf of Nixon, then, was not to be lightly discounted or the counter-offer to be too far away if the adversary had any inclination to make a deal; then, if the imaginative stroke was needed, Nixon would supply it or Kissinger would attribute it to him.* There was an added complexity: sometimes Kissinger played the tough guy, sometimes Nixon did, so the bid they presented could not always be analyzed in terms of the next steps. "I have the reputation of being a hard-line anti-Communist," Nixon stressed at one of his first Kremlin meetings, and he had made certain that Kissinger had pointed that out to the Russians in the preliminary negotiations. When Nixon pronounced that statement, Alexei Kosygin, who was created to exemplify the adjective "dour," cracked his first thin smile of the summit and replied, "We know, we know."

Nixon's greatest negotiating strength came from the fact, which he went out of his way to reiterate, that his roots were on the political right; that the traditional, conservative suspicion of a Yalta-style "secret agreement" was out of the question with Nixon at the negotiating table. At the President's direction, Haldeman had sent a memo to a handful of us making this point eighteen months before: ". . . the American people and the people of the world appear to have confidence when President Nixon talks with the Russians. They know that he can hold his own and there is not the apprehension that there has been at times when two-way conversations have been held." We knew this message came directly from the President because it was accompanied by a plea to point out "that the President never misses any of the things he's scheduled to do because of illness," a foolish example of duty-first stoicism Nixon always wanted to get across, but never did until he came down with pneumonia early in his second term.

Nixon's mission in Moscow, then, was partly tactical: to use the Soviet desire for détente as a lever to achieve peace in Vietnam; to use the pressure of the presence of world leaders in the same room to reach agreement on arms limitation that might otherwise drag on for months, or even miss the moment entirely; and to take the moment at flood tide, leading on to his own political fortunes, being President at the summit when other men had to be candidates on the stump.

It was more than tactical. The Moscow summit, culmination of three

---

* "Somebody told me you had no convictions," Henry said to me one day. I replied I had no arrests but plenty of convictions, and Henry smiled: "That's a good line. Why not call Maxine Cheshire and attribute it to me?"

years of diplomacy, a decade of shifting power balance, and a generation of positioning, could—if it went according to plan—fuse together the needs of conflicting and distrusting powers, beginning a process of cooperation so complicated and engaging that it would be impossible to separate the intertwined ganglia without too much mutual pain.

Nixon, a mystic rather than a mechanic about power, wanted to make himself a symbol of tough-minded, sentimental, dignified Americanism to the Soviet peoples, giving the Soviet pragmatists at the top more leeway to lean against generations of anti-American propaganda. The most dramatic element to the summit meeting in Moscow was that the result was not ordained. On the details, some treaties were all set to be signed, but there was no idea of what would be done about Vietnam, and there was some doubt SALT would be advanced to treaty form. Nobody could be certain how the symbolism would work out, either: whether the chemistry would lead to explosions or synergisms, whether the reaction of the press and the world would be skepticism about, or confidence in, the future of peace.

After a brief visit to Salzburg, Austria, to avoid jet lag when we arrived in the Soviet Union (I could see the President looking dangerously at the fancy outfits of the Austrian Honor Guard) the *Spirit of '76*, preceded by the press planes, landed in Moscow. We began living by our little schedule notebooks; this is a page from the first night:

MONDAY, MAY 22, 1972 - Continued
Dress for official dinner: Business suit and street-length dress.

Guests receive invitations which also contain seating assignments for the dinner. A seating chart is available in St. Vladimir Hall.

VIP AND STAFF INSTRUCTIONS

From Hotel Rossiya:

7:40 p.m.   Motorcade departs hotel en route the Grand Kremlin Palace with the following:

Sec. Rogers	Mr. Scali
Amb. Beam	Mr. Price
Mrs. Beam	Mr. Safire
Asst. Sec.	Mr. Hyland
Hillenbrand	Mr. Negroponte
Amb. Mosbacher	Min. Klosson
Mr. Flanigan	Mrs. Klosson
Mr. Ziegler	Mr. Andrews
Brig. Gen.	Mr. Codus
Scowcroft	Interpreter
Mr. Klein	Mr. Matlock

7:50 p.m. Motorcade arrives at the Grand Kremlin Palace. Party is met by a Soviet protocol official, who escorts group to St. Vladimir Hall.

From Kremlin Residence:

7:45 p.m. The following members of U.S. party attending the dinner meet in the residence and, escorted by a Soviet protocol official, walk to the Grand Kremlin Palace:

Dr. Kissinger	Mr. Sonnenfeldt
Mr. Haldeman	Mr. Walker
Mr. Chapin	Mr. Lord
Miss Woods	

8:00 p.m. The President and Mrs. Nixon arrive at the main entrance of the Grand Kremlin Palace.

Chief of Protocol Kolokolov and Commandant of the Palace Kazakov greet President and Mrs. Nixon.

The President and Mrs. Nixon are escorted up the main staircase and proceed to St. George Hall where the Soviet leader greets them.

President and Mrs. Nixon and the Soviet leader move to St. Vladimir Hall where the Chief of Protocol introduces the dinner guests who are standing in a line around the room.

8:15 p.m. Cocktails are served in St. Vladimir Hall.

8:30 p.m. The Chief of Protocol claps his hands to signal the party to move to the Granovit Hall and take their places. Dinner begins.

9:45 p.m. After dessert, the Soviet leader proposes a toast.

President Nixon responds immediately.

10:00 p.m. Dinner ends. The President and Mrs. Nixon bid goodbye to the Soviet leader and walk to residence.

VIP AND STAFF INSTRUCTIONS

9:05 p.m. Attendees at the official dinner return to residences in the same manner in which they arrived.

OVERNIGHT

In that last paragraph of the 8 P.M. entry, a good idea was introduced to us by Soviet diplomacy—the reverse reception line. "The Chief of Protocol introduces the dinner guests who are standing in a line around the room" means that the reception line remains stationary while the guests of honor move along it. In this way, the VIPs set the pace, all the reception-liners see the entire ceremony without being at the end of a line in another room, and somehow the whole thing feels more democratic with the world leaders moving around like the hands of a clock.

In Granovit Hall, its ancient panel paintings freshly retouched to give the room a modern, garish look, the President read the toast I had been slaving away at for three weeks without departing from text, evidence of the solemnity of the occasion. The Russian to my right pointed out the little window near the ceiling where the Tsarinas were permitted to look in at the stag dinners of the Tsars, while President Nixon was talking to the Soviet leaders next to a painting of the temptation of a saint.

At 4:29 A.M. on Tuesday, May 23—the first morning that an American President awoke in Moscow—a U. S. Secret Service agent was startled to see Richard Nixon, dressed casually in a maroon sports jacket, pass the agent's post on the way to a Kremlin stroll. Two other American agents were promptly alerted by radio. Joined by three Soviet KGB men, they took their flanking and following positions as the President walked downstairs and out into Moscow's early morning sunlight.

He walked past the great, cracked iron bell, ignored the Tsar's black cannon, and crossed a wide street leading to a monument with fresh flowers at its base. There, the thirty-seventh President of the United States stopped and took a long look at the statue of Nicolai Lenin, the first chairman of the Council of People's Commissars.

On the way back, using one of the KGB men as an interpreter, he stopped to chat with a Soviet soldier. "How old are you?" "Twenty-five." "You have a long life ahead of you." At four fifty-three, the President retired to his quarters, made some notes, and by five-thirty was back to sleep.

Through that first day, in private sessions and semi-public dinners, all eyes were on the interplay between Brezhnev and Nixon. Ordinarily, Nixon would let Brezhnev take the lead, responding to rather than leading the conversation. The Soviet leader, who walks with a stately, carefully controlled pace, lets himself become animated when seated. With his right hand, he conducted conversations, cigarette between index and middle finger, elbow on the table, using his hand to shape arguments and indicate nuances. Nixon, who walks stiffly, was relaxed when seated, steepling or folding his hands. Brezhnev champed at the bit while his interpreter was putting his words into English; Nixon, though six years younger than his counterpart, was infinitely more experienced in communicating across a language gulf, and spoke slowly, using a simple construction and plain words wherever possible, nodding during the translation for emphasis and as if he understood.

In such circumstances, facial expressions are important; both Nixon and Brezhnev, with pronounced and expressive eyebrows, used them to advantage. Brezhnev was adept at an eyes-widened, "so that's it!" expression, briskly nodding and projecting an air of welcome discovery, and Nixon was excellent at an expression on his face that says, "Is that so?" reminiscent of the photo of General Eisenhower when informed that General MacArthur had been fired. Both men knew all about the way to play to photographers, and constantly upstaged each other in their ostentatious deference. (The first photo they were in together, in the "kitchen conference" in 1959, is described in this book's prologue.)

Nixon, accompanied by Kissinger and NSC staff members John Negroponte and Winston Lord, went to Brezhnev's dacha on Wednesday, May 24, to talk about Vietnam. The dacha is neither rustic nor as well appointed as Camp David's Aspen cabin; like the President's retreat in Maryland, this hideaway is in the midst of a forest, with a view down a long slope of the Moskva River. At six-thirty, they went for a boat ride on the river and at seven forty-five assembled in a small room with a long table. Podgorny, Brezhnev, Kosygin, and interpreter Alexandrov sat on one side, the President, Kissinger, Lord, and Negroponte on the other—for some reason, probably to get away from the formality of other negotiating sessions, possibly to better be able to enjoy the view of the river, the President sat on the end of the American side. Henry once drew it for me. The river is on the right, down the hill:

Podgorny   Brezhnev Kosygin Alexandrov

Hill

Negroponte   Winston Lord..Kissinger President

The meeting started on a note of acrimony and steadily became worse. "Barbaric!" was the Brezhnev characterization of the mining of Haiphong harbor; phrases like "just like the Nazis" flew around the room, and before long there was yelling, table-pounding, and threats about what could happen if Soviet ships and sailors were injured by bombs or mines.

This was hardly the image of the Moscow summit that was being presented to the outside world. In public, the leaders were taking shots of vodka, shaking hands for cameras, getting along famously. In the large private sessions, the atmosphere was businesslike and formal. Here in the small room, Leonid Brezhnev was a different man. The Soviets had done their best to prevail on the North Vietnamese, they had told Kissinger, and just because they could not succeed was no reason for a barbaric act that put Soviet ships in jeopardy and endangered the lives of Soviet sailors. Nixon, who knew the extent of loss of face Brezhnev had suffered when he did not call off the summit after the Americans mined Haiphong harbor, looked stolid and impassive. Every fifteen minutes or so, the President would respond to a Brezhnev diatribe with a couple of sentences. (There are two sides to every coin: the Nixon who cannot appear warm and cozy on television was uniquely capable of appearing icily impervious to shouted imprecations from world leaders in a small room.) At one point, Nixon used an approach that Khrushchev had once used on him thirteen years before, in the kitchen conference, where Nixon had first briefly met Brezhnev. After a particularly savage blast, Nixon asked coolly, "Are you threatening, here?" When that had been translated, there was a silence; the meeting went on in a more restrained atmosphere for a few moments, and then back to the one-sided onslaught. Kosygin was especially bitter about the possibility of a Soviet ship being hit by an American bomb; Brezhnev berated Nixon for endangering détente over such a peripheral matter as Vietnam.

Then the damndest thing happened. When it was over, it was over, and they all went upstairs to a larger room, sat down and had a dinner that two of the American participants described to me later as "jovial." The contrast between negotiating with the Chinese and the Soviets could not be more extreme. In China, the mood of the negotiations and the cultural events and dinners was of a piece—correct, civilized, slightly patronizing from the Chinese side, almost serene. With the Soviet leaders, it was bombast then laughter, saber-rattling then smiles, hard work then hard drinking, going to bed when it was light then waking up when it was light and wondering where the Moscow nights were.

Brezhnev and Nixon found common ground in making Kissinger the butt of jokes, a role Henry enjoys when conducted by heads of superpowers. "Our people have instructions to settle SALT," said Brezhnev, over a brandy. "If not, it has to be Dr. Kissinger's fault." The President, with some zest, suggested: "We'll send him to Siberia—would you take him?" Brezhnev roared at this kind of sinister good humor, and said that if the negotiations failed, they would send Kissinger to Alma Ata (the Siberian town where Khrushchev had sent Malenkov after deposing him), and if he succeeded, to Lake Baikal, noted for its depth and frozen condition—not much of a choice either way. After a half-dozen vodka toasts, the Russians pretended to argue the wisdom of getting Kissinger drunk. Since he had to negotiate that night when he returned to the Kremlin, would he be a pushover if drunk, or would he get belligerent? Lots of laughs.

But Brezhnev worried Kissinger with a bit of information passed in the merriment: "We have assigned Smirnov to conclude SALT. He's never met a foreigner before." (Leonid Smirnov was a hard-line Deputy Prime Minister in charge of Soviet arms production, close to Kosygin, and an unknown quantity as far as American negotiators were concerned.) After the dinner at the dacha was over and the last toast hoisted, the Americans returned to the Kremlin and the NSC members to the negotiation at 1:30 A.M. Gerard Smith, the chief U.S. negotiator at the SALT talks going on in Helsinki, had cabled Kissinger that the U.S. delegation was not pleased with many of the concessions Kissinger had been making; moreover, the Joint Chiefs of Staff in Washington did not like them either, and might not hold still for further moves which it felt would compromise U.S. security.

Kissinger had treated Smith with contempt, more as a front man than a negotiator. The key negotiations on SALT for the past year had been conducted in the corner office of the West Wing of the White House between Kissinger and Anatoly Dobrynin; it was there that the most serious impasse had been resolved a year before, when Kissinger and Dobrynin arranged for their leaders to sign the preliminary agreement of May 20, 1971. I have been in Kissinger's office when he was on the phone to Dobrynin—kidding, at one moment, about a bottle of Russian brandy he had received from Anatoly and how the Secret Service was still looking for the transmitter in it, and then turning to a matter like the exchange of captured intelligence agents and solving the problem in a way that made it seem casual. In their face-to-face sessions, Kissinger would flatter Dobrynin (especially after he had been made a member of the Central Committee) as being tougher than the Russians that sold Alaska to the United States, and Anatoly would wish on Henry the job of being American Ambassador in Moscow negotiating an agreement.

Both of these men, operating near the highest level and seeing more to U.S.-Soviet relations than SALT, had problems with their chief negotiators at the bargaining table, where all the details of the agreements were being worked on. Dobrynin saw fit to, or was required to, fill in the Soviet negotiator, Semenov, on what was happening in the "back channel"; Kissinger saw no need to give the U.S. negotiator, Smith, more than what Henry decided he needed to know.

Not surprisingly, Smith and Kissinger came to cordially despise each other. Nixon, who always was suspicious of those "State Department, arms-control types" was happy to see the cards were being held close to the Presidential vest. Nixon could readily interpret the objections interposed by

Smith as the agreement neared its conclusion in Moscow as—in Kissinger's term—"wounded vanity." But it was Smith's expressed worry about giving away too much, concurred in by at least one member of the NSC staff in Moscow, and backed up by the Joint Chiefs with their connections in the U. S. Congress, that forced the President to take one of the biggest risks of his life.

There was some irony in the way that Nixon and Kissinger, the hawks, were pressing for a settlement, and arms-control bureaucrats, the doves, were in alliance with military men in the United States in being hesitant about too-generous U.S. terms.

At 2:15 A.M., May 25, Kissinger returned to Nixon's quarters in the Kremlin with bad news. The Soviets were adamant about not significantly limiting the size of their missile silos (which meant they could place weapons far larger than their massive SS-9s in the "holes"). Nor was there any "give" in their position on the construction of submarines—which, since the United States had no sub-building program in the works, would soon give them an enormous strategic advantage.

The President was lying on his stomach on the rubdown table, with Dr. Kenneth Riland, his osteopath, giving his aching back a massage. He asked if Al Haig, back in the White House, had checked Senator John Stennis of the Armed Services Committee. Kissinger reported that Haig had, and that Stennis was lukewarm about supporting an agreement like that. Haig had added that he was lukewarm about it himself.

"You'll be alone on this," Kissinger told the President. Nixon did not want to find himself returning to the States with an arms agreement that could be assailed as a sellout of our security interests; on more substantive grounds, he wanted to be sure the agreement he reached did indeed provide that security. Though few people realized it at the time, there was more to be lost politically in coming back with a criticizable agreement than in returning empty-handed. Politically, it would have been better to blame the Soviets for breaking off negotiations, and to take a tough stand, rather than to take the flak from the right and the smirks from the left.

Moreover, the President had the advantage of the Haiphong mining. He knew the Soviets wanted this agreement so badly that they would not sail their shoes against the wall, Khrushchev-style, at a U.S. insult. He knew, too, how important a West German agreement was to the Soviets— opening up Western technology to them when they needed it most to increase their lagging productivity—and that a Moscow summit failure would endanger that agreement with the Brandt government.

What the President did not know then was the extent of the Soviet need for a major deal on U.S. grain. The U.S. intelligence estimate about Soviet grain production was wrong; the Soviets appeared to want to make a deal, but they were excellent poker players—never revealing the desperate straits they were in, then or later, when they began to buy judiciously. As in most negotiations, each party is well aware of its own weaknesses, and can only guess at its opponent's weaknesses.

So Nixon decided to tough it out. If he failed, as Theodore Roosevelt had pointed out, "at least he failed while daring greatly." He took one of the most fateful decisions of his Presidency, and of the postwar generation, there on the massage table.

"Go to your negotiations, Henry. Do the best you can. But we don't have to settle this week."

Kissinger returned to the negotiating table at 2:30 A.M. Smirnov, meeting his first foreigner, heard the foreigner coolly describe the characteristics of Soviet weapons, which, Henry told me afterward, "was like telling J. Edgar Hoover about his most sensitive procedures—Smirnov practically had an apoplectic fit." The Deputy Prime Minister lost his temper—his remarks lost flavor in the translation—and in Kissinger's later description to the President's staff, "he didn't contest anything I said, only my right to say it." Foreign Minister Andrei Gromyko stepped in, as Kissinger kept describing Soviet weaponry to Smirnov's outrage, and asked for a fifteen-minute break. He cooled off his arms expert—or they agreed that the tactic of outrage was not working—and as Kissinger recalls, "at 3:30 A.M., with the light coming in the window, we got down to serious business." They settled the issue of the changes in the dimension of the silos to the Americans' satisfaction, but Henry did not have the authority to trade away the submarine limitation and would not budge. Smirnov would not budge either; at 8 A.M., the Soviets went to the Politburo to report and get final instructions.

Kissinger slept until 11 A.M.—this was Thursday, May 25—talked briefly with Nixon, got the slept-upon decision of the President, took a walk around the grounds with Dobrynin, and let him know the President was prepared to return to the United States without signing the SALT agreement, which had been scheduled for Friday afternoon. There was a ninety-minute negotiation on Thursday afternoon on economic matters with Kosygin and Podgorny, not discussing SALT at all—and without the participation of Leonid Brezhnev, whom Nixon suspected was having a problem with his own hard-liners, especially in the Ukraine.

So, with the most important agreement deadlocked and the Soviet top man fighting his internal battles, we all went to the Bolshoi Ballet. A member of the U.S. party who is a balletomane says that the performance of *Swan Lake* that night was only fair, and not all the top dancers were there. I was seated in the box next to the center where the President and Mrs. Nixon sat with the Podgornys and Kosygin; the theater is maintained in all its gold and red-velvet elegance, contrasting with the ostentatiously plain dress of its audience. At an intermission, the unheard-of happened— the wife of an Italian diplomat shouted angrily at the President. The man seated next to me was the head of the Soviet guard detail. He held up two fingers, two men behind me bolted out the back of the box to find out the cause of the disturbance. As it turned out, nothing disturbing was afoot, but that was the first time most of us considered the consequences of an assassination attempt on one superpower's leader in the other's country.

The American press treated the shout as no big deal; the Russian newsmen were dumbfounded. An associate editor of Pravda, in a nice parlay of Communist totalitarianism and Russian tradition, told me: "It's strange enough to hear shouts at political leaders, but at the Bolshoi, it's inconceivable."

At dinner after the ballet, Kissinger sat next to Gromyko and remained discouraged. He told Ron Ziegler to spread the word that there might not be an agreement signed the next day, and went into the next late-night round of negotiations with this instruction from Nixon: "If you don't think it's right as it stands, don't agree." Kissinger, eager to make a SALT agreement a capstone of the summit and the first term of the Administration, caught the President's mood and moved to reinforce it. "Unless we get what we want," he reports he told the President, "we shall not conclude." As he put it to Herb Klein, John Scali, and myself afterward, "Look, it wasn't just a matter of this summit—his political ass was on the line."

At 2:30 A.M., Kissinger told Gromyko it did not appear that a signing was possible for Friday. Gromyko asked about Saturday; Kissinger said no, the President was to be in Leningrad Saturday and did not want to call that trip off. Sunday or Monday, Gromyko pressed, and Kissinger said yes, if the Soviets would make a concession on the submarines to be built. (I will not go into the details of the agreement or its obstacles here; much of it is told in John Newhouse's remarkable book, *Cold Dawn*, and Henry Brandon has a detailed chapter from the Kissinger point of view in his *The Retreat of American Power*.) Nixon went to bed that night depressed; he wanted to sign an agreement as badly as the Russians did, and knew if the moment were missed, it might not soon come again; but he had set his negotiation course and was determined to stick to it.

Friday morning at ten-thirty Dobrynin came to see Kissinger; Brezhnev was back in the act; Gromyko would see the American team at eleven-thirty. At that session, the Soviets gave their position one more try, and then within twenty minutes accepted all the U.S. terms in dispute.

Both sides then had an agreement but no document. The two formal delegations were still in Helsinki and could not be expected to produce a document that night. Kissinger, determined that Gerard Smith and the U.S. delegation not be permitted to admit impediments to the marriage of true minds, worked out an agreed-upon text with the Soviets in Moscow and told them to cable it to the Soviet negotiators in Helsinki, giving our negotiators the second copy, which must have been quite a humiliation. Henry proudly pointed out that this was the first time in diplomatic history when identical instructions were sent to the two parties negotiating an agreement—and he did not add it was the perfect way to show whose handiwork the agreement really was.

As with any act of love, there was a terrific rush at the end. Shortly after noon on Friday, I told an American protocol man that I thought there would be a signing that night. He said, with a note of disdain, "They don't sign international agreements on typing paper, you know." He was wrong:

there was going to be a signing that night on foolscap if necessary. As Gromyko put it to Kissinger: "Why admit we couldn't do it?"

At one o'clock the President, who never takes a drink at lunch, told Kissinger, "We have to drink to this." He poured out a couple of glasses of vodka and both men belted down the tasty essence of Russian potatoes in a gulp.

That night, in the rush to sign, both Nixon and Brezhnev signed the wrong page of the English version; next morning, before leaving for Leningrad, Haldeman brought in another last page to sign. Everybody was a little hung over from the night before, but the President remembered to wish his national security adviser a happy forty-ninth birthday.

At that hypertense time—it was like the last stage of a close political campaign—it was hard to exaggerate the importance of all that had happened. Later, Winston Lord put it in a single sentence that Kissinger okayed and the President signed as part of a message to Congress: "Never before have two adversaries, so deeply divided by conflicting ideologies and political rivalries, been able to agree to limit the armaments on which their survival depends."

Dwight Chapin sent me a message that I had been bumped from the President's ceremonial trip to Leningrad to work on some toasts and to consult with Kissinger on backgrounders. The President wanted the story of the Moscow summit to be more open now, and was worried that the habit of secrecy would stay with us all after the necessity for some credit-taking had begun.

I hung around the President's apartment for a while, invading his privacy with some interest. He traveled with seven suits, two sports jackets, eighteen ties, and a black l'Aiglon woven leather belt. Blue and white striped pajamas hung in the bathroom, and loud blue slippers poked out from under the bed, with "presented to President Richard M. Nixon" printed on the inner soles, and his gold wrist watch, which he forgot to put on that morning, on the bedtable with "To VP RN NAWSS May 20, 1955" inscribed on the back. In the paneled study next to the bedroom, near a brass lamp with a green shade and long green fringe hanging from its edges, was the President's homework in neatly organized briefcases. Briefcase A contained the Issues Book: Volume I, Soviet Leaders; Europe. Volume II, Vietnam. Volume III, Mid East. Volume IV, SALT. Volume V, Basic Issues. In Briefcase B, Volume I was labeled Bilateral Agreements; Volume II, Dr. K. Conversations in Moscow; Volume III, Background Reading; Volume IV, Soviet Policies and Objectives; Volume V, State Department books on Austria, USSR, Iran, Poland, all the countries on the current trip. There was a bookcase with Russian books in it, but if the President wanted to turn from his homework for some light reading, there was one book in English, Dostoevsky's *The Idiot.**

---

* Nixon's reading in Russian history led him to some odd conclusions. Six months after his return from Moscow, the President was being briefed by environmental aide Russell Train about a mutual inspection project of the U.S.'s Lake Tahoe and the USSR's

Late Saturday afternoon, with the President on his way back from Leningrad—where he had come across a memorial to Tanya, whose family was killed in the Nazi siege, and whom he would use in several speeches—Kissinger was showing signs of strain. The night before, after Gerard Smith had given a confusing, defensive, and unnecessarily secretive press conference about SALT, Henry had saved the situation with a long briefing standing on a platform in the Intourist Hotel nightclub that stressed the point that security had been achieved at last. By that time Henry was physically beaten and irritated by the constant questioning that seemed to indicate a U.S. "defeat" at the negotiating table. Murray Marder, a Washington *Post* reporter who knew more than any other reporter on the trip about the SALT negotiations, had helped change the mood of the correspondents with his well-informed and generally friendly questioning— the press corps figured that if Marder wasn't furious, maybe the U.S. had a good deal.

At Bob Haldeman's insistence, Henry sat down with a few of us to fill us in on what could be said on background, since the Soviets had men hanging around the press rooms and bars with party lines they were putting out to correspondents (especially to the French reporters, whose dispatches would be read by Hanoi's delegation at the Paris peace talks). In his exhaustion, Henry was blunt: "On the sub deal, they finally adopted the essentials of my formula. Not my formula, the President's formula." On the communiqué's writing: "Say that Marty Hillenbrand will be there." (That was a reference to the Assistant Secretary of State for European Affairs, one of the few top men at State whom Kissinger respected, and an acknowledgment of Hillenbrand's presence was intended as a sop to the Foreign Service.) Why were the Russians so anxious to get an agreement? "To stop our ABM's." Was the agreement ever really in doubt? "I was sure we'd have a deal by Sunday, but, Jesus, these guys are tough negotiators." Soviet Jews? "Say nothing while we're here. How would it be if Brezhnev comes to the U.S. with a petition about the Negroes in Mississippi?" Economics? "There'll be a grain deal when Peterson gets here. The maritime deal was screwed up by the unions, and that must be handled first before we can conclude the grain deal." The President's state of mind? "Don't say he's elated; he feels mature about it." That was not so, the President did feel enormously elated, but it would not have been a good idea to take that posture in front of the other party to an agreement. When I pressed Henry on that, he snapped, "He never dances a jig." That was an unfortunate reference to Hitler's reaction at the surrender of the French, and he quickly explained, "Look, you know he has a tough situation back in Washington. Scoop Jackson will hit this hard." At that moment the President called. He was back from Leningrad, enthusiastic, and wanted to see

Lake Baikal. "Are the Soviets trying to develop tourism there?" the President asked. Train said he thought so and the President said, "Gambling, that's what would do it for them—a big casino on the lake. Tolstoy made a million on *War and Peace* and gambled it all away on cards, you know." Train didn't know what to say.

Henry, who was not so enthusiastic, but was glad to have the chance to get away from us.

The President was now most concerned with his speech to the Soviet peoples on television. ("Never say 'Russian people'" I had written to the President after admonishments from U.S. Soviet experts, "but refer to 'Soviet peoples' in the plural.") It would have an enormous viewing and listening audience in the Soviet Union, and even be telecast in its entirety in the United States, though not, as Haldeman pointed out grimly, on prime time or on all three networks. Nixon was especially conscious of the rare opportunity to reduce mutual suspicion on this telecast. For a leader of one superpower to address another superpower's population is no small potatoes. To the State Department's dismay, Nixon chose the top Soviet interpreter, Viktor Sukhodrev, to do the running translation, rather than an American translator. This in itself was evidence of trust (besides, Nixon admitted, Sukhodrev is the best in the business today) and the brilliant interpreter's performance supplemented Nixon's own hard work—obviously, nobody told Sukhodrev not to do his dramatic best.

Nixon had done his best to set hyperbole aside for this trip. Before he left the States, he told reporters "so my remarks are not with the overblown rhetoric which you have properly criticized me (for) in the past," rather a startling thing for him to say—but he had not set aside *schmaltz*, and in a speech to "folks," not to diplomats, *schmaltz* had its place.

This was not his first speech to the Russian people. In 1959, then-Vice President Nixon had delivered a speech on Soviet radio, which is still used in public speaking classes as a classic in refutational rhetoric, setting up and knocking down a series of beliefs in the minds of the audience. Nixon's 1959 talk was rational, very low key, almost legalistic in its presentation, with limited aims and clearly achieving those aims.

In 1972 he took the same theme—although philosophical differences are deep, cooperation will keep the peace—but this time made an effort to stir the emotions of millions of Soviet citizens. The speech was built on three images rooted in the Russian character. The first, the "mushroom rain" that greeted him on his arrival in Moscow, a sunshower that makes the mushrooms grow, a good omen to Russians who think of mushroom-gathering in the woods the way American suburbanites think of barbecues in the backyard. Second, a story of the traveler who wanted to know how far he was from town, and was only answered by a woodsman after he had established the length of his stride. Third, the reference to Tanya, a Leningrad heroine whose story moved Russians the way Anne Frank's moves us, evoking innocence and hope amid hatred and war.

The mushroom rain idea was contributed by Harriet Klosson, wife of the deputy chief of mission of the U. S. Embassy, who passed it to me to pass to writer Ray Price; the woodsman story came from Leonid Brezhnev via Henry Kissinger; and Nixon researched the Tanya story himself, reading a display on his visit to Leningrad. U.S. correspondents there were inclined to view the images, and the speech itself, as standard Nixon cornball with a Russian overlay; but a reporter who speaks Russian, and who watched it on television with a Russian family, reported an emotional reaction from "folks" who were Nixon's audience. The year 1959 was ancient history; now Nixon was not out to score points but to reach and move a populace that had much in common with his Silent Majority in terms of unabashed and unself-conscious patriotism, sentimentality, and the desire for a peaceful order.

Another difference that could be observed between the Nixon of 1959 and 1972 was in his readiness to ad lib. Written material was held close to hand in 1959; the kitchen debate with Khrushchev could not be prepared, but other speeches and remarks were honed and rehearsed.

In 1972 he varied his style easily. I wrote the opening toast at Granovit Hall to Kissinger's exacting specifications, and Nixon did not depart once from the text he edited (he knew "the only way to enter Moscow is to enter it in peace" would go over, and he hit it hard) nor did the Soviet leaders depart from their committee-prepared remarks. Yuri Arbatov, the Kremlin's Americanologist, seated across from me at that dinner, whispered loudly after some platitudinous line of Podgorny's, "Do you hear the steps of history walking by?" I said, "Oh, did you write that part?" and he gave me a hurt look.

But Nixon felt no compunctions about departing from his text, sometimes when he wanted to, sometimes—as when the reading light went out at the podium in Warsaw—when he had to ad lib. In Kiev, he set aside a prepared speech, seizing on a brief note I had appended to his suggested remarks about Kiev's eleventh-century Golden Gate. The President built his remarks around the similarity of experience of "two cities of the golden gate"—Kiev and San Francisco—one ravaged by war, the other by earthquake and fire, but fortunate enough to have citizens with the spirit to rise and rebuild greater than before. Appropriate; well-phrased; oratory in the grand style; done without a note.

But following that speech, this little problem came up:

After the dinner in Kiev and the toasts and the speeches, a group of Ukrainian entertainers performed for the President and Mrs. Nixon. They were wonderful, but went on and on until after midnight, whereupon the President became possessed of one of those nice, warm ideas: to set up a group picture. He said to Bob Haldeman, "Let the photographers in," turned and proceeded to do one of his favorite acts, Setting Up a Picture. Nixon was an enthusiastic composer of photos, usually big crowd scenes à la Busby Berkeley that never made the papers, but he enjoyed it and so did the people in the picture, who were later relentlessly pursued until they received autopen-autographed copies suitable for framing.

The trouble in this case was that the photographers had all been sent home in a bus two hours before. In the States, a small group remains behind in case, but in the USSR, when the photographers go, they all go and they are not soon seen again. There was the President, telling his wife to stand here and the leader of the Ukraine to stand there, putting the tall baritone next to the tiny soprano, while a look of horror slowly spread across Haldeman's face as the awkward moment neared when the truth would dawn and the President of the United States would look like a pitiful, helpless giant.

Dr. Walter Tkach, the Presidential physician, also seeing this terrible moment in the works, ran outside to his car and came back a few moments later with a tourist's Instamatic camera topped by a flashcube. When the President turned around, having arranged about twenty people to his liking, and expecting to face the assembled world photographic corps, there was his doctor with the little camera. The President smiled uncertainly; the little flashcube went off; Nixon, the smile frozen on his face, gritted, "You better shoot another, Walter," which he did. The Ukrainians noticed nothing amiss, the President was spared the egg on his face. "You've been with us for three years in case of an emergency," Haldeman told the physician, "and that was it."

There were other nervous laughs on the trip, often centered around the likelihood of Soviet eavesdropping. When the SALT negotiations reached the point when some quick photocopying was needed, Henry Kissinger held a document up to the chandelier and an imaginary lens, asking, "Could I have half a dozen of these in a hurry?" Gromyko said no, the hidden cameras in the Kremlin had been installed back in the time of Ivan the Terrible and were not sensitive enough to copy documents. That kind of banter showed a certain ease in a relationship; of course, the less significant the meeting, the more elaborate were the precautions against prying eyes and ears. The American Embassy in Spaso House contains a "clean room," a plastic room-within-a-room that is supposedly impenetrable, like the "cone of silence" in a forgotten television spy series. Chapin called a meeting there to make sure all of us were wearing our pageboy beepers (which one of the President's aides refused to do because he claimed whenever the buzzer in his pocket went off it made him pee down his leg). On another occasion, at a meeting in Ron Ziegler's suite in the Intourist Hotel, the press secretary tuned his TV set up to loud volume, as Herb Klein played his transistor radio, John Scali banged his highball glass steadily on the coffee table, and I hummed a series of Al Jolson favorites. It is to be hoped that this caused difficulty for eavesdroppers, because it certainly made it impossible for any of us to know what the hell the meeting was about.

Similarly, when I called columnist Charles Bartlett's home in Washington from Moscow, I had been warned the call was being recorded. Charlie wasn't there, but his wife Martha was, and she wanted to remind me to buy some antique Oriental porcelain when I got to Tehran. "Don't forget the china!" she yelled around the world, and I only hope Peking-oriented Soviet tappers were listening to that.

(We laughed about the tapping. A year later, after all the stories of illegal tapping by the "plumbers" and the FBI had come out, we looked back and asked ourselves if we wanted a society where it was assumed that everything you said was being overheard and could be used to blackmail or jail you. The tapping ceased to be a laughing matter.)

Tehran really did not belong on the tail-end of a trip to Moscow, but the President wanted to show his respect for his anchor in the Middle East, the Shah of Iran. With De Gaulle and Adenauer gone, the Shah was about the President's favorite statesman in the world.* After an overnight state visit, the *Spirit of '76* came back through Warsaw, scene of a tumultuous welcome for Nixon in 1956. The President sent Chapin back through the plane to tell the press aides and writers to spread the word that no similar reception could be expected—he did not want the Warsaw story to be a poor comparison to his previous visit. "And remember this, gang"— Chapin was the only person I have known who used the word "gang" with sincerity—"no Polish jokes. The first guy to make a Polish joke gets his ass shipped right back to the States. I mean, really, no foolin', the Old Man is serious about that."

He was absolutely right. Crude, cruel ethnic humor would not only have been in bad taste, but would surely be quoted and built into an incident. However, when the plane rolled to a halt at Warsaw's International Airport, and the ramp was pushed up to the door, the *Spirit of '76* stood there for ten minutes because the Polish ramp didn't fit the plane and every one of us was afraid to look at anybody else for fear of exploding in inane, undiplomatic laughter.†

Four days after we left Moscow, after the State Dinner in the beautiful Malinovsky Palace in Warsaw, the impact of the summit began to set in. The President, who had been holding himself so closely in rein, began to loosen up on the plane earlier that day. The playback of the success of the Moscow summit was coming to us in the USIA summaries as well as the President's News Summary. The AP led a dispatch: "The US and SU agreement has been scorned by Congress conservatives but praised for the most part by both liberals and moderates." Nixon knew he could contain the conservative reaction with his treaty, and was sure that only a conservative could have brought about such an agreement. Haldeman's memo of two years ago looked valid: Nixon's reputation as trustworthy in dealing with Communists, his stand-up-to-the-Russians image gained in a Moscow kitchen so long ago was invaluable in making it possible to end the arms race. "Only Nixon could have . . ." The news summary had another item of interest: "McGovern says he's pleased but 'I have to admit a certain inner anxiety about the way the so-called great powers can preoccupy themselves with arms accord and joint space efforts as important as those things are . . . while at the same time pretending that that killing in Vietnam is happening on some other planet.' "

George McGovern's dog-in-the-manger reaction was perfect for us,

---

* After Nixon's fall, the Shah wrote him a long and moving letter of condolence.

† A Polish joke told some years later went: "Question: How would Nixon have handled Watergate if he were President of Poland? Answer: The same way."

Nixon men thought. And the Washington *News* headline was typical of small-newspaper coverage: "RN Winds Up Summit in Glory."

Henry Kissinger and I walked out of the Malinovsky Palace about 11 P.M., followed by his Secret Service guards a dozen paces back, to stroll through the reconstruction of downtown Warsaw. The Poles have redone the city the way it was before World War II's devastation, and there was something to be said for not having used the leveled areas as an excuse for high-rise office buildings. We wound our way through the dark, new-old streets saying little. Henry looked back at what had happened the past couple of weeks, where the world was, where he and I were walking, and said in what struck me as honest affection, "Not bad for a couple of Jewish boys, huh?"

We talked about the book he would do someday, and the one I would do fairly soon. "Yours will be better," he assured me, "because you only have to be 90 per cent right." I recalled another walk we had taken, around the pitch-and-putt golf course in Key Biscayne in January 1970, working on the first "State of the World" message, when he had said about Bill Rogers and the State Department: "It's like the Arabs and the Israelis. I'll win all the battles, and he'll win the war. He only has to beat me once." He remembered, and said it had not changed much—one wrong step and he was finished; all the vultures would eat him up. But, he said, it was all worth it, even the backbiting, because what he and Nixon were doing really counted for something, and if they had not happened to be there at this time, who knows who would have missed the chances the President and he were not missing?

We could not know that a combination of Russian bargaining shrewdness, weird crop conditions, and bureaucratic ineptitude would make the forthcoming grain deal appear scandalous; or that during that time we were in Moscow a small group of workers for the Committee to Re-elect the President was planting listening devices on the telephones of Democrats in their Watergate headquarters; or that in the coming year the Soviet press would be in the odd position of denouncing American impeach-Nixon demands as aimed against the policy of détente that Nixon and Brezhnev had brought about. That was all as inconceivable as shouting at political leaders in the Bolshoi.

"Been one hell of a week, Henry," I said, as we came to the replica of an old square in Warsaw where members of the American party were whooping it up in a nightclub. "What does the President do for an encore?"

Henry didn't hesitate a second. "Make peace in Vietnam," he said.

PART SEVEN

MUDDLING ALONG
ON THE HOME FRONT

1. NIXON'S EHRLICHMAN

What Henry Kissinger was to Nixon in foreign affairs, John Ehrlichman hoped to become in domestic affairs. In the early days of 1971, when the "State of the World" was being fashioned in the National Security Council, the State of the Union was being launched out of the Domestic Council, containing plans for what Nixon wanted to call "The New American Revolution." In some ways, the product of Ehrlichman and others lived up to the hyperbole, adding much to the promise of the "new Federalism": revenue sharing, government reorganization, and welfare reform were all directed toward satisfying the national conscience while returning control to the states and localities through a selective decentralization.

More than anyone else close to Nixon, John Ehrlichman changed during the President's first term. In 1973, after the balding, stocky, Germanic lawyer from Seattle had finished testifying aggressively to the Senate Select Committee looking into Watergate, columnist Joseph Kraft gave his impression of how Ehrlichman had changed over the years: from a friendly, open, liberal-minded man when he brought his fine family to Washington in 1969, to the arrogant, tough expounder of the Presidential-power line of 1973. The conclusion the columnist reached was that a good man had been corrupted by Richard Nixon.

Ehrlichman changed, all right, and dramatically, but in a more complex way, as I saw it. His personal story tells a great deal about Nixon, character, Fate, and all that.

He came to Washington after having proved his loyalty and efficiency to the Nixon operation as a campaign tour director; a staff man who knew how to follow orders; a martinet in many ways, intolerant of little mistakes. (I recall coming late to one of his staff meetings during the campaign of 1968. He spotted me in the back of the room and snapped, "Safire, your Nixon pin is upside down." He was right; when I looked down, the word spelled "Noxin." "He has eagle eyes, the bastard," I said to myself.) He was junior to Haldeman, who at UCLA had been the manager of one of Jeanne Ehrlichman's campaigns for student office. Jeanne was perky, warm, poised, and intelligent, among the best of the new White House wives. Her discreet irreverence seemed at the start an odd contrast to her up-tight husband, who gave the impression of a man ready to march off a cliff if given the appropriate command.

Within one year, John began to change for the better. He showed himself to be a man of balance and compassion, the "closet liberal" on many matters; perhaps, with growing confidence, Ehrlichman was able to set aside an unnatural overlay of officiousness. He was destined to follow orders on national security matters that would bring him to a Senate committee as a spokesman for unlimited Presidential power, sounding on his way out of public life as arrogant as he appeared on his way in. Because of the manner of his departure, one would never know how much he had matured and developed, how much good work he had accomplished.

Let's begin with Ehrlichman at his early worst, in the 1968–69 interregnum, when he was still clipping along as the tour director without portfolio, angling to establish a domestic council with himself at the head but losing to a star system built around Daniel P. Moynihan, Arthur Burns, and Bryce Harlow. Haldeman told him to take charge of the "PR types" to get out the proper "line," and I received this pompous memo from him soon after I was appointed to the White House staff:

To: Bill Saphire   Date: December 16, 1968

From: John D. Ehrlichman

It has been suggested to me that we capitalize upon the work habits of the President-elect: long hours of work, delayed dinners, 18-hour days, late reading, no naps, perfunctory and very short lunch and breakfast times (frequently 5 or 10 minutes);

No time for exercise except walking to and from;

Also his make-up as evidenced by his selection of Cabinet and staff: that he is unafraid of being surrounded by brain power; that he selects bright people; that he is intolerant of stupidity; listing Rogers, Kissinger, Laird, Mitchell, Kennedy, McCracken, Moynihan as illustrative;

When he goes to Florida next week, he will carry bulging brief-cases of work; he is a voracious reader who seldom indulges in reading personal stories about himself but limits himself to reading on the issues;

In 22 years in public life, he has never singled out a critical writer for personal criticism since he has deep respect for the craft.

His television habits run to the documentary and entertainment, rather than news. He seeks news in perspective and seldom spends his time with the instant news broadcasts since he has found them to be frequently inaccurate.

His suspicion of "instant news" will bring about a removal of the news tickers and the multiple television sets from the White House.

In addition to the possibility of the foregoing as a basis for a personal line, it would be appreciated if you and Garmond and anyone else you would like to include would spend some time preparing suggestions for descriptive names for the Black Capitalism, news dissemination, listening post, youth service, and similar proposed activities.

Herb Klein should be employed as the disseminator of the lines developed and approved, and we should work out some system of regular get-togethers to insure that you and your colleagues are abreast of advance planning both from the standpoint of schedule and program. I am at your disposal for this purpose.

John D. Ehrlichman

JDE/hg

The "Garmond" referred to was Len Garment; Len and I had a talk about this note and shrugged it off. Some of it made sense—"unafraid of being surrounded by brain power" was true—but "In 22 years in public life, he has never singled out a critical writer for personal criticism since he has deep respect for the craft" was twisting a fact. I have always enjoyed crystallizing a line of argument, or a positive theme about Nixon or others that might not be perceived, but it always had to be rooted in common sense and supportable by some evidence. Privately, Nixon had often expressed such lack of "respect for the craft" that it would be boneheaded to try to sell the idea that Nixon was above the possibility of irritation by reporters.

Nixon was to repeatedly lean on his aides to stress how he never complained publicly about an individual reporter, to contrast with Kennedy's and Johnson's diatribes. Nixon felt that his refusal to complain about reporters individually in public dramatized his restraint under intense provocation by a press corps that he was convinced hated him.

Nixon's feelings about the press, and Ehrlichman's willingness to indulge those feelings, was driven home in the next memo from Ehrlichman, showing not only his willingness to follow bad orders without question, but the President's state of mind at the time (Nixon was at his best in adversity, at his worst in victory).

To: Bill Safire   Date: December 23, 1968

From: John D. Ehrlichman

Subject: Research Paper

RN requests that a research paper be developed which includes a recapitulation of the typical opposition smears of Richard Nixon back through the years, including the more vicious press comments.

John D. Ehrlichman

JDE:sw
cc: Pat Buchannan

I ignored the memo; Pat Buchanan did too, I think, and ammunition was denied those sessions in which the Nixon men would "rub each other's sores," as the President-elect liked to put it.

Ensconced in the White House, on the second floor of the West Wing, Ehrlichman began to relax a little and to separate his work from Haldeman's. They were old friends, both Christian Scientists, and both had German names—it was easy to identify them as "the Prussians," and later "the Berlin Wall," lumping them into a single entity. As they headed in different directions—Haldeman to strict staff management and Presidential public image, and Ehrlichman to public issues, a "substance man"—their banter and their relationship remained frank and friendly.

For example, there was a meeting in the Roosevelt Room at 10 A.M., April 16, 1969, with Haldeman, Ed Morgan (a deputy to Ehrlichman), Len Garment, Bud Wilkinson, and I:

Haldeman went to the fireplace, nicely stacked with wood ready to be lit, and showed us all how to light the fire. "You have to heat the chimney to get a draft," Bob explained confidently, and held a flaming piece of twisted-up newspaper up the chimney for a moment. Then he lit the paper under the logs, and the smoke began to pour into the room. Coughing, wiping his eyes, Haldeman sputtered, "Tell Higby when he comes in at seven-thirty every morning to light the fire."

As the fire blazed up, Haldeman went to his seat and tried to start the meeting. It was too hot on his back, and there was too much smoke, and he changed his seat. Ehrlichman came in the Roosevelt Room at that point, looked around in mock horror: "What's with the smoke-filled room? That's not the right image for this Administration."

"Close the door," Haldeman said. "All we need is this damn smoke going across the hall into the Oval Office."

Ehrlichman protested, "But we'll walk out of here smelling like a bunch of Smithfield hams!" He was right; in a few moments, the cloud of smoke had spread across the ceiling and was steadily descending down to head level, at which point the meeting participants would certainly choke. The subject of the meeting was my suggestion for an Administration ombudsman. I wanted to move quickly on a public interceder in the White House, but Ed Morgan, a fine man and a glutton for hard work, wanted a thorough study. Ehrlichman, sensing that Haldeman was grimly determined not to be driven out of the meeting by the smoke, and would stoically suffocate before opening the door and letting smoke blow into the President's Oval Office, came up with a fast resolution—a short study, report back in ten days, the meeting was over as far as substance was concerned, did Bob have anything else? Only then did Haldeman conclude the meeting and we all groped our way out into the fresh air.

Ehrlichman's proximity to the President meant that he was the object of the President's irritation with others. Richard Nixon never has enjoyed telling anybody bad news, firing anybody, or running down associates to their faces. This could be variously interpreted as gentility, a lack of ruthlessness that erodes executive authority, shyness, cowardice, or a reluctance to take on small confrontations with people when big confrontations with issues or institutions are so much more worthy of Presidential time. Here is a typical memo along that line from the President, directed to two aides:

June 16, 1969

PLEASE TREAT AS VERY CONFIDENTIAL

MEMORANDUM FOR: MR. EHRLICHMAN
                    DR. KISSINGER

Subject: Comment by the President (information only)

This is just a short note to inform you, at the President's request, that he doesn't think much at all of Dave Packard's response when asked what the President had meant by a "sufficiency" of arms. As reported in today's Presidential news summary, Packard merely shrugged and said, "It is a good word to use in a speech. Beyond that, it doesn't means a god-damned thing."

ALEXANDER P. BUTTERFIELD

This would be followed up by Nixon to Ehrlichman or Kissinger with "Did you tell him? What did he say? Then what did you say?"

Toward the end of 1969, the competitive reign of Moynihan and Burns in domestic policy was replaced by the rise of Shultz and Ehrlichman. Labor Secretary George Shultz had been an economist, dean of the College of Business Administration at the University of Chicago, and he was what

Nixon considered *"un homme sérieux"*—a man whose presence carried the authority of intellect and command, who would offer sensible and sometimes startling conclusions in a way that Nixon admired. Shultz became the senior domestic man, Ehrlichman the junior, but Shultz was his own man and Ehrlichman was Nixon's man—a staffer who drew his power and position from the Boss, with little independent personal authority. So Nixon would hammer on John, but treat George with deference, and once —with unintended cruelty—told a visitor that if he really wanted something done in the domestic area, to see George Shultz, not John Ehrlichman.

Despite this, or because of its accompaniment by long hours in personal conversation with the President, Ehrlichman continued to grow in prestige and mature as an executive. On January 26, 1970, the President decided to veto the HEW appropriations bill as too costly. I cooked up a veto message for television, which Ehrlichman rewrote completely, leaving a lonely sentence: "There is no good time to waste the taxpayers' money, but there is no worse time to waste it than today."

At six-thirty, two and a half hours before the President was due to go on the air with his speech, Ehrlichman called me to come to his office with Bryce Harlow to go over the latest draft. I objected to a line that said "taxes are too high," and John allowed as how that was a Presidential favorite but maybe he was wrong to imply a promise of that sort. When the President called to ask the three of us over to his EOB office right away, I snatched up my papers and made ready to make haste. Ehrlichman, however, was quite relaxed in the face of such a Presidential summons. We entered the elevator on the second floor and pushed the basement button. The car stopped at the first floor and a messenger was standing there with a large cart of mail. Every harried staffer, including Harlow and myself, hastening over to the President impatient for a draft with a deadline approaching, would have said, "Take the next car." Not Ehrlichman. He waved the man in, held the door-open button while he jiggled the cart past the door, and patiently waited for the messenger to get it out when we reached the basement.

The President was nervous. This was his first veto, and it hit right in the liberal breadbasket—funds for health and education—making Nixon seem like a skinflint taking money from the people who needed it most in the name of a vague anti-inflation effort. He was going to do it dramatically—actually sign the veto on the air—but he did not yet have his script in hand.

(An aside: When I was first assigned to this, I asked four top White House aides, "How do you veto a bill—I mean, what do you do physically?" Nobody knew, of course. Fortunately, there was an Executive Assistant of the White House who had served forever, or at least since Herbert Hoover, named William Hopkins. He said: "Sign the veto, not the bill. If the President writes anything on the bill and then signs it, it may be a law, so write nothing on the bill—not 'Vetoed, RN,' or anything like that.

Leave it alone, or else you may have a law." With the President going on TV with both documents in his hand, to set one aside firmly and then to sign the veto, I worried about a mix-up and the hooting that would follow.)

In Nixon's EOB office, Ehrlichman brought up the point about a line that read "I think prices and taxes are too high," said he agreed with me it was wrong. The President looked at me. I said we weren't about to bring prices and taxes down, just to try and not have them go up so fast. He nodded and made the cut. Almost anything that made the speech shorter was all right with him, so he could get it down to about eight minutes or twelve hundred words. Ehrlichman didn't like the use of a word, "impose," and suggested "institute"; I said "begin" was better than that, but the President liked "institute"; later, I saw we had been arguing about a typographical error—the word should have been "propose," which is the way I fixed it.

The President was both pleased and irritated because he had caught an error that all of us, including Ehrlichman and the careful Bureau of the Budget, had missed, referring to "next year's budget" instead of "this year's budget" (which projects ahead a year). With that mistake in mind, Nixon demanded we double-check every figure in the speech, a task that fell on Assistant Budget Director Richard Nathan, who had a headful of figures left over from the State of the Union message four days before. The President told me to take my master copy across the street to Rose Woods to type a reading copy; I stopped in the vestibule of the EOB office for a moment to check a fact with Nathan, then trotted over to an anxious Rose— she had just been called by the President demanding, "Where are the first three pages?"

While we were waiting on the steps of the EOB, Bryce Harlow observed to Ehrlichman: "You notice how his style is changing? His whole approach to his job seems to be different now. He wants to get much more into substance and detail and argue things out for himself. He used to rely on his staff much more for these drafts than he does now." Harlow had served as an Eisenhower speechwriter, and this difference in Presidential operation was not lost on him. Ehrlichman agreed: "You should have seen him on the State of the Union. We had a long discussion on just about every line. And he never forgets anything, which isn't always good."

We watched our television set to see the President firmly set aside the bill and sign the veto message. (Fortunately, he didn't mix them up, as he said, "For the first time, tonight, instead of signing a bill which has been sent to me by the Congress, I am signing this veto message."*)

At Ehrlichman's direction, Dick Nathan and I worked into the night to rewrite the veto message to the Congress, inserting paragraphs of the President's speech into his message draft. Whenever we called somebody for

---

* The first bill the Budget Bureau recommended be vetoed had to do with the pay of zookeepers at the National Zoo. Jim Keogh and I felt that the President's first veto should not be on a matter that would lend itself to funny editorials, and the zookeepers, unvetoed, got their raise.

information, they would say, "But I just saw the President sign the veto message on television with my own eyes," and we would tell them not to believe everything they saw on TV, the message still needed work.

Ehrlichman was careful to remain in the President's orbit, but obviously liked working with and learning from Shultz. The President felt he could make political comment to Ehrlichman with more ease, as if Shultz, coming from academe, were above politics. When both Shultz and Ehrlichman were in a meeting with the President March 30, 1970, Shultz—still Secretary of Labor—raised the question of how to pay for the increase to go to postal workers after their strike. It was to Ehrlichman that the President turned and said, "If we send up a surtax extension without going to war with Russia, nobody will ever believe us again."

At about this time—before the Cambodian incursion, before the Kent State tragedy—Ehrlichman began to make known his concerns about the posture of the Administration. He lined up against the hard-liners privately and persuasively, as can be seen in this confidential memo to Haldeman April 15, 1970:

CONFIDENTIAL

FOR BOB HALDEMAN

Contacts in depth with people on the outside, and excluding for the moment any consideration of the news magazines for this week, the content of which I do not weigh into this, I am impressed by several basic facts.

In terms of social programs, e.g. manpower training, anti-poverty, environment, health and education, we are doing as much or more than Johnson or Kennedy.

In terms of sound legislation on the domestic side, experts agree that we have made more good proposals for significant reform (draft, post office, manpower, occupational health and safety, etc.) than any for ten years.

We have loaded aboard a lot of bright, young, able people who can present the President and his programs in an excellent light.

Nevertheless, among young business executives, among municipal officials and on the campuses we are epitomized by the Vice President, the Attorney General and Judge Carswell.

We are presenting a picture of illiberality, repression, closed-mindedness and lack of concern for the less fortunate.

Even to those individuals who are conservative in their politics or their economics, credibility, fairness and openmindedness are considered to be desirable attributes in an Administration.

I do not sense any existing activity on the part of Herb Klein or, for that matter, Ron Ziegler, to respond to this dilemma.

It is not simply a problem which is manifested in polls.

The widespread negative impression on campuses and in urban areas can directly result in urban and campus unrest and I think that's where we are, coming into the spring.

The lack of understanding among young executives of the opinion-maker group is even more disturbing if it is a gauge of the penetration of our line among the literate.

I assume it is our object to make a conscious effort to broaden our political base. The Agnew-Mitchell-Carswell presentation can only result in a narrowing of the base since it appeals to only one segment of the spectrum, and repels the balance.

We are about to send up, for instance, the message on the all-volunteer army. We are about to consummate postal reform. We are about to announce further moves in Vietnam. Each and every one of these should have strong appeal for young people, for young business people and for ghetto dwellers.

I will watch with interest the efforts made to drive home the inherently popular appeal of these programs among segments of the population where we are weakest. I'll bet you there isn't a ripple.

Ehrlichman

This concern for the sensitivities of young people was the cause of what nineteenth-century novelists would call "a strange twist of Fate." Haldeman, upon receiving the memo, asked his assistant, Jeb Magruder, to come up with a "game plan" for reaching out toward youth. This was promptly, if mechanistically done, and one of the ideas in Magruder's memo appealed to Haldeman especially.

There are two dozen more of these young men and women, all of whom are bubbling over with youthful enthusiasm for the President and his programs. Why not generate more publicity here? And why not encourage, rather than discourage, this group of people to accept speaking engagements on college campuses from time to time? We're never short of invitations and a Staff Assistant to the President is a big drawing card on the campus. If thirty Staff Assistants each hit just one campus per month, we'd make 360 campuses in a year.

There are also bright young fellows in the Departments who probably have never had a column inch of publicity. John Dean,

Dick Kleindienst's aide, is an example of a sophisticated, young guy we could use.

As if unconsciously signing his death warrant, Haldeman handwrote in the margin: "Absolutely. Really work on this" beside Dean's name. See Plate 7, following page 200.

In the uproar after Cambodia, Ehrlichman led the way among White House staffers to meet and talk with agonized young people. Such action was expected of Len Garment, Ray Price, Pat Moynihan, Steve Hess, John Price, and the centrists who were considered "the libs,"* but Ehrlichman's efforts were more important, since he represented more of a piece of the Old Man, and reporters might not have expected him to be as active in this. John was sincere, too; I saw him with a group of angry young people one day, in a private session, and he was giving it all he had; they were impressed if not sold, but the fact of his attempt to communicate was more important than success or failure.

He became less the servant of the President's whims, and while not yet the chief adviser, at least the respected staff executive on substantive issues. John was called out of a meeting one day to see the President, and excused himself to his visitors. Later he said, "When I got to his office, he asked if I had been free, and I mentioned the visitors. He then told me, 'I shouldn't have called you out. Let me know when that happens again.'" Ehrlichman told that story with an affection for a boss who had turned more considerate, and for its reflection on his own changed standing.

He picked up a few hints from old hands at personnel relations in how to work with people. Since Pat Moynihan had sent champagne to the White House telephone operators on Valentine's Day, teetotaler Ehrlichman sent them boxes of candy on Mother's Day, even those who were not mothers.

When his name was misspelled—leaving out the 'h'—in *Courage and Hesitation*, a book by Fred Maroon and Allen Drury, he replied to an embarrassed note from Doubleday's Ken McCormick with this:

THE WHITE HOUSE

WASHINGTON

November 30, 1971

Dear Mr. McCormick:

It was very thoughtful of you to write me as you did about the way my name was spelled in the Drury-Maroon book.

---

* My nephew, Peter Safir, was visited by a dozen friends from Princeton who came down for the demonstrations, and stayed with him in some rooms above my garage. I would give a few of them a lift to the White House in my car in the morning, where they would demonstrate outside while I worked inside, and it gave me a good feeling.

Since the book hit the bookstores the other day, I've noticed that my mail has begun to arrive without the first "h". I had a letter from my mother today. She left out the first "h", too.

Over the weekend my wife and I talked about this and decided that you would probably be selling tens of thousands of those books and all those people would get used to seeing my name spelled that way. Undoubtedly many more people will read the book than my wife and I together know personally or correspond with. So we have decided (and our children have agreed to this) that Doubleday and Company doubtless know best. Who are we to try and fight such a big corporation with all of those presses and those bookstores?

So beginning today we have dropped the "h" out of our name like you wanted us to. Yesterday my wife went through all the kids' clothes and took out those little labels that we sewed in when they went to camp and we have ordered a whole new batch with the new spelling. It is going to cost about $9.85 plus my wife's time sewing them in again. The bank says I can get new checks with the new spelling . . .

At this stage, it was Ehrlichman—I'll keep the "h"—along with George Shultz and Caspar Weinberger, who was putting the "new Federalism" into action, pushing for revenue in the Congress over the stern opposition of Ways and Means Committee Chairman Wilbur Mills (the President was right about the chairman's holding "open hearings with a closed mind") and meeting with groups of Governors and mayors to show how the shift of responsibilities would work. While taking flak directed mainly at Haldeman for being part of the "Berlin Wall" to protect the President, Ehrlichman was actively lobbying against the President's resistance to abortion reform, against the Colson effort to provide aid to parochial schools, and as a couple of chapters herein suggest, he was a force for moderation in the reaction against busing. "We have to protect the President from his own worst instincts," John said more than once, and Colson would use that remark against him as evidence of less than total loyalty to the President.

Ehrlichman was still following direct orders with fidelity, but he had earned the right to swing a little—to resist somewhat, to have his view carefully considered, to promote a favorite project. He and Jeanne were even going out at night to civic events and dinner parties, which was considered a rarity for White House aides, though not nearly so rare as some columnists liked to say. The difference between Haldeman and Ehrlichman in the social sense was thus obvious; in the operational sense, it was more subtle: when it came to turning down Ehrlichman, the President would do it through Haldeman, but when it came to turning down Haldeman, the President would do that direct. Ehrlichman, who had been the tour manager of the '68 campaign, wanted to be the advance man for the President's trip to China in 1971–72, but Henry Kissinger did not want any White House staffer near his own level on the preliminary trips. Dwight Chapin got the job.

After a while, the White House tends to become just another office to the people who work there. Instead of getting power-crazed by virtue of living in a kind of palace, one can become power-bored by virtue of working in one. A sense of historic place is both valuable and tempering: it was Ehrlichman who pointed out that the quick walk we took several times a day between the White House and the Old Executive Office Building was the walk that Lincoln took to the office he kept in that old building when it housed the War Department. (The EOB is great. "Can't we get rid of those pipes on the walls?" I asked the decorator when I moved in, and she looked at me in horror: "You mean the antique tapestry hangers?") John dug up the Lincoln historical account by David Homer Bates: "His tall, homely form could be seen crossing the well-shaded lawn between the White House and the War Department with unvaried regularity." After that, it was impossible to trot between the buildings without a feeling of pride about the footsteps in which one was treading.

The "doodles" in this chapter and elsewhere in the book were the work of a man who was having fun, but who knew where he was and wanted to remember it. John gave me copies of his doodles to use in this book with generosity and self-deprecation; they add to the sense of "being there."

He had a strong sense of family, too. When the President was in California one weekend, Ehrlichman commandeered Camp David and invited up the Domestic Council staff with wives and children. Since I was working on a speech in the domestic area at the time, I was invited along, and could see Ehrlichman as an exuberant family man, enjoying the interplay of his own and other children and not just doing it for "staff morale." Back in Seattle when he was a zoning lawyer, he would take his family backpacking in the Washington woods, and the long hours in the White House —with weekends at the President's beck and call—were more of a burden to him than to men secretly pleased to get away from the wife and kids.

His first memo in this chapter talks stiffly about slogans. By 1972, I received a memo from Ehrlichman on the same subject that showed a new and becoming flippancy toward the packaging of issues: "As the old philosopher once said, facts are nice but slogans sell beer," it began. He enclosed a set of "key fact sheets" which described in stupefyingly dull terms the domestic initiatives of the Administration, adding: "The President suggested that I ask you to develop a slogan for each of these fact sheets as they come off the production line. We were thinking of having a slogan contest here among the messengers, secretaries and drivers but we decided to let you have a crack at it first . . ." I zinged out a couple of one-liners, he told the President his wishes had been carried out, and it was no big deal.

Meanwhile, of course, there were the occasional walks the President's confidential aide would have to take on the dark side of the moon. The "plumbers" operation came under him, and the abuse of power became Ehrlichman's area just as obstruction of justice became Haldeman's. Egil Krogh and David Young—fine, stalwart "straight arrows"—were infused with a sense of mission at getting information to stop the leaks that the President was grimly convinced were setting back peace and domestic tranquility. Krogh was Ehrlichman's protégé, from his law office in Seattle. The President personally motivated Bud Krogh to go out and get the facts on Daniel Ellsberg, which led to the mission by Howard Hunt and Gordon Liddy to break into the office of Ellsberg's psychiatrist.

Later, after the Watergate break-in conceived by those same operatives, Ehrlichman showed an apparent reversion back to his loyalty-first attitude. Perhaps that could be extenuated by the belief that an unauthorized action was being exploited by the political opposition, but his reference to loyal Acting Director L. Patrick Gray to be left "twisting slowly, slowly in the wind" was cruel, and his secret recordings of conversations with Richard Kleindienst and Herbert Kalmbach, who were hardly "the enemy," left other loyalists aghast and persuaded those two attorneys to cooperate with the prosecution.

Eavesdropping. The sneakiness did not trouble John Ehrlichman, who felt that the need for a permanent record outweighed the drawbacks of betraying the confidence of the person he was talking to. He had, after all, placed the FBI wiretaps of the newsmen and White House aides suspected of leakage in his office safe; listening in on conversations and making a recording hardly seemed to him to be immoral. Curiously, eavesdropping is the sinister thread that traces its way from early in the Administration through to Watergate. First the taps in 1969, then the plumbers, then the Mitchell-Magruder approval of the Liddy plan to eavesdrop on Larry O'Brien. Of course, the ultimate eavesdrop was the White House recording system, producing the tapes that incriminated the President and many of his men, and in the transcripts of one of those tapes made public in April 1974 was the height of eavesdropping irony: Nixon could not bear to face John Mitchell, who had authorized the wiretap of O'Brien, and passed that job on to Ehrlichman. When Ehrlichman allowed as how he would like to record that conversation, the President told him to "gear up" for it, and that he had similar equipment installed to record Henry Kissinger at times. The President was misleading Ehrlichman. The taping equipment was not in the Oval Office to record Henry on vital national security affairs, but for the purpose of recording everything—including Ehrlichman, who did not then know about the taping system operated by the President and Haldeman. The double irony on the tape was this: Ehrlichman was asking the President for permission to eavesdrop on John Mitchell, who had caused all the Watergate trouble by okaying the plan to eavesdrop on Larry O'Brien, but Ehrlichman did not know at that time that his request was being eavesdropped upon by the ubiquitous tape machine that immortalized everyone who spoke to the President. It was like one of the

Indian signs of snakes in a circle swallowing each other's tails. All in all, the eavesdropping circle was not to be believed by rational men, and the tolerance shown for it by John Ehrlichman is one of the strongest counts against the man.

"How could you do it—how could you record telephone conversations secretly?" I asked Ehrlichman at lunch in 1974 on the day after his conviction for perjury. "I never had any trouble with that at all," he replied. "As a lawyer, I did it as a matter of routine, because people have a way of forgetting what they say on the phone. And in the White House, you guys on the foreign trips would call in and I could hardly make out what you were saying, and had to play it back two or three times. The equipment is available to anybody, it's not illegal. I know you have hang-ups about it, but I never did." To this day, he will not admit the wrongs of eavesdropping, even to himself.

Just before I left the White House in early 1973, I snatched up one of Ehrlichman's doodles—of a wall sconce in the Cabinet Room—for inclusion in this book. I learned later from Steve Bull that, unknown to Ehrlichman, this was the sconce with the listening device behind it.

A passage in Herman Melville's *Moby Dick*, spoken by Ishmael, is something I look at in trying to figure out men like John Ehrlichman, enmeshed in the series of events leading up to Watergate:

> If I had been downright honest with myself, I would have seen very plainly in my heart that I did but half fancy being committed this way to so long a voyage . . . But when a man suspects any wrong, it sometimes happens that if he be already involved in the matter, he insensibly strives to cover up his suspicions even from himself. And much this way it was with me. I said nothing, and tried to think nothing . . .

At the Senate's televised hearings, Ehrlichman was the first witness to slam back hard at the Committee, refusing to concede guilt or to act penitent. He put on a tough show with chin outthrust, and his decision to brazen it out delighted Nixon supporters who were tired of getting kicked again and again. But the bland assumption that the Fourth Amendment was dead, and that the President had unlimited power to act in defense of national security, was a defense on illegitimate grounds. Coupled with his prepossessing appearance—that was always a problem with John, who was far less arrogant than most government officials in real life—the net result was to mark Ehrlichman as a neo-Fascist, and Herblock played up the anti-German slur by putting an armband around him with an "N" that looked like a swastika. That wasn't John Ehrlichman, not even in caricature. What happened to make him adopt an attitude that made such a perception possible?

Perhaps he felt he had to make a Constitutional case for a break-in that would keep him out of jail; perhaps he was told to charge directly into the

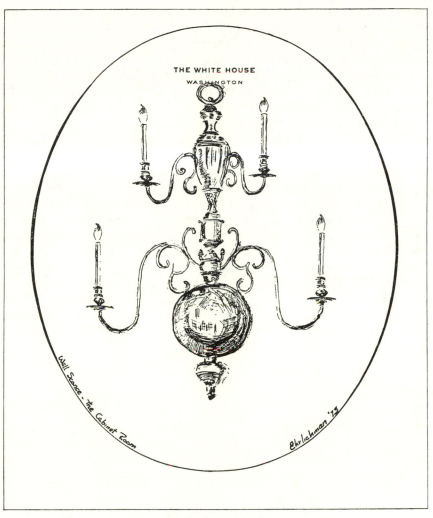

John Ehrlichman doodle.

Committee and stop its momentum at the price of his own reputation's destruction. Ehrlichman, who started out apparently so arrogant, showed humility and humor and sensitivity in the course of the Nixon first term, but left looking and acting more arrogant than when he came in.

There is tragedy in that, and the loss to public service of a man of intellect and stamina. In departing Washington, he refused to go along with the "stay away" advice to young people transmitted by a shattered young assistant to Haldeman named Gordon Strachan. Instead, Ehrlichman urged, "Come and do better." Yet, Ehrlichman was impelled to add, "You will encounter a local culture which scoffs at patriotism and family life and morality just as it adulates the opposite . . ." There it was again, the embittered "us against them," the self-isolating rejection of his attackers as unpatriotic immoralists, rather than as merely partisans, spoken by a man who discovered more about the complexities of the local culture than his simplistic parting shot revealed. In the fall of 1974, he returned to Washington for the conspiracy trial, no longer a defender of the indefensible; he infuriated Nixon by insisting his presence as a witness was necessary, and based his case on having been a protector of national security at the direction of the President. It had become "every man for himself," which can happen when "all for me" gets out of hand.

There is a lesson, too, in the slow switch from automatic press-hater at the start, willing to compile lists of vicious quotations from the past, to a reasonable man respected by many serious reporters for whom he found time to explain the less dramatic Nixon policies. Ehrlichman tried to keep up a brave front to reporters before the Senate hearings, and was asked if he intended to write a book. "I'm thinking of writing a column," he said, making conversation and trying to be friendly. "I understand there's space available." Washington *Post* columnist Nicholas Von Hoffman, who would deplore an "enemies list," crushed the banter with: "Yeah—but where you're going, you can't get it out." The face of the former Assistant to the President for Domestic Affairs went ashen, and he fell silent. Perhaps John Ehrlichman had learned the consequences of the indulgence of enmity, but not everybody had.

THE WHITE HOUSE
WASHINGTON

11-24-71   Cieline + wall detail - Minority Leader Ford's Office - Capitol Bldg -

John Ehrlichman doodle.

2. WAYWARD BUS REVISITED

Just as liberal Leonard Garment had been the central shaper of Nixon's 1970 desegregation message, pragmatist John Ehrlichman was the man on the scene as the President made his final education decisions in 1972.

In his 1970 desegregation statement, Nixon cautiously steered an ocean liner toward its port, relying for guidance not only on his own beliefs but on "input" from inside and outside government on this subject. Yale's law professor Alexander Bickel and Johns Hopkins education authority James Coleman made long and thoughtful contributions; White House advisers lined up against each other in extended argument and in the development of briefs and alternative statements; at the end of that 1970 study, Nixon decided on a responsible course concurred in by most of the government establishment and at least not opposed by most of the influential media. In this way, the President sought to defuse a potentially dangerous situation; to reassure anxious parents that the most extreme court decisions were no guarantee that their children would be bussed; and to lead the courts along a middle path, insisting on desegregation but not pressing integration.

In two short years, times had changed. The courts had not been led. The tide of public indignation was rising, and with it the gorge of the President of the United States. "Forced busing is wrong," he told me with some force in early 1972; "and I don't care if it does sound like demagoguery—I want to say so loud and clear. The courts don't understand the folks." He closed the conversation with "I happen to believe this."

In early March 1972, John Ehrlichman put out the word that the President was going to make a statement or a speech about the problem of busing, but in view of the forthcoming Democratic primary in Florida where George Wallace was making busing his central issue, the President would wait until after the primary to make known his views. Presumably, this was to ensure that he could not be accused of making the statement for political purposes, but that received as little credence as it deserved—in fact, making the statement after Wallace's victory, and after Muskie's impolitic excoriation of Florida Democrats who voted for Wallace, the President's speech gained even more of a political coloration.

I was relatively clean on busing—that is, I had not been bloodied in the scraps on the subject described in the earlier chapter and was not identified by the President as leaning one way or the other on the issue of the need for integration pressure to bring about desegregation. Ray Price, representing the President's conscience, was at work on another lengthy statement setting forth the President's closely reasoned argument against involuntary busing, at the same time reaffirming Nixon's commitment to the cause of civil rights in general and desegregation in particular; Pat Buchanan, representing the President's gut feeling, was sending in memos and draft speeches slamming the courts and the "social planners" who were dismissing the traditional values held by most Americans about neighborhood schools and substituting their own requirements for racial balance. For his speech, the President wanted a senior writer who had not been heavily involved in the subject, who could listen and not lobby, and by process of elimination the assignment fell to me. I put aside a foreign affairs assignment and drove to Camp David on March 14.

My previous stays there had been in a couple of the older, more rinky-dink cabins, but on this occasion Ray Price and I were assigned ("berthed" was the Navy phrase) in Birch, the cabin customarily used by Tricia and Ed Cox on family weekends. I slung my bag on the bed in the master bedroom and opened the closet to hang up my coat. There, to my shock and horror, were the frilly nightgowns and negligees of the President's older daughter. I slammed the door, leaned back against it, darted my eyes about and waited for something to happen. No thunderclaps. When Price came in and wondered why the only tapes for the stereo in the living room were old André Kostelanetz favorites, I opened the closet a crack and showed him the reason.

To work. The President called me at three-thirty that afternoon to outline what he wanted in detail, and the notes of that conversation might be more useful in knowing what was on his mind than a look at the carefully crafted speech itself:

"Let me give you a little guidance on the speech," he said. "Ten minutes, 1500 words. Now with regard to the tilt. The message Ray is working on, and it's an excellent job, tilts toward the reasonable approach and that kind of careful explanation is what I want to do in the written statement. In the speech proper, I want to speak to 'folks.' I've always been against busing—don't say 'forced busing' by the way, that's too obvious a code word—and now I'm going to do something about it. I want to say why I oppose it, and then put the monkey right on the back of the Congress— call for a law that stops further court orders on busing. Not a freeze, not a stay, but a 'moratorium' on all new busing.

"I want to make sure everybody knows we are not turning the clock back. Pick up some good rhetoric on that in the written message—and point out that quality education for all schoolchildren, black and white, is the thing.

"Here's the kind of thing I want to say to make it understandable. For example, when an eight-year-old child is within five minutes of a school, and could walk to school, but because of a court order to bus for racial balance he has an extra hour's ride—well, that's just wrong, there's got to be a better way. It's done in the name of ending segregation, but it's certainly detrimental to the education of that child. This has got to stop.

"Now, that's true whether the kid is white or black. White parents are worried about sending their kids into a school in a poor neighborhood, and black parents don't want to send their kids to hell and gone just so they can sit next to whites.

"Keep it simple, enough detail so that it's honest, but I want people to say, 'By God, he's saying what we believe,' because I *do*." Nixon thought about that a moment, and added: "Be sure and say we're not turning back the clock. I don't want a Wallace-type speech.

"Let's crack the extreme lower court decisions that have led us into this contradictory maze. That's made it necessary for Congress to step in.

"Start off by saying my position on busing is well known—I've always been against it. On segregation, I've always been against that, too. Now the question is, how can we deal with segregation in a way that does not result in busing?"

I pointed out that "in a way" were his three favorite words—to get out of Vietnam *in a way* that did not mean surrender, to return power to people *in a way* that did not set back the clock, to manage the economy *in a way* that would enable the free market to take over again soon, and the President added "—and the purpose of the Brown decision was better education. So we have to desegregate *in a way* that brings about better education."

He wanted to get across his sense of urgency: "High up, put that the trouble with a Constitutional amendment is that it would take too long. Even one year of inferior education is too high a price to pay. That's why I'm for—one, a moratorium on all new busing—two, improved education, with the money to fix up ghetto schools, and—three, for all agencies of Government, at every level, to carry out the spirit of this message in their actions." He put on his speech voice: " 'I have directed the Department of Justice to intervene in those cases where it is necessary to prevent busing of this nature.' And what I say to the bureaucracy isn't a suggestion —it's an order.

"I won't go into the rigamarole about Title I, nor is this the place for a long defense of Negro rights. There's no way you'll get the support of the pro-busing people. And don't take that to mean that Negroes are pro-busing—you'll see, they're not. We've got the support of the majority, white and black, on this, and I want them to know the President is strongly on their side.

"I don't have the luxury of demagoguery here, I have to be simple without being simplistic, you know? Plug the written message to Congress in the speech, I want somebody to read that. This is the most difficult damn problem that has confronted this nation in a hundred years, and we just have to come to grips with it, all of us—that's the spirit I want.

"And look, Bill—don't shop it around. I've sweated out the policy already on the message. I am the one who will decide on this."

I said he had told me not to show the big economic speech to anyone, either, and it was a lucky thing I had not taken him literally. "All right," he conceded, "I may let Ray take a quick look, but Ray and Len and Buchanan and Ehrlichman—they'll all want a crack at it. So no copies. I'll make the decisions."

After looking at my first draft that night, which was primarily a popularization of Ray's message, Nixon decided that I belonged in the group who did not quite understand what he wanted, and interposed John Ehrlichman between himself and everybody else. These were some of the comments the President handwrote in the margin of my first draft:

make it more vivid   make a stronger attack on lower courts chaos

add Spanish speaking

great majority of blacks would never be helped by busing

John Ehrlichman brought back pages of notes; Buchanan was getting his licks in, and the President would refer John to paragraphs of Pat's but wanted the speech to stay in hands that could be called centrist, or moderate, or at least opportunist.

In one notation, the President spelled out the purpose of his speech:

Some (of) our Courts have gone too far—
Time has come to call a halt—

Then, in a three-point handwritten addition, he laid out his basic position on the whole subject:

1. purpose of desegregation is better education
2. Busing as means for desegregation brings inferior education
3. There desegregation sans busing—

Interpreting the final item, "There desegregation sans busing": the President indicated, "therefore, desegregation without busing is our goal." (He always used the French *sans* for "without" in writing notes—it reminds me of the time he said Hubert Humphrey was not seen as "*un homme sérieux.*")

Ehrlichman's handwritten notes summed up Nixon's position:

> *It's wrong*
> *I'm against it*
> *I'm going to try to stop it*

Around midnight, I took Ehrlichman's notes, which outlined the President's thoughts plus selections from my drafts and Buchanan's, as well as a couple of paragraphs from Price's message, and pulled it together again for Rose Mary Woods, Sally Cutting, and Marge Acker to type. I sent it to Ehrlichman and waited.

By this time, Len Garment—who had scored so often in the original desegregation position paper two years earlier—had several substantive changes to suggest. At breakfast in Laurel cabin the next morning, Len looked up as Ehrlichman came in. "No on all three," said John, relaying the President's decisions.

Garment had given it all he could, but what he could convince Nixon of two years before—that steady pressure to desegregate was "the right thing"—did not apply in the same way anymore. Nixon saw busing as a profound personal-freedom issue, not a phony issue to be dismissed with charges that any position on it was demagoguery. Nixon knew that most lower-middle-class mothers, when they were considering moving into a new neighborhood, first looked for a school and then for a house, and felt that "the right thing" was to respect that sense of neighborhood.

Nixon had his position; it was supported by his majority; and throughout the campaign that followed, he made sure there was daylight between himself and the Democratic candidate on that subject. The President knew that the people could be led, appealed to, ordered and shamed—as had been the case in the long struggle toward desegregation, a just cause that the majority might not otherwise have joined—but when any arm of government went too far, the people would say no. Justice could not be blind to the injustices caused by the pursuit of justice—at least, in Nixon's view, not in this area.

When it came to passing a law, the Congress largely ignored the President. Some anti-busing amendments were tacked onto school aid legislation so that Congressmen could say they "voted against busing," but nothing along the lines the President had asked for was seriously debated. The rejection of Nixon's busing moratorium was no major political setback—the President sent the voters the intended message about where he stood—but Congressional reluctance to help inner-city schools disheartened the more compassionate of the Nixon men. Here were the so-called liberals of the House and Senate stanchly defending "aid to Federally impacted areas"—localities that received bonuses for school support where Federal employees were stationed, a schooldoggle that enriched some of the richest communities in the nation at the expense of the poorest—while denying emergency assistance to the public schools that needed money most.

On the busing issue, Nixon's instructions to his speechwriter in early 1972 turned out to be prescient. In 1973, Roy Wilkins of the NAACP was to say, "There is no sacrifice of racial pride or loss of education if blacks go to school with blacks . . . Black children will not suffer by attending an all-black school." Washington *Post* columnist William Raspberry, the most influential Negro writing today, commented: "It has long seemed insane to me for black people to pursue whites from this neighborhood to that and clear on out of the county because of some unspoken belief that black children could not get a proper education in the absence of white children. It struck me as educationally unsound, psychologically damaging to black children, and tactically disastrous. And it had scared hell out of an awful lot of white Americans whom it is useless to call racists."

So who won, the good guys or the bad guys? From the perspective of a liberal of the Sixties, the forces of reaction had been flirted with and then set back in 1970, and then cravenly caved in to in 1972. A liberal of the Seventies might credit Nixon with steadfastly pursuing desegregation— Negro pupils in all-black schools in the South decreased from 68 per cent in 1968 to 9 per cent in 1972—but would hastily fault him for doing it because he was forced to, not because he wanted to. However, the liberal of the Sixties, who took a sharp right turn on this and other issues in the Seventies, as so many did, might say that Nixon did sense the mood of the people, and did no damage to "the good end" of desegregation by denouncing the "bad means" of busing. In 1974, the Supreme Court, in a 5 to 4 decision with all four Nixon appointees voting with the majority, set aside a Detroit plan to integrate city and suburban schools. The busing issue was not ended, as the citizens of South Boston would discover, but it seemed as if Nixon's view would prevail.

3. HARDBALL

"Forced" busing, abortion, the denial of aid to parochial schools, and the denial of freedom to jailed Teamster leader James Hoffa were four of the matters Presidential aide Charles Colson stanchly opposed. Colson was the architect of Nixon's "new majority," and more than anyone helped the President turn away from the idealistic "new alignment of ideas" to the practical realignment of voting groups based on self-interest.

We will come to that "new majority" later. Colson was also the manager of the news, a pejorative label for the necessary task of seeing to it that an Administration does not trip all over itself in public, making five major announcements on Monday and clamming up the rest of the week. He was brisk, short-haired, and liked a short laugh; a moneymaking lawyer and former aide to Senator Leverett Saltonstall, he was used by the President as a breaker of china—that is, to upset the system of controls on substantive issues Nixon trusted to Ehrlichman, John Mitchell, and George Shultz.

Haldeman did not like Colson; he was a living "end run." Nixon liked him to the extent of placing him in the office next to his Executive Office Building hideaway, which Colson used for the most effective one-up at the White House: whenever you raised your voice in objection to a Colson idea, he would look furtively at the wall of his office, giving you the impression that he hoped you had not disturbed his neighbor, the President.

Colson had more respect for, and less animosity toward, the press than Nixon or Haldeman. He played the leakage game with gusto, and quickly learned the mechanical end of press relations better than Jeb Magruder; as a "substance man," Colson had more clout with reporters than Ron Ziegler.

The President's special counsel also practiced the game of hardball. This is a political term fairly new to the language. It means tough-minded operations; use of pressure rather than less subtle means of persuasion; the roughshod ride rather than the more publicly accepted methods of compromise; the velvet fist in the iron glove. This first declension of political activity is practiced across the country by thousands of pols; the next declension is called "dirty tricks," and the third leads to Liddy, Hunt, and prison. The practice of the first, or hardball, is metaphorically antedated in Mr. Dooley's comment, "Politics ain't beanbag." The game of politics is not for people who are unwilling to take some punishment as they dish it out.

I got along well with Colson; he made sense, he listened to reason, he could get through to the President in a hurry with a good idea and not bog you down in paperwork, he was affirmative and enthusiastic. He was productive to work with as long as you did not let him draw you into playing hardball.

Here are two incidents that illustrate the kind of game it is, and how Colson played it at the behest of the President. The episodes involve two of the most estimable men in Washington, neither of whom would be intimidated or pressured, and their reactions are evidence that gentle men can outplay the hardest hardball without adopting its tactics.

The first instance, in which I was caught in the draft, was not one of the happier episodes in my White House stint, but it taught me a lesson that is worth passing along.

A hot fight took place in the Senate in 1971 over the extension of the draft; antiwar Senators, led by Majority Leader Mike Mansfield, wanted the draft extension tabled, which would mean that Mansfield's amendment calling for the withdrawal of all American troops from Vietnam within nine months would be sent back to a Senate-House conference, and thus given a new lease on life. The President felt it important that this strategy be defeated; when an Administration supporter, Senator Gordon Allott (R., Colo.), wanted to send the bill back to conference on an unrelated issue of military pay, Nixon's agents quickly agreed to his pay demands provided he stick his amendment on some other bill and not drag the military conscription bill into conference.

A conservative Democratic Senator who supported us and opposed Mansfield on this matter told Congressional liaison aide Clark MacGregor on Thursday, September 16, a curious story. A meeting had taken place the day before of the Senate Democratic leadership, and that Mike Mansfield had laid it on the line in an uncharacteristic way, according to our source. This vote would be a test of party loyalty and—added the Senator who was our informant—Mansfield said that Senators running for office next year who needed funds should take note.

Bob Haldeman and Chuck Colson put their heads together about this. It certainly did not sound like a Mike Mansfield tactic—it was not in his nature to high-pressure other Senators—but who knew what the passions about the war in Vietnam did to otherwise mild-mannered men? Our Democratic source may have been exaggerating for purposes of his own, but he was certainly in a better position to know what went on at that meeting than the White House was, and if his report were true, the Administration could lose the key vote. With the tide turned, we could lose a few more votes in conference, and the doves would have snatched control of the war away from the President.

Colson called me, described the situation, and asked me to ask a couple of reporters to find out what had happened at that meeting. If indeed Mansfield had put the heat on, it was a legitimate news story.

I said it didn't seem like Mansfield style at all. "Granted," said Colson, "but there could be no harm done by getting some reporters to check it out." If Mansfield denied it, there was no story, and that was that—but if any part of it were true, exposure would make it difficult for Democrats to enforce party loyalty.

This seemed reasonable enough, so I called one newsman to tip him to a possible story—I couldn't vouch for its accuracy, but a Democratic Senator did warn the White House about it; that fact in itself made it worth looking into. Then I called another reporter, whom I did not know, but who, Colson assured me, would never reveal a source, and passed along the same information.

In checking it out, the second reporter ran into the first reporter pursuing the same tip and promptly decided that the far better story was in "White House rumor-mongering." He could not do that story himself, because he would have to admit publicly he was blowing a source, so he gave the story about my calls to a wire service reporter on the same beat. This was how the story broke:

REPORT 9-16 WA

WASHINGTON (UPI)—PRESIDENT NIXON'S CHIEF SPEECHWRITER WAS SAID THURSDAY TO BE CIRCULATING A REPORT THAT SEN. MIKE MANSFIELD HAD THREATENED DEMOCRATS WITH THE LOSS OF CAMPAIGN FUNDS UNLESS THEY SUPPORTED HIM ON THE DRAFT BILL.

THE SPEECHWRITER, WILLIAM SAFIRE, WAS REPORTED TO HAVE CALLED SEVERAL REPORTERS ON A "BACKGROUND" BASIS TO SAY THAT MANSFIELD TOLD A DEMOCRATIC CAUCUS THAT BLOCKING THE DRAFT BILL SHOULD BE CONSIDERED AN ACT OF PARTY FAITH.

ASKED ABOUT THE REPORT, MANSFIELD DENIED IT AND SAID HE INTENDED TO SPEAK ON THE SUBJECT BEFORE A CRUCIAL SENATE VOTE ON THE ISSUE FRIDAY.

WORD OF THE ALLEGED THREAT FIRST WAS CIRCULATED BY A REPORTER WHO SAID HE HAD BEEN CALLED BY SAFIRE. A WHITE HOUSE SOURCE QUESTIONED BY UPI SAID SAFIRE WAS CIRCULATING THE REPORT AND THAT SAFIRE BELIEVED IT TO BE TRUE.

THE RUMOR COULD AFFECT THE OUTCOME OF THE FRIDAY VOTE . . .

It was a lively story: before a critical vote, the White House, in desperation, leaking false gossip maligning the Senate Majority Leader. Was that Colson's intent? No. Was that what I would have let myself be used in doing? Hell, no. But was that the way it appeared to a journalist sus-

PLATE 17. An Elliot Richardson doodle.

PLATE 18. State Dinner, 1972, at the U.S. Embassy in Moscow: Mrs.
Nixon with Alexei Kosygin, President Nixon next to Leonid Brezhnev.

PLATE 19. January 1973: Henry Kissinger returns from Paris to the Cabinet Room to tell how he arranged the Vietnam cease-fire. (The author, George Shultz, Herbert Stein.)

PLATE 20. The President reports on his trip to the People's Republic of China.

picious of White House motives? Absolutely. And, in retrospect, that was not a farfetched conclusion.

The Nixon White House, when one of its own found his hand caught in the leakage bucket, did not take an apologetic tack. Clark MacGregor, in charge of Congressional relations and the man who was passed the information by the Democratic Senator, confirmed to the wire services that I was the one who made the calls in the belief that the information was true. Haldeman, as always in sticky situations, did not cry over spilt milk but passed the word to Ziegler to hang tough—not to back off or appear in any way to be on the defensive.

The expected flak began to materialize: Senator Alan Cranston called it "irresponsible," Senator Lloyd Bentsen demanded the President "forthwith publicly reprimand his speechwriter," adding my action was "inept, even stupid." However, nobody outdid Senator Ernest F. Hollings, conservative Democrat of South Carolina, who was supporting the Administration on the bill but wanted it widely known he felt the imputation of pressure by Mansfield was reprehensible. "It's a goddamned lie," said Hollings. "The whole story is nonsense. Completely false. Senator Mansfield said every Senator's vote is a personal matter."

The partisan blasts were the least of my concerns. I felt bad that I had been involved in the middle of a devious mousetrap play, and on top of that, that I had bungled my end. I had harmed my standing with some reporters, but I could live with that. What really troubled me was what Mike Mansfield would think.

Senator Mansfield is one of the solid islands of integrity in Washington's marshes; tough-minded but gentle, experienced and soft-spoken, he knows his mind and keeps his word, and is one of the people that raise the general level of politics. That he should have his reputation for no-pressure-tactics besmirched by a pipsqueak White House assistant was bad enough, but that the pipsqueak should be me was especially deplorable.

He turned the story off by refusing to respond. After flatly denying the allegation, and repeating the denial of a test of party loyalty on the Senate floor just before the vote, he refused to escalate the matter into a "he-impugned-my-motives" brouhaha on which he could have whipped up considerable support.

I was standing by the news ticker across the hall from my office looking at the latest takes on the story—it was getting some play because nothing much was happening that afternoon—feeling about two feet tall whenever I read some gracious, kind remark by the Majority Leader in answer to a baiting question. This was typical:

> "I just feel embarrassed for both Mr. Safire and me," Mansfield said. ". . . I don't know who the Senator was that called Mr. Safire and I don't want to know," he said. "As far as I'm concerned, the matter is dropped. It no way impinges on my friendship with the gentleman at the White House."

Mansfield said he had met Safire twice and had even been to dinner at his home. He said he regarded him as "a very good man, intelligent, with a sense of know-how."

Besides making me feel even smaller, Mansfield's restraint infuriated columnist Mary McGrory, who felt that with a little blood on the floor the doves could have carried the day:

"And a White House aide unleased a sneak attack against the majority leader. William Safire, a speechwriter for both the President and the Vice President, called up reporters and whispered that Mansfield had tried to blackmail a Democratic caucus, threatening a campaign-fund cutoff to those who voted against him.

"In the light of the morning's performance—not to mention Mansfield's history of no pressure—it was preposterous. It was also dirty pool and any other member would have turned it into a weapon to rally the club to his side, making a frightful scene and calling for a vindication of his honor.

"But not Mike Mansfield," continued Miss McGrory. "He is St. Sebastian, forgiving the marksman as the arrows rend his flesh. Instead of storming into the chamber Friday morning, charging foul play and demanding vengeance, Mansfield, as usual, spoke more in sorrow than in anger . . . Everyone else saw it as the inevitable result of a clash between a man who observes the Golden Rule and one who takes his tactics from pro football."

When the bill came to a vote, the Administration won, 47–36. The next day, Saturday, I called Mike Mansfield at home. Before I could begin my apology, he said, "Gee, I was just going to call you, to tell you how sorry I was that you were embarrassed by all this. I looked for you when I was over at the White House yesterday, and I almost went over to your office."

"You wouldn't have found me," I said, "I was under the desk." I told him that I did know for a fact that one of his colleagues had said what I told the reporters; I think the Majority Leader knew who it was and what the Senator was up to, but did not want it confirmed by name, so I did not. Then I said I was sorry as hell.

"These things happen," the Majority Leader said. "Sometimes a reporter just wants a story—don't let it upset you. Tell your wife we're looking forward to seeing the both of you soon, and tell her not to feel bad either. Forget about it."

Obviously, I have not. For the rest of my stay at the White House, I was less naïve about the kind of assignments I would take on. Nor did Haldeman or Colson ask me to grab a glove and take part in future hardball games; my ineptitude or my distaste, like an angel on my shoulder, kept me from such doings as the hardball got harder. What I had been asked to do was probably not intended as a tawdry trick, but was interpreted as that and worse. A political pro does not blanch at the use of pressure, but in this case, the proper course would have been to challenge the dissembling Senator's phony report on Mansfield without using the press as intermediary. Live and learn, from a Senator with two faces as well as from another Senator with integrity.

In the next instance of hardball, I was more umpire than batsman, but had a good chance to observe the workings of the game.

"Nixon fiddles while Burns roams" was a gag around Washington in the early summer of 1971. Arthur Burns, chairman of the Federal Reserve and the man with his hand on the faucet of the money supply, had strayed off the reservation. He was publicly taking issue with the Game Plan, suggesting that the time had come for a more stringent "incomes policy," the economists' euphemism for forms of controls.*

The President was nettled by Burns's public pressure; that was not, he believed, the best way to help him arrive at a difficult decision. Colson, who knew I admired and was friendly with Dr. Burns, said pointedly that it was Burns's guidance that got the economy in a pickle in the first place; moreover, CEA Chairman Paul McCracken was Burns's recommendation, along with George Shultz, the stoutest advocate for a free market economy in the Administration.

But Burns would not get back on the Nixon team. While never criticizing the President, he made his pessimism plain, and on July 23 told the Joint Economic Committee, "I wish I could report that we are making substantial progress in dampening the inflationary spiral. I cannot do so." In a burst of candor, the widely respected economist explained why he was perplexed: "The rules of economics are not working the way they used to . . . even a long stretch of high and rising unemployment may not suffice to check the inflationary process."

That did it. The President was piqued, and he let Haldeman and Colson know it. Haldeman had crossed swords with Burns before, in 1969; the Chief of Staff felt that Counselor Burns did not understand the staff system, and pointed to the time Burns went in to see the President alone and took up his time with such trivia as getting some pictures signed for friends. Burns thought such amenities were an important human element in government, but quickly became conscious that Haldeman controlled the door—after that episode, a third party was usually present at meetings with the President and Burns, because, as Chapin said, "who knows what he'll hand the President to sign that hasn't been staffed out."

Even so, Burns's professional approach to dealing with Nixon was the wonderment of the White House staff. In the Oval Office, arguing with Edward Morgan on a welfare matter, Burns made a long, slow presentation of a conservative point of view: "As I said in my July 8 memorandum, Mr. President . . ." The President interrupted, to speed things along: "Yes, Arthur, I read that." "But you couldn't have, Mr. President. I didn't send it in yet. I have it with me here." "Thanks, Arthur, I'll read it." The feeling among the more officious members of the junior staff was that one

---

* "Incomes policy" is a form of economic controls; "incomes strategy" is the idea of giving cash instead of services to the poor.

just did not do that with the President. Nixon said nothing, but his staff took umbrage for him.

The issue was resolved to some extent by Burns's departure for his long-promised berth at the Fed, but the staff and the Cabinet were impressed with the fact that the access to the President and the method of operation to make the President orderly were matters that were entrusted to Haldeman alone, and not even a Burns could break through.

Haldeman and Burns had taken each other's measure and dealt from then on in a frigid but polite way; Colson and Burns did not know each other. Unlike Haldeman, who respected Burns's power with the press and would allow some leeway for Burns's long-time, avuncular loyalty to Nixon, Colson saw simply an appointee with whom the President had grown irritated and who was disrupting a smooth operation, and who was helping the President's critics. He would put the heat on Burns and get him into line.

Colson stepped into a buzz saw. Burns wrote the book on business cycles; he will admit to a mistake with the confidence of a big man; he goes to the well of leakage seldom but with great effect; he rarely gets into a scrap, but when he does, he does not lose. Burns perseveres. (As a student at Columbia University, the course he found most difficult was Physical Education but to graduate he had to climb a rope and vault a bar. The young Burns spent hours every day for two months jumping over that bar until he seriously injured his arches, which is why he walks slowly today. Still, he likes to dance.) A solid friend, a fierce enemy, as Colson was to discover.

There has long been a thought noodling around the White House that the Federal Reserve was too independent; if the elected Administration gets the credit or blame for the conduct of the nation's economic affairs, then it should have the authority to decide on the money supply. As the importance of the supply of money was increasingly recognized, the idea of its control by the Fed—a body far removed from the electorate—became a matter for legitimate debate. Colson dusted off this argument and told a press aide working in Herb Klein's shop, DeVan L. Shumway, to put a shot across Burns's bow. He passed along some other ammunition (Colson later told me) which was excessive, wrongheaded, and unduly impugning of motive.

Shumway, who later became better known as the buffeted spokesman for the Committee to Re-elect the President, is a soft-spoken order-follower who draws the most onerous assignments. He did his job, and the UPI story led:

"Washington, July 27. Several advisers have urged President Nixon to double the size of the Federal Reserve Board. Administration officials also disclosed that Nixon rejected a request from Arthur F. Burns, Chairman of the Federal Reserve, for $20,000 a year pay raise. Burns currently gets $42,500." The UPI reporter wanted verification from a source higher-up than Shumway. Colson spoke to the reporter, and the story went on: "As a counterpoint to discussion of increasing the size of the Board, two administration officials said in separate interviews that Burns had asked for a boost in annual salary . . . one of the officials remarked wryly that Burns, through frequent calls for wage and price restraints, had persuaded the President that this is not the time to increase high-level government salaries." The story carried a denial from a Federal Reserve spokesman that Burns had lobbied for an increase in salary.

The next day, Ron Ziegler had to do some careful minefield-walking in his press briefing. On Haldeman's instructions, he did not confirm the story, but did not shoot it down, either. I became angry and sent Ron the following memo:

> Tactic #1 has been to float out an idea from an unnamed Administration source to expand the Fed Board. This is wrong because: (1) "court-packing," even when a court is unpopular, causes a fierce public reaction against the President who proposes it, as FDR learned to his chagrin; (2) the idea coming from an anonymous White House source, followed by your briefing this morning (dissociating the President from it without actually knocking it down) only makes the President seem to be unaware of what is going on in his own White House; (3) this will not intimidate the Fed—on the contrary, it will make them more recalcitrant than ever.
>
> Tactic #2—spreading the word through two Administration officials that Burns is bucking for a pay increase. Even if this were true, and I have no way of knowing whether it is or not, the use of a personal shot like this at Dr. Burns is cheap, shoddy, and cannot but backfire. Burns, as you may know, two years ago proposed that the President and the Cabinet—himself included—take a 10% pay cut, which we shot down and he kept quiet. To embarrass him with a charge like this now (and we have embarrassed him because he had to deny it in the UP story) only injects a note of personal bitterness in what had been a policy controversy.
>
> This is not a light jab—to a man like Burns, this is the equivalent of calling him soft on communism or much worse. And the fact that it comes from two unnamed officials must tell him that this is an orchestrated Administration plot.

Five days later, I had a visit from Dr. Martin Anderson, a colleague from the '68 campaign now teaching at the Hoover Institute and a good friend of Dr. Burns. Marty said it would be a good idea for me to "go visit Arthur." I checked with Bob Haldeman, who called back to give me three points to make to the Fed Chairman, obviously from the President, which I wrote down:

"1. The President is saddened by the degree of public disagreement with his policy made by the Chairman in recent months.

"2. The Chairman's criticism works against rising public confidence and harms economic recovery.

"3. The Chairman must not expect his criticism to go unchallenged and cannot be surprised when others suggest ways to bring monetary policy in line with the national economic policy set by elected officials."

I went to see Burns in the marble palace that is the central bank, and my report to Haldeman for the President described what happened:

> First, he let off some steam: The leak about packing the Fed was stupid, which did not distress him all that much, but the crack about his lobbying for a raise was vicious, mean and infuriating. He is being pictured as a hypocrite calling for economy while seeking a raise, and Ziegler's ambivalent response to questions did not set it to rest. He will have to live with that smear, and he is personally deeply offended. He had gone to some lengths to find the source, he said, and learned it was some fellow in Klein's operation whose name begins with "S" [Shumway], who did it at Colson's instigation. I hope Colson can sleep nights.

I passed along Burns's reaction to the President's three points. First, "it pains him to see the President saddened by his public statements, as he wants more than anything to see the President succeed," but he could not and would not back off his stabilization board suggestion. On the second point, Burns held that "confidence comes from credibility, not from making rosy statements in contravention of the facts." On the idea of taking over the Fed, my report went, "He reminded me of FDR's court-packing experience and asked my p.r. opinion of public assessment of such a fight. I pointed to the change in the importance of monetary policy since the Fed was formed, the general distrust of bankers, the appeal of accountability in monetary policy. He replied that Presidents usually felt that way in office but changed their minds afterward."

At the end of my meeting with Burns, I suggested that a growing rift between him and the President would be bad for the country, and he agreed, saying he would not publicly react to the demeaning leaks of the past week; he did not want to hurt the President.

I also sent to Pat Buchanan, who was preparing the President's briefing book for a press conference the next day, an ameliatory suggested answer to a likely question about Burns.

Haldeman, who might have been impressed with the arguments in my memo, or who might have taken this opportunity to embarrass Colson— who was beginning to spend a lot of time alone with the President—sent my memo in to Nixon. The President called me before the press conference to suggest that I get a transcript of the conference over to Arthur Burns as soon as it was ready, and proceeded to go far beyond what Burns had expected or I had hoped for:

"Arthur Burns," said Nixon, ". . . has taken a very unfair shot. Within this Administration, the Office of Budget and Management, on a reorganization plan two months ago, recommended that the Chairman of the Federal Reserve, because he basically is our central banker, should be raised to the same status of the central bankers abroad. I enthusiastically approved the idea. However, when the matter was raised with Dr. Burns by my associates, he indicated that neither he nor any other individual in a high position in Government should take a salary increase at a time that the President was going to have to take some strong measures, as I am going to take to limit salary increases in other areas of Government, including, for example, blue collar workers.

"So, consequently, while there is not any question but that the Federal Reserve position will eventually be raised to the Level I position that was recommended, Arthur Burns and, incidentally, George Shultz, who is also on this list as a recommendation of the Ash Council, Arthur Burns and George Shultz being the responsible men that they were, asked that there not be an example set by them of a pay increase which would make it very difficult for us to deal effectively and responsibly with pay increases in other sectors of the Government."

Burns's reaction to this is recorded in the final entry in this file:

August 5, 1971/

CONFIDENTIAL

MEMORANDUM FOR: H. R. HALDEMAN

FROM: BILL SAFIRE

SUBJECT: Burns

I sent the text of the President's news conference over to Arthur Burns yesterday afternoon and got a call back afterward: "It warmed my heart. I haven't been so deeply moved in years. I may not have shown it, but I was pretty upset. (He showed it all right.) This just proves what a decent and warm man the President is. We have to work more closely together now."

He said he would call me in a week or so with some specific ideas. I said I'd be available.

Years later, Colson would fervently embrace religion, and would make a pilgrimage to Dr. Burns's office to apologize for what he had done. Burns would forgive him, revising his estimate of Colson in contrition as he sadly revised his estimate of Nixon's character. Colson told Burns of a trip on the *Sequoia* during which Nixon discussed the details of putting the shot across the Fed Chairman's bow—including the idea of putting out the word that Arthur had hypocritically asked for a raise. "He did it with a smile," Colson added, twisting the knife. (I spoke to Colson about this in 1974, after he had begun serving his jail sentence; he insists it can be corroborated by two others present on that yacht ride, but neither Henry Kissinger nor Caspar Weinberger recalls anything of the sort.)

My own view of Chuck Colson, with the benefit of hindsight, is that of a True Believer deeply betrayed: he was stunned by the revelation that all his conversations with the President were secretly recorded, and then, when the transcripts were released of Nixon's conversations with Haldeman and Dean, Colson read how the President spiritually double-crossed him, brushing Colson off as a man who would "do anything," agreeing with Haldeman that Colson was "an operator in expediency." With his fundaments turning to mud, small wonder Colson turned from Nixon to God.

In 1971, of course, all that was undreamed of. That summer, Colson led the charge against Ellsberg and the Pentagon Papers; and simultaneously, an economic crisis was coming to a head. At the time of the Burns episode, it seemed to me a lucky thing that the President had dramatically dissociated himself from the hardball-players, extricating himself from a situation that then appeared to be caused by aides carrying out his orders with too heavy a hand. The President would need Arthur Burns to judge, refine, and then to help put across an economic initiative that John Connally had been cooking up.

4. THE PRESIDENT FALLS IN LOVE

"Ah wouldn't trust that feller," John Connally of Texas told the President one day about a critic of the New Economic Policy, "any further than ah could throw a chimney by its smoke!"

The untrustworthy subject of the former Governor's opinion is less significant than the fact of a vivid vermillion streak among the patches of gray—a colorful character in the high reaches of the Administration, with whom the President could while away the time, or whip up public opinion. Connally meant stimulation, excitement, and political savvy to Nixon, and his presence was what the President liked to call "a bold stroke."

"Big Jawn" came and went through the last half of the first term the way Nixon's first Budget Director, Robert Mayo, liked to call "a dose of salts." ("They don't take salts anymore, Bob," the President would reply, looking benignly at his out-of-date Quadriad member.)

"The Boss is in love" was a statement familiar to the Old Nixon Hands, because it was a process that happened periodically, and often in the spring. To be politically "in love," of course, is to have an affair of the head, to be entranced by a new face, captivated by a new subject matter: the high-intensity lamp burns brightly but not usually for long.

Nixon fell in love in 1967 with John Mitchell, and they would spend long hours together, plotting, relaxing, brooding, chuckling, dreaming. This affair lasted through mid-1970, then it receded, and the relationship became similar to the trust and mutual kindness of old flames. The affair with Henry Kissinger was different. Growing quickly in 1969 and '70, it was never really more than a warm companionship and began to wane in 1972 and remained a *mariage de convenance* until Watergate's urgency forced Nixon to clasp Henry to his bosom. Daniel Patrick Moynihan bloomed in 1969's spring, with his Disraeli books and shibboleth-shattering ideas; Nixon was in love again, we could tell by a look at the log—there was Moynihan in there for long hours, taking Nixon to the mountaintop of social psychology and showing him vistas of Rooseveltian glories.

Pete Peterson had his fling in 1970—the successful executive with a mind full of penetrating questions about international economic policy—teaching Nixon what he wanted to know about "being number one economically in the world" when the United States could no longer be superior militarily; giving the President the justification for economic "moxie" by pointing to the emergence of Japan and Germany, based on a national spirit and government-sponsored trading advantages. Peterson had a theory about relationships with the President: "The rocks in my head fill up the holes in yours," but he did not long enjoy the status of number one intellectual concubine, and was spun out to the job of Commerce Secretary when his star was already on the decline. Charles Colson, after the 1970 campaign, was a Nixon companion, too, but nothing flashy there— more a long, three-year, political affair, building a new majority together, taking up much of the time that had been allocated to the faithful Haldeman and the developing Ehrlichman, both of whom watched the rises and falls of the new loves with some jealousy, but with patience, knowing full well Nixon would ultimately come home to them. They would worry about a Colson, who was in their league; Connally was not, and they shared in the President's pleasure.

Nixon's relationship with Connally, somewhere after Peterson and before Colson, was presaged by a comment the President made to John Ehrlichman in the fall of 1970: "Every Cabinet should have at least one potential President in it. Mine doesn't."

Treasury Secretary David Kennedy, who had been chosen primarily because he was not an Eastern banker, had proved to be neither strong in the inner councils nor persuasive outside, and knew it. A good and kind man, he let the President know he would not take offense at being eased out. Nixon remembered how John Connally, serving with Roy Ash on a reorganization commission, had come to the monotonous and politically naïve Ash's rescue at a Cabinet meeting with a forceful presentation; he put Connally on the Foreign Intelligence Advisory Board, the most coveted blue ribbon panel of all, and talked to him privately a couple of times. After a while, the President confided to Arthur Burns, who knew of his search for the right man to take charge of economic affairs, in this way: "Only three men in America understand the use of power. I do. John Connally does. And"—this said grudgingly—"I guess Nelson [Rockefeller] does."

The Nixon-Connally relationship can be viewed in its most productive moments in the coming chapter on the economic weekend at Camp David, but three scenes not previously publicized illustrate something of the "Connally Effect":

Scene I: The Cabinet Room, 10:30 A.M., December 14, 1970.

The Cabinet and Republican leadership had been called together for a budget briefing. George Shultz was called on to speak first, as the President was late, and said somewhat grimly, "Paul McCracken and I will share the privilege of discussing the budget." But the President entered, junked the agenda, and came right to the point: "The purpose of my brief appearance at this Cabinet meeting today is with regard to a change in the Cabinet." He said some nice things about David Kennedy, who was going to resign as Treasury Secretary, and built up his new job as roving ambassador, which the mild Kennedy said would give him plenty of time for fishing in a variety of international streams.

"Now," the President said, "we come to the successor. I have been consulting with people on a very private basis, and you can say that the successor should be a banker. I have been told to substitute one banker for another. I don't agree. We believe in our economic policy. It is going to continue. What we need over the next two years, with partisanship rearing its head more and more, is a leading Democratic political man, as well as a man who can serve as Secretary of the Treasury. This is so we can have the benefit of his leadership in presenting economic and foreign policy in a nonpartisan light. The time has come, in the interests of the country and the Administration, that we have a Democrat in a top position in the Cabinet.

"We have a man who is a great admirer of Dave's—a man who has worked with me in the reorganization of the government—without whose efforts we would never have gotten the reorganization plan through. The man is John Connally." Nobody in the room batted an eye or made any kind of facial expression. Dead silence.

"As George and John will agree," the President continued, nodding at former Governors Romney and Volpe, "he was a fine Governor. As a lawyer, a member of the boards of several banks, not unsophisticated in the field. As I was telling John Tower recently"—in this way the President indicated he had cleared the appointment with Tower, Republican Senator from Texas, who was present—"he is coming not only as a Democrat but as Secretary of the Treasury for the next two full years." This meant Connally was not going to run for office in Texas the next year.

"Mel and Bill"—to Laird and Rogers—"I think he will be extremely helpful in the international area. We need to have stroke on the Democratic side. I would appreciate it if all the members of the Cabinet would support this appointment. We can expect some flak. Why a Democrat? Why Connally, who didn't support me in 1968? Stay away from the politics of this. At this time in the country's and the Administration's history, it is important to have a strong and vigorous political leader from the Democratic Party willing to give up his partisanship and willing to support us down the line."

John Mitchell took his pipe out of his mouth and said: "With tough sledding coming up on the domestic front, we need a source of bipartisan support—Connally could do it. This is a big plus to those willing to pay some attention to those factors. I feel very strongly about it."

The President said, "Connally said he wouldn't take it until George Bush got whatever he was entitled to. I don't know why George wanted the UN appointment, but he wanted it so he got it." (Bush was narrowly defeated in a 1970 race for Senator in Texas, partly because Connally made some ringing TV commercials for Lloyd Bentsen, Bush's opponent, blasting Bush for supporting the President on welfare reform. A few years later, Connally was indicted, Bush was Ambassador to Peking, and Bentsen was a candidate for the Presidential nomination.)

The President called on the Secretary of State for a reaction. Rogers said, "Connally is an outstanding public servant, with an interest in serving the country. I don't think we should have any reservations."

The President turned to John Tower: "This is hard for you. I am for every Republican running. We need John Tower back in 1972."

Tower said, "I'm a pragmatic man. John Connally is philosophically attuned to you. He is articulate and persuasive. I for one will defend him against those in our own party who may not like him."

Postmaster General "Red" Blount broke the tension slightly by saying, "And it's nice to get him out of Texas, too, John." Tower raised his eyebrows: "Why, that never occurred to me."

The President solicited the support of Volpe and Romney: "As Governor he was highly thought of, wasn't he?" Volpe nodded, "He is articulate" (which he pronounced "artikilat").

House Minority Leader Jerry Ford interjected: "From the point of view of legislation in the House, he'll be helpful." The President said, "With Texans especially. He won't change Wright Patman, but he'll have a good impact."

Senate Minority Leader Hugh Scott said, "This will simplify and ease many of your problems on the Hill. Connally knows where the Indian trails are, too."

The President asked, "Mel, how was he thought of at Defense when he was Secretary of the Navy?" Laird said only, "He'll be helpful at advocacy."

Going down around the table from Laird, the President looked at Senator Wallace Bennett of Utah, who got a laugh with, "I can't wait to see Wright Patman's face."

The President was laying the groundwork for the proper interpretation of Connally's appointment by the press, his welcome by the Congress, and his toleration by the Republican Party—especially John Tower's Republicans in Texas, who would remember that Connally had helped defeat their ticket just a few months before.

The next morning, somebody remembered how President Eisenhower had appointed Texas Democrat Robert Anderson to be Secretary of the Treasury in his second term; like Connally, Anderson had also been Secretary of the Navy and the situation looked fairly similar. But Nixon did not want a precedent for his bold move; he briefed Haldeman closely on what to tell the men with contact with reporters, and we received this memo signed "H" the morning after the Connally appointment was announced:

> It has been suggested that this move has a direct precedent in
> Eisenhower's appointment of Bob Anderson to be Secretary of

the Treasury after he had served as Secretary of the Navy and was a Democrat.

The analogy does not fit in any way, shape, or form, however. Anderson was a Texas Democrat who had supported Eisenhower in his campaign for election, whereas Connally was a Texas Democrat who opposed Nixon's candidacy both in 1960, when Connally supported Kennedy, and in 1968, when Connally supported Humphrey.

Anderson was appointed Secretary of the Navy by Eisenhower. Connally was John Kennedy's Secretary of the Navy as a Democrat in a Democratic Administration.

Anderson changed party affiliation and became a Republican and then was appointed Secretary of the Treasury by Eisenhower, moving from his Navy post to Treasury. Connally has been, is now, and will continue to be, a Democrat and he was appointed to the Treasury post as a Democrat from private life, not from a previous Government post.

The Connally appointment is a major bi-partisan move—the Anderson appointment was not.

I could see why the President wanted his Connally move to be interpreted as unprecedented, but this detailed refutation of a minor point seemed odd. Later, I discovered that in 1956, President Eisenhower had urged Nixon to take a Cabinet post so as to get administrative experience, rather than run again for Vice President. It was typical of Eisenhower to want his headquarters staff to have army corps command experience before qualifying for Supreme Commander. The "dump-Nixon" movement, abortively conducted by Harold Stassen, failed when Nixon refused the President's well-intentioned offer. (Both Eisenhower and Nixon then refused to call Christian Herter, who was Stassen's choice for VP, to get Herter to nominate Nixon—Len Hall had to make the call in the end.) The Herter boomlet, however, was not Eisenhower's idea. According to Bryce Harlow, an intimate of both Eisenhower's and Nixon's, the man Ike had in mind in 1956 to replace Nixon as Vice President was a Texas Democrat named Robert Anderson.

Scene II, December 15, 1970

The day after the Connally appointment, a meeting of the Domestic Council, in the Cabinet Room. The subject was the State of the Union message of 1971—the whole new Nixon domestic program, his honest effort to make a real difference in American life. Revenue sharing was its centerpiece, turning to reality the rhetoric of "returning power to the people," turning toward the return of power in the form of real money to the states and cities, with few strings attached, and sure to wrench the old relationships between pressure groups and the Congress. Government re-organization was another part, shaking up the bureaucracy to be able to better handle the less detailed function of the Federal Government. Wide-ranging welfare reform was a part of it. But the President felt the program, revolutionary as it was, did not sound like much—and boldness without the appearance of boldness is rarely better than timidity in Washington, D.C.

"Let's not kid ourselves into thinking it's a bold new program," the President cautioned. "Or that it will pass. It's not dramatic. I remember the Republican Coordinating Council back in 1966—'We shall have bloc grants'—and there's not much sex appeal here. And it doesn't trim down the bureaucracy—it just shuffles them around a bit." The President was glum about revenue sharing being treated as no different than the old "bloc grant" idea—giving money in lump sums for decision locally, rather than "categorical grants," with Washington doing all the deciding as to who gets the money under what local circumstances. That was actually what revenue sharing was all about, but on a grand scale—it hardly sizzled when served up to the public. The President explained it this way to Connally:

> "You say to the cities, now look here—here's the money. It covers all these things. We're saying to you, 'you know best.' If your property taxes are too high, and you want to cut back on Great Society programs, you can. Of course, all the social workers will fight it. But the social worker lobby is not as old as the highway trust funds. I am not saying we shouldn't fight the highway lobby, but we should know the muscle we are up against."

> Connally put in: "You're still going to raise the total money you give cities and states?"

> Weinberger: "No city will get less than they are getting now."

> Connally: "Most of those fellows in the highway lobby can handle themselves pretty well in the local areas. They will not be upset . . . But answer me this: What's your basic objective?"

> Ed Harper, of the Domestic Council staff, began the answer by saying "to get revenue sharing passed—"

> Ehrlichman cut him short: "Let's be more philosophical. We want to have a distinctively Nixon domestic program."

> Finch added: "A new affirmation of confidence in state and local government."

> Weinberger: "A new direction in government."

> The President: "When you touch a nerve like this, it's like a dentist drilling—they say it's not going to hurt but, boy, they duck fast when

you give them no categories. This is more than helping states balance their present budgets. What we will do is say, 'You will now have the opportunity to decide what to do with your money.'

"We know the social workers' reaction to the Family Assistance Plan is negative because it interferes with their world," Nixon said. "It disturbs the way they run into a house and look for the old man in the closet. Any time you take on an ingrown bureaucracy, you are taking on a vicious fight. Of course, one way to enlist them is to find them other jobs."

Weinberger: "There will be a 100,000 reduction in Federal employment."

Connally: "In 1965 there were 10 million on government payrolls. By 1980, there will be 17 million. That's local, state and federal."

Nixon: "In the health field, we will get opposition from both sides. Some people say Kennedy's bill is a $77 billion program, but if we take the other direction—ours—we take a proud profession, medicine, and make it do things in new ways. It's the same with lawyers. And I would say the same about the academics, but"—looking at Shultz—"not with you here, George. When you get to universities, you figure you are so bright, everyone else is a know-nothing.

"In the executive branch," the President complained to Connally, "we write too much. The poorest writing is done in the biggest books. There seems to be a situation these days that no book is worth anything unless it runs a thousand pages. Now I don't believe in the one-page bit, but I know when I boil down a position, I have really thought the subject through. So when you send me memos on this subject, don't go into detail on all the difficulties. Throw all the political difficulties out—we all know what they are. And don't waste your time getting out thirty thousand words of memorable prose. Say to yourselves: 'Now, if I were making the decision, what would I need to know?'

"Romney made an interesting point," the President continued, "he said, 'you know, in the automotive business they always come up with a new model every year, a new color or whatever. That's what people buy. The trouble with government is we never get a new model.' People feel that no matter who you elect, you get the same thing."

The President was speaking from the heart at this point—"more of the same" was something he had always scorned—and he identified his own difficulty in moving the bureaucracy with the average man's sense of powerlessness in affecting the government.

"Except for the executive reorganization," Nixon continued, "the one legitimate criticism of this Administration is that we managed all the programs we inherited a little better. That's not enough. There's a mystique: People need change. Change is a revitalizing, reinvigorating force. I mean change in an institution and changes in the life of a person. I lean to doing something more bold rather than less bold.

"We don't want to appear like damn fools. If we don't have the guts and the follow-through to have one victory—like on revenue sharing —we will look terrible. Of course, wherever executive action alone can make changes, we will do it.

"There's a feeling of enormous frustration that the more things change, the more they stay the same. People think, quite unfairly, that all government workers are drones. The Great Society programs had appeal because they indicated things would get better. Today people look at government—this huge monster—and wonder what difference it made. We are interested in substance, of course, but we are also interested in something new. If we are going to fight it, let's fight it hard.

"With my political sense," the President concluded, "I can tell what will happen when we hit the army engineers or the welfare workers. Everybody fights for selfish reasons; let's recognize it and get the selfish reasons enlightened for a change."

John Connally brought up the subject of the Calley trial and compared it with the bomb on Hiroshima killing millions of civilians. He was making the point that different people did different things for different reasons. "The Great Society," Connally said, "gave hope for change, but hell, if you'll pardon my saying so, Mr. President, the average person doesn't even know revenue sharing was ever even proposed. And what difference does it make if nobody knows it? I say let's run the risk. If you lose, you lose big—but what's the sense in losing small?"

The President's decision, probably made right there, was to go strong with his package, to call it "The New American Revolution," to launch its "six great goals" with all the fanfare he could muster at a joint session of the Congress. It was a powerful pitch; in the end, with the exception of the "one victory" of revenue sharing, which kept him from appearing like a damn fool, he "lost big." But he never regretted the try, or faulted Connally for urging him to go for the brass ring.

Scene III: The Cabinet Room, December 15, 1971

Bipartisan leadership meeting: Connally, who had been in the Administration exactly one year, was briefing Senators Mansfield and Scott, Speaker Albert, Joint Economic Committee Chairman Wright Patman (described by one Quadriad member as "a gentleman and a demagogue"), the President and others on the progress of his negotiations with the "Group of Ten" nations on the price of gold and trade matters.

> Connally: "The Europeans have a way of whipsawing you—they say they can't go ahead unless the Common Market agrees, but then any one of them can make sure the Common Market won't agree. So frankly, we used the Congress as our bargaining lever."
>
> The President: "We scared them with you."
>
> Speaker Albert: "Will you need Congressional action this week?"
>
> The President: "No, afterward."
>
> Connally: "No, no—don't take away our bargaining lever."
>
> Kissinger: "Pompidou said to the President he wanted a change in the price of gold. The President implied he couldn't put before Congress the recommendation prior to seeing the whole package."
>
> The President: "I said 'the Congress won't buy a pig in a poke.'"
>
> Kissinger: "That was a helluva translating problem."
>
> Connally: "We trust us more than we trust them. All of them hide behind their commitment to the Common Market—so it's extremely difficult to get all your 'coons up one tree.'"
>
> The President: "That would be hard to translate, too."

Sitting with the staff members against the wall, away from the Cabinet table, taking notes, I followed the meeting into a discussion of the best way to get a settlement with the other nations on money and trade. Connally, who had negotiated hard, said now was the time to push for a settlement. Pete Peterson, sitting next to me, gasped—he had come out of a meeting not long before, and Connally had pressed for just the opposite —to hang tough and not settle, letting the Europeans come to us. Here was Connally not only reversing field before the Congressional leaders, but doing it with enthusiasm, selling hard what he had recently opposed. Peterson found this hard to fathom: it was okay to go along with a Presidential reversal and say nothing, but to adopt the opposite argument and seek to persuade others was beyond his ken. Yet that was Connally, and a good argument could be made for that sort of loyalty: he presented his position, he lost, and instead of grumbling, since it was a matter of tactics and he had no fundamental disagreement with principle, he reversed his field and ran as hard as he could doing his job for his leader.

Nixon's Connally move was politically exciting, and he saw to it that the political man near him got his ego nourishment. Haldeman made much of deferring to Connally, and the story was circulated widely that only Connally could blast his way through Haldeman's stance in the Presidential hallway: the press enjoyed any penetration of "the Berlin Wall." After the August 15 economic weekend that marked a turnabout in policy, the President told me, "Give Connally credit. Give the whole team a play, but give Connally a big play. Did you see his press conference? What did you think? The boldness, the comprehensiveness . . ." Nixon was not worried about the limelight going to his associate; this was a good trait in the President, and most President-watchers, including the staff, thought it could not be true. But Nixon was unusually generous with credit—as he would show with Henry Kissinger—and not the least concerned when glory was being heaped on associates, especially if it kept them happy and productive.

At the 1971 Bermuda Conference with Prime Minister Edward Heath —a smooth affair after the prickly meeting in the Azores with President Georges Pompidou—the State Dinner was held aboard H.M.S. *Glamorgan.* In the captain's reception, Nixon spotted the Prime Minister standing quietly in a corner talking to no American. The President's caught Connally's eye, jerked his head over toward Heath, and continued talking to Sir Alec Douglas-Home, as Connally smoothly crossed the room and began to chat with the PM (at that conference, the only problem we had was in making conversation). After the dinner, I slipped the President a note with the motto of the Welsh ship that was our host, since Nixon was a sucker for mottoes in after-dinner speeches; sure enough, in his toast, he said, "I found that the motto of this ship is 'Aim for the Highest.' That just happens to be the motto of the Secretary of the Treasury, too." Connally blushed demurely and said to reporters later that the President must have meant that he had been aiming for the highest adjustment in currency rates.*

Opposites attract; that was obvious. Nixon was the loner, Connally the extrovert. One man endured a press conference, the other enjoyed one. Nixon was a memo man, Connally a briefing man. One would do his best studying from the written word and the other from the spoken word. Connally was supremely confident of himself and his good fortune, Nixon was sure only that you got what you deserved if you fought for it, and could never quite believe he had it.

Connally's advice was usually to take the chance, to press the luck, to go for broke: "Sometimes it's not *what* you decide but *that* you decide." When Nixon wanted someone to urge him to mine the harbor at Haiphong, he turned to Connally and heard what he wanted to hear. Nixon was ready to take some even bigger gambles than Connally would, but much less often, with long stretches of safe-playing in between. The two politicians used each other, fully aware of the other's usage: Nixon needed a new tool and a persuasive voice, and Connally needed a new forum and a new lease on political life. Each agreed that Connally would make a more suitable successor to the Presidency than Agnew.

Connally, as a successful politician turned successful businessman, had an insight to contribute to Nixon: that the businessman of today was a far cry from the entrepreneur of old who resented government interference.

---

* British Commander J. C. Appleyard-List, seated next to me at that dinner, was most instructive in other ways, too. When Heath said, "To the President of the United States," which was followed by Nixon's "To the Queen," he coolly pointed out to me that Heath should have said: "To the President of the United States *of America*" and Nixon should have said: "To *Her Majesty* the Queen."

Most business managers, Connally understood, were ready to trade away too much economic freedom for stable labor demands, figuring "uncertainty" to be worse for business than government controls. Shultz and Stein resisted this practical resignation of the modern managers, on the theory that controls ultimately stultified an economy and sapped initiative; Nixon tended to listen to their evocation of virtue, since it was his own inclination, but Connally taught him where the hidden business support was for the step he hated to take. (There was some poignancy, years later, to Nixon sailing down the Potomac on the *Sequoia* with Connally in 1973, trying to get his former Treasury Secretary to advise him to freeze wages and prices, because Nixon needed a dramatic move so as to appear "Presidential." Connally went along and let himself be talked into giving that advice, and probably knew it was a mistake—but there were certain appeals to which this obstinate, opinionated man could not say no.)

In the 1972 Presidential campaign, the President sent the speechwriters a copy of a Connally speech, with this covering note: "It has the grabbers and the quotable lines. It has no wasted words or high blown rhetoric, but makes all the points. It is high level, hard hitting and simple." We all went up to a screening room to see Connally's speech as he had taped it for television, and the professional admen in the room were stunned by its impact.

"That's some pitch," said one of the image-makers, "who wrote it?"

"Aram Bakshian, I think, with a big help from Big Jawn."

"Fantastic. And the way it came across—who did we get to play Connally?"

Only Connally could play Connally, and he played him most of the time. He knew his own strengths, and Nixon's too—when I told the President I intended to write a book, Nixon quickly suggested: "Talk to Connally and to Moynihan—they understand me best." That was interesting, I thought: two Democrats, two colorful and stimulating men, two former aides no longer close, seen by Nixon as his best interpreters.

"I brought him in from the Texas League," the President told a delegation of citizens about his Treasury Secretary one day, and warmed to his baseball metaphor. "Sometimes he singles, sometimes he doubles, and he often gets a home run. Furthermore, when a ball comes at his head, he knows how to duck."

Since Connally bedazzled and enthralled Nixon, there was a tendency to think that the Texan knew how to size up a situation and react to it even better than the Old Pro. Connally was better than Nixon at press conferences, more at ease in any dealings with the public; in the Cabinet Room, however, the relationship was that of an avuncular producer and his star. Even in public, there could be seen evidence of a sophistication and sensitivity in Nixon that was not in Connally. Here is a petty example of the two of them, along with Vice President Agnew, reacting to similar circumstances.

The scene is the Kennedy Center's Concert Hall, the night of the special performance conducted by Eugene Ormandy on the eve of the Second Inaugural.

Concert-goers know that it is improper to applaud between movements of a symphony or concerto; one is supposed to preserve the mood of the music and withhold applause until the conclusion of the work. But many members of that audience were not experienced in concert-going; they bought tickets because it was the thing to do that night of Inaugural weekend and besides, the President would be there.

At the end of the first movement of Grieg's Piano Concerto, most of the audience burst into applause for soloist Van Cliburn. From my orchestra seat I craned my neck to see who was doing what in the Presidential box.

John Connally was clapping enthusiastically. Regular concert-goers in that audience knew immediately that he did not know the right thing to do.

Earlier, between movements of Beethoven's Fifth Symphony, Vice President Agnew had sat stonily, his hands resting in his lap, ostentatiously not applauding. That, too, was a mistake (and of all things, on the elitist side); though the concert-goers would approve, the majority of the audience that looked around wondered why the Vice President did not join in—didn't he like the performance?

Only Nixon handled the situation with understanding. He did not applaud at first, reassuring other classical music lovers that he was a man who knew what was proper, but after a couple of moments, as eyes turned to him from around the hall, he joined in the applause, so as not to have the people applauding wondering about him, or about their own gaffe.

That is one meaning of "Old Pro." I was not the only one who noticed this little byplay; Bob Haldeman had also turned in his seat to see what his Boss would do in the circumstances, and when the Nixons joined in the applause, he grinned widely, shook his head, and started to clap as well. The applauding Connally looked at the President too, probably wondering what in hell took him so long to make up his mind.

With John Connally, Nixon had what he wanted: not only a Cabinet with a "top Democrat," but a Cabinet "with at least one potential President." Later, Nixon toyed with the idea of appointing Connally Vice President after Agnew's fall, but Mel Laird, pressing for Jerry Ford, scotched that. The stars of Nixon and Connally crossed again in 1974, when the Texan was indicted for taking graft on the same day the President was charged by the House Judiciary Committee for abuse of power. But that, as T. S. Eliot might say, was in another country. In 1971, Connally took a large part in decisions made atop one of the Catoctin Mountains on the weekend of August 13–15, as Nixon's economic policy reached its crisis point.

5. THE ECONOMIC SUMMIT

"Circumstances change," said President Nixon to his economic advisers before the meeting on Friday, the thirteenth of August, 1971, began. "In this discussion, nobody is bound by past positions."

Least of all, he might have added, himself. One past position was a fierce opposition to wage and price controls; in every economic speech I had ever worked on with him, there was a boilerplate paragraph on the horrors of wage and price controls, how they would lead to rationing and black markets and a stultifying government domination of the economy. Other past positions included all the proper obeisances to "free trade" (textiles and steel excepted where campaign promises had been made) and to "protecting the value of the dollar" a general term that included a hearty pooh-poohing of changes in the price of gold. Two years before, as part of his tax reform package, he had proposed and signed repeal of the investment tax credit.

Larry Higby in Haldeman's office had called me on Thursday to suggest I hold myself available for the weekend, on an unidentified subject. On Friday he told me to get a bag for the weekend and take a car out to the Anacostia helipad, but not to tell my wife or my secretary where I was going.

The decision on timing was taken suddenly, largely at the urging of Treasury Under Secretary Paul Volcker who foresaw crisis in the international money markets. John Connally was called back from a weekend in Texas. Economic aide Peter Flanigan was caught in a storm at sea, missed the weekend's meeting, and was kicking himself for the better part of a year. Four days before, Chairman Paul McCracken of the Council of Economic Advisers had advised Cabinet members, "The inflation news of the past few months has not been encouraging. The Inflation Alert will be expected to evaluate the implications of that for the future."

I called the motor pool for a car and was told I would be doubled up with Herbert Stein of the Council for the trip to the helipad. Herb was the author of the only book on economics I had ever read all the way through

(*The Fiscal Revolution*, University of Chicago Press, 1968, with an introduction by George Shultz) and one of the few practitioners of what Carlyle called "the dismal science" to be able to explain economic ideas in straightforward English prose.

As the car pulled out of the ramp of the Executive Office Building, I reminded Herb that I had once bought his book for cash and asked him what was up for the weekend. "This could be the most important weekend in the history of economics since March 4, 1933," he intoned.

We rode for a while in silence as I tried to remember just what FDR did on entering the White House four decades ago. It came to me.

"We closing the banks?"

"Hardly," Herb chuckled. "But I would not be surprised if the President were to close the gold window."

I did not have the foggiest notion about what the "gold window" was, but did not want to reveal this ignorance to Stein unnecessarily or to push him for more information that would be officially vouchsafed to me later. On the helicopter headed for Camp David, I was seated between Stein and a Treasury official. When the Treasury man asked me what was up, I said it struck me as no big deal, that we would probably close the gold window. He leaned forward, put his face in his hands, and whispered, "My God!" Watching this reaction, it occurred to me that this could be a bigger deal than I thought, so I turned to Stein and asked, "How would you explain to a layman the significance of the gold window?"

"It's the suspension of the convertibility of the dollar," he shouted in my ear over the sound of the chopper. "Anybody knows *that*," I shouted back with an offended look, "but how would you put it in one-syllable words?" Herb answered, "I wouldn't try. That's why you're along."

Which was true. The President wanted a "generalist," a nonexpert, to draft his economic speeches; it was a way of forcing experts to set aside jargon in the presentation of economic affairs and of putting economic positions in their proper political and social context. There was an element of defense in it, too. More than once the President told a roomful of economists to "put that in simple terms so Safire can understand," and then he listened carefully as they explained it to me.[*]

The "gold window," I later learned, was the willingness of the United States Treasury to exchange gold for dollars at the fixed price of $35 an ounce, thereby making the dollar "as good as gold" in international trade. With this gold window open, all other currencies had a fixed standard to which to relate; if it were to be closed—if we ended our willingness to con-

---

[*] Dr. Arthur Burns had reviewed an economic speech I wrote in the '68 campaign and commented in his W. C. Fields voice, "You must have gotten an 'A' in economics." When I didn't reply, he looked at me over the rims of his glasses and asked, "You did fairly well in economics, then?" I continued silent; he took off his glasses and looked bleakly at the Candidate's chief economic writer: "You *took* economics, didn't you?" When I shook my head, he sighed and looked at the brighter side: "At least you won't have a lifetime of preconceptions to overcome."

vert dollars to gold—then currencies would have to relate to each other and a whole new world economic order would have to be established.

There was to be a meeting of the Quadriad with the President at 3 P.M. Friday. The announcement of this meeting of the Secretary of the Treasury (John Connally), the Director of the Office of Management and Budget (George Shultz), the Chairman of the Federal Reserve (Arthur Burns), and the Chairman of the Council of Economic Advisers (Paul McCracken) at Camp David did not cause much of a stir; the President had met with them before and no news came out of it. However, the presence of Paul Volcker, the Treasury Under Secretary for Monetary Affairs, and Peter Peterson, the head of the Council on International Economic Policy, would have alerted some newsmen that something was up on the international front; the presence of Stein and me could have signaled a likely speech or statement, which was why we were smuggled up on the q.t.

Nixon recognized the historic nature of the meeting and directed us all to the guest book, signing it himself and having us do the same. (See Plate 9, following page 296.) He motioned Connally to sit on his right.

The necessity for secrecy was underscored by the President as the meeting began in his living room in Aspen Cottage, with its picture-window overlook of the Catoctin Mountains. "One of the reasons we are holding this meeting at Camp David is for security," Nixon said sternly. "There are to be made no calls out of here. Our ability to act has already been compromised somewhat. Between now and Monday night, when we announce our decisions, everyone here is to button his lip. If you do have to talk to somebody, you take responsibility for the leak.

"The best structured way for us to go about this is to have John present to us as a group what he has talked about to several of us privately."

Treasury Secretary John Connally ticked off the series of actions:

—on the wage-price front, a freeze, to be followed by some kind of restraint afterward.

—to stop the hemorrhaging of the balance of payments, an import tax, or border tax. And "we close the gold window."

—to stimulate jobs, reinstatement of the investment tax credit, and the removal of the excise tax on automobiles. ("For every 100,000 cars we don't sell, we lose 20,000 jobs.")

The President followed quickly with: "I would like to add this. One, with tax relief as proposed here, there would have to be budget cuts as well. Increasing the deficit at this time would be a mistake. Two, your wage-price restraint, as I understand it, would be one that would work for a brief period—maybe ninety days. You could not take it off without something to go into its place. We ought to do that thinking now."

The President's crisp presentation slowed as he began getting into the problems ahead: "About closing the gold window—we cannot know fully what effect it will have. We all need more education on the import tax, whether to do it unilaterally or go to Congress, selectively or across the board, and then, of course, how to get rid of it when we want to. Next, we have to consider what kind of machinery should be set up to enforce a wage-price freeze—escalator clauses, hardship cases, all that. And what kind of Board is to do so."

He called on George Shultz to analyze the import tax picture, along with the special problem of textiles. Of the group assembled, Shultz had been the strongest voice against wage-price controls; Burns had been calling for an "incomes policy" for eight months, and McCracken had reluctantly moved in that direction early in the summer; Connally wanted prompt and bold action soon after he joined the Administration in February. It was Shultz, and to some degree Stein, who counseled "steady as you go"—that inflation was slowly but surely coming under control, that unemployment had peaked and would come down in an incipient recovery; two months before, at a Camp David meeting, their view had prevailed and the decision was made to wait and look at the monthly statistics in the months ahead.

The international monetary situation changed the picture entirely. Gold was pouring out of the U. S. Treasury at an alarming rate, and on Thursday afternoon, the British asked for a $3 billion "cover" for all their dollar assets. All agreed that action was called for there, but the President insisted that when he moved it would be on a comprehensive, across-the-board basis. Nixon was not about to stick his thumb in the dike and wait for another hole to appear elsewhere. He wanted a whole new dike.

Philosophically, Shultz and Stein could live with this—"circumstances change" was the President's escape hatch—besides, they were good soldiers and their special abilities were never more needed. The meeting was not without its tension, however. The following portion of my notes includes some technical matters, but gives the flavor of the afternoon's five-hour discussion:

> The President: "George, address yourself briefly to the rather intriguing question of textiles." (This was the first time the President smiled in the meeting.)
>
> Shultz: "You don't have that authority under the trade acts. There is always the 'trading with the enemy' act—that will enable you to do anything."
>
> The President: "No. That smacks wrong from the point of view of international leadership, and I don't want to corrupt my national security power. My long-range goal is not to erect a 10 per cent barrier around the U.S.—that would be retrogressive—but to set a procedure that lets us go up and down with room for negotiation.
>
> "If we could move on the authority," the President continued, "and at the same time close the gold window, we then provide the basis of negotiation. It gives you more stroke.
>
> "The people who say they can relax now and sell a lot of stuff to these 'dumb foreigners'—heh! The foreigners are not so dumb."
>
> Discussion centered on ways to correct the imbalance of the ex-

change rate. Connally pressed for a border tax on imports for its shock value and political impact.

The President: "We don't confront a theory, we confront a fact. We can fiddle around with an exchange rate but [Ways and Means Chairman Wilbur] Mills is coming in with an import surcharge. I had to sign a leaf-raking bill the other day—but when you can't stop it, find the least objectionable way to rake leaves."

Burns: "I would go for a border tax, provided you expressly stated it was temporary. You can extend it. I am afraid that if you impose a tax without a time limitation, it could be termed aggressive."

The President: "Does that bother you, John?"

Connally: "We ought to 'suspend' rather than repeal tax agreements, and we should say it is on a temporary basis, but we shouldn't make a specific limit like six months."

Burns: "At the right moment I want to question the judgment of closing the gold window."

The President: "Let's talk about it right now."

Burns: "No. Let's finish with the border tax first."

Shultz: "I'll get together a plan with price changes and revenue estimates, and with the impact directly on the textile problem."

The President: "Paul (McCracken), you and Pete work with George."

McCracken (to Connally): "You want to close the window and let the dollar float in addition to a border tax?"

Connally: "It's more understandable to the American people to put on a border tax. I know it's inconsistent; you are right. But the tax may make a change in the exchange rate possible."

The President: "Arthur, your view, as I understand it, is why is it not possible to do all the things that get at the heart of the problem and then go to close the gold window if needed. The Treasury objection to that is that reserve assets will be depleted quickly."

Burns: "I think they are wrong. If they are right, you can close it a week later. You will be doing something dramatic—a wage and price policy, a border tax. You will order a cutback in government spending. These major actions will electrify the world. The gold outflow will cease. If I'm wrong, you can close the window later . . ."

The President: "Wouldn't they retaliate on the tax, too?"

Peterson: "If you announce you have a balance of payments problem, other countries cannot retaliate under GATT."

Burns: "If we close the window, other countries could double the price of gold. We are releasing forces that we need not release. I think Paul Volcker should go ahead and start negotiating with other countries on a realignment of currencies."

The President: "If we do all these things, speculators may say 'Next they'll close the gold window,' and there would be a run."

Burns: "*Then* you would close the window. What's to lose by waiting?"

The President: "The argument on the other side is that domestic opinion would not give it a chance. In reading over the years on this subject, I have never seen so many intelligent experts who disagree 180 degrees. George and others like the floating idea. Arthur says to get in a good negotiating position and then deal. But you risk appearing that your actions didn't work." . . .

Connally: "What's our immediate problem? We are meeting here because we are in trouble overseas. The British came in today to ask us to cover $3 billion, all their dollar reserves. Anybody can topple us—anytime they want—we have left ourselves completely exposed. There is no political risk—Reuss wants you to do it." He showed a batch of clippings about Democratic Congressman Henry Reuss's support of this idea.

Burns: "Yes, this is widely expected. But all the other countries know we have never acted against them. The good will—"

Connally: "We'll go broke getting their good will."

Volcker: "I hate to do this, to close the window. All my life I have defended exchange rates, but I think it is needed."

Connally: "So the other countries don't like it. So what?"

Volcker: "But don't let's close the window and sit—let's get other governments to negotiate new rates."

Connally: "Why do we have to be 'reasonable'? Canada wasn't."

Burns: "They can retaliate."

Connally: "Let 'em. What can they do?"

Burns: "They're powerful. They're proud, just as we are." . . .

The President: "What I have in mind for a speech is this: I believe that when you have a lot to say, you don't have to say a lot.

"I'm thinking of a speech of ten minutes—concise, strong, confident. Not a lot of stuff whining around that we are in a hell of a shape."

Peterson: "Let's get competitive. Businessmen will like that."

The President: "Technology! 'I have asked the Secretary of the Treasury to submit to me other tax proposals to encourage the development of technology.' That kind of thing. Pete, what do you think the reaction of 'folks' to closing the window will be?"

Peterson: "They will worry."

The President: " 'The President has assured the devaluation of the dollar. The dollar will be worth less.' The media will be vicious. I can see it now: 'He's devalued the dollar.' "*

Burns to Volcker: "What will happen to the price of gold?"

---

* Nixon was wrong about that. Partly because of the way he faced up to devaluation, partly because wage and price control was being called for by Democrats and largely because a bold stroke is a good story, the media handling of his necessarily complex speech was both skillful and responsible.

Volcker: "Everybody who speculates in gold will seize on this to make a mint. We have to come up with a proposal to demonstrate gold is not that important. Maybe we should sell some."

McCracken: "People's reaction to closing the gold window would be negative. On the other hand, they will see it as part of a program of strong action on wage-price matters."

Volcker: "There is a certain public sentiment about 'a cross of gold.' "

The President (making a face): "Bryan ran four times and lost."

Connally: "We don't have a chance unless we do it. Our assets are going out by the bushel basket. You're in the hands of the money changers. You can see the result of this action will put us in a more competitive position."

Burns: "May I speak up for the 'money changers'? The central bankers are important to you. They would be pleased at this action, short of closing the window."

As Connally and Burns went at each other, the President made some notes and summarized: "Let's consider the decisions. The important thing we have already decided, and on the GATT basis. The border tax is not too damned aggressive, just aggressive enough.

"The wage-price part we have decided.

"Budget cuts—we're pushing back Family Assistance, postponing Revenue Sharing and setting a goal of a 5 per cent cut in personnel—White House staff included. Symbolically that's very important. The average person doesn't think the Federal employee out of work is unemployed. He doesn't think he is employed anyway . . ."

"We can cut five to seven billion dollars," said Shultz, the Director of the Office of Management and Budget, who had been tipped weeks before to be ready.

The President: "The difficulty is this: Say you get five or six billion on savings. Then add a billion or so on the import tax. I'll take a surprising view for a political man. It's almost an article of faith that you cannot give tax relief to business without giving relief to individuals. It's a fact that Congress will push up our proposals on tax reduction in any event. We will call it the employment tax credit. The businessman will not give a damn what it's called as long as he gets it."

Burns: "Maybe the Jobs Tax Credit. Make the tax credit high for the first year—10 per cent, and then 5 per cent afterward."

Haldeman (from the back of the room): "Great!"

Burns: "Also, I would add in the personal tax break."

The President: "You are too softhearted, Arthur, to be a banker."

Burns: "I have not been at it long enough. I would also suggest a token reduction of the budget deficit."

The President (to Volcker): "How much do you think the import tax would bring in?"

Volcker: "A billion and a half to two billion."

The President: "Be as honest as you can, but get the two billion. Let's talk about the freeze. George?"

Shultz: "(1) An across-the-board freeze is best. (2) An atmosphere of crisis is necessary. (3) The life of the freeze must be short and (4) how do you stop it when you start?"

The President: "Particularly if it is working."

Shultz: "A freeze will stop when labor blows it up with a strike. Don't worry about getting rid of it—labor will do that for you."

The President: "The shorter it is, the more chance for success. What worries me is putting the economy in a strait jacket under the control of a bunch of damn bureaucrats for any length of time."

Shultz: "In your statement you should show that we will use this period to stop inflation in its tracks. And we will settle other problems as we go on. We have to come out of this with a tripartite board: three public, two labor, two management, to set criteria and to be able to spin off problems to subcommittees."

Burns: "I agree."

The President: "Though we are not bound by previous positions, in the light of circumstances, one thing we do not want is permanent wage and price control. That's got to be hit right on the nose."

Burns: "George Shultz and I talked philosophically but never in detail on wage and price stabilization. There is remarkable similarity between George's thinking and my own. I would have a three-month freeze, which would have shock value, and give us time to work out the machinery for dealing with stabilization. I would add Congressional leaders to the commission to develop our plan. This would insure their political support. And there would be the distinct threat that if management and labor cannot agree, something would be imposed upon them."

Shultz (shaking his head): "The President must maintain control."

The President: "Arthur, if you were suggesting this in January of 1973, I would agree. But you would no more get the Democratic leadership to participate than fly. On the other hand, they want a bipartisan group of Senators to go with me to China—no way. It cuts both ways. On wages and prices they would see we would be trying to put the monkey on their back."

Talking politics, the President was surefooted. He quoted his chief rival: "Muskie said, 'What we must do is to go back to the prosperity and high employment of the past two Administrations.' I said, 'Pick 'em—6 per cent unemployment with Kennedy or less than 5 per cent unemployment with war.' " The President paused, sighed and said, "There must be a better way to do the damn thing. After eight years of the New Deal, in 1940, there were nine million unemployed. It took World War II to get us out of the depression. We have to find a way—I know this gets away from free market thinking, to which I am attracted—to stimulate the American economy in peacetime to the great ventures that will provide full employment. John, that's what we want out of our tax system."

The President then sketched out the speech he wanted to make on television: "It is always well to start with Subject A. The U.S. at long last enters an era of peace, which we all welcome. But in another sense, peace brings challenges—a newly competitive world. The question is, is the U.S. going to strive to be Number One economically? Competition we welcome—we wish them well—but we hope to do better.

"Let's look at ourselves," Nixon said. "First, we are moving from war to peace with its effect on unemployment. We have to take action to employ those laid off in defense plants and the armed forces. Second, as international speculators attack our dollar, the balance of trade is suffering and that means that jobs are going down. What can we do? There is nothing to be frightened about. We are still the richest nation in the world. We are not going to allow the American dollar to be torn down. (1) An import tax. (2) Investment tax credit. (3) Stop the irreversible heritage of war—inflation. We have made some progress but not enough. We need action—inflation robs the working man. He's on a treadmill.

"The American people must give their moral support to this effort. What can you do? Labor, support the freeze. Businessmen, invest. Consumer, buy. All of us get off our butts. In a crisis you don't flounder around. We are a great country. We will deal with it. Fifteen hundred words. Pete, Herb, I want you to work with Safire on this. John has a draft." (Connally handed it to Safire.) "Arthur, you could help in a special way. It would be appropriate for you to be in on it."

Burns: "Mr. President, I'll help in any way I can."

The President: "Safire here will be the editor. I can't do a speech by committee, so he will go over the various parts with each of you."

Burns: "How about doing this Sunday night instead of Monday night?"

There was a general discussion at this point on the timing of the speech. The President felt that Sunday night might generate an atmosphere of crisis. Volcker felt that Monday would be a hellish day in the money markets. I didn't think the whole program itself could be pulled together until Monday night, but if it could, Sunday night would not be more of a crisis atmosphere than Monday.

Shultz then organized the work, assigning different groups to different subjects—Connally and Volcker to tax policy and monetary affairs, McCracken and Stein to the wage-price freeze, and his own men to the budget cuts.

The President: "When you background on this, put 75 per cent of your effort into TV. John, you take the lead with George. With business types, here's where Arthur and the others have enormous stroke. I have not had anybody working for me in the press area who understood the value of TV."

Burns: "I can take care of informing the central bankers."

Peterson: "State knows about this meeting this weekend and wants in."

The President: "I want this kept secret. In Congress, talk to Mills and Byrnes just before the speech—don't bother with the Foreign Relations types. You have Banking & Currency, Appropriations—that's George Mahon—just by telephone. That's the way we did the China thing. Inform about a hundred top business people and labor. The details can be worked out by the staff.

"Hell," the President said, looking to me, "we could do this speech tomorrow night. The problem is not in writing a speech—but in doing the program right. Rushing it through, just to save a couple of billions in gold on Monday does not appeal to me. We have got to be damn sure we know what we are doing before we get stuck with it.

"There will be other international developments that will surprise you in the next few months because I haven't told anybody." The President had the Peking and Moscow summits up his sleeve. "The one thing that is sure to come on this—why didn't we tell the press beforehand? Say—'Why, if we had told you, you would have told the world and we would have lost all our gold.' Now I just want to get together with the Quadriad and Volcker."

The others, including myself, left at this time (7 P.M.). The Quadriad and Volcker stayed on with the President to discuss Burns's disagreement about gold convertibility. After that meeting, I was told by Volcker to do my draft of the speech assuming we would close the gold window.

After the Quadriad meeting, the President remained alone while the rest of the group dined at the Laurel Cabin. The no-phone-call edict was still in force, raising some eyebrows of men who had shown themselves to be trustworthy repositories of secrets, but 6'8", dour Treasury Under Secretary Volcker explained a different dimension to the need for no leaks: "Fortunes could be made with this information." Haldeman, mock-serious, leaned forward and whispered loudly, "Exactly how?" The tension broken, Volcker asked Shultz, "How much is your budget deficit?" George estimated, "Oh, twenty-three billion or so—why?" Volcker looked dreamily at the ceiling. "Give me a billion dollars and a free hand on Monday, and I could make up that deficit in the money markets."

Even as we kidded around, the men in the room knew that Volcker was undergoing an especially searing experience. He was schooled in the international monetary system, almost bred to defend it; the Breton Woods Agreement was sacrosanct to him; all the men he grew up with and dealt with throughout the world trusted each other in crisis to respect the rules and cling to the few constants like the convertibility of gold. Yet here he was participating in the overthrow of all he held permanent; it was not a happy weekend for him.

I was seated next to Arthur Burns at dinner, who told me, "You know, I argued pretty strenuously against the gold move—that's the only difference I have with the whole policy. But even on that I don't feel so cocky—nobody can be sure. When it was decided, I told the President he would have my wholehearted support." In the general discussion at the dinner, the need for a press conference the day after the President's address became apparent. I began to raise the kind of questions that would arise, and John Connally, seated at the foot of the table, began to answer them forcefully. In a few minutes, we had slipped into a mock press conference, my role as nasty reporter with snide questions, Connally's as Administration spokesman. Thinking up mean and dirty questions is easy, especially armed as I was with the understanding of some of our weaknesses, and I began to thoroughly enjoy flaying the Secretary of the Treasury. One probe particularly forced him into a corner, and I thought I had him, but he skillfully countered with "You're pretty good on the questions, Safire—how are you on the answer to that one?" Herb Stein, who turned out to have the answers to everything that weekend, stepped in to save the situation.

As this rehearsal was going on, Ehrlichman kept slipping out of the room and returning. Later, I was called away from the table to take a telephone call from the President, who did not want to be with us, but wanted to know exactly what was going on. "Ehrlichman has been telling me of the contribution you're making," Nixon said. "That's good, ask all the tough ones. Tell Connally to hit interest rates in his briefing; I don't want to exhort bankers in my speech. Tell McCracken and Shultz to downplay rent control. We're doing it, but I don't want to screw up the housing boom—too many jobs depend on it. You're sitting next to Arthur? You know, Arthur is a fine man. Really, a fine man. Tell him I said that." I did so.

I went back to my cabin after dinner and wrote most of the night so that I could have a draft early enough for Rose Woods to retype and show the President at breakfast. At 7 A.M. Saturday, I walked over to Rose's cabin, Witch Hazel, and was surprised to find her furiously typing away. "Is there another speechwriter up here?" I wondered. She nodded and pointed toward Aspen, the President's cabin.

At 3:15 A.M., I later learned, the President arose and decided he would do his own speech. He filled both sides of three sheets of paper with notes, then dictated a memo to me—a thorough first draft of the speech—into his recording machine. At five forty-five, he put on a robe and walked out of Aspen into the swimming pool area holding the dictation tape in his hand, startling a Navy chief who was surreptitiously taking a dip in the Boss's pool. The President said good morning and asked the panic-stricken chief to take the tape over to Rose Woods's cabin and leave it inside the screen door. The extent of the chief's embarrassment was shown in his response to his Commander-in-Chief: "Yes, ma'am!" The President thought that was funny enough to tell to Chapin later that day, with the stricture not to pass it along because he didn't want the swimming sailor to get into trouble.

All the President's speech notes, by the way, were taken from his bedroom desk and given me by the President with a generous "Here—you keep them as a souvenir," but I knew his largesse in this area gave archive-conscious Haldeman apoplexy, so I turned them in to Rose for inclusion in the Nixon library someday. When Haldeman came after me with blood in his eye—"turn those notes he gave you in immediately!"—I was actually able to shoot back a reply that made him look sheepish, not a frequent Haldeman expression at that time.

At 7:30 A.M., Rose handed me my memo from the President. The top page:

August 14, 1971

MEMORANDUM TO SAFIRE

FROM THE PRESIDENT

Following is a rough draft of the structure of the Sunday night speech. I believe is the best approach rather than to start the gobbly gook about crisis of international monetary affairs, the need for sacrifice, etc. which seemed to be the thrust of Volcker and to a lesser extent Peterson,

The text begins as follows:

Good Evening. I have addressed the nation a number of times on ending the war. Because of the progress we have made toward achieving that goal, this Sunday evening is an appropriate time for us to turn our attention to the challenges of peace.

America today has the best opportunity in this century to bring a full generation of peace and what we have not had in the past 10 years a new prosperity without war. To achieve either of these great goals requires not only bold action, bold leadership but greatness from a great people.

Prosperity without war requires action on three fronts. More jobs for Americans; dropping the rise in the cost of living; protecting the value of our dollar against the international speculators who have launched a massive attack against it.

I retired to Old Birch, my cabin, to conform what I had written overnight with what the President wanted; his draft and mine, not surprisingly, were not all that different. Nixon had finally gone to bed, but before retiring left word with Haldeman which was duly passed on to me: "Be sure Bill understands that I have definite ideas in my draft. On form, the outline is right: the structure is jobs, prices, sound dollar, with two steps on the dollar—import tax and the gold window. Use gutsy rhetoric and keep the feeling—only correct it on the technical fronts. Show the other people only the sections that concern them, don't circulate the drafts. I want it to be a surprise." And then the clincher: "I don't want this brittle and beautiful, but brutal and effective. Sunday, not Monday. Ten minutes."

I told Haldeman that was all very well, but if it was going to be ten minutes, then I would have to cut what the President had written in half. Haldeman deadpanned, "Then I guess he meant twenty minutes." (It was an article of speechmaking faith with Nixon that the American people, poised to switch to *I Love Lucy* reruns, would give him only ten minutes to say his piece on television. He spoke at a rate of about 125 words a minute; ten minutes meant a 1,250-word speech, which is long for a station break but too short for a substantive speech. His constant pressure to "keep it short" reduced the temptation to wordiness, but all his aides fought him on the ten-minute deadline. Only Henry Kissinger had the courage, however, to take a three-page draft that had come back with the President's order to "cut it to two pages," and hand it to a secretary with a laconic "Type this on two pages.")

I gave my draft to Rose to type for the President—it was about noon on Saturday—and headed for Laurel for lunch. There the three task forces were barreling ahead: Shultz and his deputy, Caspar Weinberger had directed the Budget men two weeks before to come up with contingency plans for a severe cut in outlays, and they were ready; Treasury's Volcker, along with the Federal Reserve's Burns, was working on how to spring the news of the decision on the international banking community, and setting up the technical cushions to absorb the shock; McCracken and Stein, the economic advisers, had done plenty of thinking beforehand on how they would approach wage-price stabilization and were now ready to lay out freeze plans. Shultz had divvied up the work load logically.

A prodigious amount of work can be accomplished by putting a group of decision-makers in three adjacent rooms, leaving the connecting doors open, cutting off incoming phone calls, and setting a deadline. Arnold Weber,* an assistant director of OMB who only wanted to return to his professorship at the University of Chicago, but who was destined to run the freeze, and Herbert Stein, who mournfully described himself as the only man to work for the U. S. Government on postwar planning through three wars, turned out to be both workhorses and mines of information. (Weber later referred to the owlish, bespectacled Stein as "Dr. Strange-price.") In the absence of bureaucracies, the men assembled at Camp David looked inward and to each other for judgment and ideas; facts would be checked out the next day, Sunday. Should the Cost of Living Council have veto power over the decisions of the Pay Board and Price Commission? In the normal course of Washington planning, such a question would trigger weeks of debate, memoranda, supporting data, and interdepartmental meetings; here at Camp David's Laurel Cabin, Weber got up, went

---

* Weber was one of the few who fiercely resisted the temptation to classify documents, whether "eyes only" or merely "administratively confidential." I once received a communication from him marked "Teeth Only."

to chew it over with Connally in one room, the two of them walked in to see Shultz in the other room and together they reached a conclusion (no on day-to-day decisions, yes on the long run). That kind of free-wheeling interchange happened dozens of times; we were winging it, but that was the only way it could have been done, and the quality of the work turned out depended not on the size and depth of departments but on the intellectual grasp and organizational ability of the men in the cabin. The implications of slamming a lid down on the American economy were staggering; its responsibility was sobering; interdependence was absolutely necessary, and there could be no prima donna stuff. It was also more fun than any of the men there had ever had in their lifetimes.

A couple of speechwriting problems of mine were cleared up at lunch. The "accelerated investment tax credit," as it was called in the early stages, seemed to sound like the name of a fast grab by fatcats to me, and I suggested the Job Development Tax, which was accepted. But Paul McCracken, whose orderly mind always liked to call things exactly what they were, persisted in calling the Cabinet-level group being established to stabilize prices and wages "the Cabinet Committee on Wage-Price Stability." I wanted to call it the Cost of Living Council, which would have a certain popular appeal, and laid it on the line to Paul: "The President prefers Cost of Living Council, but he says that if you or Connally object strenuously that I should cave in and call it what you want." McCracken smiled and threw up his hands, Connally said, "What the hell, it's his Council, let him call it what he wants," and the Cost of Living Council was born.

After much of the work had been done on the "fact sheets"—which were ordinarily summaries of programs, but in this case were the program outlines which would later be filled in by staffs of economists and budgeteers —Stein wrote a spoofing Fact Sheet along the style of the Ten Commandments, which, oddly, turns out to be an excellent summary of the substance of what went on during that historic weekend:

Herbert Stein
8/16/71

Fact Sheet

On the 15th day of the 8th month the President came down from the mountain and spoke to the people on all networks, saying:
I bring you a Comprehensive Eight-point Program, as follows:
First, thou shall raise no price, neither any wage, rent, interest, fee or dividend.
Second, thou shall pay out no gold, neither metallic nor paper.
Third, thou shall drive no Japanese car, wear no Italian shoe, nor drink any French wine, neither red nor white.
Fourth, thou shall pay to whosoever buys any equipment ten

percent of the value thereof in the first year, but only five percent thereafter.

Fifth, thou shall share no revenue and assist no family, not yet.

Sixth, whosoever buyeth an American automobile, thou shall honor him, and charge him no tax.

Seventh, thou shall enjoy in 1972 what the Democrats promised thee for 1973.

Eighth, thou shall appoint a Council of Elders to consider what to do for an encore.

Pete Peterson suggested, perhaps facetiously, that the 90-day freeze be extended to 100 days, to evoke memories of FDR. Cap Weinberger shot that down by pointing out that the "hundred days" phrase originated in the time between Napoleon's return from exile in Elba and his defeat at Waterloo.

The President reviewed the draft, pronounced himself generally pleased, but was not happy with the way I handled the problem of devaluation of the dollar. Volcker felt that there was no dollar devaluation, technically speaking, that our action was to force other currencies to revalue upwards, and we would be better off refusing to accept devaluation as a valid description; but my worry was that the President would finish his speech and afterward the commentators would say, "In effect, devaluation!" The viewer would then wonder why the President didn't tell him about that. With credibility in mind, I explained away devaluation in my draft; my gut reaction was right but I did not go far enough. Seated by the pool the next day, the President wrote out a passage that met the problem head-on. To see the passage in Nixon's own handwriting, see Plate 10, following page 296. It is translated here:

Let me lay to rest the bugaboo of devaluation.

Will this action reduce the value of the dollar?

The long term purpose and the effect of this action will be to strengthen the $—not weaken it.

Short term—the $ will be worth buy less—

But ifu overwhelming majority who buy American products in America—your $ will be worth the same tomorrow as it is today—

Saturday night, about eleven o'clock, a tired George Shultz came by my cabin to look over the budget portion of the speech. I asked him to read the whole thing, contrary to the President's instructions, because I wanted to cut down the possibility of error (and if you couldn't trust George Shultz, the whole country would be in the soup). He promptly caught a misstatement, already cleared by Treasury, that might have proved embarrassing. When I told the President in the morning that his desire for surprise among his aides was not as important as having a deeply knowl-edgeable person go through the whole speech word by word, he agreed and made the perfect choice for the final review: Herb Stein. As usual, when you challenged a Presidential fiat with a good reason, the President would adjust his position.

At midnight, Arthur Burns, trudging along in his snazzy Camp David windbreaker (the President later gave us all one of them with our names and the date sewn in) rapped on my screen door. He suggested a few judicious changes, striking out the denunciation of the "international money changers," and I walked him back to his cabin in the cool summer night.

Strolling through the moonlit woods in a Presidential retreat on a his-toric weekend is conducive to reminiscence, and Dr. Burns recalled the time he was adviser to another President: "The intra-Administration scraps seemed more intense in the Eisenhower days. I had written what I con-sidered to be a pretty good economic report when I was chairman of the Council of Economic Advisers in '56—as a matter of fact, a superb eco-nomic report—but George Humphrey called me to say it wouldn't do, it sounded 'socialistic' to him.

"Humphrey got to all the moguls"—Burns used the archaic word, "moguls," with zest—"in the Cabinet, and they lay in wait for me at the next Cabinet meeting. I didn't lift a finger to enlist support. I was de-termined to be absolutely calm about the whole thing. I thought I was looking suitably calm as we went into the Cabinet Room to talk to the President about the economic report, until President Eisenhower said to me, 'Why are you carrying two pipes in your hands, Arthur?' I looked down, and sure enough, I had a pipe in each hand, so I said, 'I came well prepared, Mr. President.' The upshot was Eisenhower backed me and Humphrey backed down."

George Humphrey, as Treasury Secretary, dominated the Eisenhower Cabinet on domestic affairs, and I wondered about the future of Secre-tary Connally. "A forceful and ambitious man," said Dr. Burns, "I think he'll help the President." Burns was pleased and proud about the way Nixon was handling the situation this weekend. The President's approach of thinking each element through, permitting time for discussion, asking all the penetrating questions, insisting on a comprehensive solution, and making decisions in a way that enlisted everyone's support—whether they agreed with all the decisions or not—was mature and deserving of respect. "He's a President now," said Burns. "He has a noble motive in foreign af-fairs to reshape the world, or at least his motive is to earn the fame that comes from nobly reshaping the world. Who can say what his motive is? But it's moving him in the right direction."

The next morning, Sunday, the President posed for pictures in his living room with all of us, carefully positioning everybody for this group portrait. Riding back to Laurel in one of the electric golf carts, Haldeman said, "It's good he does that. Otherwise somebody plunks himself down next to him and years later historians think he was the most important adviser there." Connally was on his right in the formal picture.

The group went back to the White House at 2 P.M. while the President continued to hone his speech. Rose Woods and I remained behind with him to turn out the reading copy. He had one change that troubled me: entitling the new approach the "New Economic Policy." I had a nagging feeling it was not original, but I could not pinpoint my objection. It turned out to be Lenin's slogan, and caught a few snide comments, but the Communist connotation soon dropped away, and it became a useful handle.

The other word changes were revealing of Nixon as a writer and molder of public opinion. His desire to be (as he told Haldeman to inform me) "brutal and effective" was now modified as he came toward the moment of facing the nation on television; his changes were all in the direction of toning the rhetoric down. Thus, "tough competition" became "strong competition," "march" was changed to "move forward," "a decisive stroke" to "decisive action." The formal "the American people" became the informal "every American," and the stern "let us never forget" he changed to a more positive "let us always remember."

In the peroration, I had changed Peterson's pitch for a "competitive spirit" from an ad-lib talk he had recently given to businessmen to "the competitive urge," to give a more elemental and emotional emphasis; Nixon changed "urge" back to "spirit" because he wanted to give the impetus an idealistic connotation. This is how his reading copy looked, and with phrases numbered, laid out by Rose Woods for ease of phrasing:

1. A nation, like a person, has to have a certain inner drive in order to succeed.

2. In economic affairs, that inner drive is called the competitive spirit.

   (1) Every action I have taken tonight is designed to nurture and stimulate that competitive spirit, to help us snap out of that self-doubt and self-disparagement that saps our energy and erodes our confidence in ourselves.

      1. Whether this nation stays number one in the world's economy, or resigns itself to second, third or fourth place;

      2. Whether we as a people instill our faith in ourselves, or lose that faith;

      3. Whether we hold fast to the strength that makes peace and freedom possible in this world, or lose our grip—all that depends on your competitive

spirit, your sense of personal destiny, your pride in your country and in yourself.

We can be certain of this: As the threat of war recedes, the challenge of peaceful competition increases.

1. We welcome competition, because America is at her greatest when she is called on to compete.

   (1) And no nation has anything to fear from our competition, because we lead our competitors on to new heights for their own people.

As there always have been in our history, there will be voices urging us to shrink from that challenge, to build a protective wall around ourselves, to crawl into a shell as the rest of the world moves ahead.

1. Two hundred years ago, a man wrote in his diary:

   (1) "Many thinking people believe America has seen its best days."

      1. That was in 1775, just before the American Revolution at the dawn of the most exciting era in the history of man.

2. Today, we hear the echoes of those voices preaching a gospel of gloom and defeat, saying the same thing:

   (1) "We have seen our best days."

      1. Let Americans reply:

         (1) "Our best days lie ahead."

As we move into a generation of peace, as we blaze the trail toward the new prosperity, I say to every American:

1. Let us raise our spirits.

2. Let us raise our sights.

3. Let all of us contribute all we can to the great and good country that contributes so much to the progress of mankind.

4. Let us invest in our nation's future.

5. And let us revitalize that faith in ourselves that built a great nation in the past, and will shape the world of the future.

On the helicopter back to the White House, he practiced the speech to himself, fiddling with some last-minute changes, and then could not resist telling me: "You know when all this was cooked up? Connally and me, we had it set sixty days ago."

In terms of his economic approach, the President had hoped all summer he would not have to put into action the plan that "Connally and me"* had cooked up; in political terms, however, he knew it would stun his critics and befog the issue that could best be used against him. Nixon hated to do it, but he loved doing it.

Stein had been right; the weekend at Camp David turned out to be the most important in economics since 1933. The President, when he acted, did not take half measures or limit his incursion into the free market system to a Parrot's Beak of controls. Without visible regret, certainly without apology, he moved across a broad front in a series of actions that changed the economic landscape of the world. "Circumstances change" and so must policy to meet them; lamentations and excuses are not called for.

This unencumbered attitude of the President's permeated the free market men around him. When later in the week I asked Herb Stein for a point sheet on why the controls would not lead to "rationing and black markets" as we had always direly predicted, he sent it along with this quotation from *Macbeth*:

> "I am in blood
> Stepp'd in so far, that, should I wade no more,
> Returning were as tedious as go o'er."

Was it all worth it? Was the trip to this summit necessary? Stepping in so far toward actively managing the economy, Nixon would have to take further steps into that morass.

From the international side, he had done the right thing: the drain on U.S. gold reserves posed a real emergency calling for an immediate remedy, and the comprehensive action he took—the "Nixon shocks"—made it possible for the hard-bargaining Connally to change the position of the United States in world trade. With currencies realistically realigned, U.S. exports had a competitive chance, and began moving out to redress an artificially created imbalance.

On the domestic side (which we may look at separately, but which does not exist independently of our international economic activity) Nixon made the right short-term political move, running off with the Democrats' clothing, being bold and decisive and Rooseveltian, doing just what he said he hated to do: "grandstanding." He was also trying something different when the other road he had been running up seemed to lead to both unemployment and inflation. For nearly three years, he had resisted

* See Plate 12, following page 296, for a photo of "Connally and me."

putting politics ahead of the economic instincts of the free-market men, but when Arthur Burns started pressing for controls, the politics then gained an economic intellectual underpinning. What was popular might also be right—who really knew?—and it was worth a try.

"Only Nixon" could have done it: by his obvious and genuine reluctance to interfere with market forces, with his sincere and announced intent to stop managing the economy as soon as inflationary expectations had been wrung out of it, and by his long wait until nearly everybody else was advocating controls and could not then sabotage his effort, he was able to take the plunge and bring most of the nation along with him. George Shultz went along to help and to learn; economist Milton Friedman said the international moves were right and the domestic moves were wrong, and from this distance, it appears that Friedman was right.

For the United States economy resists management: when prices of a product are held down by fiat, producers say they are not going to work for nothing and shortages come about: baby chickens are slaughtered on television, causing children to cry and editorial writers to rethink their exhortations to clamp lids on the economy. Nixon's economic summit produced a sense of action, and temporarily helped induce a lessening of the pressures of inflation; the natural force of the boom that was going on soon began to chew into the unemployment figures, making the August 15 moves look even better; it appeared in 1972, around election time, that Nixon might even achieve his goal: "a new prosperity without inflation and without war."

In 1970, with prices not increasing so fast, all the public attention was fixed on rising unemployment—economic policy was thus a failure. In 1973, with unemployment down and the average worker's real income up, food prices shot up alarmingly—and economic policy, going through its fourth phase of management, was considered a failure. By 1975, unemployment was again on the rise, but inflation had reached a rate that seemed impossible in 1971. After a time, long after Nixon, the American people are going to learn to live with partial success—some unemployment and some inflation—and the experience of the President who went into the price control business against his every instinct will be useful. His timing was right; he had the best advisers; he acted in an across-the-board way that gave meaning to all his individual actions; he had no other reasonable choice. The fault, dear Brutus, lies not in the actions of our leaders, but in ourselves, when we demand that government regulate our working lives without intruding on our freedom.

6. AD LIB

When the President held on to his draft of the State of the Union message in early 1972, refusing all comment until the last minute, the speech-writers asked Haldeman what was going on. Seated at the head of the staff table in the Roosevelt Room, he slumped back in his chair and ran a pencil through his crewcut: "I dunno. This may be the first extemporaneous State of the Union message in American history."

In due course, the President sent back the message with his fixes and suggestions, but his willingness to flirt with deadlines was based on his ability to ad-lib. There could be no extemporaneous States of the Union, but there could be—and were often—speeches set aside, or only portions read, while the President said what he had in his mind. If one takes "ad lib" to mean far more than a spontaneous quip, but a method of communicating with a crowd—then I submit Richard Nixon rates a place in the pantheon of American political ad-libbers.

When a speechwriter, with an especially straight face and sincere expression, suggests to his friends that they pay special attention to this speech or that passage, soberly adding, "You know, the President wrote that himself," he is really saying, "Here is one of my better efforts, but I am too loyal and true-blue a ghost to ever admit it." The writer thereby not only buttresses his reputation for having a passion for anonymity but gains fame. This is known as ostentatious self-effacement, and it works its oily way far more effectively than less subtle forms of aggrandizement.

From time to time, however, a speechwriter comes across a line or an entire speech that he admires and has not written himself; indeed, he considers it damn near as good as if he *had* written it himself. His immediate reaction is, "I will have to congratulate one of the other speechwriters"; if he does, and if the response is, "Thanks, but when I said the same thing to Ray, he said he thought you did it," a suspicion crosses his mind that perhaps the President came up with it himself.

The truth is, of course, Nixon did a great deal of it himself, especially what is referred to as "remarks"—those toasts or informal speeches that make a great impression upon those in the room with him and go largely unnoticed outside. Writers gave him "notes" for these affairs—historical sidelights and any appropriate anecdotes—and he used a small percentage of that material as the basis for some of what he said, but by and large the remarks sprang from his own experience and his ability to extemporize.

People around President Nixon knew this to be true, which is one reason why he tolerated the public exposure of his speechwriters. We were never hidden away in closets by a speechreader fearful of revelations that his thoughts were composed by others. Nixon was capable of writing his own speeches and sometimes did; he was even more capable of giving his own without writing down anything. Because Nixon's writing and extemporizing ability was well known to President-watchers, in and out of the White House, there was no need to pretend that he personally turned out the torrents of requisite prose that filled the twelve hundred pages a year of *Public Papers of the Presidents*. Because Nixon often proved he could ad-lib, his writers never had to skulk around.

In terms of graciousness, dignity, propriety, and the kind of modest eloquence that makes guests comfortable and guests of honor glow, Nixon acting as host or master of ceremonies was the best in the business. Yet he was widely ridiculed as not knowing where to put his hands, ponderously making every other sentence "perfectly clear" while guiltily darting his eyes and wiping the sweat off his upper lip, supposedly incapable of making the small talk that puts people at ease. That was the caricature accepted as gospel by people who never saw him in action in person. But many of those who have, including political opponents, will admit that Nixon on a platform was one of the most adept speakers to have practiced the art in our time.

"To err is Truman," cracked Martha Taft, and President Nixon was not immune to the occasional placement of his foot in his mouth. The statement that Nixon considered murderer Charles Manson guilty before he had been convicted was gleefully front-paged by the Los Angeles *Times*, and Nixon's use of the word "bums" to describe demonstrators who burn down buildings was stretched into his supposed characterization of all college students. After flubs like these, Ziegler would say the President "misspoke himself," an odd locution meaning "he didn't mean to say that," but the critical reaction following any error was loudest from those who complained most about the President not having enough press conferences, where the possibility of anyone's making a slip is greatest. Nixon's public speaking slips were remarkable in their rarity, considering the extent to which he spoke off the cuff and without notes. (The story about the fighting line he delivered in the '60 campaign—"America cannot stand pat," which he changed to "stand still" after getting a glare from his wife—is unfortunately apocryphal.)

Most of my friends look at me with suspicion and incredulity when I claim that Nixon is the best extemporaneous speaker in American politics. Nixon? That string of banalities? That wound-up plastic man waving his arms? Those simplistic slogans? The foul-mouthed, unintelligible man of the transcripts?

Yop, that's the man. First, there is a difference between a no-script stump speaker and a genuine extemporizer; most politicians can memorize a ten-minute pitch, which becomes known as "the" speech, and deliver that without notes. John Kennedy was superb at that, and at not messing up the cadence of his speech by trying to make it different all the time—in the index of his collected speeches of the 1960 campaign, for example, there are hundreds of references to Abraham Lincoln, and almost all were about the same quotation. Robert Kennedy, like John Lindsay, was a master at the honed-down outdoor stump speech, but it was "the" speech.

Nixon, who held fast to "the" speech in campaigns, and had a "the" speech for young people built around "what's right with America," could also extemporize on other occasions—and that is what separated him from most political speakers.

Nixon always thinks about what he is going to say beforehand, and he sometimes thinks about how to improve his spontaneous style. Early in 1968, I wrote him a letter about his speaking style, its pros and cons:

What's right about the Nixon style?

1. Structure. A typical Nixon speech has a beginning, a middle and an end. ("Tell 'em what you're gonna tell 'em, then tell 'em, then tell 'em what you told them.") Deeper than that, it goes somewhere—it sets out to make a point and then takes logical steps to reach that point. It sets out to persuade, to make a case. It can be outlined to reveal its progression. This is the hardest kind of speech to write, rejecting temptations to eloquently digress.

2. Conversationality. It is designed to be heard rather than read. The vocabulary can be understood by most people. The thoughts are broken up into medium sized sentences, interspersed with short sentences for emphasis, to allow an audience to grasp each thought.

3. Audience contact. From the self-deprecating humor at the start, to the applause lines throughout, to the stirring and often anecdotal peroration at the conclusion, there is an awareness of the people listening and an effort to relate to them. (Note: FDR's fireside chats showed that this speaker-listener contact need not be tossed aside if an audience is not present to laugh or applaud. Technique is different for a media presentation, but not at the expense of contact and real communication with the listener.)

4. Contrapuntal construction of phrases. Most famous example of this is Kennedy's "Ask not" line. Nixon style uses it often, as "the man of thought who will not act is ineffective; the man of action who will not think is dangerous." Using a semicolon as a fulcrum, balances two phrases with key words inverted.

5. The internal monologue. Asks rhetorical questions seldom; asks specific questions often, as "Why do I say we must make sure there is no reward for aggression? First . . ." This alerts the audience as to what is to follow; what follows is the numbered answer: "The third reason why . . ." Makes it easy to follow the argument.

What's wrong about the Nixon style? (Obviously, this letter is being written in the Nixon style.)

1. Over-use of verbal signals and the trappings of structure. Too much obvious structure makes a speech legalistic or makes an audience feel it is being babied. The numbered and "here's why" approach smacks of Madison Avenue commercials. Abuse of the structural strength turns it into a weakness, which Russell Baker parodied last Sunday.

2. There seem to be three reasons for everything.

3. Obvious hedging. Too much use of "on the other hand" and "at the same time".

4. Tut-tutting. Bending over backwards not to seem like it is going for the jugular in personal criticism, a holier-than-thou tone sometimes creeps into the Nixon style and elicits a "where-does-he-come-off" reaction.

5. Willingness to accept military or academic jargon: "Meaningful" negotiations, "viable" alternatives, "options" for choices, "at this point in time" for right now, clutter up the style and show a lazy acceptance of clichés.

If you feel your hackles rising at this point, you have a good idea how any writer instinctively resents and resists criticism of his style, which is why the amalgamation of your speechwriting team's way of writing into the Nixon style must be handled with care.

If a speech should have a theme that can be expressed in a single sentence; if a speech should have a structure that can be outlined on a single page; if a public figure should present himself consistently as the product of his own thought in his own way—then the time is ripe for you to weld your three brilliant individual writers into communicators of Nixon thought in Nixon style.

The preceding paragraph is pure Nixon style. It is a complex thought, broken into its component parts; it summarizes the theme of this letter, and it is written for spoken delivery. But the technique should be used only once in three speeches.

Nixon's only reply to this critique was, over the course of the next five years, an occasional "You won't like that, I know, but I want to do it." He did, however, eschew "at this point in time," which ravaged the discourse of his subordinates, and tried to steer clear of the vogue words of academe, like "meaningful," "viable," and "ambivalent." (I could never get him to stop saying "vitally important," which came to his lips at relatively unimportant occasions.)

If I had to write that critique again, I would certainly add "Too much self-pity." He found too much pleasure in recounting how the fashionable people would never appreciate what he did, a part of the "us v. them" syndrome, and would lay too much stress on the courage it took to pursue the unpopular course.

Most of what is right and wrong in the Nixon style can be seen in the following remarks ad-libbed to the Cabinet at a private dinner on January 20, 1972. There is banality there and there is a make-the-best-of-it sentence that goes "what we lack is demagoguery," when he really means he wishes he could sell like Jack Kennedy. But there is a sincerity, a shape, and an eloquence to it that makes these after-dinner remarks a perfect example of Nixon on his feet; and offers a rare self-evaluation that was shared with too small an audience.

Here is the only whole speech in this book, chosen by a speechwriter because it was not written, and is worth taking the time to read:

This is January 20, 1972, and tonight the fourth quarter begins. The football analogy tells us that the fourth quarter really determines the game. That was really the problem with the Redskins, you know. They were great in the first half, but in the fourth quarter, they didn't quite have it. So the game is determined in the fourth quarter in a sense, but only in a very narrow sense, in terms of winning the immediate game. Whatever happens in the fourth quarter, I think that all of us have got to understand that what we have done and what we will do will last and is worth doing.

I was talking with Pat and Bryce and to Bob Dole, here, about how I really get in the mood for writing a speech. For perhaps three or four days before a major speech, like the Inaugural or the State of the Union or a major foreign policy speech, I try to get totally away from the subject and to put it in the perspective of history—in terms of this country, its place in the world, what we mean and all the rest.

I'm not going to recommend that all of you do what I did before this speech, but I will say that Pat Moynihan is somewhat my mentor in terms of telling me what I should read. He doesn't think I am too well educated, so as a result, a while back he sent me a group of books to read. What surprised him was that I read them. I am an inveterate reader, as I know all of you are. I'm not quite sixty, but after fifty you wake up late at night—1:00-2:00—and then for two or three hours you read. Perhaps I have read more than almost anybody in this room. Not simply those things that have to do with tactics. They don't really matter. But things that have to do with strategy, with ideals, they matter very much. I was thinking in terms of the Cabinet in the things that I read. Not only in preparing this speech before the Congress, but for this dinner. The things that really mattered were a couple of books that Pat Moynihan sent to me and urged me to read. One was Blake's Disraeli, *a classic biography, and another was Lord Cecil's* Melbourne, *another classic biography. These were two very different men, but two men very much alike in one sense: they were magnificent politicians, and so immediately the fashionable set today would say, "Ah, politicians. Bad." Because to the fashionable set that would mean they didn't believe anything—it would mean they had no ideals, and ideals are all that matter.*

All of us know, of course, that ideals are enormously important. But the pages of history are full of idealists who never accomplished anything. It was these pragmatic men, the Melbournes and the Disraelis, who maybe didn't feel anything very deeply—that is what the historians say, although who knows, why question their motives?—who had the ability to do things that other people only talked about. They left an imprint on 19th century Britain, one we have inherited in terms of reform, that will be effective not only for a century, but for centuries to come.

We in this Cabinet, and this Cabinet family, have been charged with being a group of gray men and women, pragmatic, practical, non-idealistic. So be it.

I believe in some things very deeply, and I know from having talked to all of you around here, many of you individually, every one of you individually from time to time, that you believe in some things very deeply. What we lack is demagoguery. What we believe in is not the show of idealism, but getting it done, doing something, making progress in areas where it has never been made before.

I would urge you some time, when you wake up in the middle of the night as I do, to pick up Cecil's Melbourne *or maybe Blake's* Disraeli *and read it. You'll find very interesting things. You think we have problems. You should read about the problems in 19th century England! The important thing was that through all those problems, the intrigue (and it is a fascinating, magnificent story) clearly apart from all the rest, out of it all came, in a slow, tortured, some call it muddling along, but nevertheless, successful way, an inexorable drive toward a better system of government—toward more representative democracy, if I may use that term in its best sense, toward more representative government, if I may use that term in its best sense, than we had ever had before. We have that under these two men—Melbourne and Disraeli.*

Not that I or any of you are like Melbourne or Disraeli, but in this room tonight are a group of dedicated men and women who for three years have taken a lot of hard shots, who have taken a lot of heat, who believe very deeply, I am sure, in what is best for this country. You sometimes wonder if it is worth it, will it work, does the rhetoric really matter more, because as you look at the press, the media, and the rest, you sometimes realize that doing things, accomplishing things, doesn't get that much credit. It may seem that what really matters is encompassing it all in beautiful phraseology and the rest.

Let me put it in very direct terms. On this occasion, three years after we came here, we have to think in terms of what has happened that would not have happened if we had not been here.

In the field of foreign policy—leaving out the very anguished problem of Vietnam, where we think we have done very well and we will bring it to an end—in the field of foreign policy, if we had not been here, then without question there would not have been any progress toward opening the world, toward a new relationship, with no illusions, not only with Mainland China but with the Soviet Union.

This does not mean we are less anti-Communist than we were. It does mean that we recognize as I said earlier today, that where there are great differences between great powers, we have to determine whether we are going to allow events, by reason of our not moving on them, simply to go on down the track until they explode in an inevitable nuclear confrontation—or whether we do something about it. So we have done something about it. We may not succeed, but we will have tried, and for that reason those who stand in this room, four years, eight years, twelve years from now will look back and say because we were here, the possibilities of peace in the world are brighter—peace not in the sense of a naive idea that all people are going to love each other and that all people are going to get along and that our differences are only because of misunderstanding, but peace in the sense that there are differences that will inevitably continue, that as long as we live, there is going to be hatred in the Mideast and hatred in South Asia and perhaps very great differences between the Communist world and the non-Communist world—but that at least during this period, something new happened. We changed the game, and as a result of our changing the game there is a chance, not a guarantee, but a chance that people can live together, talk together, disagree, but not fight, that they may survive. This we will contribute.

On the domestic front—oh, there is so much we would like to do, in terms of welfare, the problems of the cities, the problems of reorganization, the problems of health and all the rest. And how disappointed all of you must be. All of you in this room who have worked so hard and believe so deeply, and feel that so little progress has been made. But just think, if you had not been here and if we had not presented the initiatives we have presented, very little would have been done. Oh, there would have been a lot of talk, a lot of beautiful rhetoric. But rhetoric raises people's hopes, then dashes them, and results in the violence and frustration which we inherited when we came here.

So now, here we stand. Putting it in the sense of these very profound biographies which my friend, Mr. Moynihan, sent to me, we are not going to make the world perfect. There will not be peace for all time, as H. G. Wells thought there would be if everybody just got educated. There will not be a situation in which everyone will instantly be raised up, become responsible and all the rest. This is an imperfect world. There are imperfect people. We are not perfect. But the great thing about it is that here we are after three years, and in the field of foreign policy and the field of domestic policy, we have this magnificent opportunity to make the world safer, safer for all the generations to come. We may not succeed, but we will have tried. We have a magnificent opportunity at home to make this country more governable. We must realize that when we came here many had lost faith in the ability of this country to govern itself. I'm not sure we have restored it, not yet, but I am sure that if we had not been here, much less would have been done.

What I am finally saying to you is that in this room are a group of very dedicated men and women, who with great devotion and great selflessness have thought of this country and its place in the world, and have the thought that we are only here for about four quarters—maybe longer, but you can only assume the 4th quarter. But in those four quarters, let us be sure that nothing was left undone that could have been done to make this a more decent country, in terms of our relations between ourselves and in terms of all the infinite problems we have.

I simply want to say, as one who has seen government for 25 years, who has no illusions, who is considered to be totally pragmatic and by many totally political, I make an admission, I say it very unashamedly. You see, I happen to believe very deeply in this country. I think it is a great country. I think it is a good country. I know that if America fails, peace and freedom in this world will not survive, and I know that the men and women in this room, by what we do, have the opportunity to see that America succeeds—succeeds in making this difficult problem of representative government work in America; succeeds in the field of foreign policy; succeeds not in the sense of a phony idealism, but with a pragmatic view toward the problems in the world. I realize that because we were here for these four years, America is a better place in which to live, the world is a safer place in which to live, and

*whatever happens after that, whatever happens in the election, really
doesn't matter. We can all be very proud, and I am very proud of everybody in this room.*

The person who believes Nixon to be a cloyingly pious, deceitful opportunist, or even one who considers him a mildly jingoistic old square,
might be put off by a reading of the foregoing. In cold print Nixon's words
do lack the ironic emphasis of understatement. Yet the same readers who
react to the transcript of a cool man being emotional with a "that's a bit
thick" expression would—in the room where it is being delivered—have
an entirely different reaction.

Nixon as President had his own commanding presence, to which was
added the aura of being the most famous person in the world, and he was
right there in front of you. The setting was a high-ceilinged formal room
of the White House, a place where patriotism is allowed a little more leeway as an acceptable emotion to display, and—this is important—he stood
there without a note, saying what came to his mind right then and there
in a simple, direct, colloquial yet dignified way. When he paused to gather
his thoughts, your attention did not wander; you thought along with him,
and felt satisfied when he said the appropriate thing, which is what you
would have said if you had been standing there, and if you were so practiced an orator that you knew when not to "orate." More often than not,
people disposed to dislike Nixon left one of those ad-lib performances
thinking they had Nixon wrong, and wondering why he didn't come across
that warmly and sincerely on television.

The secret to Nixon's success in a small group was the key to his failure
in reaching a more sophisticated audience on television: He was far better
at speaking to real people than he was at speaking to "the" people. People
in a room react; he could feel it and bounce off it; because he knew he was
good on his feet, he put his audience at ease.

On television, however, the sense of place was missing, and he froze
into what he thought he was supposed to be. While the majority of his
audience was probably comfortable with the uncomfortable Nixon, the
people who always voted against him not because of what he stands for,
but because they just cannot stand the way he stands, winced at what they
took to be labored piety and simplistic argument. Many of the same people
—exposed to the ad-libbing Nixon in the flesh—would freely admit to being
amazed, as I have heard time and again.

In the example chosen in this chapter, Nixon is quoted verbatim in a
private meeting with his Cabinet. Obviously, I was not there scribbling it
all down; in this case, I had heard about the extemporaneous speech and
asked Alex Butterfield if the Signal Corps had recorded it. He said they
had, and a copy had been sent to those present; on occasions like these,
it was assumed that the event would not be lost to history. That was what
the taping system was really supposed to be about—to capture speeches
like these, authentic history with no motive of eavesdropping—but, like

so many projects, the taping was carried through in a way that went beyond all sense of proportion and ultimately cost Nixon his job. The "fourth quarter" speech has been included here not only for its substance, or the point it makes about his speaking style, but also as a sample of what the President must have had in mind when he signed his political death warrant by approving the taping system.

"On the domestic front—oh, there is so much we would like to do . . ." The way he intended to do it was in mobilizing the support of "us," the new majority. And he did, for a brief moment, bring off what few of us thought would ever be possible.

PART EIGHT

THE NEW MAJORITY

"We'll be doing some big things with the Cabinet soon," the President told me late one night after a speech in December 1970. "Not only a few new faces, but a total reorganization. Make it smaller. Eight men is all a manager can really handle.

"Reorganization, revenue sharing, welfare reform—we want to put it all together, crack it hard in the State of the Union. Give the country back to the people. Oh, the bureaucrats will go right up the wall.

"Get the word out, we're not afraid of controversy. Oh, they'll say, 'What about "Bring Us Together"?' That's fine about patriotism and all the great goals, and we should never stop reminding everybody about that. But all the people aren't going to come together, old and young, black and white, rich and poor—not on the bread and butter issues where interests are different. We can't pretend to want to unify everybody, we've got to build our majority."

1. THE TWO-IDEOLOGY SYSTEM

The most far-reaching and ultimately self-destructive political decision Richard Nixon made during his first term was to abandon the role of President as party leader, and to infuse his "new American majority" with an ideological fervor.

"Abandon the role of President as party leader" is a sweeping statement. But the "only Nixon could" theme applies: just as only a hard-line anti-Communist like Nixon could undertake the opening to Red China with political impunity, only a man with a hard-earned reputation as party loyalist like Nixon could fold up the "Big Tent" philosophy. Only a proven political pragmatist could purge the party to suit an attitudinal discipline.

What is the test of party loyalty? Simply put, it is the willingness to endure the presence of people of different viewpoints under your own banner; if your ideological opponents are in the majority of your party, you give them your support and your vote, even if they are not as much to your liking as the candidates the other party puts forth.

Such loyalty is derided as slavishness and a selling-out of convictions by the pure in heart, but the route to political power in a two-party system is to go along with the majority of your party, not cheering but not bolting, so that when you achieve a majority in your party, you can rightly demand loyalty from your intra-party opponents and so defeat the outside opposition. Benjamin Disraeli had that in mind when he said, "Damn principle —stick to your party!"

Without respect for party loyalty, you have a Goldwater campaign of 1964 or a McGovern campaign of 1972—that is, hardly any campaign at all. Nothing is more certain in politics than the crushing defeat of a faction that holds ideological purity to be a greater value than compromise.

In 1968, Nixon's policy had been to support all Republican nominees— some more than others, but nominally all. In 1970 the policy changed— Wyoming Democratic Senator Gale McGee, for example, a liberal but a hawk, was not actively opposed; when Vice President Agnew passed through Wyoming, the instructions directly from the President to those of us on the trail were to go through the motions of supporting the Republican in the race but not to sink our teeth into McGee's hide.

In the case of Republican Senator Charles Goodell, Nixon succeeded in helping the voters of New York to purge a man the President viewed as a political apostate. The President hedged a little on this, pointing out that if Goodell had any chance to win, he would have refrained, and the presence of a third-party candidate, Conservative James Buckley enabled him to gain what the President called "an ideological seat," but the meaning of the purge was not lost on dovish or liberal-leaning Republican Senators who might need Nixon support someday.

After that campaign, Nixon prepared to launch his "New American Revolution," which John Ehrlichman had been working on for more than a year. The NAR (whose title was soon dropped because the initials happened to be those of Governor Nelson A. Rockefeller) was the culmination of the centrist "new Federalism." This veering-away from the traditional tenets of conservatism irritated the True Believers of the right on the White House staff and concerned the President.

Exactly halfway into the first term, Haldeman sent a few of us the identical memo:

January 18, 1971

CONFIDENTIAL

MEMORANDUM FOR: MR. SAFIRE

FROM: H. R. HALDEMAN

The President received the attached memorandum from one of his strong Conservative supporters and found it very interesting.

As you can see the writer is quite troubled by some of the directions that the Administration is taking.

The President would like very much to have at your earliest convenience, your comments, analysis and thoughts regarding this memorandum.

Attachment

CONFIDENTIAL

The "strong Conservative supporter," I found out later, was Pat Buchanan; the title of his polemic was "Neither Fish Nor Fowl." I will excerpt from it liberally here because it shows Nixon's interest in controversy within his staff. More important, Buchanan's thesis probably reflected the President's conservative gut feelings even as he was actively espousing a more centrist position in his State of the Union and Budget messages.

We suffer from the widely held belief that the President has no Grand Vision that inspires him, no deeply held political philosophy that girds, guides and explains his words, decisions and deeds. The President is viewed as the quintessential political pragmatist, standing before an ideological buffet, picking some from this tray and some from that. On both sides he is seen as the text book political transient, here today, gone tomorrow, shuttling back and forth, as weather permits, between liberal programs and conservative rhetoric. As someone put it, "the bubble in the carpenter's level."

Left and right, both now argue aloud that the President, and his Administration, do not take decisions on the basis of political principle—but on the basis of expediency; that ours is "ad hoc government," which responds only as pressures mount from left or right. Neither liberal nor conservative, neither fish nor fowl, the Nixon Administration, they argue, is a hybrid, whose zigging and zagging has succeeded in winning the enthusiasm and loyalty of neither left nor right, but the suspicion and distrust of both.

The impression among sophisticated conservatives—now being conveyed to the rank-and-file—is that the President, subsequent to the harsh (and unjust) criticism of his 1970 campaign, has moved leftward in force to cover his exposed flank.

The "full employment budget," the open embrace of an "expansionary deficit"; the public confession that "Kent State and Jackson State" and the defeat of FAP, were his greatest "disappointments," the admission "I am a Keynesian now"; the enthusiasm for both FAP and for the forthcoming FHIP—these are part of a pattern left and right have both recognized.

A close examination of the early returns, and the projected returns, from the President's recent moves seems imperative before the President sets his compass on the course indicated in that conversation. The State of the Union and the Budget mark the point of no return.

Over the course of two years, but especially in the last month, the President has conspicuously abandoned many of the *sustaining traditions* of the Republican Party, traditions Richard Nixon rode to triumphant success in 1968 over the defeated "programmatic liberalism" of the New Deal.

Two brief examples. In both "reducing the size of the Federal Government," and "balancing the Federal Budget," the President has swept these traditions aside with an ease and facility that must have astonished millions of Republicans who have held them as articles of faith for forty years.

On his statements and positions of recent weeks, *the President is no longer a credible custodian of the conservative political tradition of the GOP.* Can one seriously imagine in 1972 those little old ladies in tennis shoes ringing doorbells in Muncie for "FAP," "FHIP" and the "full employment budget."

In the profit-and-loss statement drawn up from the President's move left, we must not overlook the inevitable and considerable loss in morale to the tens of thousands of party workers, the backbone of the GOP, one of the hinges on which the 1972 election will surely swing. The President once rightly identified the Left as the home of the True Believer in the Democratic Party and the Right as the home of the True Believer in the GOP. With Richard Nixon on the ticket, the troops of the Democratic Party will be out in force; where will the troops of the GOP be?

The President's recent moves—if publicized widely nationally leave the Republican True Believers without a vocal champion. One has to guess that this political vacuum will not go unfilled, that the old political faith will not go unchampioned for long.

Though a minority nationally, many millions of Americans hold fiscal and political conservativism as gospel—and the President's rapid moves have taken him further to the left in a month than the average Republican travels in a lifetime.

Further, in shedding some of the sustaining traditions of the GOP, we have donned the garments of the same "programmatic liberalism" the President scorned as outdated in 1968. Regardless of our rhetoric about "cleaning out the Federal Government" and "returning power to the States, cities and the people," the Federal Government under the Nixon Administration has grown to a size to dwarf the Great Society. What Great Society program—with the insignificant exception of the Job Corps camps—has been abandoned?

Rather than draw up our own yardstick of success and failure, we have willingly invited judgment by the old measures of the old order. Thus, we proudly point up that we are spending more for "human resources" than for "defense resources." (Most Republicans would argue that Federal spending for "human resources" has proven a failure, and there should be less, not more.) We publicize statistics on how much "integration" has taken place under President Nixon; we argue that our welfare program provides a guaranteed income for families and is bigger and better than anything they have offered; we underscore how much more rapidly we are bringing Americans home from Vietnam and the rest of the world; we congratulate ourselves on each new cut in the defense budget. In short, we ask our adversaries in the media and the academy to judge us on how well we are doing in reaching objectives which liberals—not conservatives—have designated as the national goals.

When the suggestion even surfaces that the President may be disenchanted with OEO, and perhaps ready to scuttle it, Rumsfeld and

Carlucci rush to Capitol Hill to swear our eternal fealty to the organization.

Truly, the liberals went swimming and President Nixon stole their clothes—but in the process we left our old conservative suit lying by the swimming hole for someone else to pick up.

As my own concern with whether the President wins in 1972 is of a piece with my concern for the President's place in history, I have to view the sharp leftward move in disappointing terms.

The President is now abandoning an historic opportunity, the opportunity to become the political pivot on which America turned away from liberalism, away from the welfare state—the founder of a new "Establishment." While the course of a "conservative President" would be more difficult by far, and politically more risky, it would seem a preferable course historically if only because the President would be assured an unoccupied niche in America's history books and a following of millions of men and women to honor his memory.

After observing what liberal journalists, liberal academicians and liberal historians are doing to the most liberal New Dealer of them all, Lyndon Johnson, I cannot think that they will be paying much grudging tribute to the accomplishments of liberal-come-lately Richard Nixon. One wonders who will be writing our epitaph.

In the passage that began "Rather than draw up our own yardstick," Buchanan made a good point about Nixon's willingness to accept liberal rather than conservative goals. To an extent, this was my doing, since much of the quotable prose in the Budget Message that year was mine, and I had a hand in the philosophical rhetoric of the State of the Union and the Economic Report of the President, all of which blossomed forth in a three-week period near the start of 1971.

With a certain zest, I began the Budget Message with a fine Democratic cliché: "To the Congress of the United States: In the 1971 budget, America's priorities were quietly but dramatically reordered: for the first time in twenty years, we spent more to meet human needs than we spent on defense." George Shultz and Cap Weinberger liked that opener, and the President bought it as punchy, political, and understandable, something he did not expect to see in the Budget messages. Buchanan, however, recognized it for what I intended it to be: an acceptance of "their" goal, not necessarily "our" goal, in a document that would be the basis for all our "talking papers" and game plans. I believed then, and do now, that Nixon delighted in accomplishing what his predecessors could not in "reordering priorities"; Buchanan believed, and probably still does, that the President should have felt guilty about cutting the defense budget and allowing the controllable domestic portion to rise.

I responded to Haldeman's memo inviting comment on the anonymous Buchanan's "Fish Nor Fowl" polemic in part as follows:

How many people think the way he does?

This is the work of the intelligent conservative ideologue, who gives his elitism away with the crack at "the booboisie in the hinterlands" that admired the President's TV Conversation.

He represents the intellectual aristocracy of the conservative movement, reflecting the spoken opinions *but not the attitudes* of most people who identify themselves as conservatives.

Most conservatives are more worried about unemployment than about the intellectual ideal of a balanced budget. They will say they support a balanced budget, but they will vote against an Administration that endangers their jobs. When it counts, the pocketbook takes attitudinal precedence over the ideology—in most cases.

William Buckley and his intellectual following may represent established conservative thinking, but do not represent the gut feelings of the majority of people who accept the label "conservative" in their voting patterns. Similarly, many of those who call themselves liberals read Max Lerner or the New Republic fervently and yet dig their heels in against local school integration. Let us not be misled into thinking the great majority of voters are ideological purists.

The writer of the memo is aware of this: "While the course of a conservative President would be more difficult by far, and politically more risky," he would be assured a following of millions to "honor his memory"—after he lost the next election. In fact, however, Goldwater went that route and the honor of his memory is tempered by the conservatives' displeasure with a loser . . .

Aside from the desire to turn the next election into a Viking's funeral, what is the writer's biggest misconception?

Old-fashioned purism. The left is the left, and the right is the right, and never the twain shall meet. A choice not an echo. I disagree; I believe there is a breaking-up of the old battle lines between liberal and conservative (interesting that the American Conservative Union calls its newsletter "Battle Line") and a churning about of ideological patterns. In this transitional era, with liberals and conservatives joining to praise ecology and decentralization, the political center is the place to be, and orderly change is the something to be for.

The New Federalists, neither leftists nor rightists, led by George Shultz and John Ehrlichman programmatically, and egged on by Ray Price and myself rhetorically, won the battle. Buchanan, who spoke for one of Nixon's most elemental moods, almost won the war, until the Watergate agony forced a relaxation of ideological discipline.

Why did Nixon circulate the Buchanan "Fish Nor Fowl" plea if he had already decided to stay firmly in the middle of the road—or, as he preferred, to take a "new road" headed neither left nor right?

First, Nixon had an affection for most of the conservative values, even though he knew he could not win with them, and he wanted to keep reminding himself and his staff that he was irritating conservative support with his liberal-ish moves.

Second, Nixon throughout his political career had always been fairly progressive in domestic affairs, though his ardent anti-Communism gave him a conservative coloration. (One big change in his views was on education, from "You know, I'm a real nut on education," a comment he made to his writers in 1968, which was transformed to "the trouble with this country is that the education being given the 'leadership class' is taking all the spine out of them," a remark in 1972.)

Third, Nixon liked any reorganization plan that resulted in fewer people reporting to him directly.

Fourth, and most important to him, he wanted to take on the Washington Establishment frontally, and the only way he could do that was by identifying himself with Establishment goals—saying, simply and accurately, that the only way to achieve a better life for more people without alienation was through a return of power to localities, and the more efficient use of the power that remained in Washington. Better means to the same goals.

The President said as much to the group gathered in the Cabinet Room at noon on January 27, 1971, as he reviewed his reorganization plans: "Offense is the best defense, and this new setup is an attack on the Establishment. I'd like the first man here willing to defend the status quo to stand up." Nixon looked sharply around the room. Nobody stood up. (Several of us ground even more deeply into our chairs.) Somebody suggested that Wilbur Mills, who ran House Ways and Means like a personal fiefdom, might not go along with revenue sharing. "I know," the President replied dryly, "he's willing to hold open hearings with a closed mind. But you have to understand—we are the only part of the Establishment that has the capability of renewing itself. We can keep 'em off balance."

The legislative initiatives of the "New American Revolution" moved slowly in 1971. General revenue sharing was grudgingly passed, "special" revenue sharing was delayed; government reorganization was stymied by the Congress, and some of it was put into action by the President acting alone; and welfare reform was killed primarily by liberals, who wanted not only a whole loaf but one baked to their exact specifications, and was then abandoned by a Nixon who heard Buchanan loud and clear. Nixon saw the liberals of his own party "more interested in making headlines than in making history," as he put it, and regardless of party turned more and more toward the people with whom he could feel congenial politically: in domestic affairs, people who resented the "welfare bums," and in foreign affairs, the people who sided with him against those who would "sell out, bug out, surrender."

By the summer of 1972 the decision had been made to spend the campaign kitty on re-electing the President, and not to share much of it with Republican candidates in local campaigns. A few of the Old Nixon Hands could not believe this; we remembered how Nixon tried to get Rockefeller in 1966 to make a contribution to the campaigns of some Republican Congressional candidates in Iowa; we believed that the real strategy was to hold on to the money as long as possible, and then when local races needed it most (and when the close ones could be separated out for special help) the President would be the financial hero to Republicans who had a chance of being elected regardless of ideology. We were mistaken.

Instead, what amounted to the "Schorenstein Rationale" was put forth. Hymie Schorenstein was a Brooklyn district leader in the Twenties who refused to spend a nickel on local campaigns, sending his collections instead to the campaign of Franklin Roosevelt for Governor. "You ever watch the ferries come in from Staten Island?" he asked his pleading candidates. "When that big ferry sails into the ferry slip, it never comes in strictly alone. It drags in all the crap from the harbor behind it." After a dramatic pause, Schorenstein would conclude, "FDR is our Staten Island Ferry."

So Nixon was supposed to be the Staten Island Ferry; the money spent on the Presidential campaign, Clark MacGregor was told to argue, would build up a landslide so huge that weak candidates would be swept in; in other words, the local candidate would benefit more from not being helped financially. (When Watergate broke, shortchanged Republican candidates landed with some glee on the President's neck, and his "selfishness" was privately cited as the reason in many cases.)

As the President prepared for his press conference on October 3, 1972, he wrote a note to himself in his press briefing book: "Generally support Republican candidates, no blanket endorsement of all candidates—where a Dem supports policy, I shall not campaign against him." "Campaign against" was written in and "oppose" was crossed out, as the President clung to a fine distinction.

All party-loyalty pretense was dropped in the case of Senator James Eastland of Mississippi, crucial to the campaign on the mildly annoying Watergate affair and a stanch supporter throughout the first term; the Republican running against him was made to feel like a pariah. Nixon's policy, then, became to support his friends and punish his enemies regardless of party. Of course, a Republican had a far better chance of support than a Democrat of the same ideological ilk, but the fervor would be absent. Why was this not the cause of a great outcry from party regulars? Because the tilt was in the conservative ideological direction, and those were mostly the party regulars. The party's liberal wing was so debilitated, especially with Rockefeller moving rightward, and the record of the Republican liberals in the Goldwater campaign so lacking in party loyalty, that any protest would have seemed ridiculous.

Besides, Nixon still had the Cheshire Cat's lingering image of a loyal party man. He had carried the banner as Vice President during the off-years when Ike was serenely above the battle. He had done right by Barry Goldwater; he had helped pick up the pieces in 1966—who could say Nixon had not helped the Republicans when they needed it most? With this protective coloration, he could take a political stance that would have infuriated party officials had it been struck by Eisenhower or Rockefeller. Nixon hurt the party? Never.

But he did, perhaps because he felt he was playing for bigger stakes. He was trying to turn the United States away from the ever-bigger government of the past forty years, and away from the undertow of isolationism that followed war-weariness and self-doubt. To do this, he felt he needed more than the support that the Republican Party plus some swing voters could give him. He needed a sea-change in political alignment, the kind of change Roosevelt brought about in 1932 and 1936, transforming the groups not in various "movements" (civil rights, antiwar, hippie) into a movement all its own.

Nixon saw in the quiet abandonment of party loyalty, a higher loyalty —the ability to build a new majority based on the principles so long espoused by the largest part of the minority party, and by so doing to reconstitute the Republican Party as a majority party. Put negatively, he wanted to purge the party of its nonmajoritarian elements; put positively, he wanted the Republican Party to be the "party of the open door," welcoming hawkish or conservative or disillusioned Democrats and independents who would make up tenfold for those he considered the screwballs (Lindsay, Riegle, McCloskey) who would be banished to where they could be comfortable.

Perhaps Nixon thought he had to rise above the party to pull the party up, sound enough practice for any President, but the addition of ideological tidiness to the formula caused great mischief. In 1973, CBS correspondent Dan Rather listened sympathetically to Senator Barry Goldwater's ruminations:

"The thing that bothers me," said Goldwater, "is here I have spent over a third of my life trying to build the Republican Party, adding my little bit to it, having been successful in the South and in the Southwest, and then all of a sudden, as I near the end of my time in politics, I wonder— what the hell's it all been for? Here we are just drifting around. More independents than Democrats or Republicans. And we need a two-party system . . . I get up in the mornings and I think, oh, well, what the hell, what can you do?"

Sadly, nodding sagely, the New York *Times* and the Washington *Post* both printed the texts of this public agony of a real Republican. In fact, however, Goldwater did more than any man to narrow the base of the Republican Party. By exalting the True Believers, he drove out the moderates and liberals, and richly deserved the drubbing he received. In reaching out for the South with a sectional appeal, he lost everything else, setting an example of the politics of exclusion that should have flashed a red light for every Republican for generations.

Goldwater proved you cannot build a party by sticking gamely to conservative principle and waiting for the nation to come to see the wisdom of your ways. Nixon proved you cannot build a party by centering a national election on the head of the ticket alone, or by relying on the popular revulsion toward social manipulation or long-haired hippies to be institutionalized in local party affairs.

In June 1972, Nixon was explaining to Buchanan in a memo the difference between right-wing extremists and left-wing extremists: "The right wing would rather lose than give up one iota as far as principle is concerned. The left wing's primary motivation is power. They are always willing to compromise their principles in order to get power because they know that without power they cannot put their principles to work."

Nixon made this point in a kind of embittered admiration of left-wing opportunism and impatience with the right wing's willingness to go down in purifying flames. If only the opportunism could be exposed, he thought, the left wing would be discredited or the right wing inspired to emulate their example—either would do, to even things up. A hopeful note to me was that it showed Nixon certainly did not count himself among the right-wing extremists, but the distressing note was the President's obvious acceptance, even at that late stage of his political life, of a simplistic left-right schism, and his identification with the right wing.

Four years before, working with him on a speech that we felt would provide some catnip to political columnists, I drafted a few ideas about "a new alignment," an approach to divergent groups not through the customary bloc-building special interest appeals, but through certain common denominators like the desire to get Big Government out of their lives. Nixon added to the title; I objected, saying that would make it unwieldy; he said no, it was important. So the title became "A New Alignment for American Unity." As it turned out, the unity he was seeking was not a national unity, but a factional one, and in fact he did unify his New Majority and helped create the New Minority. But the two-ideology system, backed up in this case with cultural and psychological divisions, only added to the us-against-them separation, fomenting distrust, fear, and occasionally hatred on both "sides." Ideological tidiness intensified division; what had been healthily fuzzed up in the two-party system now became focused, and, like a magnifying glass left in the sun, started fires that had never been as fierce before.

That wasn't his plan. Certainly Nixon was partisan, out to win, but by winning he felt he could build a generation of peace in the world and ignite a spirit of self-reliance in the American character. His "New American Revolution" or "New Federalism" would have fit that plan, but along the way, the us-against-them syndrome led to a demand for a two-ideology system, rather than a two-party system. His most vitriolic opponents pushed him in the direction his own combative instincts wanted him to go; the Pentagon Papers case led him into an overreaction that led to his most fundamental mistakes; when the lid blew off, there were no troops to rally. Republicans, shortchanged, were angry at him anyway; conservative True Believers, toward whom he was turning, lashed out at him to pay him back for past ideological impurities; the moderates in the party took heart at his buffeting; and the New Minority quaffed the wine of vindication.

The Silent Majority went underground; it did not entirely break up, because its centripetal force was too great to permit even Watergate and the Agnew scandal to change its character, but it no longer had its rallying point. A political party offers a home, but an ideology offers cold comfort after the battle. Nixon and his loyalists found that out as they began to rebuild after their 1972 victory shriveled to defeat. The experiment with a two-ideology system had ended, and as Nixon said when mod Quarterback Joe Namath tearfully if temporarily quit the Jets in 1970, "Good riddance!"

2. NIXON AND THE CATHOLICS

We were sitting around the Oval Office with the President one February day in 1970 wondering what big new issue would come up to replace the environment in media and public interest.

None of us doubted that the environment issue, which had been captured by faddists and turned into an unassailable crusade by editorial writers, would be abandoned by all of them as soon as something sexier came along—leaving the Nixon Administration to carry the fight in the face of growing opposition from consumers (pollution devices drove up prices) and labor. Carry the good fight on against pollution we would, doing what was right to clean up the air and water, feeling sorry for ourselves all the way as the fashionable-issue set traipsed off with public attention on some fresh, newsworthy endeavor.

The Outs would get all the political mileage and idealistic lift out of the "quality of life" and leave the Ins with the damn sewers and the strenuous slogans of Theodore Roosevelt about conservation. In that vein, we rambled along, "rubbing each other's sores" as the President put it, but nobody felt too bad about the burdens of the Ins—after all, you could someday begin a chapter with "We were sitting around the Oval Office with the President one February day . . ."

"Shelter," said I, reaching for a trendy term to describe that old, drab subject, housing. When interest in the environment tapered off, my argument went, housing would replace it. FDR had put it first in his Second Inaugural Address, surveying "one-third of a nation ill-housed, ill-clad, ill-nourished . . ." The housing industry was in recession, which augured a slump no matter what the other figures said; the resentments were rising about integrated housing in the suburbs; we were trying to hold down the traditional public housing which had so often become instant slums or quickly belied their "low-income" intentions; the HUD bureaucracy was proving difficult to penetrate, scandals had already been uncovered and more were sure to come—the whole subject seemed to me ripe for the customary discovery, viewing with alarm, embrace, passionate involvement, instant solution, and quick boredom of the concerned dilettante. At the same time, it offered the Nixon Administration an area to move in sensibly: to increase the supply of new housing through stimulation of the private sector, and to introduce new building materials and methods opposed by the building trades unions. (They were against us anyway, and their wage demands were the worst of all.)

The President didn't see it that way. "Health," he said, "that'll be the most important domestic concern of the immediate future. My intuition tells me that's coming on big. I told HEW we ought to get ahead of that, we should be sure to have a good health program all our own, increasing the supply of doctors and medicine rather than jacking up the demand. Which reminds me—Bryce, where do we stand with the HEW appropriation?"

Harlow said the education message was being held up pending the President's possible second veto of the HEW appropriation. "What if we veto the continuing resolution?" the President asked. "Then, Mr. President, the entire agency would expire." The President allowed himself a luxurious moment to contemplate that impossibility, then turned to education.

Nixon had just met with parochial school leaders; before that, he had sent word to me to stiffen up the private school portion of the education message. "It's vitally important that private schools survive," he added now, getting animated and more specific. "They're in a helluva crisis, schools closing at the rate of one a day. Colson has some of the assignments; I want to work on imaginative assistance to private schools. Dig out the speech in the campaign that I made about private schools." He remembered a statistic. "Why, in Philadelphia, there are a quarter of a million students in public school, the same number in private school, and it costs four times as much to educate the public school students."

Then why, I asked, had Commissioner James Allen of HEW's Office of Education cut down the request for Title II aid, providing books to parochial schools? "Because it doesn't go to the school bureaucracy, that's why," Nixon replied. "Damn HEW wants to hang on to control." When Buchanan added that HEW officials blocked other attempts to aid non-public schools, the President's feet came down off his desk and he pulled his swivel chair up to the desk top, and he barked, "Blocked it! It should be done tomorrow! We'll knock it out of the education message and give them a sock in the puss with a separate message—we'll save those private schools one way or another.

"What is it about those guys, anyway?" the President wanted to know. "One day they're blocking something deliberately, the next they're forgetting to do something I made a commitment to do. We put out a message last year about one- to five-year-olds, the First Five Years of Life idea—and then nothing happens, they don't do anything about 'em. When we were growing up, my mother—more than my father—" Nixon broke off and started again. "Why, before we ever got to first grade, we learned to read.

There were Mexicans at the school we went to, and I skipped a grade, not because I was any smarter, but because my mother taught me to read at home. The Right to Read is important as hell. And nothing happens." He slumped back in his chair, adding a non sequitur, "I think TV hurts reading. Look at my kids, at Key Biscayne or San Clemente, the TV is almost never on. Not that they're any smarter, they're just interested in other things." Haldeman pointed out that some television could teach pre-school children to read, and the President said to me, "You think we should spend more on educational TV?" I said damn right, provided we could develop new sources of programming. He shrugged to show he'd have to be sold on that, he didn't want a fourth network with the same cultural and political biases he saw in the commercial three.

"I keep telling the educators," the President said, "they have to think about what kind of generation they're creating. Read about what's happening at the University of Manila—that's our school system all over again. Riots, anti-American parades—just like Harvard." His irritation dissolved: "That's what I tell Kissinger. He doesn't quite go along, he says, 'Vell now, Mr. President,' but they'll get to him before long."

The President, as he often did after letting a conversation trail along in a desultory way, presented a rundown of the reasons for the support of private schools, which fitted closely with his own political instincts: they provided a yardstick by which to measure public education's effectiveness; educated some five million children who otherwise would have to be taught on tax money; offered diversity in education; added their own religious and moral instruction which, if that is what parents wanted, was to be encouraged rather than denied. Nixon was aware of the arguments against: the need to separate church and state, the possibility of evading desegregation through a false use of "freedom of choice," the problem of providing support without having control of the use of funds. The paradox was that the customary supporters of a strict construction of the Constitution were adamant for a liberal interpretation of the Constitutional strictures against the establishment of a state religion. There was no doubt in the President's mind about where he stood: in favor of aid to private schools, through provision of transportation and textbook costs if Constitutionally possible, through a tax credit if not.

How much politics went into that decision? It would be foolish to say none—John Kennedy, for example, to overcome the bugaboo of Popery, had to take a clear position against parochial school aid. It showed he would withstand Catholic pressures and thereby helped cool Protestant suspicion. Nixon knew that his position on "parochaid" would be appealing to what is loosely and misleadingly called the Catholic vote.

Ever since the "Bailey memorandum" of 1956 purported to show how a Catholic could be elected President—and was proved accurate in many ways in 1960—the notion of getting the largest religious minority in America to vote as Catholics has intrigued politicians. In Nixon's White House, several aides dealt with aspects of that question in varying ways: Peter

Flanigan, a Wall Streeter with a Benedictine education and long-time relations with the "powerhouse"—the Archdiocese of New York—was the one most directly in touch with the hierarchy and the Vatican; Charles Colson, a Boston Episcopalian who was the man most concerned with Catholic groups; and Pat Buchanan, the conservative speechwriter and a product of a Catholic parochial school and a Jesuit high school in Washington, D.C., best understood Catholic theological discourse. Along with Rose Mary Woods, the President's personal secretary, who made it to Mass every Sunday morning no matter what part of the world she was traveling in—these were Nixon's Catholic antennae, receiving signals from a bloc that had long since split and whose larger section had become switchable.

Since New Deal days, about three out of four Catholics were registered as Democrats. But more than half the Catholics voted for Eisenhower in 1956, and then switched back for Kennedy, voting nearly 80 per cent Democratic in 1960. Now it was apparent that an ideological schism was developing and affecting voting patterns.

In the fall of 1971, a memo on the Catholic vote prepared for Ken Cole was sent on to John Ehrlichman and then in to the President. Since in 1960 Catholicism as an issue was settled by the election of Kennedy, the memo argued, it was no longer advisable to appeal to Catholics *as* Catholics—"the major issues among Catholics are not related to Catholicism but rather to general economic and social conditions. Catholics seem to be concerned with tax levels, tax increases and general problems in the environmental area." The analysis warned against irritating Protestant groups by pressing for aid to parochial schools and added, "Furthermore, the parochial aid issue is complicated and many Catholics may either contribute to the decline of these schools, or are relatively unconcerned about the problem. The same may be said for Catholic clergy. A 1970 Gallagher Presidents' Report Survey found that 35.4 per cent of the active Roman Catholic priests affirm that the Church should discontinue or abandon its schools."

Buchanan read this and went right through the roof. Terming it "remorseless nonsense" and angrily demanding to know why it had been sent to the President without critical comment, he made his point to Ehrlichman, Haldeman, and Colson, which they dutifully passed up top. Buchanan divided Northern Democrats into "New York *Times* Democrats" and "Jim Buckley Democrats" and wrote: "When RN comes out for aid to parochial schools, this will drive a wedge right down the Middle of the Democratic Party. The same is true of abortion; the same is true of hardline anti-pornography laws. For those *most against* aid to Catholic schools, *most for* abortion, and an end to all censorship are the New York *Times* Democrats. And those most violently *for* aid to Catholic schools and *against* abortion and dirty books, are the Jim Buckley Democrats.

"Rockefeller, in coming out for parochial aid, has recognized this. In 1970 he won over Catholic Democrats in greater numbers than ever—while his upstate Protestants grumbled about aid to Catholic schools, but they 'had no place else to go.'"

The last shot—"no place else to go"—was the conservative Buchanan's revenge. For years, during the liberal emphasis on welfare reform, the conservatives within the Administration were told that the Nixon followers on the far right would have to hold still and stick with RN because they would have "no place else to go." Then Buchanan added: "The one-third of priests who are not interested in Catholic schools probably contain the one hundred per cent of Catholic clergy who either endorse or 'understand' what the Berrigans were trying to do. What I am saying is that there is a deep division in the Catholic community. We should be working the Catholic social conservatives—the clear majority . . ."

Essentially, Buchanan—with Flanigan and Colson in agreement—was saying that it was a good idea to go for the largest segment of the Catholic vote with conservative stands on issues of interest to them as Catholics—abortion, pornography, parochaid. A somewhat different point of view —to appeal to conservative Catholics in generally conservative terms, but not taking positions on issues that might turn off Protestants—had been made as well. Which course did the President choose?

Neither and both. His decision on these matters was not primarily based on "what will this do for me with conservative Catholic Democrats" or "which Protestants will this offend." He never had to make the decision of appealing to Catholics *as* Catholics or rejecting such an appeal; instead, he followed his personal instincts on these matters. In the past, he had ducked the issues ("local option" or "for each person to decide"). Now, with at least a political offset or at best a political advantage to public exposition of his long-held views, Nixon could sound off. Most of the time, he identified with the antipermissive, authoritarian views of much of the Catholic social conservative majority. The political arguments, pro and con, removed the barriers to his speaking out or encouraging other Administration spokesmen to do so.

In the campaign of 1968, Nixon had limited his antipornography statements to a blast at obscenity, already set outside the bounds of free speech by the Supreme Court. In his first term, he could blaze away at the recommendations of the Johnson-appointed Commission on Pornography. This did not take much courage; pornographers do not have supporters, only customers. His position earned Nixon the contempt of the people who already were 100 per cent against him, which bothered him not a bit, while it built support among social conservatives.

On abortion, since the issue first arose politicians took refuge in "local option," and Nixon ducked it that way early in his Administration. The abortion issue is on a different order of magnitude from other so-called Catholic issues—many Catholics are convinced that abortion-on-demand is nothing less than legalized murder. Suddenly, on April 3, 1971, to the amazement of Flanigan and Colson, the President directed military hospitals to reverse rulings made the previous year aimed at liberalizing abortion, and added "the country has a right to know my personal views. From personal and religious beliefs I consider abortion an unacceptable form of population control. Further, unrestricted abortion policies, or abortion on demand, I cannot square with my personal belief in the sanctity of human life—including the life of the yet unborn."

A year later, Buchanan suggested to Haldeman that the President send a letter to Terence Cardinal Cooke in New York reiterating his views on abortion and commending their campaign to work for repeal of the state's recently liberalized abortion laws. John Mitchell approved, the letter was sent and released by the Archdiocese on Buchanan's okay, to the embarrassment of John Ehrlichman, who was the main contact with Nelson Rockefeller and who had been told the letter was personal and private. Rockefeller, taking a politically risky stand against abortion repeal, was understandably angry, and the New York *Times* denounced "a President openly working through a particular church to influence the action of a state government." Buchanan was not penitent; from his standpoint, the right people were angry at him. The President felt right about it, and may have been influenced by the strong sanctity-of-life argument put forth by his daughter Julie. In the months that followed, the President wanted to make his position known more widely, but was restrained by Colson and Ehrlichman, who felt the point had been made and we should let the issue lie. Flanigan felt that what had been a philosophical principle on the President's part had been made to seem like a stand taken only for political advantage, which conservative Catholics would not like.

Philosophically, the President felt that unrestricted abortion was further evidence of a society granting approval to irresponsibility, and that pornography was another example of permissiveness gone wild, leading to moral decay and the decline of Western civilization. My own view, which was not actively solicited after my first couple of press briefing book comments, followed the libertarian rather than the traditionalist root of conservatism—that is, the government should butt out of the individual's life wherever possible, and the decisions to buy smut or to abort a birth should be made by the individual. It was one of those situations where there was much to be said on the other side, and where conservative consistency could carry you to different conclusions. When the Supreme Court struck down abortion restrictions in 1973, the President shook his head and prepared to answer any questions with a grim support of the rule of law.

On the issue of aid to parochial schools, libertarians could agree strongly with the President's position: diversity was the essence of Federalism, new and old, and there was nothing the public school system needed more than the stimulus and criterion of a private system. Did aid to parochial schools erode the separation of church and state? Of course it did, to some degree. If that erosion ever became a dangerous degree, it would have to be faced and turned around—but it was not now as much a danger as the stultification and uniformity of education. Nixon issued a statement supporting parochaid in Pittsburgh in October 1968, and was made an enthusiast after a meeting Colson arranged with Bishop Bernadine, head of the U. S. Catholic Conference in February 1970.

After that meeting, the President told Colson, "Break all the china in the White House if you have to—I'll back you up, but I want a plan on how we rescue the parochial schools on my desk Monday morning." The President did one of his slow burns. "Think of it. Those people—they're real believers. They don't teach because it's just a job—some of those nuns risk getting raped, and yet they go ahead and teach in the poorest neighborhoods. And they teach fundamental values, things I believe in, not like some of these screwball progressive education groups. Find the money to get their Title II funding for libraries doubled, to one hundred million, and by Monday."

Colson was an abrasive, straight-ahead ex-Marine who liked working directly for the President; he filled a need for Nixon, who wanted an intermediary other than Haldeman to push John Mitchell and John Ehrlichman. On most of the Catholic issues, Mitchell and Ehrlichman differed with the President; Colson was to be the goad.

Through Colson, the President ordered John Mitchell to file an *amicus* brief in the *Lemon v. Kurtzman* case being argued before the Supreme Court, permitting State aid to private schools. Solicitor General Erwin W. Griswold point-blank refused to file such a brief himself, because he believed the President's position was unconstitutional. The President told his special counsel to make sure the Justice Department filed that brief. Colson leaned hard on Mitchell to do so, which the Attorney General did not in the least appreciate. Grudgingly, he filed the government's support of the principle of State aid to private schools, and was not surprised when the Supreme Court, including two Nixon appointees, struck down the principle, 8 to 0. This left only the tax credit route open, which the President vowed to pursue.

The President had appointed a Commission on School Finance, headed by Neil McElroy, which was about to come out with a report against State aid to private schools. However, there was a subcommittee on Private School Finance, headed by Dr. Clarence Walter, president of Catholic University, which, not surprisingly, disagreed. The President arranged that the subcommittee report become public knowledge first, and the full commission's report appeared as a kind of rebuttal.

Support for parochial school aid received a boost from an unexpected quarter. Orthodox Jews in middle-class urban areas who could not afford the trek to the suburbs, and who were worried about an influx of blacks and Puerto Ricans, turned increasingly to their own parochial schools. The preservation of the local Hebrew school became a crucial matter to some Jews, and split a group that had traditionally stood against any remote possibility of a lowering of barriers between church and state.

To sum it up, Nixon felt comfortable in publicly allying himself with conservative "Catholic causes" because he believed in them and he saw they could help him build his majority. He was struck by the number of labor union leaders who were in the group that Buchanan characterized as "Buckley Democrats"; after a meeting with labor leaders in the White House, the President observed in some wonderment: "If we had held a Mass there, 90 per cent of them would have hit the rail."

The President had the taste and the good judgment, however, not to make any blatant, direct appeals for a Catholic bloc vote. When he accepted an invitation to address a Knights of Columbus convention, he looked over remarks prepared by a new member of the speechwriting staff, a Jesuit priest who had run for the Senate from Rhode Island, John McLaughlin, and set most of them aside as too obviously a reach for Catholic support. Buchanan was asked for the next draft, and that True Believer sallied forth against the detractors of America, defended the morality of the war in Vietnam, and concluded with a ringing patriotic peroration that would have warmed a lot of hearts.

Ray Price objected. The day before, on Sunday, August 15, 1971 the President had gone on national television to explain his economic plan and appealed for bipartisan support. "To engage in a slugging match on your first appearance since the speech could seriously undercut its impact," Price wrote the President. "It would break the spell and shatter the mood." A couple of hours before the Price memo reached him, however, the President had already called me with much the same instructions:

"I'm going to send over to you, which I would like you to do for me, a thousand-word draft of Father McLaughlin's and one of Buchanan's on the Knights of Columbus for tomorrow night in New York.

"I want fifteen hundred words at the outside. In McLaughlin's draft, pick up all the fine things about the Knights. Buchanan's has bite—too much—but there's some good hard-hitting stuff in his, down to earth, and we need some of that, but it is a little rough. Meld them together, and then play off the theme of last night: America today is entering a new era of peaceful competition. We have announced bold action. And then take off from the end of the speech last night.

"I'll say this—you don't have to put it in—but I am the first President to address the K of C. That's significant in itself." I took that to mean he wanted to veer away from the obvious tack and to compliment the audience by ignoring its special interests. Buchanan, watching me banging away in a hurry—the President had said, "Let me say there is no problem in getting it back to me, seven or eight o'clock tonight is all right"—chipped in some careful language in support of parochial school aid. (The jealousies of 1968 about who-wrote-what had long since vanished; a few months before, Buchanan had been given a Vietnam draft of mine to instill more of a hard-line feeling.)

The President went golfing that afternoon with William Rogers, his first outing on the links in more than a year—shot a 52 on the first nine holes, then improved to a 42 on the second nine, and he felt pretty good about that—ate an early dinner, and went to work on my draft. By 10 P.M., he had sent me his rewritten version, incorporating some last-minute suggestions of Ray Price's as well. There was a passage about how it is not easy for the working man to forego a wage increase, or a businessman to hold the line on prices, which Nixon gave this lift:

> But if the temporary sacrifice of each of these will result in stopping the rise in the cost of living for all Americans, this is a great goal—worth sacrificing for.

I took a final crack at a draft, gave it to the unsung denizens of the basement of the EOB to type up overnight, and sent it to Nixon before breakfast the next morning. He made further changes—he wanted this speech to be just right—and he gave it to Rose Woods to type his reading copy, admonishing her to show all his changes to Ray Price and me before inclusion, to give us a chance to object. We had no fixes on his fixes.

In his delivery of the speech in the Waldorf-Astoria's Grand Ballroom, Nixon took the pulse of the audience and proceeded to work in and out of the prepared text, ad-libbing as the spirit moved him but sticking to the structure he had worked on. This is an effective form of presentation, and moved the audience in the room; at the same time, the AP and UPI leads contained both the point and the tone he intended, as the President's News Summary showed:

Wire Reports on
THE PRESIDENT'S SPEECH TO
THE KNIGHTS OF COLUMBUS
August 17, 1971

RN has opened a two-day, nation-hopping tour with an appeal for public support of his new economic policies. He said, "If the temporary sacrifice of each of these Americans will result in stopping the rise in the cost of living for all Americans, this is a great goal worth sacrificing for." RN was given a two-minute ovation when he endorsed introductory remarks by Cardinal Terence Cooke, calling for aid to the nation's parochial schools. The President said private and parochial schools are closing at the rate of one-a-day. He declared: "we must resolve to stop that trend and turn it around." and he added: "You can count on my support to do that." (AP)

* *

RN paid special tribute to the late Vincent Lombardi. "I talked to him on the phone just a few days before he died," RN said. "I said, 'Coach, you've had millions of people rooting for your teams but never so many as are rooting for you now.' He said, 'Mr. President, it's a tough battle, but I can tell you I'll never quit fighting.' What America needs today is that kind of fighting, that kind of competitive spirit." RN won resounding applause from the more than 1,000 delegates when he pledged his help to parochial schools suffering heavy financial burdens. (UPI)

* *

Did all this pay off at the polls for Nixon? The Gallup figures are impressive: Catholics, who had voted against him 78 to 22 per cent against Kennedy in 1960, who had voted against him 59 to 33 per cent against Humphrey in 1968 (ex-Wallace), voted *for* him 52 to 48 per cent against McGovern in 1972. There are thousands of modifiers that should be built into those statistics, but the result, after all the qualifications are granted, is that Catholics who were social conservatives—or Democrats who were trending conservative and happened to be Catholic, if you prefer—switched to Nixon in droves.

To hold that Nixon wooed and won the "Catholic vote" in his first term, however, would be mechanistic. He sensed and identified with the feelings and value judgments of a great many people who had been his former political opponents. He exploited that identification with gusto (critics would say shamelessly) drawing strength and personal confidence from the evidence of the success of his new alliances, which emboldened him to be himself. In so doing, he touched all the right bases of self interest—appealing to Catholics on the "Catholic issues"—but not in an overbearing way that would alienate people who would otherwise be for him. Above all, he did this in a manner consistent with a rejection of "special interests" politics.

Now, hold on a minute—how could he appeal to special interests while denouncing special interests? Here's how: His primary concern, frequently expressed, was the general interest. Where a special interest conflicts with the general interest, he would take a position against the special, and if this were accompanied by wrist-to-forehead protestations of political derring-do, he could get away with it. If, however, the special interest was consistent with his view of the general interest—then he not only supported it but made a big deal out of it. Some special interests of a majority of Catholics—to help parochial schools, to restrict abortion, to crack down on pornography—fit into Nixon's general belief that permissiveness was gnawing at society's underpinnings. Parochaid fit not only into Nixon's preference for diversity, but echoed his distrust of a school establishment he felt was more concerned with adjustment than excellence, with using education as a tool of social engineering rather than as an aid to each child's self-reliance. In each of these instances, support of the special interest was, in Nixon's view, in the general interest.

But he could not, in consistency or in modern politics, say, "I'm for your special interests so you should be for me." Instead, after letting it be known that he stood with them on what concerned many of them most, he called for them to make the sacrifices he demanded of all Americans, placing country before self, public interest in restraining inflation before personal interest in wage boosts—in all, the unpopular road to popularity, the work ethic in political action, the self-denying, sometimes self-pitying, path to a landslide. Richard Nixon could certainly be as calculating as Kennedy or as manipulative as FDR, but in this situation, on the issues of greatest concern to Catholics, he followed his instincts.

To Nixon, theology was a peripheral interest, but he told Colson one day, "I could be comfortable being a Catholic." Catholicism intrigued him with its comprehensiveness, the stability it offered, the requirement of total acceptance of the faith.

"Pat," he asked Daniel Patrick Moynihan one day in 1970, apropos of nothing, "you're Catholic, aren't you?" Moynihan nodded yes. "You believe in the whole thing?" The tone of the question was respectful, but Moynihan was never the reverent type. "Not only that, Mr. President," he replied, cocking his head at Haldeman and Ehrlichman—both Christian Scientists—"I even believe in doctors."

3. NIXON AND THE JEWS

For a man whose statesman-hero of the nineteenth century was Benjamin Disraeli; whose hero as a lawyer, especially on the right to privacy, was Louis Brandeis; whose model of a strict constructionist Supreme Court Justice was Felix Frankfurter; whose favorite writer of fiction was Herman Wouk; who, upon becoming President, named a German Jewish immigrant named Henry Kissinger to be his foremost foreign policy adviser and an Austrian Jewish immigrant named Arthur Burns to be his chief domestic counselor; who later placed one Jew, Herbert Stein, at the head of the Council of Economic Advisers, and another, Leonard Garment, at the head of his double-every-year commitment to the arts and humanities, and named another, Ed David, to be his chief science adviser; for such a man, in the midst of a popular landslide against an opponent weak on the two issues most critical to the Jewish community, to win nearly four out of ten votes cast by Jews is amazing—amazing not that he won *only* four, but that he won as many as four, almost double his total in 1960 and 1968, since—as everyone used to say—Jews don't trust Nixon.

For those puzzled by this phenomenon, as well as for those who thought the last sentence would never end, there is a simple explanation. In 1972, hundreds of thousands of Jews switched to Nixon, or abstained from voting their Democratic habit, not because they liked Nixon more but because many of them came to adopt his positions on the issues that became most important to them. Let us see how it came to pass.

Nationally, the "Jewish vote" should be insignificant: this 4 per cent of the population could hardly affect the popular-vote totals. But the complicated American electoral system, which people with neat minds would like to reform, has a way of preventing a tyranny of the majority. Jews make a difference in New York, Illinois, California, Florida, Ohio, and New Jersey—traditionally the "battleground states." The Electoral College, so often derided as anachronistic, gives great weight to minorities.

Moreover, as Nixon pointed out to several of us in 1968, Jews are in the habit of voting, increasing their significance in the critical states by nearly half again. On top of that, every new Jewish vote Nixon could get was really two votes, since it usually meant the reduction of a vote against him. Traditionally, the Jewish vote for the Presidency ran about four-to-one Democratic, but candidates for state races like Rockefeller and Javits would get as high as 35 per cent, indicating that there was room for a 10 per cent turnaround, enough to swing a key state in a tight election.

Back in 1960, running against Kennedy, about the only thing Nixon had going for him was Herb Klein's name. Some people thought Klein was Jewish, which he was not. (Herb, in his bland way, never denied it.) Nixon did badly, garnering about 20 per cent of the vote in 1960. In 1964 the Goldwater campaign sliced even this meager percentage in half, and Nixon wound up in 1968 with about 15 per cent against Humphrey.

In that campaign, as Republicans were accustomed to doing, Nixon sought some traction in the Jewish community with his long-time strong support of Israel, but he was resigned to defeat on that. Nixon knew that the Democrats would promise as much if not more, and Israel was not a "switcher" issue.

Nixon had a speaking date with B'nai B'rith in Washington, D.C., on September 8, 1968. The day before, in Pittsburgh, I was banging out a speech about Nixon's position in regard to the Middle East. The paper I had been given to work with seemed to me unduly evenhanded, a position that would make it seem Nixon was pulling away from Israel in order to become a broker between Arabs and Jews. Therefore, in lieu of a pledge to maintain a balance of power, I drafted: "Israel must possess sufficient military power to deter an attack; sufficient power means the balance must be tipped in Israel's favor."

That, I thought, was a clear-cut stand for the Republican candidate. Ray Price and Pat Buchanan thought so too, but also thought it was crass, unconscionable, and wrong-headed. Worst of all, they were convinced it would pose a policy problem for Nixon after he was elected. I had already lived through one Nixon election campaign in which we woke up on Election Day afflicted by a list of "if only's," so I posed this question: "If we're going to slap the Israelis in the face, why did we pick the B'nai B'rith convention to do it at?" More important, I felt that whatever experts were advising Nixon on this matter happened to be wrong, and not just in terms of American politics. If the Arab nations were "equal" to Israel in terms of arms, they would keep trying to overrun Israel until they succeeded. We argued heatedly about this, with Ray deploring "grandstanding" and Pat reminding me that Nixon had erred once before on a quick comment about Middle Eastern affairs, when he predicted that the war that had broken out in 1967 would last a long time, since neither side had the power to achieve victory. (That was not a prediction we could brag about in view of the way people later referred to that episode as the "six-day war.") We put our disagreement up to the Candidate for decision.

Nixon was his own foreign affairs expert, and after listening to our differing opinions, wrote in a qualifier—"As long as the threat of Arab attack remains direct and imminent"—and then went with "sufficient power means the balance must be tipped in Israel's favor." An exact balance, he explained, would invite miscalculation, and "for that reason—to provide Israel a valid self-defense—I support a policy that would give Israel a technological military margin to more than offset her hostile neighbor's numerical superiority." There was another fight over the words "more than" before "offset," but Nixon was firm—he had made the decision and was not about to fudge it. Then, to me, he added, "You'll see, there won't be a single vote in this for me. They'll cheer and applaud, and then vote for the other guy, they always do. But we're right on the issue, and it wouldn't hurt to say so."

I had to smile at Nixon's four-square use of a phrase that my mother so often used, accompanied by a shrug—"it wouldn't hurt"—but he turned out to be right. He ran ahead of Goldwater's total, but behind his own record in 1960, winding up in 1968 with 15 per cent of the Jewish vote.

To my knowledge, Nixon's policy toward Israel was only once influenced by American political considerations. In early 1970, at the time of the visit of French President Georges Pompidou, the Jewish War Veterans demonstrated in several cities. In New York, one demonstration especially upset Madame Pompidou, who overreacted and threatened to go home. Mayor Lindsay and Governor Rockefeller were loath to offend the Jewish groups in New York with a strong response.

That night, March 1, 1970, my wife and I were having dinner at the Haldemans' home in the Kenwood section of Chevy Chase, Maryland, with the Len Garments, the James Keoghs, and the Alex Butterfields. The Haldemans did not entertain too frequently (there's the understatement of the chapter) but did so warmly and graciously—the home movies shown after dinner, taken by Bob on every Presidential trip and at every State occasion, were in focus and historic—and the four hours spent there not only gave us some indication of Haldeman's relationship with the President but of the President's reaction to what he considered improper pressure.

After the first of five calls that evening, Haldeman said to Garment in a good-humored way, "The President is hopping mad at the Jews today, with all their demonstrations against Pompidou. Never seen that before—he usually likes you guys." With each succeeding phone call from an increasingly frustrated, miffed President, Haldeman passed along the message at the dinner table: "I want a statement from Kissinger on my desk at 9 A.M. . . . ."; then, "I don't want to see any more Jews about Israel in my office for at least—I don't know how long"; and then, "Let 'em get their planes from Rockefeller and Lindsay!"

Haldeman did not take any of Nixon's expostulations seriously; the President needed an outlet for his irritation, Haldeman was that outlet, and he knew the President would be amazed and disappointed if his closest assistant took any action on the basis of what the President said while letting off steam. Time enough the next morning to ask the President,

"Did you really mean that?" and the President would look at Haldeman severely and ask, "What idiot suggested that?"

Garment was having difficulty swallowing his food, however, and each cheery report from Haldeman about the President's blowing his stack at the demonstrating Jews depressed him further. Len excused himself, went to the phone in the kitchen and passed the word to American Jewish leaders as well as Ambassador Yitzak Rabin of Israel—a cool general who had shown Nixon around Israel in 1967 and for whom Nixon had the highest regard—that the President was concerned about domestic Jewry's intrusion into diplomacy, and especially by insulting a guest of the U. S. Government.

The next morning, Haldeman did not remind the President of any of his "orders" of the evening before, because Nixon had a better idea. He would fly to New York himself, substitute for Vice President Agnew at a luncheon (a historic first), let Lindsay and Rockefeller see what it was like to be a responsible statesman, and show Pompidou how he understood the trials of a President whose wife was upset.

Ambassador Rabin and the U.S. Jewish leaders did what they could to restrain the counterproductive demonstrations. I helped edit a statement being drafted by Jewish leaders denouncing extremism, which was duly reported to Nixon, whose anger cooled. He admired the Israelis, especially Rabin and kept applying the word "moxie" to them, a sure sign of the highest approbation.

Petulantly, Nixon wanted some outlet for his pique at the Pompidou-picketing affair, and Haldeman found the least consequential: a hold on all routine messages to Jewish dinners, yearbooks, and bar mitzvahs. When Rita Hauser passed along one of these requests and received no action, she suspected that somebody was doing something silly, and promptly complained to John Mitchell. The Attorney General picked up the phone to the White House and started the flow of congratulatory messages moving again.

Linking the attitude of Jews toward Nixon and vice versa to a separate subject like Israel is unfair and often exaggerated, but the link exists. "They're not ashamed to be patriots," Nixon once told his Cabinet, and his admiration for the nationalism and guts of the Israelis rubbed off onto his attitude toward Jews in America. He could see, too, the anomaly in the position of many Vietnam doves regarding Middle Eastern policy, and did not hesitate to exploit it. We would often write in reminders that a strong stand in Asia affected our credibility "in the Middle East and elsewhere" and the "elsewhere" was only to make the point seem less like a hard knuckle being twisted in Jewish spines.

Word would filter back to Nixon of the quiet way Yitzak Rabin calmed criticism of U.S. foreign policy in those influential circles in which he moved. When American troops made a commando raid into North Vietnam to try to rescue POWs and the raiders found no prisoners, the effort was derided; at one Georgetown dinner party, it was wryly suggested to

Ambassador Rabin that the United States should have subcontracted the job to the Israelis, who are more adept at commando attacks. Rabin was not amused, and replied only, "You left your calling card up there," a remark that Nixon men promptly passed on to the President.

Because Henry Kissinger was Jewish, he stayed out of the forefront of Middle Eastern policy-making; this was convenient to the President, who was glad to give Bill Rogers an important area to get his teeth into. Kissinger kept in touch with Middle East tensions through Joseph Sisco, Assistant Secretary of State, who sharpened his negotiating skills needed for Arabs and Jews by operating between Rogers and Kissinger. Secretary Rogers, who troubled American Jewish leaders with a tendency to seem evenhanded in the Middle East, produced a fairly successful policy in that area, helping to bring about a cease-fire that lasted for a time, if not a peace. Nixon would intercede from time to time, usually with a pro-Israeli "tilt" in supplying jets, and the President personally took command of the U.S. action in turning back the Syrian tanks crossing into Jordan in 1970. Within the Nixon White House, admiration for the Israelis was once expressed casually by Henry Kissinger: "There'll be no more ten-year wars. The Israelis have it right—if you can't win a war in six days, the hell with it."

When Henry Kissinger made one of his rare gaffes, using the word "expel" in regard to the Soviet presence in the Middle East, he asked that the President back him up on the use of that word in his forthcoming press conference. This was the recommended answer by Kissinger, edited by Buchanan:

SOVIET PRESENCE IN EGYPT

Q.   Mr. President: A high White House official has been quoted as saying this government's policy is to "expel" the Russians from the Middle East. That, coupled with your TV interview, has in the eyes of some undercut your Middle Eastern Peace initiatives. Can you tell us if it is indeed American policy to "expel" the Soviets—and whether you think our peace efforts have been damaged by your television remarks?

A.   America's objective in the Middle East is peace. All our efforts are directed toward making progress toward the kind of settlement that will bring a durable peace to that region.

Along with other top level officials of this Administration, I have spoken of the dangers inherent in the Mid-East Situation—as part of the background of the new United States initiative. Those dangers are the strongest arguments I know for making that initiative successful.

As for Soviet combat forces in the UAR, we view their presence there with concern—even though it is claimed they are there in a strictly defensive role. If that is indeed the reason for their presence—then they can be withdrawn when there is a peace settlement. Again, it is that settlement toward which our efforts are being made today.

(PJB/HAK)

The word expel was used in that context—and as all statements by White House spokesmen, fully reflected my views. (HAK)

Nixon did not go for that last point; as Plate 13, following page 392, shows, he wrote instead: "Not expel by force—but by peace settlement."

Perhaps because of the rising respect for Nixon as a firm friend of Israel, the ire of many of my own friends and relatives in 1970 was raised against Spiro Agnew, as the embodiment of all that was illiberal and repressive. They could finally accept Nixon as President—after all, he had been President for a year and the world had not come to an end—but the thought of Agnew as only a heartbeat away made their blood run cold, especially after the media stopped treating him as a buffoon ("if you've seen one slum, you've seen 'em all") and started monsterizing him ("effete snobs," "rotten apples"). The same people who used to say, "I can understand your being a Republican, but to work for Nixon—" in time said to me, "I can understand your working for the President, but to write speeches for Agnew—"

Ever since Agnew's cordial "fat Jap" remark was twisted into a racial slur, the Vice President was sensitive about any ethnic references ("Personally, I'm a Greek—I mean, I'm Grecian"). In November 1971, on his way to a television interview, he passed another interviewee, Pentagon Papers distributor Daniel Ellsberg, in the hall; on the air, the Vice President said, "Dan Ellsberg is in the lobby Xeroxing a salami sandwich." The Anti-Defamation League of B'nai B'rith promptly got in touch with the White House—"an awful lot of people took offense at the remark and communicated their distress concerning it to us." Garment looked at this and wondered to me, "Are my ethnic antennae losing their sensitivity?" I said no, and suggested we buck the complaint along to John Volpe, in case he felt the remark was anti-Italian salami. But it was a serious complaint, so I sent it to Art Sohmer, the Vice President's chief of staff, with the notation "It's easy to see an ethnic sensitivity to Ellsberg, but this complaint, in my view, is hypersensitive, and I would file and forget," which he did.

Concerned that the counterattack on Agnew would center on anti-intellectualism, with the follow-up likely to be anti-Semitism, I made every effort to identify those who tried to shout down speakers as anti-intellectual (rarely covered) and ostentatiously used big words that sent reporters scurrying to unabridged dictionaries (always covered). The use of alliteration came in this symbolic category, and the sibilant syllables sizzled.

Yom Kippur, the sacred Day of Atonement, always comes up smack in the middle of a political campaign. The Jewish members of a candidate's staff, if they are nonobservant, go discreetly into hiding, or, if they are observant, spend the day in synagogue. In 1968, I told Nixon I could not stay and hear him deliver his "American Spirit" speech in Williamsburg because I had to get back for Yom Kippur ("You go all the way, the cap, the shawl, and everything? Good for you!"). In 1970 I told Art Sohmer and Vic Gold, then Vice President Agnew's press secretary (both Jewish), that I had to cut back and would rejoin the campaign in thirty-six hours. I flew cross-country, made it to temple just before sundown, slumped into a seat next to my wife, and listened to the rabbi's sermon begin with an admonition "not to let our country be divided and polarized by those who use the technique of alliteration." That's all I needed; the "nattering nabobs of negativism" was not a sin I had come to atone for. Ambassador Rabin, also in the congregation, caught my eye and may have had a talk with the rabbi afterward.

Two years later, however, the mood of much of that congregation (and the sermon as well) had changed. Agnew was no longer such a symbol of repression; to many, he had become a symbol of impatience with the excesses of the counterculture and an affirmation of authority to stem the tide of "permissiveness." Black anti-Semitism was a problem; the "limousine liberal" charge hit home as well, annoying liberals who could not afford limousines, including many Jews; crime was reaching into the streets of neighborhoods of the upper middle class, and its immediate containment outweighed the need for a search for "root causes." And for the first time, a significant difference was discernible between the two candidates on the support of Israel, with Nixon looking strong and McGovern weak. There were a couple of sleeper issues as well.

Sleeper-switcher number one was an offshoot of a different strategy: aid to parochial schools. As we have seen, this was of primary concern to the Catholic hierarchy, who convinced the President of its rightness (diversity in education supported New Federalist doctrine, insofar as there was doctrine) and its relevance (many of the best schools in ghetto areas were run by Catholics). But Orthodox Jewry, too, had a deep interest in parochial schools, especially since public schools in poorer Jewish neighborhoods were running down.

Although there can be no direct cause-and-effect relationship established and religious conservatism is a cousin to political conservatism, in 1972, fully 75 per cent of the Hasidim voted for Nixon—and the school issue was at the forefront of their concerns.

An even more pervasive sleeper-switcher was summarized in the scareword "quotas." To many Negroes, a quota is a newly opened door, but to most Jews, a quota is a sign on a closed door that says, "Stay in your place."

In the Fifties, Vice President Nixon, with Eisenhower's Labor Secretary James Mitchell, worked out the first "affirmative action" requirements in hiring for government jobs; later, with George Shultz as Labor Secretary, President Nixon approved the "Philadelphia Plan" to put economic pressure on construction unions who barred blacks. The requirement was not a hard-and-fast "quota"—it was elaborately euphemized as a "goal," with flexibility for unusual circumstances—but it waddled and quacked enough like a quota for it to be so adjudged. This did not affect many Jews. A standard ambition for a Jewish family was to see the son become a member of a profession, not a construction laborer. Therefore, this quota, helping give Negroes a fair chance for the first time in a field of little concern to most Jews, was seen not as a threat but as a good and liberal thing to do.

Quotas on educational opportunity were something else. When I went to Brandeis University in 1972 to spend a day with Max Lerner's classes, one point driven home by students whose views were in a drearily recognizable pattern had to do with the quotas imposed by HEW on aid to higher education: "Does the President realize that unless you're a black or a Chicano, you are not sought after now on faculties?"

The American Jewish Committee wrote to both Nixon and McGovern asking their views on quotas, and received the expected denunciations of the concept from both—at that point, the Democrats were not worried about black sensibilities on that score. But I felt that McGovern was vulnerable to a direct charge: that he, who had won the nomination by organizing the convention on quotas for youth, for women, and for blacks, was "the quota candidate."

The President agreed, and nailed him on that theme in one of his key campaign addresses:

> In employment and in politics, we are confronted with the rise of the fixed quota system—as artificial and unfair a yardstick as has ever been used to deny opportunity to anyone.
>
> Again, as in many attacks on basic values, the reasons are often well-intentioned. Quotas are intended to be a short-cut to equal opportunity, but in reality they are a dangerous detour away from the traditional value of measuring a person on the basis of ability.
>
> You cannot have it both ways: You cannot be for quotas in limiting political opportunity and against quotas in limiting economic opportunity.
>
> The basic idea of quotas is anti-ability wherever it is applied.

Wherever this matter was discussed—and it was always discussed before Jewish groups—the Democrat's line of defense became, "What about your Philadelphia plan?" An answer that says "you're another" is weak; the fact that Jews were not threatened by the Philadelphia plan gave that Democratic defense a shadow-boxing quality. (And, unfortunately, we dropped our pressure on construction unions too soon.)

In essence, educational quotas in the early Seventies pitted one minority that had made it against another minority that had not—an unfortunate and even tragic development straining a traditional alliance. "Open admission" to city colleges meant a good break for many blacks at the expense of quality education for many lower-middle-class whites, including Jews; busing was important too, and is dealt with elsewhere in this book; and housing also became an area of ugly confrontation.

Moreover, for the first time, the Nixon campaign was openly trying to get Jewish voters to switch, and the very fact of the effort was news. Neither Len Garment nor I liked the publicity the effort received after a while —the accent was on "Jewish money" being collected by Detroit industrialist Max Fisher and New York financier Bernard Lasker—and that kind of thing was not, to use an old expression, "good for the Jews" or for Nixon. We tried to play it down and did not succeed.

Thus, several new factors were going for Nixon: the turning rightward of many Jews, the undertow caused by the competition of minorities, and the exploitation of the quota issue. But there was always the indefinable suspicion on the part of many Jews that "Nixon just doesn't like Jews." If he didn't like intellectuals, and he didn't like New Yorkers, and especially since he had to know that most Jews didn't like him—then, *ipso facto*, he had to harbor secret anti-Semitic tendencies. As proof of this, my friends would point to the fact that Nixon had "abolished" the Jewish seat on the Supreme Court and had not appointed a Jew to his Cabinet.

I discussed this feeling, in passing, a couple of times with the President. In 1972 the Cabinet complaint was quickly turned aside—no Cabinet officer had the power of a Kissinger or a Burns, both Nixon appointees. But the Supreme Court seat was not so easy: Brandeis and Frankfurter were his idea of great judges, and while Jews were only 4 per cent of the general population, they were reportedly over a fourth of the population of lawyers. Nixon shook his head—he could no more appoint a man because he was a Jew than he would *not* appoint him because he was a Jew. But didn't he apply a "representation" criterion with Haynsworth and Carswell? That was different: a Southerner belonged on the Court because so much of what the Supreme Court had done in recent years so profoundly affected life in the South. As far as Nixon was concerned, there was no "Jewish seat" or any other racial or religious seat. He would not feel in the least defensive about that point. On the contrary, he felt the time of tokenism had passed.

All the publicity about the Nixon campaign being interested in the Jewish vote was useful only in showing some Jews, who needed to feel wanted before crossing the street, that Nixon did indeed want their vote. The overt ethnic effort might lead a logical observer to conclude that Nixon's campaign went after Jews in the traditional bloc manner, adding them to the other blocs like Catholics, Mexican-Americans, etc. But the more than doubling of Jewish support was an exodus traceable to currents deeper than ordinary ethnic interest: to street crime and the demand for a toughness in law enforcement that would have seemed illiberal in the Sixties; to a regrettable but real resentment at black "ingratitude," and black advancement at white (not only Jewish, but white generally) expense; to the themes of anti-elitism and anti-permissiveness stirred first in 1970 by Agnew; to the affirmation of the "work ethic" lauded by Nixon over the "welfare ethic" he attributed to the Democrats.

These were attitudinal and ideological inroads into a group that used to be a sturdily recognizable bloc, assisted by strong special-interest appeals—on Israel and Soviet Jewry—but primarily dealing with the right-hand side of the hyphen in the phrase "Jewish-Americans." Similarly, in dealing with the much larger "Catholic vote," Nixon's touching of all the bases of special interest surely helped, but the general themes had the greatest effect.

Did Jews swing toward Nixon because he surprised them with his progressive programs and foreign policy initiatives, or did they swing because the Jews themselves moved rightward?

Norman Podhoretz, whom I quote here only slightly out of context, suggested the former in the September 1972 *Commentary*:

> In the course of his career as President he has done more and more to deserve, if not the affection of liberals, then at least a diminution of their dislike. He has proposed a guaranteed annual income, he has instituted wage and price controls, he has withdrawn half-a-million men from Vietnam, he has enunciated a foreign-policy doctrine involving a lesser degree of American intervention in international disputes, he has visited Communist China, he has negotiated an arms-limitation treaty with the Soviet Union and possibly also (if such surprising developments as the move toward unification of the two Koreas and the departure of Soviet troops from Egypt are anything more than coincidence) the beginnings of a long-range political settlement. On balance, surely, it makes more sense for Nixon's old supporters in the conservative camp like William F. Buckley, Jr. and Richard J. Whalen to feel betrayed (which indeed they seem to do) than it does for liberals to go on hating him as much as they seem to do. Nevertheless liberals do go on hating him, less perhaps than they used to but still much more than, on the record, they rationally should.
>
> And if this is the case with liberals in general, it is also the case with Jews, who are still one of the most liberal groups in the country.

I disagree; Nixon's liberal moves (and they were considerable, though well disguised) won few liberal Jewish votes, but his conservatism, and the lower-middle-class Jews' reaction against involuntary busing and Government-pressured integration of suburbs, won him far more.

The reaction of Jews in Forest Hills, New York, against the construction of Federally financed housing that would have brought an influx of low-income blacks into their neighborhood, was seen by liberal commentators as a sorry backlash by a group that had traditionally sided with the civil rights movement.

Debating a Nixon spokesman at a meeting of the Zionist Organization of America, Frank Mankiewicz, McGovern campaign director, gave a gutsy defense of the classically liberal position: "While concern of Jewish groups over quotas is most understandable, one would hope the flame of justice raised in Sinai has not been snuffed out in Forest Hills." That was a profile in courage by any account, and he paid for it in votes.

But what liberals failed to understand, and what Nixon men grasped instinctively, was the view from the position of the Forest Hills resident: for most of them, Forest Hills was a place they moved to from the city. This represented their last stand; on an income of $10,000 a year with small savings, they could not do what other whites did when confronted with poor black migration—that is, move out to the suburbs. When they objected to Government-inspired integration, they did not see themselves as bigots, and they did not relish listening to wealthier liberals, who had escaped the ghettos, call them bigots from the safety of the suburbs. In 1972, Jews did not change their habits to vote their economic interests—most Jews who lived on Park Avenue remained loyal to the Democrats, despite their economic interest—but many Jews did vote their social interests, viewing Nixon as a defender of those social interests.

Len Garment's relationship with Nixon had its ups and downs. At the outset, in the law firm in 1966, their association went from professional to personal; they liked and respected each other, and might not have expected to. In the White House, Len was never family—not in the Haldeman-Ehrlichman-Ziegler-Chapin group that monopolized the President's company—but he was always treated with somewhat more deference than the others in the outer-inner circle. He had a White House car, a title of "special consultant" that put him up over the special assistants in the order of protocol that Haldeman meticulously laid out in the Federal Register, and the status of resident liberal conscience on civil rights matters. Len and I would go to Georgetown dinner parties, thinking that we would never have our loyalties questioned by the other Old Nixon Hands, although both of us—"sophisticated" New York Jews—were probably considered by Nixon "a little brittle" for the crunch. Nixon knew that Garment was an important counterweight in the White House and was not winning enough battles to keep him in for any length of time, so the President would accede to every request Garment made for funding the National Endowments for the Arts and Humanities, doubling the funding every year. This astounded much of the cultural community—which, by and large, despised Nixon—and had no political mileage in it for Nixon. Len espoused the cause of Federal aid to the arts skillfully, stressing to the President the need for symphonies out in the heartland,

and Nixon kept astounding a succession of budgeteers by overriding their cuts in Garment's arts and humanities requests.

After his first year in the White House, including a triumphant "Evening with Duke Ellington" that rocked the place with the most fun it had there in many years, Garment felt himself moving farther away from the center, as did others. The President's interest in winning the Jewish vote in 1972 was a stimulus to Garment, and he treasured a note from Nixon on Election Night that enthuses, only slightly inaccurately, "We even carried Brooklyn!" But his power after the first term was diminished, until the Watergate revelations broke in April 1973; suddenly, not being too close to the center became an asset, and Nixon—the man who specialized in survival—turned to his old law partner to help him survive. Even then, however, Garment could not get through to Nixon at a crucial moment: the President knew Garment's advice would be to fire Haldeman and Ehrlichman immediately, so he did not permit Garment access to the Oval Office, and—fatally—temporized.

Garment, pushing along Henry Kissinger, had another assignment in 1972, which came to fruition in 1973: to make it possible for Soviet Jews to leave the Soviet Union. The "plight of Soviet Jewry" was no phony issue; the Soviets had been willing to inundate Israel with older emigrants who would be dependent on the state, but imposed an impossibly high departure tax on trained, educated citizens who wanted to leave. This was akin to asking for ransom, and American Jews reacted angrily; Nixon's reaction to this reaction was just the opposite of his feelings about the demonstrations against Pompidou. He believed the Jews were right to stand up for their fellow Jews, and that the Soviets were making a mistake in allowing this to stand in the way of East-West détente.

Garment ran delegations in to see Kissinger and the President before and after the Moscow summit; the Nixon men impressed on the Jewish leaders the need to let the Soviets back off without losing face. Kissinger kept pointing out that they were not telling us to solve our own race problem before dealing with them.

The Jewish leaders who met with Nixon came away with the impression that he would be a good negotiator for the Jews in the Soviet Union; that he knew the power game, and would play his hand well. One, a lifelong Democrat and an active McGovern supporter, told me after coming out of a meeting with Nixon in early April 1973, "This may be the only thing I trust him about."

The trust was fairly placed; the rate of departure of Jews from the Soviet Union increased to about 35,000 per year, though many individual Jews continued to be harassed within the USSR, along with dissenting Soviet citizens who had no organized group lobbying for them on the outside. Nixon passed along the heat he was getting from U.S. Jews to the Soviets, who dickered grudgingly; it was much the same as Nixon's use of Mansfield's pressure to "bring our troops home from Europe" on European leaders. When Nixon in 1973 named Henry Kissinger to be Secretary of State—the first immigrant and the first Jew in that job—the U.S. Jewish community worried that his own background might cause him to lean over backward in favor of the Arabs, or to press the Soviets less determinedly; they were more on target in their concerns on the latter, because Kissinger did not want détente jeopardized by the admission of impediments like internal policy to the marriage of true minds. In a decade, the pressures on U.S. policy had changed; liberal Democrats and internationalists, including many Jews, had felt before Vietnam that the moralizing of John Foster Dulles was insufferable, and that he should stop talking about "godless Communism" and get on with the business of relieving tensions. After Vietnam, and after the situation of Soviet Jews came to the world's attention, liberal Democrats wanted to charge a higher price for the détente the Soviets seemed to want—a change toward more freedom in Soviet society, including the freedom to leave—and the first Jewish Secretary of State found himself in a position quite different from Dulles', arguing that the object of U.S. policy could not be to affect the internal doings of adversaries or friends.

When war broke out in the Mideast again in 1973, Nixon reacted the way American Jews and Israelis expected him to: by quickly moving to make certain Soviet arms shipments to the attacking Arabs were offset by U.S. arms shipments to Israel. This time, however, Arabs threatened oil cutoffs to nations helping Israel, and the United States found itself alone —the NATO countries and Japan had too much to lose to join any peacekeeping effort. Nixon, with Kissinger now his Secretary of State, came through on all previous commitments, risking a confrontation with the Soviets. When U.S. forces around the world were placed on alert after what Kissinger interpreted as some suspicious Soviet moves, Nixon was accused of manufacturing a crisis to distract attention from his Watergate woes. Certainly the war and ensuing tension called attention to Nixon's strong suit, foreign affairs, but the idea that he played politics with nuclear weaponry was an indication of the savagery with which he was being attacked at home.

At that time—in September–October 1973—Jews in America suffered their greatest cognitive dissonance in regard to Nixon. They hated him for Watergate, but they loved him for Israel. In Washington, D.C., the leaders of the Jewish community, active in Democratic politics (usually in the camp of Senators Ted Kennedy or Henry Jackson) were especially torn. It was decided to get Kennedy to put out a statement deploring suspicion about the President's motives about the security alert, and to shut up otherwise, which was done. The general feeling was reflected by an antiques dealer in New York, who told me he had a son in Israel and was reading a copy of the New York *Post* about missing tapes: "They ought to impeach him, the bum," adding "—but they better not try."

In the end, Nixon found himself being defended by a group led by a feisty rabbi, Baruch Korff, whose views were strongly disavowed by the overwhelming majority of Jews in America. Ironically, the June 23, 1972, tape that was finally released showing Nixon's participation in the initial cover-up of the break-in at Watergate also contained what could only be interpreted as a vicious slur at Jews as "left-wingers" who populated the arts field. Arthur Burns felt especially incensed about ethnic slurs on the tapes; Garment, Stein, and I all felt that sinking sensation in an especially personal way. It simply did not fit in all we knew about Nixon's attitude toward Jews, and it fit perfectly with most Jews' suspicions of latent anti-Semitism in Nixon, which all of us had worked so hard to allay. Did the President, in private and away from the Jews he had appointed, lump what Henry Kissinger had come to stiffly call "my co-religionists" into a cliché category of lefties and artists? Apparently so; were it not for his penchant for eavesdropping, it would have remained his secret, and his associates who were Jews would have been convinced that Nixon's feelings were those he expressed by his actions.

Before that revelation, all of us had observed that Nixon treated Jews in America as a voting group to be wooed along the normal lines of self-interest, but more importantly, along social-issue lines that had nothing to do with the usual appeals; in that, he was singularly successful, although the gain he made in Jewish support was probably the first to be lost in the revulsion after Watergate. Nixon treated the Israelis with a special affection, springing from an appreciation of their patriotism and the work ethic in action, and from his gratitude for their support of his politics at home and his hawkish policies in Vietnam. As a result, Israel had the best friend it ever had in the White House and Nixon had a friend in the Israelis. And Nixon treated the relatively many Jews around him with no Jewish consciousness on his part—there seemed to be no plus or minus to being a Jew in the Nixon White House, which is the best way for it to be.

A good indication that Nixon's public attitude led to an end to edginess throughout the government came in some byplay at a meeting of bankers in the Federal Reserve board room in late 1972. To my mind, it shows not only was there no Jewish-Gentile tension in the Nixon Administration, but there existed a healthy consciousness of difference.

The board room at the Federal Reserve Board is one of the most impressive rooms in Washington, high-ceilinged and somber; the men who attended this meeting were suitably impressive, the WASP establishment on the money side, gathered to discuss Phase III—the workings of the economy after most controls were lifted.

Federal Reserve Board Chairman Arthur Burns, pipe in hand, gray hair parted in the middle, settling into the fourth year of his fourteen-year appointment, spoke out in his convincing Vermont twang for a stringent target: to lower the rate of inflation to a point under 2 per cent a year. Herbert Stein, chairman of the Council of Economic Advisers, disagreed —he thought that 3 per cent was more realistic. Burns shrugged expressively, and turned to the bankers present for support. To his surprise, the conservative men around the long table were not with him; they tended to agree with Stein.

Burns then told one of his favorite anecdotes. When he served as Eisenhower's CEA chairman in 1958, he met with David Ben-Gurion in Israel and asked him if he listened to the advice of his own economists. Ben-Gurion, according to Burns, said, "Never." Why not? "They only tell me what is impossible—and then I have to go out and do the impossible."

Having made the point in this captivating way that a lower inflation rate was the proper target, Burns placed his pipe in his mouth and let the message sink in.

"But Arthur," said Herb Stein into the silence that followed, "in this case we're dealing with Gentiles." After a split-second's delayed take, the assembled bankers broke up in laughter.

4. THE WORK ETHIC

In the late summer of 1971, the President looked over a draft of a Labor Day speech and questioned the use of a phrase: "The 'work ethic.' You think anybody listens to this intellectual stuff?"

The "work ethic" was to catch on and become familiar to a wider circle than read the New York *Review of Books*; so much so, that in the 1972 campaign, looking over a draft of a radio speech on his philosophy of government, the President said, "Instead of this intellectual stuff, maybe we should be concentrating on the work ethic."

Richard Nixon has always been a card-carrying intellectual, at home with abstractions. But he liked to call his writers "you intellectuals" and to strike a folksy pose; he knew just what he was doing, we knew, and he knew we knew. It was a way of reminding us that he was not about to go high-hat, that he was well aware that he did not draw his political strength from the intellectual community. His folksy credentials reasserted, he would then call for specific historical research. ("Arthur Krock sent me a little book once that was a collection of Woodrow Wilson speeches; it was twenty years ago, but Rose will know where it is . . .")

To understand Nixon, it helps to understand his approach to the work ethic in a variety of terms:

—In personal terms, it is what he remembers of his parents: "If a job puts bread on the table, if it gives you the satisfaction of providing for your children and lets you look everybody else in the eye, I don't think that it is menial. Scrubbing floors, emptying bedpans—my mother used to do that—it's not enjoyable work, but a lot of people do it. And there is as much dignity in that as there is in any other work to be done, including my own."

—In terms of his own political history, it is the man who was born with a potmetal spoon in his mouth fighting a Rockefeller for the nomination and a Kennedy for the Presidency.

—In patriotic terms, there is the pride that "hard work is what made this country great" and "this country was built not by what Government did for people, but by what people did for themselves."*

—In social terms, there is the resentment felt by the worker at the share of his income taken from him to care for the nonworking.

—In political terms, there is the understanding that a Republican, long stereotyped as a tool of the fat cats, can identify with the lower-middle-class workingman on matters that finesse the customary economic arguments.

The concerns of the working "ethnics" gave rise to Nixon's articulation of the work ethic. In embryo, it could be heard in his "forgotten Americans" speeches in 1968; he later went to these people as the Silent Majority on November 3, 1969; he sent Spiro Agnew out to speak to them and rally them in the 1970 campaign; he detailed Charles Colson, his White House special counsel, to cultivate the "hardhats" who were supporting him and rebelling against the "limousine liberals" in 1971; and he was standing there with his bushel basket when George McGovern shook the Democratic apple tree from root to branch in 1972.

A short, perceptive Assistant Secretary of Labor named Jerome Rosow was the one who started people within the Administration thinking about the new worries of workingmen with an April 16, 1970, memorandum to Labor Secretary George Shultz titled, "The Problem of the Blue-Collar Worker."

Rosow opened by pointing out that any concern for the blue-collar worker included two million blacks "who share many of the same problems as whites in their income class. This non-white group also shares the same concern as white workers for law and order and other middle-class values." His nonracist position staked out, Rosow then put his finger on their economic problem:

Lower middle income Americans—people with family incomes between $5,000 and $10,000 a year—were caught in a squeeze like no other part of the population. As their children reached their teens, and family budget costs reached their peak, the income topped out: they reached a plateau in their capacity to earn. Worse, although money wages had gone up by some 20 per cent since 1965, inflation had taken it all away, leaving them embittered and confused.

These seventy million Americans were fearful of violent crimes, now spilling into the suburbs; concerned about their seniority and status being taken away by the overdue rise of minority groups; resentful at being forgotten because they were not as helpless as welfare recipients; and wor-

---

* That contrapuntal phrase, used by Nixon more than any other in the 1968 campaign and later during his Presidency, was taken from a speech by George Romney. Political tradition permits this lifting of a phrase coined by a primary opponent or a supporter; George McGovern's best 1972 line about tax reform, "The rich businessman can deduct his three-martini lunch, but you can't deduct the price of a baloney sandwich"—was taken from Florida's Governor Reuben Askew. Pride (of authorship) goeth before a fall (campaign).

ried because their lack of education made it hard to escape from their economic and social problems. They were prone to take their frustrations out on minorities.

Rosow also pointed out this item about working people, which was an eye-opener to white-collar politicians and bureaucrats on the White House staff: "All blue-collar workers, skilled or not, have been denigrated so badly—so harshly—that their jobs have become a last resort, instead of decent, respected careers . . ." This touched a nerve in Nixon, and after a meeting with Urban League officials, he told George Shultz and me: "Let's get moving on a program about the dignity of work."

With no special deadline or forum for a speech on the subject, a "dignity of work" speech percolated quietly on a back burner. I mentioned it to the President during a stay in San Clemente in the spring of 1971, and he had some good advice: "Get away from the Washington crowd. You shouldn't be talking to the reporters or the opinion leaders to get the feel of this. Read some of my mail from real people. Go out and talk to some people yourself, break out of the cocoon."

I rented a car and drove up north of Los Angeles, into the Santa Ynez valley, spending a couple of nights in a trailer camp, identifying myself accurately enough as "a writer" and chewing over the subject of work and why-work? with friendly types whom the President would identify as "the people who elected us." Frankly, it had been a long time since I had shaken a calloused hand, and the thoughtful answers I heard stayed the onset of creeping elitism. There was one man, a tourist from Ohio, talking in wonderment about his son: "My own kid takes food stamps from the government. He goes to school, he lives with a few other kids and they all put in for food stamps, for welfare. And they got it. Doesn't bother him a bit, to be on welfare. I can't understand it. You want to eat, you work. If you're a cripple, you go on welfare—but if you can work, you work. My own kid . . ."

Somebody within the cocoon—I think it was Henry Hubbard of *Newsweek*—put me onto "the Protestant ethic," and I pulled a couple of books out of the Library of Congress back in Washington. The originator of the phrase was Max Weber, a German Marxist of the late nineteenth and early twentieth century whom I had vaguely heard of as the man who applied the word "charisma" to political leadership.

Weber saw the Protestant (sometimes called Puritan, or Calvinist) ethic as the embodiment of economic evil—as he subtitled it, "the spirit of capitalism." In medieval times, the accumulation of wealth was looked upon as sinful, but Calvin and the Puritans took it instead to be praiseworthy, evidence of God's favor to an individual's undertakings. Combined with an asceticism and disfavor of outward displays of wealth (which only piled it up more, since spending it was frowned upon), the idea of work for work's sake became an "ethic." A rising middle class seized upon it as a challenge to the notion that leisure or contemplation was an end in itself. This, said Weber, was the pernicious "spirit" that drove capitalism, infusing its *petits bourgeois* practitioners with the fervor that sanctified selfishness.

In one of those quirks of semantic history, the "Protestant ethic" soon lost the pejorative connotation Weber intended for it and acquired the sincere, hard-working, positive connotation to people who believed in free enterprise and the development of individual character.

I submitted a draft speech in June, but other events requiring other speeches crowded out the "dignity of work." The weekend of August 15 at Camp David came and went, and with it came wage and price controls, suspension of the convertibility of the dollar, and a thorough dose of economic castor oil. In the aftermath, there was Labor Day—and the opportunity to pick up the theme of the "competitive spirit" needed to advance the interests of the American worker and investor.

So the "work ethic," after its long gestation, was given its Nixon articulation, in a form the President liked and used much too rarely: the national radio speech. The President avoided any mention of "Protestant" and concentrated on calling it by a nondivisive monicker: the work ethic.

"As the name implies," the President said, "the work ethic holds that labor is good in itself; that a man or woman at work not only makes a contribution to his fellow man, but becomes a better person by virtue of the act of working.

"The work ethic is ingrained in the American character. That is why most of us consider it immoral to be lazy or slothful—even if a person is well off enough not to have to work—" The President wrote in here: "or can avoid work by going on welfare." He rejected the siren song of those who would preach it to be immoral or materialistic to strive for a higher standard of living, and asked, "What's happening to the willingness for self-sacrifice that enabled us to build a great nation, to a moral code that made self-reliance a part of the American character . . . ?" In plain words, he then went into some fairly advanced thinking on management's personnel policies, about incentives, refresher careers, and the avoidance of dehumanization. The telling line was "We must give more respect to the proud men and women who do work that is all too often considered 'menial.'" Thinking of his mother, Nixon wrote in: "Let us recognize once and for all that no job is menial if it leads to self-reliance, self-respect and individuality."

The first work ethic speech, as the President expected, went largely unnoticed. Columnist Max Lerner, who has an eye for sociology in politics, was about the only writer who noticed: "President Nixon's Labor Day sermonette," Lerner wrote, "on the work ethic, was addressed not only to the traditional audience of union members but also to the South and Midwest, where the language of the work ethic is politically warming, and to the whole middle class which feels that honest work has gone down the drain."

The work ethic, as espoused by Nixon, who believed in it with all his heart, was the crystallization of a vague feeling that there had to be an answer to *The Greening of America* and other tracts that seemed to say that no self-respecting mind would settle for calloused hands. In a few months, it began to be talked about in intellectual circles, and later merited an "essay" in *Time* magazine, proof that the work ethic had made the big time.

The AFL-CIO's George Meany noticed, too.

5. LABOR REWARDS ITS FRIENDS

George Meany and Richard Nixon were diametrically allied. That is, they respected and admired each other and did not like or trust each other. Their vision of America in the world was the same: hard-line, hang tough, be number one. Their vision of government in American society was opposite: Meany for central government performing more social services, Nixon for the diffusion of power and the arrest of governmental growth. On the gut issues, the social issues, they identified with working people in much the same way: traditional, conservative, worried about the effects of permissiveness, quick to sense the barbs of real or imagined snobbery. Nixon was an ideological partisan, Meany a party partisan, and every time their paths crossed, the clearing looked later as battered and churned up as an elephants' mating ground.

In this romance between Nixon and labor, two of Nixon's closest aides were the go-betweens. George Shultz was the friend and golfing partner of Meany, and often a sparring partner as well—boring in, taking occasional shots, clinching and hanging on, never winning or losing or wanting to do either. Charles Colson was not the emissary to Meany, but to the even more conservative side of the labor movement; these were the construction trades headed by Peter Brennan, the maritime unions so dependent on government subsidy, and the independent Teamsters, headed by James Hoffa's successor, Frank Fitzsimmons.

Nixon had a long background in labor. With Jim Mitchell, Eisenhower's Secretary of Labor, he had settled a steel strike, and was familiar with the left-right split in the labor movement on domestic matters (pro civil rights, pro activist government, except when it came to breaking down racial barriers in unions and economic barriers in trade). He figured labor would continue to oppose him on party lines, as Democrats against him as a Republican, and oppose him on economic matters, because they couldn't be angry at themselves for cost-pushing inflation. But Nixon was anxious to exploit the possibility of support on the matter that mattered most, foreign affairs.

That's where the hardhats came in. After Cambodia and Kent State in the early summer of 1970, Nixon desperately needed some expression of grass-roots support, and New York construction trade leader Peter Brennan delivered: 100,000 workers marched down Broadway, the television networks had to cover it, and Nixon felt that helped turn the tide. At about that time, unruly construction workers beat up several Vietnam protestors on Wall Street, which was also heavily covered; when the President welcomed hardhats to the White House, the antiwar movement sought, with some success, to picture the President approving mob violence when it supported him.

The irony was that of all people, the construction workers had been given the hardest time by the Nixon Administration. They were the perfect example of wage-push inflation, getting raises at the rate of 17 per cent a year in the largest of all American industries, and in that industry—alone—did the President approve a wage-price stabilization board. When voluntary agreement was not forthcoming, the President suspended the Davis-Bacon Act, an archaic law passed in the early Thirties requiring contractors to pay "prevailing" wage rates to all workers in an area—in effect, the Act put a floor under the highest wage being paid, to the benefit of the union, removing the cost benefit to the consumer of competition. As Labor Secretary Jim Hodgson put it in a Cabinet meeting at the time, "Rescinding Davis-Bacon got their attention the way a two-by-four gets the attention of a mule." As a result, the construction unions led the labor movement in moderating demands, and Nixon let them have their cherished Davis-Bacon back later on.

In 1969 the construction unions were the target of the most courageous, if short-lived, civil rights action undertaken by the Nixon Administration—the Philadelphia Plan, a series of "goals and timetables" to bring blacks into mostly white construction unions. Assistant Secretary of Labor Arthur Fletcher, a dynamic black who transfixed a Cabinet meeting when he pleaded his case for black economic achievement, saw this effort as the keystone of the Administration's commitment to "helping people help themselves." Later, this ran into Nixon's objections to "quotas," and although George Shultz tried his damndest to explain the difference between goals and quotas in terms of vastly different degrees of coercion, most of the zip went out of that integration effort after the hardhats marched in support of Nixon on the war. By 1971, Charles Colson was warning the President, "Meany thinks . . . we are trying to destroy the building trades through wage controls and especially through minority hiring practice requirements. Every speech by Art Fletcher sends Meany up the wall."

Throughout 1970, Nixon applied the successful Rockefeller formula to labor leaders—invitations to the White House, flattery, all the little attentions that count for prestige back home. Came the 1970 elections, and labor proceeded to clobber the Republicans, causing Colson to write Haldeman on Election Day:

In view of Meany's performance over the last two weeks, I realize that the conventional wisdom will now say he is a lost cause. By persisting in a contrary view, I realize that some will also say that I have lost my mind . . .

Regardless of the outcome of today's elections, the Democrats will remain on the isolationist tack. Both McGovern and Muskie will be trying to outdo each other in wooing new left money and support. They will have learned from the social issue that they cannot stray too far to the left on law and order, but I believe they will continue to the left in foreign policy. I do not believe Meany could support for President a Democrat of the new left committed to the new isolationism.

While I realize that Lovestone tends to give me the rosy view, Jay did report to me that in a quiet, very private conversation, Meany told him that the only nationally known Democrat on the scene at the moment that he, Meany, could support in 1972 would be Scoop Jackson . . .

The liberal press will make the most of Meany's support of the Democrats in this election. They already have played it up big saying that despite the public romance between Meany and the President, Meany went all-out to beat us; the honeymoon is over, etc. Obviously, the press would like to create open hostility between the Administration and organized labor. We shouldn't be taken in by it. We must continue after the leaders and the rank and file.

Treasury Deputy Secretary Charls Walker made the case that we recognize Big Labor as our political opponent and blaze away at it in substance as well as rhetoric, including labor reform legislation. Colson hung in there in a memo on December 8:

According to Gallup, we received one-third of the blue collar vote in 1968. Yet 54% of the blue collar vote approves of your handling of the Presidency today (notwithstanding the depressed state of the economy). It is obvious that any improvement over 1968—even as much as 5% to 10%—could be decisive in a number of key industrial states.*

Colson, while having to explain away the AFL-CIO's thumping support of Democrats despite patient efforts to woo them away, could point to the election of James Buckley in New York, the conservative candidate for Senator, who was helped mightily by the longshoremen and by Peter Brennan's construction workers. The President reserved judgment; on

---

* By coincidence, according to Gallup, 54 per cent of union members and their families voted for Nixon in 1972. That 20 per cent jump was a large part of the landslide.

March 8, 1971, he wrote Colson a realistic assessment, based on his emerging "us v. them" attitude:

> I think it is very important that we get across to the leaders of the labor movement, particularly in the construction trade, the Teamsters, etc., who are our friends, the fact that RN is with them all the way and is going to do everything he can to find a way to help them.
>
> RN has no use for the UAW leadership at the top or the left wing people who are head of the Garment Workers Union. They are basically not only hopeless Democrats, but also hopeless pacifists, as distinguished from Meany who is an all out Democrat, but a great patriot. We simply are not going to make many points by trying to get along with the congenital left-wingers of the labor movement. We might make some points by trying to appeal to those leaders in the labor movement who basically are conservative in their views and because they are conservative, probably ask for far more than they should get at the bargaining table; but who potentially are our friends if only we can keep a line of communication open to them.

At a Cabinet meeting on March 26, 1971, the subject was inflation, and Paul McCracken went over all the alternatives from mild "inflation alerts," pointing the finger at excessive increases and hoping publicity would keep them down; to a wage-price review board using moral suasion only; to comprehensive controls.

The President gave a clear indication that he would not move halfway. If he decided to go, he would go whole hog. "The idea of a wage-price review board is wrong," Nixon told his Cabinet flatly. "I will not go for something so temporary. Either we bite the bullet or else. I know it would make everybody feel better for a while—maybe three months before an election—but everybody should stop talking about it because it isn't going to happen. Don't ever put on any cosmetics that will come off before the girl sees the boy."

Warming to the subject of halfway measures, such as an Executive Order creating a review board with guidelines but no enforcement teeth, the President said: "Let's understand something. Business and labor don't do anything because they are concerned about the national interest. That doesn't mean they're bad people—when I hear a businessman say, 'I'm doing this for the public interest,' boy! I get my stock out of that company." He explained why the construction industry was different: "Why will a wage-price review board work in construction and not any place else? Because you can stick Davis-Bacon to them. A review board will not work unless it can do something. If we really look hard-nosed at this, in the long run the best thing for this sick construction industry is to keep the recision of Davis-Bacon going. It's an abortion, passed long ago for different reasons, and if we really wanted to strike at union power, we would keep the suspension.

"On the other hand," the President continued, looking at Jim Hodgson, "here's the argument for the Executive Order: this is not our only pot. The mitigating effect on wages of an Order in the construction industry would take a little steam out of price increases in other areas. Second, we may have to go to wage-price controls someday if all else fails. Jim, make it clearly understood to the construction trades that sure, we like the demonstrations by the hardhats, but they have to know our next step is not to beg them to comply but to reinstitute the suspension of Davis-Bacon with a vengeance. Do you buy that?"

Hodgson nodded. "I get the message. The leaders can actually use that clout so they can pass it on to their membership."

The President cautioned the rest of the Cabinet not to think of the construction unions as typical: "In this industry we have the weapon of Davis-Bacon. It won't work anywhere else—we don't have that weapon. Most people are good not because of love, but because of fear. You won't hear that in Sunday School, but it's true."

As an aside he added, "One of the interesting things about talking to George Meany—at seventy-five this guy's got backbone, guts, and all the things a lot of our businessmen lost years ago." When a Cabinet member broached the idea of a review board again before the meeting ended, the President handled it with some sarcasm: "The timing would be important —so that the impotence of what we did would not be discovered until after the people voted." There was a nervous laugh around the table.

Exactly four months later, and two weeks before he decided to impose wage-price controls and suspend the convertibility of gold, the President outlined his views on labor to John Connally, George Shultz, Bob Haldeman, John Ehrlichman, and Charles Colson. Connally wanted a get-tough approach on wages that would offend labor, sweetened with a get-tough approach on trade legislation that would appeal to labor; Shultz disagreed strongly, holding that we should be stressing productivity gains and avoiding confrontations with labor's leadership.

The President said that two-thirds of our society is made up of working people and their families, the other third "the so-called governing elite"— editors, business leaders, academicians, etc. When it came to standing up for the country in its time of need, giving the country its great strength, it was the people who "offer their backs and their brawn"—the working two-thirds—who could be depended upon.

During the recent Vietnam crises, the President went on, his only real support came from that working two-thirds, most of whom had never gone to college, in contrast to the other third, "the elite, which has been showing signs of decadence and weakness. The more that people are educated, it seems, the more likely they are to become brighter in the head but weaker in the spine."

The group that used to be called the leadership class, he held, no longer had the character that the nation so desperately needed. Examples were the "new managers": not the two-fisted entrepreneurial types like his old friend, Elmer Bobst, but the men who were ready to "paint their tails white and run with the antelopes." The country was going through a great moral crisis—"a crisis of character"—the farmers, the hardhats, and others who worked with their hands seemed to represent to Nixon "whatever is left of the character of this country," not the leadership class.

Men like Meany, Fitzsimmons, and Brennan, the President said—"hard-boiled Democrats"—in times of national need showed the character and the strength that was so necessary. Regardless of politics, Nixon concluded, it was vital to continue to recognize and work with these men, and not to attack the unions.

Connally saw that most of this Presidential rumination was directed at him; the Treasury Secretary backtracked, making it clear that when he talked about "taking on labor," he meant not labor generally, but perhaps one or two individuals, the way Roosevelt had done so successfully with John L. Lewis.

The President came at his point another way. "The new arrogance of some young people" bothered him. He gave as an example a young man who had come to the White House with his father, and who acted embarrassed at the older man's poor grammar when addressing the President. And yet, Nixon pointed out, "the young man's education was obtained only because of the hard work of his father."

This conversation, between the President and some of his most intimate advisers, reflected deeply held views about character and moral fiber. Years later, in more politic form, the same theme deploring the abdication of the leadership class was to recur in interviews, particularly with Saul Pett of the AP and Garrett Horner of the Washington Star-News just after his re-election. But in this meeting the President's concern about a "crisis of character" was being expressed to the men at the center of power; he was not putting anything on for the benefit of a wide audience. It can be assumed that this was how he really felt.

After the August 15 blockbuster freezing wages and prices, which is narrated in another chapter, Nixon's relationship with labor was ambiguous; as George Shultz predicted, coming out of a meeting with Meany and steelworkers leader I. W. Abel, "They'll denounce us, but they'll work with us." Meany obviously felt he had to fume and sputter, not only to negotiate the best deal in the way of guidelines and tripartite arrangements, but to lay the basis for stalking out later when controls became intolerable, which was only a matter of time.

Shultz found encouragement in that attitude; he was worried about controls becoming too popular, which could result in the end of collective bargaining and the free market system. Government management, he feared, would sap initiative the way it had done in the railroad industry. The ultimate protection against this, Shultz knew, was not philosophical purity, but the refusal of the unions to go along.

As the ninety-day freeze was coming to an end, the President called me in to work on a speech announcing Phase II. We were in his EOB office on October 7, 1971, and the President observed: "We may have a good villain in Meany. You see that picture on both the covers of *Time* and *Newsweek*, with the cigar and the scowl? I like Meany—as a man, I'd take him to most businessmen, but he's the perfect symbol of the old politics."

I recalled a mission Nixon had sent me on in 1969, to get Thomas E. Dewey's advice in his law office in New York. Dewey had requested that the President send him an aide to listen to a central point he wanted to get across: that "every President needs a villain." To FDR, the villain was the "economic royalists," and to Truman it was "special interests"; Dewey recommended that Nixon make inflation his villain, dramatize his fight against it, and put every unpopular action he had to take under the umbrella of helping the housewife fight the rising cost of living. The President nodded, recalling the advice, which he had not taken: "Dewey forgot that you have to focus on a person, or a group of people. We'll see about Meany. In a way, I'd hate to."

The following month, Meany stepped up his campaign against controls, focusing on the absence of controls on corporate profits (which were then at a twenty-year low, compared to all-time highs for wages and prices). The President, with Meany in mind as the potential villain, and assuming labor would support the Democratic nominee in 1972—Humphrey, Kennedy, Muskie, or Jackson (he saw no chance of McGovern)—decided to beard the lion in his den, at the Bal Harbor, Florida, annual AFL-CIO Convention.

Nixon informed labor's leadership that he would like to address their convention, which they could not turn down. When the White House asked for the opening day, Meany refused—that was the day of his own opening address and he would be damned if he would share the headlines with the President. The labor leader's voice boomed throughout the coffee shop in which he took the call: "Who the hell does he think he is?" (Haldeman smiled when he heard that: "Class," he said.)

As expected, Meany insulted the President at the convention in Bal Harbor going to great lengths to make certain his snubs were made public. Henry Cashen, Colson's chief aide and later his law partner, phoned in the details—a seat for the President in the second row on the platform (which he ignored), the banishment of the band just before the President's entrance so "Hail to the Chief" could not be played, and the comment by Meany as the President left the hall, "Now for Act II." The President's interest paralleled the AFL-CIO's interest in showing the extent of the snubs, and at Haldeman's signal, Colson orchestrated the tut-tutting. John Connally, who may not have needed orchestrating, called Meany's behavior "boorish." (I suggested a battle cry, "Remember Bal Harbor," but this was dismissed as unsuitably lighthearted.)

The following spring, as Shultz had predicted, the labor members of the Pay Board, including Meany but not including the Teamsters chief, Frank

Fitzsimmons, decided the time had come to storm out. In response, I drafted a statement for the President containing a lead he liked: "Ever since taking office, I have made it plain that fighting inflation must be everybody's job. Yesterday, George Meany walked off the job." He reviewed the specific case—a longshoremen's settlement—and wrote in "the pay board is right and Mr. Meany is wrong." Then he asked me to use my judgment in getting other views, and I went to Shultz and Connally. Both cautioned that the President would be breaking his own rule: the Board had been set up to insulate the President from individual decisions. Connally added, "But hell, if he wants to say it, he can."

On the phone to the President: "Connally said it was okay? Then that's what I'll do. I really want to crack 'em on this. I can always duck another one later—say it's too complicated, or whatnot. I want to nail Meany to this one, though."

He wrote in another line, using a fact I didn't know he had: "I shall not be deterred from that course by the disaffection of a few union leaders who represent only 17 per cent of America's 80,000,000 wage earners."

When I had my final draft, I told Haldeman I would run it past Colson, Shultz, and Herb Stein. Haldeman's reply was instructive of his assessment of where the power lines lay: "On something like this, Connally is more important than everybody else combined."

For a time, it seemed to members of the White House staff that the 1972 campaign would be fought with George Meany the villain; certainly that November convention was the low point in the strange affair between the mutually admiring antagonists. But George Shultz, who genuinely admired Meany, kept playing golf with his friend in Washington, and Colson stayed in touch with Jay Lovestone and Peter Brennan, hoping for a break.

Then, in August 1971, Senator Henry Jackson made a speech to a New York labor group, which was not especially well covered, but came to the attention of the President. Nixon sent it to his speechwriters and a few other aides for careful study—not only as an example of hard-hitting speechwriting (one author was Ben Wattenberg, co-author of *The Real Majority* which defined "the social issue") but as a good indication that the best villain lay elsewhere.

Scoop Jackson's speech opened by lacerating our economic "gameplan" and denouncing the Nixon Administration's heartlessness toward the poor, to establish the speaker's partisan, anti-Nixon credentials. Then he came to the heart of the matter:

> The working people are also under attack from the left fringes, by people who would like to take over the Democratic Party. If this takeover were to succeed, the Democratic Party will lose in 1972 and be in deep trouble for years thereafter.
>
> There are some people in the Democratic Party, who, intentionally or not, have turned their backs on the working man. They are either

indifferent to him or downright hostile. Their cocktail parties abound
with snide jokes about "hardhats" and "ethnics." They mouth fashionable clichés about how workers have grown fat and conservative with
affluence, and how their unions are reactionary or racist . . .

Jackson also put his finger on another concern: "I am also very much
disturbed by the way the absolutists on the left are perverting the environment issue into an attack on working people . . . Stop economic growth,
they say. Turn off technology. Shut down factories. Turn workers out.
Turn back the clock to a simpler, agrarian age . . . Can we clean up our
social and physical environment with a nineteenth-century technology and
dirt farm economy?"
On that final point, the President—who was mindful that his Administration had done more than any other in attacking pollution—put it simply
to me in connection with a speech of his own: "In a flat choice between
smoke and jobs," said Nixon, "we're for jobs."
We watched Jackson, who could have been a real threat to Nixon, fail
to get to first base in the Democratic nomination race; and then, to our
amazement, the break came.
Nixon's political, new-majoritarian dream came true in the person of
George McGovern, who was anathema to George Meany, and to many of
the fairly prosperous, work-ethic workers that organized labor represented.
On the "us-against-them" scale, Meany officially supported "them" as
Democrats, but he wasn't one of them; McGovern was "them" personified.
Shultz's contacts with Meany became more frequent, but the Treasury
Secretary kept his conversations with his friend private, and as far as I
know sent in no memos that could compromise the relationship. But after
the acceptance speech in Miami—a rambling effort that broke all his own
rules for organization and length—the President was briefed by Ehrlichman on what Meany and the top Meany lieutenants were passing along
through friends in the labor movement:

> They have come to be enthusiastic supporters of our busing posi-
> tion.
> We should have more to say about taxes. Property tax relief is not
> of great interest to labor union members, but they care about the rich
> people who don't pay a tax—somebody getting away with something
> annoys them.
> Don't talk about defense in terms of jobs—our people know that
> jobs are involved, talk about national security.
> You're right on with being dead set against amnesty.
> McGovern was a dumb cluck to come out for right-to-work for
> teachers. He just can't count—there are a lot more parents than there
> are teachers. Don't argue philosophically about the right of public
> employees to strike. Just say you're the first President to really recog-

nize public employees' collective bargaining, with the postal workers, and you like to solve problems without strikes.

Come out for the Supersonic Transport again and don't forget the maritime workers, either—your platform takes good care of them.

Don't worry about vetoing legislation like the water quality bill. Our members won't object to that; they don't want to be put out of jobs by environmental kooks anyway.

Don't overplay your accomplishments on inflation. Say you've made some progress but you're not satisfied. Run against inflation, don't run on the basis that you've solved it.

Stop pitching directly for the support of Democrats. It makes it seem like you're trying to break up the Democratic Party. You'll get more Democrats to vote for you if you don't remind them about being Democrats, or suggesting that you are a threat to the long-term continuance of the Democratic Party.

Don't look at the polls that say you're way ahead; go out and fight for your re-election.

In a nutshell, that was organized labor's advice to Richard Nixon at the start of his re-election campaign. The advice made sense, the way labor leaders usually make sense in private. It did not belabor the obvious, such as labor's preference for Nixon over McGovern on just about every foreign policy matter.

Meany and his men did not say anything to Nixon about unemployment. In public, nothing so moves a speaker to a labor audience as the plight of the "army of the unemployed," but in private, generalized unemployment is far down labor's list of problems as long as it does not bite deeply into union payrolls in the form of heavy layoffs.

A word about the demagoguery of unemployment. Each percentage point of unemployed is about 800,000 people. When unemployment stands at 6 per cent, about 4,800,000 people are out of work, or to round it out rhetorically, "nearly five million American workers cannot find work under this Administration." Pictures come to mind of breadlines, breadwinners coming home empty-handed, a large segment of the population scraping up breadcrumbs amid the general prosperity.

That is not the way it is. The first question to ask is "compared to what?" Compared to the Kennedy years, 6 per cent unemployment was just about the average. Compared to the Johnson years, when the Vietnam build-up started the defense industry sopping up the unemployment pool, the 6 per cent figure is about 2 per cent higher—or about 1,600,000 people.

Next to be asked is "who are those people?" In the decade of the Sixties, more and more young people and women seeking part-time and full-time employment entered the job market; breadwinner unemployment, jobs for heads of households, stayed about the same between the early Sixties and the early Seventies.

Of course, Nixon never tried to make this argument—only a political idiot would even seem to "defend" unemployment. And whenever a story came out saying "unemployment stayed the same this month, but teenage unemployment rose" the writer did not add "that means that non-teenage, or adult, unemployment dropped." It would only show fat-cat heartlessness to discuss unemployment in any terms other than outrage.

The most Nixon could do was to repeat ad nauseam that two million people were taken out of the armed services and defense plants (which happened to be the increase in unemployment) and hurriedly add that we saw in that no excuse—as Paul McCracken liked to put it, as long as one person who wanted a job did not have it, society had unfinished business. (Not a word about the people who had quit their last job because they did not like it, which would always mean there would be unemployment, because this is a free country.)

With all that said, let me hedge a little. The trade-off between inflation and unemployment is no inexorable law of nature, and economists and manpower experts can work together to narrow the gap between price stability and more than "normal" unemployment. But it is a sticky problem, and nobody has yet figured out how to hold down inflation without "slowing down" the economy—which is called a recession (sh!) and results in increased unemployment, and is roundly denounced by people who denounce you all the harder for runaway inflation. Labor leaders are realists and blaze away at unemployment figures with a good understanding of the demagoguery involved.

The two million unemployed (I'm taking the difference between the 4 per cent "full employment" unemployment, and the 6 per cent it was running in 1972, and adding a few hundred thousand for fairness) was the defense that liberals used against a subject that touched working people in their resentments and in their pride: the "work ethic." As explicated at some length in a previous chapter, the work ethic was the spirit of economic self-reliance, the morality that said nobody was entitled to something for nothing unless age or infirmity made them dependent.

Unemployment was used—speciously, in my view—as the standard riposte to the work ethic appeal. "The way to cure such degradation," went a typical editorial in the New York *Times,* "is not to preach sermons about 'the work ethic' but to help people get jobs." Sounded sensible, but it begged the question: did the increase of ten million people on the welfare rolls in a period of surging prosperity signal a shift away from the traditional values of reward for work, no reward for no work?

Nixon knew he had a central issue here, not just for the campaign, but in the building of his new majority, the shoring up of "the American character," and the reaffirmation of national purpose. He was serious about that, and was not about to let a phony counter-argument like "first end all unemployment before talking about the work ethic" stop him. On Labor Day, 1972, the President wanted his speech "run past" labor's top leadership before delivery (nobody uses "cleared with" since "clear it with Sidney Hillman" backfired on FDR). The top echelon of the AFL-CIO and the Teamsters made some changes and Nixon expounded upon his theme:

> The work ethic tells us that there is really no such thing as "something for nothing," and that everything valuable in life requires some striving and some sacrifice. The work ethic holds that it is wrong to expect instant gratification of all our desires, and it is right to expect hard work to earn a just reward. Above all, the work ethic puts responsibility in the hands of the individual, in the belief that self-reliance and willingness to work make a person a better human being.

> The welfare ethic, on the other hand, suggests that there is an easier way. It says that the good life can be made available to everyone right now, and that this can be done by the Government. The welfare ethic goes far beyond our proper concern to help people in need. It sees the Government, not the person, as the best judge of what people should do, where they should live, where they should go to school, what kind of jobs they should have, how much income they should be allowed to keep.

> The choice before the American worker is clear: The work ethic builds character and self-reliance, the welfare ethic destroys character and leads to a vicious cycle of dependency.

One labor leader who looked over the President's Labor Day draft, Frank Fitzsimmons of the Teamsters, changed a line that read "The welfare ethic goes far beyond giving money to people in need" to read "beyond our proper concern to help people in need." Another labor leader, who was identified in memos to the President on this speech only as "the man with the cigar," objected to a line calling for "working people to make their decision not out of habit, but out of conviction," commenting, "I know what he's getting at, but don't insult the workingman." The cigar-chomper also beefed up a paragraph on neighborhood schools. Labor Secretary Jim Hodgson spotted a potential gaffe: the word "merit," he said, had an anti-seniority connotation, and we changed it to "ability." In talking about quotas, McGovern flubbed the nuance and talked about "merit," making us preen in savviness.

The AFL-CIO stayed neutral, which was in itself a ringing endorsement of the President whom labor had deliberately insulted only a year before. The majority of union members and their families voted for Nixon, a sea-change in voting habits. He won his mandate, and expressed his gratitude by appointing Peter Brennan, head of the hardhats, to be his third Labor Secretary. Nixon would be convinced, at the start of his new term, that much of what he could accomplish would be due to the support of his carefully cultivated new friend, the blue-collar worker.

Nixon and his new friend's leader were not strange bedfellows—they admired each other, respecting the same values. George Meany, walking out of George Shultz's office one day after discussing some Pay Board matters, saw a small picture of the President and Mrs. Nixon on Shultz's table. The labor leader gestured to the picture with his cigar. "There's a great gal," he said. "Terrific. She comes through nice."

Keeping in mind that affinity, and the good advice proffered to Nixon in the fall of 1972, the extent of the change in atmosphere within one year —and the realistic fickleness of an interest group—can be measured by what George Meany had to say to his annual Florida gathering in October 1973; which led to a national impeach-Nixon campaign: ". . . this Administration has cast a dark shadow of shame over the spirit of America. After five years of Richard Nixon, this great and once-proud nation stands before the world with its head bowed—disgraced, not only by its enemies abroad, but by its leaders at home."

With brilliance, panache, subtle understanding, and nefarious connivance, the new majority had been fused together, destined to hold sway for one election year; then, after Watergate, Meany would decide he had a good villain in Nixon, and the carefully built coalition would be smashed to smithereens.

But in his ad-lib "fourth quarter" speech to the Cabinet on the third anniversary of his Presidency, Nixon had high hopes for what he could do with the support of the practical power-brokers of his new majority. "It was these pragmatic men, the Melbournes and the Disraelis, who maybe didn't feel anything very deeply—that is what the historians say, although who knows, why question their motives?—who had the ability to do things that other people only talked about."

Did Nixon himself "feel anything very deeply"—besides a defiant respect for "us" and a fierce contempt for "them"? He was a loner, in the best and worst sense of that word; few people got to see the private man, which was the way he liked it. This is a good time, before his gain and loss of a great mandate, to see what Nixon was like alone on that Catoctin mountaintop.

PART NINE

THE PRIVATE MAN

1. THERE IS A THERE THERE

Gertrude Stein, whose enigmatic lines like "a rose is a rose is a rose" made her famous in the Twenties, caught the spirit of characterless communities by saying of Oakland, California, "There's no *there* there."

That is what has long worried many people about Nixon: they saw him as the political man, the born trimmer, the zigzagger and flipflopper, the constantly moving target. Liberals admire conservatives who would rather be right than President, provided they stay right and do not become President. In other men, changes of position over a period of years might be described as realistic or flexible, displaying an ability to grow and move with the times. In Nixon, such changes were often seen as the most arrant expediency. His adoption of what George Shultz called "the full employment budget"—deficit financing, to stimulate a sagging economy—was perceived by conservatives not as an awakening but as a sellout. The single most frequent charge made about Nixon was that he was "unprincipled," made by right-wingers who wanted him to be as conservative as they imagined him to be, and by left-wingers infuriated by the way Nixon subsumed their best ideas in developing his own "New Federalist" approach. A "man without principle" is the classic attack on any centrist, because from whatever direction the criticism, the critic will gain perverse satisfaction from finding the oasis to be a mirage—that there is no "there" there.

Nixon's character traits are deep-rooted and have resisted tremendous buffeting over the years; they may not be all good character traits, and, as Nixon would put it, "some may not be fashionable these days," but it is misleading to pretend that the stresses that come to the surface in 1973 were merely those—in FDR's phrase—of "a chameleon on plaid."

As we will see in the chapters of this section that follow, Nixon is a suspicious man who is an essential optimist, a contradiction in terms but a complexity that exists in him: people will always be out to get him, he thinks, but things will get better. He is a fiercely loyal friend and protective family man, always a good character trait, but he overreacts viciously to attacks on those close to him and lashes back. He seeks his "peace at the center," in the Quaker term, in being alone, which may be the most secure place in the midst of a storm, though he frequently spoils that with his lapel-grabbing insistence to all who will listen that he is cool in a crisis.

Nixon held to principles of self-reliance and no-something-for-nothing which he and his wife learned the hard way. He applied those personal experiences to policy, just as he consistently applied his personal resentments at snobbish slights he has suffered over the years to the institutions whose favor he knew he would never receive. Nixon has suffered more than most men, and enjoys thinking about how he has suffered more than most men: this has made him strong and stubborn, willing to change his mind when he espies a changing situation but rarely to change his attitudes about life and people.

If it is all this simple, then, why could pre-Watergate Americans not agree on who was the "real Nixon"? Because Nixon himself befogged the portrait of the private man, partly because he wanted to, and because he saw his character the way he would like himself to be: the John Ford hero. He is not—and a John Wayne would be a terrible President—but the fact that Nixon thinks he is makes up part of his character. As Gertrude Stein might put it: *to the real Nixon, the real Nixon is not the real Nixon.*

Miss Stein would have left that line deliciously obscure, but let me detract from it with some interpretation:

All his public life, Nixon tried to present to the public the reverse of an Oliphant or David Levine caricature. He wanted to be seen as upright and true, long-suffering and pious, cool in crisis, beset by Lilliputians and despised by aristocrats, fashionably unfashionable, a man of the people who never forgets the folks, and above all—up there on a mountaintop to make the great and lonely decisions, disdaining the importunings of his aides to cave in and give up and take the popular road, instead taking the action needed to give the nation back its "driving dream."

That's how he thought people should see him, and he struck that pose all too often to counter the caricature of devious, sullen, self-serving opportunist that had been thrown at him for half his lifetime. He considered it necessary to crack back at tormenting mudslingers with an easy-to-grasp, contrary answer: that he stood pure and unsullied and deserved not only the faith but the sympathy of the fair-minded person. There is justification in the tendency of a man who has been often called a lie to insist that he is the truth, pure and simple, no complexities to confuse the refutation, fighting used-car-salesman hyperbole with I-have-what-it-takes hyperbole. The desire of office-seekers to present themselves as nigh-perfect is rooted in ancient history—the word "candidate" is from the white toga worn by Roman candidates to symbolize purity—and is bolstered by modern advertising psychology. In presenting himself as he believed others want to see a leader, Nixon became President of the United States, then won re-election in one of the greatest landslides in our history—ample evidence, he was certain, that he was right to present himself the way he did.

THERE IS A THERE THERE

And yet, and yet. "O wad some Pow'r the giftie gie us"—not so much to see ourselves as others see us, but to let others see ourselves as we are. To some extent, the transcripts of Watergate conversations revealed the petty, vacillating side of Nixon; or the ugly side, as he ran down his loyal associates; or the human side, as he tried to get Haldeman to stop briefing him on international economics after a Watergate revelation with "I don't give a shit about the lire."

One night when I was in Camp David—the President was not there— I jotted down some notes of what it might be like to hear the Real Nixon, in all his layers, turning to a television interviewer and saying: "Look, I can't put myself in a nutshell and neither can you. I'm as vulnerable as anybody. When that minister at Justice Black's funeral took advantage of a President's respect for a dead Supreme Court Justice to lecture me about civil liberties, I blew my stack; and when an eight-year-old kid at a posthumous Medal of Honor presentation saluted me, I choked up and had to stop the ceremony until I could get hold of myself. But a public man should not let himself slop over, he owes it to himself and his people to maintain his dignity in public. So I control myself as much as I can, and that's a lot. Now take it from the other way around—I also push myself to show I care, even when my natural instinct is to shy away, like when I plunge into a crowd to get my cufflinks torn off. When I'm naturally emotional, I consciously move to cap it, and when I'm naturally reserved—Quakers hold it in, as a rule—I consciously move to let it out. That way I don't appear either all-emotional or all-intellectual, and the truth is that I'm neither. Now you want to know if I'm essentially mean and vindictive or essentially kind and generous. That's a stupid question, because almost everybody is both: I get a real kick out of cracking the permissivists, who run the country down and hate me and all the decent values I represent, and I enjoy treating the press with cool contempt, because that's the only way to make them respect you. I play to win, and if I'm not such a good loser or a good winner, it's because I'm better at playing than I am at winning or losing. I think it's wrong to get on the defensive, or to let your opponents know they've hurt you, or to apologize except when you absolutely have to. Jack Kennedy, who was a master at manipulating the media, was right when he said, 'Forgive, but never forget.' On the other hand—and I know you think I say 'on the other hand' too often, and I don't blame you for that, that's your job, to criticize and find fault—on the other hand, I treat the people I work with with the utmost consideration. No phony crises, no unnecessary middle-of-the-night phone calls. People stick with me for many years, not the way it was with LBJ. I have a great family, and we're very close—that's to Pat's credit, and there's a woman others have underestimated for years, but not me. Most of all—and I'm sorry for you if you think this sounds so corny—I love this country. I'm proud of all it stands for. I know all the things that are great about it. I believe that if we each relied more upon ourselves, we'd be better people for it, and we could get away from the drift toward the welfare state and laziness, and something-for-nothing, and the-world-owes-me-a-living—that's the real danger. Then, with really equal opportunity—a guarantee of equality at the starting line but not at the finish line—the people who wanted to work hard would do well and the lazy would fall behind, and we'd get that competitive spirit going again that built this country. I really believe I can position this nation in a generation of peace, and there doesn't happen to be anybody else around who can do it. I'm a lot more of an idealist than people think I am, even though I say it often enough, but it takes guts and nerve and the ability to play poker for big stakes. If I had my ducks, I'd rather be admired than loved—it's possible to be both, Eisenhower showed that, but that's not in the cards for me—and I wish the goddam media would let people appreciate what I'm trying to do."

No Molly Bloom, he—that stream of consciousness would never flow past Nixon's dam. Richard Nixon never said the foregoing—it is not a direct or indirect quotation. Yet it is what I believe went through his mind, and if spoken freely would have achieved a wider appeal than the two-dimensional reverse caricature that he was convinced people want in a leader. Of course, it is easy enough to say that he would be better off letting his complexities and doubts and virtues all hang out—that could be called the popular thing to advise—but would it work? Would it effectively counter the cartoon of the cold, power-hungry opportunist, or the hard evidence of recordings of his worst moments with his least temperate colleagues? Nobody can say for sure.

Nixon has been and intends to remain a loner: a keeper of his own counsel, a sharer of his thoughts with a tightening circle of friends. That is what helped make the exposure of his intimate conversations so painful and so dismaying. "Loner," applied to a picture of John Kennedy walking pensively down a beach, is a romantic word, evoking the burden and the challenge of personal leadership; applied to Nixon, the word seems to gain a sinister connotation, as if the person describing Nixon as a loner wonders what dangerous thoughts this man is mulling over. (When Nixon introduced me to Len Garment with a note early in 1968, asking him to fold Safire into the "issues group," the Candidate wrote, "I know he is somewhat of a 'loner' but . . ." and then he gave me a nice sendoff. To be called a loner by Nixon is something.) To Nixon, then and now, loners are not especially good to have around; someone who will be "one of us" is better; but he is certain that the one who can and should be a loner is the man at the center.

After Watergate, "team player" suddenly acquired a groupthink connotation, and a loner was the thing for a staffer to be. But Nixon did not swing with the trend: he wanted to be alone, surrounded by a small team of men who essentially agreed with each other, and would see to it that his carefully deliberated decisions were carried out.

There is a contradiction in a man who is afraid of nobody and is at the same time afraid of everybody, but the vulnerability of leaders has been with us since Achilles grew a heel: Nixon's ideal of "peace at the center" often means only the absence of disagreement at the center, and after he became President he tended to draw a tighter circle around himself.

Although he would lay on the sentimentality with a spatula in public, invoking patriotism in an unabashed and sometimes excessive way, he would dole out the sentimentality sparingly in private. On the anniversary of his first year in office—January 20, 1970—late in the afternoon of that cold day, he pushed the buzzer on his Oval Office desk that brought in Rose Mary Woods and Bob Haldeman. In the gathering dusk, Nixon had not turned on the lights in the office, and was standing with his topcoat on before walking down the outdoor corridor to the Residence. Nixon nodded to his two oldest associates, each of whom cordially despised the other, and lifted the lid on the silver music box on his desk: the ridiculous object dutifully tinkled out "Hail to the Chief," getting a little slow toward the end. The President shut the box, said only, "Been a year," and walked through the open French doors into the night; end of celebration.

In an early chapter of this book, "The Man at the Wilson Desk," a layer of Nixon's cake is described as the observer-participant, the man who is his own backseat driver. This is closely akin to another layer of the private man: Nixon is a reflective man, in more than the thoughtful sense of that word. He reflects the people whom he chooses to be near him, and in that way can don a personality by opening a door. In the presence of a George Shultz, he reflected interest in the great domestic goals of shared power, free markets, more personal liberty; in the more frequent presence of a Bob Haldeman, Nixon reflected the memories of his media-bureaucracy-establishment enemies, real and imagined; with a Len Garment, Nixon was a lover of the arts; with a Bob Finch, he reflected a political analyst. He drew his coloration from the men he was with, which can be read as the mark of a devious or shallow person, but was Nixon's way of expressing his own complexity. When he wanted to be Woodrow Wilson, he sent for Ray Price; when he wanted to be Herbert Hoover, he sent for Cap Weinberger or Herb Stein; when he wanted to be Eisenhower, he sent for Bryce Harlow; when he wanted to be an FDR majority-builder, he sent for Colson. When he didn't want to be anybody but himself, he sent for Bebe Rebozo.

Does this mean that if Nixon had not been surrounded by Haldeman, Ehrlichman, Mitchell, and Colson, and instead had been ringed with Garment, Klein, Shultz, and Price, that all would have ended well? Of course not: Nixon was a reflective man, but he reflected those he wanted to reflect, when he wanted to reflect them. He peopled his office himself, and was the captive of nobody; he made his fate the extension of his character.

Kidding around, Len Garment once said Nixon viewed himself with a detached retina, and I think he meant that The Man had the uncanny ability to step outside of himself and coolly misread the man he observed. In looking at Nixon the private person in the next few chapters, we might keep in mind the oxymoronic nature of the man we study, the alienated commitment, the reflected man who chooses the mirror he wants to reflect himself in, and thereby illuminates his good and bad character. Almost everybody has dreamed of himself as the broadcaster of his own heroics, taking microphone in hand to excitedly recount the exploits of that star down on the field, himself, first getting pleasure out of being an articulate hero of a reporter, then doubling the pleasure as a taciturn hero of a participant. It's a daydream, and Presidents have daydreams too.

Nixon, however, was convinced—as we shall see after his "peace with honor" cease-fire—that if he did not provide the after-the-game analysis, nobody would do it for him. That was the reason for his assertively immodest estimates of his worth in interviews, his insistence of his calm under fire. "I have what it takes" is not something that a man who has what it takes should have to say, but Nixon felt uninterpreted, and was convinced his qualities would be forever dimmed under the media's bushel.

Ironically, that is what caused him so much grief. The ubiquitous tapes, the true record of all that was going on, was the extreme example of a Nixon determined to leapfrog the biased commentators. By recording everything, he thought he could enable historians to explore his Administration as never before, thereby earning him a place in history as a strong, perhaps even greater than "near-great" President. Nixon was Icarus, the recordings his secret wings to fly him up above the petty criticism of envious men; when the Watergate heat was applied, the fixative gave way, the wings fell off, and into the drink he plunged, an epic example of the impudence of trying to manipulate history's judgment with something as burdensome as the whole story.

Nixon was tenaciously protective of those he loved. The man who could not manage the news in the way he wanted understood the need to manage the flow of news to his wife, and saw to it she was not upset with the most vicious of the blasts against him. He was a family man, giving to and drawing strength from his loved ones, especially Julie, tender and hopelessly old-fashioned about birthdays and anniversaries, even celebrating un-birthdays. "Let's make tonight a special night," he'd tell his daughters, and then do something dramatic, like suddenly going to a Mexican restaurant, or remembering how his mother loved corsages—remember corsages? —and seeing to it that all the wives of POWs at a dinner were presented with corsages.

But the natural man, the private man, Mr. Nice Guy, one part of the truth about him, is not the part to be seen, which is in the nature of things. Before the fall, he guarded his family privacy more than most, not only for safety's sake but because he was resigned to not being "liked" and thinks the human touches take away from being at least respected. Accordingly, he decided to trade away warmth for "leadership mystique" and wound up with not much of either.

The analyst in Nixon—and there is one, able to size up a situation or a person in a hurry—is not applied to himself, because it keeps getting caught up in the manipulator in Nixon; the prestigitator of international events was all thumbs when it comes to manipulating the strings of his own marionette. He tries to appear to be what he thinks people want him to appear to be—an Eisenhower personality with Roosevelt's activism—but might he not have been better off letting the impulsive, emotional, comball, political Nixon come through? Probably not: Whenever he did blow his stack, of course, shoving Ron Ziegler, or abusing the press, he was accused by his closely watching critics of losing his grip, and then he redoubled his efforts to present that calm-in-crisis front. When he was controlled, they said he was phony; when he was open, they said he was crazed; instead of taking a damned-if-I-do and damned-if-I-don't attitude, he let it get to him. So he presented what he thought was the safest, most dignified, most respectable side as his whole front; after a while, he came to believe that was the whole front. Which is why, to the real Nixon—the one who inspired trust in his associates and love in his family—what Nixon saw to be the real Nixon was not the real Nixon.

2. ALONE TOGETHER: PAT NIXON

Before the post-pardon illness slowed him down, Richard Nixon was a man who insisted he had never had a headache in his life. He was proud of never having missed a day's work due to illness in his first term, despite some colds and sore throats that might have caused other Presidents to curtail their schedules, and would frequently tell Bob Haldeman to pass this on to several of us in a wistful attempt to construct a counter-mythology.

On the other hand, as a favorite saying goes, Richard Nixon also insisted he had hay fever, and fled Camp David on occasion to escape the rising pollen count, but his physician, Dr. Walter Tkach, told us flatly that the President does not have hay fever or anything like it.

So is Nixon a stoic or a hypochondriac? The answer is both; and nowhere is his Yin-Yang nature better revealed than in his courtship of Patricia Ryan. His impulsiveness was illustrated by his proposal of marriage to her on their first date ("love at first sight," acted upon with such alacrity, is about as rare as never having had a headache); but that spontaneity was replaced by the calculation and perseverance of his two-year courtship, including occasions when he transported her to social engagements with other men. He is unabashedly sentimental. The strip of beach their San Clemente home overlooks today leads to Dana Point, where he proposed to her, parked in an Oldsmobile coupé; and yet, when they walk along the beach today, she goes happily barefoot and he wears a sensible pair of moccasins. ("Ollie," I said to photographer Oliver Atkins early in 1968, "these are great pictures of the family, but how come Nixon is wearing shoes on the beach? Everybody else is barefoot—Pat, the girls, they like the feel of the sand between their toes." Atkins shrugged: "I'm sorry, I suggested he take his shoes off for the pictures, but he wouldn't—he's the kind of guy who wears shoes on the beach.")

Nixon enjoys the crackle and smell of a wood-burning fire, and indulged this old-fashioned yen in the summertime by turning up the air conditioning, which offended the former Pat Ryan's thrifty soul and gave the natural fire an unnatural setting. Such minor anomalies are part of the Nixon character. But a major anomaly, and one that disturbed and irked the President, was in the way his wife was perceived by the public.

Pat Nixon is a woman revered by tens of millions of Americans for the wrong reasons, and treated with condescension by millions of others for different and equally wrong reasons. She is not the way she tries to appear and she is not the way others have tried to make her appear.

The President dictated some notes to Rose Mary Woods about his wife one day in 1971, with the request that I brush them up and pass them along as his comments to a woman's magazine. I did, but Nixon's raw notes show better than the polished version his frustration at the inability of others to see her as she is, or appreciate her as he does.

"The thing that has bothered me most," Nixon dictated, "is the attempt to build the idea that she is 'too good to be true.'" His tone was defensive: "They criticize her because she happens to have the virtues that are no longer 'fashionable'—that is, she was an orphan at an early age and worked her way through school; she has great character and determination and is not the type of person who makes a fool of herself in public in order to get attention." As he went on defending her, he was defending what "they" said about him as well: "I have also been bothered by the criticism that she doesn't have warmth and that, of course, is easily answered by anybody who knows her at all. Her impeccable conduct abroad and at home under all sorts of difficult circumstances is indispensable in a First Lady.

"Mrs. Nixon, of course," the Nixon notes go on, "as most women do, takes much harder the criticism of her husband than her husband himself does. The critics don't bother me, even though I have had the most unfriendly press in history, it has never bothered me, but it deeply bothers Pat and my daughters. They see it in personal terms whereas I see the press totally in impersonal terms." In protesting too much, the President revealed his hypersensitivity to the press, and I edited it out; it is included here to show the Nixon feeling of family solidarity against the world, with the press as the quintessential representative of the hostile outside world.

Thelma Catherine Patricia Ryan Nixon, born on the eve of St. Patrick's Day, redhead and popular girl in her youth, is wife, partner, and friend to her husband, and shares his prejudices and scar tissue. She is not the saccharine, square Helen Hokinson lady that itsy-poo magazine writers tend to substitute for the real woman, nor the plastic woman that unfriendly writers have made fun of, slamming her for being "too good to be true."

"Pat Nixon's face is a private face:" wrote her husband's cousin, "Friendly Persuasion" novelist Jessamyn West, "by bone structure, by its owner's temperament, by her punishing and cruel experiences as a girl, by the reason of thirty years of political exposure." And the former First Lady is smaller than most people expect: "I guess she weighs 100 pounds," her husband told some women reporters. "When I first met her, she weighed more. I used to know her dress sizes . . . I think now she wears an 8 to a

10. And when I first met her, she wore a 12, and one time even a 14."
She is smaller now than when I first met her in 1960, perceptibly so; more
attractive and chic, but certainly more frail, which results in the paradox
of her seeming at once more at ease and more on guard. She has had a
harder life than most women and she is not looking forward to getting
hurt anymore.

Pat is womanly—children hug her hard without urging, and kids are not
bad at rejecting phony ladies who want to use them in photographs—and
she's politically hip. Strolling through Antoine's Restaurant in New Orleans, after a campaign stop in 1968 for ostensibly sentimental reasons—
the Nixons have always gone back there and know the owners well—she
smiled at a woman reporter who was coming toward her and said out of
the corner of her mouth to me, "Watch out for this one—I've read her
stuff, and she doesn't like us." The smile never disappeared as she handled
the reporter cagily.

To the Old Nixon Hands, especially in the years in New York, she was
another of the Old Hands—good-humored, loyal, easygoing, a warmly wink-
ing hostess at the annual get-togethers in their 810 Fifth Avenue home. I
would go to Nixon's law offices at 20 Broad Street and find her helping
Rose Mary Woods man the telephones. She was "Miss Ryan" to callers—
the presence of a wife in a business office would have seemed out of place—
and when one man said he was especially anxious to speak to "someone
really close to Mr. Nixon," Pat assured him that she would get the message
to somebody "really close."

On a campaign platform, she had the ability to sit there through it all,
looking interested and proud, as he delivered lines she had usually heard
before. He was not averse to taking advantage of the misperception of
Mrs. Nixon by a lot of the "folks," as the perfect "little woman," and he
used that image to warm up some audiences. Occasionally, however, he
would kid around:

"In 1952 when we were in Salt Lake City," he told a Cleveland crowd
in 1968, "Ivy Baker Priest was introducing my wife Pat and she was giving
her all the build-up that you give to the wife of a candidate.

"She was saying Pat was a fine mother and a wonderful campaigner. Then
she said, 'Now, my fellow Americans, it is my great privilege to present to
you the next wife of the Vice President of the United States.'"

After the expected laugh, Nixon added under his breath, "You think
that is funny here, you should have heard the reaction in Utah."

In the White House, there was a time when all the image types would
pull their beardless chins about Mrs. Nixon's "Project"—that is, something that she would become identified with, as Mrs. Kennedy had become
known for her redecoration of the White House, and Ladybird Johnson
with the beautification of America. "Voluntarism" was the thing, and we
envisioned her traveling the country like a new Florence Nightingale, re-
awakening the spirit of volunteer service; Mrs. Nixon did some of that,
and some traveling—a goodwill mission to Africa on her own was most

successful—but she was not about to be made into an Eleanor Roosevelt or a Jackie Kennedy. She had a good sense of her own identity—essentially wife, mother, and hostess—at the White House. "She steels herself for the public bit," the President told Jessamyn West, "and like other people when they're doing what doesn't come naturally, she puts up an extra bold front . . . Pat's idea of a joyous afternoon is the freedom to walk quietly along the edge of some deserted beach."

Duty, then—"stern daughter of the voice of God"—is what put her in public, and she didn't complain. She was a politician's wife and she did her job, although after the re-election she decided to spend less time in public, urging the girls, particularly Julie, who is more outgoing than Tricia, into that role.

One fairly important job of the wives of heads of state is "sitting next to." At a State Dinner, visiting diplomats and the wives of host nation diplomats are inflicted on each other for at least an hour and a half; if neither is a practiced conversationalist, the result is an extraodinarily long evening. President Nixon, introducing a day-long briefing of the wives of Administration officials on domestic policy, pointed out the importance of the "sitting next to" function in Washington, not only in making conversation with diplomats, but in putting forth opinions to opinion leaders and journalists who, for the length of the dinner, are a captive audience. He was right; the job that Administration wives can do at dinner parties has long been overlooked or patronized.

In Moscow during the 1972 summit, Pat Nixon was seated between Alexei Kosygin and Leonid Brezhnev at the return State Dinner given by the United States at its embassy in Spaso House. See Plate 18, following page 488. Brezhnev, to her left, had nobody between him and President Nixon; the two leaders spent most of the dinner talking to each other, leaving Mrs. Nixon with Kosygin, a man who has an undeserved reputation of being one of the dourest dinner partners in the world.

Maria I. Soukhanov, a "Voice of America" broadcaster who was Mrs. Nixon's interpreter, translated for both; the result was a classic example of "sitting next to" conversation. Kosygin began with a formal discussion of the kinds of things to be seen on a future visit, when the schedule would be less confined to work; her report on impressions of Moscow; then to a fairly erudite discussion of Soviet theater, Kosygin preferring the plays of Gorky to the productions of Na Taganka, an avant-garde company popular with young Russians.

Kosygin then looked around for a piece of bread. There was none; getting at his needs indirectly, Kosygin asked Mrs. Nixon if she liked Russian black or white bread. She went into the appropriate rhapsodies, then stage-whispered across Brezhnev to her husband: "No bread?" The President shrugged and passed a plate of nuts which Mrs. Nixon offered Kosygin to nibble on; he laughed and said now he knew why the Americans had so much grain in surplus—because they didn't eat bread.

The ice broken, they discussed honey-tea and samovars, subways in Moscow and the subway underway in Washington, the Orlov diamond in the Kremlin collection, and the noise of the fire engines outside the Soviet Embassy in New York. She turned Kosygin to reminiscence of his youth in Petersburg (Kosygin used the name for Leningrad which was in use when he was born there) and working in Novosibirsk; she had been briefed on Novosibirsk by her husband, who had been there in 1959. Kosygin made sure she knew that it had been called Novo-Nikolaevsk prior to the Revolution.

Here is an account of the conversation that shows a First Lady doing her job—nothing dramatic, but a bit of flavor that rarely makes the reporting of great events:

Mr. Kosygin, squinting at the guests in the dining room, brought attention to "the lady journalist in the yellow dress." Mrs. Nixon identified her as Helen Thomas of UPI. Mr. Kosygin began a critical discourse on the activities of the (Western) press. Mrs. Nixon explained that this is a result of the competitive system, innate in our society. This woman in the yellow dress, continued Mr. Kosygin, is a real go-getter. Mrs. Nixon agreed. Mr. Kosygin suggested that the Western press be more concerned with facts as they really occur; he also alluded to some reporters as rather negative elements.

Mr. Kosygin asked how many women we have in the U. S. Congress. Mrs. Nixon replied: one Senator and five in the House of Representatives. Mr. Kosygin interrupted, stating that women careerists in the U.S. are arrogant, ambitious, merciless, whereas in the Soviet Union, women deputies, who make up about one third of the total number, are serious, studious, and reasonable officials. Mrs. Nixon pointed out that most American women have not previously had great political aspirations and consequently there was a small percentage of women in the U. S. Congress. Mr. Kosygin said Soviet women deputies are astute and relatively unemotional in their jobs, which he found quite a contrast to American women-careerists. Back to some women reporters he had observed, Mr. Kosygin continued, they are like "kamennye meshki," translated literally as "rock bags." Mrs. Nixon said, however, that the American reporters do their job as they see fit; they present diversified points of view.

Mr. Kosygin launched into a discussion as to the mercantile (commercially oriented) character of Americans. He said that when he is confronted with malicious people, and he places many correspondents in this category, he either leaves the scene or responds reciprocally with arrogance and determination. Good people, on the other hand, produce a completely different effect. Their goodness influences others, he said. Mr. Kosygin continued for a while on the good vs. the bad. Mrs. Nixon said she absolutely agreed with his last statement: she wished there would be more feelings of benevolence, good will, and friendliness among all the peoples of the world.

Mrs. Nixon later mentioned her compassion for the Russian people who suffered greatly during the last world war, especially for Leningraders, who died and perished during the blockade—Mr. Kosygin said he was there, and it was a dreadful experience.

Like most nonplastic couples, Mr. and Mrs. Nixon occasionally rub each other the wrong way. She has a fetish about neatness in the home, but he likes to see their Irish setter, King Timahoe,* lying on the brocade sofa; she will let him know how she feels about it, and it has an effect. When the private office in the Executive Office Building was newly decorated, a beige silk ottoman was placed in front of the easy chair. Going over a speech, the President wanted to stretch out; he went to the bathroom, came back with a towel, and spread it over the new silk before putting his feet up, undoubtedly because his wife made him feel guilty about ruining furniture. After a while, the restraint wore off.

He, on the other hand, has a fetish about punctuality. At the Western White House in 1970, they were due to leave by twelve-fifteen, and the schedule called for them to meet at the helipad: he would leave from the office, she from home. At twelve-ten, as he started to leave the office, the word came to delay departure, Mrs. Nixon and Tricia needed five more minutes. To teach them a lesson, Nixon continued on his way out, and stood tapping his foot at the base of the ramp of the chopper while the two-way radio of Secret Service agents crackled with a horrified: "The President is waiting for Mrs. Nixon, he is not boarding, he is waiting at the ramp and looking at his watch!" She heard this, took her own sweet time and arrived about ten minutes late.

These are the tensions that certify a normal, close relationship; she makes an effort to take his mind off his work at dinnertime with news that will amuse or stimulate him, and never wears a black dress—he had enough of that in his Quaker childhood. In times of stress, he would flatly forbid her to read the newspapers or look at the television news, which she accepted with relief. Julie would then tell her what she needed to know.

She has come to symbolize to her husband the modern Frontier Woman: the work ethic and its achievement, the half-hidden pain under a professional coiffure and a tasteful outfit, the loyal homebody to the older generation and the stiff object of scorn to the Nixon-haters, the woman who has always knocked herself out for her man's career, putting him first, looking forward to the day when she can put on a pair of slacks and a sweater and walk the beach barefoot, even if he insists on wearing his shoes.

The Nixons reflect something Americans need, both as symbol and as

---

* Before they were married, she would take care of his Irish setter, also named King. (Timahoe was added to the current dog because it would be inappropriate for a President of a democratic nation to have a dog with a regal name, but the family calls him "King" anyway.) On the President's desk in the EOB is a small china statue of an Irish setter, which he gave Pat Ryan to thank her for taking care of his dog long ago, and which she put back on his desk as a reminder of the old days.

truth: a close family life. Nixon detractors shied away from the Nixon Family like Count Dracula at the brandishing of a cross (my metaphors occasionally get extreme) and for good reason: a man with a lifelong help-meet and well-raised kids, who bring in upright in-laws, can't be all bad. Like it or not, the American First Family from 1969 to 1974 carried many of the same responsibilities for exemplary behavior as the British Royal Family, reassuring citizens that stability and togetherness is the norm and not the exception. Nixon generously gives all the credit here to his wife (perhaps expecting the listener to say, "Oh, but you must have had a lot to do with it too") but the fact is that Pat Nixon does deserve all that credit, and it is a pity that she was seen by so many as only the carica-ture of her strong and admirable character.

3. BEBE

Charles G. "Bebe" Rebozo makes the perfect companion for a man who likes solitude, because being with Bebe can be almost as good as being alone.

The Presidency, as John Kennedy pointed out, is not a good place to make new friends; and when Wendell Willkie asked FDR why he kept Harry Hopkins so close to him, President Roosevelt replied:

"Someday you may well be sitting here where I am now as President of the United States. And when you are, you'll be looking at that door over there and knowing that practically everybody who walks through it wants something out of you. You'll learn what a lonely job this is, and you'll discover the need for somebody like Harry Hopkins who asks for nothing except to serve you."

Bebe was an old friend; of Cuban descent, Rebozo was a self-made millionaire who exemplified the success of the work ethic, making his small fortune in real estate and banking in Key Biscayne, Florida. He and Nixon came to know each other in 1951 and their friendship matured during Nixon's wilderness years of the Sixties.

Bebe always felt protective of his celebrated friend. Walking down the Key Biscayne beach in 1966, I spotted Nixon and Bebe through the picture window of one of the large Mackle houses on the beach; I went in, chatted awhile and Nixon announced he was going in the ocean for a dip. He did; Bebe fidgeted in his chair for a couple of minutes, then excused himself. "He shouldn't be in by himself," he said, and went out to the water's edge in case Nixon, a strong swimmer, should start to drown. Later, there were Secret Service men for that.*

With Bebe, Nixon made his first profitable investments, highly leveraged land speculation, but his feeling for Bebe was based on far more than a profitable association. Rebozo was a man's man, and a kind of bachelor uncle to the girls; he wore well as a friend, and, above all, he brooded well.

* When Presidents swim in the surf, two Secret Service men take up bobbing positions farther into the ocean.

One might assume the ability to brood is inconsequential, but to take long, somber, resentful thoughts and turn them carefully over in one's mind for hours on end is no mean achievement, especially if accompanied by an ability to switch moods suddenly to accommodate a friend. Bebe worshipped Nixon and hated Nixon's enemies.

Nixon had brothers, but Don Nixon was always a problem, and Ed Nixon, whom Richard Nixon loves, is nearly young enough to be his son. (Ed is a likable and gentle man, devoid of ruthlessness but with an admirable streak of pride. He wanted to give his brother and sister-in-law a housewarming present when they moved to New York, but he was short on cash; since Ed was a hi-fi buff, his brother Dick went with him to a hi-fi store, and bought a thousand dollars' worth of equipment, which Ed then spent a day installing in the new Fifth Avenue apartment, the labor being his gift.) Bebe, the same age as Nixon, a divorcé, became the operative brother, the man who could be "there" without having to be addressed, noticed, or otherwise attended to.

However, this good friend and necessary companion reinforced Nixon's worst prejudices about "them." He hated the press, as a bunch of prying, hostile threats to the privacy and the future of his friend. In the early days Bebe talked of "cowboys and Indians" and said that I qualified as an Indian because I actually enjoyed the companionship of reporters. In a sense, his distrust was not misplaced: some of the press proceeded to take after Bebe, poking into the business affairs of this mysterious man so close to the President.

Newsday, a daily on Long Island, New York, in particular, went after Rebozo and former Senator George Smathers in a six-month investigation in 1971. The series was displayed prominently, but without the results the publication had hoped for in terms of hard facts of scandal. This exposé of Rebozo infuriated Nixon, as well it might. It's my belief that the only reason for sifting Rebozo's every deed in life, and treating his story as that of an influence-wielding near-criminal, was his long friendship with Nixon. Afterward, the President made it plain to Ron Ziegler that *Newsday* was to get nothing, not even the normal courtesies extended similar news outlets. Ordinarily, these Draconian strictures soon atrophied, but not the one against the publication that hit a man solely because he was a good friend. Robert W. Greene of *Newsday*, who supervised the team that conducted four hundred interviews of Rebozo's friends and enemies, became the object of an Internal Revenue investigation, a certain abuse of the power of government overreacting to a possible abuse of the power of the press. When Ziegler was making up the list for the China trip, he called me in as he tried to figure out a legitimate-looking way to exclude *Newsday*, on the basis of circulation, or geography, or previous trips, or size of bureau in Washington. Nothing worked, so I guessed aloud that a *Newsday* correspondent would have to go to China, and Ron looked at me as if I were benighted: "No way—we don't mention the name *Newsday* within thirty feet of the President."

A good argument can be made that the press focus on a President's friends is not only unfair, but harmful. It is good for a President to have people with whom he can relax and to whom he can blow off steam, but hostile public scrutiny is a high price for any man to pay for friendship. However, there was no excuse for retaliating the way Nixon did. President Kennedy was foolish to cancel his subscription to the New York *Herald Tribune*, but President Nixon's reaction to *Newsday* after their Rebozo series was worse than foolish.

When Senate Watergate investigators asked Rebozo about a suspicious cash contribution from the Howard Hughes organization, Bebe explained how he received $100,000 in two installments and kept it for three years in a safe deposit box. Nixon critics smelled a rat, suspected a slush fund for the personal use of the President. When lawyer Herb Kalmbach fanned these suspicions, Rebozo soon found himself blinking unhappily in the spotlight. Worst of all, in many voters' eyes, was the use of campaign funds to help the President purchase earrings for his wife; that kind of simple graft was not denied, and left a bad taste all around.

Nixon, who could take press attacks without a public display of anger, could not take it when it came to the attack on Bebe. Again, as in the *Newsday* case, he overreacted, and ruined a good press conference during the Mideast crisis with a flare-up against television commentators, damaging his own cause by showing how he could be upset by criticism.

As with Kissinger and Rogers, Haldeman and Rose Woods, Mitchell and Colson, there were jealousies in any personal relationship with the President. Bebe became jealous after a while of Robert Abplanalp, the millionaire aerosol valve cap inventor who often entertained Nixon and Bebe at his Grand Cay estate in the Bahamas. This man with the unpronounceable, near-palindromic name financed the purchase of Nixon's San Clemente estate; Bebe wanted 10 per cent of the action just to stay close to it. When the time came to disclose the details of the deal, it was Bebe who held out for secrecy until Abplanalp convinced him to step aside and sell the Rebozo percentage to him.

Bebe wasn't always secretive and brooding; he could be warm, generous, and unfailingly loyal, and his smile was the most ingratiating thing about him. "A very mercurial guy," said George Smathers, a close friend. "Some days he loves the world, other days he's suspicious of everybody." Bebe was never going to blab, so he could be the butt of jokes, the recipient of offhand confidences, and sounding-board for assessments of individuals that the President could vouchsafe to no other man.

And the President could kid around with him. When they went up to Camp David together, the President always let Bebe choose the movies the whole family would see. One night they were watching one of Bebe's choices which was somewhat out of the ordinary in terms of Camp David evenings: *Hammersmith Is Out*, with Elizabeth Taylor and Richard Burton, rated R. As sex, violence, and profanity started splashing around, there was no thought given to changing the picture—the President watched any film through to the end, no matter what—but Nixon started ribbing Bebe: "Your kind of movie, Bebe?" "This is your idea of family entertainment?" "So *that*'s why you picked this movie!" Rebozo watched glumly throughout, a little embarrassed about showing this sort of thing to the Nixon women, but kind of enjoying the movie and the whole situation. When it was over, he announced sheepishly, and in truth, "I thought R stood for "Regular."

Toward the end, Bebe fit into a special group of associates of kings referred to by Francis Bacon in his essay on friendship as *participes curarum*: "sharers of their troubles." Bebe was the cause of some of those troubles, though not any of the major ones; he remained loyal to his friend through hubris and adversity, which is what some friends are for.

4. HIDEAWAY

"During the summer of 1942," wrote Samuel Rosenman in *Working with Roosevelt*, "when the Allies were still on the defensive and Roosevelt was sorely beset by multitudinous problems, he set aside for himself in the Catoctin Hills in Maryland a simple weekend retreat . . . a number of rudely constructed, small pine cabins, each of two or three rooms . . .

"The President had selected the place because it was only about a two-hour drive from Washington, and was cool enough and secluded enough to afford him a two-day surcease from the depressing heat and humidity and the unending pressure of official business and visitors in the Capital . . . He nearly always brought a few guests, generally people whom he knew well and who knew him well, and knew his ways of working. Whether he was thinking, playing solitaire, or arranging his stamps, they never interrupted him with conversation."

For a man who spent most of his adult life struggling to get to the White House, and much time after his re-election struggling to stay in the White House, it was ironic how little Nixon liked to spend his time there.

His first escape hatch was the office suite set up in the Old Executive Office Building, the great rococo relic across West Executive Avenue from the West Wing of the White House. The idea of locating another Presidential office there was a masterstroke of management. All the aides who could not be accommodated in the few offices of the West Wing no longer felt themselves to be far out in left field in the EOB. After all, we told our friends, not only did the EOB offer more spacious quarters than over in the "high-rent district," but the President himself preferred it as a place to think and write. Whenever I passed the President's EOB office with a visitor, I found myself saying, "That's really where he spends most of his time," and one day discovered it was true. Nixon took every Wednesday, for example, as his day for privacy—no visiting firemen, no "photo opportunities" in the Oval Office, no Cabinet or Leadership meetings—and the place he holed up, often with Ehrlichman, Haldeman, or Colson, and frequently alone, was the EOB office.

Then there was the Florida White House at Key Biscayne, a two-hour jet flight from Washington and, if Florida skies were cloudy, a good jumping-off spot for the Caribbean islands. Good for weekends, especially in the winter. Not bad politically either—Nixon had always carried Florida.

A third escape hatch was San Clemente—"home" to the native Californian—probably the best weather in the United States, and access to a long stretch of beach. That was for extended stays, and a communications complex was built on Government property nearby. The name "Western White House" was chosen with care to show that a country could be run from California and not just the East Coast, a jab at Eastern establishmentarianism.

But as the years went by, it was FDR's "Shangri-la"—renamed Camp David by President Eisenhower after his grandson, who would become Nixon's son-in-law—that became the most practical place for a retreat. Close enough for a thirty-minute chopper ride and a spur-of-the-moment decision to go; close enough for a visit not to be called a vacation; yet far away from what the President called "that goldfish bowl" of an Oval Office to give him a sense of change of place. Few men willingly work at home.

The change is real. The Camp David air smells different, the dress is informal, the security is better hidden, the vista is breath-taking, and there you are on top of a mountain, closer to God or whatever it is that moves people about mountaintops.

After his re-election, Nixon decided to stop feeling guilty about slipping up to Camp David so often, and told reporters: "I find that here on top of a mountain it is easier for me to get on top of the job." Nixon's aides asked themselves: good or bad? There was the danger of the illusion of aloofness (which Nixon, not his aides, wanted), and the grandiose likening to Moses on Mt. Sinai; there was the more substantive danger of the-cat's-away-the-mice-will-play in Washington, D.C.

But the public-opinion benefits were there, too. The American people like fresh air, and they appreciate a change of pace. Compared to the pomp and ceremony of the White House, a good museum to visit, many of them like the seeming contrast of a rustic cabin in the sky. I say "seeming" because the President's cabin at Camp David is far from rustic. It is a beautiful home, complete with pool, sauna, and movie projection booth, that most people would consider luxurious. Rustic it is not. (The cabin where the writers stay is rustic.)

That was a lapse in taste of Nixon's, by the way. Brought up to be a frugal man, the hero of working people who could not throw money around, Nixon—at Haldeman's urging—"improved" Camp David to its detriment. A hideaway should be a hideaway, not a Catoctin Hilton, and Nixon's building program up there smacked of the sumptuous spreads of the nouveau riche. FDR, born to wealth, appreciated rusticity; Nixon, born poor, appreciated a heated swimming pool right out front. (Camp Hoover, the hideaway of President Hoover at the headwaters of the Rapidan River, is now used by the White House staff, but not the President; it is an outdoors kind of camp, not a piece of the indoors placed in an outdoor setting.) Two strange images come to mind in connection with Nixon and nature: first, of that heated swimming pool, sending up clouds of vapor in the cool mountain air, and second, of that crackling fire in the Oval Office during the hottest days of the summer with the air conditioning turned up high. He liked a swim and he liked a fire, and the President of the United States could defy the seasons to have them.

Nixon thought that the most important public opinion benefit that flowed from his withdrawal to mountaintops and remote beaches was the sense of mystery that Charles de Gaulle had written about. A certain reserve, a dignity, was an integral part of leadership. He wanted to seem slightly out of reach without seeming in the least out of touch.

A weakness in Nixon was the way he used this supposed need for being once-removed to conceal his instinct for indirection. He did not like to do things head-on, personally putting his identity on the line, unless it was a matter of State—then it was not himself that he was using to confront, it was himself as President of the United States. That's a little fuzzy. Let me give some examples of indirection, or unnecessary aloofness.

There was a time in the mid-Sixties when Nixon lost his sense of indirection. Since he was not in or near power, there was no need for a shield; he could take rebuff without considering it a challenge to his authority; Nixon could speak more frankly, without worrying about overpowering or embarrassing his listeners.

In the eight years between the Nixon Vice Presidency and Nixon Presidency, he grew accustomed to the simple, direct actions of a plain citizen. Before, as Vice President and later as candidate for President and Governor, telephone calls would always be placed for him; as a practicing lawyer, he relearned the technique of dialing for himself. In 1967, meeting in New York with the two Californians who had worked on his 1960 and 1962 campaigns, Bob Haldeman and Bob Finch, Nixon mentioned that he ought to call a certain friend in Chicago. Finch, elected Lieutenant Governor of California the year before but who reverted to aide psychology whenever he was with his old boss, said, "Want me to get him on the line for you?" Nixon said no, picked up the phone and dialed, spoke to the answering switchboard, then the secretary, then to the man he wanted. Finch's eyes popped; he rarely saw Nixon as an ordinary mortal. "In the old days," Haldeman told me in 1968, "for two weeks we'd hear the Boss say, 'Why doesn't somebody call back Karl Mundt?' Hell of a difference now."

In the Presidency, the directness disappeared and the sense of indirection returned, in more than telephone habits. When Ehrlichman advised him to pick up the phone and give an order himself, Nixon would sometimes say, "Who could we get to turn Mitchell off on this—Connally?" He would resist the possibility of rejection. I had the assignment of getting Arthur Burns's agreement in 1971 to head a committee to regulate interest rates. Burns telephoned the President, presumably to discuss it with him; Nixon asked me to take the call first, because "If Arthur wants to do it, I'll talk to him. I don't want to talk to him if he doesn't. I'm not interested in the reasons why not." I then asked Burns if I could tip the President to the direction of his thinking before they spoke. The Federal Reserve chairman was shrewd enough to reveal his willingness to serve. I then told the man screening the President's calls (Alex Butterfield, that day) that the Burns call was one the President wanted. The happily unrejected Nixon then talked to Burns, concluded his business, and choppered off to Camp David.

Camp David is a good place for a President to exercise a right that every other citizen takes for granted: he can take a walk alone. Though never far away from Nixon, the Secret Service was not dogging his heels; since the whole area was secure, he was free to roam by himself or with somebody he wanted to talk to in complete privacy—not even the goddam tape machine could reveal what was said.

Sitting in the corner of a small room with a fireplace and with a long view was also conducive to thought, though Nixon found it necessary to protest that he did not often look out the window—"it's too distracting." In the Fifth Avenue apartment in the Sixties, he had a favorite chair in the corner of a den, with a fireplace and a view of Central Park. That chair went with him to the Lincoln sitting room, a historic cranny upstairs at the White House with a fireplace and a view of the Ellipse and Washington Monument. In San Clemente, the second-story den is a small aerie, again with a fireplace, and a view of the Pacific. At Camp David, there is a small den behind the bedrooms with a fireplace and a picture window looking over a long valley.

Psychohistorians might confidently explain this recurrence of womblike small rooms, fireplaces, and long views, but it is the kind of atmosphere most men find conducive to quiet concentration and—if they could afford it—would choose for themselves. Nixon could, and did. When, on winter mornings at Camp David, the branches of all the trees for miles around are a filigree of ice, twinkling and dripping in the sunshine, a visitor has to think that such a sight brings out the better angels of one's nature.

During the '72 campaign, when the strategy was to show the President at work as President and not as campaigning Candidate, I suggested to appointments secretary Dwight Chapin that the President not spend so much time at Camp David. The place to be "at work" was the White House —specifically, the Oval Office—not some Catoctin mountaintop, as inaccessible as De Gaulle's home at Colomby-des-deux-Églises. The remoteness of Camp David contributed to the charge of "the isolation of the President," a standard, year-round shot at every President, but one that became troublesome in a campaign. Besides, there was no hiding from the White House press corps the difference in activity in official Washington after the President's white-topped helicopter spirited him away from the Executive Mansion.

Chapin, always respectful of the opinions of other members of the staff to whom he turned for recommendations on every move of the President's, duly jotted down my reasoning in his notebook, then looked up and asked: "Do you want to be the one who tells the President he can't go to Camp David? Because it sure as hell isn't going to be me."

Chapin had a point: Nixon liked to work by himself ("in isolation" has a more sinister sound) and resented the advice of friends who told him his style could be criticized, therefore he should change his style. Certainly Nixon was too "remote" for most tastes, and surely his secretive nature caused him and the nation much unnecessary grief, but hideaways like Camp David have little to do with it. Nixon could isolate himself in a crowd or even a permanent floating meeting in the Oval Office. He viewed the criticism of Presidents getting away from what Harry Truman called "the big white prison" as petty and mean-spirited, and he was right—the symbol was not the problem. If Nixon cut himself off from needed and unwanted advice, it did not matter if he did it in a Cabinet room or atop a mountain.

Camp David, as well as the seaside, was good for Nixon because it provided an atmosphere that fed his natural optimism. The impression one had of Nixon was often of a man smiling determinedly in the face of adversity, practicing being optimistic but not really being an optimist. That is not so, and that is a secret of Nixon's strength of character at the lowest moments.

Take the movies, for example. At Camp David, as we have seen with Bebe Rebozo's choice of films, Nixon relaxed often by watching motion pictures in the darkened living room, the kind of luxury a poor boy from Yorba Linda revels in. The kind of movies John Ford used to make are his favorites, and historical epics—*A Man for All Seasons, Young Winston, War and Peace.* Sometimes he was moved by a more avant-garde movie like *The Last Picture Show,* but the ones he asked for again were *South Pacific* and *Carousel,* and he has been heard to say, "We haven't seen *Around the World in 80 Days* in a long time." Working until five, an hour's swim, dinner, a movie, and to bed—that was a Nixon Camp David day. When it came to the movie, he would be loyal to whatever had been chosen. His daughter Julie once told me: "No matter how terrible the first reel is, he always thinks it will get better. 'Give it a chance,' he'll say. Oh, we sat through some real lemons. Bebe would fall asleep, Mother and Tricia would tiptoe out, but Daddy would stick with it. 'Wait,' he'd say. 'Wait—it'll get better.'"

5. JULIE

My favorite Nixon has always been Julie Eisenhower. She is like her father without a dark side—that is, she is loyal, alert, considerate, virtuous, intelligent, and sensibly impulsive. That may sound like a version of the Girl Scout pledge, but most people who watched her speak up for her father in the worst of times would agree that Julie is not only all that, but is pluckier than any member of her family, including her father, in opening up to people.

I followed Thomas E. Dewey up the stairs of the Marble Collegiate Church in New York to Julie's wedding to David Eisenhower. The usher asked Dewey which side he belonged on—bride's or groom's. Dewey stopped, dumbfounded. "Both!" he burst out and the usher led him to the Nixon side.

The marriage of his younger daughter to General Eisenhower's grandson was especially gratifying to Richard Nixon. He liked the boy, who was straightforward and square; he recognized the political usefulness in having an Eisenhower in the family; and he must have felt that there was some justice in life, because Eisenhower—perhaps without meaning to—had treated the Nixons condescendingly during the 1952 campaign and his time in the White House. In the "Nixon Fund" crisis, Eisenhower (and Dewey) had not been especially stalwart, in Nixon's view; the Vice Presidential candidate turned the tables on them by refusing to resign on television, asking instead in the "Checkers" speech that viewers send their cards and letters to the Republican National Committee. That neatly finessed Eisenhower, who quickly became aware that Nixon had taught him a lesson in the politics of survival.

In 1956, Eisenhower had not firmly turned aside Harold Stassen's dump-Nixon movement, letting it be known instead that he had suggested the possibility of another Cabinet post to his Vice President; Nixon grimly held on, and did not forget. In the campaign of 1960 the magic Eisenhower name and personality was not used to its full potential. A story was put out that Mamie Eisenhower had asked Candidate Nixon not to press Ike because the retiring President's health was failing. This was a useful alibi, and put Nixon in a self-sacrificing light, but it was not true. Julie and I were talking about this one day in 1973, sitting in the yellow Oval Room upstairs at the White House, and she said flatly: "Mamie says that story isn't true about her asking my father in the 1960 campaign not to call on Ike so much because of his health. My father had said to Ike, 'It's got to be my own campaign,' and Ike was not the sort who would look beyond that— he'd just figure that was the way my father wanted it. And I'm sure Daddy felt that way, that it was his own campaign, but he was also too shy to ask for more help." I think this means that if Eisenhower had said, "Dammit, Dick, I want to get out there and campaign for you," Nixon would have acquiesced happily, but he did not, and the Nixon Presidency was postponed eight years.

In reflecting about Eisenhower, Nixon always told his aides that Ike was too willing to cast aside men who had proven their loyalty if they threatened to cast a shadow on his own rectitude. Ike was too selfish, Nixon thought—not enough "heart."

At any rate, the relationship between Eisenhower and Nixon was not all "that's my boy"—and it was a little too much of that, for Nixon's taste —but in the years in the wilderness of New York, the relationship improved, a note of deference slipping into Ike's avuncular posture, and by the campaign of 1968, the former President wanted to do whatever he could. By this time, and especially with Ike's grandson and Nixon's daughter getting along so well, all past tensions were best set aside, and Nixon would bring up Eisenhower's name in every campaign speech, pointing out how the Eisenhower Administration "ended one war and kept us out of others." Past slights were suffused in a golden glow, and a mutual respect and affection at last arose.

In 1972, I wrote the captions in a short book with Julie Nixon Eisenhower, called *Eye on Nixon:* a series of photographs taken by the official White House photographer Oliver Atkins and his staff, selected by Julie. She would come into my office in the EOB, like a young woman who wanted to help, not like a princess sweeping into the office of her father's aide. And she had good taste in photographs; I recall one picture of her mother talking to a Vietnamese soldier in a hospital. Pat Nixon had a beautiful, sympathetic expression but her outstretched arm was bare and the art director pointed out that its wrinkles made her appear old. Since we were not retouching pictures, he assumed it would have to go. Julie said no, "my mother is a sixty-year-old woman, and this picture tells what kind of a person she is with somebody she feels for," and the picture went in.

Because the pictures were good and the captions not reverential—in fact, some feature writers were surprised that the text in a semi-official book included a few spoofs at the Old Man—it was not panned as an idolatrous picture book about Nixon would surely have been. When it was published, in the interoffice mail came the only formal, handwritten letter I ever received from the President:

6-23-72

Dear Bill—

I was delighted to see Helen Thomas' high praise of your captions in "Eye on Nixon"—

More important Julie thought you were *terrific* to work with!
Many thanks—

RN

The note was Julie's doing, of course, and evidence of what she calls her
father's shyness comes in the indirection of his praise. Instead of saying he
liked the book about himself, Nixon wrote that he liked the way Helen
Thomas of UPI wrote about it—praising the praise, staying once removed
from commenting at all on a book about himself.

Brief, affectionate notes are often exchanged in the Nixon family. "If
you're shy," Julie says, "it's hard saying some things. And my father knows
that a note means more, too—it shows he cared enough to put it down on
paper." While others are reluctant to show the sentimental side of Richard
Nixon, for fear of revealing private matters or of not being believed, she
does not hesitate: "Of course he's sentimental. He saw some beautiful
roses growing in San Clemente, and he brought them back here to the
White House and gave some to Mother, some to me, some to Rose Woods
and Marge Acker, and the receptionist at the EOB office.

"He's sentimental about the memory of his family, too—he really loved
Hannah, his mother. But he's proud of his father. 'He didn't have polish,'
he says, 'but he had guts.' One night, at the dinner table, he was telling
about him, and he said, 'He was a helluva guy . . .' and he didn't say a
thing for a while.

"Then, of course, there was the time Mother dropped a bowling ball on
his toe. He got very angry, I mean it really hurt, and a week later his toe-
nail fell off. But after the first few minutes, when he was limping around
just furious, he got more angry at himself for losing his temper. For the
next week he couldn't have been more considerate and thoughtful to
Mom."

Julie is a sensible young woman, but never gives the impression of calculation; she's spontaneous, likely to dart out of the room to get something,
not worried about whether it's dignified or not to run down the hall. Julie
insists she gets her own impulsiveness from her father: "He'll say, 'Let's
do something special tonight, let's make this a special night.' Or, 'Tonight's
an anniversary of something, let's go out and celebrate.' There was the
time after Cambodia, when all the campuses were closed, and he said to
David and me, 'I want to have you here.' After the Cambodia speech, we
went up to the Solarium on the third floor—Bebe, Mother, David, and me.
He took phone calls, and when David told him he heard that Willy Brandt

had been defeated in Germany, he put in a call right away to Kiesinger, I think it was, to congratulate him. The trouble was, David was wrong, Willy Brandt won. That was embarrassing. David felt terrible for giving Daddy the wrong information, especially since he just picked up the phone and called—he's impulsive that way."

President Nixon would take a call from Julie any time of the day or night. I was working late on a foreign policy address with him toward the end of 1969; the phone rang in his private office in the EOB, he listened a moment, then went into a ten-minute analysis of our Latin American relations. When he hung up, I wondered if that were Kissinger or Rogers wanting to put the topic in the speech—no, he said, Julie was going to be interviewed the next morning for a USIA broadcast. "He's very good about suggesting what to say," Julie recalls. "Small talk, too—you know, he's not the way people say, he's really good at small talk. I'll call him and say, 'I'm going to speak to the Kiwanis Club in Columbus, what are your reminiscences?' and he'll say, 'Tell them when I was in Kiwanis in Whittier, I was program chairman, and when I couldn't find a good guest I'd wind up speaking myself. So tell them you sympathize with the Kiwanis program chairman, that they scraped the bottom of the barrel and came up with you. That'll go over'—and it did. The audience loved it."

The Nixon family gets together at the dinner table, and the Nixon women are conscious of the President's desire to put aside his cares when he eats. "He gets irritated when unpleasant things are brought up at dinner—that's the wrong time to talk about that kind of thing." One of his first actions in the White House was to remove the telephone from the dining room; in LBJ days, phones were everywhere. "Helene Drown, an old friend, once brought in a gag phone that she concealed under her blazer." Julie gets up to act out the story. "She pushed a button inside her coat and it rang like a regular phone. My father glared around—who put the phone in the dining room?—and then Helene pulled out the gag phone and held it to his ear, like this, saying, 'It's for you.' He wouldn't take it—said, 'Tell them I'm not in'—until he realized it was a gag, since the wire was coming out of her blazer. He was a little embarrassed that he was so taken in."

Julie will tell a story like that with genuine delight; because she is outgoing, and because she seems even more impetuous than she is, the younger Nixon daughter became a favorite of the press. Tricia, on the other hand, is more like her father in dealings with people outside the normal circle of family and friends: "reserved" is the word used in a friendly way, "cold," "aloof," "Dresden doll" are the characterizations of the less than friendly. But Tricia, the elder, is far less sophisticated than Julie, using that word to mean worldliness rather than aloofness. In an interview, Tricia would say publicly about the press: "You can't underestimate the power of fear. They're afraid if they don't shape up," which she learned at her father's knee, but which is hardly a point to make in public. In the same circumstance, Julie would filter her own response through some innate sense of decorum in discourse. Tricia gives the appearance of guard-edness, Julie of spontaneity, but it is Julie who rarely says the criticizable thing. That is why, when the Nixon family went into seclusion after the Watergate revelations, it was Julie who carried the burden of the family presence in public appearances and press interviews.

Her strongly held views—against abortion, for example—were pressed in private to her father, but rarely touched on in public. As natural and genuine as she is, she is a politician's daughter: "I believe in more women in Government, and so does my father. He's been grooming a woman for the Supreme Court, you know—I can't say who, but he's been promoting her along, and one day . . ."

Julie's significance in the Nixon story, and one reason for this chapter, is this: here is a young woman whose good sense, grace, and goodness were not acquired in a vacuum. She was, at least in part, the product of an en-vironment dominated by Richard Nixon. Admittedly, some fine parents have terrible offspring, and some terrible parents produce saints, but most often young people reflect their parents' strengths and shortcomings. Julie is evidence that the Nixons' ideas of family life help to develop good chil-dren and fine young adults. She is a glimpse of what her father could have been to others if he did not indulge himself in narrowing his own circle to the trusted, distrusting few.

Julie Eisenhower herself is everything a man could want in a daughter: not just a girl to be protected and strengthened against partisan blasts, but one to become a source of strength when an inner circle crumbles; if part of judging a man's life is to examine the sum of his human relationships, young Mrs. Eisenhower is one who speaks eloquently in Richard Nixon's favor.

In May 1973, Julie Eisenhower spoke of the days after the full force of the Watergate scandal had broken, of the depression around the house and the relationship between her parents: "Mother and I did feel kind of cut off. In Cambodia, Haiphong, and all, we were all in it together, as a family, but this time he was on his own. The other times he'd call us, but this time we'd call him to say hello. He's an upbeat person, no matter how tense a situation gets, and I'd never seen the Gloomy Gus part of him that people talk about, never before.

"He didn't try to cheer Mother up, and that was very rare. In Key Bis-cayne, around five in the afternoon he'd go for a swim, and come back not saying anything and after dinner he was feeling low. You know how Mother is, always thinking of other people, she wanted him to know that we were with him all the way, but he was just closed off.

"I felt he wasn't giving her enough credit for having such confidence in him, so during a movie I sat next to him and said, 'Mother's trying so hard to make things right, and you don't realize it. It's hard for her too.' He just said, 'I guess so,' and all through the movie I felt horrible that I had blurted that out, he didn't need any more burdens from us, but then after it was over he turned to me and said, 'You're right, it's hard for her too. I'll try.' And he did."

White House photographer Ollie Atkins took a memorable picture of Julie in her father's arms just after he had told the family of his decision to resign. It was in the third-floor California room of the residence, and the family was eating dinner on trays, reluctant to look out the windows at the crowd gathered along the fence on a death watch. Throughout the first week of August 1974, with the end inexorably approaching, the Nixon family—especially Julie—urged the President not to resign, to fight it out though the impeachment process, as his staff—led by lawyer James St. Clair and Chief of Staff Al Haig, with the quiet backing of Fred Buzhardt and Len Garment—was leading him toward resignation. The Nixon women did not want him to quit for a simple reason: they knew if he did quit, he would surely collapse and perhaps will himself into the grave.

"Do you think the staff can be kept in line?" Julie asked one of the speechwriters. He allowed as how the troops could be rallied, at least for a time, if the President was prepared to make an abject confession of cover-up guilt. Julie knew that would never happen. She took her dread with her to dinner upstairs that night of August 7, and told me the next afternoon: "Get Ollie to tell you what it was like. You know Daddy, with his sense of history, he wanted a picture, so he sent for Ollie."

Atkins entered a room filled with four tearful women (Mrs. Nixon, the two daughters, Rose Mary Woods) and three extremely glum men (the President and his two sons-in-law). Ollie's lopsided, amiable appearance—and the recollection of his presence at the happiest of times—broke the tension, and the family shouted a welcome. Nixon started arranging the family for a picture, in that way he had of stringing everybody out in a line, as Rose ducked out of the picture, behind the photographer, as she always did. The Nixons locked arms together and posed while Ollie flashed a few; spirits up, smiling bravely, like a daguerreotype of Tsar Nicholas and his family. Then, the moment the group broke up, Julie broke down, and the President grabbed the bravest Nixon to him, much as he had done in defeat fourteen years before.

PART TEN

MAN IN THE ARENA

After the Nixon defeat by John F. Kennedy in 1960, the Nixon cadre of loyalists were sent a clay replica of the life cast of Abraham Lincoln's right hand. It was my job to buy the replicas, have them packed and sent out to about a hundred of the Candidate's most important supporters. Every damned one arrived in the mail broken. To placate the group while I had a new batch of Lincoln hands made, I borrowed an idea from my old boss, Tex McCrary, and sent out a parchment with this Theodore Roosevelt quotation on it:

> It is not the critic who counts, not the one who points out how the strong man stumbled or how the doer of deeds might have done them better.
>
> The credit belongs to the man who is actually in the arena, whose face is marred with sweat and dust and blood; who strives valiantly; who errs and comes short again and again; who knows the great enthusiasms, the great devotions, and spends himself in a worthy cause; who, if he wins, knows the triumph of high achievement; and who, if he fails, at least fails while daring greatly, so that his place shall never be with those cold and timid souls who know neither victory nor defeat.

I liked that quotation; to fail "while daring greatly" took a bit of the sting out of defeat. In a Nixon speech in 1965, we used it again; and in 1974, the departing President would turn to it one last time. The passage can be seen many ways. Tom Wicker, in his novel *Facing the Lions,* used it to show how arrogance could be ameliorated by manliness, at least in admiring eyes; in a Broadway play, *That Championship Season,* the Roosevelt passage was used to show how pitiable the pretension of the strenuous life could be. In bowing out, Nixon's use of the passage was as his predecessor in office had intended it: a justification of the good fight, and a hard-to-criticize note of defiance in defeat. At any rate, whatever beauty is beheld in the "man in the arena," it made a good souvenir.

After the Nixon victory in re-establishing himself as a force in the Republican Party in 1966, I hunted around for another souvenir—unbreakable, this time—to send to the stalwarts. The choice was a "Churchill crown," the British coin commemorating the greatest Englishman of the age, set in lucite and sent with an appropriate reminder that the idea of achieving peace by throwing a small nation to the wolves was—in the Churchill words that Nixon had often quoted in that campaign—"a fatal delusion."

After his 1968 election to the Presidency, Nixon sent the standard Inaugural Medal to friends (I had grimly vowed to stay out of the souvenir-selection business forever). At Christmastime each year after that, the gift to White House staff was a large Christmas card suitable for framing: a painting of George Washington the first year, followed by Jefferson, Lincoln, and Theodore Roosevelt. The painting selected in late 1973 was James Monroe, leaving the final three paintings of the second term to be Wilson, Eisenhower, and—I guess—the plan was to have Nixon at the end.

But after the 1972 campaign, the gift sent to political supporters was a cheesy, tasteless chunk of transparent plastic on a walnut-and-plastic stand with this card:

"THE PRESIDENTIAL STAR"

THE ORIGINAL OF THIS DESIGN, A GIFT FROM AMBASSADOR WALTER ANNENBERG, WAS SCULPTED IN CRYSTAL BY STEUBEN GLASS AND NOW OCCUPIES A PLACE OF HONOR ON MY DESK IN THE OVAL OFFICE. THIS REPLICA COMES TO YOU WITH MY SPECIAL APPRECIATION FOR YOUR HELP AND SUPPORT IN THE 1972 CAMPAIGN, AND WITH EVERY GOOD WISH FOR THE YEARS AHEAD.

Richard Nixon

Perhaps another shattered right hand might have been more appropriate. As it was, the Presidential star was apt enough, for that star proceeded to plummet from the political firmament at a rate that had never before been seen.

Nixon had entered office less popular than his three predecessors; he had less to lose, yet after his popularity reached a peak after the election victory and the achievement of an honorable cease-fire in Vietnam, in 1973, it dropped in Gallup's ratings by forty percentage points in a six-month period. Harry Truman had even less support at one point, but his erosion was more gradual; the disappearance of Nixon's mandate was more sudden than any in our history.

According to Nixon, this was brought about by the incessant pounding by the television commentators on the "deplorable Watergate matter." The increased impact of mass communication on a massive change of mind cannot be discounted, but the sense of betrayal, distrust, and revulsion that grew in so many minds was based first on admitted fact—the "White

Q: Sir: Are you going to cooperate with the Ervin Committee's investigation of the Watergate?

A: First, I would emphasize that it is certainly our intention to cooperate with the Select Committee of the Senate, provided only that the hearings are not diverted from a genuine legislative purpose.

However, I must say that I was disappointed that the Democratic majority in the Senate voted to organize the Committee on a partisan basis, rejecting the request for equal representation for both parties, as is the case in other select committees, like the Senate ethics committee.

As a result of that decision, we have a situation where a Democratic majority has the power to control completely a Senate investigation aimed at Republicans. Since the Democrats can set the rules, and act as investigator, judge and jury, there is an obvious need for political restraint.

(Moore/Dean/JE)

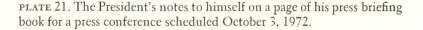

PLATE 21. The President's notes to himself on a page of his press briefing book for a press conference scheduled October 3, 1972.

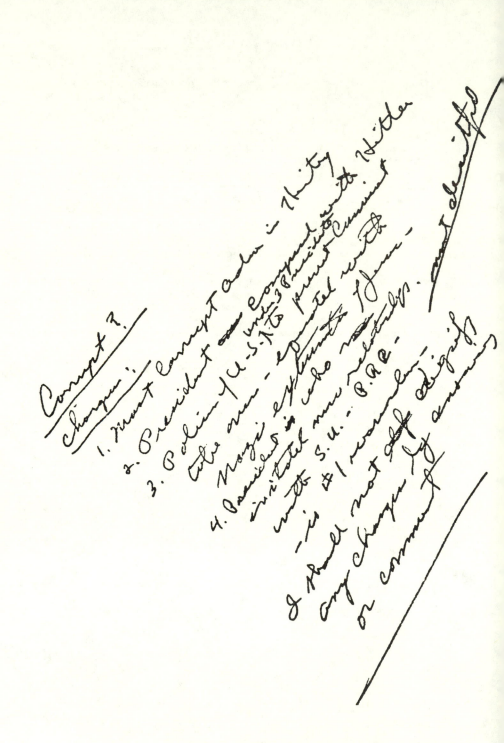

PLATE 22. In his October 1972 press briefing book, President Nixon prepares himself to defend charges of corruption.

Q: Sir: Is there any truth to rumors of a rift between you and your foreign policy adviser?

A: Not only this President but the American people owe Dr. Kissinger a debt of gratitude for his contribution in negotiating this honorable peace. As for our relations, my high regard for him remains what it has been for the four years we have worked together.

(PJB)

(+) He has advised & supported every action I have taken

PLATE 23. In a February 1973 briefing book, President Nixon puts to rest reports of Dr. Kissinger's disagreement with the Christmas bombing of Hanoi: "He has advised and supported every action I have taken."

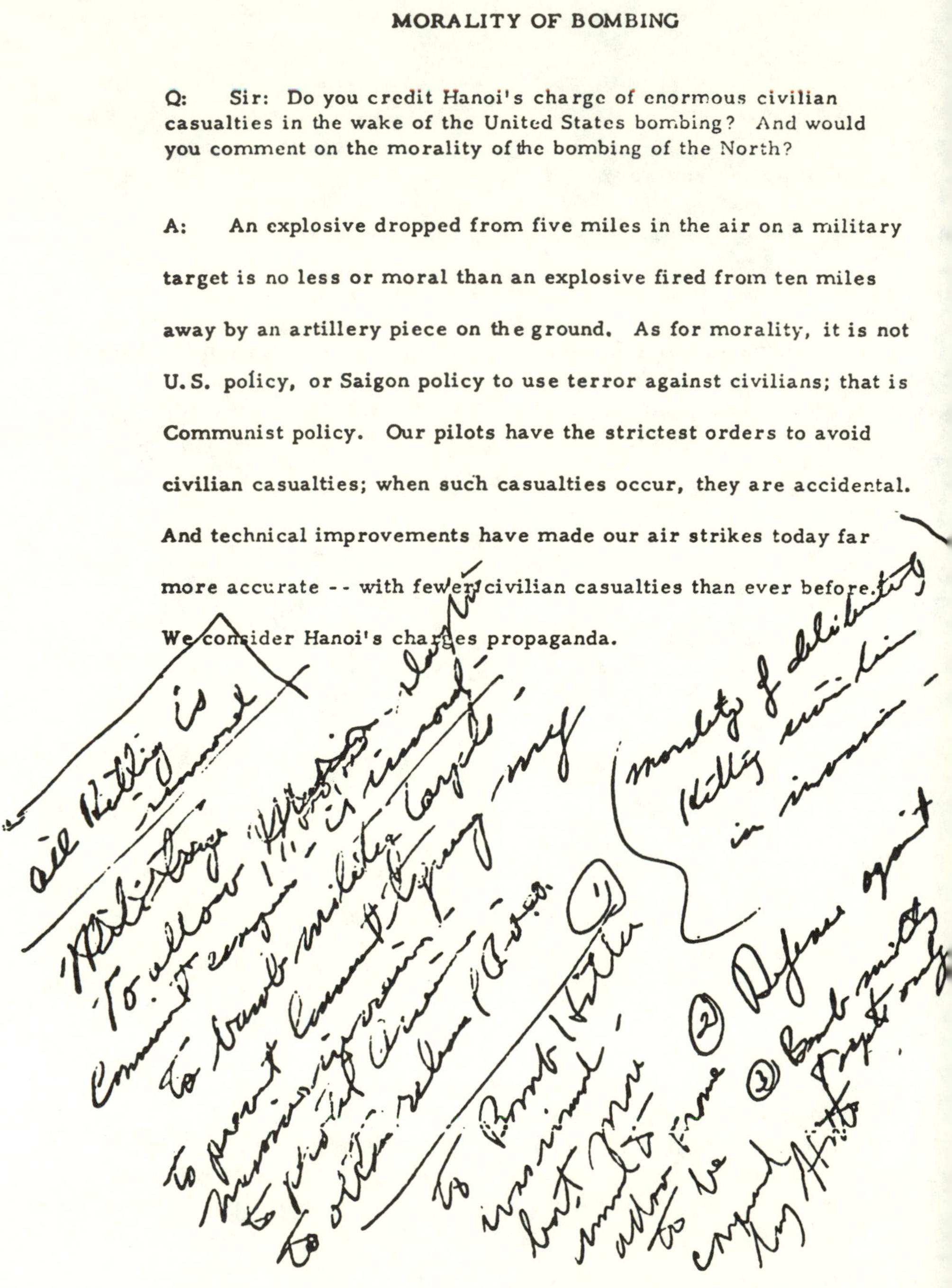

Q: Sir: Do you credit Hanoi's charge of enormous civilian casualties in the wake of the United States bombing? And would you comment on the morality of the bombing of the North?

A: An explosive dropped from five miles in the air on a military target is no less or moral than an explosive fired from ten miles away by an artillery piece on the ground. As for morality, it is not U.S. policy, or Saigon policy to use terror against civilians; that is Communist policy. Our pilots have the strictest orders to avoid civilian casualties; when such casualties occur, they are accidental. And technical improvements have made our air strikes today far more accurate -- with fewer civilian casualties than ever before. We consider Hanoi's charges propaganda.

PLATE 24. In a February 1973 briefing book, President Nixon prepares an answer on the morality of the Christmas bombing.

House horrors" were real—and helped along by an underestimation by the President of the size and momentum of the public disapproval. Watertight doors kept springing open. First the Watergate burglars were forced to talk; then the President's counsel turned against him, and finally—when Watergate seemed to be finally contained, with the country getting bored and the worst of the charges against the President unsubstantiated—the existence of the tapes was revealed, leading to a renewed hunt for evidence, the firing of the first special prosecutor, and the first serious actions toward impeachment. Overnight, it seemed, as in a Shakespearean tragedy, all his conquests, glories, triumphs, spoils were shrunk to an exaggeratedly small measure.

As the President kept giving way, making concessions that would have appeared generous and openhanded if done in timely fashion, but which seemed inadequate and desperate done under immense pressure, people who had worked with him before wondered not so much what had happened to bring about Watergate—that could be figured out—but what had happened to the Nixon ability to defuse a dangerous situation. Was this the Nixon who walked out to the Lincoln Memorial that night after Kent State's tragedy to talk to young people, who turned aside Brezhnev's wrath that day at the dacha with icy calm? Or was this the other Nixon, the man who lashed out at the Senate after the Carswell rejection, whose tirade at leakers stunned his aides at the time of the Pentagon Papers publication?

Nixon's return from Moscow in 1972 was akin to Napoleon's return from Moscow in 1812. Both men suffered their worst setbacks right after their greatest triumphs. After Nixon's summit successes—and they were remarkable—the combination of steady planning toward a New Majority and the sheer luck of the choice of an opposition candidate provided Nixon with the biggest victory a President could hope for. On top of that, after the most searing moments of decision about Christmas bombing, and the most savage criticism likening him to a barbarian, to achieve peace with honor in Southeast Asia—that was too much satisfaction at one time for Nixon. Always at his worst in victory, the double triumph over his adversaries at home and abroad doubly blunted his reactions to the ominous, murderous swinging-back of the pendulum.

I do not have much to add about the "bizarre incident" at 2600 Virginia Avenue, but in this section, as in some of the earlier parts of this book, there is the attempt to answer the questions "Why? When did it all begin?" And the question posed to everyone who ever worked in the Nixon Administration, "How could you not know all about Watergate and its cover-up?" which was best answered by Counselor Bryce Harlow's plaintive "They didn't trust me to do wrong right."

From the summer of 1972 to the winter of 1973, we board the steepest, fastest roller-coaster in American political history, where Nixon surely proved, in Theodore Roosevelt's words, "his place shall never be with those cold and timid souls who know neither victory nor defeat."

1. THE FALL OF JOHN MITCHELL

John Mitchell viewed his second campaign assignment as the broad high-way back to a lucrative and honored private life, and accepted it thinking that 1972's campaign would be like 1968 all over again, only easier.

But this time, Bob Haldeman was determined to have effective control of much of the campaign; Chuck Colson had been assiduously building his "new majority"; and Nixon wanted Mitchell for a role like that of Len Hall's in his 1960 campaign: chairman and reassuring symbol.

Patterns are usually followed in political intrigues. Mitchell wanted a protégé of his own, Harry Flemming, to be his campaign deputy; this was shot down after a while, and Jeb Magruder, whom Haldeman had first put in as Herb Klein's deputy to take over the communications operation, was transferred to the job of being Mitchell's second in command. After the campaign, Magruder would be dependent on Haldeman, not Mitchell, for his future job. It was clear to the White House staff that the substitution of Magruder for Flemming meant that Bob Haldeman was running the '72 campaign, and that the President, through his chief of staff, would carry out the pledge made after the '70 effort: "When I am the candidate, I run the campaign." But Nixon wanted Mitchell there, possibly as a check on Haldeman, more likely as a check on himself, and as a comforting figure to local politicians.

Haldeman's Magruder was the immediate cause of the downfall of John Mitchell; the underlying causes can be found in the chapter about Mitch-ell's rise in an earlier, happier portion of the book. In the handsome young cosmetics marketer from California, Mitchell saw only his monitoring by Haldeman, not real trouble. He was shatteringly wrong.

Jeb Magruder was the Game Plan Man; for Haldeman, he would reduce ideas and general orders to specific and often mechanistic Game Plans, with assignments, follow-ups, and analyses of results. He was eager, har-ried, confident, optimistic, and usually over his head. "I have an antidote for you," he said to me one day, and went on to tell me what might be better described as a pointless anecdote. He found conspiracy delectable, and would refer in whispers to "H", which was the way Haldeman signed his memos, but Magruder was too bright-eyed and bushy-tailed—a cliché he liked—to be considered any kind of threat by the likes of John Mitchell. What Mitchell overlooked was the fact that Magruder was one fine salesman.

Pat Buchanan and I were on the receiving end of a Magruder sell one day in October 1972; we had taken Jeb aside in Pat's office to find out what was really the story of Watergate. "Look, I can be honest with you guys," he told us, "but it can't get out of this room." His story was believable in its unbelievability: the campaign was awash with money. There were at least twenty men Magruder channeled money to, "including this guy Liddy, who came with the best credentials from Ehrlichman and Krogh, and who really didn't ask for much"—outsiders wouldn't understand it, but 200 G's was peanuts compared to the money that was flying around. So, Magruder said, he gave it to him, the results of some "investigations" came in, and who knew Liddy was off on a half-baked scheme breaking and entering Democratic headquarters with a crew of Cubans? The way Magruder told it, the story was strangely believable; Pat and I swallowed it whole, and we were not the only ones to gulp it down; anybody who had worked in a national campaign near the top knew how far from control the people two levels away really were. That was Magruder's "Liddy cut-out" story, which very nearly fooled everybody; only the pressure of long prison sentences put on James McCord and Howard Hunt by Federal Judge John Sirica—that nice, patriotic little judge who favored my wife with a swearing-in at the Vice President's office not long ago—peeled the veneer off the Magruder story.*

Mitchell, as the story began to seep out in April 1973, talked to me—newly ensconced at the New York *Times*—on the telephone about Magruder: "Who would have thought that All-American boy, with that nice wife and the great little kids, would turn out to be such a viper?" It was late at night and Mitchell had been drinking; though his voice was slurred, he knew enough to concentrate on the "White House horrors" that preceded Watergate, for which he felt he did not bear responsibility. Mitchell was saying that he had bought the plan to bug the Democrats at the behest of Haldeman's man Magruder, with the added pressure from Colson to dig up the dirt, and in the knowledge that break-ins and tappings along these illegal lines had been going on undetected for years.

Before the Ervin Committee, the former Attorney General had to adopt the attitude that the "cover-up" was a necessity for the preservation of the Republic; he seemed ridiculously loyal, playing the role of the good soldier. He did not implicate the President; he had to take the accusatory questioning, including the posturings of Senator Lowell Weicker (R., Conn.),

---

* The week before he went to jail, I sat next to Magruder in the steam room of the Federal City Club, and reminded him of that October day. He grinned at the recollection: "You guys really lapped that one up, didn't you?"

without striking back, looking like the grim absolutist who would have done anything to save the country from George McGovern.

Mitchell could not say what I will bet he was thinking: "Sure we did a few things with surveillance in '72, just as we were on the receiving end of surveillance in '68. If you guys can't take it, you shouldn't dish it out. And stop being so supercilious—you know there were real threats of violence in San Diego, where the convention was supposed to be—maybe you remember Chicago in '68, where real people got hurt. And you know some anti-Nixon demonstrations were planned in Democratic headquarters in '72. So we moved to stop it—and also to penetrate the opposition camp the way it's been done since time immemorial, but nobody objected when LBJ did it to Goldwater. And the way the press is on its high moral horse —remember the way NBC bugged the Republican Convention with a hidden mike in 1968, and how it treats stolen documents not as stolen goods but as liberated truth?" Mitchell did not take that combative, everybody-does-it line, not because he did not want to, but because he would have been destroyed by it—and staying out of jail became the important goal.

Nor did Mitchell talk as a political man, like this: "When something goes wrong in a campaign, you hope for the best and move to cut your losses. Maybe it will blow over. Maybe something else will happen to steal the headlines. You tell a few people you trust to handle it, you don't go into detail, and the thing usually works itself out. You don't run to the President and say, 'Let's put everybody who works for you in jail,' just because some idiot down the line got a little careless. People's whole careers are at stake. Did the press get into an uproar when Clark Clifford and Abe Fortas tried to get the newspapers not to print the Walter Jenkins thing in 1964? Can you imagine what would happen if I had tried to get the cops to take Bob Haldeman's name off a police blotter after an offense like that and then tried to get the papers to hush it up?

"No," the political Mitchell might have been thinking, "it's not a dishonorable thing to try to contain a situation, to keep people's lives from being ruined, to keep the opposition from making it into a big mudball. The moralizers have a habit of looking back and saying, 'You should have done this or that,' when you broke the law. Well, Jack Kennedy broke some international law outfitting an invasion of Cuba, and a few hundred men lost their lives—nobody talked of impeaching him for that. And Bobby Kennedy used the Justice Department to get Jimmy Hoffa and Martin Luther King, and nobody's casting aspersions on his memory. And Teddy Kennedy left the scene of an accident, that's a crime, and a life was lost— he's not being impeached or tried for trying to 'cover it up' afterward. For God's sake, put this in some perspective—there, on the spot, at the time, your reaction is to limit your liability, to narrow your losses, to see that nobody else gets hurt, that this relatively little thing doesn't become a weapon to upset and reverse the will of the people, and to ruin a good President who was not at fault."

I'm mind-reading there, not quoting from anything Mitchell said to me. In all, it is not a very good case to explain away the obstruction of justice, but probably was what went through John Mitchell's mind as he sat alone in his apartment in 1973 with a bottle of Scotch, going broke on lawyers' fees, reading about his mentally shaken wife's latest phone calls. He saw himself, surely, as a man who did his duty, who was unfortunately lax in letting somebody else come in and run what should have been his show, who did his best to ameliorate the effects of a bad break (the "cover-up"), and who, when the chips were down, decided not to try to save his own skin by blaming it on somebody else, but manfully absolved the President from any participation whatsoever and so ran the risk of ruin and jail.

Nixon, whose taped decision not to "second-guess Mitchell" was the last straw that brought down his Presidency, is not especially grateful. He remembers that little of this would have stuck to him had it not been for John Dean, who was one of Mitchell's men, and he thinks—I'm guessing again—that Mitchell should have had the good sense not to take chances like that for so little potential gain (the 1969–70 wiretaps and 1971 plumbers' operations, in Nixon's mind, were for a noble motive and excusable).

The rise and fall of Mitchell, and the varying relationship he had with Nixon over a brief five-year span, tells a lot about people's perceptions of men in Government. When he was seen by too many stereotypists as only "the heavy," the anti-black Southern Strategist who would repress the downtrodden, he was also "the rock" on some good, progressive projects and the steadier of the ship on some good appointments. When he was seen as "the new Mitchell," in late '70, as the old pro who would never conduct a campaign the way Nixon did, and the fine fellow with that remarkable wife, he was also signing bundles of wiretap authorizations (which he could not remember afterward), making a disastrous recommendation on a judge, and bemusedly watching his wife's public adulation send her 'round the bend. And when he reappeared as the heavy in 1973, condemned by the right-minded, righteous, and right-wingers for being both stupid the year before and unable to grasp the enormity of what had happened after it had all come out—then, perhaps, he deserved a little understanding along with the scorn.

On a personal level, I can say, "He was always nice to me," before adding, "but the son of a bitch bugged my telephone." Similarly, one can say, "He helped the President reach his most courageous foreign policy decisions in the Jordan crisis and in Cambodia," and "He had a lot to do with electing Nixon in the first place," before adding, "but he did not understand why public men are given public trust," and "He thought the nation's chief law office was above the law." Allowing room for these ambivalencies, some judgments can be made about his relationship with his former law partner:

Mitchell was wrong too often. He was unconcerned with the details of administration that can make or break an Administration. He began to believe his press notices about toughness and tried to live up to them, and then tried to change them too late. He lived in a world of us-against-them, and saw opponents as implacable enemies, reinforcing this tendency in the President and having it reinforced by him. Mitchell's candidate, his rocket ship and his undoing, Richard Nixon, at first tried to loyally lock arms, and then—in 1973—to make him the scapegoat. As Mitchell might explain it, Nixon was not disloyal to a friend soon enough—but when the President tried to jettison him belatedly, Mitchell fought back. Nixon's original assessment of Mitchell was correct—he was a "heavyweight"—not quick enough to block a blow, too proud to take a dive, too ready to make his own rules.

2. THE CAMPAIGN THAT NEVER WAS

Playwright Arthur Miller, in an unnoticed speech in support of George McGovern entitled "Politics as Theatre," cued the closing curtain for his chosen candidate with this line: "We are not casting the Moses to lead us out of the desert, but the chief officer of a bank in which we are all depositors."

That was sound political analysis. If the nation were in a depression, the Democratic candidate's moralistic fervor and promise of the redistribution of wealth might well have caught fire, but 1972 was a time of prosperity. Unemployment was coming down, and it is always the trend rather than the level of unemployment that has a newsworthy and political effect; politicians are less fearful of the votes of the actually unemployed than the votes of the many more who are worried about losing their jobs. Inflation? Recognized as a problem by the Ins only because not to do so would seem callous, but inflation was far less rampant in the United States than in other industrial societies throughout the world, and thanks to a recession-induced rise in productivity in the early Nixon years, the standard of living of the average worker was once again on the rise. The political truth is that candidates are rarely beaten by inflation, the bad by-product of good times, but are often beaten by recession, the correction of inflation.

Moreover, Americans wanted stability after years of shocks—"not experiment, but equipoise" as Harding would have bloviated—and that is what Nixon was giving them, not what McGovern promised them. Respect, dignity, competence, confidence, and the fact of peace rather than the talk of peace—most of "our boys" had come home and the draft was ending—that is what Nixon offered "four more years" of, not the graduate students' delight that passed for a Democratic Convention.

Yet there was something else Miller had written that sent a chill through the few of us in the White House who read it: "If Mr. Nixon produces one fundamental effect it is his defensiveness, his caution, even his suspiciousness. Of course he speaks of confidence and bids us to share it, but this in theatre is what we call acting against the words. The human truth is not in what he is saying but what his body and soul are doing and it is the latter—the actor rather than the script, which penetrates to the people."

If by "acting against the words" Miller meant that Nixon did not mean what he was saying, then that was the standard "you can't trust him" charge and unimportant. But what was provocative was the possibility that Miller sensed that Nixon did mean what he said, but that a subconscious message came through at the same time. In politics, was the actor more important than the script? As a scriptwriter, I had to hope not, but I was aware that when Nixon was standing up there saying what was right with America, exuding confidence, he was also getting across an indelible impression that he darkly suspected all that was wrong with America, and we had all better watch out for "them."*

Such intimations are set aside by the affirmative person with "I guess somebody just walked over my grave" and forgotten. For the truth was that the play was the thing, not just the actor, and Richard Nixon was producer, director, star, and—above all—author (of his scenario, if not his actual script). The "campaign of 1972" is not contained in this chapter, any more than the campaign was in the motions Nixon went through in the fall of '72. The chapters in the New Majority section—the appeals to the Catholics, the Jews, the workingmen—tell about the real campaign, to which was added the perfectly timed foreign policy achievements in the spring of 1972. Nixon's last campaign was his least campaign. He had "come up to speed," in the latest bit of early-radio jargon around the White House, and was now cruising in.

Nixon deserved to win big. Many of the people who criticized him as a matter of course were confronted by the need to say "compared to what?" and Nixon was the better choice. Personalities aside—forget Arthur Miller —Nixon had earned his re-election, for several reasons:

—He had delivered on most of his promises, to cool down the country, to "end the war," to restore "respect for America." And, as sternly promised, he had appointed a new Attorney General.

—He delivered, too, on the more intangible promise of "only Nixon could have." He had withdrawn from overextended positions and commitments in the world without abdicating responsibility or losing the world's respect; we remained a "great power"; and as the head of such, Nixon was able to achieve agreements and begin processes that would have been considered the wildest kind of "campaign oratory" if he had promised them four years before. That is generally accepted; not yet understood amid power-grab evidence is the way that administrative power in domestic affairs began to be redirected, as promised, away from Washington and back to localities, which "only Nixon" was inclined to do. His reputation as a

---

* Miller was author of "After the Fall," which inspired my lawyer-agent, Morton Janklow, with the title of this book.

hard-liner and tough guy helped him achieve the former; his position as a moderate and centrist enabled him to begin the latter.

—He aggressively asserted the will of the people. This is what gets the dander up of many who say he held the people in contempt, or that he pandered to the worst instincts, or darker side, of the American people. The "worst instincts" are often the attack term for the values and ideals of the majority that are not held by the minority—and the majority does not merely reign, the majority rules in a democratic system. Nixon was tuned in, instinctively and intellectually, to his new majority and here was where Nixon fused together all three of his psyches—as person, partisan, and President. He sensed the spirit of powerlessness, alienation—the resentment at being pushed around—in "folks," and moved to show more respect for the majority's feelings. His position on busing was not a crass and unnecessary exacerbation of tension, but a response to a feeling of good, unbigoted people that they were being pushed too far too fast.

As Barry Goldwater was Lyndon Johnson's gift of the gods, George McGovern was Richard Nixon's. McGovern's essential message was "I'm 'them.'"

Because McGovern made it possible to etch the contrast most sharply, all Nixon men were rooting for him to be the Democratic candidate through the primaries. Did "dirty tricks" played by Donald Segretti throw him his victory? Of course not; he earned it, Muskie blew it, and to rewrite history otherwise would be a dirty trick in itself. Early in the year, when McGovern was a forlorn hope, I would run into campaign director Frank Mankiewicz at a dinner party, and he would complain that the Republicans were firing all their blasts at the other Democrats, why not McGovern? I would do my best to slip in a publicity-giving shot at McGovern from time to time, but like the pundits, none of us in the White House thought he had much of a chance.

Neither did Nixon. He thought, after Muskie faltered, he might be running against Hubert Humphrey, and when that campaigner missed his chance, the President sent him a private, handwritten note that shows Nixon was not a superpartisan all the time (or he never really considered Humphrey one of "them"):

July 15, 1972

Dear Hubert,

As your party's convention
comes to an end I know
how deep your disappointment
must be.

You can take comfort in
the fact that through the
years you have earned the
respect of your opponents
as well as your supporters
for being a gallant warrior

As I am sure you will
recall after Churchill's defeat
in 1945 his wife tried to
console him by saying
that maybe it was a "blessing in disguise

Churchill answered – "If
this is a blessing it is certainly
very well disguised."
   You must feel as
he did. But like him –
you have many years
of service ahead.
   As friendly opponents
in the political arena
I hope we can both
serve our parties in a
way that will best
serve the nation
                Sincerely
                RN

Pat joins me in sending
our best to Muriel & to you.

Haldeman, overreacting to Mitchell's criticism of the 1970 midterm campaign ("like he's running for sheriff") wanted Nixon to be so far above the battle as to be out of it, emulating Lyndon Johnson's 1964 tactic of having his Vice President, Humphrey, appear to run against the Republican Presidential candidate, Goldwater. After the Democratic convention Larry Higby (even Haldeman was above the battle) sent this request:

HIGH PRIORITY

August 7, 1972

MEMORANDUM FOR: BILL SAFIRE

FROM: L. HIGBY

Now that the dust has settled, the opposition Vice Presidential candidate picked, and the opposition candidate making it clear what his line of attack is going to be, Bob asked that you put together a *brief* memo that lists your thoughts as to what our four best issues will be for the fall campaign, and what the opposition candidate's four worst issues are—i.e., the things *we* want to hit him on.

Then, put yourself in the role of the opposition candidate and looking at it from his point of view, list what you feel are his four best issues and what our four worst issues are from his viewpoint or the issues he will be hitting us on.

Please forward your thoughts by 2:00 p.m. Tuesday, August 8th.

Here was my reply, which summed up what I thought then and do now —although there had been a break-in at Democratic headquarters and Larry O'Brien was doing what he could to make a big thing of it, I was fairly certain it was no campaign issue. I was right; after a flurry of publicity, it died before Election Day. These were the real issues:

August 9, 1972.

MEMORANDUM FOR: LARRY HIGBY

FROM: BILL SAFIRE (dictated from London)

RE: Campaign Issues

A. *Our Best (Positive)*
  1. Nixon will bring peace that will last.
  2. Nixon stands for the values most Americans believe in.
  3. Nixon stopped the rise of crime and disorder.
  4. Nixon is bringing about prosperity in peacetime.

B. *Opposition's Worst (Negative)*
  1. That's your money they want to redistribute.
  2. They would appease their way into another war.
  3. They represent only the extremes and not the majority.
  4. Millions of investors in stock market securities would suffer if they won.

C. *Opposition's Best (Positive)*
  1. The average man will get a better deal through tax reform.
  2. The war would end right away.
  3. A spirit of compassion would bring the country together.
  4. They would change priorities to spend money on people and not war machines.

D. *Our Worst (Negative)*
  1. Nixon the captive of special interests and fat cats.
  2. Nixon's secret war chest conceals embarrassing donations.
  3. Nixon broke his promises on the war and is strictly an opportunist without principle.
  4. Nixon has shown he doesn't give a damn about the cities.

As it developed—or did not develop—the Nixon noncampaign of 1972 posed some amusing problems. McGovern was vulnerable on having supported Henry Wallace in 1948, after that former Vice President had bolted the Democratic Party and ran as an independent against Harry Truman. It was important to McGovern that he persuade Democrats now not to bolt, and this 1948 Wallace third-party activity could hurt him. But we knew that a portion of Eugene McCarthy's strength in New Hampshire against Johnson in 1968 came from people mistaking him for Senator Joe McCarthy—on that analogy, would not attacking McGovern for supporting Henry Wallace in 1948 be interpreted by some as his having been for George Wallace? It is to laugh, right? Wrong. Nixon's managers laid off the Wallace thing after they thought about it.

With that sort of silly problem engaging too many minds, it occurred to Ray Price, John Ehrlichman, and me that this campaign might be a good opportunity to go back to the technique so successful in 1968—the thoughtful radio address—for an articulation of the President's position on a variety of issues. We were clobbering McGovern so unmercifully on defense policy, welfare (his baby bonus of $1,000 was a good populist try, but it gave too many experts a chance for a day in the spotlight to denounce it), and the "competence" issue, that I wanted to use the campaign to get us off and running into the second term. Besides, like most Old Nixon Hands, I felt out of it; the campaign was something going on across the street and down the block, well organized, humming along, frighteningly well financed, detached. My only real contribution to the committee had been a recommendation to stress Nixon's incumbency in its title. When Jeb Magruder came into my office in late 1971, the President had not yet publicly chosen Agnew as his running mate again. (He had made his mind up in September and was prepared to say so in a press conference for three months but nobody had asked him.) Magruder said, "We can't call it 'Citizens for Nixon-Agnew' because that announces Agnew, and we can't call it 'Citizens for Nixon,' because that will be seen as throwing Agnew overboard, so what do we call the committee?" I remembered the 1966 Rockefeller campaign in New York, when the slogan was "Governor Rockefeller for Governor" ("It's either that," press aide Harry O'Donnell had argued, "or Nelson Rockefeller for Nelson.") and I suggested, simply, the Committee to Re-elect the President. "That's the best you can do?" Magruder inquired. I started to remind him that I was charging clients $90,000 a year for advice when he was selling pancake makeup for a local cosmetics house, but then I thought for a moment: any acronym problem? You always have to watch that. C, R, P. Democrats would have to try to stick an "A" in there to make fun of it, which would be in bad taste and they wouldn't try that; if you made it C, R, E, P, using the "election" as a non-hyphenated capital, you would have a french pancake, and that's even too effete for snobs. It would be safe, solid, and stress the incumbency. And so CREEP was created.

Labor Day was selected for the first of the radio speeches, and I wrote it during the convention in Miami to draw the contrast between the programs and the attitudes of the two candidates, stressing the difference between the now-familiar "work ethic" and my new "welfare ethic," launched for the occasion. The President agreed to begin using the word "paternalism" in his acceptance speech, and to make it part of his stump speech, such as it was, because there was an identifiable difference between the paternalistic and the individualistic way of governance. Besides, "paternalism" was the perfect "ism"—everybody was against it, from kids who didn't like their fathers telling them what to do, to union fathers who didn't like companies telling them how to live.

The most important speech on his political philosophy, which Nixon delivered on October 21, 1972, was directed to a radio audience and a press corps that was not buying philosophy that year. James Reston of the New York *Times* spotted it, saw it as essential Nixon, and devoted some space to it a couple of times. Nixon worked hard on that speech. "In certain campaigns," he told me as we started to polish it, "only programs separate the candidates. But in this one, we're more apart on philosophy—and a man's philosophy determines how he will decide something that's not currently before us. I dictated some of this to Rose, she'll show you."

He suggested I take a crack at "this elitist business," and continued: "You know, that's why they don't like the ethnics, the people who use poor grammar—they believe that all that's required for leadership is education, but of course that's wrong. Leadership requires character, and too much education today destroys character. Fortunately," the President added as an aside, "I had a good education, but that didn't keep me from understanding 'folks.' " I said I didn't think a hard shot at elitism was called for here. "You mean that's an Agnew word?" He agreed even as he asked the question; his instruction was to explore the leaders' responsibility to reflect the "will of the people" most of the time, and to lead it when a course was chosen that was not "popular." Nixon wanted to get a point in about the arrogance of the educated: "Try this:" he dictated, " 'people who have had the advantage of a superior education think that gives them the right to lead.' Well, the hell with that, education's more of a liability these days." Nixon had come a long way since early 1968 on that subject. As a candidate, he had told his writers then, "I'm a nut on education. Balance the budgets on a lot of things, but when it comes to education, I'm a nut about it. Always voted for education appropriations." But as President, he felt in 1972 that the academy had turned elitist and defeatist, and that the strength of character necessary for leadership could best be found usually in people not exposed to debilitating Establishment thinking. That certainly presents a startling contrast to the picture of a prairie populist versus an Establishment defender which some people had about McGovern and Nixon. Nixon's position on the failures of education would not be seen as populist, but anti-intellectual; not as admiring of the potential of the disadvantaged, but as suspicious of the attainments of the advantaged; I suggested he stay away from it. The point was boiled down in the speech to: "The advantage of a superior education should result in a deep respect for—and never contempt for—the value judgments of the average person."

I sent the President a draft, and received my cover note back with these comments:

THE WHITE HOUSE

WASHINGTON

October 12, 1972

MEMORANDUM FOR THE PRESIDENT

FROM: BILL SAFIRE

RE: 3rd Draft Radio Speech on Political Philosophy

All the changes you inked in the first two drafts are in this. For accuracy, the "hundreds of thousands of demonstrators" do not descend on "Washington," but on the "national leadership," to encompass demonstrations in other cities.

Per your telephone instruction, I added a paragraph rejecting the notion of a leadership class. However, this is done in a muted and upbeat way; the point about elitism and intellectual snobbery can be made without laying you open to charges of being anti-intellectual.

I did not use the "character quotient" idea, because "intelligence quotient" does not refer to a person's education, but to his capacity to learn -- a man denied a high school education can still have a high I.Q. So I didn't think a contrast worked.

You added the word "alien" twice -- repeating an alien philosophy and later an alien paternalism. I suggest "far-out philosophy", leaving alien paternalism at the end.

Red Flag: We could bill this as "the new American majority speech," as it goes into that heavily at the end, but the addition of "American" makes the initials NAM. Big business connotation. Maybe we'd be better off with your acceptance speech phrase -- new majority.

The central idea in the speech was this:

A leader must be willing to take unpopular stands when they are necessary. But a leader who insists on imposing on the people his own idea of how they should live their lives—when those ideas go directly contrary to the values of the people themselves—does not understand the role of a leader in a democracy. When he does find it necessary to take an unpopular stand, the leader has an obligation to explain his stand to the people, solicit their support, and win their approval.

Good questions were raised in that speech by the President. When should a leader lead and when should he follow? How shall the "consent of the governed" be established? Other questions flow from it: Edmund Burke is frequently quoted for his courageous "Your representative owes you, not his industry only, but his judgment; and he betrays instead of serving you if he sacrifices it to your opinion." But Burke lost his next election. Was the father of conservatism too much of an elitist? How can we have egalitarianism reflected in representative government and still make it possible for a minority of one to turn a tide?

In the meantime, Nixon put his foot in it. Talking to Washington *Star* reporter Garnett Horner two days before the election, the man who was on the threshold of inundating paternalism with a landslide at the polls chose exactly the wrong figure of speech in discussing the work ethic: "The average American is just like the child in the family. You give him some responsibility and he is going to amount to something. He is going to do something. If, on the other hand, you make him completely dependent and pamper him and cater to him too much, you are going to make him soft, spoiled, and eventually a very weak individual."

Nixon's groggy critics quite understandably used that to turn the paternalism charge against him. To me, that was a Presidential mistake worse than saying Charles Manson was guilty before he was convicted, or denouncing "these bums . . . blowing up the campuses." The President, as Ron Ziegler liked to put it, misspoke himself; in truth, he zapped himself.

Figures of speech notwithstanding, the perception of rising resentment against elitism, the temporary takeover of the Democratic Party by a minority elite (40 per cent of the convention with postgraduate training v. 4 per cent of the population at large), the deliberate development of social elitism into political paternalism, which then became an object voters could strike down and gain satisfaction therefrom—all this enabled Richard Nixon in 1972 to shake off the "captive of interests" charge, to blast apart the "party of the people" appeal of the opposition, and to build his majority of "folks."

If the reader wants to know the basic approach of Richard Nixon to the business and the art of governing, read the whole October 21, 1972 speech. Though he did not always say all he meant, he meant all he said in that speech and hardly anybody heard. Whose fault? His own, for not considering it a duty to get the message across on prime time television; his countrymen's fault, supporters and critics alike, for not taking the trouble to find out something to upset a few stereotypes or start some thinking.

While this high-domed palaver was going on, so was a Democratic campaign of sorts. The McGovern men later claimed that they lost it really on the Senator Eagleton affair. The revelation that the Vice Presidential candidate had gone through shock treatments for mental depression some years ago, and his subsequent dismissal from the ticket, crippled the momentum of their campaign, they said. Arthur Miller had put it differently: "Our values were tested and the outcome was we could trust a man who might or might not be corrupt, but we could not trust a man who had known despair. It was the kind of test which Warren Gamaliel Harding would have passed with flying colors, but which Abraham Lincoln would certainly have failed." That's dramatic—Miller's a dramatist—but the Eagleton episode touched Nixon, as a man who was once a Vice Presidential candidate himself and who had been told by Tom Dewey just before the 1952 "Checkers speech" to "get off the ticket." Nixon felt that McGovern had done just what the editorial writers of the New York *Times* and Washington *Post* told him to do—caved in on Eagleton, because "the unsophisticated masses" could not be trusted to understand mental problems in a potential leader—which was typical of the weakness of McGovern. Eagleton could have been a wild card in a previously stacked deck—an emotional pull on a great many people who liked scrappy, spunky men— and Nixon thought it was a McGovern political blunder to drop him. Moreover, in the Nixon political morality, abandonment of a close associate was a mortal sin, no matter what the provocation; had Agnew been discovered to have had a history that had required shock treatment, Nixon would have rallied to his side—wrongheaded though that may have been.

Life magazine published a picture of Senator Eagleton with his son, taken the year before on a visit to the President's office, and Nixon reacted with a handwritten letter to the boy:

Personal

THE WHITE HOUSE

WASHINGTON

August 2, 1972

Dear Terry—

When I saw the picture in *Life* a week ago I was reminded of our meeting at the White House when your father introduced you to me after I signed the Construction Safety Bill. I thought you might like to have a copy of the White House Photographer's picture of that meeting.

I realize these past few days have been very difficult ones for you and the members of your family. Speaking as one who understands and respects your father's decision to continue to fight for his party's nominees and against my administrative policies, I would like to pass on to you some strictly personal thoughts with regard to the ordeal your father has undergone.

Politics is a very hard game. Winston Churchill once pointed out that "politics is even more difficult than war, because in politics you die many times; in war you die only once."

But in those words of Churchill we can all take some comfort. The political man can always come back to fight again.

What matters is not that your father fought a terribly difficult battle and lost. What matters is that in fighting the battle he won the admiration of foes and friends alike because of the courage, poise and just plain guts he showed against overwhelming odds.

Few men in public life in our whole history have been through what he has been through. I hope you do not allow this incident to discourage or depress you.

Years later you will look back and say "I am proud of the way my dad handled himself in the greatest trial of his life."

Sincerely

Richard Nixon

P. S. I hope your arms are completely healed

RN

That was a nice thing for Nixon to do, and it was not done for the publicity—there was none. In his reply to the President, Terry Eagleton wrote, "Do you know what my Dad said when he read your letter? He said, 'It's going to make it all the tougher to talk against Nixon.'" That thought might have occurred to the President, but this was no tight campaign where every lever had to be pulled: the gesture was Nixon doing a natural, thoughtful thing, which he did more often than most people realized. (Makes you think, too—which lever did Senator Eagleton pull down in the privacy of that voting booth?)

Warm notes to Humphrey and Eagleton's son, what's going on here? What happened to the old partisan Nixon, to us-against-them? First, as men defeated and scorned by "them," Humphrey and Eagleton became, at least temporarily, the likes of "us." More important, the campaign ended when McGovern won the nomination, and Nixon's attention was more on the Paris peace talks than the opposition candidate's television talks.

The President made some campaign appearances and swings, like the kind of cameo role a top star will play for fun and to keep his hand in, but he turned most of the campaign over to "surrogates." At a Cabinet meeting in July, when someone referred to McGovern's proposed military cuts, the President turned to Defense Secretary Melvin Laird, who had said to some laughter that he intended to make only nonpolitical trips to defense bases telling them what to expect if McGovern won, and Nixon said: "I know one base he'd keep—Portsmouth, New Hampshire. Everyone promises to keep Portsmouth. I promised." The President pointed to HUD Secretary George Romney, who had spent a brief time in 1968 campaigning up there: "You remember, George, we all promised it. It's the most inefficient naval base we've got, but I promised to keep it. Is it any better now, or should we get rid of it—don't answer!" Nixon urged the Cabinet surrogates to refrain from name-calling, but to campaign on the issues and attack what McGovern had said originally, never his corrections; also to refer to "McGovernites," not Democrats; and to expect the media to help McGovern "get well."

I went along on a cameo tour of Westchester, New York, with the roaring tour buses passing the lonely, defiant McGovern signs held by people who seemed frightened by the motorcade's noise; the President stopped the procession at one point, greeted an elderly couple who had a "Welcome, Mr. President" sign, and assured them that there would be no amnesty for draft dodgers, which he felt was a powerful issue and which he was uncompromising about. We wound up in Pocantico Hills, home estate of Nelson Rockefeller, and the two staffs mingled in the Playhouse there. "A tennis court with two fireplaces!" breathed Ziegler, at the elaborate indoor sports facility.

While the Governor and the President went off to reminisce, plot, or fence, I saw an interesting tableau. On the mezzanine overlooking the cathedral-ceilinged entrance hall, framed by an archway, Rose Mary Woods sat talking with Ann Whitman. In the bosoms of those two active, lonely women were reposed just about all the Republican secrets of the past twenty years. Mrs. Whitman had been President Eisenhower's secretary, and after he left the White House, Governor Rockefeller's; Rose had been with Nixon all that time, her relations with Ann Whitman changing with the fluctuations of fortunes of both women's bosses. Both knew what power was, and what losing power felt like; Rose understood the fact that Ann had never been through the political hard knocks, but had entered at the top with Eisenhower, and was sensitive to slights. When Nixon had come to New York in 1963, Ann had come over at night from Rockefeller's office to help Rose answer VIP mail, as a volunteer, until the time when it appeared their two bosses might become competitors again. Because Haldeman knew that Ann Whitman had provided an opportunity for staffers to "end run" Sherman Adams, Rose Mary Woods was blocked from the office that Presidents' secretaries have traditionally used. The two ladies in the archway—intensely loyal, dignified, fiercely secretive—went unobserved by the officious staffs mingling below, but those two keepers of the keys had little in common with them and much in common with each other. (Their paths were to cross again, as Rockefeller's secretary was moving down to Washington as Nixon's was moving out.)

The noncampaign of '72 will be remembered chiefly because of what was going on in the way of furious fund-raising, dirty tricks, break-ins and bugging—all, hard to believe, at the time matters of little import to the Candidate or most of the people in the White House. We will come back to Watergate in a moment—we cannot avoid it—but it may be useful to think of the election of 1972 as having been decided in the Nixon campaign of the previous two years. "The new majority" was already organized; CREEP's campaign was a mopping-up operation, largely ignored by the Candidate and most of his men, who were smugly concentrating on what they could do with the mandate they would surely receive.

All that previous work, the real campaign, paid off. Richard Nixon, who had in 1960 lost by the smallest margin in history, and then won in 1968 by not much more, won this time in a landslide. The political language is wedded to catastrophe: tidal waves of support, prairie-fire and whirlwind campaigns, floods of returns to candidates hoping that lightning will strike, leading to avalanches and landslides, and all were used to describe the success of the campaign that never was. Even Barry Goldwater in 1964 won five states; even Alf Landon in 1936 won two; McGovern was reduced to Massachusetts and the District of Columbia, and whatever critics had said about Nixon's strategy over the past four years, it had worked. The people were with him. McGovern helped, but there are those of us who think a more centrist Democratic candidate would have lost by half as much—which would still have been a resounding Nixon victory.

When *Newsweek* columnist Stewart Alsop, flying to the Republican Convention with Nixon, asked the President what he would do and how he would conduct the Presidency without the impetus of another election facing him, Nixon disappointed him. He did not rise to the occasion in the way Alsop thought he might. I suggested the President come back to that point, and this is the way the President answered Alsop in his October 21 address: "A few weeks ago, one of the Nation's most perceptive journalists asked me what I thought it would be like to be a second-term President— free to govern with no thought of another election. Actually, he was asking one of the deepest questions of all: Would I do what I thought was best for the people, or would I do what the people thought was best for themselves?

"Fortunately, what the new majority wants for America, and what I want for this Nation basically are the same.

"But a profound question deserves a thoughtful answer.

"In the years to come, if I am returned to office, I shall not hesitate to take the action I think necessary to protect and defend this Nation's best interests, whether or not those actions meet with wide popular approval. I will not begin at this stage of my life to shy away from making hard decisions which I believe are right.

"At the same time, you can be certain of this: On matters affecting basic human values—on the way Americans live their lives and bring up their children—I am going to respect and reflect the opinion of the people themselves. That is what democracy is all about."

That fairly hifalutin' way of phrasing it reflected the Nixon view of what a President must do. What Nixon actually said to Alsop, however, was not only more Nixon-like in expression but illustrates some self-knowledge. It summarizes his enormously successful but disastrously

detached noncampaign, and indicates a reason for his forthcoming mal-
treatment of victory:

"It's always good to have the whip on your back."

In a few weeks, Nixon would lash out at the losers, in an unbecoming
display of temper at not being credited properly with making peace; in a
few months, they would come back at him with a flaming sword and cut
all his victories away.

After the election, however, the re-elected Nixon called in his staff and
spoke with them warmly and gratefully. That meeting in the Roosevelt
Room on November 8 was reported as a session in which he coldly
cleaned house, but the mood was considerably different from that.

"I have been very proud of this staff, which has been accused of lots of
things," the President said. "The charge most often heard has been that it
is efficient. We can plead guilty to that." He spoke of the forthcoming
difficulties with an opposition Congress, and asked us all to think about
our futures in or out of Government: "Everybody here as he examines his
office, should go at it with the feeling that there are no sacred cows. We
will tear up the peapatch in the Cabinet, not in terms of individuals but
in terms of the Cabinet as an institution. Now is the chance to clear out
the dead wood without having to pander to bureaucrats who say we had a
razor-thin margin."

President Nixon had an affirmative, youthful look about him that day,
a far cry from the bleary-eyed victor of four years ago. "I expect that we
will have a much more productive four years ahead," he predicted. "I expect there are those who say, 'Leave everything as it is.'" There were those
dopey "those whos" again—wrong as usual. "That was the mistake of the
second Eisenhower Administration. Change is necessary. Perhaps Presidents shouldn't serve more than four years—I am not ready to advocate
that until the end of this term." Small chuckle, then he turned to his favorite Prime Minister:

"Disraeli, at the age of sixty-eight, became Prime Minister for the second
time, defeating Gladstone after Gladstone's enormous success in reform-
ing the British Government. Disraeli's description of Gladstone was 'an
exhausted volcano.' That's true, in life, in sports, in politics. After a burst
of creative activity we become exhausted volcanoes . . . It is the responsibility of a leader, despite our victories, to see that we not climb to the top
and look over the embers that once shot their sparks up into the sky." He
was waxing a little grandiloquent here, hooked by his historical allusion,
but he wanted to say hail and farewell to many of us in as nice a way as he
could. He would not personally fire anybody, but many members of the
staff would be moved out into the agencies, leaving, he hoped, a leaner,
more manageable White House staff. "What would you like to do?" he
asked us. "Whatever you decide, we will always regard the people in this
room as members of the first team. You made possible what was recorded
last night, but it happened long before." He was right about that. When
the President left, having acted against the words, Haldeman stepped in to

do some dirty work—asking for the written resignations. Henry Kissinger slipped out at that point, murmuring, "I have already submitted my resignation in German, the adjectives are at the end." Haldeman, alertly, reminded him, "It's the verbs that belong at the end, Henry—you don't even know how to construct a German sentence." Then Haldeman, who would not have the chance to do this when his own moment of departure unexpectedly came so soon afterward, bid farewell to his compatriots in a modest and moving way: "This is a unique White House staff. There has been a sense of teamwork and dedication to the man and the cause that has been beyond belief. It may be presumptuous of me to say this, but I want to thank you for the chance to work with you."

3. BIZARRE INCIDENT

Waiting for the President to come into that hail-and-farewell meeting the morning after 1972's Election Day, Henry Kissinger turned to Peter Flanigan, who had just said something about the McGovern ineptitude and joked: "If McGovern had kept after the Watergate, he would have made wiretapping popular." There was an appreciative chuckle at Henry's remark from the whole staff; the break-in at Democratic headquarters must have been one of those madcap escapades that some low-level crazies tried to pull off, which Democratic chairman Larry O'Brien tried to exploit and dismally failed. Even the Washington *Post* had given up beating that dead horse, and in the final weeks before the election, dropped the story completely.

The "cover-up," as it was later called, had temporarily worked; the blunder had been retrieved. It had all cooled off, the election was over, and things were working out. Then Federal Judge John J. Sirica started handing down provisional sentences of thirty-five years in jail. Men who thought they had a deal with a well-paid year of incarceration suddenly saw themselves locked up for life with the keys thrown away, and Watergate started to unravel.

But it was not as simple as that. "If only" does not apply. If there had not been a botched-up break-in at Democratic headquarters, there surely would have been another Watergate, another incident that would have exposed the train of crimes done under the guise of "national security" or "domestic security" or just plain security. The illegal snooping train had left the station in early 1969, and could not be recalled; the process would have surely come to light sooner or later, and its ultimate revelation did not depend upon a single unlucky break or aberration.

Watergate has come to mean the Nixon Administration's illegal wiretapping, illegal surveillance, illegal burglary: the government's unlawful use of the law. Events in the chain: the use of illegal FBI wiretaps against Administration officials and newsmen in 1969 through 1971; the jobs assigned to private detective Jack Caulfield and others to break into columnist Joseph Kraft's home, and perhaps others; the employment of the "plumbers" group, headed by Egil Krogh and David Young, employing Hunt and Liddy and the group of Cuban-Americans, to break into the files of Daniel Ellsberg's psychiatrist; the series of break-ins at Watergate Democratic headquarters and anything else planned along those lines during the Democratic Convention; the obstruction of justice called the "cover-up."

Watergate as a label, ought not to include "dirty tricks," coercive fund-raising, or charges involving ITT, milk lobbyists, and grain dealers—all, if they are scandals, scandals of a different nature and magnitude. "Watergate" is conscious Government policy to break the law in the belief that the perversion of civil liberty is necessary to uphold the civil order or the political regime.

Whose fault was Watergate? Nixon's, of course, but that is not said as if his assumption of guilt makes him a brave and responsible—though not really guilty—executive. Nixon's own decisions brought Watergate about, and there is no tiptoeing away from that. The root decision to put in the wiretaps on newsmen was his, with Kissinger, Haig, Mitchell, Ehrlichman, and Haldeman right with him. The approval of the Huston burglary proposal was Nixon's; the motivation of Krogh to "get" Ellsberg was Nixon's. Richard Nixon put the rock in the snowball with the wiretaps, packed it firmly with snow with his approval of the Huston plan, rolled it along the ground with the Ellsberg motivation, and watched it go over the rise of the hill, Hunt and Liddy trotting alongside. From that point on, it was out of his hands. That loud crash when the snowball, by now an unstoppable monster, hit the glass doors of an office building may not have been the President's doing; he was not guilty of all those crimes; but they were all his fault.

Why? Who needed it? How could he have been so stupid? What did they possibly hope to gain? The reason why most people at the White House did not "know" about the train of illegal events was because it was held to a group that could keep a secret: perhaps a dozen men, plus the FBI (which is not a sieve when leakage does not serve its purpose).

The reason why most people at the White House, and most others as well, did not believe the Watergate break-in at Democratic headquarters was White House-controlled was because it appeared to be for such a stupid purpose: Larry O'Brien's phone? At such risk? By such dunderheads? To anybody not in the know about the meaning of the presence of Hunt and Liddy (graduates of the plumbers operation) the act defied logic; it was ludicrous; it was too horrible to contemplate; *ergo*, it must have been an aberration of some fools.

Those relative few who did know about Hunt's and Liddy's previous bag jobs, including the President and Haldeman and Ehrlichman, put two and two together the moment the headquarters break-in fiasco made news. They did know that those were "our boys" in the clink.

Nixon never made a "decision" to cover up the Watergate burglary any more than Truman made a decision to drop the A-Bomb on Hiroshima; both were the natural result of decisions that had been made before them. In Nixon's case, a decision could have been made to condemn Mitchell, Magruder, Haldeman, and everybody connected with the break-in, but that would have meant exposing the previous work of the plumbers which would also go clear back to the wiretaps of newsmen. Unless one were to decide that the entire chain was reprehensible, which Nixon was obviously not prepared to do, then there was no decision to be made other than to "cover-up." That is hard to understand in retrospect, when we can see that the Presidency hung on his "decision" when confronted by the news of the participation of his top staff in the break-in; and there can be no doubt at all about the wrongness of his action in both moral and tactical terms. In context, however, the cover-up was the logical, inevitable next step in the terrible procession, and it worked—at least, for about eight months.

Let us linger awhile at the moment of falsity. With good reason to suspect the worst of your most loyal supporters, who are only doing it for you, how do you react? In similar circumstances, would Harry Truman have turned on Harry Vaughan, Dwight Eisenhower on Sherman Adams, John Kennedy on Robert Kennedy, Lyndon Johnson on Bobby Baker or Walter Jenkins or Marvin Watson? In at least a couple of cases, they might have reacted as Nixon did, wincing and not wanting to know all the grisly details, "correctly" telling the investigators to pursue their investigations—angry at stupidity but grateful for past services rendered, doing the least legally possible and hoping for the best, taking refuge in the knowledge that other Presidents have gone through much the same worries with the men closest to them. In political real life, one does not necessarily put one's life on the line to protect a supporter, but one does not often climb on rectitude's high horse to prosecute him to the fullest extent of the law. Most things like this are forgotten. When it came out that Sherman Adams was deeply in trouble with Internal Revenue in 1961 for great wads of income taken in the Fifties, President Kennedy checked with General Ike, who got old friends to raise the money to bail Adams out of trouble; over Internal Revenue's objection, no prosecution was undertaken, and none of it surfaced for a decade. Things often blow over; don't panic; that's what people on the scene often think. Should they? Was Nixon remiss? Of course they should not, and of course he was. But not many people try to put themselves in his shoes, to understand—they want to justify all their past suspicions, or put as much distance as possible between themselves and their past leader by being more Catholic than the Pope.

Nixon's mistake, at that moment of falsity, was in putting political loyalty—first to Mitchell, later to Haldeman and Ehrlichman—ahead of his oath of office. His instinctive reaction was to obstruct the FBI investigation by using the CIA not just out of loyalty, but because Nixon had so much of his own to hide in earlier, related plumbings and tappings. He made an unforgivable decision in moral terms, then compounded it in tactical terms: first, by recording his lawbreaking, and second, by not destroying the tapes before they had become evidence.

A fearful symmetry becomes apparent. The savage protection of secrets led to the shattering of Presidential confidentiality; the cover-up of the Watergate entry resulted in Nixon being naked to his enemies. In hindsight, a pattern of consistency on Nixon's part emerges: all he did in the next two years, from firing Archibald Cox to falsely pleading executive privilege before the Supreme Court, were the actions of a man striving to protect the telltale tapes from the eyes of investigators. Those who believed Nixon did not "know," myself included, focused on the ultimate "big" cover-up—the payment of hush money to Howard Hunt, which Nixon was ambiguous about—and not on the initial "little" cover-up, obstructing the FBI investigation, which the tape of June 23, 1972, revealed Nixon as a participant. And no Nixon supporter, True Believer like Buchanan or moderate and loyalist like Len Garment, would have dreamed that the President could lie consistently to the American people over an eighteen-month period—and especially in the knowledge that the proof of his lying might someday be produced.

Nixon never gave any thought, after the initial break-in, to blowing the whistle on his men. Here was his press briefing book, prepared by Pat Buchanan on the basis of ignorance of the facts in the matter, for June 19, 1972, with the President's notes on it:

-3-

[handwritten annotations across top: "He understated" ... "Bigger business" ... "alleged" ... "at everybody"]

Q: Sir: Would you agree with Mr. Ziegler that this is only a "third-rate burglary?"

A: The thrust of Mr. Ziegler's remarks, with which I fully agree,

is that a White House briefing in Florida is not the proper forum to

be making judgments about an alleged breaking-and-entering in

Washington, D. C. I agree with that. Nor do I think it is the business

of the President of the United States to be characterizing criminal

charges made in a District Court.

Q: Sir: Have you talked with Mr. Colson about this matter or with
the former Attorney General or Mr. Ehrlichman?

A: Gentlemen, the information about this matter has come to me

in the same way as other information. There is no extraordinary

channel set up; there is no special White House investigation of this

matter. The matter is being handled by the proper authorities; and I

have no further comment upon it.

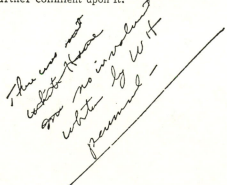

[handwritten note: "There was not what the gave no involvement white by WH personnel —"]

His immediate inclination, obviously, was to go even further than Ron Ziegler in characterizing the break-in at the Watergate as a "third-rate burglary," to saying, "He understated it—bizarre business—*attempt* at burglary." Then the President wrote for himself: "There was no involvement whatever by White House personnel."

By the time the President worked on his October 3, 1972, briefing book, he was taking the offensive, noting:

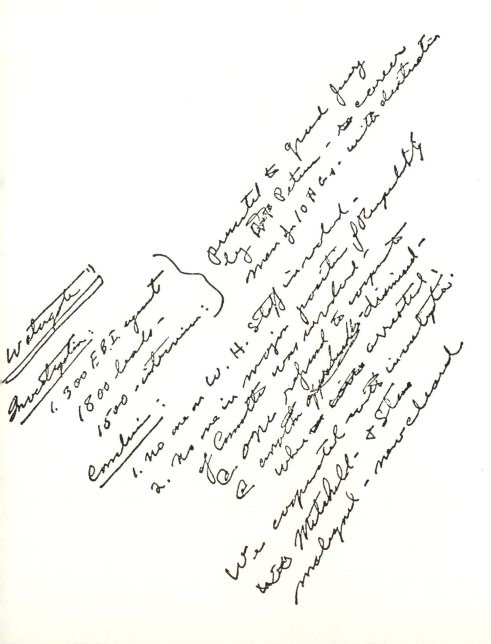

Watergate

Investigation

1. 300 FBI agents	Presented to grand jury
1800 leads	by Petersen - career
1500 interviews	man for 10 AGs - with distinction

Conclusion

1. No one in W. H. Staff involved

2. No one in major position of responsibility
   of committee was involved
          one refused to cooperate
          another dismissed
          when arrested

We cooperated with investigation/Mitchell - & Stans maligned - now cleared

Then—still Oct. 2, 1972—Nixon stepped up the offensive, collecting all the charges made against him, and, by exaggerating, minimizing them. Plate 22, following page 632, shows how he wrote out his defense against charges of corruption, which are set in type here:

Corrupt?

Charges:

1. Most corrupt administration in history

2. President compared with Hitler

3. Policies of U.S. under 3 Presidents to prevent Communist take over—equated with Nazi extermination of Jews

4. President who initiated new relationsip with S.U., P.R.C. is #1 war-maker most deceitful

I shall not dignify any charges by answering or comment

I happened to have the foregoing notes because Pat Buchanan, who ordinarily prepared the press briefing book, had a death in the family in March 1973 and I was asked to substitute for him. In doing that job, the briefer was supposed to anticipate all the likely questions, ask the various agencies and staffers to submit suggested answers, and then rewrite those answers in one hundred words or less. Nearing deadline, I found myself bogged down in questions and answers on the Vietnam cease-fire, unable to do justice to the few possible questions on Watergate, which was a dead issue anyway, I thought. Through Richard Moore, I asked John Dean for his updated Q and A on Watergate; it was run past John Ehrlichman and came to me in the form which you can see on Plate 21. The Nixon handwriting on that plate reads:

> Welcome a fair — objective investigation even handed — [illegible] of both parties

> We cooperated with grand jury — F.B.I. will cooperate with hearings, within guidelines for privilege — I shall answer [illegible]

> [illegible] unfortunate — did not follow Ethics of equal representation

> one party investigates other — glad to see Senator Ervin intends to avoid partisan[ship] & investigate both parties

Q: Sir: Will White House staff members be permitted to testify, or will you invoke executive privilege?

A: This subject will be fully covered in my policy statement-on

Executive privilege to be released this week. If there are requests

for appearances by White House staff members, these will be considered

in accordance with the guidelines contained in that statement. These

guidelines will also reflect the traditional practice of past Administration.

(Note: If the statement on Executive privilege has not yet been issued, it could still be referred to as a basis for the same answer as above.)

(Moore/Dean/JE)

Another page from the briefing book, with Nixon's handwriting:

Q: Sir: Are you still confident that there was no White House involvement by Mr. Chapin or anyone else in the Watergate affair or the espionage-sabotage operations?

A: Mr. Dean's report concluded that no one currently in the White

House (and that included Mr. Chapin) was connected in any way with the

Watergate incident. That conclusion still stands, and you will note it

was not contradicted in any other proceeding, such as the FBI investigation,

the grand jury investigation or the trial itself. As to the media reports

of alleged political espionage and sabotage, Mr. Ziegler has responded

to those on a number of occasions and I stand by what he said.

(Moore/Dean/JE)

I glanced at the answers, found them short enough, did not bother to rewrite them or ask a lot of other questions, and so—with thanks to the angel on my shoulder—avoided a brush with cover-up. Later, whenever the question "Did the President know?" was raised, I thought of that briefing book entry, as the President was systematically informed by his counsel that nobody in the White House was involved. Of course, Nixon did know from Haldeman, and probably Mitchell, at the start—the irony was that the middle level was keeping it from him, and he would make that long delay of John Dean in telling him about the "cancer on the Presidency" the keystone of his defense.

So Richard Nixon, who had hung tough in Vietnam and achieved the peace he sought "with honor"; who had hung tough at the Moscow summit and was rewarded with what seemed then like a good SALT agreement; hung tough once again on Watergate and hung himself. There have been plenty of books about Watergate, the most offensive of which was the transcript of the Presidential tapes; the reader who wants to take instruction from the way President Nixon disgraced himself has ready access to mountains of material and needs no more from me. One point, though, to show how Nixon played out his string: an hour before Nixon went on television to resign the Presidency, quoting Theodore Roosevelt's "man in the arena . . . who fails while daring greatly," I had dinner with a couple of White House lawyers who had spent the final week urging Nixon to step down. Since the President had replayed the tapes three months before—well in advance of the House Judiciary Committee's hearings— why, wondered one lawyer, hadn't the President told his attorneys and made that information public earlier, rather than at the worst possible moment? The other lawyer said that he had put that very question to the President, who had replied: "If it breaks it all up now, it would have broken it all up three months ago."

Nixon's last year in office was spent playing for time, hoping for a break, delaying as long as he could, always living with the knowledge that his guilt could be established, thinking he was watching a bad movie, and saying to himself, "Wait—it'll get better," as it got worse.

Why did Nixon permit the tapings of himself in the first place? Because he was convinced left-leaning historians would try to deny him his place in history; because he wanted to write memoirs better than Churchill's; and because he was sure he would have the same total control of his tapes as Kennedy and Johnson had of theirs.

Why didn't he destroy them when Alex Butterfield revealed their existence to the Ervin Committee? Because Nixon thought that such an act would make him look guilty, because he did not realize how bad the tapes' transcripts would appear in cold print, and because he was certain the wall of Presidential privacy could not be breached. Although it might not have been "destruction of evidence" since the tapes were not then subpoenaed, and although a rationale could have been put forth for the protection of a President's private conversations, the public burning of the tapes would have been a confession of guilt, and guilt is one thing Nixon never has admitted.

To this day, Nixon cannot understand why he was pilloried for acts that he considers no different than those condoned by his predecessors, from "bag jobs" by the FBI to wiretaps and to spying on political campaigns (1964 and 1968 leap quickly to his mind). And the actual decision that brought him down—to use the CIA to block the FBI investigation of the Watergate break-in—was, he still feels, a legitimate act to prevent disclosure of related national security surveillances.

If only he had not been forced to conceal the other "horrors"; if only he had not made it possible for his pursuers to prove him guilty with the poetic justice of his tapes; if only, if only. In time, the grisly deception will be seen in the light of great achievements, but those who invested their lives in the causes he shared will never forget that Nixon failed, not while daring greatly, but while lying meanly.

This book deals with Nixon before the fall. For a time after his re-election, Watergate was not even a shadow on his mandate. He had bigger things to think about than third-rate attempted burglaries. Nixon had a long-postponed rendezvous with peace.

4. CHRISTMAS BOMBS

Working in the White House, you sometimes find out big things in little ways.

The President and Henry Kissinger were meeting at Camp David a few weeks after the election and pessimism was pervading the reports out of Paris. One could feel the doves getting ready for an all-out assault on Nixon's "duplicity" of promising "peace is at hand" just before an election, and then backing away from it after the landslide.

I had one of the hard-to-find sets of *Messages and Papers of the Presidents*, from Washington through Hoover, which sat on my office bookshelf and was available to the researchers whenever they needed it. One of research chief Ann Morgan's new recruits poked her head in my office and asked to borrow some of the *Messages and Papers*. As she started to stagger out with eight volumes in her arms, I asked what she was looking for.

"I need to find out what previous Presidents have said when peace came. Ray Price needs it for a statement."

A "Peace Speech" was in the works; that was good to know. But then, between Election Day and the end of 1972, negotiations seemed to go from bad to worse; the North Vietnamese were "stonewalling," after having tried to force a quick agreement just before the election which President Nixon—and especially President Thieu felt lacked the needed safeguards. And for the first time in the four-year history of the negotiations, there was talk of a "rift" between Henry Kissinger and his boss. There was hardly a newscast you could turn on without hearing the words "stonewalling" and "rift."

In 1969, during Henry Kissinger's pre-celebrity stage, the White House staff wondered who would run foreign policy, Kissinger or Bill Rogers. In 1970 and '71, during Henry's celebrity stage, his colleagues were impressed, beguiled, even inspired by his mastery of the bureaucracy and incipient mastery of events. In 1972, when Kissinger became a superstar, Haldeman came to the realization that the competition for #1 Peacemaker had never been between Kissinger and Rogers (as I had been certain) but between Kissinger and the President. No longer did Haldeman and Colson shake their heads in wonderment at the Kissinger Emergence, providing sparkle and color and intellectual zest to the White House staff; they had to deal with the Kissinger Situation.

The Situation had a dynamic all its own, and the central character, a conceptual frameworker who believed in shaping events rather than reacting to them, could not always shape this one to his satisfaction. The more powerful Kissinger was credited with being, the less powerful it seemed he would be likely to remain; since he preferred the fact of power to even such a heady experience as the appearance of power, he tried to cap the gusher of public attention most of the time. When both *Time* and *Newsweek* chose him for their covers, he asked me, only half in jest, "Do you think I can survive this?" "Nope," said I cheerily, about 75 per cent in jest, "but what a way to go." Almost compulsively, Henry passed this exchange along to Hugh Sidey of *Life*, who—along with columnist Joseph Alsop—was a close journalistic confidant.

On the Saturday before Christmas, 1972, a quiet day, I dropped in on Henry, who was going over the Christmas cards he had received as he watched the Oakland-Pittsburgh football game on television. He was convinced, he told me, that a few of his esteemed colleagues were attempting to do him in. "They saw the negotiations were leading toward a peace," Henry said. "They decided to be sure it would be recognized as Nixon's doing and not Kissinger's so they put out word that the President was restraining me from giving away everything. Then, when the negotiations fell through, there they were, they couldn't blame me and it only made the President look bad." He seemed amused that bureaucratic rivals—Haldeman-inspired, he was certain, which meant that it came from the President himself—were hoist on their own petard.

On television, a beefy Oakland linebacker blitzed, and the little Pittsburgh quarterback was buried. I shook my head at the screen: "He really caught it that time." Henry smiled a smile of satisfaction. "I knew he would." Between plays, I asked, "Why did you say 'peace is at hand'?"

"I had to say that, because we had just backed away from an initialing the document, and Hanoi needed to be reassured that we were about ready to sign."

"At least you didn't do it to mislead the American electorate," I assured him.

"So they'll say I was naïve," Kissinger mused.

"Better naïve than devious."

"Not in this job."

Talk of a "rift" between the President and Kissinger was now bruited about with a vengeance. There was no rift in immediate policy between the President and his national security adviser. There was plenty of rifting going on between Henry and the White House staff, which would hardly be worth a mention but for this: when the President, with Kissinger's active concurrence, decided to recommence the bombing of the North, and especially Hanoi, Henry let some friends pass the word that Dr. Kissinger, anguished and humane, did not agree with the President's decision. On December 30, James Reston wrote in the New York *Times:* "It may be, and probably is, true that Mr. Kissinger as well as Secretary of State Rogers and most of the senior officers in the State Department are opposed to the President's bombing offensive in North Vietnam. And also, that Mr. Kissinger would be more willing than the President to take a chance on signing the ambiguous truce terms on October 26." That hit hard: for the first time, Kissinger was suspected of saying one thing to the President, and then walking away from him to protect himself with the liberal press. If true, that was no "rift" or some bureaucratic backbiting: that was an assistant's disloyalty to the President at a time of great stress, when he was raining bombs at Christmastime, and meant that Kissinger's career at the White House would soon be finished. I put it to Henry directly. Did he tell that story to Reston? "No," he insisted, "I haven't spoken to him since we were in Paris." Then how did he get that impression? "Not from me. I supported the President's decision before and after. I canvassed for the bombing."

An appropriate page from the President's briefing book, with a suggested answer written by Pat Buchanan, reads:

> Q: Sir: Is there any truth to rumors of a rift between you and your foreign policy adviser?
>
> A: Not only this President but the American people owe Dr. Kissinger a debt of gratitude for his contribution in negotiating this honorable peace. As for our relations, my high regard for him remains what it has been for the four years we have worked together. (PJB)

Underneath, the President scrawled, "He has advised and supported every action I have taken." See Plate 23, following page 632.

On the next page of that briefing book, in answer to "What did all the terror bombing of Christmas accomplish?" Kissinger had suggested: "The idea that we engaged in indiscriminate carpet bombing of populated areas is a myth. (FYI: 1300 civilian deaths in a two-week period.) Throughout this conflict, U.S. bombing has been directed against military, not civilian targets, and that was the case in December." The President wrote this instead:

> *our* motive—to end this war on honorable basis
> 1) Cambodia, May 8 contributed to
>   that
> 2) In December
>   1) They backed away

on P.O.W. (condition)
on D.M.Z. (could be no peace)
          (right to invade)
    on supervising group
2) war could go on for months
3) we resumed bombing of military targets
4) Negotiations began seriously.

Earlier, the President had jotted down some thoughts about a matter
that troubled many Americans, troubled him, and was made especially
poignant at Christmastime: the morality of bombing. The question was
never asked, but on Plate 24, you can see some rough notes made by Nixon
on what the answer would have been. The translation of his handwriting
is below:

all killing is immoral
To allow slaughter
Communist conquer—11,000,000—is immoral
To bomb military targets
to prevent Communist tyranny—my
mission
to protect Americans
to obtain release of P.O.W.s
                    (morality of deliberately
                    killing civilians in invasion)

1) to bomb Hitler
was immoral
but more immoral to allow   2) Defense against
France to be   3) Bomb Military
conquered   targets only
by Hitler

Henry Kissinger, meanwhile, who had managed to convey the impression to his media and academic friends that he was less than enthusiastic
about the Christmas bombing, steadily assured his White House colleagues
that such impressions were being spread by misinformed friends of his who
were not privy to his thinking. This was perceived as duplicity by Haldeman, especially, who had watched in wonderment as Kissinger had
changed from shadowy *éminence grise* to resplendent *éminence rouge*,
and was bitter about the way the new Richelieu could keep friends in the
press while participating in decisions that brought down media wrath on
Nixon. Kissinger had a way of expressing anguish visibly that Nixon could
never capture; his approach to the media was selective and flattering, something that ran counter to Nixon's cool-contempt theory. As long as Nixon
needed him as a negotiator, and—more important—as a media bridge,

Kissinger was safe; as soon as that need disappeared, Kissinger would be dispensed with.

A realist, Henry made plans for the inevitable moment. He remembered the way the President kowtowed to him the month before the Peking summit, and then practically ignored him in the week before the trip took place. Because Kissinger cheerily professed to be a megalomaniac, his coterie took that to be impossible; in fact, he was a realistic megalomaniac. During the final Vietnam negotiations, Henry had kidded Ambassador William Sullivan (whose name Kissinger had once passed to the FBI for tapping) about his "mock-toughness"; when Henry decided to stay away from the final signing ceremony, leaving that to Secretary of State Rogers, Sullivan kidded Kissinger back about his "mock-humility."

"When do you think I should leave?" Henry asked me in his office, on that Saturday, January 27, when Rogers was in Paris signing the document he, Kissinger, had negotiated and initialed. "Twice I was deserted by the White House staff—first on India, and now this November-December. I have to bat 1,000 per cent, and nobody can do that. I've been on the high wire doing a somersault for four years now, and I'd like to get out before I break my neck.

"I think I'll have to stay another six months," he ruminated mournfully, pacing around his office, "to break somebody in. I'll have to do that someday, and it might as well be while Nixon is President. Here at the White House, though, not at State." Henry could melt any heart; I asked him what he would be doing at 7 P.M. that evening, when the cease-fire officially took effect. "I will be at home," he said. "I will raise a glass and say, with amazement in my voice, 'Peace *is* at hand!'"

5. PEACE WITH HONOR

"In war, resolution . . ."

Nixon filled that prescription of Winston Churchill's. For four long years, under varying degrees of pressure, the President had held resolutely to his goal of "peace with honor" (Disraeli's phrase, used as a 1916 campaign slogan by Woodrow Wilson), which meant the recognition of the right of self-determination in South Vietnam, with no coalition government imposed that would be a figleaf to cover quick takeover by the North.

"*. . . in defeat, defiance;*" Nixon had shown that, too, most notably in his 1962 "last press conference" as he lashed back at an unfriendly press corps with an embittered "You won't have Nixon to kick around any more." In Vietnam, after the 1971 attack in Laos showed a weakness in the South Vietnamese forces, Nixon issued orders to "hang tough." After the North Vietnamese had launched their all-out victory drive in May 1972—when the covers of news magazines were entitled "The Spectre of Defeat" and the attacks on his policy by antiwar columnists, commentators, and Congressmen were at their most intense—again Nixon's reaction was defiant. He mined the harbor at Haiphong, gambling that the Russians would not call off the summit conference, won his gamble, and prevented the loss of the Vietnam war.

"*. . . in victory, magnanimity;*" That's where Churchill and Nixon part company. The terms Nixon was able to extract from the North Vietnamese were no military victory in the war—that had been abjured as an objective long before he became President—but the cease-fire agreement of January 1973 was a stunning and visible victory over his critics at home, who would readily have settled for what Nixon considered surrender. Did Nixon, in his hour of triumph, firmly set aside the temptation to gloat, to rub his opponents' noses in their own "bugout" proposals?

No. He had been vilified by a great many people for a long time. He had been compared to Hitler by Senator McGovern several times (which Nixon used, rubbing salt in his own wound, playing off the excess), and had been marched upon and burned in effigy by tens of thousands of students. The bombing of Hanoi in December 1972, which Nixon was convinced would be the only way to bring the war to an end, was called "war by tantrum" by James Reston, "senseless terror which stains the good name of America" by Joseph Kraft. His sanity was called to question by Republican Senator William Saxbe of Ohio: "The President has taken leave of his senses." (Not usually a forgiving man, Nixon appointed Saxbe to be Attorney General one year later.) Having thus been portrayed and cartooned as a maniacal warmonger by people ordinarily considered responsible observers and participants in political affairs, and having been undefended by articulate or influential voices, he felt his old gutfighter's urge to strike back.

On January 23, 1973, three days after his second Inaugural Address (which was his second best Inaugural Address), the President asked the networks for air time at 10 P.M. to announce the initialing that day of a cease-fire agreement, the final signing to take place in Paris the following Saturday. The announcement, prepared with the help of Henry Kissinger and Ray Price, was formal and restrained; the meetings that immediately preceded the television speech, however, were tense and revealing.

At seven-thirty that evening, Haldeman assembled the group that was most in touch with press in the Roosevelt Room; across the hall from the Oval Office Haldeman sat in his customary chair, at the end of the long table with his back to the burning fireplace, the FDR plaque to his left and a Remington portrait of Teddy Roosevelt leading the Rough Riders up San Juan Hill to his right.

"Dr. Kissinger will or will not be joining us shortly," Haldeman opened, being decisive about an imponderable, "and the point of this meeting is to get guidance on what would be productive to have said by others after the President's speech."

Kissinger entered as if on cue, back from Paris that day with a fresh haircut and an initialed peace agreement. See Plate 19, following page 488. "We initialed an agreement today," he said with quiet and justifiable pride, "which will be signed on the twenty-seventh, that meets the objectives that the President laid out on May 8 and January 25."

"The people here," Haldeman interrupted, "can get the details from your press conference tomorrow, Henry. By the way, that's been moved back from noon to 11 A.M. because of Johnson's funeral. We're concerned here with reaction to the President's speech."

"Let's be careful what we say," Kissinger cautioned, "we don't want the North Vietnamese Foreign Minister to leave Paris without signing the agreement next Saturday. If Le Duc Tho claims victory, so can we, but let's wait until after the twenty-seventh."

"What about hitting critics in the U.S.?" Pat Buchanan wanted to know.

"It's okay to hit critics in the U.S. in general terms," said Kissinger, "but I don't want it to turn into a test of manhood with North Vietnam this week. So avoid saying we beat them or that the bombing worked."

Haldeman: "The obvious attack on this speech is going to be: 'This is the same thing we had in October, so why did you have to go through with the worst bombing in the history of the world?'"

Kissinger: "The document from which the President has been working is the one North Vietnam put out on November 26, which was slanted to their point of view. So we are getting a bonus. The comparison will not only show the advantages we have worked out since the October agreement, but the difference between the October agreement and the North Vietnamese version of that agreement.

"You will recall," the National Security Adviser went on, "that the conventional wisdom in early October was that the chief obstacle to a settlement was in maintaining Thieu. They said that no settlement was possible without a coalition government. *Time* or *Newsweek* already had a coalition cabinet chosen. Compare the latest published Communist proposal, September 11 of last year, with the agreement. By his steadfastness and his willingness to make lonely decisions, the President has prevailed. So tonight I think we should show restraint and simply applaud the President's fortitude. Saturday, after the agreement is signed, we can gear it up a little more.

"I am not concerned about hitting U.S. critics but don't claim military victory," Kissinger continued. "That will cause Hanoi to claim it, Saigon to claim it."

Haldeman said: "It's the victory over the critics that concerns this group."

Kissinger: "The only way we will keep North Vietnam under control is not to say that we are out forever. We don't want to dissipate with them the reputation of fierceness that the President has earned. This is a hairy business. If we can keep the peace for six months, then a new attack would require a positive decision for new aggression.

"As I see it, there are three lines of attack against us: One, We could have had this settlement four years ago. Two, What we had last October was good enough. Three, It was only the pressure of the doves that made us do it.

"All of this," Henry added cryptically, "is part of a bigger maneuver which is still under way, and we don't want to ruin that for short-term gains." He looked at his watch, blanched, and hurriedly left the meeting.

With Henry gone, Haldeman asked Buchanan to read a statement he had drafted that was to represent the Administration line. It started with a good summary of the peace terms, then veered into a political philippic: "The credit for tonight's announcement belongs to the silent majority who stood with the President . . . Time and again, in defense of his policies against relentless, harsh, and vitriolic attack from the Left, he stood his ground and repeatedly made the crucial decisions, the result of which is tonight's peace with honor . . ."

Buchanan was reading it matter-of-factly, without passion, but the passages were sure to jump out of the printed page. I started to squirm, looking around the room to see if anybody else was registering dismay, but the faces were impassive. "Had the President's opponents in Congress prevailed," Buchanan went on, ". . . Americans would today be witnessing a bloodbath on an unprecedented scale, the victims of which would be those Vietnamese who placed their confidence in the word of the United States. The difference between what the President has achieved, and what his opponents wanted, is the difference between peace with honor, and the false peace of an American surrender."

There was a moment of silence after he finished reading the draft position, broken by Chuck Colson's enthusiastic "That was great!"

"It's the whole wrong approach," I said. "For Crissake, the President made peace, let's enjoy it—why do we have to declare war on our critics all over again?"

"You don't think they'll be hammering away at us?" Haldeman shot back. "You don't think they'll be trying to make this peace look bad and take every violation of the cease-fire and say that it's proof that there is no peace at all?"

"That's when we counterattack," I insisted, "but let's not smack anybody right off the bat. We've got a peace, let's be gracious about it, it'll throw 'em all off balance."

Haldeman shook his head, murmuring, "That would mean he'd do it himself." I pressed for clarification—"What's your point, Bob?" Haldeman did not want to make his point in the open meeting, but with all eyes on him, he could not duck: "If this line is not put out by others, the President will do it himself and that will be far worse." He wanted to get away from debate, which was unlike Haldeman; contrary to the impression he gave outsiders as a martinet, he usually welcomed debate. I knew I could count on a lot of support around the table if the decision about the Administration line were still appealable. "You're making a strategy decision that will affect reconciliation in the country, the President's ability to lead, the whole approach to the Congress in the State of the Union," I said, looking around the room. "It's worth talking about."

"There's the 'sore winner' problem," Ray Price agreed, then fell silent. Buchanan countered: "The Far Left has been banging away at us for years and they were wrong. It's because of them that this war lasted longer than it should have. Now is the time to nail them to the wall." True Believer Buchanan, as always, was consistent, forthright, and articulate; no shilly-shallying.

I was being a yes-butter. I had agreed with Nixon's Vietnam policy in general, I believed that North Vietnam's hopes for American collapse were fed by marches on Washington and thus prolonged the war, and I sympathized with the President's normal, human desire to take a swat at whatever had been buzzing around his head while his hands were occupied, but I thought that magnanimity—forced and phony, if need be—would be more useful in carrying out the President's domestic program than an indulgence in natural reaction. I took a cheap shot at Buchanan: "Some liberals were with us on this, Pat, so drop the stuff about the Left—you want to hit Scoop Jackson tonight?" Buchanan smiled, acknowledged the point, and drew a line through the ideological reference in his statement.

Some support materialized for magnanimity. John Scali, scowling more than usual, said: "The moment of peace is no time to go out and kick your critics in the teeth. Men of reason will ultimately decide that this peace was a great achievement. Let's not get on the defensive and feel we have to go after our critics with an axe."

"The President would take your line, John," said Haldeman, "if he has the luxury to do so. But as Herb Klein here knows," he said in a reference to the 1962 press conference, "if he doesn't have that luxury, he will go. It's for the men in this room to give him that luxury of staying above the battle." This was the same point Pat Moynihan had made in his farewell address to the White House staff two years before: because there was no effective "second order of advocacy," the President himself had to stay in a combative stance most of the time.

"We cannot let our critics establish that Vietnam was an immoral war," Haldeman went on. "It may have been badly handled at times, but it was a war fought for the right reason to the right result." He leaned forward and ran his hands through his crewcut. "The toughest line of all to sell will be that the bombing brought them back to the table, but it happens to be true. Eighty per cent of the American people think that Hanoi is flattened, but it's sitting there fat and happy—by their own account they had less than two thousand casualties, which is what you'd get with precision bombing of military targets."

Dick Moore, who could see what was motivating Haldeman, wondered if it would not be possible to try to get some critics to admit they are wrong. Haldeman nodded solemnly and told everybody to get two critics to turn around: "Safire, you start with Mankiewicz and Braden." When someone asked who would bell Senator Saxbe's cat, Haldeman replied with a self-mocking "Nobody's allowed to talk to him even to ask," and got a short laugh.

Colson brought the meeting back into focus: "Safire's question was answered, then. An attack on critics is a necessity."

Ken Clawson quickly amended that: "But not a Kamikaze attack, trying to destroy everybody who disagreed with us."

I grumbled that we were making a big mistake, and Haldeman concluded in this way: "If Dean Sayre rings the church bells at the National Cathedral tomorrow morning, I will say you were right." Sayre, a frequent critic who had helped stage a "counter-Inaugual" concert, was hardly going to toll the bell the next day, and Haldeman could say he told me so. The meeting in the Roosevelt Room broke up at 8:25 P.M., in time for a few of us to hurry across the hall to the Cabinet Room.

The new Cabinet applauded the President's entrance. Henry Kissinger and a few other White House aides were present, and it soon began to dawn on me that the black hat I had drawn on Haldeman in the previous meeting might have been a bit unfair.

The President was irritable and made no effort to hide it. He was not stepping up to a crisis, which required calm and the infectious quality of confidence, he was announcing a peace and felt he could let the strain of the past few weeks show in his face and voice.

"This will be a brief meeting," the President said. "Its purpose is to be sure that in the eyes of the world and the nation, the Cabinet is informed before the announcement at ten o'clock tonight." Lest anyone there made the mistake of thinking he sought the judgment of his Cabinet, he repeated: "This will be a *pro forma* meeting, as will be the meeting with the legislative leaders next.

"I will announce at ten o'clock that we have concluded an agreement to end the war and bring peace to Southeast Asia." After reading the official statement, Nixon added: "What this agreement does and the protocols connected with it ensure, to the extent they ensure anything, is that my conditions of May 8 are met. Return of the POWs; accounting of the MIAs; an internationally supervised cease-fire; withdrawal of forces; right of the South Vietnamese to determine their own future without outside interference. All these conditions have been met. The cease-fire begins Saturday. In terms of what this means for Cambodia and Laos and so forth—since this will come up at the leaders' meeting, I want Henry to take a minute on that."

Kissinger was startled; he had not expected the President to discuss the "bigger maneuver" at all. Speaking from his seat against the wall, not at the Cabinet table, he said: "The essential thing about what this means for Laos and Cambodia is that we are not to talk about it. We have strong reason to believe there will be a cease-fire in Laos within fifteen days. It could be jeopardized by an excess of talk here. In Cambodia a *de facto* cease-fire will emerge. The situation there is somewhat messier than in Laos. The degree of formality is greater in Laos, but we have understandings in regard to both of them."

> President: "And after a great deal of pulling and hauling, the government of South Vietnam is totally aboard."
> Kissinger: "Thieu is going on TV half an hour after you, Mr. President."
> President: "Between now and the cease-fire, there will be heavy fighting—we have to assume that—with both sides grabbing everything they can. After a cease-fire there will be violations—in this kind of war with no front lines that's to be expected, too. That's why the supervisory crew is so important. How many did we wind up with Henry, 1100?"

Kissinger: "1160, Mr. President."

President: "One question will be, 'when did we believe the peace was going to work?' After a torturous ten days of negotiations in December, negotiations reached total deadlock. Not on a few details, but total. The North Vietnamese were stonewalling. Probably until they could see what Congress would do. Then we [the President avoided saying that he ordered renewal of bombing] resumed our May 8 policy, then they responded. Henry arrived in Paris on the eighth of January."

Kissinger: "On Monday the eighth, the first day was brutal in every respect."

President: "As Bill [Rogers] knows, Henry's message on the first day said, 'Here we go again.'"

Kissinger: "I told them I would have to leave on Wednesday. On the next day, the President's birthday, we made advances. On the technical side an unbelievable pedant had been in charge before then, but he was replaced and everything began to move. I sent the President a cable on his birthday to the effect that they have broken our hearts before, but I thought they were on the right track."

President: "I sent a cable back: 'Let's not get too optimistic, but that's the best birthday present I ever had.'"

Kissinger: "I went back last night. With respect to the agreement there were three things to be done which were settled quickly. They were determined to settle today."

President: "As a sidelight, I thought because of President Johnson's death they would want a little more time and I thought it might help, if they wanted it, it would be all right with us."

Kissinger: "But when they were ready, were they ready! We couldn't have stopped them from settling today. Of course, as testimony to the confidence we have established over four years, they took the English translation home with them lest we slip in a different page."

The President turned to Laird: "Without Vietnamization there would have been no settlement. Our own military actions played a decisive part in this peace."

Then Nixon said to nobody in particular: "Settlement was not made easier by the totally irresponsible actions of the Congress. They passed resolutions calling for a settlement that would have settled for far less than we got. To many people, the so-called Mansfield Resolution—prisoners for withdrawal, which was the least irresponsible of the irresponsible resolutions—would have been a good deal. But the people who understood best were the wives of the POWs who knew we didn't fight this war just to get our POWs back.

"The difficulty of the Mansfield Resolution was that it would have ended the war for us, but the war would have continued for the fifty million people of Indochina. By achieving a peace with honor, we stopped the war for the Indochinese people and have enabled the Indochinese people to settle their own futures.

"It's been a long, difficult period. The critics said, 'Why don't we just get out—it's Johnson's war, not yours.' Well, it wasn't Johnson's war nor Kennedy's war. I have not engaged in that kind of rhetoric. Certainly there were mistakes in the conduct of the war, but whatever happened we have now achieved an agreement that achieves our goals and especially the right of people to settle their own futures. We knew what we stood for as a country and that will mean a lot in the future.

"If the U.S. didn't prove to be responsible in this war, if we ended it in defeat—the Chinese would never have considered us worth talking to, the Russians wouldn't consider us worth talking to, and the Europeans, with all their bitching, would never consider us reliable allies.

"We have to be responsible—and that's what this peace is all about."

Shultz (as the President turned to leave): "Quite an achievement, Mr. President."

President: "It was no Republican achievement. I have as much contempt for Republicans who would have cut and run as I do for Democrats who have done that. It could never have been without a lot of good Democrats, like Pete Brennan's people who were with us when some of the elitist crowd were running away from us. Thank God for the hardhats!"

I followed Haldeman out of the Cabinet Room, past the Oval Office, to his Williamsburg-style office in the corner.

Bob motioned for me to shut the door and sit down. "Did you notice," Haldeman asked, "on the way out of the meeting, Bill Rogers said to him, 'Don't you do it. Let us do that'? Bill understands. The Boss is great in adversity, but he's always had this problem handling success." Haldeman, who knew how to handle Nixon better than anybody, felt that the only way to stop him from attacking his critics at the moment of peace was to promise him that it would be done by proxy. That was why Nixon's peace announcement at 10 P.M. was restrained, relatively understated, and Presidential. I felt bad at that point for having baited Haldeman before so many of his associates. "I didn't want to see a dozen guys go out with a franchise to blaze away at the opposition," I explained. "That's almost as bad as the Boss doing it himself."

Haldeman made a wry face: "We're not that good, you know that. Maybe 20 per cent will happen, probably 10. I hope somebody gets something across so it can get in his news summary."

Three days later, Barry Goldwater issued a White Paper detailing all the predictions of disaster made by the President's Vietnam critics, from McGovern's June 14, 1972, statement that "if we continue under the Nixon policy, we're not going to see our POWs again" to Senator Edward Kennedy's December 27 somber "We cannot read about the heavy bombing . . . without a deep and despairing sense that peace is not at hand." As might be expected, Goldwater's release sank without a trace. Kenneth Crawford, a wise old editorialist whose column had been dropped by *Newsweek*, explained in the Washington *Post* why Nixon's dream of hairshirted critics was foolish: "Critics can console themselves with arguments that the bombing didn't do it or that it should have been done sooner or that, in any case, it won't prevent an ultimate Communist victory. They will never admit that they were dead wrong this once, as who ever does? The Nixonites wouldn't if the shoe were on the other foot, as it has been at times along the way. Crow just isn't edible in public places."

A few days later, at the first press conference he had held in many months, the President's black mood surfaced:

"Mr. President, do you have anything specifically in mind to help heal the wounds in this country . . . the divisions over the war, and specifically, anything down the road much farther in terms of amnesty?"

The President: "Well, it takes two to heal wounds, and I must say, when I see that the most vigorous criticism or, shall we say, the least pleasure out of the peace agreement comes from those who were the most outspoken advocates of peace at any price, it makes one realize whether some want the wounds healed. We do.

"We think we have taken a big step toward ending a long and difficult war which was not begun while we were here, and I am not casting any aspersions on those Presidents who were in office who can no longer be here to speak for themselves, for the causes of the war. I am simply saying this: that as far as this Administration is concerned, we have done the very best that we can against very great obstacles, and we finally have achieved a peace with honor.

"I know it gags some of you to write that phrase, but it is true, and most Americans realize it is true, because it would be peace with dishonor had we—what some have used, the vernacular—'bugged out' and allowed what the North Vietnamese wanted: the imposition of a Communist Government or a coalition Communist Government in South Vietnam. That goal they have failed to achieve. Consequently, we can speak of peace with honor and with some pride that it has been achieved."

Was it just his pique showing? In a week, most piques peak, then subside; a week is a long time to stay piqued. The parting shot Nixon took at his war critics had to be more than a venting of Presidential spleen, done because nobody else was getting the point across. There

had to be another reason, some tactical justification, for Nixon's controlled use of his temper.

I think it had to do with this:

In the election, his "us-against-them" strategy had proved extraordinarily successful; through the Christmas bombing and the period
of letdown when it seemed peace was illusory, he lost his momentum.
Nixon feared the erosion of his mandate if he did not reassert his
identity with the majority—and the best way to do that was his surefire technique of "themnity"—to point over there at the previously
noisy minority.

He was going to fight them and beat them on impounding funds,
because the Congress could never get together to work out a sensible
budget themselves—if they did, so much the better, but it could never
happen without the President's forcing the issue.

He was going to fight them and beat them on "executive privilege,"
because that was a phony issue, tossed at him to hamstring his foreign policy by the new isolationists.

He was going to fight them and beat them, too, in wrenching
power out of the hands of Washington bureaucrats and returning it
to states and localities and the private sector, knowing full well that
he would be paradoxically denounced for seizing too much power
himself in making the transition.

I told you so, he told the press, and he reminded them that the
press had been the wrongest of all. He enjoyed doing it, but he did
not do it strictly for enjoyment, he rubbed it in because he did not
want the country to lose sight of his villain.

This all happened on January 23, 1973, around the time former detective John Caulfield was meeting at Counsel John Dean's request with de-
fendant James McCord to try and talk him into keeping quiet. That night,
the President wrote a letter to Mrs. Lyndon Baines Johnson, widow of
his predecessor, in a somewhat shakier hand than usual:

THE WHITE HOUSE

WASHINGTON

January 23, 1973

Dear Lady Bird,

I only wish Lyndon could have lived to hear my announcement of the Viet Nam Peace Settlement Tonight.

I Know what abuse he took — particularly from members of his own party — in standing firm for peace with honor.

Now that we have such a settlement, we shall do everything we can to make it last so that he and other brave men who sacrificed their lives for this cause will not have died in vain.

Sincerely

Richard Nixon

A couple of weeks later, the President was feeling better, and with the bitterness of victory behind him, he invited his new Cabinet and a few departing staffers to breakfast in the State Dining Room. At that breakfast, he was to say, "Seventy-three can be and should be the best year ever." He meant it.

6. THE BEST YEAR EVER

Breakfast in the White House's State Dining Room is a treat. The eggs are fluffy, the bacon and sausages just crisp enough, the sweet rolls freshly baked, the flatware elegant, the hushed service of the white-gloved black butlers reminiscent of a bygone day. The White House calligrapher does your name on a place card that makes you feel almost guilty about stealing it, but you do.

A couple of years before, when the President told aides he wanted to speak to Congressmen at breakfast, he added pointedly that the staff should keep back and let the focus rest on the Congressmen. Chapin and Butterfield took this to mean the staff should not get breakfast at all, and so informed John Ehrlichman, who was scheduled to speak to the Congressmen with the President that morning. The snubbed Ehrlichman did not try to scrounge a cup of coffee; he sat stonily in the next room, joined by George Shultz, who sympathized and, as an old Secretary of Labor, knew the power of solidarity. When the silly staff-keep-back caveat was lifted, Alex Butterfield went around like the mother of the bride at a wedding, saying, "Eat, eat!" and the White House staff was thenceforth permitted to eat with the guests.

No such flap existed the morning of February 8, 1973, at the start of the new term.

"Okay, Ollie," the President called to his photographer, as Ollie Atkins stood on a chair to get the official picture with all the new faces, "send us the pictures and the bill."

The President was in an expansive mood; he had averted the danger of exhausted volcanoes, and he wanted to get his new term under way with a fresh mandate and no Vietnam cross to bear. He had good reason to be optimistic. He called upon Roy Ash, who had replaced Caspar Weinberger as Director of the Office of Management and Budget (Weinberger went to HEW as Secretary), for a briefing on a big issue at the time, the impoundment of funds. Ash used the euphemism "reserves" for impoundment—the President's refusal to spend money appropriated by the Congress—and as usual, put his audience to sleep. The President moved in to make the point to the rest of the group, soon to go out and speak at Republican Lincoln Day dinners.

"Here's the lead we were trying to get out in our briefing on this," the President said. "The amount reserved, or impounded, which Congress says is unconstitutional, is one-half the amount a Democratic Congress reserved in 1967 with LBJ. The point is that the Congress always appropriates and overspends, and the President has the responsibility to say no—if we spend this money and don't raise taxes, it would be inflationary. Or, if we spend this money, we will have to raise taxes.

"What the President is trying to do when he doesn't spend money the Congress has appropriated, is not to bite the Congress but to say no to tax increases and price increases.

"On the vetoes that will be coming up, I am not just going to say I am vetoing this or that bill. I am going to say, 'I am vetoing a price and tax increase,' neither of which the people want. You have to put it down their throats just like that. Don't argue the Constitution—just say that Congress wants to spend money that would result in a tax and price increase."

John Ehrlichman made a presentation on everything from tax reform to disaster relief. The topics really never seemed to change; when "aid to Federally impacted areas" came up, Elliot Richardson, seated next to me, murmured, "In 1957, my first meeting in Government was about impacted aid."

The President had something to say; he moved the briefing along, then rose, pushed his chair in front of him as a makeshift rostrum on which to rest his hands, and made a speech. It was not as good as the fourth-quarter speech he made to the Cabinet a year before, but it was less self-pitying, and had a snapper at the end that nobody who was in the room would forget. The tape was unavailable to me, but I think I have a good part of it in my notes.

The President and Ehrlichman continued the discussion along these lines, including tax reform. The President: "To put it another way, we have been operating under the concept of the full employment budget. Actually, that has meant we have been running big deficits. I have had to burn up a lot of old speeches because we were against that sort of thing. But this budget is based on the assumption of maximum growth of the economy. The idea of some that if we 'just grow more, we would have the money' is baloney. There's no way to get the money by growing faster. The economy last year grew 6½ per cent—that's full steam.

"Now in terms of speeches out there," Nixon continued, "concentrate on three things: jobs, taxes, prices. Peter Brennan is right. His people are interested in jobs. It's taken us years to get the unemployment curve down. Breadwinner unemployment is now at the lowest point since 1965, 2.4 per cent. What's involved here is your prosperity. We are fighting for a policy that frankly spends a lot of money. What about the poor? Are we heartless? On education, on housing, on health, we have increased spending over the past four years by 300–400 per cent. That's no austerity budget. What we are doing now, though, is paring out the programs that haven't worked.

"Always bring it back to the gut issue," Nixon insisted. "Most people don't want college professors subsidized, they want them fired. And lots of the time, they're right. The average person is interested in his own job, his own prices, his own taxes. Think of the people out there in that country, sitting there at their TV sets, trying to make ends meet. If you argue it on specific issues, like if you care about people affected by this or that program, we lose. But if you do it our way, that this is a tax-increase Congress, we win.

"Seventy-three can be and should be the best year ever. Congress represents the special interests trying to force the President to spend money. But helping their pet special interests doesn't help the general interest, including, if I may say so, the general interest of the special interests.

"In terms of pure politics, we are really taking on our own friends. We are knocking the farmers. Well, that's a little demagoguery to hold you for the moment. Let's move on.

"Another issue not to be defensive about is this: I notice the columnists say we have a 'super Cabinet' and a 'regular Cabinet.' That's a lot of baloney. Thick or thin, no matter how you slice it, it's baloney. We have a committee of Cabinet members to coordinate matters that cut across departments, but this new system does not downgrade anybody. There is no 'super Cabinet.'

"Now, about the press. You have handled yourselves well. Don't be afraid. Talk to members of the press particularly when you go out to the country. The press out there aren't supposed to be as smart as the press here in Washington, but don't you believe it. They will ask about real issues, not phony issues.

"On network programs like *Face the Nation* or *Meet the Press*—coordinate with Ziegler; not about what to say but about which people go on and when.

"Go out and make your speeches—we're not a closed Administration. The same is true of social events, to the extent you can stand it, move around in this town. Of course, if you have a choice of hostesses, give the ones on our side a break once in a while. But don't be defensive—go out, see them. The people out there want to be in with big shots.

"Remember that anything you say at a social event is news. If there's no press there, the hostess will get on the phone the minute you have left, so remember, it's all on the record. Now, reporters will come in to see you, they'll say they want to help you. They'll say they won't attribute anything to you, they'll ask you to tell them on a personal basis, as friends, what they want to know, and I say to you—*don't tell 'em.* Your best personal friend in the press owes his first allegiance to a story.

"When you are going out socially, assume everything is on the record and you will do well.

"In dealing with Congress, don't limit yourselves to talking to Republicans. Remember, some Democrats support us better than some Republicans do. Bill Rogers has to have breakfast with Fulbright, but he knows he can talk differently to John Stennis.

"Be very open, it will disarm them. Invite them down. And get them in social situations where you can talk substance with their wives as well.

"At committee hearings you have been taking a beating and a battering. You may get discouraged, particularly if you went in with other ideas. But there are a lot of very decent people in Congress really trying to get the facts. You may wonder, is it worth the candle? Well, it's a different way to have fun.

"I want all the new members of the Cabinet to know this, for the next four years, whenever you speak out, *you will be backed 100 per cent. If a slip occurs, you will not find Ziegler saying the President disagrees.*" That was quintessential Nixon. "The worst thing would be to be timid.

"I was talking to King Hussein of Jordan. When he was sixteen years old, an assassin shot his grandfather, and he ran after the assassin and got shot himself. He made the point—if people throw rocks at you in a parade, you cannot sit down and look for protection. *The moment a leader shows timidity he encourages people to go after him.* People can sense when a leader is timid and they automatically attack. Remember, you are a member of the President's Cabinet. Try to be conciliatory when others are conciliatory toward you, but when the other side doesn't want to heal wounds, fight 'em—you get more respect.

"On foreign policy our opponents have become strangely silent. This is temporary. They only attack when they think you are going to fail. When you have a success, they will try to forget it as soon as possible. On the other hand, I remember we talked about Eisenhower's foreign policy successes all through 1956.

"I am not suggesting that peace is certain or that we do not have lots of problems, or that the world is totally safe. But if ever an Administration can point with pride to foreign policy success, we are that Administration. We are painting on a bigger canvas, now that we are including China. We have got to claim the credit—we have to stand up there and cram it down their throats.

"When you are on a TV program, and they say afterward, 'Gee, that was helpful,' you have failed. They are only happy when they have embarrassed you and then they have a story. Remember, if the story doesn't come out with your fact in it, you have failed. When you are on TV get off their subject and move to your own."

Secretary of State Rogers was primed at that point to say a few things about the President that Nixon could not say about himself. Bill Rogers rose: "We can use our foreign policy successes to our advantage in all fields. Government is too complex to understand all its workings, so it usually comes down to this: Do you have a policy? Do you have the courage to carry it out? Is it successful?

"Let's not worry about being accused of being orderly or managerial or gray," Rogers continued. "People want their Government to govern. Remember that the President is the recognized world leader in the cause of peace and all we did was against the opposition of the Congress and the most influential part of the media. We know what we are doing, we have the courage to carry it out, and we have been successful.

"I had an interesting conversation with Pompidou which we cannot use publicly. He had been critical of the President during the bombing. He was quite apologetic about what he had said, and then he said he had been to Moscow recently, and he expressed concern that we were being too friendly with the Russians. That was because in a discussion with Brezhnev when Pompidou asked for something, Brezhnev replied, 'I'll have to talk to President Nixon about that.' That gives you some idea of the standing of the President among the world's leaders . . . I can't remember a time when the President had more support."

The President took over from there. "We will have a Cabinet meeting on energy within four weeks. That cuts across everything. There will also be another one after that on trade. In the meantime, the various Cabinet committees will meet. I hope you will participate as principals and not send your assistants. Bring them along, though, your deputy has to do the work while you are out making the speeches.

"The last point is on a personal matter.

"You have been under a barrage lately. If you think that's tough, remember we have had some pretty rough moments in the past four years. Before my November 3 speech in 1969, according to the Washington *Post*, there were ten million people marching around the White House. On the media, it's important to separate reporters from columnists, although in these days of advocacy journalism it isn't easy.

"As I say, we have had some tense moments. The Mideast wasn't easy —there was that infiltration in Jordan that had us up a few nights. Vietnam had its ups and downs and when the record is out, we will see that those who claimed to be most for peace prolonged the war.

"Perhaps you saw on TV the funeral of the last man killed in Vietnam. I didn't go to the funeral to exploit that event, but we had the family come in here. Mrs. Nolde looked about thirty-five years old, with her four boys and a girl, and other members of the family. You would think after the funeral she would be all broken up. But she carried herself like a queen. I told her I got lots of letters about how wonderful Mrs. Johnson was at the President's funeral, how she handled herself with dignity, but she had had years of preparation for that. Mrs. Nolde had never been in the glare of television. And I said to her, 'You have been a First Lady every moment since your husband died.' Then the kids came by—the seventeen-year-old boy with a red, scraggly beard—if he had not been a member of the Nolde family, I don't know if the Secret Service would have let him in, but he was a great kid. Really proud of his Dad, and it was kind of a mover for me."

The President paused at some length here, recalling the moment.

"Then the sixteen-year-old daughter came through. You might expect her to be crying, but she was not crying. She said to me, 'Mr. President, could I kiss you?'"

The President stood there for about fifteen seconds, and finally said, "Well, anyway . . ." After another pause he added, "You see, that's what it's all about."

Then he strode quickly out of the room and the breakfast was over.

EPILOGUE

"What Presidents are remembered?" Nixon ruminated aloud one night. It was about midnight, toward the end of his second year in office, and we were working on an economic speech launching "the new prosperity" to the Chamber of Commerce. Nobody else was around, the President felt like talking, so Manolo Sanchez kept bringing coffee into the Executive Office Building private office as Nixon ticked off the Presidents who are remembered, and the underlying reason why.

"Jackson fought the banks. Lincoln fought the war. Cleveland fought the Congress, and Teddy Roosevelt fought everything. In our time, Wilson and FDR were controversial men, Presidents who had to fight hard. What they all did mattered to history.

"Of course, the times they lived in were turbulent. McKinley lived in good times, and he was loved and honored in his time. Eisenhower the same. But the times we're in, these aren't the smooth times. These are the times of great controversy, and I'm not afraid to step up to controversy.

"Ray Price understands the mystique, the aura of the Presidency. Remember the speech on that, back in '68? One of the best. Read De Gaulle on the mystery of power, the power of mystery. He understood that better than anybody."*

I said I thought he was carrying the aloof, mysterious leader bit a little too far. FDR was mysterious, but he was human. Anecdotes about Roosevelt abounded, and Americans who loved him or hated him at least thought they knew him as a person, not as a remote resident of the fenced-in White House. But with Nixon, I suggested, the danger was he would become totally depersonalized—the plastic, hollow man that his

* "There can be no power without mystery. There must always be a 'something' which others cannot altogether fathom, which puzzles them, stirs them, and rivets their attention . . . Nothing more enhances authority than silence. It is the crowning virtue of the strong, the refuge of the weak, the modesty of the proud, the pride of the humble, the prudence of the wise, and the sense of fools . . ." Charles de Gaulle, *The Edge of the Sword.*

critics always maintained he was. It seemed strange, discussing this so clinically, as if we were talking about a third person; but Nixon often looked at his friend, RN, that way.

"We don't disagree about that," he said, lighting a pipe. (The pipe would soon go out, and he would poke around in the bowl with a pencil, cleaning out mainly unsmoked tobacco. To Nixon, a pipe was like Kennedy oratory, a beautiful promise unfulfilled. A cigar after dinner was different.) "You can be human and still have the mystique. The thing is, you have to be considered an *homme sérieux* by other people. Romney and Volpe, for example, they know how to sell, and they run their departments a hell of a lot better than a lot of people ever thought they would, but they aren't regarded highly. They're good men, men with real character, and it's a pity—I don't suppose there's anything they can do about that, it's the way you are perceived by others."

He got up and walked around the long, high-ceilinged room, fiddling with the glass racks of pictures of his family. "But you're right, it's the man, not the machine people care about.

"We have people here doing a great job, right down the line. John Davies runs people through the White House the way nobody else ever has.* The dinners, the 'evenings' are all better than Kennedy ever had. Haldeman's got things arranged so that the paper doesn't clog up and orders get carried out. The NSC, the Domestic Council, those are big improvements in running the country—but that's not what counts in people's eyes. It's the man."

He seemed resigned to that fact, and to the notion that nobody would ever transmit what he was like out to the public. He reminisced about a visit he had made to Poland in 1959: "There was a steel mill on the itinerary," he said. "The Polish diplomat who was my escort officer—a brilliant fellow—turned me over to the plant manager for the usual guided tour. The manager was especially proud of the new machinery in the plant, and he told me all about what it cost and how it speeded up the process. He got a little impatient when I stopped to shake hands with the workers around whatever machine he was showing off. In the car on the way back from the mill, the diplomat said something I've always remembered. 'It's not hard to find men who understand machinery,' he said. 'Our trouble is we don't have enough men who understand men.'" Nixon looked back to see if I had written that down, and was glad to see I had.

Kissinger and the glittering machinery of the National Security Council came to the President's mind. "Henry's a genius, he really is—a genius—but he's in love with the machinery. He doesn't see the mystery, not yet,

---

* Davies was the Special Assistant who handled White House tours, and was followed in 1971 by Michael Farrell. In Nixon's time, the number of White House visitors rose to 1.5 million a year. And the tourists had more to see, including a newly reinstated Map Room and garden tours. The President liked the way his staff showed off more of the house to more people. It was one of those few improvements in operation that one could actually see.

maybe he will, about the man and how important it is to get that out. He and Haldeman, I think, were taking notes in a meeting I had with De Gaulle. They got everything down of substance. But then De Gaulle said, in a kind of an aside, 'All the countries of Europe lost the war, but only two were defeated.' They never wrote it down. And that's the one thing I'll never forget from that meeting."

The President gave up on the cold pipe and nibbled the stem of his glasses. "We don't really get the word out, about what it's really like around here. There's a liberal bias in the media, I know all that, but it's really our own fault. You think of Truman—a fighter. Eisenhower—a good man. Kennedy—charisma. Johnson—work. Me—what?" He looked at me for an answer, and the only thing I could think to say was, "Competence. Sorry about that."

He smiled ruefully, having made his point and not liking the point he had made.

"Hell, if all we do is manage things 10 per cent better, we'll never be remembered for anything. Republicans are supposed to manage things better, after Democrats break new ground—that's the old cliché. We have bigger things to do."

Did he get to do those bigger things? What, besides being the first President forced to resign in disgrace, will Nixon be remembered for?

He wanted to be remembered as a controversial President, and he will surely have that wish. Nixon was the one who cut against the grain of most Establishment thought in the nation, who caused juices to flow and glands to salivate, who took too much pleasure in winning and caused his foes too much pleasure in his losing. The enshrinement of "us against them" was both the reason for his landslide and the cause of his corrosion.

As a President, he wanted to amount to something. "What they all did mattered to history," and what he did, he wanted to matter. He had both a sense of history and a sense of destiny. "Only Nixon could have" done, at that moment of our national life, much of what he brought to pass. He fought a four-year war of his own in Vietnam, paying the price in inflation and unrest, so that he could realistically reshape the American position in the world. The Nixon summits will be topped by ensuing summits, and détente will be followed by tension, but his understanding of how the subterranean stresses of power in the world were moving helped him move with them, direct some of them, and perhaps avert an earthquake of war. Historians tend to give points to leaders who think in generational terms, and may credit Nixon, more than any other American President so far in this century, with both a world view and a world vision. He knew the new limits of American power, and moved to withdraw from places and commitments where we were overextended, but he had an earthy faith in the economic power of the American system and the character of the American people, and moved to sweep back the war-weary wave of isolationism that had engulfed Wilson. Nixon consciously presided over the end of the "postwar world" and craftily helped shape—to the specifications of his vision—a somewhat safer peacetime world.

As he swam hard against the tide of popular opinion in foreign affairs, retaining an activist place in the world, he floated easily with the tide of popular opinion in domestic affairs, hoping to reduce the Federal bureaucracy's tendency to dominate every facet of American life. His critics in both cases wanted him to do exactly the opposite. That's why they doubly despised his policies, and why Nixon could say, in the words of Franklin Roosevelt, "They hate me—and I welcome their hatred!"

Presidents are not remembered for slowing down trends; Nixon's economics will be remembered chiefly for what they teach future Presidents not to do, and his revenue sharing (he should have called it power-sharing) will be recalled with some gratitude by the creative, powerful mayors of tomorrow. He sped the pace of desegregation even as he railed against "forced busing," doing the inherently right thing in the apparently wrong way, but both sensing and thinking through the conflicting claims to rights of individual freedom.

He patterned himself after Charles de Gaulle, above all others, and was too conscious of the need to create a myth. By surrounding power with mystery, Nixon believed he would gain a momentum and fashion a shield in times that called for unpopular actions. But the myth that comes to mind is that of Phaëthon, who insisted on driving the chariot of the sun around the earth for a day, and nearly scorched the world until Zeus removed him from the driver's seat with a thunderbolt, leaving his sisters weeping tears of amber. The poet Ovid, in treating this theme, wrote of "failure while daring greatness"; the same thought, in nearly the same words, recurred through Nixon's life in Teddy Roosevelt's "man in the arena," who failed while daring greatly after having tasted the triumph of high achievement. The savage irony is that Nixon not only failed to create the myth he thought would help him, but his effrontery in the attempt enabled the forces he so darkly hated to create a myth of their own about him, as if he were evil incarnate. Myths can be useful, and satisfying, and add lore to a folk, but Nixon's experience shows they should be centered exclusively on creatures of fantasy.

His stupidest blunder: he will be remembered by Presidents to come for the damage he did to the confidentiality of the Presidency—something Nixon desperately wanted to protect—by his mindless decision to tape-record everything surreptitiously. The inexorable tape machine, put in place so as to be able to set unfriendly historians straight in years to come, was an invasion of the privacy of his associates that backfired horrendously, bringing him down in disgrace.

Nixon's most penetrating perception: that there was a Silent Majority, neither guilt-ridden nor self-flagellating, which could be awakened to the fact of its strength. In standing for and articulating its values—the work ethic, the affirmation of pride in "what's right with America," the relentless optimism of people who say, "Wait—it'll get better"—Nixon cut against the grain of established opinion leadership and did necessary battle against debilitating pessimism and the war-weariness that might have led to a dangerous post-Vietnam isolationism.

His most unexpected contribution: active sponsorship of the arts and humanities by the Federal Government. Each year, he would redouble aid to cultural institutions at Leonard Garment's urging, and in the long run, the results may turn out to be the sleeper in history's judgment of the Nixon legacy.

His greatest failure: to rally and inspire, to give his countrymen what Ray Price called "the lift of a driving dream" to replace the nightmarish decade of riot and war. Instead, as Woodrow Wilson put it, "we were very heedless and in a hurry to be great": he let his obsession with secrecy draw him over the brink into invasions of privacy and the perversion of law, and every assessment of him will forever be stained with the word "Watergate."

His greatest achievement: he was in the end what he wanted above all else to be—a peacemaker, which better men who were Presidents often failed to be. To make peace and to start the world toward laying down its arms is no mean achievement, especially if it is, in Nixon's vision "a peace that can last."

His most profound personal success: he came back. No man of our time suffered such slings and arrows and came back to outrage Fortune. Whenever a future politician is depressed, whenever a loser feels lost, he can think of Nixon, who scribbled a note to himself about Ted Kennedy after Chappaquiddick: "A man is not finished when he's defeated, he's finished when he quits." But there turned out to be another side to that coin: Nixon did not know when to quit. He knew that we "wanted to believe," but did not believe we wanted to know.

His personal failure: he was concerned too much with how he would be perceived, occasionally creating a mask that became the man. "Truman —a fighter. . . . Kennedy—charisma. . . . Me—what?" Me—Character, was what he wanted, but Character is something you are; it projects itself, it is not something you or your aides project. The dismaying truth to those who know Nixon is that underneath the imitation-oak-grained formica veneer is solid oak, beneath that phony image of character *is* character: a confidence in his vision, a love of his country, a desire to be remembered as somebody who mattered because he rediscovered our faith in ourselves—and was not afraid to affirm it at a time when affirmation seemed out of date.

Motive? When speaking to his Cabinet about Melbourne and Disraeli, Nixon cautioned against lightly ascribing motives to men we cannot know. And Arthur Burns said, "He has a noble motive in foreign affairs to reshape the world, or at least his motive is to earn the fame that goes with nobly reshaping the world. Who can say what his motive is? But it's moving him in the right direction." Before Nixon made it back, he would tell us, "*Being* President is nothing compared to what you can *do* as President."

When Kissinger called Melvin Laird "a devious man, but when cornered, a patriot" he was describing himself and the President too—lions and foxes all, as political scientists from Niccolò Machiavelli to James MacGregor Burns have said leaders must be.

A moment ago, I wrote of Nixon's success in coming back. Unable now to punctuate any comeback of reputation with an election victory, perhaps his will be the last laugh when, doddering and revered, he is welcomed back to the White House by his daughter, the President, or some other mind-boggling dénouement equally laced with irony.

This book was written at a time when the President of the United States was flat on his political back, and the nation was uncertain about his resignation, impeachment, and stability, and it was concluded after Nixon became the first American President to be shamed out of office. "There may be some understanding and perspective someday," he told a friend as the year of his resignation drew to a close, "but it will take a long, long time. I'm a fatalist."

When he finally quit, Nixon had no guarantee of a pardon from the man he had chosen to succeed him; he had set aside the kind of plea bargaining Spiro Agnew had engaged in as unworthy of a President. Just after midnight of the night he made his man-in-the-arena resignation address, Nixon told several old friends—with the combination of genuine courage and cloying self-pity that ennobled and marred so much of what he said throughout his life—"some of the best political writing has been done from jail." That was vintage Nixon—self-consciously gutsy, but gutsy nevertheless—and though it cost his successor dearly, it was right that the first President to be driven from office be spared the ordeal of a show trial.

We have not yet come to the time of what Woodrow Wilson called "sober second thought"; the record is still open, as are the wounds; Nixon is too soon judged in anger or explicated in defensiveness. He will be remembered more for what he did than what he was. He was more Caesar than Hamlet, for good and for bad, and if one ex-ghost can paraphrase another: leave him to history. At least he learned the lesson of his downfall, and in his farewell at the White House, passed along the hardest-earned advice of any man's life: "Those who hate you don't win unless you hate them—and then you destroy yourself."